Political Corruption

ARNOLD J. HEIDENHEIMER
Washington University

Political Corruption

READINGS IN COMPARATIVE ANALYSIS

HOLT, RINEHART and WINSTON, Inc.
New York Chicago San Francisco Atlanta
Dallas Montreal Toronto London Sydney

To Pat

Library of Congress Catalog Card Number: 77–108574
SBN: 03–077815–8
Printed in the United States of America
9 8 7 6 5 4 3 2 1

Preface

There are some varieties of political interaction that contemporary scholarship has made vivid and comprehensible for students, even as there are other forms of political behavior that have been so neatly measured for storage as to discourage the attention of nonspecialists. Political corruption, however, is a phenomenon that has been neither neatly measured nor illuminated by much highly visible scholarship. It belongs to a third category of political phenomena that has been subject to academic attention only occasionally. Most members of established academic disciplines have left the investigation of political corruption to journalists and other purely descriptive or impressionistic writers. Because systematic studies of it have been relatively rare, political corruption has been one of those subjects consigned to limbo by the "map makers" of the contemporary social science establishment. One consequence is that university graduates are often no more knowledgeable about it than are less highly educated readers of the daily press.

Perhaps this collection will serve to put the subject and some related methods of analysis more securely back onto the social sciences map. In any event, I hope that it will make evident that there exists a respectable, and even rich, body of scholarship that is built upon various theoretical underpinnings, and which has evolved many findings and hypotheses that can serve as the basis for further research. Certainly I discovered a larger and more substantial variety of studies than I had dared to expect when I first started combing the literature in connection with a course on political corruption that I conducted at Washington University in 1968. Many of the findings have remained unintegrated, but this seems to be largely due to limited contact among individual scholars working within a variety of disciplines. Hopefully, this volume will serve to strengthen such interdisciplinary contact. Many of the selections' authors share the editor's identification as a political scientist, but others are anthropologists, economists, historians, lawyers, sociologists, and publicists.

Most readers drawn to the study of political corruption will probably want to investigate topics that are immediately related to their main interests. I kept this in mind when devising the major organizational framework of the book, and I hope that the utilization of both structural-analytical and political-geographic categories will allow the most efficient use of the materials. This organization, readily seen on the contents page, should aid the scholar or teacher in locating those materials of personal interest. To facilitate additional research, footnotes of all readings have been retained.

The second major organizational dimension of this volume is broadly cross-cultural and comparative. As definitions and ways of coping with corrupt practices vary from culture to culture, part of the incentive for achieving deeper insights into how norms are related to behavior in different social and political settings may be gained from cross-cultural studies. For this reason, the readings I have selected deal with Western as well as non-Western systems for the modern period. To maintain some contextual continuity I have concentrated on four broad cultural-political areas: Two of these, Western Europe and the United States, represent the Western tradition, and the other two, South Asia and Africa, encompass societies whose indigenous traditions are non-Western. In my introductory essays I have sought to indicate how comparative analyses might be developed, but these should be regarded merely as one scholar's very modest first steps.

While most of the selections in this volume have previously appeared elsewhere, a number have been especially translated for inclusion. As each author brings his own value system to his analysis, I trust that the bias of any one author will be balanced out by those of the others. Since nationality seems to affect the values brought to bear on analyses, it seems pertinent to point out that whereas about half the authors are Americans, others are British, Dutch, German, French, Swedish, Indian, Philippine, Ghanaian, and Singaporean.

In the face of limits to my own qualifications, I found invaluable the judgment, counsel, and assistance of students, friends, and colleagues. Particularly appreciated was the indispensable assistance extended to me by Marcia Cline and Dr. Michael Libal, and later by Martin Baach. Numerous colleagues who offered valuable advice and critical suggestions include Professors Walter Dean Burnham, David Chalmers, John A. Gardiner, Harold D. Lasswell, Rene Lemarchand, Victor T. LeVine, John Kautsky, and Robert Salisbury. I would also like to acknowledge the translation work of Peggy Hofmann and Karl Kurtz. Finally, I would like to note the great encouragement provided by my editor, Herbert J. Addison, who nursed this volume along with commendable dedication.

A. J. H.

St. Louis, Missouri
March 1970

Contents

PART 1

The Context of Analysis

Part 1 of this book is generally preliminary in nature, providing the basic tools, critical standards, and background information that will enable the student to approach and evaluate the subsequent readings with the proper perspective. Thus the three chapters that comprise the first section contain reading selections that approach the subject of corruption from different but equally fundamental points of view.

DEFINITIONS, CONCEPTS, AND CRITERIA (CHAPTER ONE)

Any attempt to analyze the concept of corruption must contend with the fact that in English and other languages the word *corruption* has a history of vastly different meanings and connotations. In some eras, for instance the 1900s in the United States, corruption was one of the most frequently employed terms in the political vocabulary. According to a critic contemporary with this period, Robert C. Brooks (see Selection 6), party orators, journalists, reformers, political philosophers, and historians "stigmatize[d] in this way transactions and conditions of very different kinds . . . [with] little disposition to inquire into the essential nature of corruption and to discriminate in the use of the word." The only connotation that the many usages of the word *corruption* had in common in this period was that it was somehow the antithesis of *reform, rationality,* and the demands of the public weal.

Thus, even the more thoughtful and objective writers of this earlier era would have been nonplussed had they read Samuel Huntington's judgment (Selection 50) in a 1968 publication that "corruption may thus be functional to the maintenance of a political system in the same way that reform is." As is implied in Huntington's usage and elsewhere in the contemporary social science literature, the term *corruption* has developed a more specific meaning with regard to kinds of behavior and a much less polarized meaning with regard to ethical connotations. At times, indeed, it is employed in a context that is almost totally value-free, as in this passage (from Selection 52) by the economist, Nathaniel Leff:

> Corruption is an extra-legal institution used by individuals or groups to gain influence over the actions of the bureaucracy. As such the existence of corruption *per se* indicates only that these groups participate in the decision-making process to a greater extent than would otherwise be the case.

VARIETIES OF MEANINGS

A careful examination of what past and present writers seem to have intended when they employed the term *corruption* in political contexts reveals an even broader catalog of usages and potential ambiguities. Some reasons for this become more apparent by referring to the *Oxford English Dictionary,* where we find that only one of nine commonly accepted definitions for the term is applicable to political contexts: "Perversion or destruction of integrity in the discharge of public duties by bribery or favour; the use or existence of corrupt practices, especially in a state, public corporation, etc."

The *OED* categorizes the nine meanings of corruption as follows:

1. *Physical*—for example, "The destruction or spoiling of anything, especially by disintegration or by decomposition with its attendant unwholesomeness and loathsomeness; putrefaction."

2. *Moral*—the "political" definition already given comes under this category. Another definition in this category is: "A making or becoming morally corrupt; the fact or condition of being corrupt; moral deterioration or decay; depravity."

3. *The perversion of anything from an original state of purity*—for example, "The perversion of an institution, custom, and so forth from its primitive purity; an instance of this perversion."

The present usage of the term *corruption* in political contexts has obviously been colored by the meanings in the "moral" category, and in earlier times usage was frequently colored by the meanings in the two other categories, especially by those in the third category. Thus the author of a nineteenth-century encyclopedia article entitled "Corruption in Politics" developed his discussion essentially in terms of meanings derived by way of Montesquieu from Aristotle, who, for instance, conceived of *tyranny* as a "corrupted" variant of monarchy.[1]

CONTEMPORARY SOCIAL SCIENCE DEFINITIONS

The variety of definitions employed by contemporary social scientists interested in corruption fortunately does not cover as wide a span as those given in the OED. Among them we can identify usages that seek to define corruption in terms of one of three kinds of basic models or concepts. The largest group of social science writers follow the OED definition and relate their definitions of *corruption* essentially to concepts concerning the duties of the public office. A smaller group develop definitions that are primarily related to demand, supply, and exchange concepts derived from economic theory; while a third group discuss corruption more with regard to the concept of the public interest.

Public-Office-Centered Definitions

Definitions of corruption that relate most essentially to the concept of the public office and to deviations from norms binding upon its incumbents are

[1] "Corruption in Politics," *Cyclopaedia of Political Science, Political Economy, and U.S. History,* I. Chicago: Rand McNally, 1882, pp. 672–674.

well illustrated in the work of three authors—David H. Bayley, M. McMullan, and J. S. Nye—who have concerned themselves with the problems of development in various continents. According to Bayley's definition of the word (Selection 54),

Corruption, while being tied particularly to the act of bribery, is a general term covering misuse of authority as a result of considerations of personal gain, which need not be monetary.

M. McMullan (Selection 32) says that

A public official is corrupt if he accepts money or money's worth for doing something that he is under duty to do anyway, that he is under duty not to do, or to exercise a legitimate discretion for improper reasons.

J. S. Nye (Selection 58) defines corruption as

. . . behavior which deviates from the normal duties of a public role because of private-regarding (family, close private clique), pecuniary or status gains; or violates rules against the exercise of certain types of private-regarding influence. This includes such behavior as bribery (use of reward to pervert the judgement of a person in a position of trust); nepotism (bestowal of patronage by reason of ascriptive relationship rather than merit); and misappropriation (illegal appropriation of public resources for private-regarding uses).

Market-Centered Definitions

Definitions in terms of the theory of the market have been developed particularly by those authors dealing with earlier Western and contemporary non-Western societies, in which the norms governing public officeholders are not clearly articulated or are nonexistent. Leff's definition, cited earlier, would fall into this category, as would the definitions of Jacob van Klaveren and Robert Tilman. Van Klaveren (Selection 2) states that

A corrupt civil servant regards his public office as a business, the income of which he will . . . seek to maximize. The office then becomes a "maximizing unit." The size of his income depends . . . upon the market situation and his talents for finding the point of maximal gain on the public's demand curve.

Robert Tilman (Selection 7) holds that

Corruption involves a shift from a mandatory pricing model to a free-market model. The centralized allocative mechanism, which is the ideal of modern bureaucracy, may break down in the face of serious disequilibrium between supply and demand. Clients may decide that it is worthwhile to risk the known sanctions and pay the higher costs in order to be assured of receiving the desired benefits. When this happens bureaucracy ceases to be patterned after the mandatory market and takes on characteristics of the free market.

Public-Interest-Centered Definitions

Some writers feel that the first set of definitions is too narrowly conceived and the second set too broadly conceived. They tend to maintain that the embattled concept of "public interest" is not only still useful but necessary to illustrate the essence of concepts like corruption. Carl Friedrich, for instance, contends that

> The pattern of corruption can be said to exist whenever a power-holder who is charged with doing certain things, i.e., who is a responsible functionary or officeholder, is by monetary or other rewards not legally provided for induced to take actions which favour whoever provides the rewards and thereby does damage to the public and its interests.[2]

Arnold A. Rogow and H. D. Lasswell (Selection 5) maintain that

> A corrupt act violates responsibility toward at least one system of public or civic order and is in fact incompatible with (destructive of) any such system. A system of public or civic order exalts common interest over special interest; violations of the common interest for special advantage are corrupt.

WHOSE NORMS SET THE CRITERIA?

The definitions employed in the first and third of the categories just discussed directly raise the question encountered in all normative analysis: Which norms are the ones that will be utilized to distinguish corrupt from noncorrupt acts? If the definitions are public-office-centered, then which statement of the rules and norms governing public officeholders is to be employed? If the definitions are public-interest-centered, then whose evaluation of the public's interest is to be operationalized? Definitions couched in terms of market theory appear to bypass this problem, but in fact they do not. They too imply that somewhere there is an authority that distinguishes between the rules applicable to public officials and those applicable to businessmen operating in the free market, or that there are certain characteristics that distinguish a "black market" from the free market.

Political scientists of an earlier generation tried to deal with the problem of norm setting with reference to the legal rules provided by statute books and court decisions. Thus behavior was judged by James Bryce to be either permissible or corrupt in accordance with the criteria established by legislators and judges:

> Corruption may be taken to include those modes of employing money to attain private ends by political means which are criminal or at least illegal, because they induce persons charged with a public duty to transgress that duty and misuse the functions assigned to them.[3]

[2] Carl J. Friedrich, "Political Pathology," *Political Quarterly,* 37 (1966), p. 74.
[3] James Bryce, *Modern Democracies,* II. New York: St. Martin's, 1921, p. 524.

But most contemporary social scientists would echo the skepticism that Robert Brooks articulated in 1910 (Selection 6) as to whether legal definitions alone would suffice:

> Definitions of corrupt practices . . . found in every highly developed legal code . . . are scarcely broad enough to cover the whole concept as seen from the viewpoint of political science or ethics. The sanctions of positive law are applied only to those more flagrant practices which past experience has shown to be so pernicious that sentiment has crystallized into statutory prohibitions and adverse judicial decisions. Even within this comparatively limited circle clearness and precision are but imperfectly attained.

The author of the article on "Corruption, Political," in the *Encyclopedia of the Social Sciences* agreed that "the question of formal legality . . . is not the essence of the concept." The normative judgments that should be used as criteria, he thought, were the judgments of the elite: "Where the best opinion and morality of the time, examining the intent and setting of an act, judge it to represent a sacrifice of public for private benefit, then it must be held to be corrupt."[4]

The definition suggested by Senturia raises numerous problems, namely those related to the difficulties of identification, operationalization, and uniqueness. Although social scientists often select particular elite groups with reference to status and other criteria, few claim to have developed specific techniques for identifying in any society a sample that would represent "the best opinion of the time." Even if this were accomplished, Senturia's particularistic emphasis would require that this fairly large body of elites serve as a jury for each particular case. Their findings, in effect, would relate only to their society of that particular era.

A consensus of the "best opinion" in a time and place, such as Britain in 1960, could presumably establish criteria beyond which private-regarding behavior would be considered corrupt in the contemporary setting. However, it would then be impossible to compare either the extent or the varieties of political corruption between the situations prevailing of Britain in 1960 and in 1860 because of the uniqueness of the suggested definition. This difficulty would apply equally to attempts to compare, say, bureaucratic corruption in nineteenth-century Russia and twentieth-century Chicago. Another difficulty in relying too much on any one elite opinion is that the incumbent elite may change drastically as the result of revolution or decolonization. Thus, in the course of decolonization, the criteria by which the colonial rulers had punished corruption among native officials and subjects were radically diluted within a short time when the opinion of the postcolonial native politicians de-emphasized many of the taboos that had been attached to private-regarding behavior. Still later, in many African and Asian countries, behavior that was widely accepted by the ruling politicians one

[4] Joseph J. Senturia, "Corruption, Political," *Encyclopedia of the Social Sciences,* IV. New York: Crowell-Collier-Macmillan, 1930–1935, p. 449.

month was heavily stigmatized the next month after spartan-minded officers successfully carried through a coup d'état.

WESTERN VERSUS NON-WESTERN STANDARDS

If one does not accept the criteria established by law or the norms of a small elite group as delimiting political corruption, how far can one go in delineating the relevant norms with reference to the standards of a more diverse set of reference groups and codes? At present this problem presents itself most directly for those social scientists who have sought to analyze corruption in developing countries where mores rooted in two very distinct milieu govern the standards of political and bureaucratic behavior. David H. Bayley (Selection 53) has outlined the resultant problem posed for the objective investigator:

> It not infrequently happens . . . in developing non-Western societies that existing moral codes do not agree with Western norms as to what kinds of behavior by public servants should be condemned. The Western observer is faced with an uncomfortable choice. He can adhere to the Western definition, in which case he lays himself open to the charge of being censorious and he finds that he is condemning not abhorrent behavior, but normal acceptable operating procedure. On the other hand, he may face up to the fact that corruption, if it requires moral censure, is culturally conditioned. He then argues that an act is corrupt if the surrounding society condemns it. This usage, however, muddies communication, for it may be necessary then to assert in the same breath that an official accepts gratuities but is not corrupt.

Given this alternative, authors like Bayley prefer to build upon the "Western denotative meaning of corruption," even in analyzing non-Western systems. This "imposition" on the rest of the world of Western standards in evaluating behavior may well be, at this stage of research and theory building, a prerequisite to meaningful comparative analysis of political corruption phenomena. In general terms (more with regard to bureaucratic than to electoral corruption) there probably does exist today a broad consensus among Western elites and non-elites as to which kinds of behavior are clearly conceived of as corrupt. This consensus has gradually developed over the past century as will be traced in the subsequent section. But the norms embodied in a definition such as that of Nye, quoted earlier, are surely built upon more than the personal preferences of a small clique of academic political moralizers. It is highly probable that any elite or even mass survey of attitudes in Western countries would result in overwhelming support for the proposition that the kinds of deviations from public rules and the kinds of self-regarding behavior that are included in Nye's definition should be labeled corrupt, and guilty practitioners stigmatized accordingly. Writers such as Bayley admit that this consensus is limited rather than universal, but they argue that the norms expressed by it are the only ones that can possibly be applied cross-culturally and that we should go ahead and do so. In further defense of his strategy, Bayley argues that:

the intelligentsia, and especially top-level civil servants, in most underdeveloped nations are familiar with the Western label "corruption," and they apply it to their own countries. . . . It is not unfair, therefore, to make comparative statements between West and non-West based upon Webster's definition. Such judgements will be readily understood by the nation-building elites in most developing countries.

THE EVOLUTION OF PUBLIC-OFFICE CONCEPTS AND RULES (CHAPTER TWO)

The conditions that cause similar forms of private-regarding behavior to be perceived as corrupt in contemporary Western societies and as perfectly acceptable in many non-Western settings may be analyzed in terms of concepts derived from the definitional approaches discussed in Chapter One. The approach emphasized in Chapter Two is centered on the public office concept. The general relevance of this approach lies in the fact that officials and the general population in most contemporary Western systems recognize the self-denying inhibitions associated with institutioned public-office roles; in non-Western societies such self-denying inhibitions are far less frequent. It therefore becomes significant to attempt to trace how in the process of modernization and bureaucratization in Western societies the holders of public offices came to be subject to norms and rules that were scarcely applicable to their predecessors.

The crucial significance of the degree of institutionalization of the public-office concept was recognized by Joseph Senturia. After defining political corruption as "the misuse of public power for private profit," he added an important caveat: "Not all acts which benefit the office-holder at the expense of the people are corrupt, else the term would include all taxation by an absolute monarch to provide accustomed luxuries for his family and court, all sacrifices and gifts given to the priestly class in theocracies."[5] Where a position of political power was regarded as the fruit of inheritance or property rights, the attempt to distinguish the private from the public responsibilities of the officeholder is doomed to failure. The selection of articles in Chapter Two was guided by the aim of illustrating how, in the process of modernization, distinct public responsibilities were gradually built into the public-office concept, how earlier property claims to office were gradually disappropriated, and how bureaucratic concepts of the office were introduced in varying ways in European and American political systems.

The drawback of the public-office-centered definition is that it virtually forecloses discussions of corruption in prebureaucratic systems. Thus those scholars who seek to apply the concept of corruption in such contexts tend to utilize concepts developed from one of the alternative definitions. Jacob van Klaveren (Selection 8) and Bert F. Hoselitz (Selection 9), for example, tend to employ

[5] Joseph J. Senturia, "Corruption, Political," p. 448.

market-centered definitions with which, as economic historians, they are intimately familiar. Their articles are included both because of their inherent merit and because they may serve to illustrate attempts to discuss the incidence of corruption somewhat independently of the norms developed through bureaucratization.

PUBLIC OFFICES IN PREBUREAUCRATIC SYSTEMS

In framing his definition of the public official's position within modern bureaucratic systems, Max Weber stressed contrasts to practices in prebureaucratic systems, which serve as a key take-off point for this discussion:

> Legally and actually, officeholding is not considered ownership of a source of income, to be exploited for rents or emoluments in exchange for the rendering of certain services, as was normally the case in the Middle Ages. . . . Rather entrance into an office . . . is considered an acceptance of a specific duty or fealty to the purpose of the office in return for the grant of a secure existence. It is decisive for the modern loyalty to an office that, in the pure type, it does not establish a relationship to a person, like the vassal's or disciple's faith under feudal or patrimonial authority, but rather is devoted to impersonal and functional purposes.[6]

Among the varieties of premodern, prebureaucratic systems the most important was that based upon patrimonial domination. The Inca society, discussed by Jacob van Klaveren, clearly fits into this category, although the degree of control here exercised by the ruler over the economy was much higher than prevailed in most historical patrimonial systems. (For a deviating interpretation see Murra.[7]) Under patrimonial systems a ruler could legitimately engage in a self- or family-centered distribution of the national income to the extreme of the Inca model, but whether or not he tried to do so, no one could seek to challenge his decision making as illegitimate or corrupt. For the patriarchal ruler knew no distinction between his authority over his household and that over the rest of his realm. He wielded his power at his own discretion, unencumbered by rules, insofar as he was not limited by tradition or by competing powers.[8] The ruler's officials and officers were likewise unencumbered by any rules other than the changeable ones embodied in the ruler's instructions. If the officials diverted many resources to their private ends, they were not breaching any rules, unless these were embodied in atypically specific instructions from the ruler himself. In that case deviance constituted insubordination rather than corruption. We would therefore agree with Van Klaveren that "by definition, corruption does not occur" in the Inca and other systems based upon pure patrimonial domination.

In feudal Europe the problem was not that all constitutional and economic power was centralized in one ruler but rather that offices had come to be per-

---

[6] Max Weber, *Economy and Society,* III. New York: Bedminster Press, 1968, p. 959.

[7] John V. Murra, "On Inca Political Structure," in Verne F. Ray, ed., *Systems of Political Control and Bureaucracy in Human Societies.* Seattle: American Ethnological Society, 1958, pp. 30–41.

[8] Weber, *Economy and Society,* p. 1007.

ceived as properties rather than being associated with assigned duties. As the "appropriation" of offices progressed, the ruler's power fell apart into various powers, which became the property of various privileged individuals. As Weber argued, "Whatever traces of (an objectively defined official duty) there are disappear altogether with the treatment of the office as benefice or property."[9]

PUBLIC OFFICE AS BENEFICE OR PROPERTY

The appropriation of benefices to officeholders was seen by Weber as characteristic both of the feudal system and of the early modern patrimonial-bureaucratic state. The feudal period was most strongly associated with *landed benefices,* which assigned office land for the incumbent's own use in the manner of a fief, thus giving the benefice holder and his heirs great autonomy from the ruler. Under early modern patrimonialism there was some reassertion of the ruler's control, but this period was characterized by the widespread and continued use of fee benefices, under which the ruler assigned to a favorite or to a purchaser the right to receive certain fees due him from his subjects. Thus the office could also become hereditary in the family of the original favorite or turn into the patrimonial possession of the purchaser.

Through the institutionalization of the landed benefice system in the feudal period, many royal officials were turned into landed nobility, whose rights to their offices came to be regarded as inalienable fiefs or as the personal property of the incumbents. The factors that shielded the nobility against any possible charges of mismanagement of office also held for the prince. "Just as the individual holders of fiefs and benefices and the other possessors of appropriated powers exercise their authority by virtue of privileges guaranteed by the prince, so his own power is considered a personal privilege, his prerogative, which should be recognized and safe-guarded by the fief-holders and other power-holders."[10] Otto Hintze argued that during this period the office became increasingly an annex of the fief, to the point where the fief was regarded as the essential attribute of which the official powers were mere appendixes. Of course the king had to have some officials who would help him carry on his own duties, but even these officials did not usually regard public office as a career. As late as the fifteenth century public officeholding tended to be only a temporary phase in the life of a knight or cleric, at the conclusion of which he hoped to be rewarded with a fief or a "living."[11]

In the early patrimonial-bureaucratic state the practice of remunerating officials by means of fees had the effect of making the officials' income largely dependent upon his "rapacity and ingenuity." It is thus seen by Koenraad W. Swart (Selection 10) and others to have been "very irrational" from the perspective of developing a responsible administrative instrument. However, says Swart,

---

[9] Weber, *Economy and Society,* p. 1040.
[10] Weber, *Economy and Society,* p. 1086.
[11] Otto Hintze, "Der Beamtenstand," *Soziologie und Geschichte.* Göttingen, 1964, pp. 66–125.

"the system . . . had great advantages in a society in which it was difficult to check on local officials because of a widespread dishonesty, relatively large distances, and a primitive administrative technique. In this way much accounting and transferring of money was avoided, and the official was interested in the execution of his duties." Bert F. Hoselitz (Selection 9) emphasizes the same explanation in more systemic terms when he notes that the redefinition of the public office in terms of property concepts strengthens the goal-attainment as against the integrative functions of the officialdom.

THE GROWTH OF A PERMANENT OFFICIALDOM

Changes in recruitment patterns that occurred as the result of the decline of the feudal system and the reassertion of central patrimonial authority led only very gradually, and by no means unilinearly, to tighter definitions of the nature of public offices and of the duties and norms incumbent upon those who hold them. Starting in the sixteenth century, budding officials began to be recruited more from academically trained young men, bourgeois as well as aristocratic, who entered consciously into life careers as "royal servants." However, due mainly to the prevailing system of remuneration, public office remained in many respects a species of private enterprise. Although they received fixed salaries, the royal servants remained, in Prussia and elsewhere, "the legitimate collectors of elastic and often very lucrative emoluments of office," which entitled them to the private appropriation of a certain share in the fees, collected both on behalf of the ruler and on behalf of the municipal and ecclesiastical treasuries within their jurisdictions.[12]

Van Klaveren, who in contrast seeks to make his definition of corruption applicable to the feudal and early modern periods, perceives the newly developed civil service as soon comfortably nesting in next to the privileged positions that the older "intermediary groups," such as the nobility and the patricians, who had established for themselves in the estate society. Since Van Klaveren attributes to intermediary groups an inherent tendency to "nurture" corruption, he sees the new career civil servants as joining other estates in attempts to exploit the people and to appropriate public wealth to their own ends. Their rise in influence merely results in "a rechanneling of corruption-incomes in favor of civil servants and courtiers."

Van Klaveren's attempt to develop theoretical concepts applicable to corruption by combining models from political and economic theory is an interesting one, although we cannot agree entirely with the way in which he elaborates them. Thus he seems to go too far when he argues also that corruption, by definition, cannot occur in "constitutions built upon popular sovereignty." By positing that in democracies "civil servants are only executive instruments of the people's will," he places himself in a situation where he has to argue that logically the instruments cannot exploit their masters. This may be logically defensible, but

[12] Hans Rosenberg, *Bureaucracy, Aristocracy, and Autocracy: The Prussian Experience, 1660–1885*. Cambridge, Mass.: Harvard University Press, 1958, p. 103.

it is empirically refutable. By linking corruption to the duties of the public office, it is possible to speak theoretically about corrupt practices under *all* kinds of constitutions where the concept of the public office has been reasonably developed.

The Sale of Offices

In many parts of continental Europe the reemergence of a powerful merchant class and the growing importance of a highly developed money economy soon resulted in something like a "refeudalization" of large parts of the career officialdom. For in order to meet pressing financial demands, rulers adopted, to varying degrees, the practice of selling offices (*venalité des offices*), which became objects of trade and exchange. The purchasers of these offices served in them as a matter of right, and thus the king was prevented from choosing his officials on the basis of their ability or reliability.

Royal rulers during this period of absolutism were still not subject to any significant constitutional rules that limited their choice of alternative techniques for achieving the goals of the state. Had they been subject to such rules, they would have run as much chance of being accused of corruption for selling judgeships as do contemporary American Presidents for appointing large campaign contributors to ambassadorial positions. For once the sale of offices became officially regulated so that the proceeds flowed into the treasuries of the king and the state, they ceased to constitute a drain of public resources toward private-regarding ends. The king used the proceeds from the sale of offices to meet the costs of military campaigns, just as contemporary parties use financial contributions to meet the costs of election campaigns, and both procedures are seen as goals asserted to be related to the public interest.

Bert Hoselitz (Selection 9) doubts whether, "under the conditions existing in sixteenth- and seventeenth-century Europe the saleability of offices had any significant impact upon the degree of corruption in government." Like Van Klaveren, then, he perceives that excessive private-regarding resource extraction during this period can be conceived of in terms of "corruption." From this perspective the main question is: Which group of officeholders would tend to be relatively more conscientious and relatively less greedy—those who received their office because they were favorites of the king or those who purchased their office from the king? Montesquieu was one of a number of reform-minded writers of the time who actually supported the sale of public office over other methods of appointment, because "chance will furnish better subjects than the prince's choice."[13] Thus, whereas today the venality of office is considered a form of political corruption, it was then perceived as a check on corruption. Jeremy Bentham, who saw the British aristocracy as being particularly prone to self-indulgence, also favored the sale-of-office principle, because he believed that it would allow more of the wealthier and more moral middle-class types to have access to high government posts.[14]

---

[13] Charles Secondat de Montesquieu, *The Spirit of the Laws.* New York: Hafner, 1949, p. 69.

[14] Jeremy Bentham, "The Rationale of Reward," *Works,* Vol. 5. Edinburgh, 1863, pp. 246–248.

Appointments in Exchange for Parliamentary Support

By comparison with contemporaneous practices in France, fewer offices were sold and more were given away by the crown in eighteenth-century Britain. This was primarily due to the fact that the British monarch's ministers had an overriding concern that their French equivalents did not have to face up to: they had to maintain pro-Government majorities in an elected parliament. In Britain it was not so much administrative posts as seats in the House of Commons that had acquired a quasi-proprietary character—"they were a valuable inheritance or a costly acquisition from which proper returns were expected."[15] Some members ensured their reelection through tiny electorates by personal favors or family influence; others felt themselves primarily responsible to small cliques or powerful patrons in their respective constituencies. By the early eighteenth century the promise of government jobs had become a main means through which pro-Government members of Parliament rounded up marginal voters in their boroughs. By the time of the accession of George III, in many boroughs "few extensive electoral interests could be maintained except with the help of Government patronage lavished at the recommendation of the borough patron."[16] These practices were long legitimatized by "a universal belief that the politically active portion of the community had a legitimate claim to maintenance by the State, just as the medieval knight had a claim to maintenance by the lord."[17]

The crown, that is to say the king's personally appointed ministers who managed the Government for him, possessed four different kinds of influence through which it could sway House of Commons members and other politically powerful individuals: money, patronage, honors, and "imperceptible influence." Ministers could employ funds from the government budget as "side-payments" because there was still no clear-cut distinction between public property and the private property of the king, and because Parliament possessed practically no control over expenditures. Honors, contracts, and commissions in the army and navy could also strengthen the crown's hand, but as Samuel E. Finer (Selection 12) writes, "these loaves and fishes were not enough, by themselves, to keep the constitution working. The public service was a fourth basket of spoils . . . and . . . it could, up to a point, be expanded at need, to meet the exigencies of a political crisis."

THE BUREAUCRATIC CONCEPT OF THE PUBLIC OFFICIAL

What kings gave they could in theory somehow or other take away. In actual European practice it took a number of centuries before their successors were effectively able to expropriate the offices that their ancestors had sold or

[15] J. Donald Kingsley, *Representative Democracy*. Yellow Springs, Ohio: Antioch Press, 1944, p. 26.
[16] Sir Lewis B. Namier, *The Structure of Politics at the Accession of George III*, 2d ed. New York: St. Martin's, 1957, p. 169.
[17] Kingsley, *Representative Democracy*, p. 26.

swapped away. Max Weber[18] sees this process of expropriation of the officials as "a complete parallel to the process through which the small, independent producers were deprived of the ownership of their tools and equipment." Where the one group was deprived of the means of production in favor of the capitalist, the others were deprived of the means of administration in favor of the ruler. Finally, in the course of the nineteenth century, the concept of the public office as private property disappeared and was replaced by the concept of the office-holder as bound to the norms and rules of the bureaucratic system of which his office was a part. An essential financial prerequisite for this change was a radical revamping of the remuneration system. With Prussia and Revolutionary France leading the way, European states abolished all manner of benefices as income sources for civil servants and replaced them with regularized money salaries. By custom an official received an income sufficient to support a standard of living appropriate to his social position, but the differential favoring the higher officials eroded in the course of the century. Whereas in 1800 the highest French officials received salaries that exceeded those of their lowest subordinates by 100 : 1, the ratio was to decline to 25 : 1 by 1900, and to 6 : 1 by 1960.

The Prussian Example

Compared to parliamentary England and autocratic Russia, Prussia under the Hohenzollern monarchy had already in the eighteenth century drawn "far sharper lines between private assets and dynastic funds, private persons and public officials."[19] New concepts of authority, allegiance, and public responsibility helped to develop in the Prussian administration massive barriers against bureaucrats bent on engaging in business for profit. These barriers had been created in part by three successive Prussian monarchs, who were exceptional by European standards in devoting their total energies to the affairs of state and thus set examples that helped them demand equally unstinting sacrifices from their civil servants. Other German states and Austria followed this pattern of adopting highly bureaucratized constitutions.

In Germany the distinction between tenured civil servants (*Beamte*) and other more varied kinds of private employees was maintained through the careful nurturing of legal and status differences. Thus the remuneration paid to civil servants (*Besoldung*) was distinguished terminologically from the salaries paid to other kinds of employees (*Lohn, Gehalt*). An article on *Besoldung* in the *Staatslexikon,* a mid-nineteenth-century Liberal encyclopedia, contrasts German recruitment of highly trained full-time officials with American and English patterns, but emphasizes that the more exacting requirements necessitate high levels of remuneration in order to attract sufficient numbers of able candidates to the service of the state. Bribery is characterized in its effects on the state and citizens as the most "pernicious of all crimes, equally destructive of the foundations of society as of faith and loyalty, of public morality as of from principles and a fatal danger to all superior as well as inferior goods of society." As anti-

[18] Weber, *Economy and Society,* p. 1087.

[19] Rosenberg, *Bureaucracy, Aristocracy and Autocracy,* p. 105.

dotes to bribery and corruption, the authors emphasize good moral examples set by the government leaders themselves, adequate levels of civil service remuneration ("A hungry civil servant costs the state and the citizens one hundred times as much as an adequately paid one"), and freedom of the press.[20]

Within the contexts of the bureaucratically evolved constitutions, especially in Germany and Austria, public officeholders became subject to a very far-reaching and specific set of obligations that went quite a long way toward inhibiting potential conflicts of interest between the duties of the civil servant and his personal material interests. Otto Hintze described the position of German *Beamten* as being based on a relation of service and authority of a unique kind, and spelled out the specific demands which the state made on the official:

> Not only his working capacity but in a certain sense his whole personality is claimed. He may not receive gifts, he may not exercise a profession, he may not have any side earnings at all without the permission of his superiors, as officeholder he is expected to devote all his working capacity to the state; the office is his only and exclusive calling.[21]

Germany differed from other countries particularly in regard to the strong peer-group reinforcement of official norms, such as those prohibiting unauthorized gift taking or the development of outside economic interests by the official or even members of his family.

Corruption in Russian Officialdom

The incidence of corruption is obviously a function not only of the development of norms, but also of the manner in which they are enforced. In the course of the nineteenth century the legal definitions of the duties and rules pertaining to public servants came to be quite uniform throughout the bureaucratic structures of continental Europe, and this facilitated the analytical problem of comparison at the cross-cultural level. There is a great amount of evidence that Russian officials remained very corrupt even after the majority of other countries had succeeded in developing adequate checks against most forms of overtly corrupt practices. As the Andersons point out (Selection 11): "Russia as well as Central and Western Europe had legislation prohibiting officials from becoming involved in questionable economic dealings: the difference lay in the fact that Germany and Austria enforced the law. . . ." The czars, who seemed specially lenient toward corruption among high officials and even ministers, and forgave them easily, were in this respect very different from the German rulers. Facing the much vaster problem of imperial integration with poorly developed technological and human resources, they were probably, in Hoselitz' terms, still much more preoccupied with integrative than goal-attainment functions. In fact, as the Andersons point out, contemporary apologists for the

[20] Rotteck-Welcker, *Staatslexikon,* rev. ed., p. 454.
[21] Hintze, "Der Beamtenstand," p. 72.

Russian conditions spoke very much as do spokesmen for underdeveloped countries today when they insisted that it was a mistake to impose the German system of administration upon the Russians since it "was utterly unsuited to their nature."

Public-Office Conceptions in Britain and America

The definitions of the nature and obligation of the public office have generally remained more diffuse in the Anglo-Saxon common-law countries than on the Continent. Whereas the Continental code-law countries could easily remodel their legal systems through the adoption of comprehensive codes, norms in the English-speaking countries had to be operationalized in terms of a more complex sequence of legislative and judicial acts and precedents. Thus, even in the twentieth century discussions of public officers and their duties have had to be very circuitous because "the terminology and the precedents relied upon in interpretation developed before public administration had developed its present scope and complexity."[22]

In Britain judicial decisions that serve as important precedent date back to the beginning of the civil service reform movement there, especially a 1783 decision which held that "a man accepting an office of trust concerning the public, especially if attended with profit, is answerable criminally to the king for misbehavior in his office." American and English courts have followed the same rule that the public officer, occupying a position of trust, is bound by the duties of a fiduciary. But, in MacMahon's words, "nowhere . . . has the definition of public office been more difficult than in the United States. Nowhere has judicial discussion of the matter been more recurrent, so prolix and in general so unsatisfactory."[23]

Finer's examination (Selection 12) of the sharply contrasting developments of public service rules in the two countries in the early part of the nineteenth century is highly illuminating. After the successful revolution against the British mother country, with its traditional society and the mutual obligations that it had engendered, the original American public service was spartan and honest compared to "the loaded compost heap of corrupt influence," which was Burke's characterization of its British equivalent. But soon the development of party competition developed in the United States the same incentives that in Britain had triggered the development of the "old" patronage system: administrative appointments had to be used for the purchase of electoral and legislative support. In Britain a two-party system was also developing; but in contrast to post-Jacksonian America, the administrative service became gradually severed from and insulated against party political influences. Helpful to the British reformers was the fact that the phenomenon that became most characteristic of the "new" American patronage, namely the rotation of offices as the "ins" became the "outs," had earlier not been widely prevalent in Britain because the freehold concept of office had made it legally difficult for incumbents to be "expropriated." Thus, as Finer points

---

[22] Arthur W. MacMahon, "Public Office," *Encyclopedia of the Social Sciences,* VI, p. 665.
[23] MacMahon, "Public Office," p. 665.

out, "the vices of the British system created a bulwark against rotation" and helped make Britain rather than America the ideal model for late-nineteenth-century administrative reformers.

BEHAVIORAL AND NORMATIVE PERSPECTIVES ON THE "INCIDENCE" OF CORRUPTION (CHAPTER THREE)

Most actions that are considered corrupt by norm enforcers within or critics outside a political system are basically varieties of exchange transactions. Depending on the technique employed, the transactions create varying degrees of specificity of obligation on the parts of the exchangers. Bribery is the most frequently cited technique of corruption, because it creates a very specific obligation on the part of the officeholder. The more that political exchange transactions engender specific obligations, the more they resemble the prototype of an economic transaction, which rests on a formal contract stipulating the exact quantities to be exchanged. The bribed official typically agrees to undertake or to forego a designated action in return for a designated compensation.

Other kinds of corrupt political exchange agreements are based on obligations that are more vague and that involve less specific quantities.[24] Officials may tacitly agree to extend unspecified forms of future preferment to office seekers or contractors in return for accepting extensive services that have a large but deliberately unspecific value. The more developed the economy, the less specific the benefit is likely to be. A tipoff leading to purchase of stock or real estate holdings that are likely to increase sharply in value will benefit the officeholder much more than will cash presents. Indeed, the more that political exchange resembles social exchange, the more unspecific and the more difficult to classify in terms of corruption it becomes. The more complex the network of social interaction and the more complicated and diverse the ways that tangible benefits can be exchanged, the less likely it is that particular actions can clearly be labelled corrupt. To the extent that their exchange transactions tend to be more direct, the citizens of less-developed countries are indeed somewhat one-sidedly exposed to the easy moral judgments of citizens of more developed societies.

Insofar as more politically developed societies are also more highly integrated societies, they tend to socialize their citizens against the temptations of material gain in ways that are organically related to the basic, supracultural definitions of corruption. If their strong civic and other social norms are effectively internalized by their members, they tend to give a greater subjective reality to "community

---

[24] Harold D. Lasswell, "Bribery." *Encyclopedia of the Social Sciences,* I, pp. 690–692.

interests" in terms of the preferences of their citizens. Thus sanctions in terms of guilt feelings and social disapproval may constitute costs that under certain circumstances may cause commitment to a proposed exchange relationship to appear irrational rather than rational from the perspective of the individual's self-interest.[25] By contrast, in a community like Montegrano (see Selection 13) no community interest or norms to enforce it are perceived to exist, hence the value of a bribe received would be discounted neither by guilt feelings nor by fear of moral condemnation. It is expected that an officeholder will accept bribes when he can get away with it, and indeed community lore ascribes corruptibility to officials almost *ex officio.*

Communities at various levels of sociopolitical development may be related to various prototypical types of exchange relations. In a culture that contains a money economy but where most individuals relate only to collectivities like the family or the tribe, exchanges with other groups closely follow the economic exchange model, since there is limited precedent that might have created trust that nonspecific obligations will ever be repaid. Because the gradual expansion of mutual interaction is accompanied by a parallel growth of mutual trust, there will be a tendency to enter into more exchanges that entail unspecified obligations to well-known clients and patrons whose reliability has been established. Trust in neighbors and identification with the community certainly does not increase monotonically with modernization! As the former peasant becomes an immigrant to an urban environment, whether in his own country or abroad, his environment seems very untrustworthy and he seeks relationships resembling those he has known. Gradually, then, he and his children develop greater faith in their neighbors and greater identification with the community, because the processes of social exchange generate trust in social relations through their recurrent and gradually expanding character.[26]

It is from this conceptual background that we may attempt to approach the "central question for the scientific study of the problem of corruption," which Colin Leys suggests, in Selection 1, should be posed as follows: "In any society, under what conditions is behavior most likely to occur which a significant section of the population will regard as corrupt?" However, because Leys's formulation appears overly ambitious and general at this stage of research and assessment, and the following, more modest form is suggested: "Which of the various forms of behavior that a significant portion of the population regards as corrupt are more likely to be more pervasive in one society than another, and why?"

THE FOUR TYPES OF POLITICAL OBLIGATION RELATIONSHIPS

Our analysis will be developed in terms of four types of political obligation relationships characteristic of communities examined in selections in

---

[25] Peter M. Blau, *Exchange and Power in Social Life.* New York: Wiley, 1964, p. 258. See esp. chap. 4.

[26] Blau, *Exchange and Power in Social Life,* p. 94.

this volume as well as elsewhere in the literature (see Table 1). For each type of community we will seek to show:

1. the relative prevalence of varieties of political behavior which are considered corrupt in terms of Western elite norms regarding officeholding and civic participation.

2. the severity or tolerance with which elite and mass opinions in that community regard the varieties of behavior which are corrupt by official definition.

The Traditional Familist (Kinship) Based System

The community that comes closest to illustrating the familist-based system is Montegrano, as described in Selection 13 by Edward C. Banfield. The "amoral familists" who populate this community distinguish it from kinship-based systems in underdeveloped countries around the globe in that the absence of the "extended family" traditions emphasizes the especially narrow bases of group interests. Here loyalty to the nuclear family is the only loyalty that counts. In contrast to other Mediterranean communities, upper-class inhabitants avoid entering into patron-client relationships with the poorer families. Families are jealous of their neighbors' good fortune even if it has occurred at no cost to themselves. There is not enough trust to support the kind of "political machine" characteristic of American cities, because the voters do not believe in the promises of potential bosses, and the latter have no faith that bribed voters will stay bought. Among appointed officials there is a decided lack of any sense of duty or calling.[27]

The Traditional Patron–Client-Based Systems

Illustrative of the patron–client-based type are the Sicilian and Greek communities studied by anthropologists Jeremy Boissevain (Selection 14) and J. K. Campbell (Selection 15). They exist in the twentieth century but are still the captives of belief and authority patterns rooted in the distant past. Protection is sought outside the family; but in the minds of the simpler peasants the powers of supernatural patron saints and of upper-class patrons blur into one another. Ties to powerful protectors are strong, identification with the general community still quite weak. Through the patron-client relationships, which unlike the kinship relationship is based upon voluntary choice of both parties, a strong sense of reciprocal obligation develops. Friendship ties and those to the patron in particular are viewed as the "throwing stick" that gives the extended family greater range when dealing with established authority. Out of reciprocity the family head pledges his own voting support and that of his entire family to the patron's discretion. The client maintains the dependency tie to the patron because he

[27] Other social scientists have strongly challenged Banfield's thesis that amoral familism is the prime determinant of political behavior and have questioned how representative Montegrano is of other Mediterranean areas. See especially Sydel F. Silverman, "Agricultural Organization, Social Structure and Values in Italy: Amoral Familism Reconsidered," *American Anthropologist,* 70:1 (February 1968), pp. 1–20, and S. Tarrow, *Peasant Communism in Southern Italy*. New Haven, Conn.: Yale University Press, 1967, esp. pp. 67–82.

TABLE 1 TYPES OF COMMUNITY AND POLITICAL EXCHANGE

Characteristic	Traditional Familist (Kinship) Based Systems: Within Families	Traditional Familist (Kinship) Based Systems: Between Families	Traditional Patron–Client-Based System	Modern Boss–Follower-Based System	Modern Civic–Culture-Based System
Archetypal protector	Family Head		Patron Saint	Political Boss	State (Constitution and Courts)
Prototype for political exchange relations	Family Obligation	Economic Exchange	Social and Economic Exchange	Economic and Social Exchange	Social (indirect) Exchange
Strength of community-regarding norms	—	Nil	Weak	Weak	Strong
Denotation of "patron"	—	—	Moral Ideal, Protector, Intermediary	Protector, Intermediary	Benefactor of Community (Art and Education)
Strong reciprocal basis of obligation between chief/patron and client	No	—	Yes	Yes	—
Kinship/friendship network open enough to permit independent "contacts" by client	No	Yes	No (depends)	Yes (depends)	Yes
Collective (Family) obligation for favors to its members	—	Yes	Yes	Yes (depends)	No
Clients directly follow patron-chief in political behavior	Yes	—	Yes	Yes	—
Family obligations perceived as having primary claim on officeholder	Yes	—	Yes	No	No

senses a need for protection that neither the family nor the state is able to provide. In terms of social distance the lowest officials of the state are so far above him that he needs to work through the patron in order to establish favorable contact with it.

The Modern Boss–Follower-Based System

Two types of situations illustrate the boss–patronage-based system. The first is the operation of American big-city political machines in normal (that is, not excessively scandalous) times during most periods in the first half of this century, as analyzed in the writings of A. A. Rogow, H. D. Lasswell, Daniel Bell, James Q. Wilson, and H. J. Ford (see Selections 42, 16, 30, and 28, respectively). The second situation is that of a chronically corrupt town, Wincanton, as analyzed by John Gardiner, in Selection 17, where the incidence of "dirty graft" has been a paramount issue for half a century. These communities differ from those in the preceding category by virtue of the fact that they are "wide-open" urban centers based upon highly differentiated economies in which even the greenest immigrant differentiates very clearly between a patron saint and the political boss. Traditionally legitimated social and bureaucratic elites have little direct influence here, for the machine makes the political decisions and the only important question is whether it is headed by a "game politician" or a "gain politician." Nonetheless, many aspects of the boss-follower relationship are modeled on that of the patron-client relationship in the traditional setting. As Ford wrote in 1905, practical experience in American cities showed that "political ideals . . . have a closely limited range. One soon reaches strata of the population in which they disappear and the relation of boss and client appears proper and natural . . . The bosses are no more shamefaced in talking about their grafting exploits than a medieval baron would have been in discussing the produce of his feudal fees and imposts." One of the few differences in the client's situation is that, due to the greater diversity of direct links to the larger society, he has somewhat more discretion as to which mediator to attach himself to, although he may have to move to another ward to effect the change. And most importantly, since these communities are "modern," they foster and adapt to change. Thus, whereas in the traditional patron-client setting, political exchange relationships tend to be based primarily on the social exchange model and secondarily on that of economic exchange, in these modern settings it is the more flexible and adaptable economic exchange model that tends to be dominant.

The Civic–Culture-Based System

The civic–culture-based system of political exchange relationship prevails in "clean," medium-sized towns or suburbs in America or Britain. The citizens do not feel they need to work through an influential intermediary in order to get the benefit of the laws and administrative programs. They have developed strong community-regarding norms, which are supported by viable voluntary associations who repay their volunteer activists in tokens of moral satisfaction rather than money or money's worth. Political exchange relations follow a model of diversified and indirect social exchange. Crude political reciprocity in economic terms, such as the bribe, occurs very rarely. Political obligations insofar as they are still undergirded by economic exchange techniques, assume sophisticated and respectable new forms, such as testimonial dinners, lawyer's fees, consultant contracts, and campaign funds. These communities are "clean" because the political leaders are not bound by reciprocity agreements with lower-class followers, which the latter could utilize as channels for forcing their styles of competition on the more "respectable" strata. In this setting the "patron" still exists, but only in a very attenuated and generalized function. The object of his patronage, directly or indirectly, is the community at large. It may benefit directly from his philanthropy or indirectly from his patronage of creative artists, the value of whose work to the community some rank higher than market prices recognize.

CORRUPT BEHAVIOR INCIDENCE IN THE FOUR TYPES OF COMMUNITIES

All ten types of corrupt behavior listed in Table 2 would be defined corrupt by a scrupulous upholder of Western administrative norms and civic behavior rules, and could be prosecuted in almost any North American or European country by an able public prosecutor who does not mind making enemies or appearing slightly ridiculous among his peers. What we shall attempt to show with reference to these types of corrupt behavior is their varying incidence in the four types of situations, as suggested by a loose form of content analysis of the relevant literature. Behaviors coded SOP are believed to be "standard operating procedure" in the respective locality. Behaviors coded FI are believed to occur with "frequent incidence." Those coded OI are thought to occur with only "occasional incidence." Finally, those coded OO are thought to occur without any regular pattern of incidence, with individual acts of official turpitude being no more frequent than they are in any large organization employing fallible human beings. For convenience in discussion the corrupt behaviors are arbitrarily grouped into three categories, those involving "petty," "routine," and "aggravated" corruption.

Petty Corruption

Petty corruption refers to the bending of official rules in favor of friends, as manifested in the somewhat untruthful reporting of details, the ignoring of cut-off dates, the "fixing" of parking tickets, and so on. It occurs widely in all four settings, although it is not standard practice in the civic-culture town, where it is likely to be frowned upon by purists, but taken advantage of by practical businessmen. In the boss-patronage community it is a widely engaged in practice, even among all residents of the "newspaper wards."

Routine Corruption

Some of the practices listed in the category of routine corruption do occur to some extent in civic-culture towns, but usually only in forms where

TABLE 2 THE INCIDENCE AND EVALUATION OF CORRUPT PRACTICES

Type of Behavior	Traditional Familist (Kinship) Based System		Traditional Patron–Client-Based System		Modern Boss–Patronage-Based System		Modern Civic–Culture-Based System	
	Incidence	Evaluation	Incidence	Evaluation	Incidence	Evaluation	Incidence	Evaluation
Petty Corruption								
Officials deviate from rules in minor ways for benefit of friends	SOP	W	SOP	W	SOP	W	FI	G
Routine Corruption								
Gifts accepted by public officials (or Parties) for generalized good will	SOP	W	SOP	W	SOP	W	OI	B if collectivized G
Nepotism practices in official appointments and contract awarding	SOP	W	SOP	W	SOP	G	OI	B if collectivized G
Officials profit from public decisions through sideline occupations (clean graft)	SOP	W	SOP	W	FI SOP: Wincanton	G	OI	B
Clients pledge votes according to Patron's direction	SOP	W	SOP	W	FI	G	OO	B
Aggravated Corruption								
Clients need patron intervention to get administrative "due process"	SOP	W	FI	G	OI	B	OO	B
Gifts (kickbacks) expected by officials as prerequisite for extending "due process"	SOP	W	FI	G	OI SOP: Wincanton	B	OO	B
Officials tolerate organized crime in return for payoffs	FI	W	FI	G	OI SOP: Wincanton	B	OO	B
Activists suddenly change party allegiance for pecuniary reasons	FI	W	OI	B	OI	B	OO	B
Officials and citizens ignore clear proof of corruption	FI	W	OI	B	OI	B	OO	B

Key: SOP = Standard Operating Procedure; FI = Frequent Incidence; OI = Occasional Incidence; OO = Rare Incidence, Without Regular Pattern
B = Black Corruption; G = Gray Corruption; W = White Corruption

they are sanitized through the "collectivization of the receiver." Thus campaign contributors to political party funds may win some degree of preference as contract bidders or appointive office candidates. In the boss-patronage city, on the other hand, most of these practices were either standard or widely practiced operating procedures, with most material benefits accruing to individuals. Thus, as Daniel Bell (Selection 16) points out, the wealth through which many of the Irish elevated themselves to middle-class status in American cities was to a large degree accumulated in construction, trucking, and waterfront industries, in which prosperity was largely dependent upon favoritism in city contracts. Favoritism, or the guarantee of unequal access, is of course the main lever through which the machine generated the stock of resources from which it diverted the "economic" component of the rewards extended to ward leaders and voters. The boss also used patronage powers to "pay his colleagues for obeying his orders . . . and to bribe elected officials to follow his policy lead." (See Selection 30.)

In the *traditional patron-client* settings many of the gifts received by public officials are less clearly related to specific obligations, but are standard practice in the sense that they recur almost seasonally. Thus, some Greek shepherd families give the village president each spring a gift of cheese, butter, or meat in the hope that this may "moderate his general attitude towards them in the coming months." (See Selection 15.) In return for helping them when they are in trouble, the lawyer-patron, who acts in the general role of a professional fixer, is able to promise the political support of his clients during local and national elections. The assistance of patrons is as essential in applying for a government job as it was some decades ago in Chicago, even though there is no party machine. In Sicily a former municipal employee who sought to regain his job had to mobilize two higher-class patrons before his application was given due consideration. In this setting, therefore, all the activities that would be considered "routine corruption" by official Western standards are standard procedures deeply rooted in more general social relationships and obligations.

Of course, all the syndromes noted above are also standard procedure in the amoral *familist* community of Montegrano. Because families in Montegrano are nuclear rather than extended, and because of the lack of the patron as mediating agent, the exchanges are more nakedly specific and the contracts more short-term in duration. A poor peasant votes for the Christian Democrats because the party has given him a "few days work on the roads each year. . . . If it ceased to give him work and if there were no advantage to be had for voting for another party, he would be a monarchist again." (See Selection 13.)

Aggravated Corruption

In the civic–culture-based community instances of aggravated corruption occur very rarely, if at all.

Among boss–patronage-based communities it is precisely the frequency of incidence of aggravated corruption that distinguishes "reform" periods from "scandal-ridden" ones, or "corrupt cities" from "machine cities." Thus, most of the varieties of corrupt behavior occur only occasionally in the better-run "machine cities" of twentieth-century America, but they were standard practice in the town that John A. Gardiner calls Wincanton (see Selection 17). Whereas in Chicago crime operators could intermittently purchase toleration from various police officials, in Wincanton the syndicate head controlled the police to the extent that he could use it to run rivals out of town. Corrupt mayors made it a standard practice to demand $75 gifts for the approval of building permits and $2000 kickbacks for the awarding of city contracts. The crooked police chief had to pay the mayor $10,000 for his appointment, and was allowed to recoup through payoffs from organized crime. In Wincanton, therefore, the varieties of "dirty graft" and aggravated corruption were as widespread as in any traditional community, except that the more developed state of the economy caused the amounts involved in the corrupt transactions to be much larger.

The incidence pattern of aggravated corruption in the patron-client society seems to differ in two interesting ways from the same pattern in the two other communities. It differs from the boss-patronage community in that the properly connected client can use it to tap a wider variety of services. It is unlikely that anyone in the Wincanton machine would have been of much help in establishing contact with a particular university professor, who would be far less likely to offer the client a thesis that he could hand in as his own. (In the Sicilian context these acts did constitute *political* corruption.) On the other hand, this setting appears to differ from the familist society in that some of the techniques of aggravated corruption are less widely employed. The Greek shepherds conceded that "eating money" (the acceptance of small bribes) was one of the rights of office that the village president needed to exercise in order to support his family. However, they were cautious about offering bribes to higher officials; and if they pledged their votes to a patron, they usually maintained their agreements for a decent period of time. In Montegrano, on the other hand, most of the inhabitants were sure that not only the local officials, but also those up the line to the national government, were corrupt and completely without a sense of obligation to office. This belief encouraged an almost universal tendency among both officials and citizens to ignore proof of corrupt behavior even when it was directly observed and to undertake no initiatives to cooperate with established authority to invoke sanctions.

THE TOLERANCE AND EVALUATION OF CORRUPT PRACTICES

Although behavior fitting into any one of the forty categories in Table 2 could be considered corrupt by some citizen who was particularly conscious of official norms, his interpretations would obviously be shared to a very widely varying degree by his fellow citizens. Indeed, it has been argued that if 99 percent of the community disagrees, then, although one's viewpoint is well-grounded in the applicable legal codes, the action is not considered "corrupt" in that community. It is this problem of normative evaluation that we seek to approach in terms of the shorthand notations of black, gray, or white corruption in Table 2. The evaluation "black corruption" indicates that in that setting that particular action is one which a majority consensus of both elite and mass opinion would condemn and would want to see punished on grounds of principle. "Gray corruption" indicates that some elements, usually elites, may want to see the action punished, others not, and the majority may well be ambiguous. "White corruption" signifies that the majority of both elite and mass opinion probably would not vigorously support an attempt to punish a form of corruption that they regard as tolerable. This implies that they attach less value to the maintenance of the values involved than they do to the costs that might be generated as the result of a change in rule enforcement.

One of the subtler characteristics of norm patterns in the civic-culture community relates to the "grayness" of attitudes toward petty corruption. The general elite disapproval of favoritism would tend to contain its extent, as in John Gardiner's study of ticket-fixing in Massachusetts, even though some forms of "giving consideration" persist. (See Selection 18.) This would be in contrast to the boss-patronage city, where even the reform-minded elements would tend to think that practices such as ticket fixing have to be tolerated. Attitudes toward several forms of "routine" corruption might also tend to be "gray" in the civic-culture setting, with the degree of toleration related essentially to important questions of form. The giving of gifts to public officials and nepotism may be regarded as "black," or punishable, if favors are exchanged at the level of the individual official or firm, but their equivalents are likely to be tolerated if the funds in question are "collectivized" through devices such as party campaign treasuries. Investigations often reveal that individual politicians surreptitiously cross the indistinct line differentiating "gray" from "black" behavior. Thus, in 1967, Senator Thomas Dodd of Connecticut was shown to have diverted to private use funds allegedly raised for his campaign treasury, and this relevation was instrumental in causing his colleagues to levy censure upon him.

In boss-patronage communities much of the "grayness" characterizing attitudes toward forms of "routine" corruption is likely to be associated with sharp differences between attitudes in the poorer, or "river," wards and those in the more well-to-do, or "newspaper," wards. Robert Lane and others have found that the attitude of working-class residents of large cities to reports of governmental corruption is "generally speaking a tolerant one, certainly not indignant, not moralistic, possibly insufficiently censorious."[28] Corrupt practices localized in the poorer sections are likely to be tolerated by middle-class opinion and to be strenuously resisted only when they spread into, or more directly affect, the "respectable" areas of the city. In Wincanton, surveys showed that very significant minorities were willing to be tolerant of varieties of favoritism and "clean graft," which were technically illegal; thus 35 percent thought it all right for city officials to accept presents from companies, and 27 percent had no objections if the mayor profited financially from municipal land purchases as long as the price charged was "fair." The "grayness" of attitudes in the boss-patronage city makes possible a higher threshold of enforcement beneath which multiple forms of "clean graft" and favoritism are tolerated. It is when rings of politicians and

[28] Robert E. Lane, *Political Ideology*. New York: Free Press, 1962, p. 335.

contractors expand their practices to include forms of aggravated corruption which do run counter to the values of the vast majority of the population that a "clean-up" campaign will sooner or later ensue, as John Gardiner illustrates in the Wincanton case.

In the traditional patronage-client community the attitudes toward the various forms of corruption are several shades "lighter" and more tolerant. Thus, most of the routine forms of corruption regarded as "gray" in the American city setting are viewed as "white," or quite acceptable, in this environment. The strength of informal social obligations is too great to permit significant criticism of the widely prevalent practices of nepotism and the purchase of influence. In the words of a local informant, the perception that "in Sicily all friendships are political," leads to acceptance of the fact of life that all politics involves giving preference to one's friends. There the patronage system, which Boissevain (Selection 14) likens to "a parasitic vine," weakens the rule of law to the point where many cases of aggravated corruption are considered as falling into the "gray" rather than "black" area. In Sicily, as in Greece, it is regarded as legitimate for officials to require bribes or patron intervention in order to give the peasant what should be his due according to the law. In contrast to the modern setting, where even lower-class citizens are infused with some measure of egalitarian ideology, the peasants in this kind of community accept the arrogance of officials as an almost legitimate function of their higher social status and regard it as natural that their sympathy can only be aroused through gifts and bribes.

In the familist-based system all of the types of behavior that are considered corrupt by the standards of Western legal norms are considered "white," or acceptable, by the bulk of the population. As effective community-regarding norms are lacking, attitudes will be determined in individual cases in relation to who is doing the corrupting on whose behalf. Since public affairs are conceived to be the exclusive concern of those public officials who are paid to look after them, the latter can expect little citizen cooperation, which would be a prerequisite for norm enforcement. In the face of such total apathy they, too, will incline to ignore evidence of obvious corruption, and thus join the conspiracy of silence that permits most forms of corrupt activity to have a frequent incidence or to become standard operating procedure.

CHAPTER ONE

Definitions, Concepts, and Criteria

1. What Is the Problem about Corruption?

COLIN LEYS[1]

THE "MORALISTIC APPROACH"

The systematic investigation of corruption is overdue. There are three main types of literature in English on the subject: historical studies of corrupt practice in Britain; inquisitional studies, mainly of the USA and the English-speaking West African and Asian countries; and sociological studies which deal with corruption incidentally. So far as I know no general study in English has appeared.[2] One reason for this seems to be a widespread feeling that the facts cannot be discovered, or that if they can, they cannot be proved, or that if they can be proved, the proof cannot be published. All these notions seem dubious. There are nearly always sources of information, some of them—such as court records—systematic in their way, and some of them very circumstantial (like privileged parliamentary debates). Many of the people involved are quite willing to talk. And commissions of enquiry have published large amounts of evidence, obtained by unusual powers of compulsion.

I doubt if it would really be as hard to discover the facts about corruption in most countries as it would be to find out the facts about some legitimate political matters which those involved really want to keep secret. One could even find ways of measuring, within broad limits, the scale and economic effects of some forms of corruption. Publishing the results might present difficulties, but these would only be acute if naming persons were essential to the object of publishing, which is not ordinarily the case in scientific enquiry, even in the social sciences. As anyone who has written on contemporary issues is aware, there are adequate conventions which enable events and incidents to be described anonymously or obliquely without reducing their credibility or value as evidence.

But so far very few people have approached the subject of corruption in this spirit, aiming to describe, measure, analyse, and explain the phenomena in-

1 Professor of Politics, School of Social Studies, University of Sussex, Brighton.

2 The best known English study is perhaps Norman Gash's *Politics in the Age of Peel* (London, 1953). Much of the American literature is reviewed in V. O. Key, *Politics, Parties and Pressure Groups* (New York, 1955), chap. 13, "Party Machine as Interest Group." See also *The Annals of the American Academy of Political and Social Science* (Philadelphia), March 1952, special number on "Ethical Standards in American Public Life." The wide range of reports of commissions of enquiry into colonial malpractice is indicated in the footnotes to Ronald Wraith and Edgar Simpkins' recent work *Corruption in Developing Countries* (London, 1963). While the bulk of this material is from West Africa and deals with local government, there are valuable reports from East Africa, and also from India and Malaya and elsewhere. Unfortunately I have not had an opportunity to study Professor Van Klaveren's series of articles in *Vierteljahrschrift für Sozial- und Wirtschaftsgeschichte* since 1957, referred to in his comments on M. G. Smith's "Historical and Cultural Conditions of Political Corruption among the Hausa," in *Comparative Studies in Society and History* (The Hague), January 1964, pp. 164–198.

SOURCE: Colin Leys, "What Is the Problem about Corruption?" *Journal of Modern African Studies.* 3: 2 (1965), pp. 215–224. By permission of the publisher, Cambridge University Press.

volved.[3] This is curious when one considers the word itself (corruption=to change from good to bad; to debase; to pervert); it denotes patterns of action which derive their significance from the role of value-systems in social behaviour. Similar phenomena, such as suicide, crime, or religious fanaticism, have intrigued sociologists greatly. However, the question of corruption in the contemporary world has so far been taken up almost solely by moralists.

The recent book by Ronald Wraith and Edgar Simpkins on *Corruption in Developing Countries* is of this *genre*. They are concerned with "the scarlet thread of bribery and corruption," with corruption which "flourishes as luxuriantly as the bush and weeds which it so much resembles, taking the goodness from the soil and suffocating the growth of plants which have been carefully, and expensively, bred and tended." It is a "jungle of nepotism and temptation," a "dangerous and tragic situation" in which the enthusiasm of the young African civil servant turns to cynicism, and where there are "not the attitudes of progress and development."[4]

They are aware that the "moralising approach" (their own term) involves a difficulty, namely that their standpoint may differ from that of those who do the things which they regard as corrupt. For instance, they can see that since any African who is so fortunately placed as to be able to get jobs for his relatives is felt (by the relatives at least) to be under an obligation to do so, it is peculiar to call this corrupt: "an act is presumably only corrupt if society condemns it as such, and if the doer is afflicted with a sense of guilt when he does it; neither of these apply to a great deal of African nepotism."[5]

However, they are convinced (no evidence is adduced) that the results of nepotism and all other forms of what they call corruption ("in the strict sense . . . in the context of the *mores* of Great Britain") are serious and bad; and they take courage from the fact that a small minority in most developing countries shares their ethical viewpoint. Consequently they conceive the problem as one of seeking in British history the causes which led to the triumph in Britain of this point of view, with its attendant advantages, in the hope that African and other developing countries might profit from the experience of Britain. (Over half the book is devoted to this enquiry.)

The results are, as they recognise, inconclusive, which is not surprising when one considers that this formulation of the problem ("Why does the public morality of African states not conform to the British?") contains an obvious enough answer: because they have a different social, economic and political system, and a different historical experience. The approach is not as bad as it sounds, for Mr. Wraith and Mr. Simpkins have observed the Nigerian scene with discrimination and sympathy. But the basis of the whole book is a simple faith, that corruption is what it is, namely what has been known as corruption in Britain for a long time; and it has at bottom a "simple cause"—avarice: "the wrong that is done is done in the full knowledge that it is wrong, for the concept of theft does not vary as between Christian and Muslim, African and European, or primitive man and Minister of the Crown."[6]

Emotionally and intellectually, this seems to be in a direct line of descent from the viewpoint of those missionaries who were dedicated to the suppression of native dancing. The subject seems to

[3] An interesting and ably-written exception is M. McMullan, "A Theory of Corruption," *A Sociological Review* (Keele), July 1961, pp. 181–201. The author has, however, a rather restricted conception of what corruption is, and a number of unwarrantable assumptions about the results.

[4] Wraith and Simpkins, *Corruption in Developing Countries*, pp. 12–13 and 172.

[5] Wraith and Simpkins, p. 35.

[6] Wraith and Simpkins, p. 45.

deserve a more systematic and open-minded approach.[7]

WHAT IS CORRUPTION?

Under what circumstances are actions called corrupt? It seems best to start from some examples.

1. In the spring of 1964 the (Republican) Secretary of State of Illinois died. Under the State constitution the (Democratic) Governor temporarily filled his place by appointing a young (Democratic) official to the office. Within a few weeks a substantial number of State civil servants appointed by the late Secretary of State were dismissed, and their jobs were filled by Democratic Party supporters.

2. In Chicago about the same time a controversy was taking place concerning school desegregation. Active desegregationists alleged that they were prevented from attending in force a meeting of the City Council as part of their campaign, because all the public seating was filled by council employees who had for this purpose been given a holiday by the city administration.

3. In Kampala, Uganda, in August 1963 the City Council decided to award a petrol station site to a majority-party member of the Council, who offered the lowest price, £4000; the highest offer was for £11,000. It was alleged in the National Assembly that the successful purchaser resold the plot to an oil company at a profit of £8000.[8]

4. In Port Harcourt, Nigeria, in 1955, there were people in the Town Hall drawing labourers' salaries not provided for in the estimates; they were employed on the personal recommendation of individual councillors.[9]

5. In New York City, in 1951, it was estimated that over $1 million per annum was paid to policemen (for overlooking illegalities) by a bookmaking syndicate.[10]

6. In Lagos, Nigeria, in 1952, the practice of giving an unofficial cash gift or a fee for services rendered was fairly authoritatively stated to be found

> in hospitals where the nurses require a fee from every in-patient before the prescribed medicine is given, and even the ward servants must have their "dash" before bringing the bed-pan; it is known to be rife in the Police Motor Traffic Unit, which has unrivalled opportunities on account of the common practice of overloading vehicles; pay clerks made a deduction from the wages of daily paid staff; produce examiners exact a fee from the produce buyer for every bag that is graded and sealed; domestic servants pay a proportion of their wages to the senior of them, besides often having paid a lump sum to buy the job.[11]

One thing which all these events have in common is that someone regards each of them as a bad thing. Equally, however, it is clear that at least someone else —i.e. those involved in the acts in question—regards each of them as a good

---

7 The authors display a militant ignorance of sociological theory and research, which may be partly a consequence of their reluctance to abandon their ethical absolutism, but seems more a part of the settled philistinism on this matter which is still so depressingly common in Britain. "It is always unwise" (they write of social anthropology) "to argue with exponents of this formidable science, since they have their own vocabulary, which differs from that of the ordinary man, and their own concepts, which are not readily understood" (p. 172), and they proceed to represent the main burden of the social anthropologist's contributions on the subject as being to the effect that all corruption in their sense is the African's idea of a customary gift. One is provoked to echo Campbell-Bannerman's exasperated reply to the outmoded dialectics of Balfour: "Enough of this foolery."

8 *Uganda Parliamentary Debates,* 27 September 1963, pp. 179–200, and 3 October 1963, pp. 411–21. The Uganda Government subsequently denied that any such sale had taken place.

9 *Report of the Commission of Enquiry into the Working of Port Harcourt Town Council, 1955;* quoted in Wraith and Simpkins, p. 22.

10 *Third Interim Report of the Senate Committee to Investigate Organised Crime in Interstate Commerce, 1951* (Kefauver Committee), quoted in H. A. Turner, *Politics in the United States* (New York, 1955), p. 412.

11 From the Storey Report, *Commission of Inquiry into the Administration of Lagos Town Council, 1953* (Lagos, 1954).

thing. Writers of the moralist school accept this, but they are convinced that such behaviour is always against the "public interest." But what is the "public interest"? Some substantial arguments have been put forward to suggest that the public interest may sometimes *require* some of these practices. The most famous of these is probably the American defence of patronage, as in case (1) above, and "honest graft."[12] This argument turns essentially on the view that democratic politics in "mass" societies can only be ensured by the integration of a multitude of interests and groups into political parties, capable of furnishing leadership and coherent policies;[13] this involves organisation and inducements, both of which cost money; therefore politics must be made to pay. From this point of view the political role of money is to serve as a cement—"a *hyphen* which joins, a *buckle* which fastens" the otherwise separate and conflicting elements of a society into a body politic; "the greater the corruption, the greater the harmony between corruptor and corruptee," as one candid critic recognised.[14] And Professor Hoselitz has argued that the early years of the life of a nation are dominated by these "persistent integrative needs of the society," and that

> Much of the alleged corruption that Western technical advisers on administrative services of Asian and African stages encounter, and against which they inveigh in their technical reports with so little genuine success, is nothing but the prevalence of these non-rational norms on the basis of which these administrations operate.[15]

This can be taken a stage further. The moralist school of thought may recognise that some of the activities recorded above indirectly serve these broadly beneficial purposes. But they generally assume that the economic price paid is a heavy one. For instance: "The sums involved in some of the proved cases of corruption in Africa would have brought considerable benefits to people for whom "under-privileged" is too mild a word, if they had been properly spent."[16]

But spending public money properly does not guarantee that it will benefit the poor.[17] The Uganda Minister of Information was much criticised for giving a lucrative and unusual monopoly of television set sales to an American contractor, in return for building a transmission station at cut rates: even had corruption been involved the policy did produce a television station much more quickly and cheaply than the policy adopted in neighbouring Kenya.[18] To take another example, one may ask whether the Russian consumer would be better off without the operations of the illegal contact men who derive illegal incomes in return for their aid in overcoming

---

12 See William Turner, "In Defence of Patronage," in *The Annals of the American Academy of Political and Social Science,* January 1937, pp. 22–8, and William J. Riordan, *Plunkitt of Tammany Hall* (New York, 1958). Plunkitt coined the phrase "honest graft" in a famous passage:

> There's an honest graft, and I'm example of how it works. I might sum up the whole thing by sayin': "I seen my opportunities and I took 'em." Just let me explain by examples. My party's in power in the city and it's goin' to undertake a lot of public improvements. Well, I'm tipped off, say, that they're going to lay out a new park at a certain place. I see my opportunity and I take it. I go to that place and I buy up all the land I can in the neighborhood. Then the board of this or that makes its plan public and there is a rush to get that land which nobody cared particular for before. Ain't it perfectly honest to charge a good profit and make a profit on my investment and foresight? Of course it is. Well, that's honest graft.

13 See V. O. Key, pp. 395–398.

14 M. McMullan, p. 197.

15 Bert F. Hoselitz, "Levels of Economic Performance and Bureaucratic Structures," in La Palombara (ed.), *Bureaucracy and Political Development* (Princeton, 1963), p. 190.

16 Wraith and Simpkins, p. 172; although previously they do say "The economic effects of all this [corruption] on a country may not be very considerable." McMullan also believes the economic costs are high, but his definition of economic cost appears to be somewhat Gladstonian, "A Theory of Corruption," p. 182.

17 For an interesting discussion of the general question, see C. C. Wrigley, *Crops and Wealth in Uganda* (Kampala, 1959), pp. 70–73.

18 *Uganda Parliamentary Debates,* 8 November 1963, pp. 108–112, and 11 November 1963, pp. 137–142. Corruption was alleged by the opposition.

bottlenecks in the supply of materials for production.[19] Even in the case of petty bribery or extortion, it is relevant to ask, What is the alternative? Could an equally efficient and socially useful administration be carried on if effective means of eliminating perquisites were found and all concerned were required to live on their salaries? Would the pressure for higher salaries be no greater? Could it be resisted? If it could not, would increased taxation fall on those most able to pay and would this, or reduced services, be in the public interest? To ask these questions is to realise that the answers call for research and analysis which is seldom undertaken, and that they are likely to vary according to circumstances. One also becomes aware that near the heart of the moralists' concern is the idea that the public interest is opposed to anything that heightens *inequality*. But we also have to ask how far equality and development are themselves compatible ideals. The régime most committed to both of them—the USSR—found it necessary to postpone its concern with equality in order to achieve development.[20] This is not to say that all kinds of inequality promoted by all kinds of corruption are beneficial from the point of view of development; it is merely to challenge the assumption that they are invariably bad.

But we still have not answered the question, Under what circumstances are actions called corrupt? What is at issue in all the cases cited above is the existence of a standard of behaviour according to which the action in question breaks some rule, written or unwritten, about the proper purposes to which a public office or a public institution may be put. The moralist has his own idea of what the rule should be. The actors in the situations concerned have theirs. It may be the same as the moralists' (they may regard themselves as corrupt); or quite different (they may regard themselves as behaving honourably according to their standards, and regard their critics' standards as irrelevant); or they may be "men of two worlds," partly adhering to two standards which are incompatible, and ending up exasperated and indifferent (they may recognise no particular moral implications of the acts in question at all —this is fairly obviously quite common). And in addition to the actors there are the other members—more or less directly affected—of their own society; all these positions are possible for them too.[21]

THE ANALYSIS OF CORRUPTION

The following questions suggest themselves as a reasonable basis for the analysis of any case in which corruption is alleged:

1. What is being called corrupt and does it really happen? In the case of the African Continental Bank it became clear that no one was able to formulate a clear enough allegation against Dr. N. Azikiwe showing precisely what was the rule which he had broken.[22] A precise statement is required of the rule and the sense in which it is said to have been perverted. It may turn out, as in the case of the African Continental Bank, that there is really no clear idea of what the rule is; or that there is a clear rule but that it has not clearly been broken (this was Lord Denning's verdict on the Profumo case).[23]

2. Who regards the purpose which is being perverted as the proper or "official" purpose? It may be so regarded by

19 M. Fainsod, *How Russia Is Ruled* (Cambridge, Mass., 1958), p. 437.

20 For a brief but penetrating comment on this see W. Arthur Lewis, *The Theory of Economic Growth* (London, 1955), pp. 428–429.

21 Chinua Achebe provides a fascinating selection in *No Longer at Ease* (London, 1960), pp. 5–6 and 87–88. See also E. C. Banfield, *The Moral Basis of a Backward Society* (Chicago, 1958), ch. 5.

22 See *Report of the Tribunal Appointed to Inquire into Allegations Reflecting on the Official Conduct of the Premier of, and Certain Persons Holding Ministerial and other Public Offices in, the Eastern Region of Nigeria* (London, 1957).

23 *Lord Denning's Report* (London, 1963).

most people in the society, including those who pervert it; or it may be so regarded by only a few people (e.g. state political patronage is regarded as corrupt by only a relatively small group of American reformers).[24]

3. Who regards the allegedly corrupt action as perverting the official purpose? This is not necessarily the same question as question (2) above. For example, in a subsequent debate in the Uganda National Assembly on the petrol station site mentioned above, the Minister of Regional Administrations accepted the principle that the Council ought not to accept offers lower than the official valuer's valuation of the property, but held that they were by no means obliged to accept the highest offer and that the Council were justified in preferring to give a "stake" in the city to a poor man rather than to a rich one.[25] The opposition took the view that it was the man's politics rather than his poverty which actuated the majority on the Council, and that the loss to the public revenue was too high a price to pay for assisting one individual member of the public. They also took the view that the official object should be to accept the highest bid, unless circumstances of public importance not present in this case dictated otherwise. Thus the nature of the rule was also a matter of controversy, but both sides to the dispute to some extent made the distinction between the rule on the one hand, and the question of what amounted to breaking it on the other.

4. What are the short-term and long-term consequences of the behaviour in question, both of each particular case and of such behaviour generally? The answer might usefully, if roughly, be broken into two parts: (a) objective consequences, and (b) subjective consequences. Under (a) will come such questions as, What resources are directed from what applications to what other applications? What are the real as opposed to the theoretical opportunity costs of the alleged corruption? What are the effects for income distribution? And what consequential effects are there on the pattern of loyalties, the scope of party activities, the incentives to economic activity? etc. etc. Under (b) will come such questions as e.g., What effect does behaving in this way have on the work of civil servants who regard themselves as behaving corruptly? and, What effect does observing such behaviour have on the attitudes and/or behaviour of others? etc. etc.

It is natural but wrong to assume that the results of corruption are always both bad and important. For instance it is usually assumed that a corrupt civil service is an impediment to the establishment of foreign private enterprise, which has enough difficulties to contend with without in addition having to pay bribes. This may be clearly the case, but sometimes also the reverse appears to be true. Where bureaucracy is both elaborate and inefficient, the provision of strong personal incentives to bureaucrats to cut red tape may be the only way of speeding the establishment of the new firm. In such a case it is certainly reasonable to wish that the bureaucracy were simpler and more efficient, but not to argue that bribery *per se* is an obstacle to private economic initiative.[26] On the other hand

24 Wraith and Simpkins ally themselves with the analogous minority in West Africa whom they idenitfy as "the most eminent and responsible citizens" of these countries, p. 173. It appears that Chinua Achebe should be included among these, and to this extent it is permissible to wonder how typical are the reactions of his hero in *No Longer at Ease*, who has an ultimate and profound revulsion against his own acceptance of bribes.

25 *Uganda Parliamentary Debates*, 27 September 1963, p. 187.

26 McMullan, p. 182, takes the orthodox view: "Investors and entrepreneurs are frustrated and dismayed and may find that the unofficial cost of starting an enterprise is too great for it to be profitable." Another view is that this is one method of reducing excess profits. In the case of extractive industries this has some plausibility. McMullan points out (p. 197) that "a group under harsh disability but still possessed of considerable wealth" provides the "optimum conditions for corruption" and that it is perhaps another "useful" function of corruption to enable economically energetic ethnic minorities to protect themselves.

the results may be unimportant from any practical standpoint, even if they are not particularly nice.

From such questions one may go on to pose another which is clearly the central one for the scientific study of the problem: In any society, under what conditions is behaviour most likely to occur which a significant section of the population will regard as corrupt? Some obviously relevant points are:

1. *The "standing" of the "official purpose" of each public office or institution in the society.* This involves the diffusion of understanding of the idea generally, and within particular relevant groups (e.g. civil servants or police); how strongly supported this conception is, generally, and within particular groups; and what effect distance and scale have on both these dimensions. For example, ordinary people in England did not immediately condemn the Ferranti company for wanting to keep over £4 million windfall profits on a defence contract, because it was an incomprehensibly vast sum gained in highly unfamiliar circumstances; but the same people would instantly condemn a local contractor who made a windfall profit of £40,000 on laying a drainpipe for the Rural District Council. And the "standing" of the "official purpose" of anything is also affected by the "standing" of other rival conceptions of its purpose, e.g. the computing moral claims of relatives on a civil servant who is making junior appointments.

2. *The extent to which action which perverts or contravenes such official purposes is seen as doing so*—another complex problem of research into attitudes.

3. *The incentives and disincentives to corrupt the official purposes of an office or institution.* For instance, the size of the profits to be made by bribery, or the losses liable to be incurred by refraining from it, compared with the penalties attached to being caught and exposed.

4. *The ease with which corruption (once defined) can be carried on.* This involves such things as the case of a particular type of corruption, and the extent to which ordinary people are exposed to opportunities for it (which is among other things affected very much by the range of the activities of the state).[27]

All these aspects clearly interact with each other.

[27] An official study of civil service corruption in Malaya in the 1950s found much more corruption in those departments of government which provide extensive services than in those which do not.

2. The Concept of Corruption[1]

JACOB VAN KLAVEREN

In everyday life corruption means that a civil servant abuses his authority in order to obtain an extra income from the public. This conception, however, expresses a value judgment that is altogether temporal and did not always exist. If it were possible to determine the amount of the civil servant's salary by objective measures, that is, by determining the functional value of the civil servant's performance for the achievement of the social product in its broadest sense, then a value-free definition of corruption would be possible. Since such a functional definition of the distribution of income is neither possible for private business nor for administration, this approach leads us nowhere.[2]

Alternatively, one could forget about normative-objective determinants of individual incomes and accept the results of the free-market economy. Provided that every economic subject tries to maximize his gains or his income or both, one could assume that the incomes derived from the free-market accord with functional-economic income. Given a system of free competition, where numerous buyers exchange with numerous sellers, both sides of the market are equally strong, and equilibrium is achieved where the two exchange curves intersect. However, if a monopolistic condition exists on one side of the market, the monopolist does not display his exchange curve but selects the point of maximum profit on the exchange curve of the other market side. Stackelberg correctly describes such a behavior as exploitation.[3]

Although a market economy can only operate under the protection of some public order or government, it is precisely this public sphere that represents a foreign body within the market sphere. The value of its services, and thus the income of the officials, cannot be determined via the free market mechanism. The establishment of government is an act of the whole society[4] to further the

---

1 This article evolved from a habilitation lecture that I delivered to the faculty of economics at the University of Munich on June 20, 1956. Both style and annotations reflect the original lecture form. Unfortunately there is little material to be found on corruption since the relevant events, naturally, are hardly ever documented. This is true also for those times where corruption was still legally tolerated, as I shall explain below. Much of this should thus be regarded as a tentative first attempt. Only the consideration that this is seemingly the first time that corruption as a phenomenon is examined in context and with regard to its inherent character gave the author the courage to publish this article.

2 See Vilfredo Pareto, *Manuel d'économie politique* (translation). Paris, 1909, p. 196.

SOURCE: Jacob van Klaveren, "Die historische Erscheinung der Korruption, in ihrem Zusammenhang mit der Staats- und Gesellschaftsstrukur betrachet," *Vierteljahresschrift für Sozial- und Wirtschaftsgeschichte,* 44:4 (December 1957), pp. 289–294. By permission of the publisher, Franz Steiner Verlag. Translation by Peggy Hofmann and Karl Kurtz.

3 See Heinrich von Stackelberg, *Marktform und Gleichgewicht.* Vienna and Berlin, 1934, p. 39.

4 The foundation of such a society by a "Social Contract" occurred repeatedly in the area of what is now the United States and was one of the characteristics of the so-called frontier. Probably the "vigilance committees" are most familiar to us from the Western movies. They were voluntary associations of peace-loving citizens who started by hanging the villains; this was called "to stretch hemp." Descriptions can be found in many American history textbooks. See Ray Allen Billington, *Westward Expansion: A History of the American Frontier,* 4th ed. New York, 1954 (1949), p. 621 ff.

common good; thus, government is not an end in itself but only a means, and officials are only servants of the community, trustees of the common good.[5] The salaries of these civil servants can hardly be derived from their contributions to the national product but must be determined by socioethical and historical considerations.

The line of this argument is based on the ideas of the "social contract," that is, on the ideas of the Age of Enlightenment, which led to the rise of the democratic states of the nineteenth century. At this point we already touch upon the question of the relationship between constitution and corruption that will be examined thoroughly in the next section. Suffice it to say here that the official who relinquishes this subservience comes to confront the public as an independent power invested with a legal monopoly. If he wishes, he can abuse his monopoly position for exploitation of the public by extorting for each official act the maximum reward that the subject with whom he is dealing is willing to pay. We are thus dealing with a method of exploitation by which a constituent part of the public-order sphere is exploited as if it were part of the market sphere. Thus we will conceive of corruption in terms of a civil servant who regards his public office as a business, the income of which he will, in the extreme case, seek to maximize. The office then becomes a "maximizing unit." The size of his income then does not depend on an ethical evaluation of his usefulness for the common good but precisely upon the market situation and his talents for finding the point of maximal gain on the public's demand curve.[6]

This comparison between the office and the business is particularly apt if, first, the civil servant does not obtain a salary and, second, if he himself has to finance the costs of his administration, an extreme situation, rarely found in modern times.[7] In this case there is also no public treasury, but only the civil servant's private cashbox. The situation becomes somewhat more complicated if a public treasury exists to meet the expenses of the administration, including those constituted by the salaries of the civil servants. Then the official may still act toward the individual members of the public whom he encounters as a maximizer and monopolist; nothing changes in this respect. At the same time there may occur various forms of theft from the public treasury. This also is a form of profit maximization, but it assumes a collective form. The public as a whole is exploited, because the tax payments are only partly used for the purposes of the community. Whether, in a case like this, the civil service is a one-sided monopolist, or whether the public has a sufficiently well-organized representation so that the struggle becomes more akin to that of a bilateral monopoly, depends on different circumstances, to be discussed later. Provisionally it can be said that corruption is always an exploitation of the public, which can occur only because the civil servants occupy a constitutionally independent position vis-à-vis the public.

To know from which side the initiative for corruption comes is no more important in this case than it was when we examined the relations among free-market parties. Only when corruption is made illegal does this question become important and then mainly from a criminal-law point of view, which is of no interest here. An offer of a bribe that

5 See Fritz Terhalle, *Die Finanzwirtschaft des Staates und der Gemeinden*. Berlin, 1948, pp. 17, 27.

6 In other words, he determines the reward for his services in every case according to the well-known principle of the railways' rate policy, "charge what the traffic can bear."

7 I discussed such a case in my study, *The Dutch Colonial System in the East Indies*, The Hague, 1953, p. 71. The case refers to the Commissioner of Native Affairs of the Dutch East Indian Company, who supervised coffee cultivation in West Java. He paid all costs of office and although he did not draw a salary, the estimated annual income of Commissioner Pieter Engelhardt was 300,000 guilders at the end of the eighteenth century.

seemingly comes from the public may in reality be due to blackmail on the part of the civil servant. Thus businessmen may be forced to make such offers if they want to participate with success in public tenders. But the previous existence of compulsion, is disguised by the fact that the final award of the contract, and as a corollary the identity of the briber, depends on a quasi-anonymous selection process.[8]

Compulsion, however, takes the form of naked blackmail, if everyone fulfilling certain objective criteria must pay such a fee, even when the initiative seemingly derives from the public. An example would be if all travelers who wanted to cross a frontier had to offer money to [border] officials solely in order to be processed. Hence it is not the initiative that is decisive but the given fact that corruption is rooted in the constitution, in other words, that there are no means to abolish legally these malpractices. Thus the public has to come to terms with letting the officials obtain a larger part of the national income than they are entitled to on the grounds of ethical considerations.

If corruption is illegal, it tends to appear as occasional acts of dishonesty on the part of civil servants, the initiative of which may come from either side, that of the public as well as that of the civil servants. Then the root of corruption lies exclusively in the *appetitus divitiarum infinitus,* the insatiable avarice that is one of the human weaknesses against which battle was already waged by scholastics. This, however, is not a historical problem.

Therefore, if we are talking about corruption, we must always think of the systematic form of corruption that is rooted in the constitution, *la fraude erigée en système,* as it is labeled in a French study. . . .[9]

8 Contemporaries very well understood these connections. The indictment of Lord Middlesex (1624) mentioned "tribes squeezed from customs farmers" who were "blackmailed into bribery." See R. H. Tawney, *Business and Politics under James I.* Cambridge University Press. 1958, pp. 257, 258.

9 See E. W. Dahlgren, *Les relations commerciales et maritimes entre la France et les côtes de L'Ocean Pacifique.* Paris, 1909, p. 33. The question here is the illegal trade of French vessels with Peru. This was only made possible, as Dahlgren correctly understood, because in the Spanish colonies corruption was part of the constitution. The same applied to the Spanish mother country at that time.

Power tends to corrupt, and absolute power corrupts absolutely.
—LORD ACTON[1]

3. The Sociology of Corruption

H. A. BRASZ

INTRODUCTION

Whilst browsing through the encyclopaedias in a reference library in preparation for the present paper, I was struck by the fact that a French publication of about a century ago contained a long article on corruption. This article went into exhaustive detail about corruption in British politics and in Russian bureaucracy. But not a word about France. It is easier to write about the British nabobs and the Russian concept *Shemokina Soud*—about the mote that is in thy brother's eye—than about the beam in thine own eye. And yet something will have to be said about this beam, and therefore I think it only proper to state at the outset that I propose to take the apple scandal in Paradise[2] absolutely seriously. It is this arbitrary point of departure which induces me to accept the postulate that in time corruption occurs everywhere, at home and abroad, in business, in private enterprise, and in the public service. This implies that the Dutch might be just as inclined to tolerate and profit from corruption as, for instance, the Americans or the Indonesians, Perhaps they have less reason to do so, or fewer opportunities. This postulate does not fit in with chauvinism. In the Netherlands, too, scandals involving corruption are sometimes disclosed.[3] As we shall see, the real, the essential corruption remains concealed as a well-kept secret.

A DEFINITION OF CORRUPTION

In my opinion corruption merits a place from the sociological point of view in the sociology of power. It might be very broadly interpreted as a perversion of power. Some years ago Van Doorn[4] made an attempt—in my opinion a successful one—to define the phenomenon of power; it would seem appropriate to associate our definition of corruption with his definition of power. According to Van Doorn power is the possibility, in pursuance of the purposes of a person or group, of restricting the alternative choices of behaviour of other persons or groups. We also find in Van Doorn the concepts "naked power" and "arbitrary power." He defines the former as power exercised without authority.[5] Invoking Geiger, he describes arbitrary power as a contrast to law.[6] None of these kinds

1 To be found among other places in Gertrude Himmelfarb, *Lord Acton: A Study in Conscience and Politics* (Chicago, 1952), p. 161.

2 Genesis 3:1–13.

SOURCE: H. A. Brasz, "Some Notes on the Sociology of Corruption," *Sociologica Neerlandica,* 1:2 (Autumn 1963), pp. 111–117. By permission of the publisher, Royal Van Gorcum Ltd.

3 See a survey of the convictions in the article by F. Prick, "Corruptie en politietransactie" (Corruption and Police Transactions), *Tijdschrift voor de Politie,* XII (1959), pp. 53–57, based on data furnished by the Central Bureau of Statistics.

4 J. A. A. van Doorn, "Sociology and the Problem of Power," *Sociologia Neerlandica,* I (1962/63), 3–47, see p. 12.

5 J. A. A. van Doorn, p. 24.

6 J. A. A. van Doorn, p. 23.

of power is sufficient for the further definition of a sociological concept of corruption. The concept naked power does not do justice to the furtive nature of corruption: corruption is not naked but veiled.

It is true that corruption can be placed in the category of arbitrary power, since it always presupposes the use of power to achieve a purpose other than that for which this power was granted. But not all arbitrary power can be called corruption, since arbitrary power may also proceed from (fancied) patriotism or simply from a confused state of mind. Arbitrary power, *i.e.*, injustice, will sometimes result from corruption. But carelessness and inattention may also lead to it.

Consequently, Van Doorn's concepts cannot solve our difficulty entirely. There is a need for the concept "corrupt use of power." I propose to interpret corruption in the sociological sense as meaning the corrupt exercise of derived power, or the stealthy exercise of derived power on the basis of the authority inherent in that power or on the basis of a formal competence to the detriment of the objectives of the original power and to the advantage of outsiders under the pretence of a legitimate exercise of power. Those who as subordinates, agents, and the like handle the affairs of principals are presumed to be and to act in good faith.[7] If they sever the connection and enter into the service of a competitor or enemy of the principal they may, it is true, be branded as turncoats, but they are not guilty of corruption. A necessary adjunct to corruption is the treacherous venom of deceit, the pretence of being absolutely loyal to the principal whilst in actual fact being intent on benefiting oneself and/or third parties.

We shall now give further consideration to the elements of this definition of corruption.

a. Derived power. The shopkeeper who is persuaded by a gift from a wholesaler to carry another line of goods is not guilty of corruption. He is trying to earn more, and the consequences of this attempt are for him to bear. If the new line proves to be of poor quality he will sell less of it. The shopkeeper really feels the dysfunctions of this (pseudo-) bribe. At most it can be said that the wholesaler is competing on dishonest terms, but this is not to be regarded as corruption. For the shopkeeper exercises original power as a self-employed person.

Now if this same wholesaler covertly gives the buyer of a limited company a "present" and in this way persuades the buyer to use his power-position in the company so that the latter switches to the new line, then in my opinion we are concerned from the sociological point of view with corruption. The buyer's power is derived from his principal, the company. His power has been obtained through delegation.[8] The dysfunctions of his corruption must be borne by the company.

In my opinion it matters little from the point of view of sociology whether this form of corruption occurs in a government agency or in private enterprise: it is exactly the same phenomenon in both cases. The distinction made by criminal law (still extent in the Netherlands, although abolished in a number of other countries) whereby bribes are illegal only where government officials are concerned[9] is sociologically irrelevant.

b. The derived power is exercised on the basis of the authority inherent in it or on the basis of formal competences; although the corrupt exercise of power

7 See also the description of the concept bribe in Lodewijk Salomonson, *Steekpenningen* (Bribes; dissertation, University of Leiden; Leiden, 1925), p. 5.

8 Van Doorn, pp. 36 ff.

9 For details see Salomonson. In 1906 the Prevention of Corruption Act became law in England (pp. 30 f.), in 1909 Germany enacted penal provisions in the Gesetz gegen den unlautern Wettbewerb (p. 41), and in 1919 France similarly supplemented the Code Pénal (p. 56).

is not legitimate, the power-holder can easily make it appear to be so. Appearances are to his advantage. But by making use of these false appearances he betrays the confidence placed in him. For the consequences of corruption jurisprudence uses the expressions abuse of power and *détournement de pouvoir* (in the case of arbitrariness or the exercise of power for a purpose other than that for which it was granted respectively).[10]

c. The derived power is exercised to the detriment of the objectives of the original power–holder. A tipping system is not in itself corruption as long as the tip is given as a matter of custom and the conduct of the recipient is not changed in a sense unfavourable to the objectives of the original power-holder. Sociologically speaking, passive subornation to commit an unlawful act (Section 362 of the Dutch Criminal Code) need not be corruption, although the law stamps this situation as bribery and makes it illegal as such.

d. The derived power is exercised to the advantage or to the detriment of outsiders. A characteristic feature of corruption seems to be treachery to the cause to which one pretends to be loyal. I do not believe that embezzlement for one's own benefit can be corruption in the sociological sense, since in such a case only one's own interests are put above the group's interests or those of the principal. Nor are such acts injurious to third parties. The fraud, the deceit practised in order to misappropriate moneys, especially by falsifying the books, is only indirectly diverted from the objectives of the original power-holder. Fraud is usually committed to obtain money or other benefits and the purpose of the original power-holder is not as manifestly frustrated by this as when the acts are deliberately opposed to this objective and, for instance, entail the risk that the quality of the product will suffer.

e. The most essential characteristic of corruption is to me the furtive exercise of formal authority and power under the pretence of legality. The real purpose for which power and authority are abused is always kept secret. At the same time the result of this characteristic is that the technique employed in the corruption is applied secretly, whilst the consequences of the corrupt exercise of power are also camouflaged as far as possible. Not only the event itself but also cause and effect must be veiled. The veiling of the cause may fail. Provided that the corrupt exercise of power continues for a prolonged period and remains unchanged in character, its effects cannot be entirely concealed in the long run. For the corrupt power-holder will accomplish a result which from the point of view of his principal remains at a lower level than might have been the case had he been conscientious.

A SUBJECTIVE OR AN OBJECTIFIED DEFINITION?

Wertheim [in Selection 19][11] seems to me to favour a subjective definition of the concept of corruption, an interpretation from which one might conclude that corruption is what is called corruption. For the sociologist the interesting question that then remains is under what circumstances a certain act is called corrupt. Come to that, much of Wertheim's paper may be regarded as an analysis of historical situations from the point of view of this question. He is not alone in this. Senturia has defined political corruption as "the misuse of public power for private profit."[12] But this brief definition gives

---

10 See the note by D. J. Veegens in *Nederlandse Jurisprudentie,* 1949, No. 559, and my article "Rechters en rechtspraak naar aanleiding van de woonruimtewet, 1947" (Judges and Jurisprudence on the Allocation of Dwellings Act, 1947), *Bestuurswetenschappen* (Public Administration), V (1951), pp. 289–305, 380–389, VI (1952), 28–50, see pp. 33 f.

11 See below, pp. 195–211.

12 Joseph J. Senturia, "Political Corruption" in Edwin R. A. Seligman and others, eds., *Encyclopaedia of the Social Sciences,* Vol. IV (London, 1931), pp. 448–452.

us no indication when an act should be regarded as corrupt. Well, says Senturia, that is the case when the "best opinion and political morality of the time," after an investigation of the intentions and the circumstances of the act, reach the conclusion that in this act the public interest is being sacrificed for the benefit of personal interest. But now comes the difficult part: who is to decide who possesses the "best opinion and political morality of the time"? Would that be the German weekly *Der Spiegel,* the Bonn judge Quirini, or Adenauer?[13]

I do not think that sociology can answer this question. We shall have to seek an objective criterion, and in my opinion this criterion is the furtive nature of the acts. From the ethical point of view one may think what one likes about the events in the foreign buying section of the Army Matériel Directorate of the Dutch Ministry of War (I am referring here to what is known in the Netherlands as the case of Major K.) It is also a fact that the man concerned was found not guilty of the charge brought against him (accepting a gift as a government official, knowing that this gift was offered with respect to acts of commission or omission occurring in the course of and in conflict with his duties, and having committed this offence on more than one occasion). But if the conclusions of the Koersen parliamentary committee are correct,[14] subjective elements played a part in the purchase of materials in Britain, and personal preference for a given agent was in a number of cases the main determinant in making certain decisions. The committee noted a tendency to let personal relations and interests prevail over the interests of the service. The committee also discovered that a letter (which included a suggestive remark about bribes) had not been submitted by the official concerned to his appropriate superiors for initialling. Here the furtive nature of the act is clearly apparent, at least from the sociological point of view, and it surprises me that, whilst the helmets and the gas masks from the report of the Koersen committee are mentioned as an example of corruption, the case of the Army Matériel Directorate is not. Do subjective interpretations of corruption form too strong an influence here? Is it difficult to choose between a certain section of the press and the Koersen committee in the matter of the Army Matériel Directorate? The "best opinion of the time" is to my mind reflected in the extent to which the acts were kept secret by the power-holders themselves. This reflection was stronger in the case of the Army Matériel Directorate than in that of the helmets and the gas masks.

In the latter case the Dutch conscience was troubled by the way in which government organization and industry failed. But here the Koersen committee found no secrecy, no concealment, but organizational faults and mistakes in the staffing of important services. This was, incidentally, a further aspect of the case of the Army Matériel Directorate.

CAUSALITY TECHNIQUE AND CAMOUFLAGE

I must now draw attention to an element which in my opinion does not belong in a sociological definition of corruption. I refer to the means by which the corruption is brought about: the technique of the causality. In my opinion a sharp distinction should be made between corrupt action and this technique.

Giving alms, practising charity and philanthropy by making a real sacrifice for a fellow-man, contributing to a benevolent association, and making a grant

13 See among others *Der Spiegel* for 2 September, 1959, on the Löffelholz case.

14 See the Report of the Committee Investigating Military Purchasing Policy (the Koersen committee) of 21 February, 1959, *Bijlagen van het verslag der handelingen van de Tweede Kamer der Staten-Generaal* (Appendices to the Report of the Proceedings of the Second Chamber of the States-General), Session 1958/59, No. 545. See above all the conclusions on pp. 46 f.

are not as such corruption. Even the much maligned tip[15] is not in itself corruption, but a manifestation of kindness, a voluntary gift on account of the rendering of a service for which another pays. In all these cases we are concerned with the neutral technique of giving. But the technique can also be applied to cause corruption: the attitude of friendliness which accompanies a gift presupposes the same attitude being displayed by the receiving party. And corruption can fit into the framework of this friendly and sympathetic attitude; if we analyse each individual case where a gift is made, there are often good grounds for suspecting corruption.

But a gift is certainly not the only technique of causing corruption. At least as much importance may be attached to an ideological bond which so undermines the sense of duty of the person exercising derived power that he begins to regard treason as his duty. Behaviour of this kind, which deviates so greatly from the norms of society, unfortunately does occur, so that some persons are prepared to spy free of charge on behalf of countries which can be identified with a certain ideology. The history of atomic secrets may be mentioned as an illustration of this technique of causing corruption. Other techniques are chicanery, threats of violence, or the simple bond of friendship. We therefore see in the causality technique of corruption both attitudes to which society attaches a very high value and techniques which in themselves are criminal.

Besides the concepts of corrupt action and causality technique a third may be distinguished: camouflage. Corruption itself is, by its nature, the easiest to camouflage. If the corrupt action cannot take place furtively, it cannot take place at all; anyone who nevertheless performs the action commits corruption plus, but does not remain at liberty long. It is much more difficult to camouflage the causality technique, since when all is said and done this technique consists in the performance of concrete acts, such as paying a bribe. Arising out of a scandal concerning Dutch gas-works managers in the twenties, Blokhuis has listed a large variety of ways in which a bribe may be camouflaged: tips, charity, advantages in kind such as the use of a car, a cheap holiday abroad, and the children's money-box are examples.[16]

15 For tips see Rudolf von Jhering, *Das Trinkgeld* (Brunswick, 1889), and Salomonson, pp. 2 f.

16 K. Blokhuis, gas-works manager at Middelharnis and Sommelsdijk. *Gasbedrijven, gasdirecteuren en corruptie* (Gas Works, Gas-Works Managers, and Corruption; Middelharnis, 1928), pp. 14 f.

4. Techniques of Political Graft

V. O. KEY, JR.

Certain conclusions and hypotheses may be drawn from the data which have been presented. A classification of the techniques of graft may be formulated, the functions of graft may be sketched, certain tentative remarks relative to the "causes" of graft may be offered, and some of the trends in graft and counter trends may be suggested.

THE TECHNIQUES OF GRAFT

The general scheme followed in presenting the descriptive material has precluded the formulation of a classification of the techniques of graft, but it should be obvious by the time this point is reached that there are certain common types which recur in all the activities of government. It is believed that practically all instances of graft may be grouped into several fundamental types of techniques of graft. The point may be raised that the patterns of behavior which are set forth as the basic techniques of graft involve such minute situations as to be meaningless. But in the precise analysis of social phenomena, it is necessary to break the indeterminate total situation into its component parts. It will be recalled that in the beginning graft was defined as an abuse of power for personal or party profit. It was noted that graft usually involved a relationship between the official exercising the power which is abused and some other individual or individuals and that the techniques of graft are the methods employed in these relationships plus the methods used in cases of graft involving only a single individual.

Bribery to influence official action is the most obvious technique of graft. The name which a particular payment in money or other value for this purpose takes is immaterial. Some campaign contributions cannot be differentiated from bribes.[1] Business and professional relationships may conceal bribery. When a corporation secures its bonds or insurance, for example, from a political leader, it cannot be assumed that this is done because the "boss" sells the best insurance. Any favor secured as a result of such relationships is secured by bribery.[2] Bribery is fundamentally the same whether employed in relation to legislators, administrators, judges, other public officials, "bosses" exercising their power or private individuals acting in agency positions. It is the same on all levels of government and in all functions. The act of bribery, as has been observed from

SOURCE: V. O. Key, Jr., *The Techniques of Political Graft in the United States.* Chicago, Ill.: University of Chicago Libraries, 1936, pp. 386–401.

1 Perhaps the difference arises when parties openly espouse the ends which campaign contributors hope to achieve as a result of their largesse. This occurs only when such ends are for class, group, or public interest, or may be made to appear so, rather than for patently and unequivocally selfish individual interest.

2 Legally the crime of bribery must involve persons possessing the power under the law to give what is sought by bribery. Legal fictions like this must be ignored in any realistic view. A "boss" probably would not have the legal power to grant the desired action, but actually he might have such power.

some of the instances recounted, is a matter requiring considerable skill. In the process there is often considerable preliminary negotiation in order to achieve an intimate relationship with the person to be bribed. He is given "good" and plausible reasons for doing what he is being bought to do. Sometimes advantage is taken of his financial needs, and he may be in a way "coerced" to accept. In other cases, of course, bribery is a more or less cold-blooded commercial transaction.[3]

The converse of bribery is extortion, i.e., the abuse or threat of abuse of a power in such a way as to secure response in payment of money or other valuable thing. This technique is the same whether it is exercised by a legislative coterie through a "sand-bagging" bill or by a building inspector through a trivial "shake-down." In extortion the initiative is clearly with the public official or the person exercising his power. Legislators may hold a "regulator" or a "revenue-raiser" over the heads of persons directly interested in the proposed legislation and subtly intimate that it might be put quietly away by payments to the right persons. A licensing official may threaten revocation of a saloon license if a campaign contribution is not made. A disbursing officer may threaten to delay a payment justly due if some gratuity is not forthcoming. The assessment of public employees usually takes the form of extortion although it is actually carried on with widely varying degrees of subtlety. In all these and other similar situations the behavior pattern involved is the same, although, of course, in making threats and demands for money various shades of bluntness in communication prevail.

In individual instances it may be difficult to distinguish between extortion, solicitation of a bribe and bribery. Businessmen usually claim that all their bribes are "protection" money which they are compelled to pay. Others take the view that there is really no extortion, but that it is all bribery.[4] It seems quite evident that there are both types of relationships.

"State-bribery" is a term which may be applied to those instances where control of various public properties and of the expenditure of public funds is abused —or perhaps more accurately misused— for the purpose of creating power or control relationships. Analyzed to the ultimate any instance in which one individual controls another is a power situation or relationship. Thus, state-bribery includes the control of the political organization, its candidates and to some extent its policies, by the control of patronage. A rebellious district leader or ward committeeman may discover that his printing contracts or his fire hose business has been cut off by the men "higher-up" in the organization and that it is too late to mend his ways. Control by state-bribery may extend to electors as in the employment of election officials and the hiring of polling places with the tacit understanding, if not express, that the ballots will be cast "right." This type of control may extend to the political attitudes of community leaders, such as bankers, through the distribution of deposits of public funds. The construction of public works, the distribution of subsidies may be in the nature of state-bribery, to control the electoral behavior of particular groups, territorial or functional. An executive may "buy" a legislator with an appointment. These examples are not intended to exclude others but are merely illustrative. The common element running through all of them is

3 See the brilliant article on "Bribery" by H. D. Lasswell, *Encyclopaedia of the Social Sciences.*

4 See Donald Richberg's remarks: "Frequently they mask their effort by publicly asserting the need for 'protection' from political interference. Indeed, this is such a prevalent disguise for political aggression that doubtless most of the Insulls most of the time feel assured that they only carry a sword for defense and not for attack when they lead a wealth-gathering foray."—"Gold-Plated Anarchy," *The Nation,* CXXXVI (1933), 368.

the element of control secured by an abuse—a perversion of the purpose—of the power granted to the official concerned. The object of the control need not be to influence a person with reference to his political behavior, but it generally is. The widespread acquiescence in the practice of various forms of state-bribery does not change their real nature. The relationship is without doubt one of bribery with public funds.

Another fundamental form of graft is political discrimination in the formulation and administration of law or rules of behavior,[5] that is to say, the power to make or administer law. The consideration is a political attitude rather than a payment of money or other value. Law making and law enforcing may be lumped together in this category for when law making is unequivocally employed for this purpose, as in administration, the individual case is dealt with rather than broad interests. The effect of abuse in this category may be to create lines of control within the political organization as when a ward committeeman or a district leader is permitted to operate a gambling house. The boss of the organization is certain of the support of this leader for he can order the police to close the place, if he wishes. In smaller matters the effect of this discriminatory administration of law may be to create "friends" among the electorate, as when tickets for violating traffic ordinances are "fixed." Political discrimination of this sort may come either as the result of the initiative of the official concerned or on petition of the person favored. The relationship may resemble either bribery or intimidation.

Discrimination in the administration of service functions for political purposes is a fifth fundamental technique of graft. The standards set up for the administration of services in individual cases are departed from and the criteria become political. Republicans are discriminated against in favor of Democrats in granting unemployment relief, for example. The Republican party functionary is given preference in the selection of stalls in the public markets. Abuses in the service functions may be differentiated from state-bribery in that abuses in the latter category are usually incident to some appointive or contractual relationship whereas abuses in the service activities are incident to a service relationship between citizen and government. Abuses in service relationships differ from abuses in the administration of law for in the latter a norm of conduct is applied through penal sanctions.

A final type of technique of graft may be denominated "auto–corruption." In bribery, extortion, state-bribery, and the other types which have been described, relationships between two or more individuals are involved. In auto-corruption the public official or person exercising the power of such official, boss or whatever he may be, in a sense plays the role of both parties in the other situations involving two or more persons. He secures for himself the administrative privilege which would be secured by an outsider by bribery. He awards contracts to himself, perhaps using dummy corporations, which would go to reward a contractor in the organization. He appropriates public property which might be used to reward some other member of the political organization. At times in all types of auto-corruption the gains may trickle into the political organization through campaign contributions and by various other means, but there is a fundamental distinction between this and the other forms of graft. However, in some instances auto-corruption may be a single link in a chain of individual cases which create a "ring" formation of power. The spoils are divided by individuals in their respective official positions, but the series

[5] Law is used here in the sense of a rule governing the behavior of the individual or corporate citizen. Administration is used in the sense of the application of such a rule to the individual case rather than in the sense of management.

of events bind together all the participants in the political machine. In auto-corruption cases often occur in which the personal gain far outweighs the group or party advantage. Matters of this kind, of course, have no place in the well regulated machine.[6]

In addition to these fundamental techniques of graft there are employed in conjunction with the primary methods various subsidiary or ancillary techniques, which have been described in considerable detail in connection with the various activities of government. The methods of maintaining secrecy, which is essential in most types of graft, are fairly obvious. In the first instance as little evidence as possible is created. When bribes are passed only the giver and the receiver are present, or perhaps the money passes through several hands from briber to bribee.[7] Some of the individuals through whose hands it passes may be more or less ignorant of what the purpose is. The terms of an agreement to give some particular privilege may be vague, indefinite or merely implied. Non-verbal symbols may be employed.[8] As little documentary evidence as possible is created. When payments have to be made from corporate or firm funds, false entries are made. A bribe may be charged as repairs to steamers or roadbed maintenance. Double records—one false, one true—may be kept. Dummy corporations have a multiplicity of uses. Business and professional relationships may conceal bribery. In the maintenance of secrecy much depends on the "right" relations with opposition politicians and with newspapers which might ferret out and disclose unsavory matters.

The various methods of camouflage and counter-propaganda constitute another subsidiary technique. In nearly every instance of alleged graft the accused has an explanation differing from the interpretation offered by the prosecutor.[9] The meanest sort of "steal" is sometimes transformed by the graft artist into a great deed for the promotion of the public welfare or at least a bit of harmless pillaging of the rich for the benefit of the poor. If this cannot be done, sufficient dust may be raised to create confusion and doubt. Foreign wars to allay domestic uprisings is a political theme on which there are many variations. Grafters as well as other political technicians have been thoroughly aware of this principle of politics. We have the spectacle of "Big Bill" Thompson sallying forth to kick King George "on the snoot" after his cohorts had virtually carried away the city hall stone by stone. Grafting political organizations have managed their activities as if public opinion mattered, whether it did or not.[10]

The evasion of legal requirements, such as those in civil service laws and in regulations governing the award of public contracts, is a subsidiary method which varies with the legal regime concerned. Certain types of evasion, however, recur. Legislation cannot anticipate every pos-

6 Many political leaders who do not profit in a pecuniary way themselves tolerate and bear criticism for inexpedient grafting by their followers. In the nature of things it is difficult to exercise much control over the illegal activities of the members of the organization in office, once it is agreed that the organization is out to get all it can. The unscrupulous leader must leave it to them to exercise their judgment to do what "will go" and what "won't go." If every plan for graft were submitted to the board of strategy of the organization, some of the less well considered ones would undoubtedly be vetoed. But, then, there are statutes punishing conspiracy which might be effectively applied if such an arrangement could be proved.

7 Compare the aphorism in R. E. Shapley, *Solid for Mulhooly* (New ed.; Philadelphia: Gebbie & Co., 1889), p. 59: "A man who's d---d fool enough to call in witnesses to see him take a bribe deserves the extreme penalty of the law."

8 The conversation of the corporation head and his political lawyer serving as an intermediary "could be heard by all the world and published without harm—so long as the winks, nods, and facial expressions are not shown on the screen."—Frank Kent, *The Great Game of Politics* (New York: Doubleday, 1930), p. 137.

9 The transparent saw, "It was a loan and not a bribe." "I got the money speculating on town lots in Japan." "It came from my tin box, a wonderful tin box." "My uncle, a seafaring man, gave me the money." "I won it on the races."

10 A first rate study could be made of the techniques and functions of deception in politics.

sible contingency and exceptions to the general rule are usually provided. These exceptions may be utilized to such an extent as to nullify the general rule. Temporary appointees are named under the provisions of the civil service laws providing for emergency appointments. In awarding contracts orders are divided and made under the legal provisions allowing purchases without calling for bids when the amount is less than $1000 or $500. Discretion may be abused. Thus, who is the lowest responsible bidder? General terms may be used to indicate specific things as in the manipulation of contract and purchase specifications. Probably more important than these verbalistic techniques designed to give a color of legality is the outright disregard of legislation governing the administration.

The master strategy of the political machine consists in the political consolidation of the beneficiaries of the graft system together with others who may be brought into the combination by some other appeal. Thus, graft as it has been defined may be either sporadic or systematic. The individual instances are the same in either case, or on any level of government, or in any country, but in any instance it is contended that it is virtually impossible to rule by graft alone. Other techniques must be employed to win the support of persons who do not obviously benefit as a result of graft.[11] At any rate the technique of combination of various interests into a governing bloc is not peculiar to organizations specializing in corrupt political techniques. It consists in welding together all the interests benefiting by the privileges given as a result of bribery, the receivers of state-bribes, and beneficiaries of political discrimination into the most powerful combination in the political life of a jurisdiction. It may include the suppression of opposition by methods often akin to intimidation as by a threat to skyrocket an individual's tax bill. Regardless of the techniques employed this procedure has to be consummated in order to attain and retain power. The aspect of a corrupt power combination which may be peculiar is that the combinations and alliances are effectuated by the application of sanctions and controls with compelling force directly to the individual. When some other types of techniques are employed successful combinations may be effectuated to a greater extent by group appeals. But the sole function of these power techniques is not to place a given set of individuals in power.

THE FUNCTIONS OF GRAFT

A clear distinction has been made between means and ends, between techniques and objectives. The techniques of graft have been regarded primarily as techniques of political control. The function of these political methods is to exert control or to influence somebody—to get something done. The basic techniques are practically the same in different places and at different times, but their function varies with the particular situation in which they are employed. The class of persons utilizing and profiting from the techniques of graft varies from time to time, but the methods are about the same. Thus, in a given city perhaps at one time the street railways were the chief corrupters of politicians; a little later it might be the gas interests; still later, the bus companies. In a state the railroads would run the government for a time and then turn it over to the timber and mining interests who in turn might relinquish control to the electrical utilities. These differences in personnel and objectives,

11 Many of the most important techniques of political machines do not involve graft. Thus, many voters cast their ballot in accordance with attitudes inculcated in eary childhood. The machine may control the symbols of the Republican party or of the Democratic party through graft, but graft is not necessary to secure the support of the persons who inherited their political beliefs. As long as people are simple there will be somebody to delude them.

but similarity in techniques and patterns of participants, show what is meant by the distinction between techniques, functions, ends.

The function performed or the end achieved by the use of the techniques of graft varies, of course, from time to time. The same is true for any political method. The Moscow Communists may employ essentially the same methods to retain power as the Italian Fascists, but for quite different ends. Some of the more frequently appearing functions which have been performed through the instrumentality of the techniques of graft in the United States may be indicated in brief compass.

The patronage system has served, and still serves, as the principal method of consolidating into a cohesive mass the politically effective sector of the population.[12] Within the relatively small group or class constituted of the people of political importance the control of patronage serves as a powerful means of control, of discipline, of direction. Lacking the tradition of a governing class, a socially responsible elite bound together by the ties of tradition and perhaps class interest, patronage serves to integrate the activities of individuals bound together by no other tie. It aids in the creation of class loyalties and simplifies the problem of party discipline. Other factors in the creation of party cohesion are not to be discounted, of course. The patronage system may be credited in a way with the functions performed by political parties for they have been largely financed from the public payroll. It is difficult to see how the functions carried on by parties could have been done on the same scale without some such method of financing. Almost everywhere party organizations have a permanent personnel which is paid for its services, but the funds for this purpose may come from sources other than the public treasury. American parties receive the benefit of a great deal of voluntary service, but a large proportion of the party work is paid for from the public treasury.

Various other functions have been served by the patronage system. It may be true that a bureaucracy will almost inevitably take on the color of the social structure of the nation, but the free and easy distribution of jobs has aided in the nationalizing process in the United States. The western lawyer and politician has always had an open ear to the call to serve his country in the federal service; and many of them responded to the call. Thus, through the federal and other public services has flowed a stream of individuals which, perhaps, has had its influence in creating national cohesion in a continental state surprisingly free from serious centrifugal tendencies. Patronage, of course, has been but one of many factors. The ready access to the public service to members of immigrant groups has doubtless aided in the process of assimilation and in the creation of new national loyalties. Had any successful effort been made to reserve public office for "Nordics," serious difficulties would have in all probability arisen.

Other forms of state-bribery, such as the distribution of contracts, orders, bank deposits, and tax favors in return for political services or support serve precisely the same function as the utilization of patronage to create lines of discipline in a political army. Many party functionaries are compensated for their labors with printing contracts, construction contracts, and various other types of public expenditures. These relation-

12 The concept of the politically effective sector of the population is based upon the hypothesis that a relatively small proportion of the population will operate and be immediately influential in the operation of the government. In so doing the wishes or hypothetical wishes of the masses may condition their behavior, but the actual power will be left to a relatively few. In a city this group may be the political machine proper and the persons bound to it by close ties often of a material character. In a social aristocracy based on land it may be a relatively few large landowners. In large social units it is of course difficult to define the limits of this group with any high degree of precision.

ships serve to control, just as jobs do. It is, of course, not to be denied that many of these relationships involve more of fraud, of purely personal profit, rather than group profit, but the aspect of patronage and other forms of state-bribery which stands out vividly is the fact that office, hope of office, or other immediately personal reward serves to solidify a "political" class lacking the tie of tradition or the resources necessary to sustain a benevolent oligarchy. Whether this is "right," or "just," is a matter for the professors of ethics. The phenomenon is there.[13]

Graft in the proprietary activities of government results in the creation of control relationships within the political machine. It is a means of controlling and rewarding the members of the party organization. Techniques such as bribery serve a different function. They may often be a means of solving provisionally at least conflicts of interest between social groups or between individuals and society. The wholesale bribery of legislatures by railroads in connection with rate regulation and taxation involved a dispute between carriers and shippers. The shippers were victorious in the long pull, but they were checked for years by techniques often of a corrupt character. Thus, bribery may be a means of retaining a privileged position which would otherwise have been lost earlier.[14] In the development of telephone, traction, gas and electric utilities in urban centers bribery was and is employed rather freely in various forms. This involves a conflict between the utility and its customers over rates and services, but in its earlier phases there was a bitter struggle over the issue of whether such services should be monopolistic in character. In the achievement of monopoly bribery and kindred methods played no minor role. Retrospectively monopoly appears to have been inevitable and not wholly undesirable. Thus, bribery may expedite the coming of the inevitable. In the exploitation of forests and minerals, bribery bore down much of what little opposition there was to the activities of the exploiters.

In some cases bribery has served as a technique for the achievement of accommodations between groups with conflicting codes of moral conduct. The stream of puritanism encounters powerful opposition from masses with different standards of behavior and from those who profit by catering to their tastes. Sentiment wavers. The newspapers and the churches "turn on the heat" occasionally. The community as a whole takes a hypocritical attitude. In this state of indecision and conflict the system of police graft makes possible prostitution, gambling, and other practices. It serves in a way to "regulate," control, license, and keep within bounds practices which are beyond the law. They cannot be controlled through the forms of law. Whether these problems could be dealt with without the use of bribery is another question, but there can be no doubt but that bribery has been an important ingredient in the forces eventuating in operating arrangements for these businesses.

In the administration of regulatory ordinances and laws of various types bribery has been a convenient way to avoid legal requirements which may be impracticable of application. Other rules socially desirable and applicable have been swept aside in the same way by

---

13 The emphasis here has been on state–bribery as a method of intensifying or creating loyalties and lines of control within the ruling bloc. This method may also be used in warfare between social groups with very real differences as in the use of pensions and places by the court party to control members of Parliament in England. This reflected deep seated differences in the nation. See James Burch, *Political Disquisitions, or, An Inquiry into Public Errors, Defects, and Abuses* (London: E. & C. Dilly, 1774–1775).

14 Privilege as used in American politics is a rather vague term. It could be defined as something the other fellow has which you do not have. It may be a profit or a business or financial position or "right" which is in violation of the existing rules of the game or standards of fair play. Or the constant revision of these standards may bring into the category of privilege practices or "rights" once considered legitimate.

business men too busy and impatient to spend their time in securing the formulation and adoption of more workable standards reconciling their interests and the public welfare in a "fair" manner.

As has been indicated at different points throughout the volume various methods of graft serve to control a considerable proportion of the electorate. The political organization usually attempts to dispense all governmental favors through the party hierarchy. At times the governmental officials have become so habituated to action upon the request of party officials that to secure a service involving no departure from the customary rule requires party intervention.[15] The party becomes the government. In its relations with the citizenry in distributing privileges there seems to be a tendency for relations between the political organization and other social hierarchies to be carried on between equals. A "big" business man will see a "big" party man and so on. By this method of administration of favors the party may gain the loyalty of the beneficiaries, although so little is known of the behavior of the electorate that the extent of this influence can not be estimated with any degree of accuracy.

It is not to be denied that the privileges and ends sought by the techniques of graft are almost always immediately selfish in character. Perhaps most ends achieved by political action, regardless of the methods employed, are selfish to a greater or lesser degree, but the ends secured by graft are usually more immediately and obviously so. The various functions of graft have been set forth for the purpose of suggesting that in some instances the immediate ends achieved by specific instances of graft may have more meaning when considered from a broader point of view.

15 Compare "deputantism" in France.

5. The Definition of Corruption

ARNOLD A. ROGOW / H. D. LASSWELL

A positively responsible act serves a system of public or civic order coextensive with a community context. *Deviations* from the norms of public and civic order are *negatively responsible acts* when they are performed by persons capable of education and exposed to the opportunity of acquiring the relevant norms. We say that the citizen of a democratic polity is acting in a positively responsible manner when he strives to protect the fundamental institutions and the basic pattern of value distribution within the commonwealth.

In a world of conflicting systems of public order scientific or lay observers are aware that responsible acts often conflict with one another. Thus those who are identified with public order *A* regard its spies abroad as engaged in highly responsible acts. In the perspective of public order *B,* of course, the same actors and activity are destructive.

We define a *subversive act* as a violation of responsibility toward one public or civic order on behalf of another with which the actor is actually, although not necessarily formally, identified.

A *corrupt act* violates responsibility toward at least one system of public or civic order and is in fact incompatible with (destructive of) any such system. A system of public or civic order exalts common interest over special interest; violations of the common interest for special advantage are corrupt.

In applying these distinctions, we bear in mind the difference between *conventional* and *functional* definitions. The former exist in the usage of a particular social context, such as the United States at a given period. Functional distinctions are made for scholarly and scientific purposes; ultimately they have in view all social contexts and hence define terms for comparative analysis.

Consider the phenomenon of "bribery." In functional terms we say that bribery is corrupt, since it is destructive of public order for anyone to tender or receive an inducement for the purpose of promoting special interest above common interest. Conventionally, however, the prescriptions of various public and civic systems may diverge greatly from one another. The legal code may seek to reach only the bribe-taker and leave the bribe-giver or offerer alone. In some communities only "extreme" payments or offers are considered threats to the common interest; elsewhere any payment may be forbidden.

Among many Americans bribery has the conventional connotation that wealth is involved. Our functional system of analysis, however, allows for the possibility that the inducement given or sought makes use of other values, such as power (e.g., a higher office or a voice in party councils), respect (e.g., favorable pub-

SOURCE: Arnold A. Rogow and H. D. Lasswell, *Power, Corruption, and Rectitude.* Englewood Cliffs, N.J.: Prentice-Hall, 1963, pp. 132–134. By permission of the authors and the publisher.

licity), well-being (e.g., luxurious entertainment), affection (e.g., acceptance in a family circle), enlightenment (e.g., inside dope), skill (e.g., access to advanced training), and rectitude (e.g., moral support from a cynical group).

An important and presently unsettled question is: Do all societies, whether civilizations or folk cultures, possess norms that prohibit bribery? So far as folk societies are known, the evidence is sometimes obscure, partly because of the difficulty in equating the norms of "kinship and local" systems with state systems.

Bribery is an instance of expected or realized *value gain* in a corrupt act. Some corruption proceeds, not by inducement, but by creating an expectation or realization of *avoided loss*. All values may be at stake, since corruption may be engaged in to avoid foreclosure of mortgage (wealth), to prevent a political boss from blocking renomination (power), to preclude blackmail (respect and rectitude), to avoid being beaten up (well-being), to prevent exclusion from inside information (enlightenment), to prevent disqualification as a candidate for further training and competition (skill), or to forestall loss of friends (affection).

The various participations in a sequence of corrupt conduct may have very similar or very different perspectives in regard to their own goal values.

The strategies of those who initiate a corrupt sequence of conduct are aimed at affecting expectations of gain or loss. In this context we note that expectations may be influenced by all the *instruments* of policy at the disposal of participants in the political process. Following usage, we may classify these instruments according to the degree of reliance upon symbols and signs or according to the degree of nonsign resources. *Communication* and *diplomacy* rely characteristically upon symbols and signs—the former addressing all members of the body politic, and the latter focusing upon negotiation with elites. *Economic* and *military* instruments use resources that are specialized to production or to destruction (weapons). Obviously the strategies employed may be largely *persuasive* or *coercive*. If the strategies are persuasive, the target has relatively advantageous alternative outcomes at low cost; if the strategies are coercive, he has relatively deprivational alternative outcomes at high cost.

Many other distinctions can be made for various purposes; for the present, however, it is sufficient to note the familiar difference between *commission* and *omission*.

6. The Nature of Political Corruption

ROBERT C. BROOKS

In the whole vocabulary of politics it would be difficult to point out any single term that is more frequently employed than the word "corruption." Party orators and writers, journalists, "muck rakers," and reformers all use it with the utmost freedom, and it occurs not uncommonly in the less ephemeral pages of political philosophers and historians. Transactions and conditions of very different kinds are stigmatised in this way, in many cases doubtless with entire justice; but apparently there is little disposition to inquire into the essential nature of corruption itself and to discriminate in the use of the word.

Detailed definitions of corrupt practices and bribery are, of course, to be found in every highly developed legal code, but these are scarcely broad enough to cover the whole concept as seen from the viewpoint of political science or ethics. The sanctions of positive law are applied only to those more flagrant practices which past experience has shown to be so pernicious that sentiment has crystallised into statutory prohibitions and adverse judicial decisions. Even within this comparatively limited circle clearness and precision are but imperfectly attained. Popular disgust is frequently expressed at the ineptitude of the law's definitions and the deviousness of the law's procedure, as a result of which prosecutions of notoriously delinquent officials, politicians, and contractors so often and so ignominiously fail in the courts. If once we step outside the circle of legality, however, we find extremely confused, conflicting, and even unfair states of moral opinion regarding corruption. Public anger at some exposed villainy of this sort is apt to be both blind and exacting. Reform movements directed against corrupt abuses are no more free than are regular political organisations from partisan misrepresentation and partisan passion. With all their faults, however, it is largely from such forces and movements that we must expect not only higher standards of public morality, but also a clearer and more comprehensive legislative and judicial treatment of corrupt practices in the future. For this reason it would seem to be desirable, if possible, to formulate some fairly definite concept of corruption, broader than the purely legal view of the subject and applicable in a general way to the protean forms which evil of this sort assumes in practice.

Certain verbal difficulties must first be cleared away. Chief among these, perhaps, is the extreme levity with which the word is bandied about. One word, indeed, is not sufficient, and a number of slang equivalents and other variants must needs be pressed into service: graft, boodle, rake-off, booty, loot, spoils, and so on. With all due recognition of recent

SOURCE: Robert C. Brooks, *Corruption in American Politics and Life*. New York: Dodd, Mead, 1910, pp. 41–54. By permission of the publisher.

achievements in the way of gathering and presenting evidence, it is lamentably apparent that charges of corruption are still very frequently brought forward, by party men and reformers alike, on slight grounds or no grounds at all, and also that in many of these cases no intention exists of pushing either accusation or defence to a point where a thorough threshing-out of the matter at issue is possible. In "practical politics" insinuations of the blackest character are made jestingly, and they are ignored or passed off with a shrug or a smile, provided only that they be not of too pointed or too personal a character. Very serious evils may follow reckless mudslinging of this sort. Even if the charges are looked upon as the natural and harmless exuberances of our current political warfare, their constant repetition tends to blur the whole popular conception of corruption. Insensibly the conviction gains ground that practices which are asserted to be so common can scarcely be wholly bad, since public life goes on without apparent change and private prosperity seems unaffected. If, on the other hand, the current accusations of corruption are to be taken at anything like their face value, it becomes difficult to avoid the pessimism that sees nothing but rottenness in our social arrangements and despairs of all constructive reform with present materials.

A second verbal point that demands attention is the metaphorical character of the word corruption. Even when it is distinctly qualified as political or business or social corruption, the suggestion is subtly conveyed of organic corruption and of everything vile and repugnant to the physical senses which the latter implies. It need not be charged that such implications are purposely cultivated: indeed they are so obvious and common that their use by this time has become a matter of habit. Witness in current writing the frequent juxtaposition of the word corruption, used with reference to social phenomena, with such words as slime, filth, sewage, stench, tainted, rottenness, gangrene, pollution, and the frequent comparison of those who are supposed to profit by such corruption to vultures, hyenas, jackals, and so on. Side by side with the levity already criticised we accordingly find a usage which, however exaggerated and rhetorical it may be, appears to indicate a strong popular feeling against what are deemed to be corrupt practices.

Escape from such confusion can hardly come from the accepted formulas of the dictionaries. Their descriptions or periphrases of corruption are in general much too broad for use in exact discussion. Bribery, indeed, is defined with sufficient sharpness by the *Century Dictionary* as

> a gift or gratuity bestowed for the purpose of influencing the action or conduct of the receiver; especially money or any valuable consideration given or promised for the betrayal of a trust or the corrupt performance of an allotted duty, as to a fiduciary agent, a judge, legislator or other public officer, a witness, a voter, *etc.*

Corruption, however, is by no means synonymous with bribery. The latter is narrower, more direct, less subtle. There can be no bribe-taker without a bribe-giver, but corruption can and frequently does exist even when there are no personal tempters or guilty confederates. A legislator may be approached by a person interested in a certain corporation and may be promised a definite reward for his favourable vote on a measure clearly harmful to the public interest but calculated to benefit the corporation concerned. If the bargain be consummated it is unquestionably a case of bribery, and the action involved is also corrupt. But, if current reports are to be believed, it sometimes happens that legislators, acting wholly on their own initiative and regardless of their duty to the state, vote favourably or unfavourably on pending bills, endeavouring at the same time to profit financially by their action, or by their knowledge of the resultant action of the body to which they belong, by speculation in the open market. In the latter instance they have not been approached by a personal tempter, and the brokers whom they employ to buy or sell may be ignorant of the motives or even of the identity of their patrons. Clearly this is not bribery, but equally clearly it is corrupt. The distinction is perhaps sufficiently important to justify the coinage of the term "auto-corruption" to cover cases of the latter sort.[1] Corruption in the widest sense of the term would then include both bribery and auto-corruption, and may be defined as *the intentional misperformance or neglect of a recognised duty, or the unwarranted exercise of power,*[2] *with the motive of gaining some advantage more or less directly personal.*

It will be observed that none of the terms of the foregoing definition necessarily confines corruption to the field of politics. This is intentional. Corruption is quite as possible elsewhere as in the state. That it has so frequently been discussed as peculiarly political is by no means proof that government is subject to it in a greater degree than other social organisations. One might rather conclude that the earlier discovery and more vigorous denunciation of corruption as a political evil showed greater purgative virtue in the state than in other spheres of human activity. For surely the day is gone by when the clamour of reformers was all for a "business administration" of public affairs. Since that era business has had to look sharply to its own morals—in insurance, in public utilities, in railroads, in corporate finance, and elsewhere. Revelations in these fields have made it plain that much of the impetus to wrong-doing in the political sphere comes originally from business interests. This is not to be taken as in any sense exculpating the public officials concerned; it simply indicates the guilt of the business man as *particeps criminis* with the politician. Moreover business can and does suffer from forms of corruption which are peculiar to itself and which in no way involve political turpitude. Such offences range all the way from the sale by a clerk of business secrets to a rival concern, and the receipt of presents or gratuitous entertainment from wholesalers by the buyers for retail firms, up to the juggling of financial reports by directors, the mismanagement of physical property by insiders who wish to buy out small stockholders, and the investment of insurance or other trust funds to the private advantage of managerial officers.

Besides business and politics, other spheres of social activity are subject to corrupt influences. Indeed wherever and whenever there is duty to be shirked or improperly performed for motives of more or less immediate advantage evil of this sort may enter in. This is the case with the church, the family, with educational associations, clubs, and so on throughout the whole list of social organizations. To ingratiate himself with wealthy or influential parishioners, for example, a minister may suppress convictions which his duty to God and religion requires him to express. A large proportion of the cases of divorce, marital infidelity, and childless unions, reflect the operation of corrupt influences upon our family life. In the struggle for endowments and bequests colleges and universities have at times forgotten some of their high ideals. If corrupt motives play a smaller part in the social organisations

1 Other illustrations of auto-corruption may be found in speculation by inside officials on the basis of crop reports not yet made public, and in real-estate deals based on a knowledge of projected public improvements.

2 Misperformance and neglect of duty do not clearly include cases of usurpation with corrupt motives; hence the addition of this clause to the definition. Some usurpations may of course be defended as involving high and unselfish motives, and hence free from corruption.

just mentioned than in politics or business it is perhaps not so much due to the finer fibre of churchmen, professors, and the like, as to the subjection of the more grossly gainful to other motives in clerical, educational, and similar circles.

While the possibility of corruption is thus seen to be extremely broad, our present concern is chiefly with political corruption. To adjust the definition hazarded above to cover the latter case alone it is necessary only to qualify the word "duty" by the phrase "to the state." Further discussion of the various terms of the definition, thus amended, would seem advisable.

I

To begin with, corruption is *intentional.* The political duty involved is perceived, but it is neglected or misperformed for reasons narrower than those which the state intends. Failure to meet a recognised duty is not necessarily corrupt; it may be due to simple inefficiency. The corrupt official must know the better and choose the worse; the inefficient official does not know any better. In either case the external circumstances may appear to be closely similar, and the immediate results may be equally harmful. No doubt what is often denounced in the United States as corruption is mere official stupidity, particularly in those spheres of administration still filled by amateurs and dominated by the "rotation of office" theory. Thus a purchasing official unfamiliar with his duties may prove the source of large profits to unscrupulous dealers. So far as the official himself is concerned no private advantage may be sought or gained, but the public interest suffers just the same. In another case the official understands the situation thoroughly and takes advantage of it by compelling the dealers to divide with him the amount by which the government is being defrauded, or he may go into business with the aid of office boys or relatives and sell to himself as purchasing agent. The latter are clear cases of bribery and auto-corruption respectively, but so far as immediate results are concerned the state is no worse off than with the official who was merely ignorant or careless. To one not in full possession of the underlying facts all three cases may appear very similar.

Successful corruption, however, tends to become insatiable, and in the long run the state may suffer far more from it and from the spread of the bad moral example which it involves than it can easily suffer from simple inefficiency. On the other hand inefficiency also may spread by imitation, although perhaps more slowly, since it is not immediately profitable, until the whole service of government is weakened. Moreover inefficiency may develop by a very natural process into thoroughgoing corruption. If not too stupid, the incapable official may come to see the advantages which others are deriving from his incapacity and may endeavour to participate in them. Because of his failure to obtain promotion so rapidly as his more efficient fellow-servants, he may be peculiarly liable to the temptation to get on by crooked courses. Practically, therefore, inefficiency and corruption are apt to be very closely connected—a fact which civil service reformers have long recognised. It would also seem that the two are very closely connected in their essential nature, and only a very qualified assent can be given to the doctrine that inefficiency, as commonly understood, is morally blameless. To be so considered the incapable person must be entirely unaware of his inability to measure up to the full requirement of duty. In any other event he is consciously and intentionally ministering to a personal interest, be it love of ease or desire to retain an income which he does not earn, to the neglect of the public duties with which he is intrusted. Now, according to the definition presented above, this attitude is unquestionably corrupt. It is, however, so common on the part of both officeholders and citizens that its corruptness is seldom recognised.

II

Political *duty* must exist or there is no possibility of being corruptly unfaithful to it. This statement may seem a truism, but the logical consequences to be drawn from it are of major importance. Among other things it follows that the more widely political duties are diffused the more widespread are the possibilities of corruption. A government which does not rest upon popular suffrage may be a very bad sort of government in many ways, but it will not suffer from vote-buying. To carry this thought out fully let us assume an absolute despotism in which the arbitrary will of the ruler is the sole source of power.[3] In such a case it is manifestly impossible to speak of corruption. By hypothesis the despot owes no duty to the state or to his subjects. Philosophers who defend absolute government naturally lay great stress on the monarch's duty to God, but this argument may be read out of court on the basis of Mencius's dictum that Heaven is merely a silent partner in the state. The case is not materially altered when responsibility under natural law is insisted upon instead of to the Deity. Now since an absolute despot is bound to no tangible duty, he cannot be corrupt in any way. If in the conduct of his government he takes account of nothing but the grossest of his physical lusts he is nevertheless not unfaithful to the principles on which that government rests. Viewed from a higher conception of the state his rule may be unspeakably bad, but the accusation of corruption does not and cannot hold against it.

Conversely corruption necessarily finds its richest field in highly organised political communities which have developed most fully the idea of duty and which have intrusted its performance to the largest number of officials and citizens. The modern movement toward democracy and responsible government, beneficent as its results in general have been, has unquestionably opened up greater opportunities for evil of this sort than were ever dreamed of in the ancient and mediaeval world. Economic evolution has co-operated with political evolution in the process. There is a direct and well-recognised relationship between popular institutions and the growth of wealth. It is no mere coincidence that those countries which have the most liberal governments are also today the richest countries of the world. With their growth in wealth, particularly where wealth is distributed very unequally, materialistic views of life have gained ground rapidly. Thus while the liberal development in politics has opened up wide new areas to the possibility of corruption, the corresponding development in the economic world has strengthened the forces of temptation.

Viewed in this light it must be admitted that our representative democracy with its great international obligations, its increasing range of governmental functions, its enormous and unequally distributed wealth and its intense materialism, is peculiarly subject to corrupt influence. This does not necessarily mean that the republic is destined to be overwhelmed by selfishness. It does mean, however, that we cannot rest secure upon the moral achievements of our ancestors and the institutions which they have transmitted to us. We must develop a more robust virtue, capable of resisting the greater pressure that is brought to bear upon it.

But even if it be conceded that there is a greater measure of successful temptation among us than in the European nations which twit us with corruption as our national vice, it does not follow that we are inferior in political morality to

[3] Mr. Seeley has shown, of course, that no actual despotism, so-called, really conforms to this conception, but for purposes of argument, at least, the assumption may be permitted to stand.

these, our self-appointed moral censors. Reverting to the illustration of vote-buying, it is evident that we could stop this particular form of corruption at once by the simple and obvious, although practically impossible, measure of abolishing popular suffrage. Assuming, for the sake of the argument, that this could be accomplished, we might readily find ourselves burdened with greater political evils than venal voting—for instance, the development of an arrogant oligarchy and the growth either of a sodden indifferentism or of a violent revolutionary spirit among the masses. A large percentage of Prussian citizens of the poorer classes sullenly refrain from voting, nor are they in the habit of selling their votes. Presumably some of them would be venal if they had the opportunity, but the plutocratic three-class election system makes their political influence so minimal that their ballots are not worth either the casting or the buying. Neither do Prussian municipal officials engage in boodling, but the ascription of superior virtue to them on this account must be tempered by a knowledge of the fact that the local government of the country is kept closely in leading strings by the state. Paradoxical as it may seem, it is none the less true that political corruption implies the existence of political virtue; it implies trust in the performance of duty, widespread obligation to perform it, and confidence that in the great majority of cases it will be performed in spite of the derelictions that such conditions occasionally entail. If monarchies are less corrupt than democracies, it is also true that monarchies do not repose so much faith in the fundamental honesty of their citizens as do democracies. At least they do not put it to such severe political tests.

7. Black-Market Bureaucracy

ROBERT O. TILMAN

BLACK-MARKET BUREAUCRACY

Modern bureaucracy closely resembles the mandatory pricing model of market economics. Price schedules are fixed by the government for both costs and benefits, from the point of view of the seller (the bureaucrat), as well as from that of the buyer (the client). The amount of time expended in shopping and completing a transaction is also determined largely by the government. Ideally this pricing mechanism should function independently of supply and demand factors. For example, air-wave channels suitable for television broadcasting are limited, the applicants are numerous, and the rewards of television broadcasting are high. Nevertheless, a modern bureaucracy is expected to make these difficult allocations on standards that are not affected by supply and demand. Parking places are scarce in any urban area and the demands for them are great, but the meter charge should be the only one the motorist has to play if the ideal of modern bureaucracy is to be met.

Often, however, bureaucratic systems fail to live up to these ideals. Demand far outpaces supply, policing becomes lax, and the result is a black market in government services. Whether it involves something as expensive as fur coats and free vacations for high administrators, or as modest as a fixed ticket at a local precinct, we know this bureaucratic black marketeering as administrative corruption.

Corruption, as I have employed the term here, involves a shift from a mandatory pricing model to a free-market model. The centralized allocative mechanism, which is the ideal of modern bureaucracy, may break down in the face of serious disequilibrium between supply and demand. Clients may decide that it is worthwhile to risk the known sanctions and pay the higher costs in order to be assured of receiving the desired benefits. When this happens, bureaucracy ceases to be patterned after the mandatory market and takes on the characteristics of the free market.

This shift from one pricing model to another can, of course, occur anywhere in the world, but I would argue that the developing countries are more vulnerable than the developed ones. The bases of my argument are both cultural and economic. First, there is the question of the cultural setting, which a number of social scientists accept as the principal cause of corruption. In an environment where there is little or no social stigma attached to bribery, nepotism, etc., the threshold for bureaucratic black marketeering is much lower and the problems of policing are multiplied. Second, with expectations and demands rising rapidly, particularly in the urban areas of the new states, it is difficult to retain anything approximating equilibrium between supply and demand. Third, given the predominance of govern-

SOURCE: Robert O. Tilman, "Emergence of Black-Market Bureaucracy: Administration, Development, and Corruption in the New States," *Public Administration Review*. 28:5 (September–October 1968), pp. 440–442. By permission of the publisher, American Society for Public Administration.

mental activity in the new states, and the corresponding low level of activity in the private sectors, clients with demands unsatisfied by the mandatory pricing system of the government bureaucracy are likely to have fewer nonofficial alternatives open to them than would be the case in the more developed states. Finally, the very magnitude and complexity of the older economic and political systems means that any given transaction will have relatively less impact on the system than will a similar transaction in a less-developed country. In this sense the benefit from a transaction in an underdeveloped country is relatively greater, and thus the transaction becomes more important.

PRICING ON THE BUREAUCRATIC BLACK MARKET

Administrative corruption exhibits many of the pricing characteristics of the economic free market. Certain services, for example, are likely to be highly inelastic, while others, those less essential, have greater elasticity. The elasticity curves for wheat and fire protection in the United States are probably very similar. The demand is almost constant since bread and fire protection are both seen as necessities and not luxuries. While an increase in the supply may lower the price, this in turn will not greatly stimulate additional consumption. Conversely, however, rising prices occasioned by decreasing supply will not sharply reduce consumption.[1] While one might be able to continue this analogy and suggest government services that respond to market forces in a manner similar to transistor radios (where supply, demand, and price are intimately interrelated), it is my own belief that most bureaucratic services are far less elastic than light consumer goods on the economic market.

Here I am, however, making two assumptions that need to be acknowledged. First, I am presuming no change in the intrinsic values of the services, a subject I shall discuss in the following paragraph. Secondly, I am presuming that the upward communications of the political system are good enough to permit the government to know what kinds of services its citizens consider to be essential. If either or both of these assumptions do not hold, it is likely that the demand curve for such services will more nearly approximate the demand curve for transistor radios than that of wheat.

One must also consider the question of taste and intrinsic value, both of which affect demand and influence the shape of the elasticity curve. Liver was in little demand and prices remained stable and low until it was discovered to be effective in the treatment of anemias. As people began to eat liver as a prophylactic against anemia, tastes changed and liver became a popular food. Demand increased and prices rose accordingly. A similar thing happened in the Philippines in regard to citizenship. Prior to 1954 Philippines citizenship for the Chinese community had little intrinsic value and there was little demand for it. As a result it could usually be obtained through the mandatory market system, and, if not, the costs of obtaining it through the free market bureaucracy was relatively low, probably in the neighborhood of 1000. However, in 1954 the Philippine legislature passed the Retail Trade Nationalization Act[2]

1 In Manila, during the great fire in the Chinese section of the city in 1963, fire protection, however, proved far more elastic than suggested here for the United States. In the face of a rapidly expanding demand these scarce services became available only if the shop owners provided some incentive money for the fire companies (and, as I was frequently told, "cash only; no checks"), and as the fire got worse the price went up. According to frequently mentioned but unconfirmed reports, one enterprising merchant "hired" a Quezon City fire company to protect his store, which at the time was on the fringe of the fire, only to lose it to a higher bidder as the fire drew nearer.

2 The Nationalization of Retail Trade Act, which was introduced annually in the Philippine Congress until it was finally passed in 1954 is only the most striking example of many moves that had the effect of increasing the intrinsic value of citizenship. For a general discussion of the several measures see Frank H. Golay, "The Nature of Philippine Economic Nationalism," *Asia,* No. 1 (Spring 1964), pp. 13–30.

which prohibited an alien from expanding any retail business, opening a new one, or passing his own on to his children. Citizenship suddenly had a much higher intrinsic value and the demand for it rose sharply. As the demand rose, so did the price. The process of obtaining citizenship was pushed almost completely out of the mandatory pricing system and into the free market, where the price has now risen about ten-fold.

The examples of pricing mentioned thus far involve real disequilibrium between supply and demand, but there can be other cases where shortages of supply are caused more by strictures in the bureaucratic pipeline than by actual shortages. The end result, of course, is likely to be the same. Whether gratifications are difficult to obtain because of short supply or because the bureaucratic machine is clogged up, the resulting disequilibrium creates a situation conducive to the shift from the mandatory-pricing model to the free-market model, as Malaya discovered in the 1950's.

Although the Federation of Malaya (1948–1963) was relatively free of administrative corruption, the Commission on Integrity in the Public Services concluded that "bribery and other forms of corruption are practiced in all the vulnerable departments." Generally speaking, these "vulnerable departments" were those where a service was being provided for clients that could be handled more expeditiously or efficiently by the bureaucrat provided he could somehow be induced to put out the extra effort or to change his scheduled order of priorities.[3] In the last years of existence of the old Federation of Malaya many allegations of corruption were made against one of these vulnerable departments—the department concerned with the alienation of land.

During World War II and the period of the emergency (1948–1960) the alienation of public land to private ownership fell hopelessly far behind. Ample land was available, but time and manpower were not adequate to cope with the task at hand, and thus supply (in this case effective supply) and demand fell into severe disequilibrium.[4] The outcome was not surprising. Until the government simplified and rationalized its alienation procedures, and until adequate personnel became available, black-market bureaucracy flourished at the lower levels of Malaya's field administration. Land could be gotten by needy farmers, but the delays built into the mandatory-pricing model made it worthwhile for those who could afford it to tap the free-market mechanism despite its higher cost. But, the more the farmers availed themselves of this alternative the higher the price went since the bureaucrats still had only a limited amount of time to devote to the complexities of land administration.

---

[3] Federation of Malaya, *Report of a Commission to Enquire into Matters Affecting the Integrity of the Public Service* (Kuala Lumpur: Government Press, 1955).

[4] The extent of this disequilibrium is detailed in Federation of Malaya, Land Administration Commission, *Report* (Kuala Lumpur: Government Press, 1958), especially para. 110. Between 1958 and 1960 this disequilibrium grew considerably greater than the some 200,000 outstanding requests for land reported by the Commission.

CHAPTER TWO

The Evolution of Public-Office Concepts and Rules

8. Corruption as a Historical Phenomenon

JACOB VAN KLAVEREN

Corruption as a historical phenomenon is, to the best of my knowledge, a problem that has never been dealt with systematically. The reason probably is that corruption has not been regarded as a problem. This point of view is completely justified as long as corruption is only perceived as a series of accidental acts of dishonesty on the part of civil servants. He who examines this subject more carefully, however, recognizes that the phenomenon occurred much more frequently prior to the French Revolution and that it was almost constitutionally determined. In this paper too, corruption shall be examined as an [unwritten] part of a political constitution.

CONSTITUTIONS[1] AND CORRUPTION

There are two types of constitutions under which corruption, by definition, does not occur—namely in the case of monarchy when interpreted as absolute one-man rule, and in the case of constitutions built upon the idea of popular sovereignty. Thus in this respect one could say *les extrêmes se touchent.*

First we shall discuss the Inca state as the closest approximation to the model of absolute monarchy. Here all the resources of the country were claimed for an economic plan that served the glorification of the ruler and the sun cult. Since there were no productive factors left untapped, it was impossible for civil servants to divert more revenues than were already allocated to them by the king in the economic plan. The incomes of civil servants and the people were precisely determined according to social position. This even affected nutrition patterns, numbers of wives, and the quality of the clothes that were distributed. A governor of the Inca caste received vicuña clothes from the public storehouses, while the people's clothes were made from llama wool. The people walked; the Sapa Inca and the high civil servants of Inca origin were carried in sedan chairs.[2] Thus

1 Of course, we do conceptualize "constitutions" as referring not only to written constitutions or to those that were framed by a deliberate act of legislation, as many adopted since 1789 have been. Administrative principles are of far more importance, particularly during the *ancien régime,* when they were never developed *ad hoc.* Numerous Asian and Latin-American states today possess written constitutions that tolerate corruption no more than do our own constitutions. Yet corruption in these countries is systematized and goes back to superordinate, unwritten principles of administration. The author had the opportunity to observe the functioning of such a political system during his stay as university lecturer at Chulalongkorn University in Siam in 1950–1953.

2 For a discussion of the Inca state's economic system see particularly P. A. Means, *Ancient Civilizations of the Andes.* New York, 1931, chap. VIII, and Louis Baudin, *L'Empire socialiste des Inka.* Paris, 1928.

SOURCE: Jacob van Klaveren, "Die historische Erscheinung der Korruption, in ihrem Zusammenhang mit der Staats- und Gesellschafsstruktur betrachtet," *Vierteljahreschrift f. Sozial u. Wirtschaftsgeschichte,* 44:4 (1957), pp. 294–302, 312–318. By permission of the publisher, Franz Steiner Verlag. Translated by Peggy Hofmann and Karl Kurtz.

everyone received an appropriate income, and to claim more constituted an offense against the Sapa Inca and the sun cult. This distribution of the national income to the furthering of the commonweal was based on ethical and religious values, but was centripetally oriented toward the glorification of the Sapa Inca and the sun.

It will be intelligble without more ado that this *ex-ante* distribution of the national income by means of an economic plan in a natural economy . . . could be realized rather easily. This task becomes more complicated in a money economy. The presence of money is a symptom of the existence of an exchange economy, which is not to say that an exchange economy could not also exist without money. In an exchange or market economy, quasi-anonymous forces determine the extent of employment and the distribution of the national income. It could only be confirmed afterward, but not regulated in advance whether all productive forces of a nation were really utilized fully and for what ends, and whether every social group obtained the income deemed appropriate on ethical grounds. Only through the techniques of modern economic policy is it possible nowadays to determine in advance not only the size of the national product but its distribution. In this process the market economy is regulated and the functions of money are to a large extent eliminated or at least influenced into a desired direction through a public monetary policy.

These modern possibilities were still unknown at the beginning of the twentieth century and are even nowadays not available for the less-developed countries. Thus if we posit an absolute monarchy existing simultaneously with a money economy, we could assume for the abovementioned reason that it would be impossible to carry out a patriarchal distribution of income on the Inca model. The monarch could obtain from the people through taxes what he deems necessary for himself and the public civil service, but he would always be lagging behind developments by one phase. Although he is not able to dictate to his subjects what constitutes appropriate income, he can compellingly prescribe the income appropriate to the civil servants and penalize all cases of corruption. To this extent the monarchy has a beneficial effect on the broad mass of the population. This is not to say, however, that the monarch will always act in this manner. It is possible that he might allow his civil servants to maximize their income in dealing with the public.[3] However, this would loosen the relationship between the civil servants and the monarch's decision-making power. The civil service hierarchy would disintegrate into a number of "maximizing units," each with its own interests, and would thus become unre-

3 This tended to be the case in the Muslim states, which is partly explained by the fact that the emirs, the caliphs, and the dignitaries recruited from the upper social classes were Arabs, whereas the people had been conquered by force of arms and had then turned to Islam. However, the distinctions persisted, even though the conquerors, as the result of mingling with harem women of all nationalities, ceased to remain pure Arabs. At any rate, a close union between people and princes proved infeasible, so that the intermediary castes, originally also of Arab origin, were able to prevent the establishment of an absolute monarchy. They formed an intermediary group with a goal of its own, which to a large extent succeeded in making its offices hereditary but which also fell apart into cliques and parties whom the emir could use for his own purposes. Domestic politics were thus complex and difficult to keep track of. The emir let his governors and civil servants largely go their own ways, but when they had sucked themselves full, he pressed them like a sponge. To illustrate this we refer to a dialogue that took place between Emir Abdurrhaman II of Cordoba (822–852) and a high official, as noted in an Arab chronicle. Emir: "Je voudrais couper la tet de celui qui sais avoir une grosse fortune a notre détriment et qui n'en verse rien au tŕesor." Mohammed-ben-Said (turning pale since he felt that the reference was to himself): "Ma fortune, je l'ai acquise par l'économie!" The outcome was that Mohammed donated part of his fortune to the emir, thus saving his own life. For this interesting dialogue see Louis Bertrand, *Histoire d'Espagne*. Paris, 1932, p. 82. These were the prevailing conditions in the entire area from Morocco to Yemen, which can be learned of Dimacqui's vademecum for merchants as well. See G. H. Bousquet, "L'économie politique non européano-chrétienne: L'exemple de Dimachqui," *Revue d'histoire economique et sociale*, 1957, p. 15.

liable for the execution of the national policy.[4] The more developed the monarchy, the greater its corruption-checking tendency, to the point that corruption disappears completely in an absolute monarchy, as in the case of the Inca state.

We shall now discuss the other polar situation. Let us assume that the common good is not found in an almost metaphysical way by a sovereign prince in the sense similar to Rousseau's *volonté générale* but is ascertained by an expression of opinion by the people. Let us assume further that the popular will is genuinely reflected in the nation's policy. Thus there incontestably exists a situation of popular sovereignty, and the civil servants are only executive instruments of the people's will. It goes without saying that it can never be the people's will to be exploited by the civil servants, and this is just the inevitable consequence of corruption. Therefore, the people will precisely prescribe the income appropriate to the civil servants and will not tolerate corruption. As a result corruption can never be rooted in the constitution and can only occur as occasional acts of dishonesty.[5]

What we have described here are two extreme ideal types, which will never be fully realized. However, the contrast between them should make evidence which circumstances determine whether corruption is built into the constitution. Corruption is built on the underlying principle that the people are subjected to the control of officials. Thus there exists a regulating principle, which gives to the officials and other intermediary groups a public existence with a purpose of their own. We divide these intermediary groups into those that are created by the monarch, that is, the public officials, and those which have autonomous origins, that is, the traditional intermediary groups. Among the latter are the landlords but also the urban patricians. Without a monarchy there would be no royal civil servants but only the civil servants who serve traditional intermediary groups. These have, however, been historically less significant than the royal civil servants; therefore, we shall pass them by. Similarly, among the traditional intermediary groups we will consider only the urban patricians.

These intermediary groups have rights of their own. The people exist not only for the king, but also for the intermediary group. The monarch may adjust to letting these intermediary groups claim what they regard as their due portion of the national income. It is obvious that relevant opinions may diverge, in which case tensions may occur. There may ensue a struggle around the distribution of the national income, which takes place in a field encompassed by a conflict triangle

4 One may speak of feudalism as a horizontal decomposition of the state, which disintegrates into a number of quasi-independent territories. Corruption, on the other hand, leads to a vertical decomposition of the civil service, which was created precisely to centralize state powers. The colonial policy of Charles V of Spain provides a good example. Shortly after the Conquest the conquistadores tended to develop into a powerful landed caste, which to a large extent threatened to isolate the native population from the monarch. Charles now endeavored, with more energy than caution, to inhibit the distribution of these estates, the so-called *encomiendas.* This led to the uprising of the Pizarro brothers in Peru in 1544, and the attempt to dissolve the *encomiendas* failed. However, the still undistributed parts of the country now came under the supervision of civil servants, the *corregidores.* Soon the emperor realized that he did not have command over the colonies by these means either, since the *corregidores* intercepted the natives' tributes without penalty and blackmailed them in every possible way. To put an end to the thievery from the treasury Charles at last sent royal treasury officials to the colonies in 1550, but they converted themselves as well into quasi-owners of their offices. Thus Charles had to recognize that even with the help of civil servants he was unable to maintain tight control over the colonies. Under Philip II the aggressive policy toward the *encomiendas* ceased altogether. See Silvio Zavala, *La encomienda indiana.* Madrid, 1935, pp. 54, 63, 173, and L. Simpson, *The Economienda in New Spain 1492–1550.* Berkeley, 1929, p. 112.

5 Act XII of the Declaration on Human- and citizen Rights of the French Revolution says: ". . . cette force [publique] est donc instituée pour l'avantage je tous et non pour l'utilité particuliere de ceux a qui elle est confiée."

whose pillars are the monarch, the civil service, and the urban oligarchy. The intermediary forces tend to nurture corruption, whereas the monarchy tends to check corruption. However, the intermediate groups do not necessarily stick together; on the contrary, quite often the civil service is created by the monarch during the struggle with the traditional intermediary groups. There then tends to ensue a rechanneling of corruption incomes in favor of civil servants and courtiers, although the total amount of corruption incomes may well decrease.

In his study *Deutsches Städteleben in der älteren Zeit* (*German City Life*) Gustav Schmoller[6] emphasized the corruption-checking effect of the monarchy. However, he exhaustively discussed the tendency of intermediary groups to further corruption only where blame was attached to the city oligarchy. This, of course, is due to the topic of his study but is also significant for his mentality. Corruption by civil servants is only mentioned where an honest historiography cannot avoid it. It is his major concern to correct those historians who, influenced by the Enlightenment, had viewed the "free" cities as "democratic" communities whose character had supposedly been aborted by the encroachment of the Prussian princes. Schmoller is perfectly right to correct this widely prevalent but erroneous idea and to point out that these very cities were breeding places of oligarchic despotism and corruption and had no claim to being considered democratic.[7]

This error is, by the way, very widespread, and is reflected in the title of a study by Pirenne, dealing with *Les anciennes démocraties des Pays Bas* (Paris, 1922). At the end of the eighteenth century there were in the Netherlands several thinkers influenced by the Enlightenment, who praised "grand pensionaries" Johann van Oldenbarneveldt and Johann de Witt, who fell victims to the hostility of the House of Orange, as martyrs in the struggle against tyranny. In reality, however, these proud patricians were the last to be concerned with the promotion of popular influence.[8] Even Cunningham falls into this error in his thorough and learned study *The Growth of English Industry and Commerce*, in which he asserts that democracies are more often corrupt and inefficient than are autocratic governments.[9] This, however, is impossible since democracy—as we have seen—is without corruption by definition. If, on the other hand one recognizes that Cunningham identifies democracy with the rule of parliament, then this statement carries more truth. One sees here that the conception of "democracy" was already completely diffuse by the end of the nineteenth century, although its identifying characteristics can be precisely determined on the basis of an exact analysis of the ideas of the Enlightenment.[10] Therefore, we prefer to avoid this expression as far as possible, and to speak instead of constitutions that honestly reflect the people's will. If one identifies democracy with the government of parliament, as Cunningham does, then the Magna Charta, which the English nobility extracted from John Lackland in 1215, could be regarded as the beginning of English democracy, since Parliament was founded then. That would be incorrect. While correcting Cunningham in this regard, one may otherwise agree with him since he is stating only what

6 Gustav Schmoller, *Deutsches Städteleben in der älteren Zeit.* Bonn and Leipzig, 1922.

7 Gustav Schmoller, p. 232. See also his *Umrisse und Untersuchungen zur Verfassungs-, Verwaltungs- und Wirtschaftsgeschichte.* Leipzig, 1898, p. 250.

8 See P. J. Blok, *Geschichte der Niederlande* (*Ubers.*). Gotha, 1910, VI, p. 387.

9 See William Cunningham, *The Growth of English Industry and Commerce,* II. 5th Ed. Cambridge, 1912, p. 19.

10 This was brilliantly done by Leonard Woolf in his not-well-enough-known study, *After the Deluge.* London: Pelican, 1937.

has been extrapolated above, namely that intermediary groups tend to further corruption. His reference is primarily to the rural squires that were then dominant in Parliament, so that particularly for the period after 1688 one may speak of a "squirearchy." However, for Prussia, which is examined by Schmoller, and with respect to the Netherlands, the city oligarchies are more significant. Schmoller maintains that the kings, by integrating the cities into the Prussian national state, rid them of "oligarchic corruption" and extended to them an "honest and well-regulated administration." However, he feels forced to admit some reservations, particularly for the age of the soldier-king Frederick William I (1730–1740). Schmoller admits that the groups from which the civil service was recruited were not at all "ethically pure," and that a decay of the civil servants' morality must be noted during the reigns of Frederick the Great and Frederick Wilhelm II, although this did not lead back to the nadir marked during the reign of the Great Elector (1640–1688).[11]

We must contradict Schmoller as well if he thinks that his description of the situation explains a gradual transition from an "oligarchic corruption" to the—in our sense—"honest" City Regulation of 1808.[12] The later reform is, in our view, rooted in the Enlightenment, which penetrated Prussia after the defeats of Jena and Auerstaedt, even though the intellectual instruments of the reform, the "educated bourgeoisie" which had grown considerably during the eighteenth century, could not participate in the country's government to a great extent until after 1848. Thus it becomes clear that Schmoller's benevolent monarchy and his spontaneous rises and declines of morality will not carry us very far. These are not accidental events; we are concerned with a new epoch of intellectual and cultural history, the Age of the Enlightenment, which affected the constitutions of Europe.[13]

Such an optical illusion could not arise with regard to the Netherlands, where the Orange Stadtholder had to flee to England in 1795. The democratic reform party, the "Patriots," had already carried out a type of French Revolution in 1786. However, they were defeated by the hurriedly summoned Prussian forces in 1787, causing their leadership to flee to France. Strongly influenced by Jacobin thought, the exiles returned with the French troops in 1795, took over the government, and established the Republic on modern foundations.[14] One of their leaders, the lawyer Herman Willem Daendels, went as governor to Java and accomplished there what he described as the "sincere and honest political rule of the Netherlands." He established good official salary levels and forbade all forms of corruption, whether at the expense of the

11 Gustav Schmoller, *Deutsches Städteleben,* p. 232; Derselbe. *Umrisse und Untersuchungen,* pp. 250, 308.

12 Gustav Schmoller, *Deutsches Städteleben,* p. 232.

13 Likewise, the "honest" administration in Bavaria was only installed after the French successes. See Hans Schmelze, *Der Staatshaushalt des Herzogtums Bayerns im 18. Jahrhundert.* Stuttgart, 1900, p. 186. Schmelze tends to attribute the corruption that was widespread before this time to the nonexistence of an established salary and pension system. But this point of view is a naïve one. High salaries and pensions are in themselves insufficient for the establishment of an honest administration, as shall be shown below. Likewise, Lawrence Stone, who generally has a good understanding for phenomena of corruption, does not comprehend this decisive point when he writes about the government of Queen Elizabeth: "Lacking the financial resources or the educational media to produce an honest and efficient bureaucracy." See Lawrence Stone, *Sir Horatio Palavicino.* Oxford, 1956, p. XV. Precisely the higher civil servants, who generally derived the biggest advantages from corruption, normally received pensions the size of which was determined by the king on the basis of varying considerations. Thus Edmond-Jean François Barbier, *Chronique de la Regence,* II. Paris, 1857, p. 16, with respect to such a case: ". . . on retranche a cent pauvres familles des rentes viagères . . . ; on donne . . . de pension a gens qui ont été dans grands postes, dans lesquelles ils ont amassés des bien considerables, toujours au depens du peuple. . . ."

14 See I. T. Brugmans, *Sociaal-economische Geschiedemis von Nederland, 1795–1940.* The Hague, 1961, p. 16.

state or of the natives. One European civil servant who did not take the sudden reversal seriously and continued to extort from the natives was executed; thus was "honest" administration established.[15]

MONARCHY AS A CHECK TO CORRUPTION

This section maintains that the tendency of monarchy to check corruption was little developed in Europe during the *ancien régime,* perhaps least of all in England. . . .

THE TENDENCY OF THE INTERMEDIARY GROUPS TO ENCOURAGE CORRUPTION

As we have already pointed out, "corruption lay," so to speak, "in the middle."[16] The intermediary groups were the breeding places for corruption. This is generally true for both the traditional intermediary groups and the civil-servant class created by the prince. This distinction gradually disappeared, especially when the civil service was mixed with representatives of the traditional intermediary layers, as was the case in most countries. The only remaining distinction was that the city oligarchies to which we limited ourselves were organized in a collegial manner, whereas the civil servants' underlying structure was hierarchical. Therefore, the internal relations were not quite the same. Of course, the civil servants were quite often organized collegially in "boards," but this was only true for each step of the hierarchy. To begin with we shall overlook the differences and concentrate on the general conditions that are true of both groups.

Every intermediary group has the tendency to set itself apart from the lower ones, thus developing a specific social and economic consciousness. It regards itself as a specific entity of a higher social order that has the right to place itself on a higher economic level than the masses, not on the basis of any specific service to the community but because of its mere existence. But even when its members indulge in notions of their own usefulness to the community, they think of a more or less metaphysically based common good and are inclined to consider their privileged position as a requisite for the divine order. This kind of "service" is not exactly what is demanded by a truly sovereign people.

This was the mentality of Tolstoi's Count Vronsky, who supported the principle of promptly paying a gambling debt to a friend, but thought that one should kick a tailor out the door for his boldness when he time and again appeared to claim payment for his work. He would complain bitterly if this tailor asserted his legal rights; equality before the law was anathema to these strata. In 1768 this same opinion was expressed by the Scottish nobleman who called the

---

15 Details may be found in the study by the veteran director of the archives of the Dutch East India Company in Batavia, F. de Haan, *Priangan.* 4 vols. Batavia, 1910–1912, particularly Vol. 1, p. 461. See also J. van Klaveren, *The Dutch Colonial System in the East Indies.* The Hague. 1953, chaps. X, XI, XII. In Europe the conversion to "honest" administration cannot be precisely identified; but in the colonies corruption occurred quite openly precisely for the reason that it occurred at the cost of foreign people who had been conquered for exploitation. Hence the conversion was most obvious here. More details and also a summary may be found in my forthcoming textbook *General Economic History 200–1760,* esp. in chap. 25.

16 Wilhelm Roscher, *Naturgeschichte der Monarchie, Aristokratie, Demokratie,* Munich, 1933 (1892), p. 147, describes the aristocracy as "the most self-serving of all three forms of government." It is striking that this important economist never examined the effects the forms of government have on the distribution of income. The above quotation, however, shows a latent understanding for the relationship. In my view the physiocrats' preference for absolute monarchy can only be explained because they realized the tendency of the intermediary strata to encourage corruption. This fact is generally known, although not yet explained. Sismondi comes close to an explanation when he writes: "Ils révéloient les abus effroyables sous lesquelles le peuple était écrasé; mais en général, plus ennemis des corps privilegiés que de l'autorité royale, ils sembloient, par leurs principes, favoriser le despotisme." See H. C. L. Simonde de Sismondi, *Histoire des Français,* XXVIII. Paris, 1821–1844, p. 483.

businessmen who reclaimed Lady Caithness' furniture "a set of low-lifed creatures."[17]

Of course, these were noblemen, but the intermediary groups of lower origin were no different. The Dutch city patricians were always on the same level as the hereditary nobility, and they were truly convinced that they ruled by divine right.[18] John Evelyn noted with satisfaction in his diary one day that on the previous Sunday the priest had praised the differences of rank and position as being divinely ordered.[19] This mentality is evidenced by many other references. But the remarkable thing is that those civil servants who advanced by virtue of their own skills, but who were not of noble origin, assumed this view. For example, Samuel Pepys[20] succeeded in gradually achieving a more or less equal position among the members of the Naval Board of which he was the secretary. He proudly noted that day when he, like the others, kept his hat on during a conference without any objection from the other gentlemen. Soon he bought himself a sword and a carriage with two beautiful horses.[21]

Thus the intermediary groups were not totally closed, particularly not the civil service, since the work had often to be done by an ambitious member of humble origin like Pepys. Nevertheless, it can be regarded as closed, since such outsiders were assimilated at once. This mentality of the middle groups gradually led its members to believe that they were entitled to a certain conventionally conditioned way of life and the corresponding incomes. It is important for us to note here that the already mentioned standards were rather vague. Even among contemporaries and colleagues there must have been some uncertainty about the rights due to them because of their position. This uncertainty had the effect—and this is what concerns us here—of continuously increasing the demands but never of decreasing them. The tendency of the demands to spiral—and thereby the corruption, too—can be observed among both the civil servants and the city oligarchy. No one wanted to fall behind his colleagues either in his outwardly visible way of life or in the less noticeable size of his income. Thus, even when corruption was thoroughly accepted, there was an astonishing amount of secretiveness, with the result that only little material can be found for these periods as well.

The demands of the intermediary groups were sometimes pushed to a higher level by the shocklike effect of external conditions, for example, by the spread of French fashion during the era of Louis XIV or by the growing acquaintance with Oriental luxury goods. Chinese porcelain, japanned goods, or art objects made out of ivory spread more rapidly the more one believed that he had to keep pace with everyone else. There is no need to emphasize that the women

17 We quote this passage at some length because it is so characteristic of the spirit of the *ancien régime:* "My Lady Caithness is harassed in a most barbarous and inhumane way by a set of low-lifed creatures she has had the misfortune to have dealings with. Upon Saturday last her Ladyship's furniture was all sequestrated and carried away by one Pett an uphosterer, for a debt due him." The letter has been published by Leonard Woolf, *After the Deluge,* p. 75.

18 See P. J. Blok, VI, pp. 199, 203 ff.

19 See John Evelyn, *Diary II,* p. 47. Evelyn's opinions were clearly revealed in the following incident. As he was returning from Italy through Switzerland to the North with a number of gentlemen, a dog belonging to one of his companions killed a goat. When the poor shepherd asked for compensation, he was refused out of hand as being ridiculous. However, at the next village the company was stopped and forced to compensate for the loss and to pay a small fine as well. Evelyn called this "an affront" and complained about the "ill-treatment we had received for killing a wretched goat." See John Evelyn, *Diary I,* pp. 231, 233 f. It should be pointed out here that Evelyn had an honest, humane, and even noble character.

20 Samuel Pepys came from a family of estate managers in Cambridgeshire. After the Black Death these "villici" appeared as tenants (farmers). See Sir John Clapham, *A Concise Economic History of Britain.* Cambridge, 1951, p. 115, p. 202. Pepys' father was a tailor in London.

21 See Samuel Pepys, *Diary I,* pp. 128, 132.

were primarily responsible for this. A comparison between the way of life of the Dutch patricians and the English gentry during the seventeenth and the eighteenth centuries shows a very significant increase of demands as well as of income gained by corruption.[22] On close inspection this would certainly be found to be the case in every country. Schmoller[23] has already pointed to an increasing closure in Prussia of the civil service, which became a caste at the same time, as well as an increase in corruption after the death of the simple soldier-king Frederick William I (1713–1740). Undoubtedly, the predominance of French and courtly culture during the reign of Frederick the Great influenced this development. It is clear that the king's way of life had great influence. The courtiers all tried to copy this way of life in miniature, but they had to make sure that they kept their distance, just as it was generally between inferiors and superiors. What was considered an "appropriate" distance was not clear and depended on the superior.[24]

It will be obvious that not even high salaries were a prophylactic against corruption in view of these spiraling demands and the prevailing attitudes. This was particularly true because it was not just *income* that was at stake but the building of a *fortune* in a relatively short period of time in order to allow one's descendants to live the life of gentlemen without having to work.[25] It is hard for us to imagine the high demands made by the intermediary groups of that time. From our point of view, the salaries cannot be considered low. That is, they were rather average by our standards for the lower civil servants; for the higher officials they were nominally almost as high as today's but, of course, much higher in purchasing power.[26] Samuel Pepys made £350 a year. It should be realized that an excellent cook earned £4 a year with room and board, or that a clever widow got by on £6 a year and was still able to give alms.[27] With an

22 At the beginning of the seventeenth century the way of life of the Dutch patricians was not much different from that of the petty bourgeoisie. A hundred years later, however, they owned villas, saloons, and gardens in the style of Le-Notre, and often married into the hereditary nobility, who receded in the background. See P. J. Blok, IV, p. 112 and VI, pp. 101, 199. For England we refer to the cases of the Duke of Marlborough and Lord Chancellor Somer, which we will discuss further below. Thus two contradictory developments are to be observed: on the one hand an increasing degree of corruption and on the other a significant growth of the educated bourgeoisie, the carriers of the Enlightenment, who insisted on an "honest" administration. This inevitably led to a shocklike confrontation which took place during the French period. The transition is difficult to recognize in England, where—from my point of view—it had already taken place prior to the French Revolution during the financial reforms of Pitt the Younger (1784). However, I am still trying to prove this assumption.

23 See Gustav Schmoller, *Deutsches Städteleben*, p. 232.

24 Compare the careful manner in which Samuel Pepys imitated the gentlemen's habits and the satisfaction he got when he succeeded. History noted some transgression of the proper distance, particularly in the case of important persons. This aroused both the envy of colleagues and the wrath of princes. The "colleagues" ruined Lord Chancellor Hyde, whose magnificent Dunkirk House supposedly caused him to make the prophetic statement: "This house will one day be my ruin." See Samuel Pepys, *Diary II*, p. 233, notation of the editor. In France the splendid palace of the superintendent Nicholas Fouquet invoked the wrath of the young Louis XIV, which led to his own overthrow, although the skids were greased by Colbert.

25 We want to illustrate this with only a few examples. Thus Lawrence Stone, *Sir Horatio Palavicino*. Oxford, 1956, p. 271, mentions that Palavicino had bought the estate Babraham from a Robert Taylor. He was a protégé of Lord Chancellor Burghley (also spelled Burleigh) and "had made a handsome fortune as teller in the Exchequer." John Evelyn, *Diary II*, p. 118, reports that in passing he once visited Viscount Hereford, who had fallen out of favor in Ipswich, and he says, "Whilst he was Secretary of State and Prime Minister he had gotten vastly, but spent as hastily, even before he had established a fund to maintain his greatness." Of Will Hewer, Samuel Pepys' friend and dependent, John Evelyn, p. 323, reports: ". . . Mr. Hewer, who got a considerable estate in the Navy. . . ."

26 This is a widespread phenomenon. See Wilhelm Roscher, *Naturgeschichte der Monarchie, Aristokratie, Demokratie*, new ed. Munich, 1933 (1892), p. 311.

27 For these figures see Samuel Pepys, *Diary I*, p. 352, and John Evelyn, *Diary II*, p. 244. From this it appears that the civil servants' salaries were so high that large amounts could be saved for old-age pensions. Naturally, Pepys did not have to live like a cook. Note, however, that households with an income of £50 or an estate of £600 were classified as "substantial households" according to a census taken in London in 1695. See Roger Mols S. J. *Introduction à la Démographie historique des villes*

income of £350 a year Pepys' fortune increased annually by about £1000.[28] The many figures he notes in his diary show, furthermore, that he was only one of the smaller officials. A high income in itself did not serve the purpose: there had to be some pressure for honesty, which increased at the same rate that the morals and opinions of the time increased in favor of corruption. Only a tyrant could provide order here.

THE FORMS OF CORRUPTION

This section establishes two broad categories of practices: (1) fraud or graft at the expense of the treasury and (2) extortion of the subjects. It is argued that once corruption is tolerated both forms must come into existence. . . .

THE INSTABILITY OF THE SYSTEM OF CORRUPTION

This section tries to ascertain how the profits of corruption were divided: (a) between the colleagues of oligarchical bodies and (b) within the official hierarchy. The lack of precise standards led to frictions and generally unstable equilibria of corruptional systems. . . .

---

d'Europe du XIVe au XVIIIe siècle, II. Louvain, 1954–1956, p. 94. However, Pepys was able to make the £600 necessary for a comfortable existence in less than a year because his fortune increased by £1000 annually. We must remember that Pepys, who did not belong to high society, did not have high expenses. Nevertheless, he spent more than his salary, that is, more than £350 per year. Even though the salaries were sufficient to build up considerable reserves while living quite well, the high officials often received lifetime salaries. Thus Admiral Lord Sandwich received £4000 a year for his entire life. Corruption, however, was flourishing among the highest classes. Thus it is clear that high salaries and pensions in themselves are not sufficient to inhibit corruption.

28 John Evelyn's remark in 1703 shows how differently corruption was looked upon then: "This day died Mr. Samuel Pepys, a very worthy, industrious and curious person, none in England exceeding him in knowledge of the navy, in which he had passed through all the most considerable offices . . . all of which he performed with great integrity." See John Evelyn, *Diary II,* p. 371 f. Of course, it must be considered that Pepys insisted on delivery of good quality and correct amounts by the suppliers though he certainly cheated the Treasury by way of padded accounts. This can be discovered from his own notes as well. He deprecated other officers of the Navy Board who collaborated in the supply of bad materials to the shipyards. John Evelyn, *Diary II,* pp. 152, 167, writes of Sir Stephen Fox, a paymaster general in time of war, who was allowed to keep "a moderate allowance" of the soldiers' pay thanks to the prompt payment, ". . . an able and honest man" and describes his fortune of £200,000 as "honestly got"!

9. Performance Levels and Bureaucratic Structures

BERT F. HOSELITZ

In a paper published almost three years ago, I suggested hypothetically that the overall historical course of a society could be interpreted as passing through several phases of secular evolution; that it is first confronted as a major functional requisite with problems of solidarity or integration, then with those of systemic goal attainment, and finally with those of adaptation.[1] In more concrete terms, in its initial period a society is concerned primarily with problems of determining who are its members and how they are related to one another. We note these integrative concerns in the formation of simple societies, but also in newly constituted nation-states, e.g., the countries which emerged after the First World War out of the shambles of the Austro-Hungarian Empire, or more recently the newly independent nations which had shaken off the colonial yoke. In the course of time integrative concerns tend to become less pressing; methods of solving the needs of the solidarity sector tend to become routinized; and systemic goal gratification comes to occupy the first place among the needs of the society. Only at a late stage of development do adaptive needs come to occupy a principal place, but their supremacy, except in relatively crisis-free situations, is constantly threatened by the pressure of meeting the collective goals of the system. It is, of course, not maintained that this schema presents a full description of the evolution of social systems through time. In particular, it is not maintained that any of the needs, integrative, goal attainment, or adaptive are ever absent, but merely that during different phases of the development of a society different sets of needs tend to predominate. This phasing, on the whole, follows a course of evolution in which primary concern with solidarity is replaced by goal attainment, and this latter by adaptation as the major problems faced by a society.

If we apply this schema to the study of bureaucracies, we find that in societies in which integrative needs predominate, administrative behavior is strongly influenced by these integrative needs. In fact, in little differentiated societies administrative functions are often performed by institutions located primarily in a sub-sector of social action in which the maintenance of solidarity is paramount. Hence, it is not

1 See Bert F. Hoselitz, "Economic Policy and Economic Development," in Hugh G. J. Aitken, *The State and Economic Growth,* New York, Social Science Research Council, 1959, pp. 333 ff.

SOURCE: Bert F. Hoselitz, "Levels of Economic Performance and Bureaucratic Structures," in Joseph La Palombara, ed., *Bureaucracy and Political Development.* Princeton, N.J.: Princeton University Press, 1963, pp. 188–196. By permission of the author and the publisher.

surprising at all that Fortes and Evans-Pritchard point to segmental lineages as the carriers of administrative functions in certain African societies. And we find that even on a much higher level of differentiation administrative functions are performed by structures which have strong integrative admixtures, or are institutionalized primarily with reference to the integrative, rather than to the goal-attainment needs of the society. For example, in the patrimonial bureaucracies of the early Middle Ages, described by Weber, the performance of public office was basically subject to the integrative action system. Thus under European feudalism, at a time when integrative needs appeared predominant, the holding of public office was a function of the solidarity structure. I refer to the period during the ninth and tenth centuries when the various political entities in Europe began to be formed, many of them arising, in part, out of the consolidation of territories reconquered by a local magnate and his followers from the retreating barbarians. It was the time when counties and, in some instances, dukedoms or even petty kingdoms began to emerge. A public office was held in those days, at least ideally, as a fief. It was exercised in the particularist interest of its holder, and through this interest his integration into the solidarity structure was assured. The very definition of an administrative position as a fief shows the close connection of the public office with the solidarity structure, since the fief itself was the object merely of establishing a relationship between lord and vassal. The major nexus of classical European feudalism was the tie establishing a solidarity structure throughout society.[2] This interpersonal relationship often established the social status of the vassal. Hence the exercise of an office was tied to the ascriptive position of this individual in the social structure. In other words, the granting of a fief to which was tied a public office not only established the right and the charge to execute the administrative task, but also defined the social rights and obligations of the holder of the office vis-à-vis his lord, as well as vis-à-vis the public at large. What mattered most in the context of building an administrative structure by this means was not so much the constitution of a bureaucracy, but rather the fulfillment of the integrative needs of a society in process of formation.

Feudalism changed greatly in the course of its later evolution. Much of what had been real in its early phases became a pure formality later. But even in its earlier stage, it was a relatively highly formalized system, with elaborate ceremonial and extensive and explicit legal sanctions. But similar structural relations, also with primarily solidarity-forming or solidarity-enhancing functions, based on some form of ascriptive norms may be found in many fairly differentiated, nonindustrial societies. Superficial observers who have studied the social and economic relations of many traditional societies, have found extensive feudal elements in them. Though they have, on the whole, employed a vague and ill-defined concept of feudalism, they have sensed correctly that all social institutions in these societies were still strongly influenced by the persistent integrative needs of the society and that ascriptive, rather than rationalized, achievement-oriented, norms determined the behavior of persons entrusted with administrative functions. Much of the alleged corruption that Western technical advisers on administrative services of Asian and African states encounter, and against which they inveigh in their technical reports with so little genuine success, is nothing but the prevalence of these

2 On the nature of European feudalism, see Marc Bloch, *Feudal Society*, trans. by L. A. Manyon (Chicago, 1961), esp. Part IV, pp. 145 ff. On the connection between public office and the grant of a fief, see the extensive literature on *Ministeriales* and *Dienstlehen;* an abbreviated statement may be found in F. L. Ganshof, *Qu'est-ce que la Féodalité?* Bruxelles, Office de Publicité, S.C., 1947, pp. 137 ff.

non-rational norms on the basis of which these administrations operate. Moreover, as we have seen earlier, when we discussed the case of dual bureaucracies, the very existence of these structures, based on ascription and survivals of the phase of integrative predominance, constitutes a contrast and results in a clash with the rationalized achievement-oriented bureaucracies of the central government—or at least some of its branches.

The process of bureaucratic modernization in developing countries seems, therefore, to be tied up closely with the struggle for greater national unity, and, above all, the decrease, destruction, or fundamental modification of particularist tendencies still prevailing in these countries. Political modernization in the new nations of Asia and Africa implies, among many other things, a transfer of a person's loyalty from a small, particularistic group to a large entity, ideally the entire nation. In some societies this process takes place stepwise as, for example in India, where linguistic groups and linguistically defined states intervene between the small particularist group (caste, tribe, or village community) and the nation as a whole. There exist similar interstitial structures in other countries, e.g., Nigeria or Indonesia, which plainly acknowledge this federated character, but we find them even in countries which do not officially acknowledge them. In these latter the struggle against the nuclei around which particularist sentiments can crystallize is much sharper.

The demands of economic development in all these countries require the elimination or effective reduction of particularist loyalties and action based upon them. For if the human and non-human resources of a country are to be allocated optimally, strict principles of efficiency, rather than familiarity or other forms of personal and local preference, must rule in the assignment of economic and occupational roles and similar contractual relations pertaining to allocation of resources. But local, tribal, and linguistic particularisms stand in the way of this process of generalization of interpersonal economic relations in a developing country and hence the pressures for economic development tend to support the struggle against them. But, as we have seen earlier, particularistic loyalties are also at the bottom of these political sentiments which prevent the development of an achievement-oriented rationalized bureaucracy. As Dr. Wagner pointed out, in the passage cited earlier, a political unit in segmented (i.e., strongly particularistic) societies may be defined in "terms of consciousness of unity and interdependence," i.e., in terms of loyalty towards and identification with a more or less narrow group of individuals. It is this segmented structure of political organization with strong admixtures of kinship, i.e., ascription-oriented features, which militates against the establishment of specialized political (and among them also specialized bureaucratic) institutions.

Hence the requisites imposed on a society by the pressures for economic development are parallel to those made by the demands of political and especially administrative modernization. The protective shelter of predominantly integrative functions in the existing institutions must be modified or abolished, and institutions with differentiated functions in the adaptive and goal attainment subsystems of the society must take their place. This is the basic meaning of social-structural differentiation in modernizing societies.

There is still a final point that needs to be discussed, since it is tied up with those mentioned so far, and that is the relationship between the bureaucracy and the development of a money economy. As we have already seen, Max Weber regarded the presence of a money economy as a prerequisite for a rational system of bureaucracy, and again in the discussion of the feudal, patrimonial bureaucracies of early medieval Europe, we found that by granting a public office in the form of a fief, the office tended to become exercised in the particularist economic interest of the holder. In more concrete terms, a person who received, say, a tax collection job as a fief, was supposed to gain his income from part of his receipts, and other more strictly administrative posts were granted often with a piece of land attached from which the public official was expected to provide for his livelihood. As Weber argued, this system tends to produce pressures fostering the breakup of the bureaucratic structure, but also to force upon the official the role of entrepreneurial tax farmer. Hence, in systems such as these there is a strong conflict between the bureaucracy becoming institutionalized in the adaptive as against the goal-attainment sector.

We know that medieval feudalism, in the course of its development, made the fief inheritable. This established progressively a proprietary interest of its holder in the landed property attached to it, but often also in the office itself. In some cases the office provided an income in and of itself, in others it determined the social status of the holder, and in still others it gradually became, as we shall see, an object of trade and exchange. For once a proprietary interest in an office had been established, it was only natural that whoever controlled it should regard it as a good which could be bought and sold. Even if the holder of the office wished to pass it on to his son, it had to be evaluated so as to compensate other children accordingly. But since, in the last resort, an office was held not in the holder's own right, but from his superior lord, the lord—in most instances the king—wished to share in the transaction, regardless of whether the office was to be passed on by sale, inheritance, or dot. The venality of office thus arose in a context in which in the realm of public administration, goal-attainment, and adaptive system problems occupied a somewhat ambiguous position but in which gradually the natural economy had given way to a money economy, and in which it became customary to transfer property—including property in certain privileges and rights—by sale or inheritance.[3]

With the expansion of a moneyed class of traders and the simultaneous growth of a territory controlled by a monarch, conditions are established in which possibilities for demand and supply of new offices are created. For the buyer of an office it holds out not only a continuing source of income, but in a society in which the holding and exercise of an office are as yet regarded as a privilege of the nobility, the acquisition of an office also means an advancement in social status. For the crown the sale of offices provided a new, previously untapped source of revenue, especially in times of fiscal emergencies. It was this coincidence of interests on the part of important social groups, the rising entrepreneurs and the court, which caused the saleability of offices to become a widely practiced procedure. And although it was perhaps most highly developed in France, it was also common in the sixteenth, seventeenth, and eighteenth centuries in all other European countries and their colonies, as well as in the Ottoman Empire and China.[4]

The institution of sale of public office fitted very well into a social system in which goal-attainment needs tended to predominate, but in which on the institutional level clearcut structures concerned solely with meeting these needs did not yet exist. At the same time, as yet no sharp distinction was made between the attainment of systemic goals

3 See G. Pagès, "La venalité des offices dans l'ancienne France," *Revue historique,* CLXIX 1932, pp. 477-482.

4 See K. W. Swart, *Sale of Offices in the Seventeenth Century,* The Hague, Nijhoff, 1949 (Selection 10); also Martin Göhring, *Die Aemterkäuflichkeit im Ancien Régime,* Beriln, Verlag Dr. Emil Ebering, 1938; and J. H. Parry, *The Sale of Public Office in the Spanish Indies under the Hapsburgs,* Berkeley, University of California Press, 1953.

and the private goals of members of the social and political elite. It is, therefore, no wonder that in the early stages of the formation of centralized national states the practice of the sale of offices became widespread and that, with few exceptions, all administrative and municipal offices, and often also military and naval commissions, could be obtained only by those who were willing and able to pay for them or who inherited them.

But the sale of public offices ceases to be a useful instrument of recruiting and remunerating a civil service if the systemic goal-attainment problems tend to diverge from the private goal-gratification needs of the social elite. Though a system of sale of offices is intrinsically subject to corruption, it is doubtful whether, under the conditions existing in sixteenth and seventeenth century Europe, the saleability of offices had any significant impact upon the degree of corruption in government. The alternative method of selecting bureaucrats which was then common—the granting of offices to favorites—was no less conducive to the exercise of corrupt practices and was no more capable of attracting genuinely qualified persons to public service. This point was stressed sharply by Montesquieu, who favored the sale of public office over other methods of appointing civil servants, because, as he said, "chance will furnish better subjects than the prince's choice." But he preferred this method of recruiting a civil service also, because he regarded it as an orderly means of advancement in the social scale, assuring thereby a rendering of "the several orders of the kingdom more permanent."[5]

I have presented in some detail the case of venality of public offices, as it was practiced in European countries, particularly in France, during a period in their social development when the elaboration of fully institutionalized structures in the goal-gratification sector was as yet incomplete and when, especially in structures performing administrative tasks, integrative and adaptive needs played an important and occasionally even overpowering role. But although the concrete facts in the distribution of administrative positions and the recruitment to bureaucratic service vary in non-European societies, they all pass through related or analogous phases in their process of political modernization. In China, for example, the sale of offices became quite common under the Ch'ing dynasty and reached its widest extension during the nineteenth century.[6] In other countries it was never much in vogue, but the method disavowed by Montesquieu of selection by a superior, often on the basis of ascription, was not infrequent. In still other places, there existed numerous other traditional forms of recruitment of public servants, which all exhibit, however, the common feature of being associated with ambiguous and highly undifferentiated institutions in which integrative and adaptive needs play as prominent a role as those of the systemic goal-gratification sector.

All these systems of bureaucratic structure, recruitment, and remuneration then appear to be suited to societies in the process of transformation from a phase in which integrative problems predominate to one in which systemic goal-attainment problems become most urgent. But with the accomplishment of this transformation the sale of offices, or any analogous form of constituting the civil service, ceases to be a suitable method, not so much because of the possibility of corruption which these systems entail, but because of their inefficiency in procuring bureaucrats who owe primary loyalty to the optimum attainment of systemic goals.

5 Charles Secondat de Montesquieu, *The Spirit of Laws,* translated by Thomas Nugent, Book V, Chapter 19, Quest. 4, New York, Hafner Library of Classics, 1949, p. 69.

6 See P. C. Hsieh, *The Government of China, 1644–1911,* Baltimore, Johns Hopkins University Press, 1925, pp. 106 ff.

Moreover, the control by the centralized authority over the composition of the administrative structures is rigorously limited in a system in which office holders have either proprietary or ascriptively sanctioned claims on their jobs. Thus in the various countries of Europe in which economic development actually took hold, various institutional patterns were designed to eliminate the sale of offices and to replace this form of social action by one better suited to the needs of optimum goal attainment.

Let us once more take France as an example. There the crown was confronted with the dilemma between a serious loss of revenue if it abolished venality of public office, and inefficiency in administration if it retained it. A way out was found by robbing the offices which remained for sale of their administrative significance and introducing a series of new offices whose incumbents were selected on the basis of their fitness for the job rather than their ability to pay for it. In other words, the way out of the dilemma was found by rejecting both principles of selection examined by Montesquieu and by replacing them by a third, the recruitment of a centralized bureaucracy on the basis of achievement norms. In this way the *intendants* and their assistants gradually replaced the *parliaments* in the administration of France. The final step in this drama was taken when, in the memorable session of August 4th, 1789, all the three estates, moved by a spirit of generosity and national unity, sacrificed some of their privileges on behalf of the national welfare. The third estate, i.e., the representatives of the wealthier classes of the bourgeoisie, offered as their contribution the abolition of the venality of office.[7] Though this step was regarded as a sacrifice of a privilege at the time it was taken, it logically fitted into the overall historical development of the interests of the third estate. For it subjected the governmental bureaucracy to the same principles of rationality and achievement orientation which came to prevail during the nineteenth century and after in the institutions of the adaptive sector. And the bourgeoisie, more than any other social group, occupied the most responsible positions of leadership and decision making in this sector of social action.

---

7 Cf. Swart, p. 17.

10. The Sale of Public Offices

KOENRAAD W. SWART

Sale of offices was a phenomenon which was common to many countries in Europe, Asia, America and Africa, but which was not prevalent everywhere in the same forms or to an equal degree. Sometimes offices were sold for only a few years, in other cases for lifetime, or even as inheritable property. Offices could be sold by the governments, as in despotic countries, by ministers or other prominent people, as in the English departments, or by the officials themselves, as in the English army. Offices were also sold both by the government and the officials, as was the case in France. In most countries sale of offices was a more or less official institution, but there was a considerable difference between countries, such as France, England and Spain, in which the buyer of an office acquired a piece of property almost as secure as real estate, and states, such as China and the Ottoman Empire, in which every official could be deprived of his office by a caprice of the prince. The legal aspect of sale of offices was most pronounced in France where offices were regarded as immovable property.

In France, sale of offices also penetrated in more departments of government than anywhere else: in Spain, for example, the system was not followed with regard to the more important posts of government; in the Curia Romana, where the highest positions were sold, the total number of offices was small compared with that in France; in China the status of the mandarins bore much similarity to that of the French officials, but offices were normally acquired here by passing competitive examinations, and only in exceptional cases could be bought.

The similarities between sale of offices in the various countries are as important as the differences. The origin of the institution everywhere dated back to the Middle Ages if not to earlier periods. The peak was generally reached in the seventeenth or eighteenth century. It was in all countries abolished when modern political institutions became powerful. This historical phenomenon, occurring on a world-wide scale, had everywhere similar causes and similar effects. This will be evident when this institution is examined in its political, social and economic setting.

The most widespread of all factors contributing to sale of offices was the practice of remunerating officials by means of fees, or other payments made by the population. Until recently it was very common for officials to receive no salary, or only a small one. Instead, the judicial official demanded fees, the financial agent imposed taxes, and the military commanders held the population for ransom. The size of the income of the official, therefore, largely depended on his rapacity and ingenuity. He was financially almost independent from the central government.

The system of remunerating officials

SOURCE: Koenraad Walter Swart, *Sale of Offices in the Seventeenth Century*. The Hague: Martinus Nijhoff, 1949, pp. 112–127. By permission of the author and the publisher.

by means of fees is very irrational. All the proceeds from the offices should be accounted for by the official, and sent to the central government, which pays the official according to the importance of the duties he performs. The system, however, had great advantages in a society in which it was difficult to check on local officials because of a widespread dishonesty, relatively large distances, and a primitive administrative technique. In this way much accounting and transferring of money was avoided, and the official was interested in the execution of his duties.

It is obvious how this system easily changed into farming, or selling offices. If the fees increased, the remuneration of the official would become so large that it was fair that he should pay a part of it to the government or to the person who had nominated him. The only prerequisite was a certain degree of economic prosperity. Offices could not be sold unless people existed who were willing and able to buy them. If trade and commerce flourished, the fees from the offices would increase and this would in its turn, influence the degree of eagerness of the placehunting. Moreover, people would not be able to pay sizeable sums for offices if a considerable degree of capital forming had not taken place. In societies with a primitive economy, therefore, sale of offices did not develop.

The same conditions were the basis for the system of farming out taxes, which was followed in so many countries in the past centuries. It is not a mere coincidence that in countries in which sale of offices was general, such as France, Spain, Turkey and China, farming of taxes was also a firmly established practice.[1]

In some states, notably in the Ottoman Empire, remuneration of officials by means of fees was the main cause of the sale or farming of offices. In these countries, however, an element was lacking which largely contributed to the development of sale of offices elsewhere, *i.e.*, the conception of public office as private property. Offices could only be considered as freeholds if the official had a more or less permanent status and was independent in a political as well as in a financial respect.

The conception of public office as private property is typical of rather primitive societies,[2] and generally does not develop in bureaucracies, in which the officials are usually dependent on their superiors. However, the societies in which the possibilities of control were limited and aristocratic forces powerful, the officials often succeeded in extending their rights. It was common for officials, who were originally instituted as dependable agents, soon to become appointed for life, and almost independent of the prince. This trend went farthest in the feudal system in which officials developed into sovereigns, but a certain feudal character was inherent in many offices, secular as well as ecclesiastical, which were created by the princes in the later centuries of the Middle Ages. The aristocratic society of this age did not yet draw the distinction between public office and private property as sharply as today.

The officials of a bureaucracy ruled by aristocratic principles were often no longer appointed by the prince. Sometimes the officials themselves had the right to nominate their successors, or their offices had become entirely hereditary. In other cases courtiers or high noblemen had a decisive voice in granting offices, or the patronage of offices belonged to ministers or superiors in office.

---

1 W. Lotz, *Studien über Steuerverpachtung. Sitzungsberichte der Bayerischen Akademie der Wissenschaften,* Phil.-hist. Abt. 1935, 4; W. Lotz, "Revenue Farming," *Encyclopaedia of the Social Sciences,* XIII (1934), 359; K. Bräuer, "Steuerverpachtung, Steuersubmission," *Handwörterbuch der Staatswissenschaften.* 4th ed. VII, 1126; P. Roux, *Les fermes d'impôts sous l'ancien régime* (Paris, 1916); H. Sieveking, *Genueser Finanzwesen. Volkswirtschaftliche Abhandlungen der Badischen Hochschule.* Vol. 1, No. 3 (1898), 41.

2 R. H. Lowie, *Primitive Society* (London, 1921), 230–231, 263–265, 310–313.

Offices of this kind were sought because they brought prestige and honor or because they were very lucrative. True ability was not required for the execution of these offices and the nomination was made according to criteria which had little to do with the merit of the candidates. These offices were often held by deputies and could, therefore, easily be cumulated. These types of officials were not always held responsible for the performance of their duties. Many of them looked upon public service as a commercial enterprise and shamelessly extorted the population.

The freehold conception of public office developed in a combination of bureaucratic and aristocratic forms of government, which was typical of the Western European kingdoms during the later Middle Ages. The civil services of France and Spain, which were organized during a period in which the feudal forces were still powerful, showed all the characteristics of an aristocratic bureaucracy; in England this type of official lingered on well into the nineteenth century. These conditions also existed, to a certain extent, in China, at the moment when the feudal society was replaced by a state governed by officials (300–200 B.C.) and in the Curia Romana at the beginning of the fifteenth century.[3]

If offices are considered as private property, it is natural for them to be sold, but under the rule of aristocracies sale of offices often occurred to only a limited extent, because the number of offices was small and many other forms of jobbery were preferred. The aristocratic bureaucracies, however, in developing the freehold conception of public office, paved the way to the systematic sale of offices by absolute princes.

We have seen how the rise of absolutism was often connected with the introduction of sale of offices: in China sale of offices was embarked upon by the absolute princes of the Ch'in and Han dynasties; in Rome it became firmly established under the despotism of the later Roman Empire; in England it was introduced by the powerful kings of the twelfth century; and above all it flourished during the European absolutism of the sixteenth, seventeenth and eighteenth centuries.

On the other hand, the representatives of the people, the Parliament, the Cortes, and the States-General, usually opposed this policy, and in the Dutch Republic and in England, where absolutism did not triumph, sale of offices was practised on a much smaller scale.

Yet, as has already been argued, absolutism was in principle more opposed to than in favor of the medieval, or aristocratic conception of public office, on which sale of offices was based. Absolute rulers whose policy was more or less consistent, such as Philip II of Spain, Colbert, and King Frederick II, have, therefore, attempted to abolish sale of offices.

Absolute governments exploited an institution, which was in essence incompatible with their ideal of a reliable body of officials, only because of financial or political necessity. Lack of means to defray urgent expenses, especially those in connection with wars, was the main cause leading to sale of offices. In France, sale of offices was introduced during the wars in Italy, and was practised on the largest scale during the wars of the seventeenth century. In Spain, sale of offices was embarked upon during a war against the Moors and was most frequently resorted to during the many wars against France. One war, that of the Spanish Succession, led to sale of offices in such different countries as France, Savoy, Prussia, Austria and the Dutch Republic. Also in China wars were one of the mainsprings of sale of offices.

The princes would have preferred to use methods less damaging for their

3 Göller, "Hadrian VI und der Aemterkauf an der päpstlichen kurie," *Vorreformationsgeschichtliche Forschungen*. Suppl. bd., Munster, 1925, 376.

authority, but the possibilities which the rulers of the seventeenth century had at their disposal were still very limited. Their greatest drawback was that unlike governments in modern times, they could not issue loans without assigning a special part of their income as security for the interest. The Dutch Republic was probably the only state of the seventeenth century in which public debts in their modern form were already common.[4] In other countries sale of offices was one of the expedients which had to fill this need. The difference was in many cases nominal rather than actual, because the offices had often an entirely honorary character; but people who were not willing to subscribe to loans, were sometimes very eager to buy an office.

In introducing sale of offices as a systematic policy, princes were also motivated by political considerations. Sale of offices put an end to favoritism and intrigue inherent in oligarchies; in fifteenth century Spain, for example, sale of offices was used to restrict the corrupt power of the urban aristocracies and in France, the *Paulette* was said to have been introduced in order to prevent political appointments by the nobility.[5]

The middle classes often supported the royal policy, because they looked askance at the aristocracy granting all offices, and they obtained a fairer share of the spoils of office under the new system. Moreover, offices could never be sold on a large scale without the existence of a rich class who was willing to buy them. In many cases, notably in city governments, the initiative to introduce sale of offices came from this part of the population. They introduced the system into the French, Flemish and Zeeland cities during the Middle Ages, and into Hamburg in 1684. It was the same part of the people who pressed for public sale of offices in the towns of Holland in 1747 and 1748.

Many factors were influential in bringing about systematic sale of offices: a bureaucracy ruled by aristocratic principles, remuneration by means of fees, a flourishing of trade and commerce, a powerful middle class, an absolutist government which had no other means of meeting its financial emergencies than that of resorting to desperate expedients. These circumstances did not exist to the same degree in all countries which I have discussed; in Germany, the middle classes were not powerful and the economic life was only slightly developed; in Spain, the government was not entirely centralized and the economic life was not very prosperous; in the Dutch Republic and in England, the social and economic conditions were favorable to the development of sale of offices, but in these countries absolutism was thwarted and no large bureaucracies existed; in the Ottoman Empire, and to a less extent also in China, the aristocratic principle was not represented.

Only in France were all the factors which furthered sale of offices strongly developed. There existed no other European state of the size of France in which absolutism was so firmly established; on the other hand, as early as the fifteenth century French officials were much less dependent upon the king than elsewhere, even than in an aristocratic country like England.[6] The economic life of France was one of the most prosperous of Europe and the French middle class was rich and numerous. Finally, as a result of the many wars in which France was involved, its financial system was entirely disrupted and all types of financial expedients had to be used. It is, therefore,

4 W. Lotz, "Staatsschulden," *Handwörterbuch der Staatswissenschaften*, 4th ed. (1926), 824–825; E. Baasch, *Holländische Wirtschaftgeschichte* (Jena, 1927), 188 ff.

5 Richelieu and the marquis of Fontenay-Mareuil, cited by Ch. Normand, *La bourgeoisie française au XVIIe Siècle*, 34–35.

6 Cf. E. F. Churchill, "The Crown and Its Servants," *Law Quarterly Journal*, XLII (1926).

no wonder that in France sale of offices reached a greater extent than anywhere else.

Whereas sale of offices has come into being under the influence of certain political, social and economic factors, it has, in its turn, also influenced the political, social and economic development. This influence was naturally much greater in countries in which sale of offices prevailed to a large extent (France, the Political States and China) than in states in which the habit was more sporadically indulged in (England and the Dutch Republic). The effects of sale of offices have always been the subject of much speculation by contemporaries. Publicists who condemned sale of offices held it responsible for all sorts of evils, whereas defenders tried to discover wholesome consequences. The passionate point of view of both groups was generally a hindrance to a correct analysis of the question.

One of the most important consequences was hardly noticed by these publicists. This was the weakening of the same royal power which had so greatly contributed to the development of sale of offices. If the king sold offices, he could no longer choose his servants according to their capacities or reliability. In France, for instance, people whose only contact with the university had consisted in the buying of a degree, became judge at a very young age. We have seen that in other countries the inability of many officials also was notorious; in many countries these officials could not be discharged. In introducing sale of offices the princes had called into existence a power which they could not check on.[7] Princes who wanted to retain control of their administration were forced to institute new officials. The French kings created the offices of intendants, officials who had not bought their offices and to whom most of the administrative functions of the *parlements, bureaux de finances* and *baillis* were gradually transferred.[8] Similar dependent agents were appointed by the kings of Spain and Prussia in the eighteenth century.

The strengthening of the independence of the officials has sometimes been considered as a wholesome consequence of sale of offices. It has been pointed out, for example, that in France the judiciary of the *ancien régime* could not easily be influenced by politicians and that the country enjoyed a considerable degree of self-government.[9] The independance of the officials found also expression in the opposition of the *Parlements* against many measures of the government.[10] It should not be forgotten, however, that the many small potentates seldom used their power for the public good. On the whole the officials were conservative and opposed to any reform of abuses which could interfere with their privileges. They were also afraid that by showing to much disobedience to the royal power they would forfeit the valuable property invested in their offices.[11] Sale of offices fostered the revolutionary spirit outside, but not inside the body of officials.

The bureaucratic abuses resulting from sale of offices were numerous; the number of offices multiplied without any relation to the increased task of the government; many of these offices were sinecures, *offices imaginaires;* other offices were held by deputies; some people

7 Emperor Anastasius made the Empire into a kind of aristocracy by selling all offices, according to Suidas, *Lexicon.* Ed. by A. Adler (Lipsiae, 1928), s.v. "Anastasius."

8 Godard, *Les pouvoirs des intendants* (Paris, 1902), 439–441.

9 Homais, *De la vénalité des offices sous l'ancien régime* (Paris, 1903), 174–175; G. Pagès, "La vénalité des offices sous l'ancien régime," *Revue historique,* CLXIX (1932), 493.

10 Ch. Normand, 266–269; Göhring, *Die Aemterkauflichkeit im Ancien Régime* (Berlin, 1938), 88, 290, 306–309; Homais, 47, 125.

11 Loyseau, *Cinq livres du droit des offices,* III, chap. I, no. 101; Ch. Normand, 17–18.

cumulated many offices; the administration of justice was slow, as the officials could in this way exact more fees. One should beware, however, of attributing all these evils merely to sale of offices. It should not be forgotten that the aristocratic bureaucracies had already suffered under the same sorts of abuses before the systematic sale of offices by the princes had started.

The relationship between political corruption and sale of offices is likewise more subtle than often assumed. Sale of offices is an aspect of corruption as long as it is not officially regulated and not all the proceeds flow into the treasury of the prince or the State, but this jobbery came to an end when sale of offices had become a legal institution. Sale of offices was defended by writers like Barclay and Montesquieu for the very reason that it had eliminated the favoritism and intrigue of courtiers and ministers.[12] Even a radical thinker like Jeremy Bentham defended his proposal for the introduction of sale of offices by this argument.[13]

Whereas public sale of offices eliminated corrupt practices as far as they concerned the *appointment* to office, the same cannot be said with regard to the *execution* of offices which had been bought. It has always been argued that people who had bought public authority would feel themselves entitled to sell it.[14] This generalization, however, is not true for all officials. There were many who had bought their offices because they wanted to enrich themselves. People who had inherited offices were likewise not much tempted to exploit their offices. The standards of the French judiciary compare favorably with those of England and Spain, although in the latter countries the judgeships never became freeholds. The most notorious case of bribery in France was committed by a judge who was member of the reformed Parliament of Maupeou (1771–1774) and who had not bought his office.[15] It was a different matter if officials regarded the purchase of an office purely as a commercial enterprise. Extortion, bribery and peculation were the usual characteristics of their administrations.

Sale of offices also introduced some useful innovations into the bureaucracies. Elderly officials who were allowed to sell their offices obtained in this way a sort of old-age pension. The purchase price paid by financial officials fulfilled at the same time the function of security for the finances under their control.

The effect of sale of offices on the financial system of a country can be compared either with that of farming taxes or with that of issuing of loans. Sale of offices was similar to farming of taxes if the offices were sold, or rather farmed, for a short period. This method might have been financially profitable to the government, although it generally increased the tax burden.[16] Sale of offices resembled issuing of loans in its result if the officials were entitled to transfer the offices to third persons or if the offices were entirely hereditary. In this case, the financial problems of the present were solved at the expense of future generations. Sale of offices, as part of an irresponsible financial policy, often contributed to the disruption of the financial system of a country.

The effect of sale of offices on the social structure of a country has not always been the same. Shortly after its introduction, sale of offices opened the public service to classes which had been

12 J. Barclay, *Icon animarum* (Francofurti, 1668), chap. 3; Montesquieu, *Esprit des lois,* V, 19 (Paris, n.d.) 61–63; Montesquieu, *Cahiers (1716–1755).* B. Grasset, ed. (Paris, 1941), 120–121.

13 *The Rationale of Reward,* II, chap. IX. Works ed. Bowring, II, 246–248.

14 Seneca, *De Beneficiis,* I, 9. Ed. by J. W. Basore in the Loeb Classical Library, CCCX (London, 1935), 30; cf. J. Bentham, and *Constitutional Code.* Works, IX, 31–32, 286 ff.

15 H. Carré, *Le règne de Louis XV (1715–1774)* (*Histoire de France* . . . , E. Lavisse, ed., VIII2) (Paris, 1909), 416–417.

16 Cf. places referred to in note 1.

excluded under the rule of oligarchies, and furthered the social mobility. This was the case in France in the sixteenth and seventeenth centuries, when by means of purchase of offices the *bourgeoisie* replaced the nobility in the government of the state. The farming out of offices in the Mohammedan countries had a similar consequence. This effect disappeared, however, when sale of offices developed into heritability of offices and new offices were no longer sold. In the eighteenth century the *noblesse de robe* in France was as closed to newcomers as any other oligarchy.[17] Moreover, sale of offices has an undemocratic feature of its own, because it confines office holding to people of means. The purchase system in the English army was advocated for the very reason that in this way the aristocratic selection of officers was guaranteed. By excluding many capable people from public office, sale of offices called into being a group of discontented intellectuals who sometimes, as in France and China, played an important part in revolutionary movements.

The economic development was also affected by sale of offices. In China, where grain was the medium of exchange, it was argued that sale of offices would promote agriculture, because people would be eager to possess grain with which they could acquire public office.[18] A similar opinion was held by Montesquieu, who maintained that sale of offices would stimulate the economic activity as the possession of money opened the road to honorable positions.[19] Actually, the influence was rather the reverse. Sale of offices stirred up the place-hunting and caused a decrease of interest in commerce and industry. In France a great part of the capital that might have been invested in branches of industry was used for buying offices and the government used the funds which it received in this way not for promoting the economic development, but for waging wars. On the other hand, groups which were excluded from holding office, such as the protestants in France in the seventeenth century, and Jews in general, have often advanced the economic life of a country.

The conclusion from the examination of the causes and effects of sale of offices is that this institution is a product of still primitive forms of administration as long as it occurs in an undeveloped form, but is a mark of decay when it is exploited by absolute, irresponsible governments because of fiscal motives. In this latter form it is a typical characteristic of politically declining societies, such as the Byzantine Empire, the Caliphate of the tenth century, the *ancient régimes* in France and Spain, and China in the nineteenth century. Systematic sale of offices deprived the government of an efficient and reliable body of officials, strengthened the oligarchic tendencies, created a discontented *élite* and disrupted the financial system. The consequence was that the political instability of the country was increased and the outbreak of revolutions furthered.

Only few publicists who discussed sale of offices defended this institution. Among them were some statesmen, such as Richelieu, wanting to justify the course of their policy, and a few financial projectors hoping to profit by the introduction of this system. Other people who upheld sale of offices were distinguished officials, like Montesquieu and Wellington, who pleaded more or less their own cause.[20] Finally, there were critics of the aristocratic society, like Jeremy Bentham,

17 Normand, 132; M. Kolabinska, *La circulation des élites en France* . . . (Lausanne, 1912), 95, 104–105, 109–110; P. Boiteau, *Etat de France en 1789* (Paris, 1861), 328.

18 J. J. L. Duyvendak, trans., *The Book of Lord Shang* (London, 1928), 64–65, 236, 253, 304; L. Wieger, *Rudiments: Textes historiques* (Paris, 1905), 421–424.

19 *Esprit des lois,* V, 19.

20 Montesquieu, *Esprit des lois,* V, 19; *Report from Select Committee on Army and Navy Appointments 1833,* 273–274.

who hoped that the introduction of sale of offices would have a wholesome influence on a political system in which the patronage of offices belonged to an oligarchy.[21]

The great majority of writers were opposed to sale of offices. They can also be divided into different groups. First, the nobility and their spokesmen, who argued that "merit," *i.e.*, gentle birth, and not money, should be the decisive factor in appointments. This opinion was voiced in France by Le Vassor, Boulainvilliers, Fénelon and Saint-Simon,[22] in Spain by Davila and Bovadilla. Most publicists who condemned sale of offices were jurists or literates. Out of the numerous writers I mention only Bodin, Pasquier and Voltaire in France,[23] Francisco de Vitoria, Las Casas and Martínez de Mata in Spain, Edward Coke, Sir Walter Raleigh and Sir Matthew Hale in England, Botero in Italy,[24] Erasmus, Hugo Grotius and Jacob van Heemskerck in the Netherlands,[25] Breckling, Moser and Justi in Germany,[26] Kochi Bey in the Ottoman Empire[27] and Wang Ghi in China. Their opinions were inspired partly by resentment against an institution which had excluded many of them from public office, partly by the conviction that sale of offices was nefarious for the State.

Another category, which had many ties with the preceding one, consisted of dissatisfied officials. They especially denounced a certain aspect of the institution, namely, the sale of new offices by the king, because this measure lessened the proceeds from the existing offices. The representative assemblies were opposed to sale of offices largely because of this consideration, although they sometimes expressed the grievances of lower classes, who suffered more than any other group under the increasing number of officials.[28] A last group of opponents of sale of offices were the princes themselves. Edward VI of England, Philip II of Spain and Frederick II of Prussia are the best known of the monarchs who condemned the institution since it was at variance with their ideal of a reliable body of officials.

This verdict of the overwhelming majority of writers against sale of offices did not achieve any result until the most important factors which had caused sale of offices ceased to exist in the eighteenth and nineteenth centuries. As early as the beginning of the eighteenth century, governments which were in urgent need of money no longer resorted to such expedients as sale of offices, but issued loans. At the same time, the system of remuneration of officials by means of fees fell into disuse as a result of the prevalence of more rational administrative habits. Finally, in the nineteenth century, when the more democratic form of government limited the influence of the aristocracy, and the modern idea of the State came into existence, the conception of public office as private property disappeared. The State became considered as a moral entity and the exercising of public authority as a duty. The official of the *ancien régime*, the *officier*, was replaced

21 Among the many works by Bentham concerning his plans of pecuniary competition see especially; *Draught of a Code for the Organization of the Judicial Establishment in France, March 1790*. Works, IV, 285ff, 354; *The Rationale of Reward*, first published in French in 1810. Works V, 246–248; *Constitutional Code*, Book II, chap. IX, section 16, 17; chap. X, section 10, art. 63, Works IX, 271 ff., 380–381: cf. also *Works*, V, 278 ff., 302 ff., 363 ff., IX 31–32; about similar plans by J. Sinclair, see his work *The History of the Public Revenue of the British Empire* (London, 1790), III, 219, 229.

22 Cf. Göhring, 299–304.

23 Cf. Göhring, 69–73, 80–81; Homais, 168–177; ante.

24 G. Botero, *Della ragione di stato libri deici con tre libri delle cause della grandezza e magnificenza delle città* (Venezia, 1589), libro I, cap. 16.

25 Erasmus Encomium morias, LV. P. de Nolhac and M. Rat, eds. (Paris, 1936), 142–143; H. Grotius, *Parallelon rerum publicarum, liber tertius: De moribus ingenioque populorum Atheniensium, Romanorum, Batavorum . . .* (Haarlem, 1801–1803), II, 8, 9, Johan van Heemskerck, *Batavische Arcadia*. 4th ed. (Amsterdam, 1663), 485.

26 J. H. G. van Justi, *System des Finanzwesens . . .* (Halle 1766), 528.

27 E. Tyan, *Histoire de l'organisation judiciaire en pays d'Islam* (Paris, 1938), 429–430, 450–451.

28 Cf. Göhring, 61 ff.; Marion, *Dictionnaire des institutions de la France* (Paris, 1925) s.v., "Vénalité."

by his modern colleague, the *fonctionnaire*. One of the outstanding representatives of the philosophy of this new conception of the State, Hegel, called the sale of government rights the most barbarous trait of a people who constitute a state.[29]

The actual abolishment of sale of offices was the easiest in those states, like the Ottoman Empire where the institution was mainly based on the remuneration of officials by means of fees. In countries where the proprietary rights on offices were firmly established, the abolishment of sale of offices were complicated by the problem of the compensation of the proprietors. At the end of the eighteenth century the following objection was, raised, for example, by Edmund Burke against a too hasty reform of the English bureaucracy:

These places, and others of the same kind which are held for life, have been considered as property. They have been given as a provision for children; they have been the subject of family settlements; they have been the security of creditors. . . . If the discretion of power is once let loose upon property, we can be at no loss to determine whose power and what discretion it is that will prevail at last.[30]

The old system, therefore, often lingered on long after the mainspring of sale of offices had disappeared. In England it was not until the end of the nineteenth century that the *ancien régime* was liquidated. In most countries sale of offices came to an end only after the outbreak of a revolution. It was the French Revolution which abolished sale of offices in France and gave a great impetus to the reform movements of most continental European states (for example, the Netherlands, Savoy, Naples, Rome the Palatinate, Bavaria and Hamburg). Sale of offices in some Oriental states, such as Persia and China, was likewise abolished as a result of revolutionary movements.

Important factors which caused sale of offices in the past have ceased to exist. On the other hand, there are today conditions, unknown to older societies, which may lead to a revival of this institution. The increased power of the State has placed into the hands of officials greater possibilities for abusing the public authority for their own profit than ever before. Naturally the eagerness to hold these offices is great so that many people may be willing to pay for them. Even more important is the increase in power of political parties which are influential in conferring offices in many states. Their position is comparable with that of ancient oligarchies. Sale of offices, if occurring in modern society, would no longer be carried on for the benefit of the State, which has other means of obtaining funds at its disposal, but for that of political parties. In this form it was practised until recently in the United States, where candidates for office often had to pay sizeable "assessments" either to the party treasury or to bosses.[31] On the whole, however, no systematic and legal sale of offices has developed in the modern state. In this respect our society, in which many other forms of political corruption are prevalent, compares favorably with those of the past.

---

29 G. W. F. Hegel, *Die Verfassung des Deutschen Reichs. Eine politische Flugschrift.* 1801/1802. G. Mollat, ed. (Stuttgart, 1935), 35.

30 *Works*, II, 101, cited by Holdsworth, *History of English Law*, X, 504.

31 M. Ostrogorski, *Democracy and the Organization of Political Parties* (London, 1902), II, 148, 157, 343–345, 352.

11. Bureaucratic Institutionalization in Nineteenth Century Europe

EUGENE N. AND PAULINE ANDERSON

In the nineteenth century European bureaucracy changed fundamentally both its role in society and its composition and character as a social institution. Instead of operating as an instrument of absolutistic control and guidance, it became a civil service, a transformation already occurring in some countries in the late eighteenth century. Three stages of change may be distinguished: an early stage in which bureaucrats were referred to as "royal servants"; a second stage in which they were called "an artificial status group" (W. H. Riehl); and a final stage in which they had achieved a "metaphysics of bureaucracy" (Alfred Weber), when they became members of a cult and worshipped their own vocation. No longer acting only as a means, they had attained a way of life sanctioned by a superhuman ideal. In some respects the bureaucracy supplanted the Church as a social institution, and its members claimed to possess knowledge surpassing that of ordinary mortals, while conforming to a code of behavior different from and superiod to that of other men.

The transformation did not occur uniformly throughout Europe, for conditions of life differed so markedly from country to country and from region to region within a country that the stages of change appeared at different times. The bureaucracy in Russia by 1914 manifested many characteristics found in Austria before 1848 or in Prussia at the beginning of the century. The trend in all European countries, however, ran sufficiently parallel to justify a comparative analysis of bureaucracies, in which, if space permitted, it would be possible to include the bureaucracies of Church, army, and finally, of large-scale business enterprise. The following study concentrates upon the bureaucracy of the state, and since this is the most important of all bureaucracies for the introduction of social change, it will treat the institution of bureaucracy as a social unit in itself. . . .

Official employment involved total personality, the entire way of life. Its implications can best be understood by analyzing various aspects of official vocation—tenure, salary and retirement rights, standards of personal behavior inside and outside office, promotion, and disciplinary action. France resisted the institutional drive of officials to develop a state or civil service with rights and duties fixed by law and treated the occupation of official like that of private businessman. The state withheld rights of tenure in law while,

---

SOURCE: Eugene N. and Pauline Anderson, *Political Institutions and Social Change in Continental Europe in the Nineteenth Century*. Berkley, Calif.: University of California Press, 1967, pp. 166–167, 206–219, 230–235. By permission.

especially after 1830, reluctantly acquiescing in the necessity of tenure in fact. It delayed recognition of the need for a pension system and allowed officials more freedom in personal behavior outside office hours than did the governments in Central Europe. The German states and Austria offered the leading examples of bureaucratic constitutions. Hintze described the position of an official in Prussia as that of "a relation of service and authority of a unique kind, and at the same time a relation of trust." The state provided for the physical wants of officials and their families, in return for which these officials must devote their entire energies to the state. An official could not receive presents or engage in any economic activity for profit without the consent of his superior. He must behave in private life with the dignity befitting his status; he was required to inform his superior of his marriage, and in some instances to obtain his superior's prior consent. No longer to be disciplined by imprisonment, he remained subject to punishment by fine, transfer, suspension, or dismissal. The relation, Hintze concluded, involved "a fund of moral feeling and responsibility: loyalty, devotion, zeal in the performance of duty on the one hand, benevolent, patriarchal care on the other."[1] Security of tenure rarely resulted from one law; rather it developed from legislation concerning various aspects of service. In 1805 Count Montgelas in Bavaria promulgated a law for the civil service similar to Napoleonic law, which in withholding security of tenure from certain categories of officials granted enough other rights to make security certain in practice. After 1848 it became customary to assure "rights of stability" to more and more officials, rights which in toto assured tenure.[2] Prussia never passed a comparable law for the constitution of the bureaucracy; but by making entrance dependent upon examinations (1808), by dividing officials into classes and subclasses (1817), by setting up a system of pensions (1825), by promulgating an orderly procedure for disciplining officials (1844), and by many other laws and decrees during the century the state fixed a tradition of tenure equivalent to security. The German Empire based its law for officials (1873) upon the Prussian system, and the reform of the law in 1907 likewise conformed to general practice in the German states. The Austrian government recognized implicitly the principle of security of employment as early as 1771 and 1781 in creating a pension system, although essential improvements making pensions adequate to need did not come until after 1848. Both Germans and Austrians abused their officials in many ways, particularly prior to the establishment of constitutional government. They early became aware of one truth, however, which the French Counsellor of State Chardon deduced from the history of the treatment of officials in his own country: "When officials request fixed and precise rules about recruitment and promotion, they plead less for themselves than for the civil service and the nation."[3] A maltreated state official did not and could not perform his duties with the devotion that Hintze had enthusiastically admired in the German official.

Toward the end of the eighteenth and at the beginning of the nineteenth century every state introduced as a means of control the annual or semiannual confidential report. Austria in the first half of the century seems to have developed the device to its fullest extent. Ignaz Beidtel, one of the officials who suffered from it, has vividly described the effects. He states that promotion depended upon the content of these secret reports, that no one was certain of advancement. The

1 O. Hintze, *Der Beamtenstand, in Soziologie und Geschichte,* (Göttingen, 1964), p. 10.

2 Albert Lotz, *Geschichte des Deutschen Beamtentums* (Berlin, 1909), pp. 524–526.

3 Henri Chardon, *Le Pouvoir administratif* (Paris, 1912), p. 119.

reports contained data not merely about performance in office but also about the entire person of the official—health, education, associations, and conduct outside office. The system, Beidtel complains, turns superior officials into despots, subordinates into flatterers and hypocrites. Within a short time an extensive protective system of favorites and dependents spread over the provinces. Mediocrities received many high positions and imposed their standards upon subordinates. Rejecting all so-called initiators of projects, all "critics," all "men of genius," all "friends of literature," all "willful officials," all "patriots," they developed within the civil service a condition of "complete repose." Ministers protected themselves by referring matters large and small to the emperor for approval.[4]

From experience Beidtel learned the imprecise nature of standards for judging the conduct of officials. A court decree of 1796, which remained in effect until 1848, stated:

> His Majesty reserves the right to dismiss with or without pension and the customary treatment those officials who make themselves unworthy of the confidence of the Emperor and the public by crime or also merely by the suspicion of questionable actions. They can never be reinstated in or proposed for official position without His Majesty's being fully informed about their dismissal and approving their reappointment.[5]

The words "crime" and "questionable actions" lent themselves to flexible definition. A decree of 1798 established as the basis for promotion that candidates should be "the most capable and the worthiest,"[6] again weasel words. In 1811, a decree stated that recommendation for promotion must be based upon the "strictest accuracy about the knowledge, diligence and moral character of the candidate,"[7] and this information of necessity derived from confidential reports about the official. Officials were forbidden to reveal state secrets, although no definition of "state secrets" existed. This prohibition, according to Beidtel, led officials to spy on one another, to initiate disciplinary action, to indulge in personal likes and dislikes; and the victim accused of revealing a forbidden fact could not defend himself without risking a further chance of disclosure. Many officials, especially in Vienna and large towns (small-town officials were too insignificant to be much affected), lived in fear that they would be reported as imparting confidential information or as being otherwise morally untrustworthy.

> An atmosphere of lies [Beidtel declared] surrounded the individual from childhood to the grave. The educated public ceased to discuss and express opinions about important affairs. Instead of conversing over serious matters, they turned to card-playing, the theater, novels and balls and to material interests. . . .[8]

The light tone of Viennese society during the entire century originated as a means of self-protection among its most important members, the imperial officials.

Although Prussia in July, 1848, abolished the requirement of secret reports, this act did not terminate the accumulation of confidential files,[9] the postrevolutionary government reinstated the old practice while requiring that reports must be based upon verifiable data. The imperial law of 1873 sought to cor-

---

4 Ignaz Beidtel, *Geschichte der oesterreichischen Staatsverwaltung 1740–1848,* Vol. II (Innsbruck 1892–1896, pp. 42–45.

5 Quoted in Beidtel, II, p. 112.

6 Quoted in Beidtel, II, p. 112.

7 Beidtel, II, p. 113.

8 Beidtel, II, p. 119–120; see also 90–91. Beidtel's judgment was confirmed by his contemporaries, Baron Andrian-Werburg, Franz Grillparzer in his *Selbstbiographie* (Stuttgart, 1887), Graf von Hartig, and by Metternich himself. See also Josef Redlich, *Zustand und Reform der oesterreichischen Verwaltung,* and Conze, *Staat und Gesellschaft im deutschen Vormärz.*

9 Dr. Ludwig Von Roenne, *Das Staatsrecht der Preussichen Monarchie,* 4th ed. Vol. III (Leipzig 1881–1884), pp. 119–120.

rect one abuse by defining as precisely as possible a "state secret" and established public, orderly procedure to deal with violations. The law declared a state secret to be a matter "whose being kept secret arises from its own nature or is prescribed," with "culpability to be decided by whether a state or a private interest is endangered by the publication or could be endangered."[10]

The need for reports arose from the nature of bureaucratic organization, and the formal practice of reports marked an improvement over the previous arbitrary action of king or superiors. Only a century earlier Frederick William I of Prussia had declared that he would "support his officials and would not believe any accusation brought against them, and still less would he condemn them before he personally heard the oral statement of the officials in the presence of the accuser." In 1786 Frederick William II in a similarly patriarchal manner had promised his officials that he "would not dismiss or cast out any upright official without cause and unheard."[11] As the number of officials expanded beyond the limit of the king's personal supervision, the government explored methods of gauging competence in office. In the late period, when absolutism stood on the defensive, moral reliability—that is, reliability in devotion to the moral principles underlying absolutism and caste structure—became more important than intelligence and efficiency. As society outgrew these forms, means of judging officials changed in favor of greater trust, of reliance upon examinations to assure the appointment of effective personnel, and development of a sense of public responsibility in both citizenry and bureaucracy. The public expected the official to perform his duties well; standards improved, and disciplinary action became exceptional. Russia, Spain, and Italy reached this stage, if at all, only at the close of the century. In 1905 the French parliament voted the most inclusive protection so far granted the bureaucrat, expressing confidence in him and in the nation when it wrote into law the following:

> . . . all civil and military functionaries, all employees and workers of all public bureaus have the right to personal and confidential communication of all notes, descriptive sheets, and all other documents composing their file, whether before being the object of a disciplinary measure or removal from office or before being retarded in their advancement by seniority.[12]

The exercise of power exposed the bureaucracy to competition among conflicting social philosophies for official support. Absolutists and conservatives hoped to instill into officials their standards of behavior; liberals wished the bureaucracy to be liberal. The Prussian law of 1852 applied to administrative officials under a constitutional regime standards of behavior and discipline that had been enforced for years under absolutism and had been applied to the official both in his official and in his private capacity. It stated that a misdemeanor occurred when an official violated his official duties; this definition appeared clear, for the list of official duties was quite precise. The law further declared that a misdemeanor took place when an official "by his conduct in or out of official duty shows himself unworthy of the respect, regard or trust that his profession requires."[13] What did this statement mean? Habitual drunkenness, for example, on the part of an official hurt his prestige and that of his position. Did support of a political party opposed to the government constitute a misdemeanor? Furthermore, upon entering

[10] Von Roenne, III, pp. 476–477.

[11] Hintze, *Der Beamtenstand,* p. 534.

[12] Alexandre Lefas, *L'état et les fonctionnaires* (Paris 1913), pp. 87–88; Maurice Hauriou, *Précis de Droit administratif et de Droit public* (Paris, 1914), pp. 645–647.

[13] Par. 2, law of Juli 1852, quoted in Von Roenne, III, p. 484.

office a civil servant took an oath of "loyalty and obedience" to the ruler and to the ruler's government. Did this oath apply to behavior outside hours of duty, to activity as a private citizen? Was the official a special kind of citizen, without civil rights such as persons not in public employment enjoyed? And what should be done in the event that his and others' interpretation of the constitution disagreed with that of king and government, as frequently happened in Prussia in the 1850s and 1860s?

In 1850 Count Manteuffel in the name of the government under the new constitution declared to officials:

I am therefore firmly determined and consider it my duty ruthlessly to dismiss from office in a legal way all those officials who violate their loyalty or do not demonstrate the courage that their position demands or are guilty of a hostile attitude toward the government.

He expected officials to

turn their attention to the public welfare and immediately oppose all manifestations and all events which are inclined to exercise a harmful influence upon this welfare. Especially must officials be conscious of the fact that they are the bearers of governmental power. They must exercise this governmental power within their official sphere of activity, not because it seems good to them or is convenient but always because their duty demands it.[14]

The courts sustained the legality of the governmental position, asserting (1863)

. . . that participation in public demonstrations and agitation against the existing government constitute a violation of the duties that their office lays upon officials. This assertion proceeds from the principle that exercise of the constitutional rights of every citizen is limited in the case of the civil servant by his official duties. Exercise of the political rights belonging to a bureaucrat may not alter the duties of office; a dispensation as to time and subject from the carrying out of official duty because of a conflict between this duty and the official's civil rights is inadmissible. Therefore the behavior of an official in political affairs must be judged from the point of view of his official duty.[15]

In the next year (1864) the court stated that "an official acts contrary to discipline if in making public his political views he opposes the measures of the government."[16]

The government enforced these judgments about the behavior of officials as private citizens in the 1850s and 1860s, again in the late 1870s and 1880s, when Bismarck demanded the appointment of "politically reliable" officials,[17] and again in Prussia in 1899, when the Hohenlohe ministry, this time upon encountering conservative resistance to one of its bills, demanded that officials in public actively support its policy.[18] At the level of local government mayors of German and Austrian towns and cities discriminated against Social Democrats. Mayor Lueger of Vienna went so far as to force city employees actively to align with his party.[19]

In spite of these abuses officials in Central Europe suffered far less from political chicanery than those in western European countries. Then and subsequently liberals and many conservatives in Central Europe vigorously protested the exploitation of officials for political purposes. Hintze denounced it as "opinion-snooping and restriction of the rights of the citizen,"[20] and the analyst of

14 Lotz, p. 435.

15 Von Roenne, III, p. 473*n*. 5*b*.

16 Von Roenne, III, p. 473*n*. 5*b*.

17 Rudolph Morsey, *Die Oberste Reichsverwaltung unter Bismarcke 1867–1890* (Munster, 1957), pp. 262–270.

18 Lotz, pp. 436–438; Hintze, *Der Beamtenstand*, p. 39.

19 Hintze, *Der Beamtenstand*, p. 72. See also Alfred Weber, *Uber die Wirtschaftlichen Untersuchungen der Gemeinden* (Leipzig, 1910), pp. 238–248, 621–623.

20 Hintze, *Der Beamtenstand*, p. 72.

Prussian law Ludwig von Roenne defended the official's right to have "another political conviction from that of his superiors and to express it in a way allowed by law." He denied that in a constitutional system of government loyalty to the head of state is in any way related to taking sides for or against the ministry. The duty of obedience relates only to the bureaucrat's official activity, and the official remains a human being and a citizen and as such is not required to leave his conscience "at the threshold of state service." The official can be expected, he continued, to do his duty loyally and in the widest sense and not to disobey the legitimate orders of his superiors. He can also be expected to support the fundamental principles of the constitution and in a constitutional monarchy to be neither an absolutist nor a republican. He cannot be required against his convictions to support the ministry currently in charge of the government or to avoid all opposition to it in situations not connected with his office. Von Roenne particularly defended the official's right under a constitutional government to freedom of the vote and condemned all direct governmental influence in the exercise of this right by the official.[21]

Questions of tenure and conduct on and off duty involved disciplinary action. In France, where offices had formerly been bought and therefore had belonged to the individual as property, postrevolutionary governments met with difficulty in overcoming the lax discipline associated with traditional behavior. In countries where the absolute monarch appointed officials, the power of discipline lay in the hands of administrative officials, with exercise of this power restrained by the right of personal appeal to the king. The importance of the matter of discipline in the years preceding the nineteenth century arose from the fact that "every official was called to his particular position and served the Monarch for a definite purpose under conditions determined by the actual office. What we today call a transfer (*Versetzung*) would then have been dismissal from one position and the conferring of a new post."[22] During the course of the nineteenth century governments devised procedures placing the power to discipline in the hands of an objective body and, in extreme cases, giving it to the courts. Prussia introduced the system as early as 1823, Bavaria for many officials even earlier (1805), Austria soon after the revolution of 1848, and France under the Third Republic.[23] The Prussian procedure of 1823 was that which other states gradually and to varying extent adopted; it prescribed that dismissal from official service must conform to definite formal conditions and be approved by a body of independent colleagues. In a preliminary hearing all the significant facts and the entire course of the career must be reviewed and the official allowed to submit a defense. The next-higher collegiate body received the report of the hearing and decided the case; in a matter involving a high official the king himself rendered the verdict.[24]

Notwithstanding its excellence, the Prussian disciplinary action had one defect: on certain questions concerning subordinate officials it placed, as in the days of absolutism, judicial power in the hands of administrative superiors. According to the law of 1853, Von Roenne wrote,

> The chiefs of those agencies that serve provincial bureaus including the Landräte could impose upon officials under them, as well as upon officials of the bureaus under these, penalties of as much as three thalers. . . . Other chiefs of lower bureaus may impose such penalties only insofar as the right to levy penalties is granted them by special

---

21 Von Roenne, III, p. 473*n.* 5*a*; 474*n.* 5*c*.

22 Lotz, pp. 399–400.

23 Von Roenne, III, pp. 481 ff. Also Ludwig Gumplowicz, *Das oesterreichische Staatsrecht* (2d ed.; Wien, 1902), pp. 187–189; Hauriou, pp. 634 ff.

24 Lotz, pp. 399–400.

laws or instructions based upon such laws. The officials appointed to the administration of the railroads by the government are given the authority to impose penalties against any of the officials under them to the extent of ten thalers. Provincial agencies are authorized to punish bureaucrats under them with money fines up to thirty thalers but cannot exact from salaried officials an amount greater than one month's service income. Ministers have the authority to exact fines equal to a month's service income from all of those directly or indirectly under them, from unsalaried officials, however, only up to thirty thalers. . . . Only those chiefs who can levy money fines against those under them can also punish them by arrest. Those whose authority to levy fines is limited to three thalers canot impose imprisonment of more than three days.[25]

An authoritarian government could easily abuse the right to punish by fine and imprisonment, and the governmental example encouraged businessmen, industrialists especially, to fine their workers. In neither case did the victim have protection except through publicity or recourse to the courts; for fear of being blackballed, few officials used this defense. After 1872 the French made a notable advance by enabling officials to appeal to the Council of State, which protected them against small but humiliating abuses and against arbitrary loss of office and other forms of punishment.[26]

Analysis of the power to transfer officials shows the importance of precise legal definition and of orderly procedure. The increasing stability of bureaucratic organization made it possible and beneficial for the government to move an official from one place to another and from one post to another. The Prussian government in 1832 established the principle that "the official in his special position does not serve the sovereign but the general interests of the state and must agree to serve wherever he is needed.[27] Thereafter appointment pertained not to a position in a particular place but to the civil service at large. The government, however, repeatedly transferred persons as a form of punishment; an official with a family of marriageable daughters might find himself shifted from Cologne, where eligible young men abounded, to a small country town in East Prussia, and at a reduced salary. The imperial law of 1873 sought justice by distinguishing between transfer as punishment and transfer in the ordinary course of administration. In the latter category a transfer involved a post of equal hierarchical rank, and the state paid the expenses of removal; in the former category, the state ignored these conditions (par. 4). France did not seriously consider introducing the distinction until nearly forty years later.[28]

The notoriously corrupt Russian officials did not improve their behavior until the latter part of the century, and even then the Russian bureaucracy remained far from perfect. Readers of Gogol are acquainted with Russian methods for extorting fees, taking bribes, acquiring what was called "sinless revenue."[29] Autocratic government allowed officials thus to supplement their wretched salaries, reserving severe punishment for political offenders. The czars seemed especially lenient toward corruption among high officials, ministers included, and forgave them easily.[30] One Slavophile explained the corrupt habits as proving not that the Russian people ranked inferior in morality to the German but that the German system of administration imposed upon Russians "was utterly

25 Von Roenne, III, p. 485*n*. 6*a*.
26 Hauriou, pp. 635 ff.
27 Quoted in Lotz, pp. 399–400.

28 Hauriou, p. 635*n*. 1.
29 Donald M. Wallace, *Russia on the Eve of War and Revolution*, ed. by Cyril E. Black (New York, 1961), p. 13. See also the remark of Chekhov, Dec. 11, 1891, "The public has no faith in officialdom," in *The Selected Letters of Anton Chekhov*, ed. by Lillian Hellman; trans. by Sidonie Lederer (New York, 1955), pp. 156–160. Chekhov, a doctor, found at the time of the famine (1891) that the public refused to contribute money for relief because it suspected that the officials would embezzle and commit "outright thievery."
30 Wallace, p. 13.

unsuited to their nature."[31] Gurko, a high official in St. Petersburg in the decades before the revolution of 1917, avers in his memoirs that "the integrity of the overwhelming majority" of his colleagues was "beyond question."

It is very possible that graft, simple and unadulterated, is practiced even less in Western Europe than it is with us, but the desire for enrichment is much more strongly developed there and is attained by other means. To hold a governmental position and at the same time to be connected with large financial and industrial undertakings is not only a frequent but a common occurrence in Western Europe. Under such conditions one does not need to resort to bribery. Bribery, a crude, primitive, and slightly dangerous method, has now been supplanted by a method more subtle and modern, one that is perfectly safe because it is undetectable. A timely notification of some impending act of the government, indirect support of some private enterprise, and a number of other very diverse ways of assisting the profits of some business or bank—these bring much larger returns than primtive, naïve, old-fashioned bribery. In the West, consequently, those who work for the government for some time or who are prominent in a political party assemble tidy fortunes.[32]

The description by Gurko of "the West" applied especially to France prior to the Third Republic. Deputy Gasparin, an advocate of reform, offered the following explanation to the French Chamber of Deputies in February 1846: "In a country in which elections are the basis of power and there are no conditions for entry and advancement in the bureaucracy, you necessarily have corruption."[33] The German and Austrian bureaucracies appear justifiably famous for their integrity. Russia as well as central and western Europe had legislation prohibitnig officials from becoming involved in questionable economic dealings; the difference lay in the fact that Germany and Austria enforced the law, which even forbade the wife and children of an official from engaging in business or professional life without permission from his superiors. If a German official were expert in forestry, mining, agriculture, or some other occupation, he could not acquire property of a kind associated with his specialization; and in 1874 the government forbade him to serve on the board of directors or the executive board of a corporation, a joint-stock company, or a mining company, or to be a member of a committee to found such a corporation unless he first obtained approval from his chief. Nor could an official accept such a membership if it brought directly or indirectly any remuneration, or any other material reward.[34] Officials must shun temptation!

The presence of a bureaucracy implied the erection of a hierarchical structure strong enough to assure efficiency and to maintain a sense of fair treatment and satisfaction among personnel. Early in the century Prussia divided officials into three main groups—upper, intermediate, and lower—according to the extent of their education. Upon taking office an individual would know his chances of promotion and would be content to remain in the class for which he qualified by education. To allow limited promotion, each group or class had three to six subclasses. The Austrian civil service organized its personnel into eleven classes, a system the Austrian professor Josef Redlich condemned. He approved

31 Wallace, p. 6. See also David Footman, *Red Prelude* (1944), p. 7.

32 V. I. Gurko, *Features and Figures of the Past* (Stanford, 1939), p. 199. Gurko appears to have been overly optimistic. Although the relative numbers cannot be estimated, Russian high officials took "old-fashioned" bribes and resorted to methods "more subtle and modern" as well, such as using confidential information to play the stock market. They liked as much as Westerners to "assemble tidy fortunes." (Von Laue, *Sergei Witte and the Industrialization of Russia*, pp. 200–201).

33 Quoted in Lefas, pp. 227–228.

34 Von Roenne, III, p. 469; see also Lefas, pp. 466 ff.; Gurko, p. 199.

the Prussian division into three classes as "extremely healthy." This arrangement, he thought, did not arouse excessive hope of promotion and divided the personnel according to existing social groups. The Austrian system, he said, made too little distinction among kinds of work; it excited false hope and discontent by implying the possibility of advance from the bottom through the hierarchy. It related the size of salary to the class, so that increase of income depended upon promotion to a higher class and not as in Prussia upon years of service. Redlich found the Prussian method more realistic than other systems and hence just.[35]

The Russian organization produced the most unfortunate effects of all. The government classified officials into fourteen *chins* or grades, and it expected an official in any one grade competently to perform any kind of service and to be able to transfer from one task to another regardless of training and experience. It shifted officials within the same *chin* from finance to transportation to education and so on. Prior to reform of the judiciary in 1864 judges needed no professional training.[36] Education speeded promotion by enabling the official to enter service in a higher *chin* than otherwise; but the continuing practice of promotion on the basis of seniority perpetuated inefficiency, "ignorance, idleness, slavery to routine and venality."

It encouraged place-hunting and the pursuit of external signs of distinction even in learning and the arts, and it discouraged disinterested creative work and individual initiative everywhere. It falsified current values, till many came to think that only those kinds of efforts were worthwhile which were recognized by the bureaucratic slaves of the autocracy and that the supreme act in life was to advance in chin and earn a safe pension, no matter how immoral the means involved.[37]

The French government never introduced a permanent constitution into the civil service. Officials complained in 1914 of the same hardships described by Balzac in *Les Employés* (1837). The disturbing effect of lack of regular procedure for promotions became aggravated by repeated reorganization of the ministries. Chardon reported in 1908 that 150 such reorganizations had occurred during the past fifty-eight years. The Ministry of Agriculture had been reorganized eighteen times, another ministry ten times in four years, the Ministry of Commerce more than a dozen times since 1881. Ministerial portfolios changed hands rapidly in the Third Republic, and each occupant sought to leave his mark upon his ministry and to install his followers by reorganizing the personnel as completely as was feasible. Napoleon III had set the best record of bureaucratic stability of any French regime; before and after his reign French officials in striving to establish the bureaucratic ideals of security of tenure and pension and regularity of promotion and professional standards were always resisted by politicians and ministers.[38]

The development of a hierarchical organization became closely associated with the question of remuneration. In most states during the first half of the nineteenth century types of payment survived from the period of personal service. The appointee to a particular office received the remuneration traditionally associated with the office. It might be in

35 Redlich, *Zustand und Reform der oesterreichischen Verwaltung: Rede gehalten in der Budgetdebatte des Abgeordnetenhauses des Reichsrates vom 26. Oktober 1911* (Wien, 1911), pp. 18–19, 27–27. Also Gumplowicz, pp. 185–186; J. Ulbrich, *Das oesterreichisches Staatsrecht* (Tübingen, 1909), pp. 96–97.

36 W. H. Bruford, *Chekhov and His Russia*, (London, 1948), pp. 92–94.

37 W. H. Bruford, pp. 93–94. See also Von Laue, *Sergei Witte and the Industrialization of Russia*, pp. 200–201.

38 See Lefas, *passim;* Chardon, *L'Administration de la France*, pp. 139–151, and *Le Pouvoir administratif*, pp. 342–345.

kind—a house, service, the use of a certain number of horses and carriages, food, and so on; or it might derive from fees paid for official papers, official approval of agreements, court services, and the like; it might also consist of preference in renting state land at a low figure. A ruler might pay one official a larger sum than he paid another official in a different location for the same kind of work. Methods of compensation lacked uniformity and regularity; officials endured inequity of pay, and some officials exploited the state to the disadvantage of others. In the early years of the nineteenth century a lesser official in Hanover could derive a large income from fees and services, for which the public paid him individually. Before 1864 in Schleswig and Holstein a judge received fees from the trial of cases and could increase these fees by protracting the cases he handled. Parsimonious Prussia abolished the abuses in the eighteenth century, as the government always needed resources; by regularizing salaries it introduced order, improved efficiency, and lowered costs. Other German states and Austria changed to a systematic procedure some time before the middle of the nineteenth century, and the French owed their modern practice of fixed salaries to the Revolution and Napoleon.

The increased number of officials resulting from expansion of the functions of government everywhere made it essential to introduce regular salaries, and the increase in wealth enabled the government to maintain the reform. New taxes became possible, from which sufficient revenues derived to sustain pay schedules. By custom an official received an income sufficient to support a standard of living appropriate to his social position. Since living costs at court far exceeded those in a provincial town, an official, irrespective of his duties, usually received more at court than if he were stationed elsewhere. As long as conditions remained relatively simple, the differences inherent in this practice did not appear unjust. Once the unifying forces of the nineteenth century became operative, especially the modern means of transportation and communication and the social transformations of the French Revolutionary movement and of industrialism, the criterion of compensation changed. Disparity between the highest and lowest salaries greatly diminished. It has been estimated that in France in 1900 the differential was one to twenty-five; a century earlier it had been one to 100; by 1950 it was one to six.[39] In Balzac's *Cousine Bette* a councillor of state and a ministerial director had a house, carriages, and a very high standard of living. In *Les Employés* a chef de bureau employed three servants. A century later such an official had one servant and rented a small apartment, although the law sometimes implied retention of a living standard of former years; for example, the Civil Code spoke of judicial audiences held by the presiding judge of a court in his "hotel" or house, but his "hotel" had become a modest apartment. Nor did the assignment of a military guard to the presiding judge of a Cour d'Assises seem in harmony with the simplicity of the judge's way of life.[40]

When the central European states introduced constitutions and parliaments, bourgeois deputies reduced the salaries formerly paid to noble officials which had enabled such officials to live "according to their social status." Relating salary to bureaucratic class ignored caste differences in living standards, making rank in official service the sole criterion. Even so, salaries were meager. The wife of General von Roon, the Prussian minister of war, in the 1860s appealed secretly to the king for funds to supple-

[39] Christian Chavanon, *L'Administration dans la Société française,* in Aspects de la Société française, A. Siegfried, ed. (Paris, 1954), pp. 165–169. Further data for salaries are contained in the article "Besoldung und Besoldungspolitik" in *Handwörterbuch der Staatswissenschaften,* II (Jena, 1909).

[40] Chavanon, pp. 167–169.

ment her husband's low and inadequate salary. German and Austrian wits characterized an official as "having nothing but having that securely," and the mass of French officials received compensation that kept them acquainted with poverty. In other states salaries were such as to stimulate the acceptance of bribes.

The rigid relation of salary to rank did not solve the problem of remuneration, for it made promotion and hence increase of salary dependent upon retirement or resignation of the next-higher official. Since the normal loss of personnel did not open enough advanced positions for those at low levels and on low salaries, in the last quarter of the century it became practice in Germany to increase salaries within a class according to the number of years of service, so that at the time of heavy educational and other family expenses an official would enjoy an increased income. By 1900 states appeared sufficiently affluent to guarantee this equitable treatment. Regularization of salary and standardization of bureaucratic service on a basis of defined ranks proved to be essential for good government. The development affords another example from this remarkable century of institutional creativity.[41]

German critics characterized an official as "German, patriotic and entitled to a pension."[42] Others praised the system of pensions as giving the civil servant a feeling of self-confidence deriving from a secure and respected position. It helped to develop esprit de corps, a sense of bureaucratic importance in relation to the head of the state and to the legislature.[43] The Austrian professor Gumplowicz justified pensions as follows:

> It follows from the protective relationship in which the official stands to the state that it is the duty of the state not only to care for the official who has become no longer capable of service but to support his survivors in accord with their status. The state can demand from its officials complete devotion to its interests and a thorough identification of their interests with the state's only if it assumes care of officials in case of their disability for further service and likewise commits itself to care for their survivors (widows and orphans).[44]

Although governments began in the first part of the eighteenth century to explore ways of assuming this duty, almost a century of experimentation passed before the most responsibly minded of them evolved an institutional solution. . . .

In the last decades of the century the bureaucracy everywhere conformed in numerous respects to the pattern of mercantilist absolutism. Many officials outside the army were still required to wear uniforms, and others preferred this outward symbol to civilian dress. On a visit to Alsace-Lorraine in 1877, Emperor William I expressed strong disapproval when he found officials in civilian clothes; such clothing did not seem suited, he said, "to emphasize the prestige of office to the people."[45] Decorations and orders appeared effective not merely in helping to compensate for low salaries but in assuring devotion to authoritarian government. Prussia had more than one hundred different classes of decorations, and the *Handbook for the German Empire* in 1890 needed more than ten pages to list the decorations that imperial officials

---

41 On the question of remuneration, see Lotz, *passim;* Hintze, *Der Beamtenstand,* pp. 147–154; Gumplowicz, pp. 183–186; Ulbrich, pp. 96–97; Redlich, *Zustand und Reform,* pp. 14–15, 19–21; Chavanon, pp. 159–170; Lefas, pp. 44–60, 235–236; Jules Michelet, *Le Peuple* (Paris, 1946), pp. 99–107; Chardon, *Le Pouvoir administratif,* pp. 133–136; Pierre-Henry, *Histoire des Préfets,* pp. 20, 32, 175.

42 Alfred Weber, p. 244.

43 J. K. Bluntschli, *Lehre vom Modernen* Staat, Vol. 1: *Allgemeine Staatslehre* (Stuttgart, 1876), p. 611.

44 On the subject of pensions and survivor benefits, see "Witwen und Waisenversorgung" and "Besoldung und Besoldungspolitik," in *Handwörterbuch der Staatswissenschaften;* Hauriou, pp. 652 ff.; Von Roenne, III, pp. 531 ff.; Gumplowicz, pp. 189–190; Ulbrich, pp. 97–98; Hintze, *Der Beamtenstand,* pp. 65 ff.

45 Morsey, p. 275.

could be awarded. Bismarck understood the value of such awards so well that he retained in his own hands power to recommend officials for them.[46] In Austria, Russia, and France—that is, irrespective of the form of government—public recognition in the form of a medal found equal favor. In addition, officials benefited socially from the special protection given them against insults and physical attack. All governments assure their officials protection against violence; but rarely has the concept of "insult" to an official been extended to the point reached in Prussia and the German Empire. To the civilian the official stood for authority, the representative of the divine-right monarch or divine-right state. The attitude of the population disclosed in *The Captain of Köpenick* resembled that toward the civil servant as well. To question, contradict, or criticize an official involved the risk of incurring a governmental suit for insult.[47]

Contemporaries judged that the quality of officials in recent decades had declined. In Germany the bureaucracy during the first part of the century had initiated economic and social developments, and in the third quarter it had assisted in unifying the country. Early in the century the private sector of society—industry, for example—had not equaled the creative activity of the bureauracy, and the ablest members of society sought outlets for their energy in the civil service. Once the new industrialism began to stir society, officials lost the initiative to entrepreneurs, scientists and technicians, political leaders, and others. Compared to the opportunities open to individuals outside governmental service, officialdom seemed less attractive. Ability preferred the freedom of private activity, and entrepreneurs soon learned how to circumvent the bureaucracy. Professor Wiedenfeld noted in 1905 that German officials, the ablest on the average to be found in all Europe, in the recent governmental investigation of the stock exchange and of cartels lost the initiative to leaders of private industry.[48]

Professor Redlich lamented the passing of traditional leadership in Austria. He attributed it partly to the "Vienna disease" of serving exclusively in Vienna and knowing nothing firsthand about the rest of the country and mastering no other language but German. Each province, he said, closed itself to officials from any other. In addition, the nationality quarrels extended into the bureaucracy, and the incursion of masses of minor civil servants into the state-owned railroads and other enterprises brought into the administrative apparatus a personnel devoid of all sense of historical social purpose.[49] The observations of Kleinwächter, a well-informed and experienced official in the Ministry of Finance, supported Redlich's judgment. Nationality conflicts, he wrote, affect the behavior of bureaucrats. Whom did an official dare to know socially? If he were German, he might be penalized by his superior or socially ostracized by the Germans for associating with Czechs; if he were in Galicia, he might receive similar treatment from the Poles for friendliness to the Ruthenians. Instead of firmness of character and loyalty to ideals, the astute official learned to be sly and to conceal his thoughts. The picture recalls the conditions on a reduced scale of Austrian officials before 1848.[50]

The problems did not pertain uniquely to Austria. The German Empire encountered great difficulty in persuading able officials from the federal states to

46 Morsey, pp. 273–274.

47 See Von Roenne, III, 491.

48 See Professor Wiedenfeld, "Das Verhältnis der Kartelle zum Staate," *Verhandlungen das Vereins für Sozialpolitik,* (Mannheim, 1905), in Schriften des Vereins für Sozialpolitik, Bd. 116, pp. 407–408.

49 Redlich, *Zustand und Reform der oesterreichischen Verwaltung,* pp. 13–14, 27–29. See a revealing case study of bureaucratic initiative and shortcomings, Peter F. Sugar, *Industrialization of Bosnia-Herzegovina, 1878–1918* (Seattle, 1963).

50 Kleinwächter, *Der Untergang der oesterreichische-ungarischen Monarchie* (Leipzig, 1920), pp. 142–144.

enter imperial service. Imperial salaries were often lower, living expenses in Berlin much higher than in state capitals, and the difficulty of contending with the Reichstag far greater than that of dealing with state assemblies. Officials in the federal states had more independence of action than under the German chancellor, and they could anticipate a wider choice of assignment.[51] Theodor Fontaine condemned the cultural decay of the upper stratum of society, inclding higher officials. "They know the *Odes* of Horace, a little Homer and a little Ovid, and sustained by this knowledge they assume the right to regard all modern endeavors in this field as 'rot.' " He cited their limited knowledge and appreciation as one of the main reasons "why we are not entirely considered as equals and are hated by the more civilized nations.[52] Max Weber went still further in declaring German excellence in the civil service a manifestation of weakness in the entire German culture.

> Even if democratically governed countries have a bureaucracy that is doubtless corrupt to some extent [he wrote], they have achieved more success in the world than Germany with its very "moral" bureaucracy. If one is to judge purely from the point of view of Realpolitik, and if in final analysis it is a matter of power . . .

then, he asked, is a private capitalistic organization in combination with a purely business bureaucracy or a state-guided system with a highly moral, enlightened, and authoritarian German bureaucracy more exposed to corruption? Which organization has the greater efficiency? He doubted whether the highly moral German civil service was able to do so much for the country as the perhaps far less moral foreign civil service, in cooperation with the private capital so much despised by some Germans, could accomplish.[53]

France, Spain, Italy, and Russia had far worse conditions than Germany and Austria. In the best governed of the four countries, France, the civil service remained inefficient, except in specific technical lines; it did not assume the initiative in developing the economy or in providing services to encourage private initiative. Since after 1880 private entrepreneurism in many lines lost its initial drive, the country lagged behind its eastern neighbor in economy, demography, and governmental activity. The bureaucracy continued to be popular as one of the few means of social mobility and as an index of social position. When the economy slowed, the civil service attracted far more candidates than it needed. Once appointed and on the way to a pension, officials everywhere succumbed to the bureaucratic temptation to make work for themselves. Italy and Spain more than France continued to be prey to the spoils system—without the justification for corruption that Max Weber perceived in Britain and in the United States.[54] Pares concluded in 1905 that "to the bureaucratic office more than to any other place in Russia we may apply the maxim that it takes three men to do the work of one."[55] The conduct of officials aroused popular accusation of dalliance, indolence, inefficiency, hypocrisy, and in countries other than Germany, Austria, and France, venality; all

[51] Morsey, pp. 256–257, 261.

[52] Theodor Fontane, *Briefe an Georg Friedländer* (Heidelberg, 1954), Letter of 14 September 1889, p. 114.

[53] Max Weber, *Gesammelte Aufsätze zur Sociologie*, p. 416.

[54] For Spain, see the remark of Jaime Vicens Vives, in *L'Histoire du 19e et 20e siècle (1870–1914): Problèmes et Interpretations historiques* (Paris, 1962), p. 397. After the restoration of the monarchy, Vives writes, the personnel of the bureaucracy changed with each ministry. Each official sought to recover during his stay in office the loss of income while out of office. Corruption reigned, and essential public services became neglected.

[55] B. Pares, *Russia between Reform and Revolution*, Francis G. Randall, ed. (New York, 1962), p. 138. For a half century earlier, see the same complaints by Nikitenko, a high official, as quoted in Richard Hare, *Portraits of Russian Personalities* (London, 1960), pp. 5, 6. But see also Gurko's defense of the highest officials, in *Features and Figures*, pp. 198–200.

countries but Germany supported too many public employees. Austria used officials with law degrees to perform tasks elsewhere adequately handled by unskilled young women. Professor Redlich offered in the Reichsrat the following example of the resulting bureaucratism:

What happens in Austria if a school employee asks the director of a technical continuation school for a payment of twenty crowns? The director does not simply reach into his pocket but sends the request to the provincial school board with a recommendation for payment. There the request is displayed and then laid before a chief official of the accounting department. This department submits a declaration; on the basis of the declaration a report of the school board to the Minister of Public Works goes forth after it has passed two to three draftsmen in the office of the school board: reporter, aprover, reviser, to express it in German. (Laughter) The report comes to the Ministry, is there exhibited—that is very important because thereby it receives a number, is sent from the departmental head to a drafting offiical for corrections. Eventually a declaration is received from the accounting department, whereupon an order is issued to the provincial school board. . . . I don't want to describe it in the blackest colors, but it can happen that before this is still another agreement with the Ministry of Finance is sought. In this case the document is sent to the Ministry of Finance, whence a ministerial decision is prepared. In the Ministry of Finance the decision is worked over by a draftsman, approved by a counsellor and reviewed by a chief of section, as a rule by Herr Baron Engel, who is everywhere where money is involved that passes at least through one hand. Now the order of the Ministry of Labor goes back to the provincial school board, is again displayed and reviewed by a draftsman, and finally the provincial school chief writes an instruction to the director of the school, in which he is apprised that the payment is refused. (Lively amusement)[56]

Critics have always and everywhere accused bureaucracies of the foregoing evils; officials seem occupationally addicted to such weaknesses, and it requires the strength of a Hohenzollern categorical imperative to act as a preventive. More important, perhaps, in understanding the character of European society prior to World War I is the change that occurred in the social role of officialdom. An Austrian official in testifying before a parliamentary committee at this time declared: "The state official of former times, who represented merely the rulers and stood before the people as an alien figure and in a sense as an enemy, has become a people's servant who does not see his purpose in unthinking but devoted execution of orders often hostile to the public interest but who understands his sole duty to be that of serving the people." Redlich countered with the view that the official "is above all there to do his duty, to obey.[57] Neither statement can be considered correct, and neither is entirely wrong. The nineteenth century appears as one of the great periods in history for exploring the role of the bureaucracy in public life. While experiencing the many new forces and institutions—modern industry, technology, science, education, urban expansion, representative government—the governments of the century could not decide where bureaucracy best fitted into so complicated a society. Redlich's conception survived from absolutism and undervalued the sense of moral responsibility required by the official in dealing with society. The ideal of the anonymous official quoted above did not take into account the presence of representative institutions for ascertaining and formulating the will of the people and the need in responsible, popular government for a loyal, reliable administrative agency to execute popular will with dispatch. His conception could

56 Redlich, *Zustand und Reform der oesterreichischen Verwaltung*, pp. 36–37.

57 Redlich, pp. 24–25.

have turned civil servants into autocratic experts, who soon would have concluded that they knew better than the people how best to serve the state.

By the close of the century the stage of development reached by any one bureaucracy varied according to the stage reached within the total national culture. Where the economy, education, and other aspects of society showed creative activity, the bureaucracy tended to be efficient; where they continued sluggish and indifferent to public welfare, officials shared these characteristics. France had devised means of protecting the population against bureaucratic abuse, though at the expense of constructive official initiative. The outstanding example of bureaucratic efficiency in service lay across the Rhine from France. No state had achieved a bureaucracy adapted to changing social conditions; none had realized the ideal of an administrative agency composed of experts and equipped with institutions for making its expertise available not merely to governmental heads but to the interested public. The ideal itself awaited future formulation. Officials who had attained to expert knowledge in the main continued to find their own ways of utilizing their skill of gauging the practicality of their plans, of achieving useful results. The bureaucracy had made less progress along this road than had parliamentary bodies, and it suffered as well from the conflict of political and social ideals in its own midst and among the political leaders whom it served.

In spite of difficulties nations with social mobility moved beyond traditional organization of the bureaucracy into exploration of institutional organizations and of procedure to meet the needs of the time. Although authoritarian in nature and attitude, by 1914 bureaucracy had begun to develop boards and commissions composed of officials and representatives of private organizations for handling matters of common interest, such as social insurance, disputes between labor and capital, and other social issues; and this eventually brought officials and laymen into working relationship on a basis of equality.[58] Legalism as the basis of bureaucratic thinking and acting began measurably to decline in favor of social science. The bureaucracy gave signs of willingness and ability to adjust to the modern world.

---

58 See Herbert Jacob, *German Administration since Bismarck* (New Haven, 1963), pp. 60–61.

12. Patronage and the Public Service: Jeffersonian Bureaucracy and the British Tradition

SAMUEL E. FINER

THE BRITISH AND THE AMERICAN ADMINISTRATIVE SYSTEMS COMPARED

British Administration, Handicapped by Its Inheritance

The U.S.A. Begins *De Novo*

When the United States Congress created the American Federal administration, 1789–1792, it was neither helped nor burdened by any legacy from the past;[1] it had to work from tiny beginnings: and so it was able to set up a system based on common sense and rationality. It was this which brought on it the praise of Jeremy Bentham. "In the central government of the Anglo-American United States, the situations in the executive departments are every one of them single-seated. Of the thirteen here [i.e. in the Constitutional Code] proposed sub-departments, some have there no place[2]; the rest are consolidated into four, each filled by a Minister, locable and dislocable by President of the State, whose power, in so far, is that of the here proposed Prime Minister. . . . In the case of the relation between the President, as above, and his immediate subordinates —the power of the super-ordinate in relation to subordinates is not only as to location, but as to dislocation, absolute: and at the accession of each President the power of dislocation is commonly exercised as to those he finds in office, and that of location, at the same time, as to new ones; in regard to each, effectual responsibility is secured by the power expressly given to him to require of each of them a report in writing in relation to all points belonging to their respective offices: and by this arrangement are produced all the good effects, the production of which is professed to be expected from Boards. . . . In English practice, this department swarms with boards. . . . Yet for many—seatedness in no one of all the several instances, can there be any necessity or use. . . ."[3]

1 Unless we are to consider the prototype departments set up under the Confederacy; in which case we simply ante-date the construction of the Federal bureaucracy, but in no way mitigate the contrast between the American *tabula rasa,* and the British incubus of tradition. See Jensen, *The New Nation,* 1781–1789, for a strong plea to regard the Confederacy's departments as the real beginning of the American public service.

SOURCE: Samuel E. Finer, "Patronage and the Public Service: Jeffersonian Bureaucracy and the British Tradition," *Public Administration,* 30 (1952), pp. 333–353. By permission of the author and the publisher, the Royal Institute of Public Administration.

2 Because they were entrusted by the U.S. Constitution to the individual *states,* and not to the Federal Government.

3 *Bentham's Works,* Bowring, ed., pp. 216–17.

British Administration in 1780 Dominated by Mediaeval Assumptions and Forms

In sharp contrast the British reformers were faced in 1780 not merely with a going concern, but one that had been going for centuries. The essential thing to notice about this British system is that from the Norman Conquest almost no office or department was ever abolished; but functions often were. By 1780 the structure resembled a coral reef. It was made up of the skeletons of innumerable offices and functionaries which had served their turn; but inside this dead structure new creatures burrowed, made their home, and turned the detritus of ages into some kind of a working instrument.

The King's Government The key to the system is to be found in the position of the Monarch. The legal prerogatives of the King as listed in the *Commentaries* of Blackstone and the *Constitution* of De Lolme were still very largely the working practice of the 18th century. The army and the navy were the *King's* Army and the *Royal* Navy. H.M. Ministers were in fact, as well as in law, the *King's* Ministers. True, they had to enter into some working arrangement with the House of Commons in order to do the King's business, but it was to the King that their responsibilities lay. Their management of the Commons was an incident to this task. "Cabinets . . . did not depend on popular mandate but poised and turned as of old on a balance, between a royal executive, groups maintained by ministerial influence, and a public opinion not yet drawn up through party systems but scattered, formless and difficult of expression."[4] The nature of the Civil List illustrates the same point. On this grant, made to the Monarch for his private use, were borne the expenses of Ambassadors and Judges.

The executive was the King's executive and it lived apart from Parliament, controlling its own internal movements, making its own intestinal arrangements—so long only as it could persuade Parliament to grant it the funds which it deemed necessary. According to Blackstone "the King has the sole power of sending Ambassadors to foreign states and receiving Ambassadors at home. It is also the King's prerogative to make treaties, leagues, and alliances with foreign states and princes. . . . The King has also sole prerogative as to making war and peace. . . . He is a constituent part of the supreme legislative power; and as such has the prerogative of rejecting such provisions in Parliament as he judges improper to be passed. . . . The King is considered in the next place as the generalissimo or the first in military command within the Kingdom. Another capacity in which the King is considered in domestic affairs is as the fountain of justice and general conservator of the peace of the Kingdom. The King is likewise the fountain of honour, of office and of privilege; he is the arbiter of commerce."[5] This apparent theorising of Blackstone was acted on to a very much larger extent in the 18th century than is commonly supposed. It was not regarded as Parliament's task to control from day to day the affairs of the executive; and for the most part such inter-meddling by the Commons consisted largely of calling for reports from time to time, and, every so often, of setting up committees of inquiry; even these being mostly concerned in the first instance with public accounts—a matter which was clearly within the purview of Parliament since the Restoration.

The King Lives of His Own Furthermore, the mediaeval notion that "the King lives of his own" still underlay the financial relationship between the Legislature and the Executive. The Civil List was in theory supposed to be the fund by which

4 *The Second Tory Party, 1740 to 1832,* by K. G. Feiling, p. 143.

5 Blackstone, *Commentaries,* Book I, Chap. 7.

all the foreign and domestic business of the Kingdom was financed.[6] Granted to the Monarch for life, once granted it was therefore free from any ordinary Parliamentary interference. Of course, it was wholly inadequate to bear the cost of government. From time to time Parliament made up additional expenses by extraordinary grants. Military expenses however, and funds to reduce the public debt, were granted by Parliament annually and as these represented an overwhelming proportion of the cost of running the Kingdom it was through control over these that Parliament could in fact, and did in fact, exert a control over Royal policy. Yet even in respect of these sums the old mediaeval notion that "the King lives of his own" was maintained in an etiolated sense: for successive Parliaments followed the will-o'-the-wisp of creating a self-balancing fund with which to meet the increased expenses of the régime. If, for example, additional sums were needed for the army, an additional customs duty might be laid on Spanish hides sufficient to meet the estimates of the increased cost. The assumption always was that costs would not continue to increase beyond that fixed point, and that therefore the income from this special customs fund could be earmarked in perpetuity for this particular item of expenditure. As a result we find that by 1780 the customs duties were paid into a number of funds, e.g. the General Fund, the Aggregate Fund, the Sinking Fund, the South Sea Fund, while upon these funds were settled the payment of certain specified and recurrent heads of expenditure. Thus, among the services to which the Aggregate Fund was applied we find "To the Officers of the Exchequer Bill Offices on their salaries," "To the sheriffs of the several counties of England and Wales for defraying their charges of taking forth their Letters Patent for their respective offices, and passing their accounts, and obtaining their quietus," "For the support of His Majesty's household."[7] This notion that it was possible to strike a balance between the income from certain taxes and the expenditure on certain fixed items so that they should become a self-balancing account, was a mediaeval notion derived from the idea that there was a fixed sum out of which the expenses of the country could and should be defrayed.[8]

Ministries as Private Establishments Another consequence of the notions that the executive was the King's, and that the King lived of his own, was that the departments were not regarded as public departments. Ministers were the King's Ministers: but the departments they managed were (largely) the private establishments of those ministers. For the most part, clerks and subordinates were paid not by salary but by fees exacted in the course of their duties. Where additional clerical assistance was needed in an office there was no reason why the Minister should not set aside part of his salary or part of his fees of office for that purpose; or why chief clerks having been appointed and paid in this fashion should not do likewise, setting aside a proportion of the fees which they received in order to pay off additional clerical assistance. There was no reason furthermore, why an officer paid at some very high salary or who received through the course of events inordinately high fees (as, e.g. the fees of Tellers of the Exchequer were

6 Idem. "The expenses defrayed by the Civil List are those that in any shape relate to civil government; as, the expenses of the household: all salaries to officers of State, to the judges and every one of the King's servants; the appointments to foreign ambassadors; the maintenance of the Queen and royal family; the King's private expenses, or privy purse; and other very numerous outgoings, as secret service money, pensions, and other bounties."

Cf. Holdsworth, *History of English Law,* Vol. X, pp. 483–485.

7 Appendix 72, 13th Report of the Commissioners of Public Accounts, 1785.

8 By the 18th century it had reduced the collection of customs and the auditing of public accounts alike to a state of complete confusion and idiocy.

increased enormously through the huge increase of payments during the Napoleonic wars) should not cease to do any work whatsoever and simply engage some hack at a considerably lower sum to do the work for him. When such action was taken the work was said to be performed *"by deputy"* and the original post, e.g. "Teller of the Exchequer," became a "sinecure."

This notion, that the establishments were the private establishments of ministers, had three important effects. In the first place, a fee system rather than a salary system developed throughout the public services. In the second place, since these fees could not be regarded as a charge on the public accounts they did not come within the generally accepted purview of Parliamentary inquiry; and for the same reason neither did the number of individuals of the establishment. And thirdly, obsolete offices were not swept away but in fact tended to multiply; the original post so as to be performed by Deputy: then the Deputy Office became so profitable as to be performed, itself, by Deputy; and so on.

Medieval Operating Procedures Finally, some branches of the public service, and neither the least numerous nor the least important, had been continued in an unmodified medieval form. The best example of course is the Exchequer which retained, in 1780, with hardly any substantial modification, the same establishment, organisation and procedure as under Edward III. The Customs which in 1797 employed some 6,000 officers out of the national total of 16,000 was a particularly glaring example of a mediaeval organisation, illustrating how the living organs of 18th century administration had to operate within a carapace of obsolete forms. Under Edward I the offices of Customer, Controller and Searcher were created. They were patent offices, originally appointed by the King or his high officers. (From the time of Henry VI the Treasurer obtained patronage.) When, as happened from time to time, the collection of the customs was farmed out to private individuals, the patent officers' role shrank to that of merely checking their proceedings. In 1671 negotiations for a new farm broke down, it was decided that the Central Government itself should once more collect the Customs, and the Board of Customs was created. It might have been thought that the Customers, Controllers and Searchers would now once more perform those duties for which they had been created; but not at all!

The Collectors, i.e. the staff of the tax-farmers, were taken over by the Crown to become Crown servants, stationed in all parts of the country, and made completely responsible for collecting the duties and returning money and accounts to the Customs Office. The Controller merely shared with the Collector the general superintendence of the ports. The Searchers continued to do certain work until, later on, the Board of Customs found that it could be done more usefully by officers called Land-waiters and Coast-waiters: and then all that remained for the Searcher to do was to supervise such goods as went for export. As to the Customers, they found themselves without any duties whatsoever. Their work was entirely duplicated by the Collector or, at all events, might have been executed by the Collector. Yet the numerous brood of Customers and Searchers continued to be appointed long after they had duties to perform: so that by 1780 there were two sets of officials in the Customs service, the working officials (e.g. the Collectors and the Waiters) and the sinecures or half-sinecure offices (such as the Customers and Searchers) which had been taken over straight from the Middle Ages. When, in 1798, the 196 sinecure offices in the Customs were abolished, George Rose, not a very fervent friend of reform, had to admit: "the management in truth, derived great advantage from the suppression of the description of offices here noticed, as the possessors of them, holding by patents, conceiving themselves amenable only to the Treasury or the King, sometimes formally disclaimed any responsibility to the Commissioners of the Customs to the manifest inconvenience, if not to the loss of revenue."[9]

In the management of the executive branch of British Government any reformer had to tackle the dead weight of centuries. The Americans on the other hand, were able to make a clean start and planned their offices on grounds of rational utility. This must be accounted as the first and overriding reason why British administration in the period under review was far more expensive and certainly not more efficient than its American counterpart.

British Administration Sacrificed to Politics

Patronage and Politics in Britain and America

The second reason for the lower standards of public management in Britain was derivative from the first. The mediaeval structure of the administration, the ease with which an establishment could be multiplied, the high degree of independence which its internal processes enjoyed from the observations and control of the legislature—all of these were advantages which the politicians were quick to seize. The administration, to borrow Burke's phrase, was "a loaded compost heap of corrupt influence."

In representative government of the American and British types, there are three conceivable political objects for which the gift or promise of places and offices might be manipulated.

i. To ensure a public service loyal to the regime.

ii. To influence the electorate in their choice of representatives.

Here we must distinguish between a situation:—

a. Where the public officials are expected and intended to be partisans, i.e., always to vote for the "friends" who first appointed them, irrespective of the political complexion of the government of the day, and (therefore) the interest of their administrative superiors.

b. Where the public officials are expected and intended to be ministerialist, i.e., always to vote as told by their administrative superiors, i.e., the government of the day, regardless of the political interests of the "friends" who first appointed them.

iii. To influence an elected legislature; by detaching Members from their private allegiances, in order to support the government of the day.

Now in respect to (i), both the United States and Great Britain, at certain times in the period under review, made loyalty to the regime a pre-requisite of appointment to public office. Washington would not appoint former Tories. In Britain also there is evidence of some disturbance in public offices after the accession of George I, to secure adherence to the new order.[10] This kind of discrimination is compatible with a very wide choice of candidates and need not prejudice the quality of the public service. This factor may be discounted as affecting the quality of public administration in either Britain or America.

In respect to (ii[*a*]) such were the political circumstances of either country at this time that the bartering of public offices for partisan support hardly arose. In Britain, as Feiling points out, "It is indeed a truth, fundamental for our pur-

[9] *Observations Respecting the Public Expenditure and the Influence of the Crown,* by the Rt. Hon. George Rose, 1810, p. 10.

[10] Cf. E. Hughes "Studies in Administration and Finance," pp. 274–276. Cf. also pp. 185–188. Hughes shows how very slight the disturbance was.

pose, that organised continuous party existed neither in the 17th nor in the 18th century.[11] It is equally true that there was no organised Opposition until the Napoleonic Wars,[12] nor was there either popular constituency or anything resembling a national party organisation. In these circumstances, there was no tendency in 18th century Britain for rival groups of politicians to promise the places of their rivals to their own friends in return for electoral support. In the Federal sphere of U.S. politics, between 1789 and 1824, circumstances were similarly such as largely to preclude this type of abuse of the patronage system. So long as Washington was in office parties were in abeyance. After Jefferson's first term the Federalist party began to dwindle away and not until 1828 did the two-party system emerge. Had this not been so, however, it is conceivable and even likely that the "rotation of office" would have developed there and then, for the short period of intense party rivalry, 1794–1804, is full of instances where patronage was bartered for political support. The defection of New York to Jefferson in 1800 was the outcome of disappointment felt by Livingstone and Clinton who had been deprived of patronage by Washington and Adams. Again, Jefferson, on acceding to power, carried out a proscription of Federalists in the public service and gave their posts to his own supporters. There is little reason to suppose that if the Federalists had returned to power in 1804 they would have acted like the Rockingham Whigs in 1765 and simply restored the *status quo ante;* the probability is that they would have carried out a counter-purge. But, fortunately, the Republicans stayed in power, and for another twenty-odd years there was one-party control of the Federal Government. Thus, bye and large, between 1789 and 1828, a situation of political partisanship did not exist in the federal sphere of American politics, and so it was not necessary for Americans to abuse recruitment for electoral purposes.

Patronage could also be manipulated to secure the return of a "Ministerialist" legislature, one that would support the administration of the day, i.e. (ii[*b*]). Now under the American constitution this kind of legislature, however desirable, is not strictly necessary; for the President, once elected, is independent and irremovable. Not so in Britain, however; for although the Monarch was independent and irremovable, his Ministers were not and it was through his Ministers that he had to carry out his policies. Consequently it was not merely desirable in Britain but *vital* that the Administration of the day should secure—if necessary in advance—an amenable House of Commons. To quote Feiling again "It was for the King to choose Ministers and though he would obviously choose them from groups strong enough to get his business done in the Commons he chose them irrespective of the constituencies. So that the process of our day was actually inverted, Ministers being selected not in consequence of, but in order to make, an election; and before 1831 there is no example of Ministers, if supported by the Crown, being beaten at the polls.[13]

Finally, once a legislature had been elected, patronage could be used to detach members from their private loyalties and to get them to rally round the administration, i.e. (iii). To this purpose patronage has been put in the U.S. of today; but we are assured by Professor White that he has found no evidence that it was so used during the Federalist

11 Feiling, p. 2.

12 The first recorded use of the phrase "H.M. Opposition" is in 1826. It was coined—as a jest—by Hobhouse. But in 1804 Fox (in a private letter) talked of "Systematic Opposition"; and it is from this date that the practice, as against the theory, of H.M. Opposition, may be dated.

13 Feiling, p. 3.

and Jeffersonian period. Such use of patronage might have prevented the frustration of Monroe and J. Q. Adams by Congress; but, however desirable, it was not absolutely necessary, because again, once elected the President was irremovable and independent. By the same token, however, the British Cabinet being dependent and removable by the House of Commons *had* to make use of patronage in order to make the 1688 settlement work.

If, then, we review these three purposes which patronage could serve (i) did not and would not exercise a marked effect; (ii[*a*]) operated only intermittently in the USA and not at all in Britain; but (ii[*b*]) and (iii) which, however desirable, were not strictly necessary to the U.S. Constitution were both central to the British political system.

Patronage Buys Political Support in 18th Century Britain

Since a compliant House was essential if the British constitution was to work, to this purpose the patronage system was necessarily subverted. Honours could buy such support, contracts could buy such support, commissions in the army and navy could buy such support; but these baskets of loaves and fishes were not enough, by themselves, to keep the constitution working. The public service was a fourth basket of spoils; and, owing to the Gothic nature of the administration it could, up to a point, be expanded at need, to meet the exigencies of a political crisis. This is, in fact, what happened.

Compliant legislatures were returned, kept or made, by (1) the granting of favours, (2) the nomination to official posts. By "favours" we mean the handing out of pensions, or sinecures or the reversions to those sinecure posts which existed in the public service. These—which were the plums of the public service—were granted for two reasons. They might be granted to individual Members of Parliament in order to get them to support a particular measure brought forward by the administration. They were in fact a good method of making a House and of keeping it. Or, they might be used to prepare the way for an electoral triumph. Given the unreformed electoral system of the day the keys to electoral victory lay in the pocket boroughs and the close boroughs. To secure victory the politician must address himself to those individuals who possessed the first, or had what was called "a political interest" (i.e. influence) in the second. To secure the support of these individuals the sinecures, the pensions and the reversions were handed out; and in return MPs who could be relied on to support the administration would be elected. The second class of patronage, i.e. nomination to working posts in the public services, was useful, not for making or keeping a House, but in the electoral process. The electorate was very small at the close of the 18th century—about 200,000–250,000. Throughout the century, therefore, the rare individuals who had a right to vote were given preference in appointment to the public service: and as public officials they were expected to cast their vote as their administrative chiefs directed. Thus at any general election there was a large block of voters in a very small electorate, whose tradition it was to vote as they were told. Furthermore, their loyalty was, traditionally, not owed to the individual Minister or patron who had secured their admission to the public service, but to the Government of the day. In practice some of these public officials were often in a predicament; for sometimes they had to choose between voting for the candidate of their original patron and voting for the candidate of the Minister of the day. Thus, in the election at Malden in 1763, the excise men were told to vote for one Gascoyn, although they did not in fact do so, but voted against him and returned his rival, Mr. Husk.[14] Similarly, in the Maidstone election of 1761 the Admiralty instructed all the freemen of Maidstone who were employed by them in the Chatham dockyards, to vote for Mr. Northern. Instead, they seem to have voted (as did the Customs and Excise officials) for a Mr. Fuller. Thereupon Fuller wrote to the Duke of Newcastle (who controlled the Treasury patronage) asking him to "protect them from censure and discountenance."[15] But on the whole these revolts seem to have been rare and the public officials who had votes played a very important role in securing the return of Government candidates. The Marquis of Rockingham stated in 1782 "That there were no less than 70 boroughs where the election depended chiefly on the votes of revenue officers"; "The Custom House alone," he said, "had 5,000 persons belonging to it besides about 2,500 more of extra tides men, etc., and the Excise at least 4,000 more, who were voters . . ." "The revenue officers, as the law now stood, not only were forced to vote for those they did not approve, but to vote against their own friends and those in particular to whom they were most obliged."[16] In his forecast for the election of 1784, John Robinson mentions the effect upon certain boroughs of the recent disfranchisement of these revenue officers by Crewe's Act of 1782. In Winchelsea, "The revenue officers having been struck off leaves scarce a good voter." In Hastings, Rye and Seaford, he says "The disfranchising bill has made great alterations."[17]

Since the harmony of the executive and legislature rested upon the making of elections and the making and keeping of the House of Commons, there was increasing pressure in the 18th century to turn more and more posts to political advantage and to barter public office for the possession of a vote regardless of character and capacity. In her study of the Customs System in the 18th Century, Elizabeth Hoon shows that there was a steady increase in Treasury patronage. Early in the century the Treasury did little more than alter some of the Customs Board's presentments: only occasionally did it recommend. Later, it recommended more frequently; and sometimes, where there were no available vacancies, it directed persons to be employed in a temporary capacity. In 1757 it ordered that notice of all vacancies must be sent to the Treasury immediately: in 1765 that the presentments to vacancies be submitted to them each week. Next the Treasury began to create many new offices "by constitution"—a form of establishment which vested complete control of the servant in the Treasury Board: and then, in 1782, they ordered that no deputies to the old Patent officers be appointed without Treasury consent. Under this regime the standards required from candidates were progressively lowered and the commissioners complained that they were drawn "from county fox hunters, bankrupt merchants, and officers of the army and navy."[18] As to the Excise officers, these had been brought under Treasury control considerably earlier in the century—between 1729 and 1736. By the later date it was all over: an Exciseman with a vote was thereafter expected to cast it as the First Lord of the Treasury directed.

Thus the exigencies of the Gothic constitution led successive governments not only to perpetuate but even to exaggerate the eccentricities and incapacities of the Gothic administration. So long as

14 Sir Lewis Namier, *The Structure of Politics under George III*, p. 116 ff.
15 Namier, p. 142.
16 *The Parliamentary History of England*, Vol. 23, p. 101.
17 *Parliamentary Papers of John Robinson*, Camden Society, 1922, pp. 80–81.
18 *The Organization of the English Customs System, 1696–1787*, Appleton, Chapter VI.

this method of working the constitution was not under attack—and it was not seriously under attack until after 1780—the structure and organisation of the administrative system could not be attacked either. Politics was supported by the nature of the administrative system; the administrative system was supported by the nature of politics.[19]

Thus we have seen first, that whereas the United States was able to start with a clear field and to build a rational structure of administration, Britain in 1780 was loaded with the detritus of ages; and secondly, that whereas the political situation in the United States from 1789 to 1828 was such that the constitution could work without seriously depressing the quality of the public servant, this was not so in Great Britain. It is to these two causes, medieval organisation on the one hand and the servitude of efficiency to politics on the other, that we must attribute the superiority of American administration in the first 40 years of the life of the Republic.

Probity and Capacity of the Public Officials in America and Britain, 1780–1830

In considering the depression of British administrative standards we must not give too much weight to the fact that in the USA those with the power to appoint had moral standards vastly different from their opposite numbers in Great Britain. It is true that Washington was particularly stern and unbending. As we have seen, "family relationship, indolence and drink" were to him an insuperable bar to public office. John Adams was equally lofty: "I should belie the whole course of my public and private conduct and all the maxims of my life if ever I should consider public authority entrusted to me to be made subservient to my views or those of my family or friends."[20] And, once Jefferson's purge of 1801–1803 was over, "the standards were high," says Professor White. "Their choice fell upon persons from the same reputable social class of gentlemen upon whom the Federalists had depended." "We need not allow favours . . . to obscure the standards that the Republicans announced and generally maintained. Their selections . . . were made within the ranks of the Republican party, but they were confined to gentlemen who were men of integrity."[21]

It is equally true that in contemporary Britain appointments were not confined to men of integrity and that numerous bad appointments were made. As late as the period 1836–1854 (by when the situation had greatly improved), many appointments were still of the very worst quality. "I have made out a return of 55 persons who were nominated by the Treasury between 1836 and 1854. Several of them were incompetent from their age. I found some perfectly unqualified. . . . One person in that list had been imprisoned by the sentence of the Court as a fraudulent debtor. . . . There was one man whom I was forced to keep in a room by himself as he was in such a state of health that he could not associate with the other clerks. . . . There was the case . . . in which a gentleman was appointed who really could neither read nor write; he was almost an idiot and there was the greatest possible difficulty in getting him out of the office."[22] Another example of the low standards in the civil service is to be found in an analysis of the results of the qualifying

19 The nature of the process has been explored in all its ramifications by Sir Lewis Namier in his *Structure of Politics at the Accession of George III* and his *England in the Age of the American Revolution*. These works are the foundation of our understanding of 18th century politics.

20 L. D. White, "The Federalists," p. 267. It must be added that McHenry did not think that Adams' appointments quite lived up to this high moral line. "Mr. Adams thought it an essential part of the art of government to apply the influence of rewards through the medium of appointments to offices to future elections" ("The Federalist," p. 267).

21 L. D. White, "The Jeffersonians" (New York, 1951), pp. 356; 367–368.

22 Report on the Civil Service, 1860; p. 176.

examinations instituted in 1855. Of 958 persons *nominated as being fit* for public office, nearly 300 were rejected by the Civil Service Commissioners, and of these rejections 206 failed in arithmetic or in spelling.[23]

Nevertheless, on a closer examination, the apparent gap between the two civil services does not appear to be quite as wide as these facts would suggest. It is commonly said that "nepotism" was one of the besetting sins of the British Civil Service at this period. Professor White, quoting Federalist and Jeffersonian Presidents, shows that they were opposed to nepotism; but his evidence also shows clearly that the senior civil servants (e.g. Nourse, Bradley and Dearbourn) were by no means averse from bringing their relatives and friends into the public service.[24] In point of fact, this is only to be expected. Why should not departmental heads very properly consider that their friends and relatives were as capable as distant and unknown applicants? Is there any reason to believe that they might not have been right?

In assessing the standards of personnel in Britain, especially in relation to the American Civil Service at this time, it must also be borne in mind that the Collectors of revenue (e.g. the customs officials) were expected to give a heavy bond before being allowed to take up office and, furthermore, that even if nominated by the Treasury they were always subject to disciplinary dismissal by their Board. In Elizabeth Hoon's study there is surprisingly little evidence of defalcation or embezzlement on anything but a very petty scale. As to the Board of Customs itself, it was exceedingly hardworking; and her comment on its record is: "for the most part administration was sound. . . . The Board made continual attempts to improve the effectiveness of the service by expanding the organisation, encouraging officers, bettering the regulation of routine business, and having regard to the danger of patent offices, fees, and the like. The commissioners, however, cannot be entirely freed from the responsibility for the poor condition of many of the ports, for the too-frequent conniving of customs officials in fraud and smuggling and for the indifferent personnel which meant a proportional degree of inefficiency."[25] Despite the just criticism contained in this paragraph it is manifest that the customs system, in the teeth of the tremendous handicaps to which the inadequate organisation and political interference gave rise, was not the weltering sink of corruption, immorality and indolence which we have been conditioned to expect.[26]

Now if we look in any detail at some of the American services during this period we shall find that despite the care in choosing public servants, the officials were not always as efficient or upright as Presidential high-mindedness would suggest. For example, after the war of 1812 there was a crop of embezzlements by public agents in the United States. Theoren Rudd, clerk of the district court in New York, absconded with 65,000 dollars of public money and over 52,000 dollars belonging to litigants before the court. John Braham, receiver of public money at Huntsville, Alabama, speculated away 80,000 dollars on the cotton market. Byas Watkins, auditor in the U.S. Treasury, embezzled over 7,000 dollars and ran away.

---

23 Report on the Civil Service, p. 283.

24 "The Jeffersonians," pp. 358–359.

25 Hoon, p. 78.

26 Indeed, she continues thus: "There was no concerted attempt at the badly needed reform of the system partly perhaps because the Commissioners' hands were tied by the limitation of their powers, *partly because of such immutable institutions as sinecures, fees and customs duties,* and partly also because eighteenth century opinion did not demand reform. . . . That the revenue was as productive as it was *despite the system which had to be enforced,* is evidence of a certain degree of judicious administration . . ." (Hoon, p. 78). The italics are my own.

Professor White comments "that these cases were as exceptional as they were conspicuous,"[27] but the fact remains that it is from isolated incidents like this —such as the Duke of York scandal in 1809 or the Melville scandal of 1805 or the existence of the "subordinate treasuries" in 1780—that the low morality of the British public service of the time has been deduced. It is a major merit of Professor White's volumes, in itself, that he has supplied a standard by which we can gauge the shortcomings of contemporary British administration. It is clear from the examples cited that even in a public service like that of the USA with its high standards of recruitment and high ideals as to public service grave derelictions could every now and then occur. And this should serve as a warning to scholars on this side of the Atlantic not to judge the 18th century British civil service by the more spectacular examples of nepotism, inefficiency and malversation: because it may very well be that if these services were inspected as closely as Professor White has examined the American, the much-paraded examples of inefficiency might turn out to be as untypical of the British public services as he has shown them to be untypical of their counterparts in the USA.

Finally, in assessing the quality of the 18th century British public service, one ought never to forget that side by side with the bankrupts, the foxhunters and the illiterates there were such notables as Abbott, Arbuthnot, Barrow, Bickersteth, Finlaison and Deacon Hume, Larpent, Rickman, Stevenson and Sir T. Murdoch: and also an anonymous mass of humbler officials whose integrity and capacity was sufficient to leaven the ineptitude of the ranker political nominations, and to carry the GPO, the Customs and the Excise to a not altogether inconsiderable measure of success.[28] Indeed any student undertaking to examine the characteristics of the 18th century public servant might well adopt, as his starting hypothesis, Sir James Stephen's classification of the Colonial Office of his day. There were, said he, a small minority of first rate intellects, experienced and devoted to the public service: a larger group of men "who performed diligently, faithfully and judiciously the duties to which they were called"; and a third group, in the majority, of those who possessed "only in a low degree and some in a degree almost incredibly low either the talents or the habits of men of business, or the industry, the zeal or the knowledge required for the effective performance of their appropriate functions."[29] A similar state of affairs seems to have characterised the public offices in the eighteenth century.

27 "The Jeffersonians," pp. 419–422.

The Pace of Invention and Reform, 1780–1830, in America and in Britain

If we are trying to assess administrative capacity, ought we to judge a system merely by what it is at one point of time: or may we not also judge by reference to what it has evolved from and what it is advancing to? From this standpoint, the British achievements from 1780 to 1830 bear comparison with the American and, indeed, may be deemed to surpass them. It should by now be clear how great was the American advantage in starting with a clear field, and in that her internal politics at this period did not necessitate, as in Britain, a continual subordination of administrative efficiency to the maintenance of political power. Yet from

28 For the G.P.O. see H. Robinson, *The British Post Office* (Princeton, 1948). For the Customs, see E. Hoon, op. cit.; for the Excise, notably the Salt Office, Hughes, op. cit. These three services made up seven-eighths of the public service at the close of the 18th century. The Taxes Office, 1799–1816, is described in A. Hope-Jones, *Income Tax in the Napoleonic Wars* (C.U.P. 1939); it shows an organisation as efficient as any described in Professor White's volumes.

29 "Papers relating to the Reorganisation of the Civil Service," 1855, pp. 72–73.

1801 onwards, as Professor White clearly shows, American administration had reached a plateau; more than that, a good deal of evidence throughout *The Jeffersonians* indicates that in many respects it was already slipping back. In Britain, on the other hand, it is no exaggeration to say that in the years 1780–1834 a revolution was accomplished in the public service. Its Gothic structure was laid in ruins and upon them was reared the massive foundations for a coherent and rational structure which the next generation was to erect.

Developments in America, 1801–1830

Of the USA during this period Professor White remarks: "The major developments grew out of the crisis caused by war. The embargo left no permanent changes in normal procedures, although it provided some extraordinary precedents, and the depression of 1819–1822 was neither long nor severe enough to leave a mark on the administrative system. The incompetence of the defence departments and of civilian administration revealed by the war with Great Britain was so impressive, however, that it caused the first major reorganisation of the federal administrative system. The principal elements will be recalled: the establishment of the army General Staff,[30] the formation of the Board of Navy Commissioners, and the reconstruction of the accounting organisation and system of accountability. Other significant reforms and developments also took place after 1815. West Point was reorganised and put on a high professional standard. Ship construction was standardised. A system of inspection of land offices was introduced, the first of its kind. The procedures of the State Department were greatly improved by John Quincy Adams. The Post Office was energised by John McLean.

"Of special importance was the establishment of professional assistance to the heads of the two defence departments by means of the General Staff of the army and the Board of Navy Commissioners. The full significance of this innovation was probably not understood at the time, since each institution was proposed and defended as a means of relieving the head of the department from an impossible burden of detail. The Secretaries did benefit to some extent in this respect, although detail kept crowding its way to their desks. Much more important was the availability of professional advice on army and navy affairs, hitherto lacking on any systematic or orderly basis. The Navy Board was particularly useful in bringing its judgment to bear on naval construction and on the management of navy yards and posts. Both agencies were successful in elaborating a body of regulations for the government of the uniformed forces.

"The State Department remained throughout the period with no professional officer to assist the Secretary. The Treasury had enjoyed the services of men above the rank of chief clerk from the beginning: the commissioner of revenue, the register, and the head of the General Land Office in particular, but like the comptrollers and auditors, they brought no relief to the Secretary in the discharge of his own duties. The Post Office had two officers of general competence aiding the Postmaster General: the first and second assistant postmasters-general. These modest advances were significant of later developments.

"The Republican years confirmed Federalist ideas about permanent service in the general government. Tenure, although not protected by law, was in fact during good behaviour, both in Washington and in the field. Clerks might end their official work in the same office, indeed in the same position in which they

30 Not a General Staff in our modern sense (created in the U.S. in 1903), but an Advisory Board who assisted the Secretary in the housekeeping and management services of the Army.

began, but the expectation of life service was high. The army and navy offered somewhat greater freedom of movement than the civilian agencies, but both uniformed services suffered reductions that forced many career officers into civilian life."[31] "The Jeffersonians in fact," he says, "carried the Federalist administrative machine forward without substantial alteration in form or in spirit for nearly three decades."

But in some respects, the standards of administration were slipping back. The Treasury, after the retirement of Gallatin, ceased to control the estimates of the other departments. The Collectors "tended to become careless in the conduct of Custom House business."[32] The State Department had become choked by domestic business which Congress declined to transfer to a separate Department of the Interior.[33] Above all, from 1824 to 1828 the high standards of recruitment hitherto characteristic of the system became subjected to an increasingly intolerable political pressure and finally collapsed with the election of President Jackson.

Developments in Britain, 1780–1830

By contrast, the British system had been almost completely remodelled since 1780, and the Reform Bill of 1832 was to provide a still greater impetus to its reorganisation.

Size and functions In 1828 the British Civil Service (excluding the law courts, the Colonies, and the Household) consisted of 22,900 persons. In 1797 there had been 16,267. The net increase of over 6000 was almost entirely accounted for by an addition of over 5000 in the Customs Service, 600 in the GPO, and 66 in the Taxes Office.

The functions of central government were at this time not greatly dissimilar from those of the U.S. Federal Government. The primary function was to defend the country and to pay off the national debt; consequently the biggest departments and the most expensive were those of the armed services on the one hand and the collection of revenue on the other. The public service as a whole may be divided into six groups. There was first the Treasury group which comprised the Treasury, the Exchequer, the Audit Board, the Land Revenue Board, the Tax Office, the Stamps Office, the Hackney Coach and Hawkers Office, the Board of Customs and the Board of Excise. The Mint, the Board of Woods and the Board of Works may also be regarded as coming within this general group. Next there comes the Army group of which the chief offices were the War Office, the Ordnance Office, the Army Pay Office, the Store-keeper's Office and the Commander-in-Chief's Office. Of the Navy group the chief offices were the Admiralty, the Navy Office, the Navy Pay Office, and the Royal Navy Hospital Board. Fourth comes a group of departments or offices which we may call the Secretariat. They represent the developments, by 1828, of the primal office of the Royal Secretary. By this time they consisted of the Home Office, the Foreign Office and the Colonial Office. The last group, miscellaneous, consisted of such offices as the Council Office and its quondam offshoot, the Board of Trade; the Privy Seal Office; and the Board of Control.

Lack of Coherence The system as a whole was still largely incoherent. It is true that Board management, in appearance the prevalent pattern, was already illusory. (In respect to the Treasury's major functions, the Chancellor was in full control. The Minutes continued to be read twice weekly to a board at which the junior Lords were present; but from 1809 no record was kept of their indi-

31 "The Jeffersonians," pp. 554–555.
32 White, p. 161.
33 White, chap. 14.

vidual attendance and the matter became more and more a formality. The junior Lords were permitted to criticise the wording of the Minutes and were sometimes set to research and report upon certain aspects of business; but by 1828 the running of the department was firmly in the hands of the Chancellor and his permanent staff.[34] Similarly, the Board of Trade, though technically a board, was, in fact, a Department administered by its President and Vice-President. The Board of Control was likewise a board only in name.)

In addition, the Secretariat, organised from the start on Bentham's principle of single-seatedness, was, between 1780 and 1830, moving into the forefront of administrative activity. Thus six of the departments, and these not the least important, were by 1828 organised on the "single-seated principle" regardless of any formal appearances to the contrary.

Yet though some of the departments were thus acquiring a coherent pattern, the Departmental Groups, with one big exception, still remained inchoate. The exception was the Treasury group, over which the Treasury was beginning to assert much more stringent control.[35] The Army and the Navy groups, however, were very loosely organised. Thus, the Secretary for War and Colonies was responsible for the size of the force and for controlling its functions abroad during war; but the Home Secretary was responsible for general military questions when the army was at home. The Secretary at War was responsible to Parliament for finance and for the contacts between the army and civilian population, but the Commander in Chief was responsible for the discipline of the forces. He had no control over troops abroad, however, and he could not move troops at home without the consent of the Secretary at War: he had no control over the supplies because arms and stores were the responsibility of the Ordnance branch, provisions the responsibility of the Commissariat, and clothing the responsibility of the Board of General Officers. All these offices approached each other by formal letter. The incoherence of the system was fully seen by contemporaries. Lord Howick's commission in 1837 produced a comprehensive plan of re-organisation, but Wellington, who was Commander-in-Chief, opposed this so firmly that no action was taken and the system continued to muddle along until the disasters of the Crimean War. The Navy was in a similar state; but reforms here were initiated by Graham in 1832.

Finally there was a marked lack of Treasury control over the whole organisation—if organisation it could be called. The Treasury's control over the estimates of its own "group" were recognised by the law and custom of the constitution, but the other departments preserved their independence jealously. Estimates for the armed services were discussed at the Cabinet level before being passed on the Treasury;[36] and in 1783 when Pitt's Public Offices Regulation Bill found its way to the House of Lords it raised cries of alarm from officers who feared that their autonomy would be curtailed. Lord Townshend opposed it because "it would give the Lords of the Treasury greater influence over the Board of Ordnance than they at present possessed." Lord Stormont (the Lord President) complained that "it gave most extraordinary powers to the Treasury and diminished the necessary power and the dignity of the other officers, in a manner very inconsistent with the duties which they had to discharge. . . . Several of the great

[34] Select Committee on Miscellaneous Expenditure, 1848: QQ. 1260; 1303; 1304; 1311: The American War of Independence and the Napoleonic Wars had thrown so vast a burden on the Treasury that Board management became impossible.

[35] *Edinburgh Review*, April 1810: Hon. G. Rose's "Observations."

[36] Select Committee on Public Monies, 1856: QQ 1173, 2199, 3170, 3174.

offices of the State had ever been distinct and independent: but this Bill gave the Treasury a painful pre-eminence over all of them, and made every one of the rest subject to its control." The Bill was defeated 40 to 24.[37]

Emergence of the Cabinet Nevertheless, between 1780 and 1834 reform had proceeded continuously on a massive scale. In the first place we must remark the rise of the Cabinet as a supreme controlling body; secondly, that the essential preliminary for Treasury control had been created; thirdly that the public offices had been largely modernised; and fourthly that there was an increasing divorce of administration from political considerations.

By 1828 the Cabinet was beginning to take its modern shape and becoming the co-ordinator and supervisor of the separate departmental establishments.[38] In 1780 the Cabinet had consisted of the Cabinet officers, the Cabinet officers *"with the circulation,"* and the Cabinet officers "with the circulation *and the Post Office*." Under Pitt's premiership a distinction was finally drawn between the Efficient Cabinet and the Titular Cabinet; and the latter withered away. Again, with the accession of Pitt, "government by departments," which had become prevalent under North's administration, began to decline. The Cabinet began to work as a team and look to the Prime Minister for its lead. The convention of Cabinet unanimity grew up: after enduring public criticism and opposition from his Lord Chancellor for nine years, Pitt insisted on his removal from the Cabinet, and this enforced resignation of Lord Thurlow in 1792 marks the beginning of the tradition of unanimity.[39] In 1821 Canning resigned from the Cabinet because he did not see eye to eye with his colleagues on the affair of Queen Caroline; and Huskisson's resignation over his vote on the East Retford Bill in 1828 further drove home this convention that a Minister ought to resign if unable to vote together with his colleagues. It is perfectly true, of course, that owing to the prevalence of "open questions" during this period, Cabinets were formed and maintained at that time in a fashion impossible today; but, nevertheless, while 1780 saw the Cabinet a mere group of departmental heads, 1828 saw it a collective unity. In this way, the British Cabinet was fast becoming an American Presidency put "into commission"; or if one prefers it, to become a collective Presidency, and the head of the executive branch. What is more, after the Reform Bill of 1832, the Cabinet was destined to go far beyond the American Presidency in its control of the administrative branch; for whereas the latter became increasingly hampered and plagued by Congressional committees and their financial pressure, the procedural changes which followed the Reform Bill in Britain

37 Parliamentary History, Vol. 23; pp. 1110–1114.

38 For a masterly summary of the present state of studies see E. T. Williams, "The Cabinet in the Eighteenth Century," *History,* XXII (1937).

This essay has been thoroughly revised, and is reprinted in *The Making of English History,* Dryden Press, New York, 1952, pp. 378–391.

39 The resignation of Richmond in 1794 seems to illustrate both the tradition of unanimity and the emergence of the efficient Cabinet, in one and the same case. Richmond was Master General of the Ordnance in Pitt's Cabinet of 1784. Ceasing to attend Cabinet meetings, he was in 1794 finally asked to resign both his post and his Cabinet office. The correspondence (Bathurst MSS., HMC, pp. 707–711) indicates:

1. That both Pitt and Richmond agreed that a Cabinet member was to consider himself as "responsible among others" for Cabinet decisions, and to give public support to them.

2. Pitt also argued that absence from Cabinet discussions was inconsistent with such responsibility for collective decisions, a view to which Richmond at first demurred, but to which he was willing to assent later.

3. Richmond excused his absences by arguing that the Ordnance was not "naturally" a Cabinet office, and hinted that he might carry on at his post while resigning the Cabinet; to which Pitt replied that the execution of these important departmental duties was "incompatible with a state that precludes confidential intercourse on *all* the points of public business."

reinforced the leadership of the Cabinet over the House of Commons, finally rendering it the undisputed head of the administrative departments.

The Foundations of Treasury Control

In respect to the second great line of reform, viz. the foundations of centralised Treasury Control, the matter is somewhat more complicated. The reforms proceeded along four lines. To begin with, such control cannot be exercised, unless the public accounts show clearly how much money comes in, how it is appropriated, and how it is being spent. This was quite impracticable under the system of 1780. By this, certain revenues were traditionally assigned to certain funds and from these funds certain payments were traditionally made; furthermore many public servants were paid by fees, not by salaries. The reform of the Public Accounts was the first requisite of effective budgeting. It began with Pitt's Consolidated Fund Act of 1787. Contrary to popular belief, this Act did not operate fully until the close of the whole Napoleonic Wars:[40] but by 1828, its intentions were being fully carried out. All income, from all sources, was paid into one single Consolidated Fund; and all expenditure was paid out of it. (Except for "drawbacks," etc., for which see below, p. 122.) Annual gross amounts of income and expenditure had been placed before the House in 1802 and balanced accounts in 1822. Though an enormous improvement on the 1780 situation, these were still incomprehensible as to detail. It was not until appropriation accounts were introduced in the generation after 1830 that the exact identification of all items of expenditure was accomplished.

A second move in the direction of effective budgeting was the modernisation of the system of receipts and payments. In 1780 these were still being effected in the ancient Exchequer by a procedure sanctioned by time and Henry I. In 1783 the old system of giving tally-sticks as receipts was directed to be abolished, and check-receipts to be substituted for them;[41] though the reform did not become effective until 1826. But by 1834 the whole Exchequer had been swept away and replaced by the Comptroller General and his small staff; and it was to him that the legality of payments of public money was now referred; while instead of the physical transfer of treasure in and out of chests kept at the Exchequer offices,[42] payments were made by book transactions on accounts at the Bank of England.

Two more reforms which increased Treasury control of budgeting were the steps leading to greater control over Estimates and those facilitating greater control of Appropriations. The latter was effected by reforms in the method of audit. In 1780 audit was in the hands of the Auditors of Imprest, or, rather, by their deputies, for the Auditorships were notorious sinecures. But the system in use was so complicated and cumbersome and slow that in 1780 there were

40 Select Committee on Public Monies (Report), 1857: Appendix I, p. 25.

41 A Tally was a stick on which notches were cut indicating the sum received; a large notch meant £1000, a smaller one £100 and so on. When suitably notched it was split in two, endwise, the Exchequer retaining one half, the other being given, by way of Receipt, to the party who had paid in the money.

42 To be strictly accurate, the procedure up to 1834 was as follows. Sums paid into the Exchequer were entered in the Teller's book and then sent to a Clerk of the Bank of England, who kept them and credited the Teller with the amount. Sums paid out of the Exchequer were paid on the Teller's instructions by this same bank clerk, who debited the Teller with the amount. "After one o'clock the Bank Clerk agrees and settles the accounts with the several Tellers, and either pays to or receives from each Teller the balance; if a large sum, in Exchequer Bills of £1000 each and the remainder in cash; otherwise in cash, in bags . . ." This farce was to keep in being the notion that the whole income and expenditure were being physically transferred into and out from the Tellers' chests. (Appendix 68, Sixth Report of Commissioners of Public Accounts, 1781).

open accounts going back thirty years: there was even one which went back to 1689. In 1785 the Auditors of Imprest were abolished and an Audit Board set up. Incapable of handling the huge sums spent during the Napoleonic War, after 1815 it steadily improved. Furthermore, its accounts were more readily comprehensible to the public. In 1780 the Auditors of Imprest were still keeping their accounts in *Roman* numerals. Now, since it is impossible to add up large sums expressed in Roman numerals with any accuracy or speed, Arabic numerals were written in by the side, and additions and subtractions were made in these; but the result was so to superimpose the Roman and Arabic numerals that neither were easily distinguishable. Furthermore, the receipts and issues were still recorded in the Latin tongue; and this was not the golden Latin tongue nor even the silver Latin tongue, nor even the language of Ulpian, but a barbarous gibberish which had evolved departmentally in the course of centuries, and was impossible for any outsider to read or understand.[43] However, in 1834 the English language and Arabic numerals were at last introduced in the teeth of a protest, "that if those proceedings were directed in future to be made in English, the present records in a few years would be obsolete and unintelligible."[44]

Despite the modernisation of the audit system it was not complete. For one thing, the sums paid into the Consolidated fund by the departments were net sums and not the gross ones; that is to say, departments did not pay in all that they received, but subtracted what were called "drawbacks" (i.e. costs of collection) and the costs of making contracts or sales of property, etc. Consequently it was hard to check whether such drawbacks were justified. In the second place, and far more serious, no departments laid an appropriation account before the House. It was discovered in 1831 that for some years past, sums voted by Parliament for one purpose to the Admiralty had been used systematically for quite different purposes. The underlying reasons were "loose estimates which did not truly represent the financial requirements of the naval service; an incomplete system of accounts, which generally could not exhibit the naval expenditure under the heads of the separate grants of Parliament; tardy examination of accounts, which would have delayed the preparation of audited returns of expenditure to a period when they would have been of no practical value; but, above all, the absence of any returns to the House of Commons upon which reliance could be placed, showing how far the intentions of Parliament had been complied with in the application of the naval grants."[45] In 1832 the huge sums voted to the Admiralty were expressed in an appropriation account by Sir James Graham; in 1846 the system was extended to the War Office, and in 1861 extended to all other votes.

The last set of reforms which conduced to more effective Treasury control was the growth of its control over departmental estimates. In 1780 the items of expenditure were to be found in three groups, viz. in the Services' estimates, in certain Miscellaneous grants, and in certain charges traditionally borne on the King's civil list. The Service estimates do not concern us here as we have seen that they were negotiated at Cabinet level before proceeding to the Treasury. Treasury control originates in its control over items of civil expenditure. In 1780

43 Cf. Select Committee on Public Monies (Report), 1857, Appendix I, p. 469.

44 22nd Report of the Select Committee on Finance: Appendix E.2, 1797.

45 Select Committee on Public Monies (Report), 1857, p. 31.

this was a minute item compared with the whole, only £80,000 out of a total of over £22 million.[46] The Treasury had controlled these estimates for miscellaneous expenditure, and in some cases had even made them up in its own offices, as far back as the Revolution of 1688, and possibly before. The more extensive control over civil items which developed after 1780 arose from the fact that by successive statutes certain items, e.g. the cost of ambassadors or judges, which had hitherto been borne on the Civil List, were transferred to the Miscellaneous Estimates and so became subject both to the scrutiny of the Treasury and of the House of Commons. The final transfer of the civil items took place in the definitive reform of 1831, as a result of which the civil list was confined to royal household expenditure and all national items were transferred either to the Consolidated Fund or to the annual Miscellaneous Estimates. Thus, by 1831 the Treasury and the Commons were made responsible for items which hitherto had been concealed in the royal civil list. But in addition to this, the proportion which miscellaneous items bore to the total government expenditure began to rise sharply during the 19th century. In 1820 there was something like £2 million out of a total of £57 millions: by 1850 some £4 million out of a total of £55 million. In this way, after the reform of 1831, Treasury control increased *pari-passu* with the increase of civil estimates.

By 1834 instead of a primitive system of finance incomprehensible either to the public or to the Treasury, reforms had been made without which centralised treasury control of departmental expenditure would have been impracticable; national and departmental accounts were either effective or about to become so; the receipts and payments system had been modernised; the notion of retrospective audit to check appropriations had been evolved at the Admiralty and was to spread to all other departments; and finally, the Treasury control of the miscellaneous estimates had been insured and was to grow with the growth of these estimates in the national budget. The sequel has a certain irony. While the British system of financial control was evolving to its logical terminus in the Exchequer and Audit Act of 1866, the US financial system stood still. The US Treasury became one department among many, exercising neither supervision nor restraint over its partners: each department submitted its own estimates to the Appropriation Committees of Congress; and no effective post-audit of accounts was developed. In 1916 an unofficial Commission of three American political scientists examined and reported on the British system; and in 1921, by the Budget and Accounting Act, the essentials of that system were, as far as the Constitution permitted,[47] introduced into the USA: A Comptroller and Auditor was appointed, and the Bureau of the Budget set up to collate departmental estimates and present Congress with a unified "executive budget."

46 A very large sum indeed was paid out to maintain the Customs Excise Service and the other Treasury Boards, but as shown above, this was recovered by these Boards in the form of drawbacks and did not appear before Parliament; but these drawbacks were controlled and challenged by the Treasury, and in this sense were, from the outset, amenable to Treasury control in addition to the £80,000 mentioned in the text. In 1854 "drawbacks" were abolished, and the Revenue departments paid their *gross* revenue into the Consolidated Fund.

47 I say, deliberately, "as far as the Constitution permitted," because the simple fact is that it has not permitted anything but a travesty of the British system to be transplanted. Congressional control of Appropriations, and its perennial jealousy of the Executive Branch have stultified any close approach to the British model. See *The President's Committee on Administrative Management* (U.S. Govt. Printing Office 1937) pp. 169–202; *The Hoover Commission Report,* 1949. (i) "Budgeting and Accounting," and (ii) "Fiscal, Budgeting and Accounting Systems." Also, "Federal Administrative Pathology and the Separation of Powers" by C. McKinley, *Public Administration Review,* Winter 1951.

Modernization of the Departments

While the Cabinet was fast becoming the effective head of the whole public establishments of the country, and as the Treasury was on the point of becoming the effective co-ordinating head at the departmental level, a third great change took place in the British public service. This was the modernisation of the public offices. We have seen that in 1780 a great number of the clerks of these offices were paid by a fee system, and that as a result, internal developments in each Ministry occurred outside the public gaze. In 1780, Lord North agreed to set up a commission to examine the public accounts, and this commission which reported between 1782 and 1786 analysed in detail the system of payment by fees and concluded heavily against it. It recommended that wherever possible they should be replaced by a salary system. There was a subsequent piecemeal development throughout the public offices, some adopting the recommendations and some not. A Select Committee of 1797 repeated the recommendations of the earlier inquiry; and this report was followed by a Treasury Circular to defaulting offices. In changing from fees to salaries the system generally adopted was to fund all departmental fees into a common pool from which fixed salaries were then paid out to all persons on the establishment. The difficulty that arose here, was that the fund itself fluctuated from year to year. Were officials to accept cuts in their salaries whenever there was a fall in the fee fund? In 1810 a statute laid it down that any such deficiencies would be made good from the Civil List, but this proved grossly unsatisfactory. In 1816 it was replaced by a statute by which any deficiencies were to be made good by a Parliamentary vote. From this point, salaries came within the purview both of the Treasury and of Parliament; and what we have hitherto called the Public Service had made the step which transformed it into the Civil Service. Quasi-private clerks and officers were now definitely public officers; henceforth Parliament's interest in cheap government and efficient government carried the reform movement forward into inquiries about the internal management of the departments and the quality of their personnel. Thus by 1830 the stage was set for the great internal reorganisation which was carried through after 1848, and which was stimulated by the gross administrative shortcomings revealed in the Crimean War.

During this period also, the dead wood was swept out of the departments. It has been seen that so long as sinecures existed and so long as politics could make use of them, so long obsolete forms and processes must continue in the public service, e.g. in the Customs or the Exchequer. From 1780 to 1834 the sinecures were eliminated. It is difficult to make an estimate of the total existing in 1780 as very often what was described as a sinecure was, in fact, an office with a very light duty; but the number of total sinecures seems to have been in the order of 600. Burke's Civil List Act of 1782 swept away 134 offices and another 144 were swept away by Pitt in 1782–1783. All these were offices on the Civil List, however. In 1783 the Exchequer Act suppressed the Usher, Tally cutters, Chamberlains, and the second-clerks in the Teller's office, and similarly the offices of the Auditor and four Tellers. In 1798 a further wave of suppressions occurred: 196 offices in the Customs were done away with and three in the Land Revenue. In 1810, there were still 242 sinecures costing roughly £300,000: but by 1834 they were almost eliminated.[48] Thus, partly by the transition from a fee system to a salary system and partly by the abolition of sinecures, the way was at last

[48] Report of the Select Committee on Sinecure Offices, 1834.

open to the reorganisation and public control of the departments and the civil service.[49]

Increasing Divorce between Politics and Administration

The last of the four major developments in the modernisation of the public service, 1780–1834, was the increasing divorce of administration and politics. In 1782 contractors were excluded from Parliament, and in that same year the revenue officers were disfranchised. In 1809, following the Duke of York scandal, an Act prohibited the sale and brokerage of offices; and another Act "to secure independence in Parliament," laid down that bribes "of offices, places and employment were contrary to the freedom of election." This last Act was made more effective in 1827 by an Act which made the *acceptance* of such bribes penal, not only the mere offering of them. These measures together with legislation which regulated and brought under public control the pension list, and others which interfered with the buying and selling of government boroughs had by 1830 destroyed the influence of the Crown. Perhaps the final proof is that Wellington lost the election of 1830.[50] By 1830, although the party in office always endeavoured as far as possible to give jobs to *its* supporters rather than to those on the benches opposite, and although patronage was helpful in ensuring party discipline inside the House, the more flagrant subordination of administrative efficiency to political considerations had disappeared; and, within the next generation, was to disappear completely.

In all these respects, therefore—the emergence of Cabinet leadership, the foundations of effective budgeting and treasury control, the modernisation of the public offices, and finally, the severance of administration from high politics—the foundations were laid for the remarkable reforms of the mid-19th century which made Britain rather than America the ideal model for administrative reformers throughout the world. If, to resume the thread of our argument, British administrative ability is to be measured by the tendency of the period 1780–1834, it stands up very well against its contemporary in America. For this, after the initial burst of creativity in the Federalist period, had settled down and in some cases had lost pace.

[49] This is to ignore the momentous reorganisation of certain particular departments, notably the Customs, the Tax Office (1785), the Post Office (1784).

[50] Cf. *English Historical Review*, Vol. LXII, No. 245: "The Waning of the Influence of the Crown," by A. S. Foord.

CHAPTER THREE

Behavioral and Normative Perspectives on the "Incidence" of Corruption

13. The Moral Basis of a Backward Society

EDWARD C. BANFIELD
WITH THE ASSISTANCE OF LAURA FASANO BANFIELD

[From a book about a village in southern Italy, the extreme poverty and backwardness of which is to be explained largely (but not entirely) by the inability of the villagers to act together for their common good or, indeed, for an end transcending the immediate, material interests of the nuclear family.]

A very simple hypothesis will make intelligible all of the behavior about which questions have been raised and will enable an observer to predict how the Montegranesi will act in concrete circumstances. The hypothesis is that the Montegranesi act as if they were following this rule: Maximize the material, short-run advantage of the nuclear family; assume that all others will do likewise.

One whose behavior is consistent with this rule will be called an "amoral familist." The term is awkward and somewhat imprecise (one who follows the rule is without morality only in relation to persons outside the family—in relation to family members, he applies standards of right and wrong; one who has no family is of course an "amoral individualist"), but no other term seems better.

In this chapter, some logical implications of the rule are set forth. It will be seen that these describe the facts of behavior in the Montegrano district. The coincidence of facts and theory does not "prove" the theory. However, it does show that the theory will explain (in the sense of making intelligible and predictable) much behavior without being contradicted by any of the facts at hand.

SOURCE: Reprinted with permission of the Macmillan Company from pp. 85–104 of *The Moral Basis of a Backward Society* by Edward C. Banfield. © by The Free Press, a Division of The Macmillan Company, 1958.

1. *In a society of amoral familists, no one will further the interest of the group or community except as it is to his private advantage to do so.* In other words, the hope of material gain in the short-run will be the only motive for concern with public affairs.

This principle is of course consistent with the entire absence of civic improvement associations, organized charities, and leading citizens who take initiative in public service.[1]

A teacher who is a member of a leading family explained,

> I have always kept myself aloof from public questions, especially political ones. I think that all the parties are identical and those who belong to them—whether Communist, Christian Democrat, or other—are

[1] The importance of voluntary associations in the United States has been explained by their function in facilitating social mobility. This explanation is not incompatible with the one given above.

Those who belong to "do-good" organizations secure gratifications (e.g., status, power, neighborly association, etc.) which have nothing to do with the public-spirited purposes for which the organizations exist. Even so, these public-spirited purposes are not unimportant in the motivations of the participants. Moreover, most of the self-regarded ends which are served do not relate to material gain, or at least not to material gain in the short-run.

men who seek their own welfare and well-being. And then too, if you want to belong to one party, you are certain to be on the outs with the people of the other party.

Giovanni Gola, a merchant of upper-class origins, has never been a member of a political party because "It isn't convenient for me—I might lose some business."

Gola does not think of running for office because:

I have all I can do to look after my own affairs. I do enough struggling in my business not to want to add to it in any political struggling. Once in office there would be a constant demand for favors or attentions. I'd have to spend all my time looking after other people's affairs . . . my own would have to be neglected. I don't feel like working hard any more. I am no longer young. [He is in his late forties.]

Those who run for office, Gola says, do so for private advantage.

They get the office, and then they look after themselves. Some take office so as to be able to say, "I am the mayor." But really there isn't much honor attaching to an office; people here don't even respect the President of the Republic. In F–, the mayor wants to be mayor so that he can keep the population down.

2. *In a society of amoral familists only officials will concern themselves with public affairs, for only they are paid to do so. For a private citizen to take a serious interest in a public problem will be regarded as abnormal and even improper.*

Cavalier Rossi, one of the largest landowners of Montegrano, and the mayor of the nearby town of Capa, sees the need for many local public improvements. If he went to the prefect in Potenza as mayor of Capa, they would listen to him, he says. But if he went as a private citizen of Montegrano, they would say, "who are you?" As a private citizen he might help a worker get a pension, but as for schools, hospitals, and such things, those are for the authorities to dole out. A private citizen can do nothing.

The trouble is only partly that officials will not listen to private citizens. To a considerable extent is also that private citizens will not take responsibility in public matters. As Rossi explains,

There are no leaders in Montegrano. People's minds are too unstable; they aren't firm; they get excited and make a decision. Then the next day they have changed their minds and fallen away. It's more or less the same way in Capa. There is lots of talk, but no real personal interest. It always comes to this: the mayor has to do it. They expect the mayor to do everything and to get everything—to make a world.

Farmuso, the director of the school district and formerly the Communist mayor of a town in another province, is earnest, energetic, and intelligent. He listed several things which might be done to improve the situation in Montegrano, but when he was asked if he could bring influence to bear to get any of them done, he said that he could not. "I am interested only in the schools," he explained. "If I wanted to exert influence, with whom would I talk? In Vernande there are six teachers in two rooms, but no money for improvements. I have talked to the mayor and others, but I can't get anything even there."

The feeling that unofficial action is an intrusion upon the sphere of the state accounts in some measure both for Mayor Spomo's haughty officiousness and for the failure of private persons to interest themselves in making stop-gap arrangements for a school and a hospital. In nearby Basso a reclamation project will increase vegetable production and make possible the establishment of a canning factory. The large landowners of Basso will not join together to build a factory, however, even though it might be a good investment. It is the right and the duty of the state to build it.

3. *In a society of amoral familists there will be few checks on officials, for checking on officials will be the business of other officials only.*

When Farmuso, the school director, was asked what he would do if it came to his attention that a public official took bribes, he said that if the bribery were in his own department he would expose it at once. However, if it occurred outside his department, he would say nothing, for in that case it would be none of his concern.

A young school teacher, answering the same question, said that even if he could prove the bribery he would do nothing. "You are likely to be made a martyr," he explained. "It takes courage to do it. There are so many more dishonest people than honest ones that they can gang up on you . . . twist the facts so that you appear to be the guilty one. Remember Christ and the Pharisees."

A leading merchant would not expose bribery, because "Sooner or later someone would come to me and tell me it would be good if I didn't."

4. *In a society of amoral familists, organization (i.e., deliberately concerted action) will be very difficult to achieve and maintain. The inducements which lead people to contribute their activity to organizations are to an important degree unselfish (e.g., identification with the purpose of the organization) and they are often non-material (e.g., the intrinsic interest of the activity as a "game"). Moreover, it is a condition of successful organization that members have some trust in each other and some loyalty to the organization. In an organization with high morale it is taken for granted that they will make small sacrifices, and perhaps even large ones, for the sake of the organization.*

The only formal organizations which exist in Montegrano—the church and the state—are of course provided from the outside; if they were not, they could not exist. Inability to create and maintain organization is clearly of the greatest importance in retarding economic development in the region.[2]

Despite the moral and other resources it can draw upon from the outside, the church in Montegrano suffers from the general inability to maintain organization. There are two parishes, each with its priest. Rivalry between the priests is so keen that neither can do anything out of the ordinary without having obstacles placed in his way by the other, and cooperation between them is wholly out of the question. (On one occasion they nearly came to blows in the public square; on another the saint of one parish was refused admittance to the church of the other when the *festa*-day procession stopped there on its route). When some young men tried to organize a chapter of Catholic Action, a lay association to carry Catholic principles into secular life, they encountered so much sabotage from the feuding priests, neither of whom was willing to tolerate an activity for which the other might receive some credit, that the project was soon abandoned.

The Montegranesi might be expected not to make good soldiers. However brave he may be, the amoral familist does not win battles. Soldiers fight from loyalty to an organization, especially the primary groups of "buddies," not from self-interest narrowly conceived.

Lack of attachment even to kindred has impeded emigration and indirectly economic development. In the half century prior to 1922, there was heavy emigration from Montegrano to the United

2 Max Weber remarked in *The Protestant Ethic and the Rise of Capitalism* (Allen and Unwin edition, London, 1930, p. 57) that "the universal reign of absolute unscrupulousness in the pursuit of selfish interests by the making of money has been a specific characteristic of precisely those countries whose bourgeois-capitalistic development, measured according to Occidental standards, has remained backward. As every employer knows, the lack of *coscienziosita* of the laborers of such countries, for instance Italy as compared with Germany, has been, and to a certain extent still is, one of the principal obstacles to their capitalistic development."

States and later to Argentina. In general, however, ties between the emigrants and those who remained at home were not strong enough to support "chains" of emigration. Hundreds of Montegranesi live in the hope that a brother or uncle in America will send a "call," but such calls rarely come. People are perplexed when their relatives in America do not answer their letters. The reason is, probably, that the letters from Montegrano always ask for something, and the emigrant, whose advantage now lies elsewhere, loses patience with them. The relative absence of emigration, as well as of gifts from persons who have emigrated, is a significant impediment to economic development. Some Italian towns, whose ethos is different, have benefited enormously from continuing close ties with emigrants who have prospered in the New World.[3]

5. *In a society of amoral familists, office-holders, feeling no identification with the purposes of the organization, will not work harder than is necessary to keep their places or (if such is within the realm of possibility) to earn promotion. Similarly, professional people and educated people generally will lack a sense of mission or calling. Indeed, official position and special training will be regarded by their possessors as weapons to be used against others for private advantage.*

In southern Italy, the indifference of the bureaucracy is notorious. "A zealous official is as rare as a white fly," a man who had retired after 49 years in the public service remarked.

"From the President of the Republic down to the last little Italian," a landowner said, "there is a complete lack of any sense of duty—especially of the sense of duty to do productive work."

The school teachers of Montegrano notably lack a sense of calling. It is not uncommon for a teacher to come late to class or to miss class altogether. At best the teacher teaches four hours a day and takes no further part in the lives of the children. An engineer from northern Italy was shocked at what he saw in Montegrano. "During the summer vacation," he said, "a teacher in the north may hold informal classes. He will take the children on walks into the country and explain a bit about nature. Or they will go on picnics and sing together. The teacher is a part of the children's lives out of school as well as in." In Montegrano, he found, teachers spend the summer loafing in the *piazza* and they do not speak to their pupils when they see them.

"Study and education," a young teacher who was himself of an artisan family explained, "has helped some people to succeed. It has helped them by giving them an advantage over the ignorant. With their knowledge, they are better able to exploit ignorance. They are able to cheat more dexterously."

With other professionals the situation is more or less the same. The pharmacist, a left-wing socialist who enjoys a government monopoly is one of the richest men in town, feels himself under no obligation to stock the anti-biotics and other new medicines which the doctor prescribes or to extend credit to those desperately in need. The doctor himself, although an outstanding man in many ways, does not feel under an obligation

---

[3] McDonald writes in a personal letter: "Since 1927 Italians who are not officially assisted may be nominated and paid for by relatives or friends resident here in Australia. Solidarity of some kind is needed for chains of such emigration to have continued 30 years. Montegrano folk apparently would not help each other. In Reggio Calabria, community solidarity is lacking yet there is nuclear family solidarity plus relatively strong identification with and participation in cliques of certain relatives selected from the kindred kinship system plus certain friends (especially *compari* and *commare*). I have found that these nuclear family-clique members are the Calabrians who form the links in the migration chains. Since cliques of relatives and friends overlap in their system, these chains are snowballing despite the lack of community solidarity. In fact, comparing the rate of growth of Calabrian settlements of the above clique-nuclear family solidarity type with Calabrian settlements of the Montegrano solidarity nuclear family type, I have found that the former grew very much faster than the latter."

to provide himself with the bare essentials of equipment for modern medical practice.

6. *In a society of amoral familists, the law will be disregarded when there is no reason to fear punishment. Therefore individuals will not enter into agreements which depend upon legal processes for their enforcement unless it is likely that the law will be enforced and unless the cost of securing enforcement will not be so great as to make the undertaking unprofitable.*

This, of course, is another impediment to organization and to economic and other development.

It is taken for granted that all those who can cheat on taxes will do so. Minimum wage laws and laws which require the employer to make social security payments on the wages of domestic servants are universally ignored.

An employer who can get away with it is almost sure to cheat his employees. If the employer is a local man, the worker can get justice by appealing to the Marshal, whose informal powers are great. Otherwise the worker is usually cheated. The new municipal building was built by contractors from Matera who paid Montegrano laborers less than the legal minimum and left town owing several of them wages for their last month's work. Since the employer was not a local man, the Marshal could do nothing. In principle the workers could appeal to a labor commission in Potenza. In practice they had to reconcile themselves to the fact that they had been cheated.

Frequently the worker is prevented by self-interest from taking his case to the Marshal. He cannot afford to be on bad terms with the employer: it is better to be cheated than to be deprived of employment altogether. Accordingly, it is the custom for the employer to pay only at his convenience. A peasant may have to go, hat in hand, to the *signore* month after month to ask politely for the dollar or two that is owed.

Mutual distrust between landlords and tenants accounts in part for the number of tiny, owner-operated farms in Montegrano. Rather than work a larger unit on shares, an arrangement which would be more profitable but which would necessitate getting along with a landlord, the peasant prefers to go it alone on his uneconomic holding. Twenty-one peasants were asked which they would prefer, to own eight hectares of land or to sharecrop 40. One said he would prefer to sharecrop the larger holding "because even if I had to be under another and to work a little harder, the gain would be much more." None of the others thought the gain from the larger holding would offset the burden of having to get along with a landlord. Their explanations showed how anxiety, suspicion, and hate make cooperation burdensome.[4]

I would prefer to be the owner of eight hectares rather than have the rental of 40 because if you are an owner no one commands you and furthermore you are not always worried that tomorrow your half may not be yours and so always under the necessity of being careful.

I would prefer to be the owner of eight hectares or even less than to work someone else's land. I've had experience with that already and it is really unbearable because the owners always think you are stealing from them.

I would prefer a little land of my own to renting 40 hectares because, as I have already said, I hate the rich who sit in the

4 Seventeen of these peasants were also asked which they would prefer, to own eight hectares or to have a steady job paying 1000 lire a day. Eleven preferred the cash wage; all but one because there would be no worry or uncertainty. Of the six who preferred to own land, two said that their incomes would be greater, two said that they would be independent of an employer, and two said that they would have both larger incomes and independence.

To the peasants, the cash wage of 1000 lire was associated with a "company" such as contracts with public agencies to do road repairs, not with private individuals. The company, the peasant feels, is less likely to cheat and is in general more dependable. One said he would prefer the wage if the employer were a company but the land if the employer were a private party.

breeze all year and come around only when it is time to divide the produce which I have worked hard with so many sacrifices to grow.

7. *The amoral familist who is an office-holder will take bribes when he can get away with it. But whether he takes bribes or not, it will be assumed by the society of amoral familists that he does.*[5]

There is no way of knowing to what extent bribery actually exists in Montegrano. There is abundant evidence, however, that it is widely believed to be common. The peasants are sure that the employment officer gives preference to those who bring him presents. They believe, too, that Mayor Spomo made a fortune by selling the communal forest without competitive bids. Better informed people say that it is highly unlikely that there is graft in the administration of the commune: its affairs are too closely supervised from Potenza. However, many upper class people agree that bribery and favoritism are widespread in southern Italy at large.

A teacher had this recollection of Fascism:

> During Fascism there was a great spirit of emulation among the pupils and good discipline. Today all this is gone; children grow up very rude and the teacher in school must always have a stick in hand because the children are fighting among themselves all of the time.

9. *In a society of amoral familists, the claim of any person or institution to be inspired by zeal for public rather than private advantage will be regarded as fraud.*

A young man said,

> If I decided that I wanted to do something for Montegrano, I would enter my name on the list at election time, and everyone would ask, "Why does he want to be mayor?" If ever anyone wants to do anything, the question always is: what is he after?

Anti-clericalism is widespread in Montegrano, and the usual objection to priests is that they are "money grubbers" and "hypocrites." In fact, the priests seem to be no more concerned with gain than are other professionals, and their level of living is no higher than that of the others. They are peculiarly liable to attack, however, because the church professes to be unselfish.

Socialists and Communists, like priests, are liable to be regarded as pious frauds. "There are socialists of the mouth and socialists of the heart," a peasant woman explained.

The extraordinary bitterness and, as it seems to an outsider, unfairness with which so many peasants accuse others of hypocrisy is to be understood, in part, perhaps, as an expression of guilt feelings.

---

[5] An interview with the Communist mayor of Grottole, another village of Lucania, by E. A. Bayne of the American Universities Field Staff, reveals the same selfishness and distrust that are evident in Montegrano.

After explaining to Bayne that the peasants of Grottole would not work together—that all wanted something for themselves—the mayor asked if the Americans would give the village a tractor. After he had been discouraged in this hope, the mayor said,

> When you leave here I will go down in the street with my people, and they will ask me, "Did you get any help for us?" And I will try to explain that you are not officials—not even rich tourists—but journalists. "Why then," they will say, "have you bought them wine and coffee with our money and now have nothing to show for it?"

At the conclusion of his interview Bayne laid a few thousand lire on the mayor's desk and asked if he would distribute it where it would do the most good. Perhaps there was a Christmas fund for children? The mayor's consternation was immediate. With politeness but with unmistakable firmness he refused.

> You do not understand my people [he protested]. If I were to accept this gift which *I* understand, those people in the street would soon ask if there had not been more and how much I had kept for myself. We have no Christmas fund, for who would contribute to it? . . .

Two years later Bayne revisited Grottole and found that the mayor had been defeated for re-election and had taken to drink. "He didn't do anything for the people and they became tired of him," someone explained. "Now we have a new mayor—this one is really a fascist. He won't do anything either."

Quoted with permission from American Universities Field Staff letters of December 17, 1954, and February 21, 1957.

As is explained elsewhere, the peasant is not unaware that charity is a virtue. Not practicing it himself, he feels some guilt therefore, and he projects this as hostility against those institutions, especially the church, which preach the virtue of charity and through which, perhaps, he would like to be vicariously virtuous.

10. *In the society of amoral familists there will be no connection between abstract political principle (i.e., ideology) and concrete behavior in the ordinary relationships of every day life.*

In Montegrano, the principal left-wing socialists are the doctor and the pharmacist, two of the town's most prosperous gentlemen. The doctor, although he has called upon the government to provide a hospital, has not arranged an emergency room or even equipped his own office. The pharmacist, a government-licensed monopolist, gives an absolute minimum of service at extremely high prices (Signora Prato paid five cents for a single aspirin tablet!) and is wholly unconcerned with local affairs, i.e., those which would have implications for action by him.

The discrepancy between ideology and behavior in practical affairs tends to discredit ideology in the eyes of the peasants. Prato was one of those who assembled in the *piazza* when Dr. Gino tried to organize a branch of the Socialist Party.

> I went a few times and it all sounded very good [he said later]. But that Spring Don Franco hired a mule to cultivate his vineyard, and I thought to myself, What can this be? What can Socialism mean? Why does Don Franco, who is such a believer in it, hire a mule instead of the ten workers he used to hire? There are ten people out of work. And it wouldn't cost him any more to use them than to use the mules.

> What ignorance! [the doctor exclaimed when he was told what Prato said]. Cultivation well done by hand is better than cultivation done with a mule. But the workers here must be watched all the time because they don't really know their jobs, and it is a nuisance to have to be on hand to keep watch. With a mule, you can at least see that the whole row has been done the same way.

11. *In a society of amoral familists there will be no leaders and no followers. No one will take the initiative in outlining a course of action and persuading others to embark upon it (except as it may be to his private advantage to do so) and, if one did offer leadership, the group would refuse it out of distrust.*

Apparently there has never been in Montegrano a peasant leader to other peasants. Objectively, there is a basis for such leadership to develop: the workers on road gangs, for example, share grievances and one would expect them to develop feelings of solidarity.

Suspicion of the would-be leader probably reduces the effectiveness of the doctor, the mid-wife, and the agricultural agent as teachers. When a peasant was asked whether she could get birth control information from the mid-wife, she replied, "Of course not. It is not to her interest that I limit the size of my family."

The nearest approximation to leadership is the patron-client relationship. By doing small favors (e.g., by lending a few bushels of grain during the winter, by giving cast-off clothing, or by taking a child from a large family as a house-maid), a well-to-do person may accumulate a clientele of persons who owe him return favors and, of course, deference. Such clients constitute a "following," perhaps, but the patron is not a "leader" in any significant sense. In Montegrano, moreover, none of the well-to-do has troubled to develop much of a clientele. One reason is, perhaps, that the leading families are not engaged in factional squabbles, and so the advantage to be had from a clientele does not outweigh the expense and inconvenience of maintaining it.

12. *The amoral familist will use his*

ballot to secure the greatest material gain in the short run. Although he may have decided views as to his long-run interest, his class interest, or the public interest, these will not affect his vote if the family's short-run, material advantage is in any way involved.

Prato, for example, is a monarchist as a matter of principle: he was born and brought up one and he believes that monarchy is best because Italy is too poor to afford frequent elections. These principles do not affect his vote, however. "Before elections," he explains, "all the parties send people around who say, 'Vote for our party.' We always say 'Yes,' but when we go to vote, we vote for the party we think has given us the most." The Christian Democratic party has given Prato a few days' work on the roads each year. Therefore he votes for it. If it ceased to give him work and if there were no advantage to be had from voting for another party, he would be a monarchist again. If Mayor Spomo has influence with the Minister of Agriculture, he should be kept despite his haughtiness and his stealing. But if Councilmen Viva and Lasso can get a larger project than the mayor can get, or if they can get one quicker, then down with him.

13. *The amoral familist will value gains accruing to the community only insofar as he and his are likely to share them. In fact, he will vote against measures which will help the community without helping him because, even though his position is unchanged in absolute terms, he considers himself worse off if his neighbors' position changes for the better. Thus it may happen that measures which are of decided general benefit will provoke a protest vote from those who feel that they have not shared in them or have not shared in them sufficiently.*

In 1954, the Christian Democratic party showed the voters of Basso that vast sums had been spent on local public works. Nevertheless the vote went to the Communists. There are other reasons which help to account for the vote (the Christian Democratic candidate was a merchant who would not give credit and was cordially disliked and distrusted), but it seems likely that the very effectiveness of the Christian Democratic propaganda may have helped to cause its defeat. Seeing what vast sums had been expended, the voters asked themselves: Who got it all? Why didn't they give me my fair share?

No amoral familist ever gets what he regards as his fair share.

14. *In a society of amoral familists the voter will place little confidence in the promises of the parties. He will be apt to use his ballot to pay for favors already received (assuming, of course, that more are in prospect) rather than for favors which are merely promised.*

Thus Prato, in the statement quoted above, attaches weight to past performance rather than to promises. "All the parties make promises," he says. "The Christian Democratic party had a chance and it has done a great deal. Why change?" And thus a writer, after describing the enthusiasm with which the new mayor was received after Spomo's defeat, remarks significantly, "We will wait and see."

The principle of paying for favors received rather than for ones merely promised gives a great advantage to the party in power, of course. Its effect, however, is often more than offset by another principle, as follows:

15. *In a society of amoral familists it will be assumed that whatever group is in power is self-serving and corrupt. Hardly will an election be over before the voters will conclude that the new officials are enriching themselves at their expense and that they have no intention of keeping the promises they have made. Consequently, the self-serving voter will use his ballot to pay the incumbents not for benefits but for injuries, i.e., he will use it to administer punishment.*

Even though he has more to gain

from it than from any other, the voter may punish a party if he is confident that it will be elected despite his vote. The ballot being secret, he can indulge his taste for revenge (or justice) without incurring losses. (Of course there is some danger that too many will calculate in this way, and that the election will therefore be lost by error.)

Addo's switch from Christian Democrat to Communist and back again to Christian Democrat is to be explained in this way. The priest in Addo was slightly mad. Some of his eccentricities nobody minded (he arrayed himself as a cardinal and required a chicken as part payment for a marriage), but when he left town a few days before the election taking with him the *pasta,* sugar, and other election-day presents that had been sent them from the Vatican, the voters of Addo were outraged. Afterward, a new priest soon made matters right.

16. *Despite the willingness of voters to sell their votes, there will be no strong or stable political machines in a society of amoral familists. This will be true for at least three reasons:* (*a*) *the ballot being secret, the amoral voter cannot be depended upon to vote as he has been paid to vote;* (*b*) *there will not be enough short-run material gain from a machine to attract investment in it; and* (*c*) *for reasons explained above, it will be difficult to maintain formal organization of any kind whatever.*

Prato says "Yes" to all who ask for his vote. Since they cannot trust him to vote as he promises, none of the parties will offer to buy his vote. The *pasta* and sugar that are distributed by the parties are good-will offerings rather than bribes. The amounts given are, of course, trivial in comparison to what would be paid if there were some way of enforcing the contract.

17. *In a society of amoral familists, party workers will sell their services to the highest bidders. Their tendency to change sides will make for sudden shifts in strength of the parties at the polls.*[6]

The sudden conversion of the secretary of the Montegrano branch of the Monarchist Party to Communism occurred because Monarchist headquarters in Naples was slow in paying him for his services. When he turned Communist, the Monarchists made a settlement. He then returned to his duties as if nothing had happened.

[6] That voter behavior in the Montegrano district is closely similar to that in much of rural Italy is suggested by the data in an undated report by the Office of Intelligence Research, based on data secured by International Research Associates, Inc., of New York, which includes "profiles" of the political situation in 76 communes ranging in size from 200 to 7000 electors and located in all parts of Italy. The communes described are those in which Communism made its greatest gains or suffered its greatest losses in the 1953 elections. The data was gathered in field interviews in which citizens were asked to explain the voting shift in their communes. The report shows that local economic issues were by far the most important cause of the voting shifts. Economic doctrine, it shows, was of little importance. National issues—e.g., monarchy, the church, foreign policy—were of even less importance. "Next to economic causes," the report says, "significant changes in the voting pattern appear to have been caused by corruption, graft, injustice (real or fancied), and failure to fulfill promises."

14. Patronage in Sicily[1]

JEREMY BOISSEVAIN

The purpose of this article is two-fold. First, it seeks to further our understanding of certain organisational aspects of patronage, an institution which has recently been given considerable attention (Banfield 1961; Boissevain 1962, 1965; Campbell 1964; Foster 1961, 1963; Kenny 1960, 1961; Mair 1961; Silverman 1965; Trouwborst 1961, 1962; Wolf 1966). Secondly, it examines some of its functional aspects and discusses factors which appear to account for its importance in Sicily, the area which provides the ethnographic data for the paper.[2]

Patronage is founded on the reciprocal relations between patrons and clients. By patron I mean a person who uses his influence to assist and protect some other person, who then becomes his "client," and in return provides certain services to his patron. The relationship is asymmetrical, for the nature of the services exchanged may differ considerably. Patronage is thus the complex of relations between those who use their influence, social position or some other attribute to assist and protect others, and those whom they so help and protect.[3] The means by which this relationship is constituted and the form which it takes differ considerably from society to society. It varies from the formal contract in East Africa between members of the dominant class and the peasants, which is usually sealed by a gift of cattle from the former to the latter and entails a series of clearly delineated, institutionalised rights and obligations for each party (*cf.* Mair 1961; Trouwborst 1962), to the less formal relationship concluded between the Mediterranean patron and his client, in which the exact nature of the rights and obligations are not clearly defined culturally. The structure of the system in the Mediterranean is thus much more difficult to analyse, for it is implicit rather than explicit. Nevertheless, common to both the formal and informal systems of patronage is the need for protectors on the one hand, and for followers on the other. Why this should be so, at least in Sicily, is a matter which I discuss later.

SICILIAN SOCIETY

Before turning to examine patronage in Sicily I shall give a summary of some of

1 I read an earlier version of this paper at the 1964 meeting of the American Anthropological Association in Detroit and I am grateful for the comments of those who participated in its discussion. Professor F. G. Bailey, Dr. A. Balikci, Dr. A. Blok, Dr. P. and Dr. J. Schneider, Dr. A. Trouwborst and Dr. A. Xibilia kindly read and criticised the manuscript.

2 The field work upon which this article is based was carried out in 1962 and 1963 and was made possible by grants from the Centro Regionale per lo Sviluppo di Comunità, the Penrose Fund of the American Philosophical Society (grant 3275) and the Co-operative for American Relief to Everywhere (CARE, Inc.), for which I am most grateful.

SOURCE: Jeremy Boissevain. "Patronage in Sicily," *Man* (N.S.). Vol. 1, No. 1 (March 1966), pp. 18–33. By permission of the publisher, The Royal Anthropological Institute of Great Britain and Ireland.

3 I have purposely used a very broad working definition of patronage, for as will be apparent from the following analysis, patron-client relations are often relations between friends.

the important structural features of Sicilian society. In particular I touch upon the island's recent violent history, the importance of the family, the socio-economic hierarchy and some local moral concepts. Following the unification of Italy in 1860, administrators from the north, notably Piedmont were sent to Sicily to make this region part of the new state of Italy and to enforce its new laws. But their task was greatly complicated by their ignorance of the local dialect and customs, notably the network of kinsmen, friends, friends-of-friends, patrons and clients that bound baron to brigand, rich to poor, and stretched from one end of Sicily to the other, providing a parallel line of communication, and at times, completely paralysing the attempts of the central government to enforce its laws (*cf.* Franchetti 1925). The corruption and banditry in Sicily became a national problem, and in 1875 the Italian parilament appointed a commission to report on the situation. Moreover, the rural proletariat, including the miners tapping the island's rich mineral deposits, continued to rebel against the appalling conditions under which they worked and lived, and further insurrections exploded before the turn of the century (*cf.* Sonnino 1925; Renda 1956).

After the rebellion of the Sicilian Fasci (1893–1894) had been ruthlessly crushed by the central government, an uneasy peace reigned while the battered workers' movement recovered. Following the 1914–1918 war the bandits, their numbers swelled by deserters from the military forces and discharged soldiers who had no desire to return to the soil, once again held sway in the Sicilian countryside. At the same time, Mussolini's strong-arm gangs set off a new wave of violence that the police and the military, in fact the government of the country, made little attempt to contain (Mack Smith 1959: 348). This period of unrest was followed in 1922 by Mussolini's march on Rome, the beginning of 21 years of oppression, poverty and war for most Sicilians.[4]

A period of unrest and violence also followed the end of World War II. Conservative political forces within Sicily, aided by *mafiosi* and bandits, the most famous of whom was Giuliano, sought to obtain the independence of Sicily from Italy and to crush the revived workers' movement and the growing pressure for land reform (*cf.* Maxwell 1956; Pantaleone 1962).

Thus for the last century, Sicily has been a land where revolution and violence have been endemic, where economic exploitation of the proletarian masses by a small upper class composed of the bourgeoisie and nobility, often aided by delinquents, went hand in hand with their control of the local and regional administration, and their manipulation of it for personal gain. In short it was, and to an extent still is, a land where the strong survive at the expense of the weak.

The central institution of Sicilian society is the nuclear family. The rights and obligations which derive from membership in it provide the individual with his basic moral code. Moreover a man's social status as a person with honour, an *omu* or *cristianu,* is closely linked to his ability to maintain or improve the economic position of his family and to safeguard the purity of its women, in whom is enshrined the family's collective honour. A person's responsibility for his family is thus the value on which his life is centred.

Other values and organisational principles are of secondary importance. If they interfere with his ability to carry out

4 The attitude of Sicilians towards the Fascist period depends in part upon their present political persuasion and their social position. Many conservative bourgeois who held positions of power under the Fascist regime, look back with nostalgia to the Mussolini era. Their more liberal counterparts do not do so, nor does the mass of the rural proletariat, which regards this period as one of oppression and grinding poverty. This does not necessarily mean that they feel Sicily would have been better off economically without the Fascists.

his obligation to his family, he combats them with intrigue, force and violence if necessary. In so doing he is supported by public opinion, even though he may be acting contrary to the law. Justice and the rule of law are not synonymous.

Because the system of reckoning kin is bilateral, each person stands at the centre of a vast network of persons to whom he is related both through his parents and through marriage. Relatives are expected to help one another. But the help one can expect from, or, reciprocally, the obligation one has to assist a kinsman, diminish as the genealogical distance between the two increases. In general it is extended to blood relatives as far as second cousins, the limit of the range within which the Church prohibits marriage. Effective recognition for purposes of mutual aid and friendship generally goes out only as far as first cousins.[5] It is strongest between members of the same nuclear family, that is between parents and their children, and between siblings. This obligation to the members of one's own natal family diminishes when a person marries and founds his own family.

Thus the Sicilian divides the world around him into kin and non-kin. The former are allies with whom he shares reciprocal rights and obligations of mutual assistance and protection. The latter are either enemies or potential enemies, each of whom is seeking to protect and improve the position of his own family, if need be at the expense of others.[6]

Sicilian society is highly stratified. Away from the few large cities the economy is based upon agriculture. Effective control over land, the traditional basis of local wealth, was until recently held almost exclusively by the rural bourgeoisie composed of professionals, shopkeepers, brokers and artisans, who do not work the land themselves.[7] These form the *borghesia* or bourgeoisie, for whom most of the *contadini,*[8] those who physically till the soil, work. The proportion of *borghesi* to *contadini* in Leone,[9] an agro-town of 20,000 in southern Sicily where I spent seven months in 1962 and 1963, was 16 to 84 per cent. Only 15 per cent of the *contadini* own or hold the land they work under emphyteutical (perpetual) leases. The rest are share croppers or landless labourers; thus they are the dependents of those who control the land.

An enormous gulf separates those who work the land from those who do not. Traditionally there tended to be a strong correlation between wealth in land and education, though expanding public education, the gradual division of the large estates[10] and the cash now being sent home by Sicilian migrant labourers working in northern Europe is rapidly modifying this neat alignment. In general, high social status attaches to wealth and to education. Low social status is accorded to those who work the land,

5 There is no socially recognised limit, as with the Sarakatsani in Greece, where the limit is set clearly at second cousin (Campbell 1964: 36). The dividing line between kinship and non-kinship for purposes of mutual aid varies with the personal preferences of the individuals concerned, and also with their socio-economic class. In general the wealthier one is the farther out the limits of kinship obligations are extended.

6 Banfield (1958) found that much the same attitude prevailed among the peasants of Montegrano in Lucania, and called it "amoral familism." But it is of course only "amoral" in the eyes of the outside observer. The people of Lucania and Sicily regard it as a highly moral attitude, and consider those who act accordingly as acting morally.

7 Very often the land was, and still is, owned by members of the nobility resident in the cities, who lease their estates *en bloc* to intendents or *gabellotti,* or in smaller parcels under emphyteutical leases (which give perpetual effective control over the land in return for a small annual ground rent) to other prominently placed members of the bourgeoisie. These in turn either employ landless labourers, *braccianti,* to cultivate it for them, or they sublease it to share-croppers, *mezzadri,* who in their turn either cultivate it themselves or employ *braccianti* to help them.

8 Technically speaking *contadini* are those who own land and work it themselves. I avoid the use of the term in this sense and employ it as do most Sicilians, as a social category to designate all those who work on the land.

9 A pseudonym.

10 The gradual application of land reform laws after 1950 has had surprisingly little effect upon this generalised picture (*cf.* Blok 1964; Rochefort 1961: 109 sqq.).

for physical labour, especially agricultural labour, is despised. The *borghesi* are better educated and wealthier. Moreover, their sons become the municipal and provincial civil servants who run the affairs of rural Sicily. In contrast, the *contadini,* who by and large work for the *borghesi,* have an inferior education and often live in grinding poverty. The contrast between the bourgeoisie and the rural proletariat has thus been not only between employer and employee, but between wealth and poverty, between education and illiteracy.

It must not be thought, however, that these broad classes are organised corporate groups. They are interest groups which are often opposed. Though the separation between them is marked, there are many lines of mutual dependence as well as many kinship links which cut across the indeterminate frontier between the two. Though most marriages take place between members of the same social class, social mobility is quite common. Thus many families have relatives in the other classes located at various levels of the socio-economic hierarchy.

This stratification, when taken in consideration with the overriding obligation of mutual aid that exists between close kinsmen, has important effects on the political life. Civil servants generally favour their close relatives, and try to derive a personal advantage from their position. Since most are members of the *borghesia,* this means that the upper classes receive preferential treatment. In northern Europe or North America, civil servants who behave in this way and who are caught are punished by law and by the pressure of public opinion, which regards as immoral and contemptible the bureaucrat who betrays the public service ethic of honesty and impartiality. But in Sicily, there is no neat correlation between what is *legal* and *moral*. It is illegal for a brother to murder the person who has raped his sister, yet this, in terms of the local system of values, is a highly moral act. In the same way, it is illegal for a civil servant to let a public contract to a person who gives him a large commission or present. But, seen from the point of view of his relatives, this act is not immoral. On the contrary, by performing it he fulfils his primary obligation to aid his own family and his nearest kinsmen. In practice this means that the civil servant is only impartial to persons who are neither relatives nor friends. Yet these belong to a category of persons whom he mistrusts and, in a very real sense, looks upon as potential enemies. Thus non-kin with whom he deals in his official capacity, unless they are introduced by a third party who is a kinsman, friend, patron or client, receive short shrift. He is not only impartial, he is so detached as to be remote.

PATRONS, CLIENTS, AND FRIENDS

To an extent, then, every Sicilian feels himself to be isolated in a lawless and hostile world in which violence and bloodshed are still endemic. Not only is he surrounded by enemies and potential enemies, he is also subject to the authority of an impersonal government whose affairs are administered by bureaucrats, each of whom is either trying to derive some personal advantage from his official position or is liable to be manœuvred against him by his enemies. The more one descends the socio-economic ladder, the farther removed people are from kinsmen and friends who wield power and who can therefore control the forces shaping their lives.

Thus the basic problem the Sicilian faces in dealing with the world of non-kin is how to protect himself from his enemies, both known and unknown; and how to influence the remote, impersonal, if not hostile, authorities who make the decisions which control his well-being and that of his family, with whom his honour and standing in the community is so intimately bound. Most resolve these problems by seeking out strategically placed protectors and friends, who, together with kinsmen, make up the personal network of contacts through whom the average Sicilian attempts to protect and advance the fortunes of his family.

He often seeks to bind an influential, professional-class patron to himself by persuading him to become the godfather, the spiritual sponsor and protector, of one of his children. This is a relationship that is not lightly entered into since it is a formal contract, solemnised in public and before God, and once concluded not to be broken. Co-godparents, *compari,* are automatically "friends," and a *compare* is supposed to favour his godchild, if not the child's father.

Before turning to an analysis of the operation of the system of patronage, it is necessary to unravel the apparently overlapping statuses of kinsman, friend and patron. I am here concerned primarily with the last two. I believe a conceptual distinction can be made between kinship, on the one hand, and patronage and friendship, on the other, although in the actual operation of the system, they overlap. Their difference lies in the distinction between the obligations of kinship and patronage. An individual is born into a kinship system, and there finds, ready-made so to speak, a network of persons with whom he has a series of jurally defined obligations. His position in the system is ascribed. Kinsmen are supposed to help each other. Thus if he asks a close kinsman to put his personal network of contacts at his disposal, this favour is accorded freely, if it is within the means of the relative to do so. By according the favour, the kinsman is not necessarily contracting a reciprocal service. The service he provided does not place the kinsman whom he is helping under an obligation over and above that which exists normally between kinsmen.[11]

In contrast to the ascribed mutual obligations which exist between kinsmen, the relationship between patron and client, or between friends, is entered into voluntarily. A favour or service granted creates an obligation which entails a reciprocal service that must be repaid on more or less a *quid pro quo* basis. If it is not repaid when requested or expected, the relationship is terminated. A person's position in a network of patronage is achieved, not ascribed, generally speaking. It should be noted, however, that the obligation created by a patron in one generation may not be called on until the following generation; hence patron-client relations often exist between families. Thus a patron may place his personal network of kinsmen, friends, patrons and clients at the service of a client or friend, but it is a calculated action which imposes a very definite obligation upon the person soliciting the favour. It is a debt that has to be repaid sooner or later. Among close kin no detailed ledger of services given and received is maintained, while such a social accounting is the basis upon which a system of patronage rests. However, because there is no clear demarcation separating kinship and non-kinship between distant cousins, the greater the genealogical distance between two persons exchanging favours, the more likely it is that an accounting will be kept. Kinship thus shades off into patronage.

While the institution of friendship, *amicizia,* exists in Sicily, it is necessary to see it in its local context in order to free it from the burden of preconceptions the outsider transfers almost automatically to the term. Given the overriding importance of the nuclear family in Sicilian society, and the distrustful attitude a person takes towards non-kin, friendship is an apparent contradiction to the principles presented above. But friendship must be qualified. To begin with, the tie between friends is always subordinate to that between kinsmen. Secondly, it is a voluntary relationship which entails reciprocal services. If these

[11] Campbell (1964: 99) makes a similar point.

are not granted, it can be broken. Because it is an unstable thing, friendly non-kin often convert their friendship into a binding, formal tie through the institution of godparenthood.

The analysis of friendship in Sicily is further complicated by the fact that the term friend, *amico,* is applied indiscriminately not only to all social equals with whom a person is in contact, but also to patrons by their clients, and to clients by patrons. All are *gli amici,* friends.

The useful distinction which Eric Wolf (1966: 10 sqq.) has drawn between "emotional" and "instrumental" friendship is very much to the point here. Emotional friendship "involves a relation between an ego and an alter in which each satisfies some emotional need in his opposite number" (10). In contrast, in instrumental friendship "each member of the dyad acts as a potential connecting link to other persons outside the dyad." The former is associated with "closure of the social circle," the latter "reaches beyond the boundaries of existing sets and seeks to establish beachheads in new sets" (12). Friendship in Sicily is instrumental. The only friendships that I encountered which might have been described as emotional were between first cousins, but there the members of the dyads used the term *cugino,* cousin, and not *amico,* friend, to address and refer to each other.[12] Actions which are patently return services rendered by a client to a patron are said to be done *per amicizia,* for friendship. In fact an informant once remarked that in Sicily all friendship is political, and quoted the proverb "He who has money and friends holds justice by the short hairs"[13] to emphasise his point. Thus in the Sicilian context, friends are actual or potential intermediaries and patrons. For when a friend is called on to provide protection or assistance—a situation which occurs not infrequently in a society such as that in Sicily in which there is great inequality in the distribution of economic and political power—the friendship becomes asymmetrical and shades off into patronage. (Pitt-Rivers 1954: 154; Campbell 1964: 232 sq.)

The present-day Sicilian normally has more than one patron, and works through the one he deems most useful in a given situation. But should two patrons come into direct competition, he must choose one to the exclusion of the other. However, as social relations become progressively specialised, and the Sicilian moves out of his relatively isolated community to deal with increasingly diverse decision makers—thus requiring functionally specific patrons—the danger of an encounter between two patrons operating in the same social field diminishes. In contrast, in the past, particularly before the first World War, rural communities were more isolated from outside centres of power and the average Sicilian was limited to patrons drawn from the local *élite.* These were persons who were in direct and continuous competition with each other. It was consequently normally not possible for him to have more than one patron.

Up to this point the benefits of a patron-client relationship have been considered only from the point of view of the client. But clients protect a patron's good name and report on the activities of his enemies. It is in their interest to do this, for the stronger their patron is, the better he is able to protect them. Favours such as reports on the manœuvring of an enemy are services which generate reciprocal obligations, thus strengthening the tie between client and patron. In a society where social prestige is measured by the resources a person can command to protect and advance the position of his family, a clientele of persons who owe services of various types is a considerable asset. It enables the patron to perform,

12 *Cf.* Campbell (1964: 101 sqq., 205, 230, 233) for an analysis of cousinage and friendship in Greece, which has many parallels to the situation in Sicily.

13 *Cu' havi denaro ed amicizia, si teni intra lu culu la giustizia.*

in his turn, a large variety of favours for his own patrons and "friends," and makes him more attractive as a patron. Thus an increase of either clients or patrons brings about an increase of the other.

Many of the services that a professional-class patron can claim from his clients are activities that a member of his social class could not perform—either because they are beneath his dignity, or because they are illegal—such as threatening or committing violence on the person or property of a personal enemy, or the enemy of some friend, or some friend-of-a-friend. A *contadino* is sometimes willing to perform unpleasant, if not illegal, services for a social superior, for it places his patron under a heavy obligation that can be turned to good advantage at a later date, possibly to help some "friend," who then becomes a client. A *contadino* with such a patron is in a position both to obtain protection and to command services. If he is astute (and ruthless) he may be able to turn selected contacts into an ever-widening network,[14] which can often be converted into political and economic power, and thus enable him to move up in the socio-economic hierarchy. Many members of the *borghesia* owe their secure middle-class positions as landowners, shopkeepers, or even professionals, to the extra-legal activities of an ancestor who started the family on its way up. The life history of the late Don Calogero Vizzini, the so-called *capo-mafia* of Sicily until his death in 1954, provides a well-documented, if extreme, case in point (Pantaleone 1962: 94 sqq.).

There are then in Sicily persons seeking protectors even as there are influential persons seeking followers. The dangers, imaginary or real, which would surround the client should his patron withdraw his support, and the need that a person has for a large and powerful clientele in his competition with his peers, ensure that both patron and client generally meet their reciprocal obligations when called upon to do so.

PATRONAGE IN ACTION

It may now be asked how a system of patronage actually operates. We have examined the structural principles upon which it rests. But what are its organisational elements? Michael Kenny has noted three basic roles in a system of patronage: patron/client, patron/patron and client/patron. A fourth logical possibility, client/client, he rules out, for by definition, as soon as one client offers the other some service, he is no longer a client (Kenny 1960: 23). But if we accept this argument, can we not also say that the role relation patron/patron is a logical impossibility, for if one gives and the other receives, is not the relation asymmetrical at any particular moment? Most persons in fact occupy roles as both patron and client. Patrons, at least in present-day Sicily, do not form a separate social category as landowners or school teachers or municipal administrators, though it is fair to say that in the past those who belonged to these social categories monopolised the links with centres of power outside the community and were thus the most important local patrons.

Relations between patrons and clients involve superordination and subordination. But by superordination I mean greater access to power, not necessarily superior social rank; though as noted, in the past, economic and political power and high social rank coincided. Today the situation is more complex. Persons who are sons of *contadino* families, and who thus have low standing in the local

[14] Banfield (1961) in his interesting study of the operation of patronage ("political influence" in his terms) in Chicago makes a similar point with regard to the trading of political favours. One regrets that he did not display the same political sensitivity in his study of Montegrano (Banfield 1958), where he reduced political activity to voting behaviour.

hierarchy of prestige, now not infrequently occupy positions of power in political parties and workers' syndicates. They are consequently able to dispense favours to and intercede on behalf of wealthy landowners who have much higher social standing. Traditional roles are reversed; economic and political superordination no longer coincide.[15]

Though the dyadic sets patron/client and client/patron are the basis upon which the system rests, a system of patronage is more than just the sum total of an almost infinite number of dyadic sets, each of which is cut off from other sets. I shall argue that essential to understanding patron-client relationships as a system is the notion that two dyads can make a triad. The key person in the system is the man in the middle, the broker, who has dyadic relations with a wide variety of persons, and is thus in a position to place two people, possibly unknown to each other, into a mutually beneficial relationship from which he derives a profit. This is the *raison d'être* of the broker, of whom there are a great variety in Sicily as in other Mediterranean countries.

It is at this point that I differ from the formal analysis of patronage presented by Professor Foster (1963). While I agree with him that each individual can be seen as standing at "the centre of his private and unique network of contractual ties," I disagree when he argues that the overlap of this personal network with other similar networks has "no functional significance" (1281). On the contrary, it is precisely because this overlap exists that we can speak of a *system* of patronage. The fact that *B* is a client of a powerful person *A* is often precisely the reason why *C* becomes *B*'s client. As Foster notes, there is no dyadic or contractual relationship between *A* and *C*. But I suggest he fails to appreciate the importance of the fact that because both the personal networks of *A* and *C* include *B, C* can work through *B* to come in contact with *A*. They are friends-of-friends, *amici degli amici,* which in Sicily, and I suggest in other societies in which patronage operates, is an important social category. The undue emphasis that Foster has placed on the dyadic contract, which by his definition binds only two persons (1281), has obscured this. Moreover, the informal dyadic "contact" between two persons is very often converted to a reciprocal relationship between two groups of persons, and is therefore no longer dyadic in Foster's terms.[16]

But to return to the two basic patronage role relations suggested above. Action based upon patronage is varied, and normally involves two other role relations at the same time, namely friend/friend and kinsman/kinsman. While there may be a direct person-to-person transaction between a client and the patron whom he is trying to influence, the manipulation of the system is not usually that simple. A person seeking to influence an important decision maker who is his social superior, but not his patron, selects a patron in his own network who is close to this person. The relationship is vertical. But his patron, the social equal of the person whom he wishes to influence, moves horizontally, possibly making use of his own kinship network in the process. Frequently a client moves vertically and horizontally by using recommendations, *raccomandazioni*. Where the person seeking a favour must move outside his face-to-face community these recommendations are often the personal calling cards of the last patron warmly recommending his *carissimo amico,* or dear friend, to a relative or a friend farther along the patronage network in the direction the

15 Sydel Silverman (1965) gives an excellent account of the evolution of patronage in Central Italy. This parallels changes taking place in Sicily, though the replacement of traditional multi-purpose patrons by functionally specific "intermediaries" has not gone as far in Leone as it has in her village of Colleverde.

16 Silverman (1965: 178) makes a similar point.

client wishes to move. The person presenting the *raccomandazione* is a friend-of-a-friend, and is helped because of that. Usually the relationship between the person being passed along and those who help him is quite impersonal: he is merely a counter in the social game played between those among whom he is passed.

I should like to give a few examples of patronage in operation. The first is that of the horizontal-vertical approach. Salvatore, a student from Syracuse who had worked in Leone, wished to come into personal contact with a certain professor at the University of Palermo in order to obtain permission to present a thesis, for which registration had closed two months before. He made a special trip from Syracuse to Leone to discuss this problem with *Avvocato* Leonardo, the Secretary of the Christian Democratic Party in the town. Six months before, while he was still in Leone, Salvatore had helped Leonardo prepare a draft of an important memorandum on the town which had been requested by the party's provincial leaders. Salvatore explained his trip by saying, *Leonardo mi doveva questa,* Leonardo owed me this (favour). Salvatore knew the lawyer was in touch with many people in Palermo and felt sure that through him he could come into personal contact with his professor.

Leonardo was willing to help and gave Salvatore a card to his cousin, the personal secretary of a Palermitan official, asking him to help. He also offered to let Salvatore copy his thesis, which he pointed out would save a great deal of bother, since it was a good thesis and had been presented to a different professor a few years before. Salvatore thanked him but replied that he wanted to do his own thesis, for the experience.

Armed with Leonardo's *raccomandazione*, Salvatore set out for Palermo. The following day he met Leonardo's cousin and explained what he wanted. The cousin suggested that he see his brother, who knew many people in the University, and in his turn gave him a card. That evening Salvatore met the brother who said that he knew the professor's assistant, and gave him a card introducing him as his *carissimo amico.* The next day Salvatore called on the assistant with his *raccomandazione* and explained his case in full, asking what he should do. The assistant replied that he could arrange matters with the *Professore* but only on condition that Salvatore make electoral propaganda in Leone and the surrounding area for the *Professore,* who was standing for the Chamber of Deputies in the election the following month. Salvatore understood and pretended to live in Leone, and not in Syracuse, which was outside the electoral district in which the *Professore* was standing, a fact which made him quite useless. The assistant then telephoned the *Professore* and made an appointment for Salvatore.

Salvatore went to see the *Professore* and explained his wish to present his thesis that June. The *Professore* looked rather doubtful, but Salvatore mentioned that he was impressed with his public spirit, and had already spoken about his candidature to several of his friends in Leone. The *Professore* loosened up at once. He indicated that the thesis should not present a problem. He then wrote a letter for Salvatore to take back to a former student of his in Leone, whom he also asked to help in his campaign.

Salvatore returned to Syracuse, via Leone, where he delivered the letter, and at once began to work on his thesis. Eventually his thesis, which was very good, was accepted and today Salvatore has his degree. The *Professore,* however, was not elected.

In his passage along this patronage network, which was essentially the network of Leonardo who placed it at his disposal, Savatore of course was momentarily in contact with Leonardo's cousins and his professor's assistant. As he was helped along not for his own sake, but because he had been passed along by a friend or kinsman, his relations with these persons were qualitatively different from the others. Leonardo did not weaken his position with Salvatore by placing his network at the latter's disposal. On the contrary he strengthened it, for thanks to him, Salvatore attained his goal, and in so doing became aware of the efficacy of Leonardo's network. Moreover, should he wish to use the network again, he would have to pass through Leonardo again in order to receive the same cooperation from the next link.

The second example illustrates what may be called the vertical-horizontal approach. Calogero, a small land-broker, wished to become a municipal employee in Leone. He based his case on the fact that he had been employed as a clerk in the Town Hall before he had emigrated to Argentina, that he was a wounded veteran of World War II (and as such should receive preference), and that he possessed the educational requirements. After a great deal of manœuvring at the local level, he succeeded in getting the Leone town council to propose his name to the Commissione Provinciale di Controllo (CPC), the body that screens the credentials of all candidates proposed for office by town councils in the province and decides whether they shall be accepted. The members of the CPC are normally subject to considerable pressure from political parties and influential persons seeking to have their candidates accepted and those of their rivals rejected. Calogero was afraid that his name would be rejected by the board because of the counter manipulation of enemies in Leone, who had their own candidate. As he had no direct contact with any of the members of the board, he worked through two patrons. The first was a former commanding officer. He explained his fears and asked for help. The major agreed to help his former corporal, and proceeded to contact one of the members of the board whom he knew personally. The second patron was a lawyer in the provincial capital whom Calogero had known for many years. The lawyer was able to contact another member of the board who was a former classmate and a member of the same exclusive social club. The pressure applied by the two patrons effectively countered the move of Calogero's rivals, and he was appointed to the post. It is interesting to note that he had retained the lawyer to represent him in much the way that any professional client might do and had paid him a fee for his troubles. Yet the relation between the two was more complicated than the impersonal market relations based on an exchange of services for cash. Calogero looked upon the lawyer as his patron, his protector at the provincial capital who was able to contact the important decision-makers as an equal and friend. The action of the lawyer was not reciprocated completely by the fee he received, for he retained a claim on the loyalty and services of Calogero, who would be more than willing to defend his name and to provide his services within the more limited social field of Leone, should he be requested to do so.

The final example illustrates the last point as well as the continuing nature of patron-client relations, for as Sicilian families are tightly united, so a service to one member is felt to be given to the group, creating a collective reciprocal obligation. One Sunday *Professore* Volpe discussed certain personal problems with me as we strolled back and forth in the village square. He had been having problems over the education of his eldest son. Both the problems and the methods used to resolve them are rather Sicilian. He suspected that one of his colleagues at the secondary school in the neighbouring town where he taught, and where his son went to school, was trying to injure him by failing his son and thus blocking his entrance to the University. This would have damaged the family's position as an important member of the professional class in Leone. He was able to have his enemy followed whenever the latter passed through Leone on his way to the provincial capital or Palermo by certain of his own clients and those of his brother, an important notary in Palermo. He was proud that his brother, who lived on the other side of Sicily, but "who has friends everywhere," was even able to obtain reports, from one of those friends, of conversations held by the suspect at the latter's social club. Both the conversation overheard and the observed contacts in Palermo of his enemy seemed to confirm his suspicion. *Professore* Volpe's brother then moved swiftly to apply counter pressure through a nameless important person in Palermo. This person then placed pressure on his client, the important decision-maker, regarding the boy's admission to University, who had been previously contacted by the patron of *Professore* Volpe's enemy. As the two brothers between them boasted a wider range of contacts and a more powerful protection than their rival, they were able to resolve the affair to their satisfaction. The son was admitted to the University.

It is of course quite possible that the entire plot to dishonour the family was a figment of *Professore* Volpe's imagination, for it was all based upon intuition and indirect evidence. The suggestions by his brother to his influential friend in Palermo were most certainly couched in allegory and allusion, as was his recital to me in which no names or specific accusations were mentioned. *Professore* Volpe believed it to be true, and acted accordingly, thereby illustrating well several of the points I have tried to make above.

But the story continues. Several months after his son was admitted to the University, *Professore* Volpe was insulted in front of most of his fellow-teachers by his old enemy. He told me that he was so angry that he had to leave the common room, but before slamming the door he had shouted at his enemy that he would have his apology. He had returned to Leone and during his evening stroll the same day met *"uno dei quelli"* ("one of them," an expression often used to allude to a *mafioso*). In telling me this, he pulled his cap down over one eye to indicate to me a *mafioso* in Sicilian sign language. This person was one of those who had helped keep his enemy under observation two months before when he passed through Leone on his way to the provincial capital and Palermo. He mentioned the insult he had received, and his *amico* said, *Ci penso io,* I'll see to it. The *amico* apparently went to the neighbouring town late one evening soon after and knocked on his enemy's door. In a courteous but tough voice—which the *Professore* imitated for me—he informed the enemy that it would be better to apologise or there might be unpleasantness. Two days later the *Professore* got a short note of apology by post. When I asked how much he had had to pay his *amico* for all his help, he smiled and replied, "Nothing, of course," and explained that the *amico* was the son of a man whom his own father, who had been important notary, had helped to keep out of prison forty years before. "He helped me for *amicizia.* Because of our father we have friends all over Sicily. They are not criminals. They are men who make themselves respected. They will help you when you need it, but . . . when they turn to you for help, you give it or . . . ," and he made the chopping motion that means the application of violence. "You help them and they help you. They give and you give."

Professore Volpe ended by saying that his son is doing well at the University and thus justified his faith in his ability and intelligence. "But his younger brother is lazy and not very bright," he observed. "He will probably be failed this year. My enemies are busy again. I must see what can be done." And muttering about the many responsibilities of fatherhood, he went off to lunch.

From the foregoing discussion and the three cases we have examined it is evident that while at the analytical level a distinction can be drawn between patronage, friendship and kinship, this distinction has little importance at the operational level. The Sicilian uses all three interchangeably to influence the outcome of decisions which concern him. Of the 18 dyadic sets based on kinship, friendship or patronage which constituted the portions of the networks that Salvatore, Calogero and *Professore* Volpe manipulated to achieve their ends, three were based on kinship, six on friendship and nine on patronage (four patron/client and five client/patron). These are summarised in Table 14.1. It is not possible to give priority to one to the exclusion of others.

DISCUSSION

The system of patronage is seen to be an essential part of the political system in Sicily, for through it individuals and groups influence the outcome of decisions which concern them. It provides a system of communication which is parallel to the official channels of the government. This is of particular importance in a society such as that in Sicily, which is highly stratified and in which positions of authority are frequently occupied by persons who belong to the upper strata of the socio-economic hierarchy. For in such a society the lines of communication through the formal system are tenuous and difficult to follow because of the social distance between those who wish to make their voices heard on high, and those who control the channels through which such messages necessarily must pass. Those desiring to communicate are faced by the rigid apparatus of a ponderous bureaucratic system. The system of patronage permits a person to contact officials on a personal basis. Campbell has remarked in describing the operation of the patronage system in Greece that "it introduces a flexibility into administrative machinery whose workings are very often directed by persons remote from the people whose fortunes they are affecting" (1964: 247). It means that the *contadini* have some way of controlling the harsh forces that surround them. To some extent then, it gives them a voice in their own destiny. It not only provides protection and facilitates communication, but may also furnish a way of moving upward in a stratified society.[17]

Beyond the individual and family levels, patronage can be seen to link entire villages to the structure of government, for the personal networks of village leaders, while manipulated primarily for personal ends, also provide the lines of communication along which village business moves upward, and provincial, regional and national funds flow downward into the village for public works and other development projects. At this level the patronage system is linked with the structure and operation of political parties (*cf.* Boissevain 1965: 120–33; 1966). This is

[17] Trouwborst (1959) and Mair (1961) have observed a similar connection between patronage and social mobility in East Africa.

TABLE 14.1
SUMMARY OF NETWORKS

Social Basis of Dyads	Salvatore	Calogero	Volpe	Total
Kinship	2		1	3
Friendship	2	2	2	6
Patronage				9
Patron/Client	1		3	(4)
Client/Patron	1	2	2	(5)
Total	6	4	8	18

a subject I shall deal with more fully elsewhere.

A system of patronage can also be likened to a parasitic vine clinging to the trunk of a tree. As the vine saps the strength of the tree, so patronage weakens government. It leads to nepotism, corruption, influence-peddling and, above all, it weakens the rule of law. And, in Sicily, because violence is still part of the social currency, it has led to the persistence of brokers who are specialists in matters of violence, the *mafiosi.* In brief, it leads to and perpetuates the very conditions which have brought it into being, nurtured it, and permitted it to develop to the point where it is perhaps the most important channel of communication.

Why has patronage assumed such social importance in Sicily?

Ties of dependency exist because there is still need for protection that neither the State nor the family is able to provide.[18] The Sicilian requires protection not only from his neighbours, who are trying to protect and advance themselves at his expense, but also from a powerful government which he feels has been imposed upon him and which he regards as corrupt. He also needs protection from the law which he not only believes can be manipulated by his enemies to his detriment, but with which he is also often in conflict because of the differing requirements of the legal system and those of traditional justice. Finally, he needs protection from the violence and exploitation that are a part of Sicilian life. It is obvious that many of the conditions which give rise to the need for protection, and hence patronage, are simply the result of the successful operation of the patronage system. Patronage is, to a very large extent, a self-perpetuating system of belief and action grounded in the society's value system.

Nonetheless, there is another important factor which I believe has favoured the persistence of patronage in Sicily. This is the continuing importance of the Catholic religion. Despite rampant anticlericalism, the Roman Catholic religion remains deeply rooted in the life and customs of the people. The many religious processions and feasts for the various patron saints are still among the most important social events of the countryside. I suggest that in such a society there is a strong ideological basis for a political system based upon patronage. There is a striking functional similarity between the role of saints as intermediaries between God and man, and the mortal patron who intercedes with an important person on behalf of his client.[19] In fact, a patron is sometimes called a *santo* or saint, and people occasionally quote the proverb *Senza santi nun si va 'n paradisu,* without the help of saints you can't get to heaven,[20] to illustrate the importance of patrons in achieving one's desires. This parallel was drawn for me by the Archpriest of Leone as he sought to explain the spiritual role of saints. He noted that just as you would not think of approaching a cabinet minister directly, but would work through some influential friend who could introduce you to the local deputy who could then state your case to the minister, so too must you not approach God directly. You must work through your patron saint who, being closer to God than you, is in a better

18 *Cf.* Marc Bloch, who sees the fact that the kinship group was not able to offer adequate protection to the individual against the violence and general lawlessness that followed the break-up of the Roman Empire as a primary reason for the development of the relations of personal protection and subordination so characteristic of feudalism. "For the only regions in which powerful agnatic groups survived—German lands on the shores of the North Sea, Celtic districts of the British Isles—knew nothing of vassalage, the fief and the manor. The tie of kinship was one of the essential elements of feudal society; its relative weakness explains why there was feudalism at all" (1961: 142).

19 Kenny also points to this functional similarity in his study of patronage in Spain (1960: 17).

20 For the Maltese version of the same proverb see Boissevain 1965 (121).

position to persuade Him to heed your prayers. The role of patron in Sicily thus receives constant and authoritative validation from the Church through the widespread cult of personal and community patron saints. It is a striking fact that in Catholic countries with a strong cult of saints, such as those in the Mediterranean area and in Latin America, there is also a political system which if not based upon, is at least strongly influenced by patron-client relations. These countries may be contrasted to Catholic societies in the north of Europe where the cult of saints is considerably less pronounced, as is the importance of patron-client relations.[21] I do not mean to suggest that there is a causal connection between the cult of saints and a system of political patronage, although there may be. But I think it is obvious that religious and political patronage reinforce each other. Each serves as a model for the other.

Thus spiritual patrons join the more mortal patrons, friends, and kinsmen who make up the personal network which individual Sicilians manipulate in order to influence the outcome of decisions and events, both natural and supernatural, which affect the well-being of their families.[22] I see the system of patronage as part of a gigantic network in which all Sicilians have a place. The average Sicilian is in contact with many others through whom, following selected strands, he is able to come into personal contact with almost every other person in the same network. He is at the same time the client of a number of patrons, each of whom normally operates in a separate social field, and the patron of a number of clients. Each of his patrons and clients have others who depend on them and on whom they depend. He also has lines which link him laterally to friends with whom he exchanges favours. He is the central point for a number of strands. The most selected strands to influential persons, and especially to persons with many clients, that pass through him, the stronger his position becomes, for his power grows in proportion to the number of appeals made to and through him. Some persons are in contact with only a few people. Others are linked directly with many above and below them as well as with equals, and serve as brokers for various types of services. Yet others, very few to be sure, are immense centres of power from which strands radiate directly to every part of the network. These are persons who occupy key positions in the political structure.

21 Wolf (1966: 18), for example, remarks on the absence among the South Tyrolese of the patron-client tie of the type discussed here. In a personal communication he informed me that the public cult of saints there appears to be less important than in the south of Italy. The feast of the Sacred Heart of Jesus was celebrated with far greater pomp than that of the patron saint of the Tyrolese village he studied.

22 In fact what I call the *patronage network* is nothing less, though it does include something more —the importance of the ties between patrons and their clients—than the *personal network* discussed by Barnes (1954: 43 sqq.).

REFERENCES

Banfield, E. C. 1958. *The moral basis of a backward society*. New York: The Free Press.

———. 1961. *Political influence*. New York: The Free Press.

Barnes, J. A. 1954. Class and committees in a Norwegian island parish. *Human Relat.* 7, 39–58.

Bloch, M. 1961. *Feudal Society*. Chicago: Chicago U.P.

Blok, A. 1964. Landhervorming in een west-siciliaans latifondo-dorp: de bestediging van een feodale structure. *Mens Maatsch.* 39, 344–359.

Boissevain, J. 1962. Maltese village politics and their relation to national politics. *J. Commonwealth Pol. Stud.* I, 211–227.

———. 1965. *Saints and fireworks: religion and politics in rural Malta.* (Monogr. Social Anthrop.) London: Athlone Press.

———. 1966. Poverty and politics in a Sicilian agrotown. *Intern. Arch. Ethnogr.* (In press.)

Campbell, J. K. 1964. *Honour, family and patronage*. New York: Oxford Press.

Foster, G. M. 1961. The dyadic contract:

a model for the social structure of a Mexican peasant village. *Amer. Anthrop.* 63, 1173–1192.
Foster, G. M. 1963. The dyadic contract in Tzintzuntzan, II: patron-client relationships. *Amer. Anthrop.* 65, 1280–1294.
Franchetti, L. 1925. *Condizioni politiche e amministrative della Sicilia.* Franchetti, L. and Sonnino, S. *La Sicilia nel 1876.* (2 vols) 1. Florence: Valecchi.
Kenny, M. 1960. Patterns of patronage in Spain. *Anthrop. Quart.* 33, 14–23.
———. 1961. *A Spanish tapestry: town and country in Castile.* London: Cohen & West.
Mack Smith, D. 1959. *Italy: a modern history.* Ann Arbor: Mich. U.P.
Mair, L. 1961. Clientship in East Africa. *Cah. Etud. afr.* 2, 315–325.
Maxwell, G. 1956. *God protect me from my friends.* London: Longmans, Green.
Pantaleone, M. 1962. *Mafia e politica.* Torino: Einaudi.
Pitt-Rivers, J. 1954. *The people of the sierra.* London: Weidenfeld & Nicholson.
Renda, F. 1956. *Il movimento contadino nella società siciliana.* Palermo: "Sicilia al Lavoro."
Rochefort, R. 1961. *Le travail en Sicile.* Paris: Presses Universitaires de France.
Silverman, S. 1965. Patronage and community-nation relationships in central Italy. *Ethnology* 4, 172–189.
Sonnino, S. 1925. *I contadini.* Franchetti, L. and Sonnino, S. *La Sicilia* nel 1876. (2 vols) 2. Florence: Valecchi.
Trouwborst, A. A. 1959. La mobilité de l'individu en fonction de l'organisation politique des Barundi. *Zaire* 13, 787–800.
———. 1961. L'organisation politique en tant que système d'échange au Barundi. *Anthropologica* 3, 1–17.
———. 1962. L'organisation politique et l'accord de clientèle au Barundi. *Anthropologica* 4, 9–43.
Wolf, E. R. 1966. Kinship, friendship, and patron-client relations in complex societies. In *The social anthropology of complex societies* (ed.) M. P. Banton (A.S.A. Monogr. 4). London: Tavistock Publications.

15. Village Friendship and Patronage

J. K. Campbell

[From a study of life in a community of Greek Sarakatsan peasants, which the author believes contains many parallels to society anywhere in the Greek provinces and in other portions of the Mediterranean world.]

Here a brief digression is necessary to consider the nature of friendship in Zagori villages.[1] Between villagers ties of friendship relate persons who are, in principle, equals. All villagers, without discrimination, possess the same legal rights in the local polity. If a man is also honourable in his conduct, a good neighbour, and legitimately born of Zagori parents, he is entitled in the social life of the village to be treated with a degree of consideration that represents a recognition of his social personality. Persons who are equal in these respects must show some concern for each other's social sensibilities by avoiding public rudeness and by a careful and courteous exchange of greetings when they meet.

Friendship begins where one man accepts a favour (χάρη) from another. The person who gives the favour will assert that he expects no return; it would be insulting to suggest that his act of friendship had a motivation. It is, however, the very altruism of the act, whether this is simulated or not, which demands a counter favour. Default destroys the friendship and provokes accusations of ingratitude. Although liking and sympathy are alleged to be the premises on which friendship between village equals is based, it would be more true to say that villagers who are able to do each other reciprocal favours sometimes discover from this experience confidence in one another. From these beginnings there may grow a relationship of intimacy and warmth. But in essence friendship of this kind remains a contractual relation, a form of co-operation in which services of various kinds are exchanged and accounted.

The network of friendships of the President or of other influential villagers becomes in reality a system of patronage. Accountancy is then more difficult because the patron is able to do more material favours for his client than the latter is able to return. But although the character of the relationship is now, in effect, asymmetrical, patron and client, because they are interacting in the context of village community relations where all true villagers are in principle equals, they continue to treat one another as if they were equals in the situation of their friendship as well. Both patron and client claim publicly that the other "is my friend." The patron says that he helps his

---

1 Friendship in Epirote villages appears to be very similar to the parallel institution in Andalusia. See Cf. Pitt-Rivers, *Mediterranean Countrymen* (The Hague, 1963), chapter 7.

Source: J. K. Campbell, *Honour, Family and Patronage: A Study of Institutions and Moral Values in a Greek Mountain Community*. Oxford: Oxford Clarendon Press, 1964, pp. 229–238. By permission of the publisher.

client simply because it pleases him to help those of his friends who are in difficulties. The client explains that he is the friend of the patron, not simply because he receives benefits from him, but because he is a good man. In short, their friendship exists within the field of village values where behaviour is evaluated against the ideals of independence and love of honour.

In the Sarakatsan community the situation is different. There is no co-operation between unrelated families and no established political authority in the shepherd community which might lead to relations of political friendship. A relationship which has many of the aspects of patronage exists between the dominant family and the other associated families in a co-operating "company," but these connexions are based on the values of kinship, not friendship. When a Sarakatsanos says "I have him as a friend," he generally means that he has established a relation of mutual advantage with a person outside the community who in most cases is in the superordinate position of patron. The use of the word "friend" by the Sarakatsanos is not here encumbered with any theory of equality or disinterested motives. The fact that in terms of power he is the weaker partner in the majority of his relations of friendship is recognized by the Sarakatsanos but does not immediately concern his pride since these people stand outside his community. On the contrary, the more effective relationships of this kind that a man possesses, the greater his prestige in the community since it proves him to be an able protector of his family and his flocks.

It is by no means certain that a President will accept any Sarakatsanos as his political client. What the President has to offer will be clear enough from the earlier description of the ways in which he can help or hinder. The chief service the shepherd is able to pledge in return is his vote and those of his family and associated kinsmen. But to accept a man as a client commits the patron to protection instead of exploitation, and to that extent it is a restriction on the free exercise of his power. A President generally prefers to assume these obligations only to Sarakatsani with some influence. Naturally, more humble families have vicarious access to his patronage through their influential kinsmen, but the intermediate link which separates them from the President's beneficence makes it less likely that their affairs will be settled with the same despatch and satisfaction.

The extent to which a President needs to enter these commitments depends, of course, on the balance of the political groupings in his village. In one village the President commanded about three quarters of the village vote, but by his generally uncompromising hostility he had driven the Sarakatsani into the arms of the small opposition party. A month before the election it appeared that he had no Sarakatsan supporters and that his cause was lost. Conveniently the election was held in November, after the Sarakatsani had departed to the plains eighty miles away. The opposition party chartered a lorry to transport, as they had calculated it, an adequate number of Sarakatsan voters to assure their victory. But, in the event, the President skilfully contrived a narrow majority by making secret agreements with two shepherd families. The five members of these families who returned from the plains, ironically enough in the lorry chartered by the opposition, were sufficient to give the President victory and a new term of office.

After the election the two families received a number of favours. In the spring the sheep of one family were short-counted by sixty and the flock of the other, which by right of the customary rotation of grazing areas ought to have gone to an area of indifferent grazing, spent a more profitable summer on the village's best grassland. In the face of the unusual solidarity of the local Sarakatsan group at the time of the election, the action of the two dissident families was described as treacherous. They were branded as "The President's men," with an overtone of meaning which implied that they were puppets dancing at the command of the master, capable even of betraying their own people. Yet as passions cooled and the months passed, evaluations changed perceptibly. At first the members of these families were unequivocally "traitors," but later they were considered merely "cunning" (by no means an entirely pejorative judgement), and eventually one sometimes heard grudging admissions of their "cleverness." For it is recognized that each family is free to seek its own protection and the political friends who can provide it. Indeed, Sarakatsani believe that in the nature of the situation favours and concessions are to be won only by some, not all families. It is, therefore, the duty of each head of family to scheme and intrigue for his own security. Only in the case of a breach of faith between kinsmen is an accusation of treachery seriously considered.

But the friendship which a Sarakatsanos achieves with a village President, or indeed with any other influential person, involves more than the exchange of specific material favours; it establishes, also, an asymmetrical relation of sociability which enhances the prestige of both men. A Sarakatsanos who has friendship with the President boldly sits down with him at the same table when he enters the coffee-shop. The President offers him a drink, he stands him a drink in return. Meeting him in the village square, the shepherd stops to talk for a few minutes about this and that. Were they not patron and client, a curt "Good day" from each side would be the extent of their social intercourse. However, it is not a relationship of equals. The shepherd belongs not only to a different community, but to a qualitatively inferior one. While the President will say of a villager who is similarly his client that this man is his friend, he will not say this of a shepherd. If an explanation in his presence is necessary, he may say, "George is a good lad, I help him," but behind his back he will simply say, "He is my man." Yet, although they are his social inferiors, the President gains prestige by being seen publicly with his shepherd clients. If he drinks with other villagers who are his supporters, this is no cause for comment. He merely keeps company with those who are his social equals and natural companions. When he drinks with four or five shepherds it draws attention to his possession of power, to his ability to hold men who do not waste their time drinking with ordinary villagers whom as a class of persons they detest and despise. The Sarakatsanos accepts his position of inferiority in the relationship because he must. He does not, as most villagers would, address the President by his Christian name; but he is not subservient in his manner. He speaks to him courteously as "President." When another person of importance comes to speak to the President, and it is clear that he is dismissed, he moves to another table, or with a "Good health, President," to which the latter replies, he leaves the shop. These are the conventional terms on which these unequal friendships are founded. What is important to the Sarakatsanos in these situations is that other shepherds who do not possess this valued link should see and envy him.

In asymmetrical friendship relations, since it is assumed that the patron has more favours to offer than the client can return, or that reciprocal favours are so dissimilar in quality that accountancy is difficult, there is often greater stability than in friendships between equals, which are very frequently bedevilled by accusations of ingratitude. Yet, even here, there are many complaints, the patron asserting that the client should be more vocal in his gratitude, the client complaining that the patron does very little in relation to the client's worth and needs, and the services he has rendered. In short, the patron wants more honour, the client more benefits.

The third widely practised method of placating or influencing the President is to present him with a gift of cheese, butter, or meat. Some families do this each spring as a matter of general policy without having in mind any particular favour. They hope that the gift may moderate his general attitude towards them in the coming months. More often, families wait until they face some specific difficulty. A gift of cheese or some other produce is delivered to the President's home and then, perhaps two days later, the gift-giver walks into the village office and makes his request. The President may be helpful or he may not. The assumptions of the giver and the recipient of the gift are not necessarily the same. The giver hopes that the gift will arouse some sense of obligation in the receiver. But the latter, if he chooses to feel that the gift was forced on him against his will, may decide that he is not obliged to feel grateful. If he intends not to grant the favour, the refusal is never direct. The many difficulties which stand in the way are elaborated at very great length. He explains that he will see what can be done, he will write to a friend in Jannina, he wants to help. In fact he will do nothing; and the original gift is not returned.

A gift is frequently offered to the President by a Sarakatsanos when he meets with legal troubles. Stratos and a number of his kinsmen were using 20 mules to transport wooden planks from a saw-mill to the road below the village where the wood was loaded on to lorries. The area for the grazing of Sarakatsan mules and horses is an hour's climb above the village and this was very inconvenient for Stratos and the other muleteers. They chanced their luck and grazed their animals at night in the little-frequented village orchards close to their loading-point. On the thirty-ninth night of their operations they were discovered by the agricultural guard who from his examination of the length of the grass and some damage to young apple trees was confident of a very successful case. Stratos was not able to claim that the President was his friend, but since he was a law-abiding careful man his relations with the President had been generally good. He begged for his assistance, explaining the extreme difficulty the group would have suffered if each night the mules had had to be released so far from the scene of operations. He managed also to mention that he would like to help the President in the current rebuilding of his house. It so happened that he had two loads of timber which he did not require. The next day, the President saw the agricultural guard and warned him that, in his opinion, it would only be reasonable to take into consideration the one night when he had actually seen the mules. For the rest, who could say? There had been high winds recently which often damaged trees, and he added that he had noticed one of the agricultural guard's own goats straying one evening in the direction of the orchards. Accordingly, the President received his wood, Stratos and his kinsmen escaped with a small fine, and the agricultural guard's dream of a triumphant case came to nothing.

Two points must be stressed about this method of influencing the President. Gifts must be presented with finesse. A man of honour is not to be crudely bought by social inferiors if he does not wish to lose prestige in the community. The shepherd must give the lamb, butter, or cheese to the President as if it were merely an expression of friendly respect, and in no way tied to the favour he is about to request. Secondly, whether in relation to these gifts of produce, or to other perquisites of his office, the limited dishonesty and corruptibility of a President is not dishonourable. "He eats money" (*τρώει παράδες*), others say with envy. But they concede that this is the right of his office. His allowance is not large, he too must live, he also has a family to support. If a favour, even where it is entirely legal, involves trouble beyond the ordinary routine duties of his office, why should he weary himself for a man to whom he is not related in any way, unless that man by a gift, or in some other way, demonstrates the esteem in which he holds him.

We have now discussed in the order of their effectiveness three ways in which the Sarakatsani attempt to influence the President of their summer village—spiritual kinship, friendship, and gifts. In principle, spiritual kinship binds a President to help the shepherd in all situations. Ideally it is a diffuse relation, there is nothing reasonable that cannot be requested, and the right to expect this assistance is sanctioned by the ritual link between godfather and godchild. Friendship of the kind established between a village President and a Sarakatsanos, is a patron-client relationship of some stability over time, and the range of favours which may be demanded is almost as extensive as that between spiritual kinsmen, but the atmosphere of calculation is more pronounced. Confidence which is ritually sanctioned in spiritual kinship is more easily destroyed in the relations of patron and client. Gifts given by a shepherd to the President generally have a specific object in view and each gift is effective for only a short period of time if, indeed, it is effective at all.

The President is not the only man with power or influence in a village; the other members of the council, the schoolmaster, the priest, other villagers of wealth or reputation may have these qualities in varying degree. When the President is particularly severe towards them, the shepherds attempt, by the same methods we have just considered, to attach themselves to other persons in the village who are known to have influence on the council, or personally over the President himself.

When the sheep of Theodoros were despatched by the President to the poorest area of grazing for the second year because of his active opposition during the elections, Theodoros did not appeal to the Nomarch against this injustice. He went instead to Vlachopoulos. Vlachopoulos is the Vice-President of the village, and the President's closest friend. He also owns the older of the two village coffee-shops which is the one more generally patronized by the Sarakatsani both for social gatherings and for the many small purchases which they make. After the bitter feelings aroused by the autumn elections there was a spontaneous boycott of the Vlachopoulos shop by the Sarakatsani and at the time when Theodoros approached him two or three weeks after the shepherds had returned to the summer pasture, only a few Sarakatsan men were to be seen drinking in the old shop. For a week Theodoros assiduously made small purchases in the shop. Finding Vlachopoulos alone one day, he took the next step by remarking that he was not a man to dwell on old scores and that he thought his return to the shop proved this point. It seemed, however, that the President was still governed by his rage and spite. This was surely unjust, and he asked Vlachopoulos if he would not intercede with the President on his behalf. Vlachopoulos agreed to do this. It is a fair assumption that he was especially pleased to see Theodoros who leads a substantial co-operating "company" and has many other kinsmen in the local group of shepherds. It was very probable that if Theodoros returned to his shop to drink, as well as to buy, the boycott would be over. This proved to be the case. Vlachopoulos persuaded the President to rearrange the grazing areas, and after a week or two of further delay to impress upon Theodoros the misguided nature of his opposition in the previous autumn, the President eventually effected the necessary changes.

A Zagori village and the local group of Sarakatsani that is linked to it through rights of citizenship, form a network of friendship relations, some of which are symmetrical and others of the patron-client variety. This network enables a man in many situations to obtain a measure of satisfaction from a person with whom he is in direct opposition. He achieves this by indirect pressure because he is a client, or friend, of the friend of his enemy. Villagers and shepherds are careful to maintain friendship links with opposed political factions and personages whenever this is possible. The implication is that there are often inherent limits on the way in which the President or other influential villagers may use their power against most individuals, since, very probably, in any particular act of victimization they are attacking the friend, or client, of one of their own friends. Only very poor villagers, or Sarakatsani with small flocks who are not attached to the co-operating "company" or more powerful kinsmen, may be treated unjustly without encountering some responding pressure through the system of friendships; for these persons, having little to offer in return, may not have patrons. But in other cases to ignore the pressures received through the system of friendships may endanger important relationships on which a man's influence and prestige largely depend. It is not suggested, however, that a man with strategically aligned friendships is secure from all injustice. On the contrary, Theodoros suffered a considerable financial loss until his friendship with Vlachopoulos rescued him from further punishment.

In the Zagori villages, as in the Sarakatsan community, a dominant feature of the social system is the isolation of the family and its struggle against other families, whether in terms of the possibility of bare subsistence or of social prestige. The more important social obligations are particular to the individual's family, and these stand in direct conflict with the weaker and more general responsibilities of good neighbourliness. The notion of service to the community (εὐεργεσία) exists, and is honoured. But the service takes a form which honours the individual, his family and the community in equal degree as, for instance, in the foundation of a church or school. Such services are never anonymous. The idea of service to fellow citizens of the same community exists also, but it remains an ideal value which is not realized in a society where familial obligations have an absolute priority. The President and councillors of the village are firstly heads of households and only secondly public servants. A President does not feel under the same moral obligation, even within the sphere of his formal duties, to help equally a close kinsman, a spiritual kinsman, a friend, and a man to whom he is linked only by common citizenship. It is suggested that in this absence, for the most part, of universally applicable values the system of village friendship and patronage in fact achieves a distribution of various facilities which, although it is never equitable, guards most families, even those of the hard-pressed Sarakatsani of Zagori, against complete exclusion. The system of friendship and patronage achieves this, not by upholding any general rights of citizenship, but, in a sense paradoxically, by an appeal to the individual and family interests of a person in authority. For without friends a man loses all power, influence, and social prestige.

16. Crime and Mobility among Italian-Americans

DANIEL BELL

I

Americans have had an extraordinary talent for compromise in politics and extremism in morality. The most shameless political deals (and "steals") have been rationalized as expedient and realistically necessary. Yet in no other country have there been such spectacular attempts to curb human appetites and brand them as illicit, and nowhere else such glaring failures. From the start America was at one and the same time a frontier community where "everything goes," and the fair country of the Blue Laws. At the turn of the century the cleavage developed between the Big City and the small-town conscience. Crime as a growing business was fed by the revenues from prostitution, liquor and gambling that a wide-open urban society encouraged and which a middle-class Protestant ethos tried to suppress with a ferocity unmatched in any other civilized country. Catholic cultures rarely have imposed such restrictions, and have rarely suffered such excesses. Even in prim and proper Anglican England, prostitution is a commonplace of Piccadilly night life, and gambling one of the largest and most popular industries. In America the enforcement of public morals has been a continuing feature of our history.

Some truth may lie in Svend Ranulf's generalization that moral indignation is a peculiar fact of middle-class psychology and represents a disguised form of repressed envy. The larger truth lies perhaps in the brawling nature of American development and the social character of crime. Crime, in many ways, is a Coney Island mirror, caricaturing the morals and manners of a society. The jungle quality of the American business community, particularly at the turn of the century, was reflected in the mode of "business" practiced by the coarse gangster elements, most of them from new immigrant famililes, who were "getting ahead," just as Horatio Alger had urged. In the older, Protestant tradition the intense acquisitiveness, such as that of Daniel Drew, was rationalized by a compulsive moral fervor. But the formal obeisance of the ruthless businessman in the workaday world to the church-going pieties of the Sabbath was one that the gangster could not make. Moreover, for the young criminal, hunting in the asphalt jungle of the crowded city, it was not the businessmen with his wily manipulation of numbers but the "man with the gun" who was the American hero. "No amount of commercial prosperity," once wrote Teddy Roosevelt, "can supply the lack of the heroic virtues." The American was "the hunter, cowboy, frontiersman, the soldier, the naval hero." And in the crowded slums, the gangster. He was a

SOURCE: Daniel Bell, "Crime as an American Way of Life," *Antioch Review*, XIII (Summer 1953), pp. 132–133, 145–154. By permission of the author.

man with a gun, acquiring by personal merit what was denied to him by complex orderings of a stratified society. And the duel with the law was the morality play *par excellence:* the gangster, with whom rides our own illicit desires, and the prosecutor, representing final judgment and the force of the law.

Yet all this was acted out in a wider context. The desires satisfied in extra-legal fashion were more than a hunger for the "forbidden fruits" of conventional morality. They also involved, in the complex and ever shifting structure of group, class and ethnic stratification, which is the warp and woof of America's "open" society, such "normal" goals as independence through a business of one's own, and such "moral" aspirations as the desire for social advancement and social prestige. For crime, in the language of the sociologists, has a "functional" role in the society, and the urban rackets—the illicit activity organized for continuing profit rather than individual illegal acts—is one of the queer ladders of social mobility in American life. Indeed, it is not too much to say that the whole question of organized crime in America cannot be understood unless one appreciates (1) the distinctive role of organized gambling as a function of a mass consumption economy; (2) the specific role of various immigrant groups as they one after another became involved in marginal business and crime; and (3) the relation of crime to the changing character of the urban political machines. . . .

II

The Italian community has achieved wealth and political influence much later and in a harder way than previous immigrant groups. Early Jewish wealth, that of the German Jews of the late nineteenth century, was made largely in banking and merchandising. To that extent, the dominant group in the Jewish community was outside of, and independent of, the urban political machines. Later Jewish wealth, among the East European immigrants, was built in the garment trades, though with some involvement with the Jewish gangster, who was typically an industrial racketeer (Arnold Rothstein, Lepke and Gurrah, etc.) Among Jewish lawyers, a small minority, such as the "Tammany lawyer" (like the protagonist of Sam Ornitz's *Haunch, Paunch* and *Jowl*) rose through politics and occasionally touched the fringes of crime. Most of the Jewish lawyers, by and large the communal leaders, climbed rapidly, however, in the opportunities that established and legitimate Jewish wealth provided. Irish immigrant wealth in the northern urban centers, concentrated largely in construction, trucking and the waterfront, has, to a substantial extent, been wealth accumulated in and through political alliance, e.g. favoritism in city contracts.[1] Control of the politics of the city thus has been crucial for the continuance of Irish political wealth. This alliance of Irish immigrant wealth and politics has been reciprocal; many noted Irish political figures lent their names as important window-dressing for business corporations (Al Smith, for example, who helped form the U.S. Trucking Corporation, whose executive head for many years was William J. McCormack, the alleged "Mr. Big" of the New York waterfront) while Irish businessmen have lent their wealth to further the careers of Irish politicians. Irish mobsters have rarely achieved status in the Irish community, but have served as integral arms of the politicians, as strong-arm men on election day.

The Italians found the more obvious big city paths from rags to riches pre-

---

[1] A fact which should occasion little shock if one recalls that in the nineteenth cenutry American railroads virtually stole 190,000,000 acres of land by bribing Congressmen, and that more recently such scandals as the Teapot Dome oil grabs during the Harding administration, consummated, as the Supreme Court said, "by means of conspiracy, fraud and bribery," reached to the very doors of the White House.

empted. In part this was due to the character of the early Italian immigration. Most of them were unskilled and from rural stock. Jacob Riis could remark in the '90s, "the Italian comes in at the bottom and stays there." These dispossessed agricultural laborers found jobs as ditch-diggers, on the railroads as section hands, along the docks, in the service occupations, as shoemakers, barbers, garment workers, and stayed there. Many were fleeced by the "padrone" system, a few achieved wealth from truck farming, wine growing, and marketing produce; but this "marginal wealth" was not the source of coherent and stable political power.

Significantly, although the number of Italians in the U.S. is about a third as high as the number of Irish, and of the 30,000,000 Catholic communicants in the United States about half are of Irish descent and a sixth of Italian, there is not one Italian bishop among the hundred Catholic bishops in this country, or one Italian archbishop among the 21 archbishops. The Irish have a virtual monopoly. This is a factor related to the politics of the American church; but the condition also is possible because there is not significant or sufficient wealth among Italian Americans to force some parity.

The children of the immigrants, the second and third generation, became wise in the ways of the urban slums. Excluded from the political ladder—in the early '30s there were almost no Italians on the city payroll in top jobs, nor in books of the period can one find discussion of Italian political leaders—finding few open routes to wealth, some turned to illicit ways. In the children's court statistics of the 1930s, the largest group of delinquents were the Italian; nor were there any Italian communal or social agencies to cope with these problems. Yet it was, oddly enough, the quondam racketeer, seeking to become respectable, who provided one of the major supports for the drive to win a political voice for Italians in the power structure of the urban political machines.

This rise of the Italian political bloc was connected, at least in the major northern urban centers, to another important development which tended to make the traditional relation between the politician and the protected or tolerated illicit operator more close than it had been in the past. This is the fact that the urban political machines had to evolve new forms of fund-raising since the big business contributions, which once went heavily into municipal politics, now—with the shift in the locus of power—go largely into national affairs. (The ensuing corruption in national politics, as recent Congressional investigations show, is no petty matter; the scruples of businessmen do not seem much superior to those of the gamblers.) One way urban political machines raised their money resembled that of the large corporations which are no longer dependent on Wall Street: by self-financing—that is, by "taxing" the large number of municipal employees who bargain collectively with City Hall for their wage increases. So the firemen's union contributed money to O'Dwyer's campaign.

A second method was taxing the gamblers. The classic example, as *Life* reported, was Jersey City, where a top lieutenant of the Hague machine spent his full time screening applicants for unofficial bookmaking licenses. If found acceptable, the applicant was given a "location," usually the house or store of a loyal precinct worker, who kicked into the machine treasury a high proportion of the large rent exacted. The one thousand bookies and their one thousand landlords in Jersey City formed the hard core of the political machine that sweated and bled to get out the votes for Hague.

A third source for the financing of these machines was the new, and often illegally earned, Italian wealth. This is well illustrated by the career of Costello and his emergence as a political power in New York. Here the ruling motive has been the search for an entrée—for oneself and one's ethnic group—into the ruling circles of the big city.

Frank Costello made his money originally in bootlegging. After repeal, his big break came when Huey Long, desperate for ready cash to fight the old-line political machines, invited Costello to install slot machines in Louisiana. Costello did, and he flourished. Together with Dandy Phil Kastel, he also opened the Beverly Club, an elegant gambling establishment just outside New Orleans, at which have appeared some of the top entertainers in America. Subsequently, Costello invested his money in New York real estate (including 79 Wall Street, which he later sold), the Copacabana night club, and a leading brand of Scotch whiskey.

Costello's political opportunity came when a money-hungry Tammany, starved by lack of patronage from Roosevelt and La Guardia, turned to him for financial support. The Italian community in New York has for years nursed a grievance against the Irish and, to a lesser extent, the Jewish political groups for monopolizing political power. They complained about the lack of judicial jobs, the small number—usually one—of Italian Congressmen, the lack of representation on the state tickets. But the Italians lacked the means to make their ambitions a reality. Although they formed a large voting bloc, there was rarely sufficient wealth to finance political clubs. Italian immigrants, largely poor peasants from Southern Italy and Sicily, lacked the mercantile experience of the Jews, and the political experience gained in the seventy-five-year history of Irish immigration.

During the Prohibition years, the Italian racketeers had made certain political contacts in order to gain protection. Costello, always the compromiser and fixer rather than the muscle-man, was the first to establish relations with Jimmy Hines, the powerful leader of the West Side in Tammany Hall. But his rival, Lucky Luciano, suspicious of the Irish, and seeking more direct power, backed and elected Al Marinelli for district leader on the Lower West Side. Marinelli in 1932 was the only Italian leader inside Tammany Hall. Later, he was joined by Dr. Paul Sarubbi, a partner of Johnny Torrio in a large, legitimate liquor concern. Certainly, Costello and Luciano represented no "unified" move by the Italians as a whole for power; within the Italian community there are as many divisions as in any other group. What is significant is that different Italians, for different reasons, and in various fashions, were achieving influence for the first time. Marinelli became county clerk of New York and a leading power in Tammany. In 1937, after being blasted by Tom Dewey, then running for district attorney, as a "political ally of thieves . . . and big-shot racketeers," Marinelli was removed from office by Governor Lehman. The subsequent conviction by Dewey of Luciano and Hines, and the election of La Guardia, left most of the Tammany clubs financially weak and foundering. This was the moment Costello made his move. In a few years, by judicious financing, he controlled a block of "Italian" leaders in the Hall—as well as some Irish on the upper West Side, and some Jewish leaders on the East Side—and was able to influence the selection of a number of Italian judges. The most notable incident, revealed by a wire tap on Costello's phone, was the "Thank you, Francisco" call in 1943 by Supreme Court nominee Thomas Aurelio, who gave Costello full credit for his nomination.

It was not only Tammany that was eager to accept campaign contributions from newly rich Italians, even though some of these *nouveaux riches* had "arrived" through bootlegging and gambling. Fiorello La Guardia, the wiliest mind that Melting Pot politics has ever produced, understood in the early '30s where much of his covert support came from. (So, too, did Vito Marcantonio, an apt pupil of the master: Marcantonio has consistently made deals with the Italian leaders of Tammany Hall—in 1943 he supported Aurelio, and refused to repudiate him even when the Democratic Party formally did.) Joe Adonis, who had built a political following during the late '20s, when he ran a popular speakeasy, aided La Guardia financially to a considerable extent in 1933. "The Democrats haven't recognized the Italians," Adonis told a friend. "There is no reason for the Italians to support anybody but La Guardia; the Jews have played ball with the Democrats and haven't gotten much out of it. They know it now. They will vote for La Guardia. So will the Italians."

Adonis played his cards shrewdly. He supported La Guardia, but also a number of Democrats for local and judicial posts, and became a power in the Brooklyn area. His restaurant was frequented by Kenny Sutherland, the Coney Island Democratic leader; Irwin Steingut, the Democratic minority leader in Albany; Anthony DiGiovanni, later a Councilman; William O'Dwyer, and Jim Moran. But, in 1937, Adonis made the mistake of supporting Royal Copeland against La Guardia, and the irate Fiorello finally drove Adonis out of New York.[2]

La Guardia later turned his ire against Costello, too. Yet Costello survived and reached the peak of his influence in 1942, when he was instrumental in electing Michael Kennedy leader of Tammany Hall. Despite the Aurelio fiasco, which first brought Costello into notoriety, he still had sufficient power in the Hall to swing votes for Hugo Rogers as Tammany leader in 1945, and had a tight grip on some districts as late as 1948. In those years many a Tammany leader came hat in hand to Costello's apartment, or sought him out on the golf links, to obtain the nomination for a judicial post.

During this period, other Italian political leaders were also coming to the fore. Generoso Pope, whose Colonial Sand and Stone Company began to prosper through political contacts, became an important political figure, especially when his purchase of the two largest Italian-language dailies (later merged into one), and of a radio station, gave him almost a monopoly of channels to Italian-speaking opinion of the city. Through Generoso Pope, and through Costello, the Italians became a major political force in New York.

That the urban machines, largely Democratic, have financed their heavy campaign costs in this fashion rather than having to turn to the "moneyed interests," explains in some part why these machines were able, in part, to support the New and Fair Deals without suffering the pressures they might have been subjected to had their source of money supply been the business groups. Although he has never publicly revealed his political convictions, it is likely that Frank Costello was a fervent admirer of Franklin D. Roosevelt and his efforts to aid the common man. The basic measures of the New Deal, which most Americans today agree were necessary for the public good, would not have been possible without the support of the "corrupt" big-city machines.

III

There is little question that men of Italian origin appeared in most of the leading roles in the high drama of gambling and mobs, just as twenty years ago the children of East European Jews were the most prominent figures in organized

---

2 Adonis, and associate Willie Moretti, moved across the river to Bergen County, New Jersey, where, together with the quondam racketeer Abner "Longie" Zwillman, he became one of the political powers in the state. Gambling flourished in Bergen County for almost a decade but after the Kefauver investigation the state was forced to act. A special inquiry in 1953 headed by Nelson Stamler, revealed that Moretti had paid $286,000 to an aide of Governor Driscoll for "protection" and that the Republican state committee had accepted a $25,000 "loan" from gambler Joseph Bozzo, an associate of Zwillman.

crime, and before that individuals of Irish descent were similarly prominent. To some extent statistical accident and the tendency of newspapers to emphasize the few sensational figures gives a greater illusion about the domination of illicit activities by a single ethnic group than all the facts warrant. In many cities, particularly in the South and on the West Coast, the mob and gambling fraternity consisted of many other groups, and often, predominantly, native white Protestants. Yet it is clear that in the major northern urban centers there was a distinct ethnic sequence in the modes of obtaining illicit wealth, and that uniquely in the case of the recent Italian elements, the former bootleggers and gamblers provided considerable leverage for the growth of political influence as well. A substantial number of Italian judges sitting on the bench in New York today are indebted in one fashion or another to Costello; so too are many Italian district leaders—as well as some Jewish and Irish politicians. And the motive in establishing Italian political prestige in New York was generous rather than scheming for personal advantage. For Costello it was largely a case of ethnic pride. As in earlier American eras, organized illegality became a stepladder of social ascent.

To the world at large, the news and pictures of Frank Sinatra, for example, mingling with former Italian mobsters could come somewhat as a shock. Yet to Sinatra, and to many Italians, these were men who had grown up in their neighborhoods, and who were, in some instances, bywords in the community for their helpfulness and their charities. The early Italian gangsters were hoodlums—rough, unlettered, and young (Al Capone was only twenty-nine at the height of his power). Those who survived learned to adapt. By now they are men of middle age or older. They learned to dress conservatively. Their homes are in respectable suburbs. They sent their children to good schools and had sought to avoid publicity.[3] Costello even went to a psychiatrist in his efforts to overcome a painful feeling of inferiority in the world of manners.

As happens with all "new" money in American society, the rough and ready contractors, the construction people, trucking entrepreneurs, as well as racketeers, polished up their manners and sought recognition and respectability in their own ethnic as well as in the general community. The "shanty" Irish became the "lace curtain" Irish, and then moved out for wider recognition.[4] Sometimes acceptance came first in established "American" society, and this was a certificate for later recognition by the ethnic community, a process well illustrated by the belated acceptance in established Negro society of such figures as Sugar Ray Robinson and Joe Louis, as well as leading popular entertainers.

Yet, after all, the foundation of many a distinguished older American fortune was laid by sharp practices and morally reprehensible methods. The pioneers of American capitalism were not graduated from Harvard's School of Business Administration. The early settlers and founding fathers, as well as those who "won the west" and built up cattle, mining and other fortunes, often did so by shady speculations and a not inconsider-

---

3 Except at times by being overly neighborly, like Tony Accardo, who, at Yuletide 1949, in his elegant River Forest home, decorated a 40-foot tree on his lawn and beneath it set a wooden Santa and reindeer, while around the yard, on tracks, electrically operated skating figures zipped merrily around while a loud speaker poured out Christmas carols. The next Christmas, the Accardo lawn was darkened; Tony was on the lam from Kefauver.

4 The role of ethnic pride in corraling minority group votes is one of the oldest pieces of wisdom in American politics; but what is more remarkable is the persistence of this identification through second and third generation descendants, a fact which, as Samuel Lubell noted in his *Future of American Politics*, was one of the explanatory keys to political behavior in recent elections. Although the Irish bloc as a solid Democratic bloc is beginning to crack, particularly as middle-class status impels individuals to identify more strongly with the G.O.P., the nomination in Massachusetts of Jack Kennedy for the United States Senate created a tremendous solidarity among Irish voters and Kennedy was elected over Lodge although Eisenhower swept the state.

able amount of violence. They ignored, circumvented or stretched the law when it stood in the way of America's destiny, and their own—or, were themselves the law when it served their purposes. This has not prevented them and their descendants from feeling proper moral outrage when under the changed circumstances of the crowded urban environments later comers pursued equally ruthless tactics.

IV

Ironically, the social development which made possible the rise to political influence sounds, too, the knell of the Italian gangster. For it is the growing number of Italians with professional training and legitimate business success that both prompts and permits the Italian group to wield increasing political influence; and increasingly it is the professionals and businessmen who provide models for Italian youth today, models that hardly existed twenty years ago. Ironically, the headlines and exposés of "crime" of the Italian "gangsters" came years after the fact. Many of the top "crime" figures long ago had forsworn violence, and even their income, in large part, was derived from legitimate investments (real estate in the case of Costello, motor haulage and auto dealer franchises in the case of Adonis) or from such quasi-legitimate but socially respectable sources as gambling casinos. Hence society's "retribution" in the jail sentences for Costello and Adonis was little more than a trumped-up morality that disguised a social hypocrisy.

Apart from these considerations, what of the larger context of crime and the American way of life? The passing of the Fair Deal signalizes, oddly, the passing of an older pattern of illicit activities. The gambling fever of the past decade and a half was part of the flush and exuberance of rising incomes, and was characteristic largely of new upper-middle class rich having a first fling at conspicuous consumption. This upper-middle class rich, a significant new stratum in American life (not rich in the nineteenth century sense of enormous wealth, but largely middle-sized businessmen and entrepreneurs of the service and luxury trades—the "tertiary economy" in Colin Clark's phrase—who by the tax laws have achieved sizable incomes often much higher than the managers of the super-giant corporations) were the chief patrons of the munificent gambling casinos. During the war decade when travel was difficult, gambling and the lush resorts provided important outlets for this social class. Now they are settling down, learning about Europe and culture. The petty gambling, the betting and bingo which relieve the tedium of small town life, or the expectation among the urban slum dwellers of winning a sizable sum by a "lucky number" or a "lucky horse" goes on. To quote Bernard Baruch: "You can't stop people from gambling on horses. And why should you prohibit a man from backing his own judgment? It's another form of personal initiative." But the lush profits are passing from gambling, as the costs of coordination rise. And in the future it is likely that gambling, like prostitution, winning tacit acceptance as a necessary fact, will continue on a decentralized, small entrepreneur basis.

But passing, too, is a political pattern, the system of political "bosses" which in its reciprocal relation provided "protection" for and was fed revenue from crime. The collapse of the "boss" system was a product of the Roosevelt era. Twenty years ago Jim Farley's task was simple; he had to work only on some key state bosses. Now there is no longer such an animal. New Jersey Democracy was once ruled by Frank Hague; now there are five or six men each top dog, for the moment, in his part of the state or faction of the party. Within the urban centers, the old Irish-dominated political machines in New York, Boston, Newark, and Chicago have fallen apart. The decentralization of the metropolitan centers, the growth of suburbs and satellite towns, the break-up of the old ecological patterns of slum and transient belts, the rise of functional groups, the increasing middle-class character of American life, all contribute to this decline.

With the rationalization and absorption of some illicit activities into the structure of the economy, the passing of an older generation that had established a hegemony over crime, the general rise of minority groups to social position, and the break-up of the urban boss system, the pattern of crime we have discussed is passing as well. Crime, of course, remains as long as passion and the desire for gain remain. But big, organized city crime, as we have known it for the past seventy-five years, was based on more than these universal motives. It was based on certain characteristics of the American economy, American ethnic groups, and American politics. The changes in all these areas means that it too, in the form we have known it, is at an end.

17. The Politics of Corruption in an American City

JOHN A. GARDINER

OFFICIAL CORRUPTION

Textbooks on municipal corporation law speak of at least three varieties of official corruption. The major categories are nonfeasance (failing to perform a required duty at all), malfeasance (the commission of some act which is positively unlawful), and misfeasance (the improper performance of some act which a man may properly do). During the years in which Irv Stern was running his gambling operations, Wincanton officials were guilty of all of these. Some residents say that Bob Walasek came to regard the mayor's office as a brokerage, levying a tariff on every item that came across his desk. Sometimes a request for simple municipal services turned into a game of cat and mouse, with Walasek sitting on the request, waiting to see how much would be offered, and the "petitioner" waiting to see if he could obtain his rights without having to pay for them. Corruption was not as lucrative an enterprise as gambling, but it offered a tempting supplement to low official salaries.

Nonfeasance

As was detailed earlier, Irv Stern saw to it that Wincanton officials would ignore at least one of their statutory duties, enforcement of the State's gambling laws. Bob Walasek and his cohorts also agreed to overlook other illegal activities. Stern, we noted earlier, preferred not to get directly involved in prostitution; Walasek and Police Chief Dave Phillips tolerated all prostitutes who kept up their protection payments. One madam, controlling more than 20 girls, gave Phillips *et al.* \$500 each week; one woman employing only one girl paid \$75 each week that she was in business. Operators of a carnival in rural Alsace County paid a public official \$5000 for the privilege of operating gambling tents for 5 nights each summer. A burlesque theater manager, under attack by high school teachers, was ordered to pay \$25 each week for the privilege of keeping his strip show open.

Many other city and county officials must be termed guilty of nonfeasance, although there is no evidence that they received payoffs, and although they could present reasonable excuses for their inaction. Most policemen, as we have noted earlier, began to ignore prostitution and gambling completely after their reports of offenses were ignored or superior officers told them to mind their own business. State policemen, well informed about city vice and gambling conditions, did nothing unless called upon to act by local officials. Finally, the judges of the Alsace County Court failed to exercise their power to call for State Police investigations. In 1957, following Federal raids on horse

SOURCE: John A. Gardiner, "Wincanton: The Politics of Corruption," in *Task Force Report: Organized Crime*. The President's Commission on Law Enforcement and Administration of Justice (1967), pp. 67–70, 74–76. For a more extended analysis see Gardiner, *The Politics of Corruption: Organized Crime in an American City*. (New York: Russell Sage Foundation, 1970.)

bookies, the judges did request an investigation by the State Attorney General, but refused to approve his suggestion that a grand jury be convened to continue the investigation. For each of these instances of inaction, a tenable excuse might be offered—the beat patrolman should not be expected to endure harassment from his superior officers, State police gambling raids in a hostile city might jeopardize State-local cooperation on more serious crimes, and a grand jury probe might easily be turned into a "whitewash" in the hands of a corrupt district attorney. In any event, powers available to these law enforcement agencies for the prevention of gambling and corruption were not utilized.

Malfeasance

In fixing parking and speeding tickets, Wincanton politicians and policemen committed malfeasance, or committed an act they were forbidden to do, by illegally compromising valid civil and criminal actions. Similarly, while State law provides no particular standards by which the mayor is to make promotions within his police department, it was obviously improper for Mayor Walasek to demand a "political contribution" of $10,000 from Dave Phillips before he was appointed chief in 1960.

The term "political contribution" raises a serious legal and analytical problem in classifying the malfeasance of Wincanton officials, and indeed of politicians in many cities. Political campaigns cost money; citizens have a right to support the candidates of their choice; and officials have a right to appoint their backers to noncivil service positions. At some point, however, threats or oppression convert legitimate requests for political contributions into extortion. Shortly after taking office in the mid-1950s, Mayor Gene Donnelly notified city hall employees that they would be expected "voluntarily" to contribute 2 percent of their salary to the Democratic Party. (It might be noted that Donnelly never forwarded any of these "political contributions" to the party treasurer.) A number of salesmen doing business with the city were notified that companies which had supported the party would receive favored treatment; Donnelly notified one salesman that in light of a proposed $81,000 contract for the purchase of fire engines, a "political contribution" of $2000 might not be inappropriate. While neither the city hall employees nor the salesmen had rights to their positions or their contracts, the "voluntary" quality of their contributions seems questionable.

One final, in the end almost ludicrous, example of malfeasance came with Mayor Donnelly's abortive "War on the Press." Following a series of gambling raids by the Internal Revenue Service, the newspapers began asking why the local police had not participated in the raids. The mayor lost his temper and threw a reporter in jail. Policemen were instructed to harass newspaper delivery trucks, and 73 tickets were written over a 48-hour period for supposed parking and traffic violations. Donnelly soon backed down after national news services picked up the story, since press coverage made him look ridiculous. Charges against the reporter were dropped, and the newspapers continued to expose gambling and corruption.

Misfeasance

Misfeasance in office, says the common law, is the improper performance of some act which a man may properly do. City officials must buy and sell equipment, contract for services, and allocate licenses, privileges, etc. These actions can be improperly performed if either the results are improper (e.g., if a building inspector were to approve a home with defective wiring or a zoning board to authorize a variance which had no justification in terms of land usage) or a result is achieved by improper procedures (e.g., if the city purchased an acceptable automobile in consideration of a bribe paid to the purchasing agent). In the latter case, we can usually assume an improper result as well—while the automobile will be satisfactory, the bribe giver will probably have inflated the sale price to cover the costs of the bribe.

In Wincanton, it was rather easy for city officials to demand kickbacks, for State law frequently does not demand competitive bidding or permits the city to ignore the lowest bid. The city council is not required to advertise or take bids on purchases under $1000, contracts for maintenance of streets and other public works, personal or professional services, or patented or copyrighted products. Even when bids must be sought, the council is only required to award the contract to the lowest responsible bidder. Given these permissive provisions, it was relatively easy for council members to justify or disguise contracts in fact based upon bribes. The exemption for patented products facilitated bribe taking on the purchase of two emergency trucks for the police department (with a $500 campaign contribution on a $7500 deal), three fire engines ($2000 was allegedly paid on an $81,000 contract), and 1500 parking meters (involving payments of $10,500 plus an $880 clock for Mayor Walasek's home). Similar fees were allegedly exacted in connection with the purchase of a city fire alarm system and police uniforms and firearms. A former mayor and other officials also profited on the sale of city property, allegedly dividing $500 on the sale of a crane and $20,000 for approving the sale, for $22,000, of a piece of land immediately resold for $75,000.

When contracts involved services to the city, the provisions in the State law regarding the lowest responsible bidder and excluding "professional services" from competitive bidding provided convenient loopholes. One internationally known engineering firm refused to agree to kickback in order to secure a contract to design a $4.5 million sewage disposal plant for the city; a local firm was then appointed, which paid $10,700 of its $225,000 fee to an associate of Irv Stern and Mayor Donnelly as a "finder's fee." Since the State law also excludes public works maintenance contracts from the competitive bidding requirements, many city paving and street repair contracts during the Donnelly-Walasek era were given to a contributor to the Democratic Party. Finally, the franchise for towing illegally parked cars and cars involved in accidents was awarded to two garages which were then required to kickback $1 for each car towed.

The handling of graft on the towing contracts illustrates the way in which minor violence and the "lowest responsible bidder" clause could be used to keep bribe payers in line. After Federal investigators began to look into Wincanton corruption, the owner of one of the garages with a towing franchise testified before the grand jury. Mayor Walasek immediately withdrew his franchise, citing "health violations" at the garage. The garageman was also "encouraged" not to testify by a series of "accidents"—wheels would fall off towtrucks on the highway, steering cables were cut, and so forth. Newspaper satirization of the "health violations" forced the restoration of the towing franchise, and the "accidents" ceased.

Lest the reader infer that the "lowest responsible bidder" clause was used as an escape valve only for corrupt purposes, one incident might be noted which took place under the present reform administration. In 1964, the Wincanton School Board sought bids for the renovation of an athletic field. The lowest bid came from a construction company owned by Dave Phillips, the corrupt police chief who had served formerly under Mayor Walasek. While the company was presumably competent to carry out the assignment, the board rejected Phillips' bid "because of a question as to his moral responsibility." The board did not specify whether this referred to his prior corruption as chief or his present status as an informer in testifying against Walasek and Stern.

One final area of city power, which was abused by Walasek *et al.*, covered discretionary acts, such as granting permits and allowing zoning variances. On taking office, Walasek took the unusual step of asking that the bureaus of building and plumbing inspection be put under the mayor's control. With this power to approve or deny building permits, Walasek "sat on" applications, waiting until the petitioner contributed $50 or $75, or threatened to sue to get his permit. Some building designs were not approved until a favored architect was retained as a "consultant." (It is not known whether this involved kickbacks to Walasek or simply patronage for a friend.) At least three instances are known in which developers were forced to pay for zoning variances before apartment buildings or supermarkets could be erected. Businessmen who wanted to encourage rapid turnover of the curb space in front of their stores were told to pay a police sergeant to erect "10-minute parking" signs. To repeat a caveat stated earlier, it is impossible to tell whether these kickbacks were demanded to expedite legitimate requests or to approve improper demands, such as a variance that would hurt a neighborhood or a certificate approving improper electrical work.

All of the activities detailed thus far involve fairly clear violations of the law. To complete the picture of the abuse of office by Wincanton officials, we might briefly mention "honest graft." This term was best defined by one of its earlier practitioners, State Senator George Washington Plunkitt who loyally served Tammany Hall at the turn of the century.

> There's all the difference in the world between [honest and dishonest graft]. Yes, many of our men have grown rich in politics. I have myself.
>
> I've made a big fortune out of the game, and I'm gettin' richer every day, but I've not gone in for dishonest graft—blackmailin' gamblers, saloonkeepers, disorderly people, etc.—and neither has any of the men who have made big fortunes in politics.
>
> There's an honest graft, and I'm an example of how it works. I might sum up the whole thing by sayin': "I seen my opportunities and I took 'em."
>
> Let me explain by examples. My party's in power in the city, and it's goin' to undertake a lot of public improvements. Well, I'm tipped off, say, that they're going to lay out a new park at a certain place.
>
> I see my opportunity and I take it. I go to that place, and I buy up all the land I can in the neighborhood. Then the board of this or that makes its plan public, and there is a rush to get my land, which nobody cared particular for before.
>
> Ain't it perfectly honest to charge a good price and make a profit on my investment and foresight? Of course, it is. Well, that's honest graft.[1]

While there was little in the way of land purchasing—either honest or dishonest—going on in Wincanton during this period, several officials who carried on their own businesses while in office were able to pick up some "honest graft." One city councilman with an accounting office served as bookkeeper for Irv Stern and the major bookies and prostitutes in the city.

Police Chief Phillips' construction firm received a contract to remodel the exterior of the largest brothel in town. Finally one councilman serving in the present reform administration received a contract to construct all gasoline stations built in the city by a major petroleum company; skeptics say that the contract was the quid pro quo for the councilman's vote to give the company the contract to sell gasoline to the city.

How Far Did It Go?

This cataloging of acts of nonfeasance, malfeasance, and misfeasance by Win-

[1] William L. Riordan, *Plunkitt of Tammany Hall* (New York: E. P. Dutton, 1963), p. 3.

canton officials raises a danger of confusing variety with universality, of assuming that every employee of the city was either engaged in corrupt activities or was being paid to ignore the corruption of others. On the contrary, both official investigations and private research lead to the conclusion that there is no reason whatsoever to question the honesty of the vast majority of the employees of the city of Wincanton. Certainly no more than 10 of the 155 members of the Wincanton police force were on Irv Stern's payroll (although as many as half of them may have accepted petty Christmas presents—turkeys or liquor). In each department, there were a few employees who objected actively to the misdeeds of their superiors, and the only charge that can justly be leveled against the mass of employees is that they were unwilling to jeopardize their employment by publicly exposing what was going on. When Federal investigators showed that an honest (and possibly successful) attempt was being made to expose Stern-Walasek corruption, a number of city employees cooperated with the grand jury in aggregating evidence which could be used to convict the corrupt officials.

Before these Federal investigations began, however, it could reasonably appear to an individual employee that the entire machinery of law enforcement in the city was controlled by Stern, Walasek, *et al.*, and that an individual protest would be silenced quickly. This can be illustrated by the momentary crusade conducted by First Assistant District Attorney Phil Roper in the summer of 1962. When the district attorney left for a short vacation, Roper decided to act against the gamblers and madams in the city. With the help of the State Police, Roper raided several large brothels. Apprehending on the street the city's largest distributor of punchboards and lotteries, Roper effected a citizen's arrest and drove him to police headquarters for proper detention and questioning. "I'm sorry, Mr. Roper," said the desk sergeant, "we're under orders not to arrest persons brought in by you." Roper was forced to call upon the State Police for aid in confining the gambler. When the district attorney returned from his vacation, he quickly fired Roper "for introducing politics into the district attorney's office."

If it is incorrect to say that Wincanton corruption extended very far vertically—into the rank and file of the various departments of the city—how far did it extend horizontally? How many branches and levels of government were affected? With the exception of the local Congressman and the city treasurer, it seems that a few personnel at each level (city, county, and State) and in most offices in city hall can be identified either with Stern or with some form of freelance corruption. A number of local judges received campaign financing from Stern, although there is no evidence that they were on his payroll after they were elected. Several State legislators were on Stern's payroll, and one Republican councilman charged that a high-ranking State Democratic official promised Stern first choice of all Alsace County patronage. The county chairman, he claimed, was only to receive the jobs that Stern did not want. While they were later to play an active role in disrupting Wincanton gambling, the district attorney in Hal Craig's reform administration feared that the State Police were on Stern's payroll, and thus refused to use them in city gambling raids.

Within the city administration, the evidence is fairly clear that some mayors and councilmen received regular payments from Stern and divided kickbacks on city purchases and sales. Some key subcouncil personnel frequently shared in payoffs affecting their particular departments—the police chief shared in the gambling and prostitution payoffs and received $300 of the $10,500 kickback on parking meter purchases. A councilman controlling one department, for example, might get a higher percentage of kickbacks than the other councilmen in contracts involving that department.

PUBLIC ATTITUDES TOWARD GAMBLING AND CORRUPTION

A clean city, a city free of gambling, vice, and corruption, requires at least two things—active law enforcement and elected officials who oppose organized crime. Over the last 20 years, Federal agents have been successful in prosecuting most of the leaders of Wincanton gambling operations. Slot machine king Klaus Braun was twice sent to jail for income tax evasion. Federal agents were also able to secure convictions against Irv Stern for income tax evasion (a 4-year sentence), gambling tax evasion (a 2-year sentence running concurrently with the income tax sentence), and extortion on a city contract to purchase parking meters (a 30-day concurrent sentence). Federal men also sent to jail lesser members of the Stern syndicate and closed down a still and an interstate dice game.

These Federal actions, however, had very little effect upon Wincanton gambling. Lieutenants carried on while Stern was in jail, and local police, at the direction of city officials, continued to ignore numbers writers, bookies, and prostitutes. As one Federal agent put it, "Even though we were able to apprehend and convict the chief racketeers, we were never able to solve the political problem—city officials were always against us." On the two occasions when Wincanton voters did solve the political problem by electing reform officials, however, organized crime was quickly put out of business. Mayor Hal Craig chose to tolerate isolated bookies, numbers writers, and prostitutes, but Stern and Braun were effectively silenced. Mayor Ed Whitton, in office since the early 1960s, has gone even further, and the only gamblers and prostitutes still operating in Wincanton are those whom the police have been unable to catch for reasons of limited manpower, lack of evidence, etc. The American Social Hygiene Association reported after a recent study that Wincanton has fewer prostitutes today than at any time since the 1930s. The police acknowledge that there are still a few gamblers and prostitutes in town, but they have been driven underground, and a potential patron must have a contact before he can do business.

If the level of law enforcement in a community is so directly tied to local voting patterns, we must look more closely at the attitudes and values of Wincanton residents. First, how much did residents know about what was going on? Were the events which have been discussed previously matters of common knowledge or were they perceived by only a few residents? Second, were they voting for open gambling and corruption; were they being duped by seemingly honest candidates who became corrupt after taking office; or were these issues irrelevant to the average voter, who was thinking about other issues entirely? Our conclusions about these questions will indicate whether long-range reform can be attained through legal changes (closing loopholes in the city's bidding practices, expanding civil service in the police department, ending the "home rule" policy of the State police, etc.) or whether reform must await a change in popular mores.

Public Awareness of Gambling and Corruption

In a survey of Wincanton residents conducted recently,[2] 90 percent of the respondents were able correctly to identify the present mayor, 63 percent recognized the name of their Congressman, and 36 percent knew the Alsace County district

2 This survey was conducted by eight female interviewers from the Wisconsin Survey Research Laboratory, using a schedule of questions requiring 45 to 75 minutes to complete. Respondents were selected from among the adults residing in housing units selected at random from the Wincanton "City Directory." One hundred eighty-three completed interviews were obtained.

attorney. Seventy percent identified Irv Stern correctly, and 62 percent admitted that they did recognize the name of the largest madam in town. But how much did the people of Wincanton know about what had been going on—the extent and organization of Irv Stern's empire, the payoffs to city hall and the police, or the malfeasance and misfeasance of Bob Walasek and other city officials? Instead of thinking about simply "knowing" or "not knowing," we might subdivide public awareness into several categories—a general awareness that gambling and prostitution were present in the city, some perception that city officials were protecting these enterprises, and finally a specific knowledge that officials X and Y were being paid off. These categories vary, it will be noticed, in the specificity of knowledge and in the linkage between the result (e.g., presence of gambling or corruption) and an official's action.

While there is no way of knowing exactly how many Wincantonites had access to each type of knowledge about gambling and corruption during the period they were taking place, we can form some ideas on the basis of the newspaper coverage they received and the geographical distribution of each form of illegality. The dice game, for example, was in only one location (hidden and shifted periodically to escape Federal attention) and relied primarily on out-of-town gamblers. The newspapers said little about it, and it was probably safe to say that few residents knew of its existence until it was raided by the FBI in the early 1960s.

Prostitutes were generally found only in two four-block areas in the city—semi-slum areas that no outsider was likely to visit unless he was specifically looking for the girls. The newspapers, however, gave extensive coverage to every prostitution arrest and every report by the American Social Hygiene Association which detailed the extent of prostitution and venereal disease in the city. A series of newspaper articles, with photographs, forced the police to close (for a short period of time) several of the larger brothels. With regard to prostitution, therefore, it is likely that a majority of the adult population knew of the existence of commercialized vice; but, apart from innuendoes in the papers, there was little awareness of payoffs to the police. It was not until after the election of a reform administration, that Stern and Walasek were indicted for extorting payments from a madam.

In contrast to the dice games and prostitution, public awareness of the existence of pinball machines, horsebooks, and numbers writing must have been far more widespread. These mass-consumption forms of gambling depended upon accessibility to large numbers of persons. Bets could be placed in most corner grocery stores, candy shops, and cigar counters; payoff pinball machines were placed in most clubs and fireballs, as well as in bars and restaurants. Apart from knowing that these things were openly available, and thus not subject to police interference, there was no way for the average citizen to know specifically that Irv Stern was paying to protect these gambling interests until Police Chief Phillips began to testify—again after the election of reformer Whitton.

Public awareness of wrongdoing was probably least widespread in regard to corruption—kickbacks on contracts, extortion, etc. Direct involvement was generally limited to officials and businessmen, and probably few of them knew anything other than that they personally had been asked to pay. Either from shame or from fear of being prosecuted on bribery charges or out of unwillingness to jeopardize a profitable contract, those who did pay did not want to talk. Those who refused to pay usually were unable to substantiate charges made against bribes so that exposure of the attempt led only to libel suits or official harassment. As we have seen, the newspapers and one garage with a towing contract did talk about what was going on. The garageman lost his franchise and suffered a series of "accidents"; the newspapers found a reporter in jail and their trucks harassed by the police. Peter French, the district attorney under Walasek and Donnelly, won a libel suit (since reversed on appeal and dismissed) against the papers after they stated that he was protecting gamblers. Except for an unsuccessful citizen suit in the mid-1950s seeking to void the purchase of fire trucks (for the purchase of which Donnelly received a $2000 "political contribution") and a newspaper article in the early 1960s implying that Donnelly and his council had received $500 on the sale of a city crane, no evidence—no specific facts—of corruption was available to the public until Phillips was indicted several years later for perjury in connection with the towing contracts.

Returning then to the three categories of public knowledge, we can say that even at the lowest level—general perception of some form of wrongdoing—awareness was quite limited (except among the businessmen, most of whom, as we noted in the "Introduction," live and vote in the suburbs). Specific knowledge—this official received this much to approve that contract—was only available after legislative hearings in the early 1950s and the indictment of Phillips in the early 1960s; on both occasions the voters turned to reform candidates.

If, therefore, it is unlikely that many residents of Wincanton had the second or third type of knowledge about local gambling or corruption (while many more had the first type) during the time it was taking place, how much do they know now—after several years of reform and a series of trials—all well-covered in the newspapers revealing the nature of Stern-Donnelly-Walasek operations? To test the extent of specific knowledge about local officials and events, respondents in a recent survey were asked to identify past and present officials and racketeers and to compare the Walasek and Whitton administrations on a number of points.

Earlier, we noted that 90 percent of the 183 respondents recognized the name of the present mayor, 63 percent knew their Congressman (who had been in office more than 10 years), and 36 percent knew the district attorney. How many members of the Stern organization were known to the public? Seventy percent recognized Stern's name, 63 percent knew the head of the numbers bank, 40 percent identified the "bagman" or collector for Stern, and 31 percent knew the operator of the largest horsebook in town. With regard to many of these questions, it must be kept in mind that since many respondents may subconsciously have felt that to admit recognition of a name would have implied personal contact with or sympathy for a criminal or a criminal act, these results probably understate the extent of public knowledge. When 100 of the respondents were asked "What things did Mr. Walasek do that were illegal?," 59 mentioned extortion regarding vice and gambling, 2 mentioned extortion on city contracts, 7 stated that he stole from the city, 8 that he fixed parking and speeding tickets, 4 that he was "controlled by rackets," and 20 simply stated that Walasek was corrupt, not listing specific acts.

Even if Wincantonites do not remember too many specific misdeeds, they clearly perceive that the present Whitton administration has run a cleaner town than did Walasek or Donnelly. When asked to comment on the statement, "Some people say that the present city administration under Mayor Whitton is about the same as when Mayor Walasek was in office," 10 percent said it was the same, 74 percent said it was different, and 14 percent didn't know. When asked why, 75 respondents cited "better law enforcement" and the end of corruption; only 7 of 183 felt that the city had been better run by Walasek. Fifty-eight percent felt the police force was better now, 22 percent thought that it was about the same as when Walasek controlled the force, and only 7 percent thought it was worse now. Those who felt that the police department was better run now stressed "honesty" and "better law enforcement," or thought that it was valuable to have an outsider as commissioner. Those who thought it was worse now cited "inefficiency," "loafing," or "unfriendliness." It was impossible to tell whether the comments of "unfriendliness" refer simply to the present refusal to tolerate gambling or whether they signify a more remote police-public contact resulting from the "professionalism" of the commissioner. (In this regard, we might note that a number of policemen and lawyers felt that it had been easier to secure information regarding major crimes when prostitution and gambling were tolerated. As one former captain put it, "If I found out that some gangster was in town that I didn't know about, I raised hell with the prostitutes for not telling me.")

Comparing perceptions of the present and former district attorneys, we also find a clear preference for the present man, Thomas Hendricks, over Peter French, but there is a surprising increase in "Don't knows." Thirty-five percent felt the district attorney's office is run "differently" now, 13 percent said it is run in the same way, but 50 percent did not know. Paralleling this lack of attitudes toward the office, we can recall that only 36 percent of the respondents were able to identify the present incumbent's name, while 55 percent knew his more flamboyant predecessor. Of those respondents who saw a difference between the two men, 51 percent cited "better law enforcement" and "no more rackets control over law enforcement."

In addition to recognizing these differences between past and present officials, the respondents in the recent survey felt that there were clear differences in the extent of corruption and gambling. Sixty-nine percent disagreed with the statement, "Underworld elements and racketeers had very little say in what the Wincanton city government did when Mr. Walasek was mayor"; only 13 percent disagreed with the same statement as applied to reform Mayor Whitton. When asked, "As compared with 5 years ago, do you think it's easier now, about the same, or harder to find a dice game in Wincanton?"; only one respondent felt it was easier, 8 percent felt it was about the same, 56 percent felt it was harder, and 34 percent didn't know. The respondents were almost as sure that Whitton had closed down horse betting; 51 percent felt it was harder to bet on horses now than it was 5 years ago, 11 percent felt it was about the same, and three respondents thought it was easier now than before. Again, 34 percent did not know.

18. Ticket-Fixing in Massachusetts

JOHN A. GARDINER

TICKET FIXING

One Massachusetts legislator, invited by a local League of Women Voters to discuss the functions of a legislator, startled the ladies by beginning, "The chief function of a legislator is to fix traffic tickets for his constituents." In a state in which most public employees are under the civil-service system, fixing tickets may be one of the few services a legislator can perform for his constituents. One state senator, hearing a safety council official propose a no-fix system, asked incredulously, "Do you really mean that I'm not going to be able to help out friends who get into trouble? There's nothing immoral about fixing minor traffic tickets." Legislators protested an earlier attempt to end fixing on the ground that it would cut down their influence, and they denied a request to increase the size of the state police force after it adopted a no-fix policy.[1]

For the policeman as well as the legislator, requests to fix tickets may well be one of the primary bases of contact with the public. Any motorist, of course, can try to talk his way out of a ticket—"I didn't see the stop sign"; "My speedometer is broken"; "I'm late for work"; and, fairly certain to anger the patrolman, "How dare you stop me? I'm a friend of the governor (bishop, mayor, chief)." But even if a Massachusetts motorist is unable to convince the officer not to write up the offense, there is still a good chance that he can avoid punishment. (The course of action will vary from city to city, depending on whether the policeman carries the Registry ticket books or is recording the facts on a departmental ticket form. In the latter case, the motorist can erase all evidence of the violation if someone in police headquarters rips up the form. If, on the other hand, the arresting officer fills out the Registry tickets on the road—in Cambridge and twenty-seven other cities in the state—the motorist's only hope is to persuade the chief to mark the ticket "warning," since chiefs and policemen fear that someone in the Registry will notice if a Registry form is completely destroyed.)

How does the process of ticket fixing work? Although your ultimate chance for success in getting a ticket fixed (termed by all Massachusetts police officers, "to give consideration") varies from city to city, the list of persons to call does not. Your best bet is to know a member of the police force that stopped you. (If you knew the officer himself, you would not, of course, have received the ticket

1 "Leglislators Support No-Fix," *Boston Herald,* March 13, 1960; "No-Fix Plan Cuts Accidents," *Boston Herald,* February 28, 1960.

SOURCE: Reprinted by permission of the publishers from John A. Gardiner, *Traffic and the Police: Variations in Law-Enforcement Policy,* pp. 118–123. Cambridge, Mass.: Harvard University Press,

in the first place.) Other persons to call are: *any* police chief in the state, any policeman in the state, a politician from the city involved, any other politician in the state, and then "friends" of any of these persons. Once you state your case to your contact ("I wasn't going very fast," "I've never had a ticket before," "I need my license to keep my job"), the pattern of communication varies. If your contact does not come from the city in which the ticket is written, he will probably call the chief; someone within the city might have a friend lower down on the force who can take care of it more quietly.

The origins of these lines of communication are lost in antiquity, but their existence is clear. The most effective intercity line of communication is through the home-town police chief. Police chiefs in Massachusetts frequently said that their "constituents" call them regarding tickets received in other towns and that they then call the other chief to ask for consideration for the motorist. The philosophy of all police chiefs seems to be this: the chief should call for his constituent, and the other chief should grant consideration, unless: (1) the Registry ticket has already been written and the recommendation made (if the ticket has been written but the recommendation not yet made, fixing involves a warning rather than destroying or voiding the ticket); (2) the offense is of a serious nature (no chief or politician is willing to involve himself in any situation involving alcohol, accidents, or *dangerous* speeding—"What if the guy later gets involved in an accident or kills somebody? I don't want my name mixed up with his," one city councilor said); or (3) the motorist was rude to the officer. The logic of the last policy is interesting: the chiefs say that they will not intervene for rude motorists because "they are showing disrespect for the law"; it would seem equally likely that they refuse because a rude motorist has got an officer mad, and the cost to the chief of fixing a ticket written by an angered officer is greater than when the officer is less personally interested in the violation or violator. In all three situations, chiefs feel no obligation to their constituents or to other chiefs. Otherwise, Massachusetts chiefs generally seem to assume that consideration will be given, several chiefs said that they would be surprised if another chief did not give consideration in ordinary circumstances.

Several things should be noted about the organization of ticket fixing in Massachusetts. The first is that the general standards used in appraising requests for fixes—the violation is minor, it is a first offense, and the motorist was not rude to the officer—are known and accepted by all of the participants in the system, and few attempt to jeopardize the system by requesting fixes that do not satisfy these standards. A former mayor in one city mentioned that every politician knows at least one person on the force to call, but "if the violation *might* be regarded as 'serious,' the fix has to be cleared with the chief first. If he decides that it is serious, he won't fix it and politicans won't touch it." A councilor added, "I just leave the message with whoever answers the phone at headquarters. If the motorist gave the cop any trouble, or if he was a bad guy (had a prior record), they'll know I don't want to have anything to do with it."

A second interesting aspect of Massachusetts ticket fixing concerns the *quid pro quo* on which the system is based. Even though, according to one probably exaggerated safety-council estimate, half of all traffic tickets written in the state are fixed,[2] it seems that money is not the reason why tickets are fixed. All policemen who spoke freely about their fixing activities were indignant at any suggestion that they or their colleagues would accept money for their services. One lieu-

2 "State's Safety Council Says 50% of Traffic Tickets Fixed," *Boston Herald,* March 23, 1965.

tenant hotly replied, "If we found that one of our men was taking money for fixing, he'd be fired immediately!" None of the evidence collected either during my study or during the three-year investigations of the Massachusetts Crime Commission (which, though it concentrated on corruption at the state level, also investigated ticket fixing)[3] revealed any instances in which money was accepted to cover up a minor traffic violation. The only explanation for this is that, since police chiefs are so willing to fix tickets on the basis of friendship or political influence, there is no reason to offer cash when stopped by an officer. If corruption in the sense of an exchange of money exists in the field of traffic-law enforcement—and there was no evidence that it does in Massachusetts at least—it would probably exist at the level of the chief rather than at the level of the arresting officer.

If money is not the basis of ticket fixing, why do policemen do it? For chiefs and men alike, fixing tickets is an easily effective form of patronage. One traffic officer described fixing as a kind of insurance. "If you take care of a ticket for a liquor dealer or salesman," he noted, "you can expect consideration when you go in to buy a suit or a bottle." Policemen distinguish sharply, it might be noted, between accepting a bribe and receiving consideration; to a policeman, accepting five dollars from a motorist is dishonest, but buying a suit for less than its list price is not. Ticket fixing also provides insurance of another sort. When asked why policemen were willing to fix tickets when called by policemen from another city, one officer replied, "Well, some day one of our men may want to take care of something in that city, so we'll fix this thing for them now."

For the police chief, fixing tickets also offers a means of maintaining cordial relationships with state and local politicians as well as with local citizens. One patrolman philosophically noted, "Fixing tickets is about the only thing that the chief can do for politicians." The chiefs in Cambridge and Malden were the statehouse lobbyists for, respectively, the Massachusetts Chiefs of Police Association and the Massachusetts Police Association; and both men appeared regularly at the statehouse to ask for legislative favors. All police chiefs must also appear before city councils and town boards of selectmen to ask for pay raises, new equipment, and so forth. Finally, since chiefs must deal with other chiefs, both socially at the monthly association meetings and professionally in conducting multicity crime investigations, they face pressure to honor fix requests from other chiefs and their friends. Some chiefs said that, unless they fixed tickets, they could not expect cooperation from other police forces on more serious matters (such intercity matters as escaped convicts or an auto-theft gang). This, of course, assumes that there is a basic feeling that chiefs *should* fix for their colleagues. A more plausible explanation involves a feeling of reciprocity—"I will not be able to fix one of *his* tickets for my friends if I don't take care of his friends who get *my* tickets. Besides, knowing the problems that I have with officials and politicians in my city, I don't want to cause him any extra problems with his officials and their friends."

3 Interview with Alfred Gardner, Chairman of the Massachusetts Crime Commission, August 3, 1965.

PART 2

The Analysis of Administrative Corruption

The underlying syndrome most pertinent to the analysis of administrative corruption has been succinctly identified by Gunnar Myrdal (Selection 22), with particular reference to the socioeconomic systems of South Asia and other developing areas. In these systems, he holds, "it has been exceedingly difficult to introduce profit motives and market behavior into the sector of social life where they operate in the West—that is in the economic sphere." On the other hand, it has there also remained "difficult to eliminate motivations of private gain from the sector where they have been suppressed in the West—the sphere of public responsibility and power." By seeking to analyze and explain the incidence of corruption within administrative structures, the authors of the selections in Part 2 are concentrating on the bureaucratic "backbone" of the public sphere. The concepts they employ build upon the historical background of Chapter Two, which analyzed the complex process through which Western societies developed techniques to contain the proclivities of officials to utilize the powers of their office for private-regarding purposes. Part 2 develops a complementary pattern by commencing with an analysis of administrative practices in the contemporary systems of South and Southeast Asia, where the incomplete institutionalization of the bureaucratic obligations of office contribute to what, in Western eyes, appears as a widespread prevalence of corruption.

THE DEPERSONALIZATION OF OFFICE

In the West the acceptance by officials of favors for themselves, their families, or friends may be regarded as instances of corruption because these officials infringe upon the principle of keeping their public and private accounts strictly separate. This separation of accounts is based upon the depersonalization implied in the rigid separation between the private household and the public office and upon the official's acceptance of formal, impersonal, legal norms as exclusive guides to the exercise of his powers. However, as W. F. Wertheim points out in Selection 19, the application of these norms "presuppose[s] a social structure in which the separation between the two kinds of account-keeping has either been carried through in actual fact, or else has been generally accepted by society as a criterion for proper conduct on the part of civil servants."

However, insofar as public offices in developing countries come close to fitting F. W. Riggs's "sala" model (see Selection 20), they are characteristically *not* structured to force their incumbents to keep clearly distinct private and public accounts. The widely used Asian term *sala* has the meaning of "office," but it also has the meanings of "pavilion," "drawing room," or "place for religious meetings." As this suggests, the official in a transitional non-Western system is subject to contradictory obligations. "The formal rules of the sala prescribe universalistic norms for the administration of the law . . . and programs of a government agency. However, family influence prevails, so that the law is applied generously to relatives, stringently against strangers." Nepotism is technically illegal, but remains a characteristic mode of recruitment. Whereas in Britain nepotism practices would now "cause a sense of guilt in both giver and receiver," in Africa "the sense of guilt on the part of the receiver would be mingled with a sense of family duty done." (See Selection 33.) Stanislav Andreski guesses that whereas in appointments to the British public service "old boy networks," family connections, and so forth might count for 20 percent and qualifications for 80 percent, in Nigeria the proportions would be the other way around (Selection 35).

STATUS, TRUST, AND SERVICE

Postcolonial Systems

Many middle- and upper-echelon officials in developing countries, especially those who have gone through periods of colonial tutelage, operate between a suprastructure of "Western" attitudes and values and an infrastructure of indigenous traditions and ethics. Suprastructure values stress technical expertise and impersonal rationality in the management of public affairs. The infrastructure values emphasize reliance and obligations toward kinship, friendship, and other primary groups. Officials were most thoroughly inculcated in suprastructure values during the latter periods of colonial rule, whereas infrastructure values were rooted in administrative traditions dating to precolonial times. There were exceptions to this pattern. Thus the Hausa of northern Nigeria had developed bureaucratic norms and "concepts" of corruption in their indigenous tradition, whereas in the Philippines and other Spanish possessions the sale of offices and other practices fostering the appropriation of offices was introduced by the colonial power.

Analyses of the development of public-office morality in former colonies in South and Southeast Asia suggest similar historical patterns. Within the traditional patrimonial systems, such as those of precolonial Burma, official remuneration was essentially based upon benefices, with officials deriving commissions from revenue collection, while custom provided that judges were entitled to fees and presents. Under colonial rule these traditions were perpetuated on a *sub rosa* basis, and as late as 1900 it was believed that in Burma up to 95 percent of the native judges and police officers took presents or bribes. But in Burma as well as in the Dutch East Indies at least the higher officialdom were gradually weaned away from such salary-supplementing practices. Indeed, by 1940 a Government Inquiry Committee reported that progress at the higher levels of the civil service showed that "Burma, if it chooses, can have as incorruptible a Civil Service as England now has, or as Germany and Austria had before the Nazi Revolution."[1]

---

[1] *Report of the Bribery and Corruption Enquiry Committee, 1940.* Rangoon, 1941, p. 9.

European and Asian commentators are generally agreed that public-office morality has declined and that the incidence of corruption has increased during the postcolonial periods after full independence was achieved. J. B. Monteiro in Selection 21 states that India saw "a phenomenal increase in the number of pedlars of influence" after independence as power was transferred to "a newer section of indiscreet public men who flouted all rules and regulations with impunity." Many officials elevated their expectation levels regarding their standards of living. Thus, Wertheim notes that preindependence Indonesian officials considered the European elite's way of life as beyond their reach, but afterward many came "to regard a life with private cars and weekend bungalows as no more than their due." In the Philippines the first wave of large-scale graft hit the nation immediately after the liberation from the Japanese occupation. Soon there developed a pyramid of grafters extending from "the petty fixers who hang around government offices," through "middle-level officials who profit from fake vouchers," to "an elite . . . whose profits from corrupt transactions with the government run into millions of pesos, but whose high positions or powerful connections render them virtually untouchable by the law enforcement authorities."[2] The fairness of linking independence to "increase of corruption" in this manner might well be challenged from the perspective of more functional modes of analyses, but it nevertheless constitutes an analytically important historical baseline.

Systems with "Hard State" Traditions

It is significant that whereas an American political scientist like Riggs feels it necessary to develop complex models of "prismatic" societies in order to analyze Asian bureaucracies, a Swede like Gunnar Myrdal employs more familar and simpler terminology. He just calls them "soft states." This concept is meaningful to citizens of countries like Sweden, Holland, and Germany, which traditionally have had "a high degree of stateness," in a way that it would not be to an American. As Peter Nettl wrote in a brilliant article:

> The concept of state in the fullness of the European intellectual and historical tradition had a life and character of its own, which was capable of affect as well as effect . . . The essence of the concept was always its impersonal nature; the state was never to be wholly identified with the individuals holding power within it. This is perhaps the most important of all the differences between those political traditions that incorporate the notion of the state and those that do not.[3]

In "hard state" political systems the state is not just a "ragtag synonym for government" but an arena of societies that has great autonomy vis-à-vis other collectivities. The integrity of civil servants in a "hard-state" political system rests primarily on their consciousness of being members of a special class, distinct from other classes in that their oaths bind them to render faithful service to the state and the public welfare. In Germany their high status led them to develop

---

[2] Orofre D. Corpuz, *The Philippines*. Englewood Cliffs, N.J.: Prentice-Hall, 1965, p. 86.

[3] J. P. Nettl. "The State as a Conceptual Variable?" *World Politics,* 20:4 (July 1968), p. 575.

disdain for the favors of other classes, to the point where, in Eschenburg's words, groups such as businessmen "did not even dare to offer them."

H. A. Brasz, a Dutch author, also enunciates a typical "hard state" view when he writes that "the best guarantee against corruption seems to me to lie in a hierarchical structure of govenrment." (See Selection 23.) Primacy of Dutch rules against private-regarding behavior is underlined by the fact that no less basic a document than the Constitution requires parliamentarians to swear that they have not and will not accept "any presents directly or indirectly from any person whatsoever." Dutch policemen, indeed, are even forbidden to accept cigarettes. Certain "soft state" practices in America cause Brasz to lift his eyebrows, and in commenting on an American colleague's investigation of American administrative behavior he is obviously somewhat scandalized by the offhand way in which the researcher took his subjects' avowals of honesty at face value. As part of postwar European sociopolitical development, the underpinnings of "hard state" practices and outlook have become somewhat eroded. Particularly in Germany the state has "softened" considerably, and Eschenburg links this phenomenon causally to the higher incidence of acts of bureaucratic corruption, which he analyzes and bemoans.

Systems with "Low Stateness" Traditions

Whereas on the Continent sovereignty became closely linked to the notion of state, this did not occur in England or the United States. The fact that public bureaucracies are the modern institutions most closely identified with "high stateness" traditions helps to explain why a rationalized public service developed so much later in these countries. Both political cultures had strong local and self-government traditions, which nourished the decentralization of power and impeded the reification of sovereignty. Particularly in the United States civil servants were denied the higher status accorded them in "high stateness" countries. As Tocqueville noted in 1831, American public officials could gain community acceptance of their authority "only on condition of putting themselves on a level with the whole community by their manners."

Both countries paid for decentralization of authority and status by having to tolerate patronage systems and widespread official corruption longer than other major Western countries. Britain dispensed with much (though not all) of this heritage with the adoption, starting in the 1830s, of a disciplined national party system and a rationalized civil service bureaucracy more on the Continental pattern. The civil service then became a major profession like medicine, the law, and the church, whose members came to accept and enforce corporate standards of ethics. Of those who entered the higher Administrative Class, only a very small number, perhaps less than 10 percent, left to take any other form of employment before retirement.

The United States, after decades of impassioned and moralistic debate, followed Britain's lead and largely copied its model legislation by introducing the "merit" system at the federal level through the Pendleton Act of 1883.

However, Congress refused to adopt those provisions of the British model that, by setting age and other restrictions on entry opportunities, and by strengthening tenure and other inducements to stay in the service, encouraged the development of a permanent body of civil servants with little or no turnover in personnel. "Our whole system abhors perpetuity," cried a senator at the time the legislation was being considered, and subsequent legislative and judicial actions tended to emasculate the "lifetime career" attractions even of the Federal service. Consequently American civil servants remained a loose and flexible social group, whose turnover and mobility remained almost as high as in the private work force. Also, lacking any special social status, American civil servants did not develop anything like the esprit de corps through which European bureaucracies policed their own ranks. This held true especially for the lower echelons of American public service, where patronage prevailed much longer. As Walter Lippmann wrote of such lower-level public officers in 1930 (see Selection 29):

> What can public office give to them except a job at a meagre salary, an opportunity to prosper a little on the side, a sense of importance in their neighborhood, and the excitement of working for the winning team? At the base of the political structure there are no adequate motives to give meaning to the conception of public office as a public trust.

OFFICIALS, PUBLICS, AND INTERESTS: THE PREVALENCE OF CORRUPTION IN AMERICA

Historians and political scientists who were shaped in "hard state" traditions frequently note and implicitly deplore the tolerance with which many educated Americans, including academics, approach problems of political corruption at home as well as abroad. Thus Jacob van Klaveren in Selection 26 recalls how at a gathering in Thailand an American comforted Thais being criticized by Europeans for the prevalence of corruption in their country by expounding uncritically about the prevalence of corruption in the United States. The American case is of universal interest precisely because America has, on the one hand, tolerated a much greater prevalence of administrative corruption than has Europe, and on the other, is so widely admired as a model by policy makers in developing countries. European advisers who, like Myrdal, argue that the new countries should give top priority to eradicating official corruption have difficulty fitting the American experience into their argument. Sometimes they offer a sinister explanation for the lack of recent research on American corruption, as in the case of Van Klaveren.

Admittedly past American writers have had difficulty in trying to pose the right questions. "How is it possible to reconcile with the good sense and business capacity of the American people the growth of governmental arrangements so antagonistic to rational principles of organizations?" asked H. J. Ford in 1905 (Selection 28). He confessed that he never found the answer. In 1914 Walter

Lippmann tried to apply a "systematic and scholarly" approach to developing "some quantitative sense of the number and kinds of acts that are called corrupt." He found this "an impossible task" and "abandoned the attempt with the mental reservation that if anyone really desired that kind of proof, a few German scholars, young and in perfect health, should be imported to furnish it."[4] In subsequent decades many German scholars immigrated to the United States, but none of them were led to this topic. So in 1959 Van Klaveren complained again that he had not found much help in the recent writings of his American colleagues on the difficult question of why corruption continued to be "systematically practiced" in the United States long after it has virtually disappeared in Western Europe.

Therefore, we shall here briefly review what lines of response the literature does contain to Van Klaveren's broad question, noting how emphases vary between writers reared in "high stateness" and "low stateness" traditions.

Premature Democratization in a "Low Stateness" Setting

Van Klaveren seeks to answer his own question by suggesting that perhaps universal suffrage was extended "too early" in a polity that had not yet become a "true nation." Since Americans did not trust public servants clearly to pursue the public or collective interest, they placed a low value on honest administration. In the egalitarian society of the Western states, in particular, the uneducated majority set the mores of "grab as grab can," and in succeeding eras of high capitalism and large-scale non-Anglo immigration these private-regarding values were perpetuated.

A "low stateness" writer like Robert C. Brooks in Selection 51 cast similar variables into a quite different equation when he compared the prevalence of vote buying and boodling in Prussia and the United States in 1910. The absence of these practices in Prussia, he claims, is due to the fact that "the local government of the country is kept closely in the leading strings of the state." He continues:

> Paradoxical as it may seem, it is nonetheless true that political corruption implies the existence of political virtue; it implies trust in the performance of duty, widespread obligation to perform it, and confidence that in the great majority of cases it will be performed in spite of the dereliction that such conditions occasionally entail. If monarchies are less corrupt than democracies, it is also true that monarchies do not repose so much faith in the fundamental honesty of their citizens as do democracies. At least they do not put it to such severe political tests.

Other Puritan reformers of the period strongly believed that virtue was polarized among the old Anglo-Saxon stock, vice among the newer immigrants; but Brooks admits that many of the "better class of immigrants must have been debauched by contact with corrupt influences."

---

[4] Walter Lippmann, *Drift and Mastery*. New York: Holt, Rinehart and Winston, Inc., 1914, p. 7.

Unworkable Institutions

Institutional weaknesses loom largest in the explanatory attempts of the earlier American writers. Ford emphasizes that the doctrines of checks and balances and separation of powers were colonial imports and that the governmental arrangements they fostered were similar to those "at the bottom of the past corruption of English politics." He recognizes that the conversion of appointive into elective posts exacerbated the problems of overlapping jurisdictions, leaving the public "with no embodiment of authority capable of giving it complete representation or of assuming full responsibility for results." That, of course, is where the boss and the machine came into the picture, and during self-righteous periods of reform Americans could focus their wrath against these objects with all the ideological momentum that propelled anarchists in "high stateness" societies to inveigh against the "state" and its beribboned heads. At most other times, however, American judgments about the individuals who operate the institutions have been remarkably charitable. James Q. Wilson in Selection 30 attributes to a widely held theory the assumption that "public officials are only human. . . They are not angels . . . and cannot be expected to be honest when others are stealing (no one wants to be a fink) and superiors are indifferent." And whereas Van Klaveren blames the low public morality of Americans for tolerating bad institutions, Ford held, in a comforting way, that "it is highly creditable to our practical capacity for government that we are able to work [them] at all."

Values: Progress at any Cost

Ford eloquently expressed a variant of "low stateness" *Weltanschauung* in the process of defending business leaders against Lincoln Steffens' criticism of their lack of support for "good government" movements of his day. He suggested that it was "better for a city government to lend itself to the operation of the forces of progress even through corrupt inducements than to toss the management of affairs out upon the goose-common of ignorance and incompetency, however honest." In an inspired flight of fancy he envisioned the judgments of future archaeologists who might evaluate the evidence of American big-city culture. "Most assuredly," he believed, they would "rejoice" that "men of affairs in our time corrupted government in securing opportunities of enterprise," for "it is better that government and social activity should go on in any way than they should not go on at all. Slackness and decay are more dangerous to a nation than corruption."

The most typical "hard state" response to this line of argument has been the suggestion that America flourished economically not because, but in spite of, its toleration of lax administrative morality. An immensely wealthy country was in this view unique in being able to afford a vast amount of waste and malinvestment. Max Weber expressed this position well in *Politics as a Vocation:*

> In America the spoils system . . . has been technically possible because American culture with its youth could afford purely dilettante management. With 300,000 to

400,000 such party men who have no qualifications to their credit other than the fact of having performed good services for the party, this state of affairs could not exist without enormous evils. A corruption and wastefulness second to none could be tolerated only by a country with as yet unlimited economic opportunities.[5]

"Folklore" and the Scale of Corrupt Practices

Revisionist historians such as Ari Hoogenboom delight in exploding the allegations of earlier muckrakers and fellow historians (see Selection 27). They suggest that many frequently cited examples of Gilded Age corruption are "of questionable validity," that historians have applied the term *corruption* "too loosely," and that "out" intellectuals blew "in" politicians up into monstrous size via use of "devil theories." Many of these criticisms are valid and follow upon Robert C. Brooks' finding that the term *corruption* was one of the most abused and ill-defined in the turn-of-the-century American political vocabulary. However, they go too far when they tend to suggest that governmental corruption was more of a problem in American rhetoric than it was in actual social and political life.

Again, however, it is a "hard state" author like Myrdal who asks that the "folklore of corruption" not be dismissed as meaningless: "This folklore has a crucial bearing on how people conduct their private lives and how they view their government's efforts to consolidate the nation and to direct and spur development. . . ." He suggests that it be studied as to whether it reflects "a weak sense of loyalty to organized society. Is there, in other words, a general asociality that leads people to think that anybody in a position of power is likely to exploit it in the interest of himself, his family or other social groups to which he has a feeling of loyalty? If so, people's beliefs about the corruptibility of politicians and administrators would be in part a reflection of what they would like to do, given the means." These reflections were written in the context of an analysis of South Asia (Selection 22), and are clearly applicable to communities like Montegrano. They may also be uncomfortably relevant to such American settings as Wincanton (as reported by Gardiner in Selection 17).

CORRUPTION IN THE PUBLIC SERVICES OF AFRICA

Many African countries seem to have taken the place of big American cities of a century ago as a prime example of situations in which corruption is so firmly "built into the constitution" that it is in practice virtually impossible to distinguish legitimate administrative functions from the "black market" bureaucracy. Norms regarding the use of public offices and approaches to definitions of the public interest that were superficially imposed by the colonial rulers have in many places been sloughed off so completely that the comments of preindependence "old hands" are in many ways very comparable to the bitter

[5] Max Weber, *Politics as a Vocation.* Philadelphia: Fortress Press (Facet Books Social Ethics Series, 3), 1965, p. 108.

Gilded Age comments by a scion of an American aristocratic founding family like Henry Adams. The parallel extends to the scope, and particularly the flagrancy, with which particular corrupt practices are carried out even at the highest levels, as though it were not necessary to disguise pilferage since potential censorious publics were nonexistent or inarticulate.

Party Dominance over Administration

The virtually "stateless" nature of the prevailing governmental superstructure in both the American and African settings is best exemplified by the total domination of party over administration. Within the context of essentially noncompetitive one-party systems, the ability of civil servants to maintain objective standards of duty to office in the face of intense party pressures has been especially low in Africa. Most African civil servants had much less opportunity to internalize Western administrative norms because in the colonial period they had been elevated to higher positions to a much more limited extent than in countries such as India and Burma. This could lead to the situation sketched by Andreski, in which "a few well-trained administrators and officers, whose indoctrination with the impersonal bureaucratic virtues had made some progress, were surrounded by half-baked new-comers, and became subordinated to politicians who had reached the top by demagoguery and huckstering."

Insofar as African politicians utilized mass party organizations to win governmental power after independence, they found it necessary to support a vast network of party employees and hangers-on. As in the American situations, some could be placed directly on the civil service payroll, but to support the rest African leaders had many fewer resources to tap than did American city bosses. Thus, whereas in the American setting rich local firms could be "squeezed" in return for franchise and license privileges, equivalent African enterprises were few and poor. The American practice of levying "assessments" on civil servants' salaries had also not proved very feasible in Africa, perhaps in part because the kinship obligations of officials left no salary remnants to be "reclaimed." Increasingly, therefore, African leaders took the easy way out by directly draining the public treasury in order to support their party networks. Thus the £14 million drained from the treasury of the Nigerian Western Region Marketing Board to support the Action Group party left that agency so impoverished that it had to borrow in order to carry out its routine functions. In Ghana, President Kwame Nkrumah was even more direct in diverting public funds and requiring "kickbacks" from foreign contractors in order to finance his party and to build up his foreign bank accounts.

Kinship Loyalties and Obligations

A crucial factor contributing to the much greater prevalence of small-scale corruption at the middle and lower echelons of African officialdom is the imposing strength of the counterconceptions regarding the purposes of public offices, which challenge the official conceptions. For traditional social obligations place the African official much more at the mercy of the demands of his kinfolk and clansmen than was the case at the turn of the century for the American municipal jobholder, whose receptivity to the requests from his family and ethnic group knew definite limits. The list of services that a successful African official is expected to provide his extended family—ranging from the finding of jobs and scholarships to the provision of feasts and lodging for visitors—is truly staggering, and attests to the strength of the counterconception that the main purpose of the successful official is to pull his family and clan up toward his status level in the modern and urbanized sector of the society. Since the official cannot begin to meet these obligations out of his salary, he must seize all opportunities to charge "black market" prices for public services. Even then, he scarcely gets a chance to build up a personal fortune, because, in Wraith's words, "he grows no richer because the more he earns, the more people he must share it with" (Selection 33).

In this context Andreski's distinction between "solidaristic" and "egoistic" graft is much more useful than Plunkitt's[6] distinction between "clean" and "dirty" graft. An official whose education was financed from the small contributions of his kinsmen obviously feels that he cannot reject their expectations of preferment when he is in a position to repay favors. In a sense he is a victim of the high status that the "hard state" colonial powers bequeathed to public positions, for an official in Tammany Hall would not have appeared nearly that much of a boon to his impecunious relatives. In the present generation only a very few officials living in the more cosmopolitan settings of the large West African cities appear to be in the position to reduce their "solidaristic" obligations. Whether they shift their energies more to the extraction of "egoistic graft" (as they do so) or reduce corrupt practices in order to approach the "Western" normative model more closely would seem an interesting question, which, like so many other aspects of this problem, published research results do not answer.

Differences between the African and Western Situations

The extensive critical discussion that followed upon Wraith and Simpkins' suggestion that African corruption might somehow evolve out of sight naturally in the way that nineteenth-century British corruption did emphasized several very vital distinctions between the two situations. One of these arises from the fact that in Africa as in other developing areas the public bureaucracy today plays a much more dominant role in the total context of society and economy than Western equivalents did in the "low stateness" societies, particularly during an era when Liberalism was at its apogee of influence. Whereas in the one setting economic development was dominantly financed through private entrepreneurial skill and capital, in Africa the overwhelming portion of development capital is funneled through the public administration. The development prospects of many African countries have been made dependent upon the attainment of development targets, and as Colin Leys suggests in Selection 34, "if the top political elite of a country consumes its time and energy

[6] Plunkitt is the Tammany politician in William F. Riordan's *Plunkitt of Tammany Hall.* New York: Knopf, 1948.

in trying to get rich by corrupt means, it is not likely that the development plans will be fulfilled." The second crucial point is well encompassed in Leys' question: Where are the Puritans to come from? Anglo-American nineteenth-century societies contained strong middle-class groups, which by virtue of religious conviction, political ideology, and social position had strong motivations to expend vast energies in relatively altruistic endeavors to reveal existing malpractices and to generate vast reform movements. Those who know Africa well find it difficult to perceive which African groups can in the course of the foreseeable future supply analogous services. To date, Puritan impulses seem only to have become apparent in the decrees imposed after military takeovers replaced large portions of the incumbent political elites. And often the military puritans, as in the case of Abboud (Sudan), Soglo (Dahomey), and Ankrah (Ghana), have had considerable difficulty maintaining their standards after a period in power.

CHAPTER FOUR

South and Southeast Asia

19. Sociological Aspects of Corruption in Southeast Asia[1]

W. F. WERTHEIM

There is often a considerable discrepancy between the significance of a social phenomenon and the attention paid to it by sociology. One greatly neglected phenomenon is that of corruption. Though a favourite subject for club conversation and newspaper headlines, it has so far received remarkably little attention from professional sociologists. As a result, the current concept of "corruption" is still enmeshed in emotional reactions and popular notions; it hardly reflects any real understanding of the historical roots and social significance of the phenomenon.

This explains how it was possible for an experienced sociologist like Raymond Aron to consider corruption in the state apparatus to be one of the most important causes of revolution.[2] He could have asked himself whether the argument should not run the other way. The truth is, rather, that in a revolutionary situation the accusation of corruption is raised because it has always proved to be an effective weapon. Clearly Aron still takes his point of departure from the popular notion that there must be a necessary and logical connection between corruption and the fall of a régime or dynasty. Yet as early as twenty-five years ago Van Leur wrote that corruption does not necessarily impair the efficiency of an administration. A corrupt régime can be quite viable and function smoothly, says Van Leur—leaving aside its "right of existence": that is not an historical question, but a political and ethical one, a value judgement.[3] Indeed, world history has known many régimes which have enjoyed periods of stability, and even of prosperity, in spite of practices that would nowadays be called corrupt—or should one even say, because of such practices? One example is the United States at the end of the nineteenth century: the army that waged the "Comic Opera War" against Cuba exhibited a "record in bureaucratic corruption, inefficiency, and bungling."[4] But if corruption flourished, so did the United States, where the Americans were in the process of realizing Adam Smith's prediction, made as early as 1776, that they would create "one of the greatest and most formidable (empires) that ever was in the world."[5]

When therefore corruption in many

1 The author expresses his gratitude to Professor Harry J. Benda of Yale University for his critical remarks and his kind assistance in editing the present text.

2 In a paper on the problem of rebellion and revolution, read at the Fourth World Congress of Sociology, Stresa, 1959.

SOURCE: W. F. Wertheim, "Sociological Aspects of Corruption in Southeast Asia," *Sociologica Neerlandica*, 1:2 (Autumn 1963), pp. 129–152. By permission of the publisher, Royal Vangorcum Ltd.

3 J. C. van Leur, *Indonesian Trade and Society: Essays in Asian Social and Economic History* (The Hague & Bandung, 1955), pp. 287–288.

4 Jacob Presser, *Amerika: Van kolonie tot wereldmacht* (America: From Colony to World Power; Amsterdam, 1949), pp. 399–400.

5 Presser, p. 406.

newly independent non-Western countries hits the headlines at home and abroad, sociologists should not be content with the shallow judgement that it is a portent of the imminent collapse of those countries, even though the prediction as such may be right. Rather should we analyse the phenomenon within its own historical setting, taking into account the social forces which brand as corruption practices which in the past may not have been experienced as such.

This brings us to the crucial question: What do we mean by corruption? In present-day language we usually associate this concept first and foremost with the readiness of officials to accept bribes. "In everyday life corruption is taken to mean that a public servant abuses his official power in order to procure for himself an extra income from the public."[6] It is true that the concept also implies bribery of persons other than public servants, *e.g.* politicians, trade-union leaders, journalists, members of the liberal professions, electors, and, most important, employees of private industry; it was largely to counteract this last form of corruption that the British Bribery and Secret Commissions Prevention League was set up. But here I shall for the most part limit myself to a study of corruption of public servants in the countries of Southeast Asia. There, owing to the rapid growth of the administrative apparatus, which sharply contrasts with the underdeveloped state of private industry, corruption of public officials is of far greater significance than any other form. With the rapid increase of limited liability companies in Western Europe, corruption in private industry became a problem of alarming proportions only from the second half of the nineteenth century onward. Administrative corruption, on the other hand, is an age-old problem which has cropped up wherever an extensive bureaucratic structure of public services has existed. Therefore, although outside the official sphere the problem is not essentially different, corruption can best be studied in its official form, which has its roots in centuries-old traditions.

According to the common usage of the term "corruption" of officials, we call corrupt a public servant who accepts gifts bestowed by a private person with the object of inducing him to give special consideration to the interests of the donor. Sometimes also the act of offering such gifts or other tempting favours is implied in the concept. Extortion, *i.e.* demanding such gifts or favours in the execution of public duties, too, may be regarded as "corruption." Indeed, the term is sometimes also applied to officials who use the public funds they administer for their own benefit; who, in other words, are guilty of embezzlement at the expense of a public body. This problem I prefer to leave outside the scope of the present paper. The specific feature of corruption in its most usual sense is that it involves two or more parties. This is also the fundamental reason why concrete cases of corruption are so difficult to trace; for there is as a rule no sign of it in the accounts of those concerned, and both parties are interested in keeping the transaction secret. Perhaps one might even see in such secrecy—as the Dutch sociologist H. A. Brasz suggested[7]—a criterion for the "corrupt" nature of a certain transaction: secrecy shows awareness on the part of those concerned that they are doing something which in the eyes of the society in which they live seems objectionable, a "corruption" of morals.

Favours from third parties accepted

6 Jacob van Klaveren, "Die historische Erscheinung der Korruption, in ihrem Zusammenhang mit der Staats- und Gesellschaftsstruktur betrachtet," *Vierteljahrschrift für Sozial- und Wirtschaftsgeschichte*, XLIV (1957), pp. 289–324, see p. 289.

7 See H. A. Brasz, "The Sociology of Corruption," Selection 3 of this volume.

or demanded by an official on behalf of members of his family or party, or of other personal connections, may be referred to as forms of corruption even if he does not directly benefit either financially or otherwise. In all these cases the crucial point is the conduct of officials who infringe the principle of keeping their public and private concerns and accounts strictly separate.

At the same time, however, this definition shows that what is nowadays meant by corruption cannot possibly serve as a universal sociological concept. For it presupposes a social structure in which the separation between these two kinds of account-keeping has either been carried through in actual fact, or else has been generally accepted by society as a criterion for proper conduct on the part of civil servants. Only then can the acceptance, or demanding, of gifts as a precondition for the bestowal of favours be regarded as a "corruption" of the prevailing standards of morality. Therefore a sociological analysis of corruption ought to be preceded by an historical treatment of the social awareness which brands certain types of conduct as corrupt.

In the above-quoted study Van Leur also wrote: "A modern, strict officialdom was only created with the Napoleonic state. Criticism of the integrity of eighteenth-century officials is thus *ex post facto* criticism."[8] Indeed, before the time of Napoleon public and private revenues were not kept separate as a matter of principle either in Europe or anywhere else in the world.

In the pre-Napoleonic period the predominant type of state, which in Asia even dates back to the pre-Christian era, was what Max Weber has called the patrimonial-bureaucratic state.

> Patrimonial relationships as the basis of political structures have been extraordinarily widespread . . . Princely possessions directly administered as territorial domains have always only constituted part of the ruler's political realm, which in addition embraces other territories which are not regarded as domains proper, but merely as subject to his political authority. . . . Whenever, then, a prince organizes his political authority . . . on the basic principles that apply to the exercise of his rule over his own domains, we speak of a patrimonial state structure. Up to the very threshold of the modern era and indeed in the modern era itself, the majority of large continental empires bear a rather pronounced patrimonial character.[9]

A particular feature of these patrimonial-bureaucratic empires is their broad agrarian basis. The peasantry produces primarily for its own needs, but part of the harvest is claimed by the rulers for the upkeep of the court and the maintenance of the urban population living in the environs of the palace. Besides this the agrarian population is required to render all kinds of services. In the process of further differentiation of functions and more rational organization involving increased clerical work and a growing hierarchy, the patrimonial administrative apparatus may take on certain bureaucratic features.[10] All the same, positions in the patrimonial structure continue to lack the bureaucratic separation between a "private" and a "public" sphere which distinguishes them from modern bureaucracy as a conceptual type. In a predominantly rural society dominated by a barter economy officials are not remunerated in money, but with a share in the produce of the land. This goes together with a far-reaching decentralization of the patrimonial rule, as the administrative pattern of the crown domains is copied in the more distant territories. Whereas the domains are subject to the direct control of the prince, the later territories

8 Van Leur, p. 287.

9 Max Weber, *Wirtschaft und Gesellschaft* (second edition, Tübingen, 1925), p. 684.

10 Weber, p. 695.

are merely under his political authority. Essentially what is found there is but a repetition of the same pattern in which the local lord maintains a court of his own by means of the tithes levied from the peasants and the services rendered by them. The peasants are not *taillables et corvéables à merci:* their tributary obligation is always largely governed by custom.[11] The local lord, for his part, in recognition of the prince's supreme authority, is obliged to pay a tribute to the latter's court, which has usually to be delivered once a year. At the same time he is required to supply the prince, on request, with manpower for large building operations or for wars. This call for agrarian manpower is usually confined to seasons in which it can be withdrawn from agriculture without much damage. Sultan Agung of Mataram (Java) used to conduct his wars, year after year, during the dry East monsoon. And in all probability the huge temples of Java were also built during a succession of post-harvest periods, as were the Chinese Great Wall and the Egyptian pyramids.

Among the large continental empires this type of conglomerative political structure was as of old the most widely adopted form; though its individual manifestations understandably exhibit a great many variations, there is nonetheless remarkable consistency in basic determinants. Even the Chinese empire, in spite of the uniformity of its officialdom, displayed, well into the modern era, these characteristics of a conglomeration of satrapies, some of them only nominally dependent, grouped around the directly governed central provinces. As in the Persian satrapies, also here the local authorities kept the revenues from their provinces in their own hands, defraying local expenditures in advance out of such revenues. The central government received nothing but its lawful tribute, any increase in which could only be affected with great difficulty and in the face of passionate opposition on the part of provincial interest groups.[12]

If the above picture of the early Asian empires, which is largely derived from Max Weber's works, is correct—and its correctness is confirmed not only by Duyvendak's study of China but also by such writers as Vella on Thailand, Schrieke on Java, and Leach on Ceylon[13] —then Wittfogel's representation of these ancient Asian empires as strongly centralized units over which the prince exercised "total power" would appear to be far removed from historical reality. Insofar as the rulers tried time and again to keep the local lords under control by force, this is not a sign of absolute power, but rather of weakness. Among the means tried to prevent imperial disintegration and to ensure the regular payment of tribute, Weber mentions the following: periodic royal tours; dispatch of confidential agents; demands for "personal guarantees" (in the form either of hostages or of regular appearances at the court); attaching sons of officials to the court as pages; putting relatives in important positions (which usually proved to be a double-edged sword), or just the reverse: appointing people of inferior class or foreigners as *ministeriales*; brief terms of office; exclusion of public servants from seigniorages over territories where they have landed property or family connections; attaching celibates or eunuchs to the court; having officials

11 Weber, p. 685.

12 Weber, pp. 710–711.

13 J. J. L. Duyvendak, *China tegen de Westerkim* (China against the Western Horizon; third edition, Haarlem, 1948), pp. 205–206; Walter F. Vella, "The Impact of the West on Government in Thailand," *University of California Publications in Political Science*, 1955, Vol. IV, No. 3, pp. 317–410; B. Schrieke, *Indonesian Sociological Studies, Selected Writings*, Part One (The Hague & Bandung, 1955), pp. 184 ff., Part Two, *Ruler and Realm in Early Java* (The Hague & Bandung, 1957), pp. 217 ff.; E. R. Leach, "Hydraulic Society in Ceylon," *Past and Present*, No. 15 (April 1959), 2–26, containing a thorough criticism of Wittfogel's theory; see *e.g.* on p. 5: "The investigator looks only for positive evidence which will support his thesis; the negative instance is either evaded or ignored."

supervised by spies or censors.[14] None of these expedients proved to be a panacea, and imperial unity was continually threatened from within by decentralizing tendencies.

This system leaves no room for corruption in the present sense of the term. In principle the local lord collects taxes and levies in kind on behalf of his own court. He does not have to render account of his income or expenditure to anybody. So long as he fulfils his tributary obligation to the satisfaction of the prince and shows no sign of rebelliousness, he is free to dispose of the assets he has collected. The limit to these is determined by tradition, which brands any increase in the charges as abuse. Transgression moreover gives rise to the danger of active resistance from the peasants. Therefore the prince arrogates to himself the right to call the local lord to account whenever he has reason to fear that the latter is becoming too independent or is endangering the continued obedience of the population by too heavy levies. In that case he will punish as "abuse" conduct which in the past may have been generally accepted as ancient custom.

> Anyone who enriched himself too much and too quickly aroused the envy and hostility of these overlords. What was considered too much or too quickly is not always clear. In any case "too much" was simply what others with sufficient influence regarded as such.[15]

Thus, although in the absence of any clear distinction between the private and the public spheres no accurate dividing line between custom and abuse could be drawn, accusations of corruption were nevertheless conceivable within this structure.

This links up with the fact that even long before the Napoleonic period certain trends came to the fore which eventually led to the emergence of new social norms. As early as the fourteenth century, Philippus of Leiden had tried, in his *Tractatus de cura rei publicae et sorte principantis*, to impress upon his prince the doctrine that he held the power bestowed upon him for the benefit of the community, and that he was obliged to exercise this power himself and not to delegate it arbitrarily to any other persons or groups. To the practice of exercising seigniorial rights for private purposes Philippus opposed a theory which boils down to the maxim "public right is public duty." Since then the development of various European empires has proceeded gradually in the direction of increasing bureaucratization, though in the *ancien régime* bureaucratic features in the modern sense did not yet predominate.

Similarly, in some Asian empires remarkable experiments were made in the direction of bureaucratization and defeudalization. For example, the introduction of the examination system in China, combined with the practice of temporary appointments of mandarins in the function of magistrate, were steps which strike us at present as surprisingly advanced. But even the examination system could not fundamentally alter the patrimonial character of the Chinese administration. Many officials still derived their income primarily from those under their control. In an economic system largely based on barter, with a poorly developed transport system, payment of officials in cash from the imperial treasury was difficult to realize.[16] How-

---

14 Weber, pp. 704–705, 708.

15 Van Klaveren, p. 322.

16 Still, from E. A. Kracke, Jr., *Civil Service in Early Sung China,* 960–1067 (Cambridge, Mass., 1953), one might deduce that in the period discussed by the author there have even been serious attempts to introduce a system of salaried officials paid from the treasury (see *e.g.* p. 83). On the other hand, even at that time "Among the most conspicuous complaints concerning officials of this period were low morale and venality, particularly in the lower ranks, traceable in large measure to

ever, in the eighteenth century new norms were coming to the fore, particularly in the European world. Increasing complaints of corruption—in France, in the Dutch Republic, in the Indies of the Dutch East India Company—do in themselves not necessarily imply that the phenomena we call corruption were becoming more widespread. They could equally well indicate that a kind of public conduct hitherto considered normal was now looked at with other, more critical eyes.

The patrimonial-bureaucratic type of state was clearly represented by the eighteenth-century Java of the Dutch East India Company. Though formally a commercial body, the Company bore in its main structure a close resemblance to a state organization. Its Java can in some respects be regarded as the successor to the seventeenth-century Mataramese empire, in which patrimonial-bureaucratic features were also apparent.[17]

In the eighteenth century the patrimonial-bureaucratic character of the Company's rule found a typical expression in the letters of the "transitional figures," Dirk van Hogendorp, to his brother Gijsbert Karel.[18] We owe to Mme Elisabeth du Perron-de Roos both the publication of this correspondence and the term "transitional figure," which stresses the fact that Dirk van Hogendorp, though himself still fully taking part in the patrimonial-bureaucratic system in the Indies, nevertheless in the course of his career developed a new sense of values, a "new conscience," which gradually made conditions from which he and others profited seem abuses.[19]

The nominal salary drawn by the employees of the Company was of merely symbolic significance. In the case of Dirk van Hogendrop it was such a trifle (80 guilders per month) that he made it over to his two unmarried sisters in The Hague, by way of pin-money. According to the Company's system employees obtained their rewards in a different way. Dirk's father had perished in a shipwreck on the way from Java to the Netherlands; probably his ship capsized as a result of being overloaded with contraband. According to Dirk's memoirs, this was quite a regular occurrence, thanks to "the corruption common to all branches of the Batavia administration and well-nigh legitimated by the detestable system of the Company to pay its employees badly, thus fostering unlimited cupidity . . ." Dirk's revenues as commissioner for the Extreme East of Java were also of a dubious nature. He excuses himself for them with the argument that "he could not live on the wind . . . Moreover such Charges had been imposed upon me that without Revenues I could not possibly meet them." Towards the end of the eighteenth century these perquisites of office were considered so normal that instead of receiving a nominal salary, an annual "office charge" had to be paid to the Company (in Van Hogendorp's case this amounted to more than four thousand rixdollars). In addition he had to pay

inadequate pay" (p. 196). The author also admits that "Many of the duties of local administration in the rural areas were carried out, under the guidance of these officials, by local functionaries who served without pay and who undertook such tasks as tax assessment, police duties, the management of storehouses, local public works, and the settlement of minor litigations" (p. 47). At any rate, it should be noted that, according to Kracke, China at an early stage "pioneered . . . in applying techniques to maintain honesty, discipline, and initiative—in other words administrative responsibility—among government personnel" (p. 1).

17 Schrieke, *Indonesian Sociological Studies,* Part One, pp. 184 ff., Part Two, pp. 217 ff.

18 Gijsbert Karel van Hogendorp became one of the outstanding Dutch statesmen. He played an important role in paving the way for the return of the prince of Orange as King William I of the Netherlands after Napoleon's defeat. His brother Dirk, on the other hand, served as a general under Napoleon, and died in exile.

19 E. du Perron-de Roos, "Correspondentie van Dirk van Hogendorp met zijn broeder Gijsbert Karel" (Correspondence between Dirk van Hogendorp and His Brother Gijsbert Karel), *Bijdragen tot de Taal-, Land- en Volkenkunde van Nederlandsch-Indië,* CII (1943), pp. 125–273, see pp. 133, 170–171.

two thousand rixdollars to the governor of the Northeast Coast of Java "in accordance with ancient custom," apart from other, similar payments. Legal and police expenditure were chargeable to his own account. All this, including his own upkeep, had to be paid for out of the same revenues that his predecessors had enjoyed, such as proceeds from "over-weight" in the levies of rice, profit from the sale of opium, gifts and fines from Natives and Chinese.

Elsewhere Van Hogendorp mentions the frequency with which such gifts are demanded from the native regents: on the arrival of the new commissioner; on each New Year's day; every time the commissioner's wife expects a baby; upon his periodical embassy to the governor general in Batavia; upon his periodical embassy to the governor in Semarang; on his departure; from each new regent he appoints. No need to ask who in the last resort had to bring in these gifts. No one could contract out of this system. Therefore, when on the basis of his new sense of values the militant "transitional figure" Van Hogendorp criticized the overlords in Batavia sharply in his "Address to the Dutch People," they were able to accuse him of the very abuses which under the prevailing system were unavoidable. This power of the central ruler to brand at will a custom as abuse fits in with the patrimonial-bureaucratic system.

After a century of growing awareness the Napoleonic reforms came as a revolutionary innovation. The French act of 17 February, 1800, created the administrative foundation of the great political edifice designed in the stern and symmetrical Empires style. "With this act," according to Presser, "Bonaparte threw a solid block of granite into the shifting sands of post-revolutionary France—not the only one, but one of the most lasting pieces. It was the well-known division into departments, *arrondissements,* and municipalities headed by prefects, subprefects, and mayors."[20] Though certainly not biased in favour of Napoleon, Presser nonetheless speaks appreciatively of the dutiful and sober conduct of the first draft of prefects. "Corruption under a dictatorship like that of Napoleon," again according to Presser, "is especially to be found at the top, within the leadership. It is centralized. It may easily go together with a high degree of devotion and disinterestedness among the lower ranks of the hierarchy"[21]—at any rate in the early days, before the rot had also penetrated further down.

The Napoleonic structure was of course not entirely new. It borrowed elements both from the Prussian state and from the reforms which immediately followed the Revolution of 1789. But the Napoleonic reforms were in any case the first to create the prototype of a state structure which Weber has called the "modern bureaucratic state." According to him, its main features are: a distribution of authority arranged systematically in accordance with generally applicable rules; a hierarchy of offices with a corresponding fixed order of procedural affairs dealt with in writing, and with minutes being kept; special qualifications for offices that presuppose a certain amount of training; the principle that an official's normal daily task should be the fulfilment of his duties, and that these various functions should be exercised according to more or less strict, exhaustive regulations that can be learnt.

As a result of this system tenure of office becomes a profession; the position of a civil servant bestows a certain social distinction; the civil servant is appointed by a higher authority, normally for life; he is remunerated in money, with a fixed salary and the right to a pension; the civil servant counts on a civil-service

20 Jacob Presser, *Napoleon: Historie en legende* (Napoleon: History and Legend; Amsterdam, 1946), p. 143.

21 Presser, p. 154.

career with a prospect of promotion according to rules of seniority, subject to the specialized qualifications required for a particular office.[22]

The bureaucratic structure, Weber holds, is everywhere a late development. It is possible only in an advanced money economy; technically it is more perfect than any other form of organization. The system aims at accuracy, quickness, written records, continuity, discretion, uniformity, strict hierarchy. One of its principles is that all cases are dealt with objectively, according to calculable rules and without respect of persons. Public and private matters are kept strictly apart, Philippus of Leiden's principle that public right is public duty being carried to its logical conclusion.

It is obvious that the preceding features are characteristic of the ideal type of a modern bureaucratic state, to which reality corresponds only in very rough outline. Thus the prefects of Napoleon's time were not entitled to a pension; and affairs were dealt with very sluggishly, since the various spheres of authority were not clearly defined, and unimportant matters had to wait for decisions at the highest level. Furthermore, the bureaucratic structure long continued to show a weakness in that the apparatus could function properly only with the safeguard of regular supervision. In the Napoleonic apparatus supervision from above was provided for, but the highest levels themselves were not subject to any supervision, and were thus exposed to the temptation of unbridled pursuit of gain. Even the institution of a supervisory body such as the Audit Chamber was no safeguard in itself; for who should keep the keepers? Not until late in the nineteenth century did the trend toward publicity in state affairs and government responsibility to representative bodies create the necessary preconditions for a serious application of the adage public right is public duty.

Still, the nineteenth-century atmosphere of modern bureaucratic government allowed the present concept of "corruption" as defined in the foregoing gradually to take shape.

Historical reality, however, never conforms to "pure types"—it always presents itself, as Max Weber put it, in mixed forms. The Netherlands East Indies government apparatus in the middle of the nineteenth century is a good example of such a mixed form, and an analysis of the situation there is the more interesting as it may lay bare the roots of present-day developments in many Asian countries. In that period once again a "transitional figure" played a part: Eduard Douwes Dekker, better known as Multatuli, the author of that famous *document humain, Max Havelaar*.[23] His difficulties and clashes with the official apparatus were partly due to the tension between a still predominantly patrimonial-bureaucratic indigenous substructure and a modern-bureaucratic European superstructure imbued with a new sense of values which was only slowly beginning to permeate that substructure.

Daendels had tried in vain to introduce the Napoleonic concept of government in Java. The Javanese princes and regents were not prepared to be demoted to the position of civil servants on the Western model and to surrender their traditional privileges as landed aristocrats. A major rebellion, commonly called the Java War (1825–1830), compelled the colonial government partly to restore the regent aristocracy to its old glory. Once more, their offices became hereditary in principle and they retained the right to all sorts of personal services from the population. Moreover they

---

[22] Weber, pp. 650 ff. (translated in H. H. Gerth and C. Wright Mills, editors, *From Max Weber: Essays in Sociology*; London, 1948, pp. 196 ff.).

[23] The best-known English translation is the one to which D. H. Lawrence wrote an introduction; it was published in New York, 1927. A new translation is forthcoming.

were rewarded, as were other groups of civil servants—including Europeans—by emoluments over and above their salaries. This extra income took the shape of a percentage of the yield of the crops, grown under a system of forced cultivation on government plantations in their districts—a typical patrimonial-bureaucratic form of remuneration. In the Priangan regencies (western Java) the so-called Priangan System was even maintained up to 1871; this system allowed the regents to keep their traditional revenues instead of receiving a salary paid by the government.

Only in an infertile area like Douwes Dekker's Lebak (southwestern Java) where government plantations were practically non-existent, did the regents and the lower-echelon indigenous civil servants have to make do with their salaries; but this was impossible if they wanted to live "in accordance with their social status." To secure the required income they stepped up the tributes and services demanded from the population to a level far above the latter's capacity. No wonder that an idealistic civil servant with a modern outlook like Douwes Dekker, who wanted to take a stand against such "abuses," could not help hurling himself against the powerful, traditional state apparatus—only to be crushed by it.

Towards the end of the nineteenth century, however, attempts were made gradually to bring the Javanese administrative infra-structure into closer accord with modern Western conceptions of government. The so-called *panchen* duties (domestic services due to native civil servants) were abolished. Henceforth the regents, and the chiefs of districts and sub-districts, were expected to live on their salaries. But this modernization failed to reach down to the foundation of the whole administrative structure, the village: the *desa*[24] headmen received no pay from the treasury and were rewarded for their services with a fixed percentage of the land tax collected by them, and with the proceeds of "official fields" which were specially allotted to them and worked by the villagers on a rotating basis. No wonder that the principles of modern administration had hardly begun to penetrate the sphere of the village economy, and that nothing was easier for a Chinese *batik*[25] manufacturer (or a European sugar-estate manager) than to induce *desa* headmen and *desa* police to round up female workers who had stayed away from work, and to return them to the *batik* factory—although they had no right to do so and the women often stayed away or absconded because of the abominable treatment they received.[26]

What was the state of affairs as regards corruption in the Netherlands East Indies administration? Towards the end of the nineteenth century in many areas conditions still prevailed which to Dutch ways of thinking were quite shocking, and which various publications have brought to light. Thus for example Opheffer mentions in one of his letters the Augean stable in the area of Rembang (central Java).[27] Dijkstra, himself clearly a somewhat odd character, wrote a pamphlet on the basis of his experience in the Lampongs (southern Sumatra), denouncing "The Corruption among Netherlands East Indies Officials."[28] In 1902 Van den Brand published a sensational pamphlet which dealt with the

24 *Desa*—Javanese village.

25 *Batik*—cotton prints made by a special technique, developed in Java.

26 P. de Kat Angelino, *Batikrapport: Rapport betreffende eene gehouden enquête naar de arbeidstoestanden in de batikkerijen op Java en Madoera* (*Batik* Report: Report on an Inquiry into Working Conditions in the *Batik* Workshops in Java and Madura; three volumes, Weltevreden, 1930–1931), II (Central Java), pp. 28 ff., 310 ff.

27 *Brieven van Opheffer* (Uplifter's Letters; third edition, Maastrich, 1944), pp. 339 ff. Opheffer was a pseudonym of a well-known civil servant, G. L. Gonggrijp.

28 J. F. Dijkstra, *De corruptie in de Nederlandsch-Indische ambtenaarswereld, of: Mr. Rhemrev als regeerings-commissaris* (Corruption among Netherlands Indies Officials, or: Mr. Rhemrev as Government Commissioner; Rotterdam, 1906).

methods used by the tobacco planters of the East Coast of Sumatra to secure the benevolent co-operation of civil servants. In general, the system was an indirect one:

> When Satan sets out to tempt, he hides his horns and carefully disguises his hooves and tail. A direct attempt at bribery is therefore rare. In the first place such an attempt is risky in itself, but what is more, it's stupid, downright stupid. The money has to reach the party concerned, but he must be able to give a plausible reason for its acceptance. . . . It is the general custom for a junior European administrative official who is transferred to another post to put up his belongings for auction. And the proceeds are largely determined by his relationship with the local planters during his—the official's—term of office. Obviously a magistrate who punishes the coolies severely at the slightest provocation, and at the same time deals extremely mildly with any offence committed by a European, is held in high esteem by his white compatriots. To express this esteem and show his appreciation of the administrator as a person, the wealthy planter gladly pays a hundred guilders for the pen with which the harsh sentence of his coolie was entered in the register. A pleasant keepsake, for sure.
>
> Look at some of the amounts that were spent some three years ago (*i.e.* in 1899) at the auction held by a civil servant who was leaving government service with a decent pension: five hundred and ten guilders for an ink stand, purchaser the chief manager of the Royal Company for the Exploitation of Oil Wells in the Netherlands East Indies; . . . three hundred and fifty guilders for a cigar-cutter, purchaser the chief manager of the Deli-Batavia Company; . . . six hundred guilders for a globe, purchaser the chief manager of the British Deli and Langkat Tobacco Company . . .

The Indonesian princes and Chinese headmen also offered incredible prices at these auctions—the princes, according to Van den Brand, "so as to be able to continue their oppression and extortion of the people"; the Chinese headmen because they controlled "the farming out of opium, pawnshops, and gambling leases, not to mention the fact that they owned nearly all the brothels."[29]

However, the *indirect* form that "bribery" takes in this case—the high prices paid at such auctions were especially intended to show the successor what he might expect if he took good care of the business interests in his locality[30]—is quite significant in itself. For in the course of the years the incorruptibility of the Indies civil service had come to be regarded as an indisputable fact. In this respect the Netherlands East Indies administration as a whole gained a reputation which closely approached that of the western European democracies. J. S. Furnivall, a noted authority on the pre-war Indies, wrote that in Java corruption was "practically unknown."[31]

He contrasted this with Burma, where during the same period corruption thrived so profusely that he devoted nearly eight pages to it.[32] His facts were primarily derived from a report published on the eve of the Second World War. The commission of inquiry doubted if among the civil servants of the two lower grades more than thirty per cent were honest. It was suggested that no less than two thirds of all police inspectors were corrupt; the excise officers were "by general consent the most universally corrupt." In the prisons "a prisoner could have anything he wanted except women; some said he could even have women." In the medical department false reports could be obtained for a consideration; ward servants deliberately treated their patients roughly if they were not paid. And so on throughout his survey of the various public services.

---

29 J. van den Brand, *De millioenen uit Deli* (The Millions from Deli; Amsterdam & Pretoria, no year), pp. 15–19.

30 J. van den Brand, *Nog eens: De millioenen uit Deli* (Once More: The Millions from Deli; Amsterdam & Pretoria, no year), p. 41.

31 J. S. Furnivall, *Colonial Policy and Practice: A Comparative Study of Burma and Netherlands India* (New York, 1956), p. 269.

32 Furnivall, pp. 170–178.

The most important source of corruption was stated to be the multiplication of all sorts of "welfare" measures which were disliked by the public. People readily made small gifts in order to escape such bothersome measures as vaccination, slaughter of diseased cattle, and building restrictions. The extension of the administrative apparatus created new opportunities for corruption. The general public was still unfamiliar with the difference between private and public interests: "even to this day the rural public frequently draws no distinction between payments to government officers which go into the Treasury, and those which do not. . . ."

One may well ask what was the reason for the difference between Furnivall's estimate of the situation in Burma and his opinion of conditions in Java. Was there a real difference? Or was it largely due to the fact that in Burma an official inquiry had been held, whereas in Java there had not been one? One should keep in mind that in general not only those who have been corrupted, but also those who do the corrupting have little cause for revealing their practices.

On the other hand it might be argued that such inquiries are the product of pressure on the part of a public that is convinced of the existence of large-scale bribery. In Burma this pressure came from nationalist politicians. No doubt Indonesian nationalists, too, would have used accusations of corruption if there had been the slightest chance of backing them up. The absence of such accusations in the often violent publications of the nationalists therefore argues in a certain sense against the existence of corruption on a large scale. Moreover corruption is furthered by a public opinion which takes it for granted that it is ubiquitous. For it is very risky to offer bribes to an official if the chances are that he will refuse them.

All the same there is enough evidence to justify the contention that Furnivall, in describing corruption as "practically unknown," idealized the actual conditions prevailing in the pre-war Netherlands East Indies. Patrimonial relationships were not confined to the *desa* economy: in the official apparatus, too, there were plenty of remnants of the traditional political structure. Thus the loyalties of Indonesian officials were still divided between state and family. To refuse a request from a member of one's family, whether for financial aid or for a job, was contrary to the moral code which still held good in Indonesian society. Hence Indonesian officials got into financial difficulties because, owing to their traditional family obligations, they lived beyond the means provided by their official salaries. The colonial government often had to overlook financial irregularities in its efforts to maintain its aristocratic props in their posts. Hence also the recurring complaints about "nepotism" among the regents.[33] The traditional Javanese custom of presenting those in high office with small gifts—a basket of fruit, a few chickens—also made it difficult to draw any sharp dividing lines. More serious abuses, judged by the standards of the public ethics of a modern bureaucracy, were not lacking either. They were found especially in the Outer Regions, where the Indonesian officials were less well trained and, more than in Java, entangled in *adat*[34] and family relations; where, moreover, the European officials, often far removed from the central authority, had to carry extremely heavy responsibilities.

Particularly in the twenties serious complaints were raised in the *Volksraad* (People's Council) about the acceptance of secret commissions—mainly in connection with contractor's agreements, for example by the State Railways. I quote from an article by D. M. G. Koch:

33 See for an attempt to justify the system: P. A. A. Djajadiningrat, *Herinneringen* (Memoirs; Amsterdam & Batavia, 1936), pp. 213–214.

34 *Adat*—custom, customary law.

Governor General Dirk Fock, who had gained the impression that corruption had deeply corroded the Netherlands East Indies administration usually so much praised for its integrity, had started a hunt for fraudulent officials and ordered a relentless prosecution of those who accepted secret commissions or committed embezzlement at the expense of the treasury. Sensational cases of dismissal from the service occurred, which created the impression that untrustworthiness had attained vast proportions and that it was creditable to take part in this hunt and to denounce people.[35]

Nevertheless Koch's statement in the same passage to the effect that the administration had a reputation for integrity is true, provided it is taken in a comparative sense by relating it to an Asian, colonial environment. Public morality was moving in a Western-bureaucratic direction, but many remnants of the traditional political structure were still there; and most important of all: insofar as the civil administration was incorruptible, this was due not so much to its Indonesian branch having been imbued with a new morality of complete loyalty to the colonial government as to a strict supervision exercised by the European authorities.

But perhaps there was also another reason why, during the first decades of this century, the phenomenon of corruption tended to disappear into the background. In the early days it was still very important for a private person to win the favour of a local administrator. Hence the collusion between planter and official to which Van de Brand drew attention—the outcome partly of solidarity among the whites, partly of the great power of the local authorities.

But the period prior to the Second World War saw an increasing concentration of business interests within large concerns whose claims could better be pressed in Batavia or in The Hague than on the spot. At the same time the influence of these concerns in government circles steadily increased. There was no longer any need for businessmen of importance to have recourse to the tricky method of bribery: they could achieve their ends equally well by legal means. When therefore in the twenties critics of Governor General Fock's régime complained that high finance was unduly favoured—the cancellation of a proposal to levy export duty on oil meant an annual loss to the treasury of well over fifty million guilders[36]—this criticism implied that businessmen managed to obtain their ends by perfectly legal means. The rubber policy during the period of the great depression, which was gravely attacked by Governor Van Suchtelen, also favoured the Western estate owners by "legal" means.[37]

At most one might speak—or rather whisper—of bribery by indirect means. But this no longer occurred on a small scale, as had been the case with the auctions on the East Coast of Sumatra at the beginning of the century. During the period of the growing power of the big concerns high officials who had served the business world well were rewarded by profitable directorships when they were pensioned off. In the public debates on the so-called Jambi affair, for example, the charge was made that a governor general and certain ministers had, in return for services rendered, been rewarded with prominent positions in the Royal Dutch Petroleum Company. In this case Minister De Waal Malefijt denied the imputation of corruption, but added:

35 D. M. G. Koch, "De zaak-Baljet" (The Baljet Affair) *De Nieuwe Stem,* XI (1956), pp. 484–491, see p. 484.

36 D. M. G. Koch, *Om de virjheid: De nationalistische beweging in Indonesië* (For Freedom: The Nationalist Movement in Indonesia; Djakarta, 1950), p. 76.

37 B. C. C. M. M. van Suchtelen, *Nederlands nieuwe eereschuld aan Indië* (The Netherlands' New Debt of Honour to the Indies; Hilversum, 1939).

Allow me to say that in general I emphatically disapprove of civil servants, who in their former posts were able to render services to a company, being offered high-salaried positions, and accepting them, even though in fact there is nothing wrong. Such offers create the impression that they are intended as a reward for services rendered, and might encourage slackness in officials who are still on active duty.[38]

So the situation began to develop along the lines described recently by an American sociologist: "Nobody any longer needs to be bribed. Every member of Eisenhower's cabinet has been a director of large corporations, with the exception of the secretary of labor."[39]

In the pre-war Netherlands East Indies a development could thus be noted which lagged behind nineteenth-century standards insofar as certain traditional elements continued to feature in the administration structure; on the other hand we also saw a typically twentieth-century development as a result of which nineteenth-century ethical standards ceased to be entirely adequate in the changing circumstances.

Against this historical background the problem of present-day corruption can now be analysed in further detail. Again I will confine myself mainly to conditions in Southeast Asia. There the world-wide phenomenon of corruption can be observed in its purest form, as it were.

Smith tells us that under President Quirino in the Philippines corruption extended from the lowest level of the civil service to the top, excepting the president himself. One could not enter government service without paying for it—small sums in the lower regions, considerable ones higher up. Criticism became so sharp that the president was forced to call a meeting to start a "clean-up campaign." But much of its effect was lost because a reporter had been listening under an open window and had overheard one of the president's closest advisers exclaim: "But what's the use of being the majority party if we can't have a little honest graft?"[40] This of course was promptly printed in the papers.

In Burma the political tensions within the large government party, which eventually led to military rule, predominantly centred around the question of corruption. Furnivall writes: "U Nu held that without drastic action to purge the party it would die a shameful if lingering death from the cancer of corruption. Others held that the remedy was more dangerous than the disease; it would entail a major operation and the patient would die under the surgeon's knife."[41] About Thailand we read: "The chief problems of the civil service at the present time are low salaries and corrupt practices," and "Corruption is probably more highly organized in the Police Department than in any other department. . . ."[42]

So if in a certain period of the history of post-war Indonesia corruption occupied the centre of attention, this was by no means exceptional in Southeast Asia. At most one might say that the country's pre-war reputation of being a favourable exception had been lost. But the situation in Indonesia during that period—covering the years from 1951 to 1957—also makes possible a closer study of the nature of post-war corruption and the form in which it appears. I

38 *De waarheid over Djambi* (The Truth about Jambi; pamphlet, n. p., 1921), p. 78.

39 Edwin Berry Burgum, "American Sociology in Transition," *Science and Society,* XXIII (1959), pp. 316–332, see p. 322.

40 Robert Aura Smith, *Philippine Freedom,* 1946–1958 (New York, 1958), p. 137. See further for an enlightening discussion of the corruption problem in the Philippines: Onofre D. Corpuz, *The Bureaucracy in the Philippines* (Manila, 1957), especially pp. 221 ff.

41 J. S. Furnivall, *The Governance of Modern Burma* (New York, 1958), p. 117.

42 Wendell Blanchard and others, *Thailand: Its People, Its Society, Its Culture* (New Haven, 1958), pp. 184, 198.

am not sufficiently familiar with local developments after 1957 (the year in which I visited many parts of Indonesia) to determine to what extent the situation in this respect has been remedied since.

First of all we have to take into account that the post-war forms of so-called corruption still frequently conceal relics of the traditional social structure. Village headmen for example are still unpaid, so that they have to maintain themselves by partly legal, partly illegal levies on the population. The patrimonial-bureaucratic substructure still influences all other sections of society, while traditional family ties continue to clash with modern concepts of morality in public affairs. Even as late as 1957 in several public services in western Sumatra it could be observed that all the personnel in one particular office belonged to a single family group: that of the office chief.

Besides these relics from an ancient past, however, post-independence corruption in Indonesia also had many typical post-war features. In the first place, under the direct influence of war, Japanese occupation, and revolution, the borderline between legal and illegal had become extremely vague and shifting. But even apart from the direct influence of war and revolution, new factors have been operating since the creation of the Indonesian Republic which promote corruption, or give it a new aspect.

One of these is the continuous extension of the duties of the public authorities. In the crisis years before the war a beginning was made with economic controls. During and after the war this process continued, as nearly everywhere else in the world, at ever-increasing speed. This gave rise to a new official apparatus exerting considerable power over the most varied sectors of the economy. Many of these services are manned by personnel without any schooling in the pre-war civil-service ethics. As in other Southeast Asian countries, the number of officials in Indonesia has multiplied: this is one of the many aspects of disguised unemployment. This leads, in turn, to serious underpayment of civil servants, which makes it not only a temptation but for most of them even a necessity to seek all sorts of supplementary remuneration.

In contrast with the extremely low level of living imposed by the salaries paid to officials is the demonstration effect emanating from the luxurious way of life of certain groups, such as foreigners and the new class of Indonesian traders and industrialists. Before the war the Indonesian officials and politicians considered the way of life of the European elite as beyond their reach. But since the Revolution much larger sections have come to regard a life with private cars and weekend bungalows as no more than their due.

Another factor which lends a new aspect to the phenomenon of corruption is that of party politics. During elections officials charged with the issue of numerous licences and permits took it upon themselves to make such favours dependent upon a donation to their party funds. The introduction of party politics has led to a spoils system—as was also shown by that conversation overheard in Manila.

Intervention by the army was regarded by many—in Burma, Pakistan, and Indonesia—as a means of putting an end to the political corruption. But experience soon taught that unlimited power in the hands of the army leadership, after an initial period of improvement, only tended to make matters worse. The regional commanders often start off with the best intentions, their action being provoked by the fact that the central government does not provide them with sufficient funds for properly discharging their duties. Thus for example it is known that the regional commander in Celebes conducted a large-scale contraband trade in copra with the Philippines in order to obtain the necessary foreign exchange. In 1957 I heard the following story: A Chinese trader from Menado (northern Celebes) told a friend in Jakarta of his intention to return to Menado. "But why, I thought you left there after the Revolution because you could do better business over here?" "Yes, in those days. But you know how it is . . . Here in Jakarta I have to tip five high officials to get a licence, but in Menado I only have to bribe one lieutenant."

Besides, in the countries of Southeast Asia business affairs are getting so much tangled up with the state apparatus that many transactions smelling of corruption are conducted by strictly "legal" methods. When representatives of foreign interests use part of aid funds for the benefit of high officials, for example by offering them expensive trips abroad, this could certainly rate as an attempt at "corrupting" these officials, though the action does not come strictly under the technical heading of "corruption."

The foregoing, mainly historical, survey was necessary because history and sociology, if they can ever be separated at all, are certainly inseparable in this case. We may now attempt to draw a number of theoretical conclusions.

In post-war conditions we find various factors which clearly foster the phenomenon of corruption, such as the moral disruption caused by war and revolution, the extension of government intervention in economic life, the low remuneration of officials, and the lure of the way of life of certain groups. Moreover the great publicity given to corruption tends itself to promote corruption.

However, there are also factors which point in the direction of changing social views and which may be regarded as indications that a new sense of values is breaking through. In the colonial era there could be no question of complete loyalty among indigenous officials in Java to a government which embodied the Western concept of the state. Under certain circumstances obligations towards relatives weighed at least as heavily. And the peasantry knew loyalty only towards their regent, hardly at all towards a central state apparatus of foreign origin.

The nationalist revolution was symptomatic of a new type of solidarity on a national basis. But this sense of unity has not penetrated deeply enough to guarantee strict loyalty from civil servants and citizens also in times of peaceful construction. The traditional particularistic loyalties are now seen to be too narrow; but an extended "quasi-universalistic" loyalty towards the Indonesian Republic is for many still too wide. Party politics make it possible for an intermediate loyalty to arise, loyalty towards a political party, which frequently overrides loyalty towards the state as a whole. Hence making the grant of licences conditional on the receipt of donations to one's party is not felt as an infringement of public-service morals. In the absence of a fully matured national conscience, loyalties also frequently attach themselves to ethnic entities: one is faithful not primarily to one's national leaders, but rather to those of one's own area or island. This lay at the root of the Nadjamuddin affair, a sensational case in what was the State of East Indonesia during the few years of federal government under Dutch control, when an ex-premier was tried for corruption without losing his prestige among his followers.

Such intermediate loyalty in conflict with loyalty to the Republic can also be due to faithfulness to a military leader under whom one has fought during the Revolution. The regional commander who maintains his own troops on the proceeds of so-called smuggling may be completely accepted by his followers. The way in which he demands levies and services from the population in his area often bears pronounced patrimonial-bureaucratic features—a relic from the past.

In contrast to these more or less particularistic loyalties a growing consciousness condemns as "corruption" actions which those concerned do not feel to be reprehensible. As in western Europe in the eighteenth century, present-day Southeast Asia is in a period of transition, during which value systems are gradually shifting. Moreover, along with the new set of values that is breaking through, much higher demands are made on the government than formerly. True, in the past many activities which in the Western world were left to private initiative, in the East were performed by the government. But this was largely done on traditional lines. The present world situation requires from the public authorities a dynamic and imaginative activity which is possible only if all loyalties are concentrated on this all-embracing social task. This new sense of values brands as corruption many formally legal instances of collusion between private persons and government officials, so that those most deeply impregnated with the new norms are even inclined to style the whole of Southeast Asian society as "corrupted."

It is this discrepancy between norm and reality, between expectations and shortcomings, which draws so much public attention to the phenomenon of corruption. The attempt to inculcate nineteenth-century standards of public behaviour into the civil administration founders on the one hand on the immature sense of loyalty of the public servant himself, and on the other on the multitude of demands made on him, which in a growing welfare state far exceed those which the nineteenth-century bureaucracy had to meet. Thus the lack of stability of the new Asian régimes is due primarily, not to the frequency of corruption, but to the discrepancy between social norm and reality—a permanent tension with a dysfunctional and disintegrating effect.

The foregoing also makes it clear why the fight against corruption in the new Asian states is such a labour of Sisyphus. In 1953 a high Indonesian official saw three possibilities: first, to shoot all corrupt officials—but that he thought too radical a measure; second, to imprison them, but that (and I quote literally) "would cause work to come to a standstill, as it is mostly minor officials that are involved" (it is interesting to learn that minor officials are more indispensable than higher ones); the third way, according to this "expert," was the best: "to introduce a new tax only payable by corrupt people . . ."[43] Apparently it did not occur to him that this would merely lead to higher tariffs . . . quite apart from the fact that most corrupt people are not in the habit of advertising their bad practices. But more intelligent experts, seeking a solution for example in stricter supervision, are also faced with insurmountable difficulties. Who is to keep the keepers? And, as we have seen above, to have recourse to a military dictatorship in the long run only makes matters worse by withdrawing government activities from public control.

All such measures fail because of their negative approach: they merely combat undesirable symptoms. The root of the evil is the lack of a more positive attachment to the government and of a spiritual involvement in its task in society, on the part both of the officials and of the whole community.

That is why the Chinese example is so instructive, for there a serious attempt has been made to encourage such a positive approach in all public servants—through education and propaganda accompanied by sharp measures against any deviation.

---

[43] *Indische Courant voor Nederland,* 24 November, 1953.

In 1951 a mass movement was started from above, popularly known as the "Three Anti's" and directed against the following evils in the public services: corruption, waste, and a bureaucratic outlook. But it is interesting that this action was soon followed by a new mass action, this time among the population and directed against similar activities regarded as harmful to the state: the so-called "Five Anti's" movement against bribery, tax evasion, fraud, theft of state assets, and leakage of state economic secrets.[44] These mass movements were accompanied by pressure on every citizen, from highest to lowest, to denounce any instance of corruption or similar abuse that had come to his knowledge—criticism and self-criticism in official terms, spying and brainwashing according to Western terminology. These campaigns moreover were conducted in an atmosphere in which Spartan simplicity, thrift, and discipline in private life were being stressed. The breaking off of practically all contact with the outside world and the expulsion of many wealthy foreign traders helped to eliminate the possible demonstration effect emanating from the way of life among social groups living in luxury.

The Chinese example also teaches us, however, that in an atmosphere of dynamic reconstruction the sharp distinction between public servant and citizen is in the process of disappearing. In the welfare state the public servant is required not only to keep public and private concerns strictly separate, dealing with the first in accordance with the prevailing legal regulations; a positive attitude and a dynamic activity in the interest of the community are also demanded of him. But the private employee, too, is no longer expected to be merely a faithful "organization man": he has to be conscious all the time of his social task in the community in which he lives, and conflicts may arise between these two loyalties.

This trend, though in many countries still quite weak, is of the utmost importance for the development of the concept of corruption. Just as in the eighteenth century a new sense of values broke through in keeping with the maxim public right is public duty, so now a new sense of values is developing that might be summed up in the adage private right is public duty. The idea of trusteeship which has recently been incorporated in all world religions and which implies that the owner in effect administers his property for the public benefit, is a clear indication that this new sense of values is not confined to Asia alone.

But in this light the situation in these Southeast Asian states which have so recently won their independence might be summarized as a tension between a past in which patrimonial-bureaucratic and particularist features strongly predominated and a universalist future aimed at socialization of the means of production. In their present condition of tension, these states cannot possibly find a secure foothold in a nineteenth-century official morality which is becoming obsolete.

44 Theodore Hsi-En Chen and Wen-Hui C. Chen, "The 'Three-Anti' and 'Five-Anti' Movements in Communist China," *Pacific Affairs,* XXVI (1953), pp. 3–23.

20. The "Sala Model" and Comparative Administration

FRED W. RIGGS

As we move toward an empirical science of public administration—as distinguished from a normative doctrine intended to guide us in administrative reform or development—we will need two kinds of knowledge: first, increasingly clear and relevant information about administrative practices, organization and history in particular countries; and secondly, more testable and tested hypotheses about causal relationships among administrative variables. Both types of knowledge should be useful in the practice of administration, but in the present context they are viewed as contributing to the growth of social, and especially political, science.

A basic tool in both kinds of inquiry—area study and theory formation—is the "constructed type" or "model." Everyone uses such models, whether implicitly or explicitly, to provide a frame of reference, "criteria of relevance," in order to select from the undifferentiated universe of sense experience the data which contribute to an organized body of knowledge. They provide the outlines around which we assemble descriptive country or area information—whether American, British, Indian, Cuban or Congolese—and they suggest relationships which we link together in our propositions, statements of causal interdependencies.

Hitherto the models upon which we have relied in political science and public administration are predominantly those derived from the study of America, Britain, and other Western countries. Because of the relative uniformity of environmental factors in all these countries, it is possible to study administrative institutions and practices as though they had an autonomous existence, apart from their environment or setting. Yet the "ecology" of public administration is as much a limiting factor as in the ecology of biological species or cities. When administration in non-Western countries is studied with the help of our non-ecological models with their implicit assumptions of institutional autonomy, or when generalizations taken from these models are applied to situations in the "underdeveloped" countries, they tend to crumble away. Hence I suggest that we need to construct alternative, ecologically based models to help us in the study of administration abroad. I make this suggestion in all modesty, quite aware that much research of value can be accomplished within the framework of the available models, especially if one makes full use of those developed by our sister disciplines, notably anthropology and sociology in which a "holistic" or ecologi-

SOURCE: Fred W. Riggs, "The Sala-Model: An Ecological Approach to the Study of Comparative Administration," *Philippine Journal of Public Administration.* 6:1 (June 1962), pp. 3–16. By permission of the *Philippine Journal of Public Administration.* Delivered at the 1961 Annual Meeting of the American Political Science Association, St. Louis, Missouri, September 6–9, 1961.

cal approach is used. However, I am persuaded of the utility of trying to supplement the existing models by attempting, consciously, to create some alternative types.

Our greatest strength lies in concepts and typologies designed for use in American and the relatively similar Western systems of government, where environmental influences are generally ignored. The social anthropologists and comparative sociologists have given us models particularly suited to the study of traditional or "folk" societies. But neither fit very well the conditions in developing countries with their mixture of tradition and industrializing-modernization. Hence I suggest our chief need is for an explicit model of transitional societies and their administrative sub-systems.

"PRISMATIC SOCIETY" AND THE "SALA MODEL"

I call one model for this purpose a "prismatic" system, not for the joy of using a new word, but because it enables me to impute to the model a limited number of characteristics, and hence to eliminate the clustering connotations that adhere to more familiar words like "underdeveloped" and "transitional."

The word itself is part of a larger system, in which polar types are used, based on definitions taken from structural-functional analysis. These terms are explained at some length elsewhere, and it would detract from this paper to repeat the discussion here.[1] Suffice it to say that the prismatic model is intermediate between a "fused," model, useful in studying traditional or primitive societies, and the "refracted" type, useful for analysis of government in advanced industrial Western societies.

Within the prismatic society one can construct sub-models for its various structures, e.g., its political, administrative, economic, social, religious. I call the administrative sub-model in a prismatic society, a "sala." The word is taken from current usage in much of Asia where a "sala" often means an office, but also a pavilion, drawing room, or place for religious meetings. I wish thereby to to symbolize the resemblance of a sala to the "office" or "bureau," which may be taken as the typical locus or "ideal type" of administrative behavior in the "refracted" model. At the same time the diffuse uses to which the sala is put suggest the multi-purpose, undifferentiated character of the "home" or "court," as locus of administration in a "fused" society, where, indeed, we cannot find a separate structure for administrative as contrasted with other functions of the society.

Heterogeneity

One of the characteristics of a prismatic society is a high degree of "heterogeneity," which is to say, a mixture of traditional, "fused" characteristics, on the one hand, and modern, "refracted" traits on the other. Hence a modern city with a sophisticated, intellectual class, Western-style offices, modern gadgets of administration, is typically found in the same country with rural villages run by "chiefs," "headmen," or "elders" whose political, administrative, religious, and social roles may be quite undifferentiated and traditional in character. The significant administrative features of a prismatic society, however, would not be brought to our attention if we merely looked for this mixture of traditional and modern institutions, even though we found plenty of examples of both.

Even more significant in the mixture might be a set of new administrative structures, different from both the traditional and modern, and product of the mixture. This new set of administrative phenomena is what I choose to call the

---

1 See, for example, "Prismatic Society and Financial Administration" in *Administrative Science Quarterly,* Vol. 5 (June 1960), pp. 1-46, and *Ecology of Public Administration* (Bombay: Asia Publishing House, and N.Y.: Taplinger, 1961).

"sala model." To repeat, the most characteristic administrative features of a prismatic society are to be found in the sala, but in the heterogeneity of a prismatic system, we will find the modern "bureau" and the traditional "court" as well as the sala. One problem of analysis in a particular situation is to find the proportions in which these structural features are mixed, and to explain the mixture. I believe that only afterwards can we manipulate intelligently, i.e., re-shape the mixture to match our goals and aspirations.

Formalism

What, then, are the essential features of the sala itself? Some are suggested by a second major feature of the prismatic model, i.e., a high degree of "formalism." By "formalism" I refer to the degree of discrepancy or congruence between the formally prescribed and the effectively practiced, between norms and realities. The greater the congruence, the more realistic the situation; the greater the discrepancy, the more formalistic.

In both traditional or fused societies, and in modern industrial or refracted societies, a relatively high degree of realism prevails. Not that complete realism ever exists. The degree of formalism in our own society is a measure, perhaps, of the extent to which we are not fully refracted, to which prismatic conditions are to be found here. Indeed, one conclusion to which I have come is that the American administrative system, especially in local government and in the more "underdeveloped" parts of the United States, is quite prismatic.

For the prevalence of formalism, to repeat, is a distinguishing mark of the prismatic system. In other words, the laws on the statute book are one thing, the actual behavior of the official is another. Not that the law is irrelevant to behavior. Indeed, the official may insist on literal performance of the law or he may disregard it utterly. What permits formalism is the lack of pressure toward program objectives, the weakness of social power as a guide to bureaucratic performance, and hence great permissiveness for arbitrary administration. Whether an official chooses to enforce a law to the letter or permit its total violation depends, presumably, upon his inclinations and his advantage.

It is easy to see that administrative discretion of this type opens the door to corruption. The client may have to pay the official to carry out the law—as in the issuance of permits, licenses, quota allocations—or to overlook violations—as in the payment of taxes.

Some implications for administrative reform should also be evident. If reform is based on a change in the law, a reorganization, re-definition of positions and duties, etc., probably no effective change in behavior will follow the change in norms and prescriptions. In a refracted model, by contrast, where a high degree of realism prevails, clearly, acceptance of a change of law or regulation can be taken as equivalent to corresponding changes in administrative behavior. Reasoning from the refracted model, the administrative specialist may conclude that similar changes in a basically prismatic system will have similar results. Were the specialist familiar with the sala model, however, he might consider such formal changes useless, and seek first to achieve a higher degree of realism, i.e., to bring about a closer approximation of practice to prescription.

Overlapping

A third feature of the prismatic model suggests even more implications for the sala, namely the phenomenon of "overlapping." By "overlapping" I refer to the extent to which formally differentiated structures of a refracted type coexist with undifferentiated structures of a fused type. In other words, it is typical in a prismatic situation for new structures—government offices, parliaments, elections, markets, schools—to be set up, but the effective functions of administration, politics, economics, education, continue to be performed, at least to a considerable extent, by older, undifferentiated structures, such as the family, religious bodies, caste and communal groupings. New norms or values appropriate to the differentiated structures are given lip-service, but the older values of an undifferentiated society still retain a strong hold. Thus overlapping implies a social schizophrenia of contradictory formal (conscious) and informal (unconscious) behavior patterns.

In neither the fused nor refracted models do we find substantial overlapping. In the refracted model, insofar as the structures realistically perform their "manifest functions," there is no overlapping. In the fused model, since there is only one major set of structures for all functions, there is also no occasion for overlapping. The concept is, perhaps, not an easy one to grasp in the abstract. I will try to illustrate it by several applications to the sala model.

NEPOTISM: THE SALA AND THE FAMILY

The sala is, formally, a locus for governmental administration. In a relatively refracted society, considerations of family loyalty are effectively divorced from the conduct of office. Indeed, the American administrative expert typically takes such a divorce so much for granted that he scarcely looks for it in studying or manipulating administrative behavior. In the sala, however, many administrative functions which were once performed openly under the aegis of familial or kinship institutions continue to be performed on this basis, but clandestinely. The new formal structures of an office are superimposed upon the family, and lip-service is paid to a new set of official norms.

One characteristic administrative result is the phenomenon of "nepotism." I do not think it appropriate to speak of nepotism in a fused society's administration. Here the family provides the formal basis of government. Positions are typically filled on a hereditary or "patrimonial" basis. It is scarcely appropriate to speak of nepotism when a king takes over by virtue of hereditary succession, but if an elected president or prime minister were to replace himself by a son or nephew, the epithet would be properly used. Similarly, we don't think of the inheritance of a small business by the son of the owner as nepotistic, but the appointment of close relatives to office in a large firm may be called nepotism.

My point is that in a fused society, hereditary succession to office is not nepotism; and in a refracted society, familial influence on appointments is negligible. Nepotism, however, is a characteristic mode of recruitment in the sala: characteristic because here patrimonialism is officially proscribed but actually practiced.

Overlapping of the family with the office occurs also in other aspects of sala behavior. The formal rules of the sala prescribe universalistic norms for the administration of the law, the general programs and policies of a government agency. However, family influence prevails, so that the law is applied generously to relatives, stringently against strangers. This becomes a matter of importance in law enforcement, the administration of contracts, purchase of supplies, enforcement of taxes, granting of licenses, foreign exchange control, import and export permits, etc. To the outside observer, the typical sala official appears "individualistic" or "anarchic" because he ranks his private and familial goals higher than the corporate goals of his agency, government or country.

"POLY-COMMUNALISM" AND "CLECTS"

In speaking of the family and kinship groupings I have over-simplified the basis of group solidarity. It is characteristic in a prismatic society for minority ethnic, religious or racial groups to become relatively "mobilized" for mass communications without, at the same time, becoming fully "assimilated" to the elite.[2] Such a condition produces several "communities" that live side by side in a relatively hostile interaction in the same society, "differentiated" in Deutsch's terms. Furnivall calls this a "plural society," but I prefer to speak of it as "poly-communal."

The development of poly-communalism has a characteristic impact on the sala. Whereas in principle a government office administers the law impartially as between or among all citizens, the sala official discriminates in favor of his own community and against members of other communities. Such discrimination affects recruitment. In other words, perhaps more significant even than nepotism is the tendency to fill positions in a sala only with recuits drawn from a dominant community. Alternatively, different offices may be appointed on a "quota basis" to the several communities, leading to mutual hostility, or noncooperation between the several agencies staffed by members of rival communities. When members of the different communities are mixed in the same office, obstacles to cooperative action also arise.

This characteristic feature of the sala is, in fact, found in America, especially in local administration in the South. The relations of the white and Negro communities of the South to each other are typical of poly-communalism. In the sala of the South, as in the sala in other countries, administrative recruitment and law enforcement predictably favor the "dominant" against the "minority" communities.

A further consequence of poly-communalism occurs in the organization of "interest groups." The refracted model leads us to picture interest groups in the form of functionally specific associations, open on a universalistic basis to all who share the group's primary goals. Such associations interact with political and administrative agencies to propose and help implement public policy in diverse functional fields.

An implicit assumption of such associational patterns, however, is open participation on a universalistic basis. In a poly-communal situation, however, group membership is typically restricted to a single community. Consequently, instead of a single chamber of commerce or trade union federation, a different chamber and federation appears for each community. The result: interest group activity is designed not only to encourage a particular policy but to apply that policy "selectively" for members of the favored community, against members of disfavored groups. Or, considered from the viewpoint of the sala, administrative recruitment and policy is oriented positively toward groups based on dominant communities, negatively against groups drawn from deviant communities.

Because these interest groups exhibit characteristics different in crucial respects from the associations of a refracted society, I think it is useful to have a special term for them. They share some of the characteristics of cliques, clubs, and sects, but none of these words exactly identifies the category I have in mind. Consequently, I have coined an expression based, mnemonically, on sounds common to these three words, i.e., *clects*. A clect may be defined as an organization with relatively diffuse functions of a semi-traditional type, but organized in a modern, associational way. Sectarian oppositional political parties and revolutionary movements in a prismatic society are typically clects. They provide their members with an alternative solidarity system to replace extended family, caste, village and religious units. They stand for a total way of life, and typically demand un-

2 These concepts were developed by Karl Deutsch in *Nationalism and Social Communication* (N.Y.: Wiley, 1953).

conditional loyalty of their members. Whereas one may belong to a variety of associations, he can belong to only one clect. Of course, not all members of a prismatic society belong to clects. Typically, only a minority do. But the clect provides a disciplined core for economic, political, religious and social action. Clects tend to be uncompromising and hostile in their relations to each other, and to the sala.

Thus we find the sala often involved in close relations with clects, or itself taking on clect-like characteristics. A particular government office or agency may be captured by a clect. Then overlapping manifests itself in unofficial orientation toward the dominant clect, despite an official mandate to serve the general public interest. An example would be an agency to regulate business conditions which favors a chamber of commerce and business men of the dominant community, at the expense of traders in "outsider" communities. Often this means that the dominant group gets special privileges, licenses, permits, foreign exchange, tax rebates. However, the recipients of these favors often do not use them, since an easier road to wealth lies in blackmarket collusion with members of the outside or "pariah" business community.

Officials in the sala also profiteer from this situation, either receiving a "rebate" or "kick-back" from the privileged clientele, or taking a "bribe" from illict entrepreneurs in the pariah community. Thus the clect-sala relationship serves to advance the special interests of an in-group as against the interests of an out-group in the same functional field, contrary to the ideal association-bureau relationship in which policy is shaped so as to advance the interests of all members of the society who share a particular functional goal or technique.

Sometimes a particular agency in the sala becomes itself a kind of clect. Once admitted, a member is treated as though he were part of an enlarged family. It becomes impossible to discipline or discharge a member, for example, just as a family would not consider expelling a member except for the most extreme reasons. Thus clect formation within the sala contradicts the achievement and universalistic norms, typical of a refracted government bureau or office. Here again overlapping means effective behavior contradictory to the prescribed norms of the sala.

ECONOMY—THE "BAZAAR-CANTEEN"

Elsewhere I have characterized the typical features of the "bazaar-canteen" as the economic sub-model of the prismatic society.[3] The bazaar-canteen is the prismatic counterpart of the refracted "market." Here typical price mechanisms are used for the exchange of goods, but they overlap with more traditional "reciprocative" and "redistributive" institutions,[4] resulting in behavior quite different from that expected in formal economic theory.

One of these characteristics is "price indeterminacy." Although there are other important typical bazaar-canteen traits, this one will illustrate the phenomenon of overlapping. In the refracted model, market conditions are assumed. Hence such aspects of administrative behavior as budgeting, salary determination, purchasing and price decisions are based on market costs and equalitarian assumptions. By this I mean that a government service which is for sale to the public is sold at the same price without distinction of persons to all citizens. The salary of officials is based on the relative value of work performed and the market cost of labor without regard to the personal identity of the incumbent.

---

3 See "The Bazaar-Canteen Model," *Philippine Sociological Review,* Vol. VI (July–October, 1958 [1960]), pp. 6–59.

4 These concepts are based on Karl Polanyi, *et al., Trade and Market in the Early Empires* (New York: Free Press, 1957).

In the sala model the same assumption is made formally, but it does not work in practice. As we have already seen, poly-communalism is typical. Hence public services are sold at preferential rates to members of the dominant community or inside clects, but at higher rates to outside clects, to members of deviant or minority communities. Often, however, a formal price is announced, from which secret deviations are made. Victims sign a contract for purchase, but pay an under-the-table bonus. Those selling to the government may receive the official rate, have to "kick-back" an unofficial percentage.

In salary determination or appointment to office, the family considerations which I have already mentioned lead to the creation of "sinecures," i.e., an official is named to a salaried position without having to perform corresponding duties, or with only minimal duties. Again, substantial "fringe-benefits" are offered to privileged incumbents beyond the official salary. Others who lack "influence" or "pull" find themselves assigned to lowly posts, denied promotion or salary increases, unable to obtain fringe benefits.

Corruption is institutionalized in the sala model. Some officials are in advantageous positions to extort bribes and other favors from clientele groups. Part of this extra income must be passed on to superiors or influential members of the bureaucracy who protect the "rackets." Outside positions as "consultants," the privilege of concurrent employment in private firms, plus other devices for augmenting income through the exercise of influence mean that the effective income and living costs of officials diverge strikingly from that officially sanctioned.

These are administrative counterparts to the economic bazaar, in which the actual price paid by a customer, after protracted bargaining, reflects not only prevailing supply-demand conditions, but also a super-imposed set of inter-personal relationships between seller and buyer. A wide fluctuation in the price of a commodity, depending upon the identity of the buyer, tends to prevail.

The canteen model refers to a situation in which uniform prices are actually charged, but prices vary widely between market-places. In some, the "subsidized canteens," prices are kept low for privileged members of an in-group; in others, the "tributary canteens," prices are raised for captive members of the out-groups.

Similarly, the sala makes its privileges available to in-group members at bargain prices, as when it seeks foreign exchange at the official rate to privileged businessmen of the dominant community. Penalized entrepreneurs of the "pariah" community are forced to buy at inflated prices in the "black-market," or obtain funds at official rates only after making informal bonus payments through extra-legal channels.

In a sense, the whole bureaucracy is privy to a subsidized canteen. Its privileges and status are a prize eagerly sought by ambitious individuals in the dominant communities. The proliferation of governmental functions, encouraged both by the first stages of industrialization and the rosy attractiveness of the "welfare state," give rise to rapid expansion of agencies, increase of offices, and conspicuous overstaffing. Yet at the same time, the economy as a whole remains poor, the national budget hopelessly unable to provide adequate salaries for all. The pitifully low salary schedule which results provides an economic incentive for capitalizing on every opportunity each encounters to augment his official salary from unofficial sources.

Whether in the bazaar or canteen form, then, price indeterminacy pervades the sala at all points where money is involved, in salaries and "fringe-benefits," contracts for purchase and supply of goods and services, in regulation of public utilities, customs and tax administration, budget making, accounting and auditing procedures, and the like.

Any analysis of the economic aspects of sala administration which accepts, at face value, the formal price structure will miss completely the effective price structure. The difficulty for analysis, of course, arises not only from the use of inappropriate models based on the assumptions of a refracted administrative bureau, but also on the formalistic discrepancy between the formally approved behavior, which is like that of the bureau, and the officially disapproved behavior, which is quite dissimilar. This consideration takes us to value systems in relation to overlapping.

21. The Dimensions of Corruption in India

John B. Monteiro

It is difficult to talk of the dimensions of corruption. As the Santhanam Committee itself admits:[1] "In the nature of things it is not possible to give even a rough estimate of the number of corrupt government servants or the amount of money or value or percentage of illegal gratification that may be involved. Statistics . . . would help in giving a measure of the prevalence of the malady. The statistical information . . . should not be taken as indicating an increase in the quantum of corruption. Increase in complaints, investigations, prosecutions, departmental proceedings, and punishment may mean more intensified fight against corruption than any increase in it. It should be also noted that all the complaints and vigilance cases do not relate to charges of bribery and corruption. Quite a number of them are in respect of other types of disciplinary offences."

Even when one approaches the statistics with an objective outlook, the figures are disturbingly large. The Government of India had 4676 complaints during the period 1 April to 31 December 1956. The number increased to 20,461 for the year 1962. The disposal of cases during the same period increased from 3716 to 16,178. At the end of 1962, there were 4283 cases pending before the Government of India. Tables 21.1 and 21.2 show the trends in this respect.

The complaints filed with the Delhi Special Police Establishment increased from 2733 in 1957 to 3847 in 1962. The majority of these complaints were signed or given personally by the complainants while some others were anonymous. Thus in 1962, of the 3847 total complaints, 2213 belonged to the first category while 1634 fell under the second category. Of

[1] Santhanam Committee Report, p. 14.

SOURCE: John B. Monteiro, *Corruption: Control of Maladministration*. Bombay: P. C. Manaktala and Sons Private Ltd., 1966, pp. 39–53. By permission of the author and the publisher.

TABLE 21.1
COMPLAINTS DEALT WITH BY GOVERNMENT OF INDIA

	Total No. for Disposal	No. Disposed of	Percentage of Disposal	Pending at the End of the Year
1956–1957	4,676	3,716	79.47	960
1957–1958	8,540	6,463	75.68	2,077
1–4–58 to 31–12–58	8,313	6,220	74.80	2,093
1–1–59 to 31–12–59	10,649	8,366	78.56	2,283
1–1–60 to 31–12–60	10,721	8,548	79.73	2,173
1–1–61 to 31–12–61	10,481	8,148	77.74	2,333
1–1–62 to 31–12–62	20,461	16,178	79.06	4,283

TABLE 21.2
VIGILANCE CASES DEALT WITH BY GOVERNMENT OF INDIA

	Total No. for Disposal	No. Disposed of	Percentage of Disposal	Pending at the End of the Year
1956–1957	616[a]	344	55.84	272
1957–1958	3,694	1,974	53.43	1,729
1–4–58 to 31–12–58	3,714	1,809	48.71	1,905
1–1–59 to 31–12–59	10,035	6,380	63.57	3,055
1–1–60 to 31–12–60	13,305	9,530	71.63	3,775
1–1–61 to 31–12–61	15,116[b]	10,973	72.52	4,143
1–1–62 to 31–12–62	19,277	13,454	69.79	5,823

[a] This figure relates only to Gazetted Officers.
[b] Out of 15,116 cases, 10,605 cases pertain to the Post and Telegraphs Directorate.

TABLE 21.3
COMPLAINTS RECEIVED AND INVESTIGATED BY THE SPECIAL POLICE ESTABLISHMENT

Year	Total	Signed or Given Personally by Complainants	Anonymous or Pseudonymous	Complaints of Minor Irregularities Referred to Depts.	Complaints Found to be False	Filed for Want of Proof	Registered as PE or RC
1957	2733	1755 (64.22%)	978 (35.78%)	556 (20.3%)	107 (3.9%)	275 (10.1%)	326 (11.9%)
1958	3310	2273 (68.67%)	1037 (31.33%)	991 (29.94%)	207 (6.25%)	539 (16.28%)	542 (16.4%)
1959	3995	2871 (71.86%)	1124 (28.14%)	1100 (27.53%)	255 (6.4%)	706 (17.67%)	614 (15.4%)
1960	2755	1475 (53.54%)	1280 (46.46%)	644 (23.37%)	75 (2.7%)	542 (19.67%)	193 (7.0%)
1961	3380	1790 (52.95%)	1590 (47.05%)	1316 (38.93%)	162 (4.8%)	1079 (31.92%)	282 (8.3%)
1962	3847	2213 (57.54%)	1634 (42.46%)	1881 (48.89%)	142 (3.69%)	813 (21.13%)	461 (9.8%)

these, many complaints were of minor irregularities and were referred to the departments concerned. It is significant to note that the percentage of such complaints increased from 20 in 1957 to 49 in 1962. In 1957 about 10 per cent of the complaints were shelved for want of proof, while in 1962 such cases amounted to 21 per cent. Besides these, the Special Police Establishment also collects information from its own sources and channels, the number of cases so compiled being 1691 in 1962. Table 21.3 gives the details of the complaints received and investigated by the Delhi SPE.

Between 1957 and 1962 the number of gazetted and non-gazetted Government servants involved in cases registered by the Special Police Establishment was 1156 and 5836 respectively. For the above period, 20 officers of the Secretariat, four above the rank of Under-Secretaries and 16 officers below the rank of Under-Secretaries, were involved. Among the engineering personnel 116 engineers of, and above, the rank of Executive Engineers and 219 below the rank of Executive Engineers were involved. There were 64 officers (other than engineers) and 120 commissioned officers of the Army. Besides these, there were officers from the Iron and Steel Controller (32), Income-Tax Officers

TABLE 21.4
CLASSIFICATION OF GAZETTED OFFICERS AGAINST WHOM CASES WERE INVESTIGATED DURING 1957–1962

	1957	1958	1959	1960	1961	1962	Total
Officers of the Secretariat of and above the rank of Under Secretary		4	4	4	4	4	20
Officers of the Secretariat below the rank of Under Secretary		3	5	—	3	5	16
Engineers of above the rank of EE	41	16	35	26	21	22	161
Engineers below the rank of EE	—	65	50	42	40	22	219
Railway Officers (other than engineers)	17	16	11	6	3	11	64
Military Commissioned Officers	14	16	26	25	17	22	120
Directors, Deputy Directors, Asst. Directors in the Departments of DGS & D, Agriculture, Archaeology, etc.	10	4	4	14	10	7	49
Controllers of Imports and Exports and Iron and Steel		6	5	6	8	7	32
Income Tax Officers	6	5	8	4	9	15	47
Excise and Customs Officers	2	6	5	5	12	16	46
Senior Officers of Statutory Corporations and Public concerns			13	11	5	18	47
Other Class I	37	27	40	21	13	29	167
Other Class II	54	17	28	30	50	34	213
TOTAL	181	185	234	194	195	212	1201

(47), Excise and Customs Officers (46), and senior officers of statutory bodies and public concerns (47). There were another 167 Class I officers and 213 Class II officers against whom cases were investigated during this period. Table 21.4 gives details in this respect.

During 1957–1962 the Special Police Establishment investigated 4669 cases against public servants involving allegations of bribery, corruption, misappropriation, and such other types of misconduct. They also investigated 771 cases of breach of import-export regulations and 75 cases against private persons and companies. During the same period the SPE laid 386 traps in which 429 public servants were caught, 16 of them gazetted and 413 non-gazetted. The SPE investigated during the years 1960–1962 nearly 300 cases of public servants possessing assets disproportionate to their known sources of income. In respect of import-export, the SPE registered and investigated cases against 451 firms involving 660 licences obtained as a result of malpractices. The value of the licences involved was Rs 2,38,24,142. Of the firms involved, 433 were black-listed.

It is relevant to note here the significant facts brought out by a recent study carried out by the Union Home Ministry on the basis of information being collected from various other Ministries and departments of the Government of India, particularly in the light of criticism in certain quarters that the anti-corruption drive was causing demoralization in the services. Despite the fact that the Special Police Establishment has taken up cases against many government servants in the past few years there has not been a single instance of an honest employee being involved. On the other hand, it is possible that many corrupt people have escaped punishment for lack of sufficient evidence. In 1963 the SPE conducted preliminary inquiries in 833 cases and 771 of these proved fruitful. The percentage of successful investigations was thus 92.6. Out of 757 regular cases in which investigation had been completed during 1963, 721 or 95.2 per cent were fruitful. No less than 87.3 per cent of the cases decided by courts ended in conviction. (*The Times of India* dated 11 October 1964.) These facts have to be kept in mind while evaluating the statistics presented in this chapter.

Commenting on the import licence rackets, the Santhanam Committee says:[2] "The fact that licences worth Rs, 2,38,-24,142 were obtained by fraud and other types of malpractices is clear indication of the extent of the problem in the licensing activities of the Government. It is common knowledge that each licence fetches anything between 100 per cent to 500 per cent of its face-value, if sold. Thus a huge unearned profit—which may be anything from rupees two to ten crores, should have been made in these transactions and it is anybody's guess as to how much of it went into the pockets of public servants." The committee cites yet another interesting case.[3] The Ministry of Works, Housing, and Supply, as it was then, had set up in 1957 a unit known as the Chief Technical Examiner's Organization with a view to introducing an internal system of concurrent and continuous administrative and technical audit of the work of the CPWD to economize on expenditure and improve technical and financial control of the works. Up to the end of December 1962, this organization detected 1593 cases of overpayment involving an amount of Rs 43,66,669. During the Second Plan period the total expenditure on construction and purchases was of the order of Rs 2800 crores. It is common knowledge that the custom of percentage is prevalent when giving out contracts for construction, purchases and sales and this is distributed in agreed proportions amongst the officials concerned. In contracts of construction seven to eleven per cent is usually paid in this manner. Thus even the assumption that only five per cent was paid as gratification on the total investment on construction and purchases during the Second Plan period, the amount involved a loss of Rs 140 crores to the Government.

The Kripalani Committee on corruption confirms similar practices in the Railways.[4] The report says:

> One sub-contractor on the Railways was candid enough to admit that the Railway contractors (including himself) made regular payments to the engineering officials on a percentage basis. The following percentage breakdown on the amount of their bills was indicated by him:

Executive Engineer	5%
Assistant Engineer	5
PWD Supervisor	5
Accounts section	2
District pay clerk	¼
Head clerk in XEN	1
Mistry/work-in-charge	1
Miscellaneous	¾
Total	20%

> It may not be so meticulously systematic as represented here but the fact of the percentages was mentioned by many witnesses, and is popularly known.

In another instance the same committee says:[5]

> The system of paying "mamul" (conventional bribe) is so universal that the givers and takers do not think it morally wrong. There was an interesting case of a

[2] Santhanam Committee Report, p. 18.
[3] Santhanam Committee Report, p. 18.

[4] *Report of the Railway Corruption Enquiry Committee*, 1953–1955 (Chairman: J. B. Kripalani), p. 48.
[5] *Report of Railway Corruption*, p. 21.

Cane Manager of a sugar mill issuing the following written instruction to the mill staff-in-charge at various sugar-cane loading centres:

The following payments will be made as noted below which please note and comply:

Station Master	–/12/–	per wagon
Guard	–/ 3/–	per wagon
Driver, etc.	–/ 2/–	per wagon
Loading charges	1/ 4/–	per 100 mds.

The rates of "mamul" may appear to be low but considering the number of wagons loaded, the amount would go into thousands. The "mamuls" were regularly paid as corroborated by the entries relating to the payment in the daily cane and cash reports of the sugar mill.

The Public Accounts Committee reported in their sixth report (Third Lok Sabha) as follows:[6]

The committee are rather alarmed at such a large number of cases of underassessment involving considerable amounts, detected in the test audit by the Comptroller and Auditor-General, when it is borne in mind that this scrutiny was limited to only a small percentage of cases in 235 incometax wards out of 1310 wards in the country. It is significant to note that the number of cases in which defects and discrepancies involving underassessment to the extent of Rs. 120.77 lakhs were discovered amounts to about 16 per cent of the total number of cases audited (i.e. 13,357 cases).

There is no acceptable estimate of tax evaded. The Income-tax Investigation Commission, in 1058 cases investigated by it, detected concealed income of the order of Rs 48 crores. Concealed income amounting to Rs 70 crores was disclosed by the assessees themselves under the Voluntary Disclosure Scheme of 1951. An unofficial estimate made by the Central Board of Revenue is that about Rs 45 crores of tax is evaded annually by assessees in the higher income groups, the evaded income being about Rs 230 crores. The Santhanam Committee comments:

We would be happy to believe that all this evasion takes place without any connivance or abetment on the part of the servants concerned. We, however, are unable to do so. It is common knowledge that some portion of the tax avoided or evaded is shared by many, including the assessing officers.

In June 1964, a businessman was "trapped" in Gujarat while giving as much as Rs 30,000 to an Income-tax Officer. This speaks for itself.

As a result of the anti-smuggling measures of the Government, goods worth Rs 434.92 lakhs were seized in 1962. "It is obvious that what has been seized does not represent the whole volume of goods smuggled in. It is accepted by all that smuggling is not sporadic or unorganized and that it is a well-organized racket and it is possible that at least some of the Customs Officials are involved in this racket either on payment of a share regularly or on each occasion" (Santhanam, p. 19).

Corruption has spread far beyond the limits of general administration to the police and even the judiciary. The problem of corruption in the police has been conceded by various police commissions. The Bihar Police Commission Report, for instance says:[7]

There is complete unanimity among the witnesses on the point that corruption exists in the police and judged by its traditional and historical background, it survives as an inveterate disease defying all administrative measures that have been adopted from time to time to tackle this problem. A well-informed and enlightened witness who has done some research in this regard favoured the Commission with his views. According to him any force like the police could be divided into two sections. The first section can be easily called the "decision apparatus"

6 Santhanam Committee Report, pp. 18–19.

7 See *Civic Affairs*, April 1962, p. 16.

and the other is the "submission or procedural apparatus." While the former takes the decision, the latter attends to procedure and is responsible for its execution. He thinks that there is far more corruption in the "execution apparatus" than the "decision apparatus." This is the type of evidence laid before the Commission by a very large number of witnesses.

The witnesses have, however, not offered any concrete picture of the extent and nature of this malady. Majority of the witnesses are of the view that the force in the lower ranks is affected with this malady and the infection is also noticed in the rank of Deputy Superintendents. The general impression seems to be that the incidence of corruption is considerable in all ranks up to the Inspector of Police, it is fair in the rank of Deputy Superintendents of Police, and almost insignificant in the rank of Superintendents of Police. This picture is also supported by the witnesses representing the State Anti-Corruption Department, and the Commission have no reason to arrive at any different findings.

Weighing various views on whether corruption has increased or decreased in the police force, the commission said:

In the view of this commission it is not of much practical value to ascertain accurately whether corruption has increased or decreased or is static; so long as it continues to exist, it is not a minor administrative problem. Witnesses have indicated various opportunities that are available for resorting to corrupt practices in the discharge of police duties and also in the internal management of the force. Most of them are so well known that this Commission does not consider it necessary to recapitulate them, but they would like to emphasize certain laxities noticed particularly in the matter of accepting presents and utilizing the services of orderlies for domestic work. In the past they were not considered as corrupt practice but in a democracy it is necessary that the superior officers set a high standard. Corruption, however, should never be judged in the narrow sense, and from the evidence that is available before the Commission it is clear that when some witnesses have said that there is a decrease in corruption they have averred to the fact that there is very much less of extortion, concoction, and manipulation at present than before.

This last sentence reminds one of the interesting but controversial strictures passed by Mr. Justice A. N. Mulla of the Lucknow Bench of the Allahabad High Court, whilst giving judgment in *State* v. *Mohammad Naim, Criminal Miscellaneous Case No.* 87.[8] He said:

If I had felt that with my lone efforts I could have cleared this Augean stable which is the police force, I would not have hesitated to wage this war single handed. . . . There is no single lawless group in the whole country whose record of crimes comes anywhere near the record of that single organized unit, which is known as the Indian Police Force.

These remarks of the judge roused such a controversy that the State went in appeal to the Supreme Court to get the "adverse" remarks expunged from the judgment. One of Justice Mulla's colleagues on the bench, while not denying the need for the strictures, expressed himself against the intemperate language used in the judgment. But, factual information collected to determine the nature of the problem would seem to warrant such an opinion.

A secret investigation carried out by the Anti-Corruption Bureau of the Delhi Police revealed that the police refused to register 65 per cent of the crime cases in the Capital. An official of the Anti-Corruption Branch had a taste of the treatment the police gave to the public when he visited a station incognito. He was manhandled when he insisted that his complaint be registered.

The high incidence of "crime burking" has shocked even police officers. To their amazement they discovered that serious crimes like robbery and burglary

[8] *Civic Affairs,* November 1961, p. 25.

were not investigated. The Anti-Corruption Branch conducted the first investigation in 21 police stations. Posing as complainants, officials went to the station to register their cases. The tests were repeated in 15 more stations. The results of the two tests are revealed in the [following list]:

Cases Sought to be Registered		*Actually Registered*
Robbery	3	nil
Burglary	2	nil
Pickpocketing	10	2
Cycle thefts	10	5
Misc. thefts	6	3
Loss of Property	1	1
Total	32	10

This fact has also been confirmed by similar investigations elsewhere. The Kerala Police Reorganization Committee, with Mr. N. C. Chatterji as chairman, in its report submitted in January 1960 has put the problem in the right perspective:[9]

> One feature prominently standing out in the police force of the country is the wide influence of corruption. It has afflicted police forces in variable degrees and has not been eradicated. The establishment of a special vigilance agency has curbed the malaise to some extent but the evil persists and has to be faced. No other single factor lowers the prestige of the force than this taint, and today when the people are zealous as never before to uphold public morals and condemn corruption, it is the duty of the Superior Police Officers to stamp it out with an unrelenting hand. Corruption cannot flourish unless there are beneficiaries who pay for the services rendered but this is no argument or justification for the acceptance or tolerance of this blight. Those afflicted by it must be searched out and removed.

The judiciary, too, is not entirely free from graft. The corruption in the judiciary does not reach up to the high level. But the court staff itself has been found to be corrupt in many cases. According to a staff correspondent of *The Hindustan Times*,[10] corruption flourished in the Tis Hazari Courts in Delhi. One had to pay anything between Rs 15 to 100 to the subordinate court staff to expedite the process of bail. This assessment is considered to be on the high side by officials. A senior official of the Delhi Administration is reported to have placed the maximum figure at not more than Rs 50 in the course of confidential discussions with magistrates. Corruption is mostly confined to lower ranks and relates to administrative matters. But there have been a few incidents which made District Magistrate S. C. Bose Mullick have second thoughts about some colleagues. He transferred a magistrate who was reported to have met with an accident while using the car of a rich man who was at one time involved in a number of cases, including one of abduction. What shocked people was that a magistrate was found to have signed a bundle of summons forms with the space, where names are filled in, left blank. The forms had been kept in an almirah in the court room. The subordinate court staff had access to the almirah.

Though most of the readers and other court staff create circumstances which make the people pay them, some are bold and direct in their approach. For instance, in a traffic offence a man approached the reader in the court to help him get away with a light fine. The reader advised him to wait, and a little later told him that he had been fined two rupees. The man paid the amount to the reader. "But what about the fine," the reader said. The man paid another two rupees.

A number of lawyers and litigants who were interviewed by the correspondent said that bribery in criminal courts began with the process of bail. Magistrates normally endorse bail applications to the police for their report. If one wants

9 *Civic Affairs*, May 1960, p. 13.

10 See *Civic Affairs*, December 1962, p. 27.

to move an application to leave the courtroom immediately, one is more often than not obliged to tip the staff. One has to follow it up when bail has been granted. The phrase "follow up" in the courts normally means to follow up with money. Otherwise the subordinate staff in courts may delay the preparation of the release warrant. The warrant must reach the jail before sunset if a person is to be released the same day. The jail rules do not permit the release of détenus after dark. A lawyer narrated an incident in which he preferred not to tip. Because he had not been tipped, a court reader did not write legibly on the release warrant the Sections under which the man had been arrested. The warrant was returned by the jail authorities for clarification with the result the man had to spend another night in the lock-up. Sometimes one has to tip the jail staff lest they carry the scrutiny too far.

Some of the presiding judges are aware of the implication of corruption in courts. But they find solace in the fact that it has only affected the subordinate staff, and at any rate it is the national character. But facts prove otherwise. In Rajasthan a Magistrate was caught redhanded while accepting Rs 11,450 from a person accused in a passport case.[11] In Bombay a magistrate was compulsorily retired on account of his malpractices. The Governor of Bihar, Mr. Anantasayanam Ayyangar created a big controversy by publicly accusing that certain judges and lawyers are in collusion over cases.

The Governor, while inaugurating the Bihar Lawyers' Conference on 3 April 1963, said:[12]

> I am afraid, in some cases people have become *persona disignata* with the judges. You just appoint this lawyer because he is a son-in-law or he belongs to this community, or if the case is transferred to some other judge, he gives up one lawyer and appoints the other. It is a disgrace to the lawyers. It is a disgrace to the judges. People were *persona grata* with this man or that man. Not only here, the cancer has spread to the districts also. As I have heard, some boy became a lawyer and wherever his father is a subordinate judge, this boy is taken. Another case has come to my notice of a sub-divisional officer having a satellite wherever he goes. It is a disgrace.

The propriety of the Governor's public statement of this kind had been a subject of a heated debate. Even the High Court Judges had joined in the public controversy. But one leading member of the governing council of the Bar Association of India seems to have known his brief well when he said:[13]

> I doubt if it would be wise for a lawyer to challenge general statements made by a Head of State in the belief that they were based on mere bazaar gossip and without being certain that they were wholly baseless and run the risk of being confronted with specific instances in substantiation of the criticism of the Governor, who had practised law for thirty years and was also the Speaker of the Lok Sabha for a number of years.

The question of propriety apart, the very fact that a responsible Governor was compelled to make such a statement publicly indicates a very unsatisfactory state of affairs with regard to the judiciary.

When we come to political corruption, that is corruption among Ministers of Government, we enter a virgin territory, explored only on the fringes. One such exploration was conducted by Justice Das into allegations against a State Chief Minister. The report of the inquiry into the Serajuddin-Malaviya affair has not seen the light of day as yet. Elsewhere, things are being hushed up. One has to go by "bazaar gossip." But the "bazaar gossip" itself is damning enough. One hears of this or that Min-

---

11 *Civic Affairs,* November 1962, p. 51.

12 *Public Administration* (Kanpur, June 1963), pp. 33–34.

13 *Public Administration,* p. 35.

ister's son having amassed wealth running into crores of rupees. There is talk of Ministers' sons and nephews getting jobs on fat salaries completely out of proportion to their merits. Yet others talk of a band of "pedlars of influence" who surround Ministers and "fix up" anything for standard rates. The list of crimes could be built up *ad infinitum.*

It is significant to note here that the Santhanam Committee, being prevented from looking into incidence of corruption in the ministerial and judicial ranks, either through the limitations of its terms of reference or special circumstances, did not feel confident to give the benefit of the doubt to these sectors.[14]

Of the judiciary, the Report said that the Committee "were informed by responsible persons, including Vigilance and Special Police Establishment Officers, that corruption exists in the lower ranks of the judiciary all over India and in some places it has spread to the higher ranks also."

On the integrity of the political leaders, the Santhanam Report said: "There is a widespread impression that failure of integrity is not uncommon among Ministers, and that some Ministers who have held office during the last sixteen years have enriched themselves illegitimately, obtained good jobs for their sons and relations through nepotism. The general belief about failure of integrity among Ministers is as damaging as actual failure."

The working of the Special Police Establishment, the Anti-Corruption Bureau, and Vigilance Sections throughout the administration has provided a sad picture of corruption. It is pertinent to remember that these anti-corruption agencies have not been working with uniform zeal, and hence the figures cited in this chapter do not tell the whole story in this sector. The involvement of higher civil servants cannot be denied.

Rampant corruption in all walks of public life has been adequately proved by the various Commissions of inquiry set up from time to time. How far has it reached in politics is a matter for conjecture, but the undenied rumours, some of which have a firm base, are dangerous enough to shake the confidence of the common man. He has reached a stage where he lacks any faith in the institutions of our country. This is a disturbing state of affairs.

14 Santhanam Committee Report, p. 108.

22. Corruption as a Hindrance to Modernization in South Asia

GUNNAR MYRDAL

The term "corruption" will be used in this chapter in its widest sense, to include not only all forms of "improper or selfish exercise of power and influence attached to a public office or to the special position one occupies in public life" but also the activity of the bribers.[1]

The significance of corruption in Asia is highlighted by the fact that wherever a political regime has crumbled—in Pakistan and Burma, for instance, and, outside South Asia, in China—a major and often decisive cause has been the prevalence of official misconduct among politicians and administrators, and the concomitant spread of unlawful practices among businessmen and the general public.[2] The problem is therefore of vital concern to the governments in the region. Generally speaking, the habitual practice of bribery and dishonesty tends to pave the way for an authoritarian regime, whose disclosures of corrupt practices in the preceding government and whose punitive action against offenders provide a basis for its initial acceptance by the articulate strata of the population. The Communists maintain that corruption is bred by capitalism, and with considerable justification they pride themselves on its eradication under a Communist regime.[3] The elimination of corrupt practices has also been advanced as the main justification for military takeovers. Should the new regime be unsuccessful in its attempts to eradicate corruption, its failure will prepare the ground

1 See India, Government of Ministry of Home Affairs, *Report of the Committee on Prevention of Corruption*, New Delhi, 1964, p. 5; see pp. 11 ff. This committee is usually referred to as the Santhanam Committee, after its chairman; we shall cite its report as the Santhanam Committee Report hereafter.

2 A few years before the military *putsch* of 1958 in Pakistan, Tibor Mende reported that: "Probably no other symptom of Pakistani public life has contributed more to the demoralization of the 'common man' than corruption." Illicit practices had reached such proportions that "their effect is likely to wipe out whatever benefits new economic projects might have secured for him." Some measures were taken by the government in response to "widespread demand for action" and "a few minor officials" were dismissed, but "they were the small culprits." (Tibor Mende, *South-East Asia between Two Worlds,* Turnstile Press, London, 1955, p. 227.)

3 "In the disorders in China since 1911 the scale of corruption had increased in a monstrous way, and reform was very much needed. The surprising achievement of the Communists was to be able to induce among their party members, who were after all thoroughly Chinese, a militant and puritanical hatred of the old system. Here was one of the outstanding instances of ideas and institutions being able to change people's character. The Communist Party set out to hunt the corrupt; it disciplined its own members savagely if it caught them; it developed a steady pressure against corruption in all the administration—incidentally attaching charges of corruption to all of whom it disapproved upon other grounds." (Guy Wint, *Spotlight on Asia,* Penguin Books, Middlesex, 1955, p. 91.)

The present writer's observations confirm the view that what has impressed the South Asian intellectuals most about China's Communist revolution has been the establishment of a strong, disciplined state, one that is scrupulously honest by South Asian standards.

SOURCE: Gunnar Myrdal, "Corruption—Its Causes and Effects," *Asian Drama: An Enquiry into the Poverty of Nations,* Vol. II. New York: Twentieth Century, 1968, pp. 937–951. By permission of the publisher.

for a new putsch of some sort. Thus it is obvious that *the extent of corruption has a direct bearing on the stability of South Asian governments.*

A TABOO IN RESEARCH ON SOUTH ASIA

Although corruption is very much an issue in the public debate in all South Asian countries, as we shall demonstrate . . . [later], it is almost taboo as a research topic and is rarely mentioned in scholarly discussions of the problems of government and planning. With regard to research conducted by Americans, the explanation might seem, at first glance, to lie in the fact that public life in the United States, particularly at the state and city levels, is still not as free of corruption as in Great Britain, Holland, or Scandinavia. But this explanation does not take us far, as social scientists in the United States, particularly in an earlier generation, never shied away from exposing corruption in public administration, politics, and business, nor were their inquiries censored. Moreover, scholars from the Western European countries mentioned have shown no greater interest than Americans in studying corruption in South Asia. Neither does the fact that Western enterprises are in league with corrupt elements in South Asia on a large scale explain the disinterest of Western scholars in the problem of South Asian corruption, for business has not been that influential in guiding research; many studies with conclusions unfavorable to Western business interests have in fact been made. For reasons we shall set forth later, the lack of investigation cannot be attributed, either, to the difficulty of finding an empirical basis for research on corruption.

Instead, the explanation lies in the general bias that we have characterized as diplomacy in research. Embarrassing questions are avoided by ignoring the problems of attitudes and institutions, except for occasional qualifications and reservations—which are not based on even the most rudimentary research and do not, of course, alter the basic approach. South Asian social scientists are particularly inclined to take this easy road, whether they are conservatives or radicals. The taboo on research on corruption is, indeed, one of the most flagrant examples of this general bias. It is rationalized, when challenged, by certain sweeping assertions: that there is corruption in all countries (this notion, eagerly advanced by students indigenous to the region, neglects the relative prevalence of corruption in South Asia and its specific effects in that social setting); that corruption is natural in South Asian countries because of deeply ingrained institutions and attitudes carried over from colonial and pre-colonial times (this primarily Western contention should, of course, provide an approach to research and a set of hypotheses, not an excuse for ignoring the problem); that corruption is needed to oil the intricate machinery of business and politics in South Asian countries and is, perhaps, not a liability given the conditions prevailing there (again, this mainly Western hypothesis about the functioning of the economic and social system should underline rather than obviate the need for research); that there is not as much corruption as is implied by the public outcry in the South Asian countries (this claim needs to be substantiated, and if it is true, the causes and effects of that outcry should be investigated). These excuses, irrelevant and transparently thin as they are, are more often expressed in conversation than in print. That the taboo on any discussion of corruption in South Asia is basically to be explained in terms of a certain condescension on the part of Westerners was pointed out in the Prologue [not reprinted here].

In our study we have not attempted to carry out the necessary research on corruption in South Asia, or even a small part of it; we had neither the time nor the facilities for an empirical investigation on this scale. The main purpose of this chapter is thus to explain why the taboo should be broken. In the course of the discussion we venture to sketch a theory of corruption in South Asia by offering some reasonable, though quite tentative, questions to be explored and hypotheses to be tested.

THE "FOLKLORE" OF CORRUPTION AND THE ANTI-CORRUPTION CAMPAIGNS

The problem of corruption, though not a subject of research, is, as we have said, very much on the minds of articulate South Asians. The newspapers devote much of their space and the political assemblies much of their time to the matter; conversation, when it is free and relaxed, frequently turns to political scandals. Periodically, anti-corruption campaigns are waged: laws are passed; vigilance agencies set up; special police establishments assigned to investigate reports of misconduct; sometimes officials, mostly in the lower brackets, are prosecuted and punished and occasionally a minister is forced to resign.[4] Occasionally committees are appointed to deal more generally with the problem of counteracting corruption.[5] following the practice established in colonial times, particularly by the British. In India and Ceylon especially, but also in other South Asian countries, the authorities have, from the start of the independence era, tried to prevent corruption, and these efforts have, on the whole, been increasing. Yet the articulate in all these countries believe that corruption is rampant and that it is growing, particularly among higher officials and politicians, including legislators and ministers. The ostentatious efforts to prevent corruption and the assertions that the corrupt are being dealt with as they deserve only seem to spread cynicism, especially as to how far all this touches the "higher-ups."

Two things, then, are in evidence: (1) what may be called the "folklore of corruption," i.e., people's beliefs about corruption and the emotions attached to those beliefs, as disclosed in the public debate and in gossip; and (2) public policy measures that may be loosely labelled "anti-corruption campaigns," i.e., legislative, administrative, and judicial institutions set up to enforce the integrity of public officials at all levels. Both are reactions to the fact of corruption, and they are related to each other in circular causation. A study of these phenomena cannot, of course, provide an exhaustive and entirely accurate picture of the extent of corruption existing in a country—the number involved, the positions they hold, and what they are doing. But it is nevertheless true that *the folklore of corruption embodies important social facts worth intensive research in their own right.*[6] The beliefs about corruption and the related emotions are easily observed and analyzed, and this folklore has a crucial bearing on how people conduct their

4 In India the number of vigilance cases reviewed is steadily increasing. See Santhanam Committee Report, Section 3, pp. 14 ff. Although the report places the statistics under the heading "extent of corruption," it makes clear (p. 14 *et passim*) that the statistics themselves do not indicate the actual amount of corruption in various branches of administration, or its recent trend.

5 The Santhanam Committee Report is the latest and the most ambitious South Asian study of corruption. The committee gives certain general judgments about the prevalence of corruption in India to which we shall refer below, but directs its main attention to establishing in considerable detail the various possibilities for corruption afforded by established administrative procedures in India, particularly in the central government, and to working out a system of reforms that would decrease corruption.

6 In the study of race relations it is the beliefs about race and the institutional and attitudinal systems of segregation and discrimination related to those beliefs that are important, not racial differences as such (see Gunnar Myrdal, *An American Dilemma,* Harper & Row, New York, 1944, p. 110 and throughout). Something similar is true about corruption, though not to the same extent, as undoubtedly the corruption practices are important, independent of what is believed about them or done to combat them. . . .

private lives and how they view their government's efforts to consolidate the nation and to direct and spur development. The anti-corruption campaigns are also important social facts, having their effects, and they are just as easy, or even easier, to record and analyze.

A related question worth study is the extent to which the folklore of corruption reflects, at bottom, a weak sense of loyalty to organized society. Is there, in other words, a general asociality that leads people to think that anybody in a position of power is likely to exploit it in the interest of himself, his family, or other social groups to which he has a feeling of loyalty? If so, people's beliefs about the corruptibility of politicians and administrators would be in part a reflection of what they would like to do, given the means.

If corruption is taken for granted, resentment amounts essentially to envy of those who have opportunities for private gain by dishonest dealings. Viewed from another angle, these beliefs about corruptibility, especially the belief that known offenders can continue their corrupt practices with little risk of punishment, are apt to reinforce the conviction that this type of cynical asocial behavior is widely practiced. The folklore of corruption then becomes in itself damaging, for it can give an exaggerated impression of the prevalence of corruption, especially among officials at high levels. It is certain that fear of bolstering that impression influenced Nehru consistently to resist demands for bolder and more systematic efforts to cleanse his government and administration of corruption. "Merely shouting from the house-tops that everybody is corrupt creates an atmosphere of corruption," he said. "People feel they live in a climate of corruption and they get corrupted themselves. The man in the street says to himself: *'well, if everybody seems corrupt, why shouldn't I be corrupt?'* That is the climate sought to be created which must be discouraged."[7]

The first task of research on corruption is thus to establish the ingredients of the folklore of corruption and the anti-corruption campaigns. These phenomena are on the surface of social reality in South Asia and therefore lend themselves to systematic observation. The data, and the process of collecting them, should give clues for the further investigation of the facts of actual corruption. Analysis of the interplay of folklore, action, and fact and of the relationship of all three to the wider problems of national consolidation, stability of government, and effectiveness of development efforts must necessarily take one into murkier depths of social reality.

THE FACTS OF CORRUPTION

With public debate quite open and gossip flourishing, the facts in individual cases of wrongdoing should not be too difficult to ascertain. The true research task is, however, to establish the general nature and extent of corruption in a country, its incursion upon various levels and branches of political and economic life, and any trends that are discernible. In this section we shall make a start on this task, but our contribution should not be considered as more than a very preliminary sorting out of problems for research. What is said is based on extensive reading of parliamentary records, com-

---

7 R. K. Karanjia, *The Mind of Mr. Nehru,* George Allen & Unwin Ltd., London, 1960, p. 61.

The Santhanam Committee Report states: "It was represented to us that corruption has increased to such an extent that people have started losing faith in the integrity of public administration. We heard from all sides that corruption has, in recent years, spread even to those levels of administration from which it was conspicuously absent in the past. We wish we could confidently and without reservation assert that at the political level, Ministers, Legislators, party officials were free from this malady. The general impressions are unfair and exaggerated. But the very fact that such impressions are there causes damage to the social fabric" (pp. 12, 13). "The general belief about failure of integrity amongst Ministers is as damaging as actual failure" (p. 101).

mittee reports, newspapers, and other publications dealing with the subject, and, even more, on conversations with knowledgeable persons in the region, including Western businessmen, as well as on personal observation. The fact that in the United States corruption has for generations been intensively and fruitfully researched should counter the notion that nothing can be learned about this phenomenon.

Concerning first the general level of corruption, it is unquestionably much higher than in the Western developed countries (even including the United States) or in the Communist countries. It serves no practical purpose, and certainly no scientific interest, to pretend that this is not so. This judgment will gain support when in the next section we turn to the causes of corruption; they are clearly much stronger in South Asia than in the other groups of countries mentioned. The relative extent of corruption in the South Asian countries is difficult to assess. There is more open discussion of corruption in the Philippines, where, in the American tradition, the press is particularly free and outspoken, than in, say, Pakistan, Burma, and Thailand under their present regimes. In India, where a moralistic attitude is especially apparent, greater concern is expressed than in Ceylon, for instance. Whether the amount of public discussion reflects the real prevalence of corruption is doubtful. On the basis of scanty evidence, India may, on balance, be judged to have somewhat less corruption than any other country in South Asia. Nevertheless, a commonly expressed opinion in India is that "administrative corruption, in its various forms, is all around us all the time and that it is rising."[8] The findings of the Santhanam Committee as to the prevalance of corruption in different branches and levels of responsibility will be reported below, in the text and in footnotes.

If a comparison is made with conditions in the colonial era, the usual view of both South Asian and Western observers is that corruption is more prevalent now than before independence and that, in particular, it has recently gained ground in the higher echelons of officials and politicians. This view, too, will gain support from our subsequent discussion of the causes of corruption. We know on the authority of J. S. Furnivall, moreover, that the Netherlands Indies was practically free of corruption in colonial times, unlike Burma where corruption was rampant except at very highest level;[9] but in present-day Indonesia corruption seems to be at least as much a fact of life as in any other South Asian country.[10] In the Philippines corrupt practices at all levels of business and administration were common in colonial times, but it is generally assumed that they have increased substantially since then.[11]

---

8 *The Economic Weekly,* December 21, 1963, Vol. XV, No. 51, p. 2061.

9 J. S. Furnivall, *Colonial Policy and Practice: A Comparative Study of Burma and Netherlands India,* Cambridge University Press, London, 1957, p. 269 and throughout.

10 In fact, a decade ago an Indonesian statesman, Mohammad Hatta, wrote: "Corruption runs riot through our society; corruption has also infected a great many of our government departments. . . . Workers and government employees, whose wages and salaries are no longer adequate for their daily needs, are being exploited by enterprising adventurers who want to get rich quickly. . . . This is why all businessmen who remain faithful to economic morality are constantly being pushed backward. Bribery and graft have become increasingly common, to the detriment of our community and our country. Each year the government loses hundreds of millions of rupiahs in duties and taxes which remain unpaid as a result of fraud and smuggling, both illegal and 'legal.' " (Mohammad Hatta, *The Co-operative Movement in Indonesia,* Cornell University Press, Ithaca, 1957, pp. 84–85.)

The situation has certainly not improved since this was written. . . .

11 An American congressional study group reported: "Those members of the study mission who had visited the Philippines previously on one or more occasions were startled and shocked to find an increase in lawlessness and of Government corruption that was more than hinted at." (*Report of the Special Study Mission to Asia, Western Pacific, Middle East, Southern Europe and North Africa,* GPO, Washington, 1960, p. 22.)

There is said to have been much petty corruption in British India on the lower level where indigenous or Anglo-Indian officials were almost exclusively employed, though in most instances Europeans were served promptly and without having to pay a bribe. On the other hand, it is commonly asserted—not only by British observers—that the Indian Civil Service was largely incorrupt. Not all Indian intellectuals agree; some maintain that in later years, and especially during the Second World War, corruption tended to spread even to this select group, including British officials.[12] In the princely states corruption was often unchecked and infested the courts of the maharajahs and the higher echelons of administration. What has been said about British India holds broadly true even for Ceylon. The French administration in Indo-China was probably never as clean as its British counterpart in India and Ceylon, but it is generally acknowledged that corruption has increased very rapidly in the successor states.[13] Thailand was always corrupt in its peculiar fashion and is thought to have become more so of late.

There seems to be rather general agreement that in recent years corruption in South Asia has been increasing. The Santhanam Committee Report speaks of "the growth of corruption" and of the need to arrest "the deterioration in the standards of public life," the assumption that the recent trend of corruption in India is upwards is implicit in the whole report. In Pakistan and Burma the military takeovers in the late 1950's undoubtedly brought major purges in their wake, but many observers—both Westerners and nationals in these countries—are found who believe there has been a resurgence of corruption, particularly in Pakistan, though the bribes have to be bigger because of greater risks.

Statements such as these should be tested by research that could either confirm or refute them; even if broadly confirmed they need to be made much more specific. As for the different branches of administration in the South Asian governments, it is generally assumed that the public works departments and government purchasing agencies in all of the countries are particularly corrupt,[14] as are also the agencies running the railways, the offices issuing import and other licenses, and those responsible for the assessment and collection of taxes and

12 This view is also expressed, obliquely, by the Santhanam Committee: "Till about the beginning of the Second World War corruption was prevalent in considerable measure amongst revenue, police excise and Public Works Department officials particularly of the lower grades and the higher ranks were comparatively free from this evil. The smaller compass of State activities, the 'great depression' and lack of fluid resources set limits to the opportunities and capacity to corrupt or be corrupted. The immense war efforts during 1939 to 1945 which involved an annual expenditure of hundreds of crores of rupees over all kinds of war supplies and contracts created unprecedented opportunities for acquisition of wealth by doubtful means. The war time controls and scarcities provided ample opportunities for bribery, corruption, favouritism, etc. The then Government subordinated all other considerations to that of making the war effort a success. Propriety of means was no consideration if it impeded the war effort. It would not be far wrong to say that the high watermark of corruption was reached in India as perhaps in other countries also, during the period of the Second World War" (pp. 6–7).

Any implication that corruption was more widespread among higher officials during the Second World War than now is probably groundless, however, and is gainsaid by the Committee in other passages; see below.

13 About developments in North Vietnam we have no specific information; that Communist regimes ordinarily stamp out corruption was pointed out before.

14 For India the Santhanam Committee Report states: "We were told by a large number of witnesses, that in all contracts of construction, purchases, sales, and other regular business on behalf of the Government, a regular percentage is paid by the parties to the transaction, and this is shared in agreed proportions among the various officials concerned. We were told that in the constructions of the Public Works Department, seven to eleven per cent was usually paid in this manner and this was shared by persons of the rank of Executive Engineer and below down to the Ministry, and occasionally even the Superintending Engineer might have a share" (p. 10).

"During the Second Plan period the total expenditure on construction and purchases was of the order of Rs. 2800 crores. . . . If it is assumed that even 5 per cent . . . is accounted for by such corrupt practices, the total loss to the excheqer is about Rs. 140 crores" (p. 18).

customs duties.[15] More generally it is asserted that whenever discretionary power is given to officials, there will tend to be corruption.[16] Corruption has spread to the courts of justice, and even to the universities.[17]

The spread of corruption among minor officials is understood to be consequent on a deterioration of the morals of some of the politicians and higher officials.[18] Both as cause and effect, corruption has its counterpart in undesirable pratices among the general public. The business world has been particularly active in promoting corrupt practices among politicians and administrators, even if it be granted that it is difficult or impossible to carry on business without resort to such practices when corruption is widespread. As the Santhanam Committee Report points out:

> Corruption can exist only if there is someone willing to corrupt and capable of corrupting We regret to say that both willingness and capacity to corrupt is found in a large measure in the industrial and commercial classes. The ranks of these classes have been swelled by the speculators and adventurers of the war period. To these, corruption is not only an easy method to secure large unearned profits but also the necessary means to enable them to be in a position to pursue their vocations or retain their position among their own competitors. . . . Possession of large amounts of unaccounted money by various persons including those belonging to the industrial and commercial classes is a major impediment in the purification of public life. If anti-corruption activities are to be successful, it must be recognized that it is as important to fight these unscrupulous agencies of corruption as to eliminate corruption in the public services. In fact they go together.[19]

Our comments concerning the importance of corruption in various branches of the economy are necessarily cast in vague, qualitative terms, as are the judgments expressed in the Santhanam CommitteReport, from which we have quoted so extensively. One important question on which the report of that Indian committee is silent is the role played by Western business interests competing for markets in South Asian countries or embarking on direct investments in industrial enterprises there, either independently or in joint ventures with indigenous firms or with governments.[20] Western

---

15 On these the Santhanam Committee Report observes: "In the Railways, besides the above [constructions and purchases], similar practice in connection with allotment of wagons and booking of parcels particularly perishables, is said to be in vogue" (p. 10).

"We were told that corruption and lack of integrity are rampant in transactions relating to obtaining of quota certificates, essentiality certificates, licenses and their utilisation" (p. 254).

"It is common knowledge that some portion of the tax avoided or evaded is shared by many including the assessing officers." (p. 19) This practice has wider effects: "Tax so evaded and avoided is kept as unaccounted money and one of the many uses to which it is put is for corrupting public servants" (p. 271).

16 Says the Santhanam Committee Report: "Where there is power and discretion, there is always the possibility of abuse, more so when the power and discretion have to be exercised in the context of scarcity and controls and pressure to spend public money" (p. 9).

17 The same report notes:

"Though we did not make any direct inquiries, we were informed by responsible persons including Vigilance and Special Police Establishment Officers that corruption exists in the lower ranks of the judiciary all over India and in some places it has spread to the higher ranks also. We were deeply distressed at this information" (p. 108).

"It is a matter of great regret that in some universities, conditions are far from satisfactory for the admission of students, recruitment of lecturers and professors and the general management of university funds" (p. 109).

18 In India, according to the report on which we have been drawing, "There is a widespread impression that failure of integrity is not uncommon among Ministers and that some Ministers who have held office during the last 16 years have enriched themselves illegitimately, obtained good jobs for their sons and relations through nepotism, and have reaped other advantages inconsistent with any notion of purity in public life. . . . We are convinced that ensuring absolute integrity on the part of Ministers at the Centre and the States is an indispensable condition for the establishment of a tradition of purity in public services" (pp. 101–102).

19 Santhanam Committee Report, pp. 11–12.

20 Of a somewhat different character is the corruption connected with grants and aid offered by Western governments. That a considerable amount of the American aid to countries like Laos, South Vietnam, and even the Philippines has been dissipated in large-scale corruption is common knowledge and, in the frank American tradition, has been reported in congressional inquiries and in the

business representatives never touch on this matter publicly, but, as the writer can testify, in private conversation they are frank to admit that it is necessary to bribe high officials and politicians in order to get a business deal through and to bribe officials both high and low in order to run their businesses without too many obstacles. They are quite explicit about their own experiences and those of other firms. These bribes, they say, constitute a not inconsiderable part of their total costs of doing business in South Asian countries. Although hardly any foreign company can make it an absolute rule to abstain from giving bribes, it is apparent that there is a vast difference in regard to the willingness to bribe, not only between companies but also between nationalities. Among the Western nations, French, American, and, especially, West German companies are usually said to have the least inhibitions about bribing their way through. Japanese firms are said to be even more willing to pay up. On the other hand, the writer has never heard it alleged that bribes are offered or paid by the commercial agencies of Communist countries. These widely held opinions are part of the social setting in South Asia, as are all the elements that make up the folklore of corruption; to what extent they mirror actual business practices should be established by the research we recommend.

There is one specific difficulty facing researchers in their attempts to establish the facts about the taking and seeking of bribes, particularly on the part of higher officials and politicians. Bribes are seldom given directly; usually they go to a middleman, whether an indigenous businessman or an official at a lower level. In particular, a Western firm, operating in a South Asian country, often finds it convenient—and less objectionable—to give a negotiated lump sum to a more or less professional briber, an "agent," who then undertakes to pay off all those whose cooperation is necessary for the smooth conduct of production and business. More generally, when a business transaction is to be settled, an official somewhere down the line of authority will often inform the Western businessman that a minister or a higher official expects a certain sum of money. Even an indigenous businessman is occasionally placed in such an indirect relationship to the bribe-seeker. As the whole affair is secret, there is often no way of knowing whether the middleman is keeping the money for himself. Indeed, he may be using the weight of an innocent person's name to sweeten the deal and increase his take. This is, of course, one of the ways in which the folklore of corruption may exaggerate the extent of corruption at the higher levels.

In research designed to establish the facts of corruption, the role of Western business interests in the spread of corruption could be investigated best by Western researchers since they would in most cases have easier access to the confidence of the bribers, while the nationals in the several countries would probably meet fewer inhibitions and obstacles in carrying out the more general study of the spread of corruption in South Asia. But more important than such a division of labor is the researchers' seriousness of intent and their willingness to cooperate with one another.

press. The writer has not heard similar allegations in relation to foreign aid given India or Pakistan. Apparently the World Bank, the International Monetary Fund, and, more generally, the inter-governmental agencies within the United Nations family have on the whole been able to avoid playing into the hands of the corrupt, except that when aid is rendered in the form of commodities—as, for instance, powdered milk given by UNICEF—part of the deliveries tend to appear on the market instead of reaching their intended destinations. The World Bank, in particular, has increasingly exerted its authority to see that its loans are used to preserve fair competition among suppliers.

THE CAUSES

The folklore of corruption, the political, administrative, and judicial reverberations of these beliefs and emotions in the anti-corruption campaigns, the actual prevalence of corruption in the several countries at different times, and the present trends—all these social facts must be explained in causal terms by relating them to other conditions in South Asia.

When we observe that corruption is more prevalent in South Asia than in the developed Western countries, we are implying a difference in mores as to where, how, and when to make a personal gain. While it is, on the one hand, exceedingly difficult in South Asia to introduce profit motives and market behavior into the sector of social life where they operate in the West—that is, the economic sphere—it is, on the other hand, difficult to elminate motivations of private gain from the sector where they have been suppressed in the West—the sphere of public responsibility and power. In South Asia those vested with official authority and power very often exploit their position in order to make a gain for themselves, their family, or social group. This is so whether that position is the high one of a minister, a member of the legislature, or a superior official, whose consent or cooperation is needed to obtain a license or settle a business deal, or the humble position of a petty clerk who can delay or prevent the presentation of an application, the use of a railroad car, or the prompt opening of the gates over the tracks. Certain behavioral reactions generally held to be outside profit considerations in the West are commonly for sale in South Asia; they have a "market," though certainly not a perfect one in the Western sense of the term.

The two differences are complementary and, to an extent, explain each other. Indeed, they are both remnants of the pre-capitalist, traditional society. Where, as often in South Asia, there is no market for services and goods or only an imperfect and fragmented one, and where economic behavior is not governed by rational calculations of costs and returns—and this is true not only in subsistence farming and crafts but to a degree also in the organized sector—"connections" must fill the gap. These "connections" range all the way from the absolute dependence of attached labor in agriculture and the peasants' relations with moneylenders and landlords, which are determined by custom and power, to the special considerations that lead to nepotism even in big business. In such a setting a bribe to a person holding a public position is not clearly differentiated from the "gifts," tributes, and other burdens sanctioned in traditional, pre-capitalist society or the special obligations attached to a favor given at any social level.

In pre-colonial times officials had to collect their remuneration themselves, usually without much regulation or control from above. As Furnivall points out in speaking about Burma:

> The officials drew no fixed salary. Some were paid by allotment of the revenue of a particular district, but for the most part their emoluments were derived from a commission on revenue collected, or from fees paid by the parties to a case. One great source of revenue was from local tolls on the transport or sale of goods.[21]

A situation then became established that one Westerner viewed as follows:

> In nearly all Asian countries there has always been a tradition of corruption. Public office meant perquisites. Officials were not well paid and had to make ends meet. The well-timed bribe—which was often

21 *Colonial Policy and Practice,* pp. 14–15. Cf. the Santhanam Committee Report's characterization of "primitive and medieval societies": "So long as the officials were loyal to the existing regime and did not resort to oppression and forcible expropriation, they were free to do as they liked. If through tactful methods, they amassed wealth for themselves or advanced their other material interests they were praised rather than censured. Often offices were hereditary and perquisites which would today amount to bribery were con-growth of the currently accepted standards of integrity" (p. 6).

almost a conventional fee—was the emollient which made the wheels of administration turn more efficiently.[22]

Even where the colonial powers in later years were able to establish a higher civil service, which was honest, well paid, and manned by both colonial and indigenous personnel—as the British, in particular, succeeded in doing—they still found it difficult to enforce rigid standards at the lower levels of administration.[23]

Traditionally, the South Asian countries were "plural societies," in the meaning given to the term by Furnivall, and under colonial rule became increasingly so. In the present context this implies above all a fragmentation of loyalties and, in particular, little loyalty to the community as a whole, whether on the local or the national level. Such wider loyalty, backed by firm rules and punitive measures, is the necessary foundation for the modern Western and Communist mores by which certain behavior reactions are kept apart from considerations of personal benefit. In South Asia the stronger loyalty to less inclusive groups—family, caste, ethnic, religious, or linguistic "community" (in the South Asian sense), and class—invites the special type of corruption we call nepotism and tends in general to encourage moral laxity. The prevalence of corruption is, moreover, one aspect of the "soft state," to which we have often referred, it generally implies a low level of social discipline.[24]

When explaining the presence of corruption in South Asia, this legacy from traditional society must be taken into account, mainly as part of social statics. But to explain the increase in corruption that is commonly assumed to have taken place in recent times, we must view the social system in dynamic terms. Many of the changes that have occurred have afforded greater incentives as well as greater opportunities for corruption. The winning of independence and the transition from colonial status to self-government were preceded and accompanied by profound disturbances. In all South Asian countries the goal of development was accepted, while the attainment of that goal was made more difficult by the accelerated growth of population, the deterioration of the trading position, and other trends. Independence greatly increased the role of the politicians. At the same time the repatriation, following independence, of a large number of officials from the metropolitan countries left South Asia few competent administrators with the stricter Western mores.[25] This

22 Guy Wint, *Spotlight on Asia*, p. 91.

23 A remarkable exception to the general rule was the Netherlands Indies. The lack of corruption there was commented on above in Section 3. It resulted from cultivating incorruptibility in the higher brackets of civil service and from leaving the old village organization as undisturbed as possible. Furnivall, after stating that corruption was practically unknown in Java, explains:

"The absence of judical corruption can easily be understood. Petty cases are settled by arbitration either out of court, or before a bench of notables with a senior and well-paid official as chairman; or they go before a civil servant or judicial officer with long service and on high pay. Moreover, the penalties imposed are so trivial that it is cheaper to be punished than to bribe a policeman or magistrate to escape punishment. Serious matters go before a bench containing at least three high judicial officers as well as laymen of good standing. It would be difficult and dangerous to bribe the whole bench. In civil cases the decision purports to follow customary law, and the people can know whether it is right; the court must justify itself to popular opinion and not to higher judicial authority. In these circumstances there is little scope for bribery." (*Colonial Policy and Practice*, p. 269.)

24 The conditions referred to so far in this section are reflected in the South Asian quest for a higher level of "morals" in business and public affairs—an improved "social climate" in which behavior patterns are judged in terms of the modernization ideals.

"In the long run, the fight against corruption will succeed only to the extent to which a favourable social climate is created. When such a climate is created and corruption becomes abhorrent to the minds of the public and the public servants and social controls become effective, other administrative, disciplinary and punitive measures may become unimportant and may be relaxed and reduced to a minimum. However, change in social outlook and traditions is necessarily slow and the more immediate measures cannot be neglected in its favour." (Santhanam Committee Report, p. 101.)

25 The dynamic factors hinted at in this paragraph are touched on in several places in the Santhanam Committee Report; see, in particular, pp. 8 ff.

scarcity was much greater and more damaging in Indonesia, Burma, and even Pakistan than in the Philippines, India, and Ceylon.

. . . [T]he extensive—and generally increasing—resort to discretionary controls is apt to breed corruption;[26] the spread of corruption, in turn, gives corrupt politicians and dishonest officials a strong vested interest in retaining and increasing controls of this type. Another contributing factor has undoubtedly been the low real wages of officials, especially those at the lower and middle levels.[27] There is also, quite generally, a circular causation with cumulative effects working within the system of corruption itself. As we have indicated, it acts with special force as people become aware of the spread of corruption and feel that effective measures are not taken to punish the culprits, particularly those who are highly placed.[28] Among the sophisticated the situation may become rationalized in the idea that corruption, like inflation, is an unavoidable appendage of development.[29] The effect of this is to spread cynicism and to lower resistance to the giving or taking of bribes.

---

26 The Santhanam Committee Report in various contexts makes this point; see footnote 2, p. 945 above. "There is scope for harassment, malpractices and corruption in the exercise of discretionary powers" (p. 45). "It is necessary to take into account the root causes of which the most important is the wide discretionary power which has to be exercised by the executive in carrying on the complicated work of modern Administration" (p. 209).

27 "We have found that low-paid Government servants are entrusted with . . . matters like gradation of commodities, inspection of mines, supervision of implementation of labour laws and awards, various kinds of licensing, passing of goods at Customs etc. While the general increase in the salaries of Government servants is a matter to be decided in the light of national economy and the tax paying capacity of the people, it may be worthwhile in the country's interest to examine whether the categories of officials who have to exercise considerable discretion in matters relating to taxation, issue of valuable permits and licences, or otherwise deal with matters which require [a] high degree of integrity, should not be given special attention regarding status and emoluments." (Santhanam Committee Report, p. 46.)

28 "Complaints against the highly placed in public life were not dealt with in the manner that they should have been dealt with if public confidence had to be maintained. Weakness in this respect created cynicism and the growth of the belief that while Governments were against corruption they were not against corrupt individuals, if such individuals had the requisite amount of power, influence and protection." (Santhanam Committee Report, p. 8.)

29 "A society that goes in for a purposively initiated process of a fast rate of change has to pay a social price, the price being higher where the pace of change excludes the possibility of leisurely adjustment which is possible only in societies where change is gradual." (Santhanam Committee Report.)

CHAPTER FIVE

Contemporary Europe

23. Administrative Corruption in Theory and Dutch Practice

H. A. BRASZ

It would seem to me that jurisprudence has long concerned itself, by its nature, with the formal aspects of the phenomenon of corruption, that is to say with the causality technique, since corruption itself is informal. Bribery cannot be defined in jurisprudence as the giving or accepting of gifts or promises.[1] For that purpose the concept of corruption, especially under the influence of the Code Pénal, has been given not only a broad meaning (rottenness) but also a narrow meaning with a legal tinge to it, namely bribery. We have endeavoured to formulate an operational concept which lies between the much too broad meaning of rottenness and the too narrow meaning of bribery used by lawyers and confined to one causality technique.

This operational definition of the phenomenon of corruption should stress its secret nature and thus the impossibility of measuring it. A statistical approach to the phenomenon of corruption is impossible. But we can try to approach it by means of a functional analysis of the groups in which corruption occurs. We can measure a few phenomena connected with corruption, such as the number of criminal convictions for bribery. Furthermore, the attitude of groups exposed to corruption can be measured against the causality techniques in a more or less experimental situation. Merton has demonstrated how a pathological phenomenon like the American political machine, with its criminal boss, can be made comprehensible in this way.[2]

Much closer to the subject under discussion is the masterly analysis by Blau of the attitude of a group of officials who were very much exposed to the temptations of bribery.[3] Among the techniques that Blau used in his analysis were participant observation and free discussion. He paid special attention to the way in which his subjects responded to those questions about bribes which evoked emotional reactions. It appeared that the camouflage of the causality technique renders it necessary to put out "feelers" before bribes are as much as mentioned, a process also described by Blokhuis.[4] For instance, a private talk is requested.[5] Before the power-holder whom one tries

1 See Sections 177 and 363 of the Dutch Criminal Code, which are discussed in detail by Hendrik Philip 't Hooft, *Omkooping van ambtenaren* (Bribery of Officials; dissertation, University of Leiden; Leiden, 1890).

SOURCE: H. A. Brasz, "Some Notes on the Sociology of Corruption," *Sociologica Neerlandica*, 1:2 (Autumn 1963), pp. 117–125. By permission of the publisher, Royal Vangorcum Ltd.

2 Robert K. Merton, *Social Theory and Social Structure* (Glencoe, Ill., 1949), pp. 73 f. (Functions of the Political Machine for Diverse Subgroups).

3 Peter M. Blau, *The Dynamics of Bureaucracy: A Study of Interpersonal Relations in Two Government Agencies* (Chicago, 1955), pp. 148 f.

4 K. Blokhuis, gas-works manager at Middelharnis and Sommelsdijk, *gasbeltijren, gas-directeuren en corruptie* (*Gas Works, Gas Works Managers, and Corruption,* Middelharnis, 1928), p. 8.

5 Of course the feelers can be extended somewhat more boldly when those concerned happen to be alone. *Cf.* Blokhuis, p. 9.

to bribe possesses proof of active bribery, he must act as if he is taking the hint. The latter act is roundly condemned as contemptible: no honourable person likes to play the *agent provocateur,* informer, or tempter. Despite the fact that the officials of the agency investigated by Blau had instructions to report any attempt at bribery to higher authorities at once, there was a rigorously observed unofficial standard that forbade this. The risks involved in provoking the direct attempt at bribery were enlarged upon in discussions among the officials, and the few of their number who nevertheless reported an attempt at bribery in accordance with their instructions were ostracized by the group. The first social function of the taboo on reporting attempts at bribery was the protection of the reputation and promotion chances of the officials against those who wanted to get in well with their superiors. But a second function of the informal norm was that it prohibited officials from acting in such ways as might be detrimental to the smooth functioning of the agency. The offer of a bribe was regarded in general as a *bona fide,* normal act by a private person. For the enforcement of the legal provisions for which the agency in question was responsible, much depended on the voluntary co-operation of the group of citizens concerned (manufacturers and managers). Reporting an attempt at bribery was an infringement of the tolerant attitude which in this case was called for in order to maintain the law.

Consequently, the officials themselves acted as judge and jury if they were offered a gift or a hint was dropped in this direction. They themselves, rather than the officially appointed government bodies, "punished" the offer by rejecting it outright, thereafter being in a position of greater authority to demand voluntary co-operation in the enforcement of the law. Their tolerant attitude was therefore essential for government by persuasion; rejecting a gift without reporting the matter to the police gave them a tactical advantage. Blau found indications that officials themselves provoked overtures so as to gain this tactical advantage.

Blau noted that in the investigation a hostile attitude was often adopted as soon as this informal norm was alluded to, whilst most officials tried to conceal as a disgraceful affair the instances generally known in the service in which, by way of exception, a bribe had been reported.

In a note[6] Blau admits that the informal norm can also be explained as a means of concealing dishonest practices. But he rejects this possibility without, in my opinion, having adduced convincing proof. For he invokes the fact that he worked together with the group of officials in question for more than three months and never heard of a legitimate practice by which the acceptance of a bribe was justified. He further points out that those officials whose honesty, in his opinion, was beyond all doubt also recognized and observed the taboo on the reporting of attempts at bribery. (Here it seems to me that Blau fails to appreciate the furtive nature and the camouflaging of corruption and the techniques which have to lead to this.) He therefore rightly excludes any assumption that all the officials of the agency were "perfectly honest."

However functional the secretiveness surrounding the informal conduct of these officials may be, and however much they act as judge and jury, I am nevertheless greatly disquieted as a citizen to find that an attempt to bribe an official in the case analysed by Blau entailed so few risks. Now it may be said that the Netherlands is not America, and that this solitary American agency is not the whole of America, but the ease with which the causality techniques in corruption can be camouflaged is closely associated with the uneasy feeling which we con-

6 Blau, pp. 241–242, note 4.

tinue to have as citizens, even though a thorough investigation carried out by the Koersen committee had found no evidence of corruption or bribery.

The practices described by Blokhuis do not differ in essence from those which Blau found. But Blokhuis ventures to estimate the percentage of corrupt gas-works managers at fifty, after having also mentioned the percentages seventy and twenty[7] Blokhuis was himself an official, Blau an investigating sociologist. And added to this is the fact that criminal statistics give us something to think about. During the years 1953–1957 there were fifty-two convictions for active bribery as contemplated in Section 177 of the Dutch Criminal Code, of which twenty-four, or 46 percent, were second or further convictions for this or other offences.[8] This rather high percentage provides food for thought. Is it above all the small group of criminals who are trying to bribe Dutch officials? Or are officials more easily persuaded to let the attempt develop into the penalized offence where this group is concerned? If the mechanism of the "feelers" and the inner resistance to playing the informer did not work in the Netherlands, then in my opinion the number of convictions for active bribery of officials (Section 177 of the Criminal Code) would be much higher than the number for passive bribery of officials (Section 363). But that is by no means the case: during the years 1953–1957 there were only thirteen more convictions for active bribery than for passive bribery of officials (thirty-nine). The offence arising out of Section 363 of the Criminal Code relates to cases of successful bribery, that is, cases which led to corruption as defined in this paper. The secret corruption did not remain secret, so that briber and the bribed were usually convicted. The thirteen cases (an average of two-and-a-half a year) in which passive bribery did not follow statistically the attempt at active bribery give some indication of the risk of coming to grief through an unwilling official when one puts out feelers about making a gift. The risk must be very small indeed, unless one assumes that the Dutch public extends feelers in a manner which is hardly *bona fide* at all.

7 K. Blokhuis, pp. 18 f.

8 Data issued by the Central Bureau of Statistics in the yearly publication *Criminele statistiek* (*Criminal Statistics*.)

MEANS OF COMBATING CORRUPTION

It must be concluded that the social means of checking the evil of corruption can be of a direct nature to only a very limited extent. It has been found that criminal law is often a broken reed. Instructions to personnel to report attempts at bribery (a means recommended by Van Poelje) must also be regarded as such.[9] Even a general conviction based on ethical grounds that corruption is to be rejected seems to me inadequate, though it is important. Of much greater importance is a mode of conduct in which the evil does not occur: an institutional behaviour both by the power-holders concerned and their public in which corruption has gained no footing.[10]

Salomonson wrote in 1925 in his dissertation on the subject of bribes that the abuse had taken root in private trade both at home and abroad and that it had swelled to an extent that could hardly be overestimated.[11] He describes in detail the alarm which the secret commissions caused in Britain (Chapter II), the *Schmiergelder* in Germany (Chapter III), the *pots de vin* in France, and the *mutor och besticknung* in Sweden (Chapter IV) around the turn of the century. Besides measures of a legislative nature against

9 G. A. van Poelje, *Bestuurskunde* (Public Administration; Alphen aan de Rijn, 1953), p. 130. "There is absolutely no reason why officials to whom such a suggestion is made should not report it at once to the mayor and aldermen."

10 Both Blokhuis and Lodewifk Salomonson (*Steekpenningen* [Leiden, 1925]), write at length about means of improvement.

11 Salomonson, p. 11.

bribes outside official circles, this evil was also combated by associations of interested parties who promised one another never to "fiddle" again and who set up an organization to track down miscreants who broke the legal ban. In 1906 the Bribery and Secret Commissions Prevention League was founded in Britain. German business followed with the Verein gegen das Bestechungswesen in 1911 and the Swedes with the Institut för bekämpande av mutor och bestickning in 1923.[12]

The Netherlands—in my opinion rightly—did not follow other countries with penal measures against bribes in the private sector. The fact that, to the best of my knowledge, no campaigns have been organized to combat corruption may be partly attributable to this. I have the impression that a whole series of formal measures, especially measures of an organizational nature, have been built into Dutch public administration to restrict the evil of corruption. This is not the place for a lengthy discussion of the constitutional and administrative aspects of these measures. I shall therefore confine myself to a fairly arbitrary selection. As regards constitutional law, Montesquieu's separation of powers and—to cite a further example—ministerial responsibility are so universally known that the mere mention of them should suffice. I might draw attention to the oath of vindication which precedes the assumption of office, whereby it is stated under oath or by a declaration in lieu of such an oath that no bribes have been given to obtain the office.[13] This means was to be found as early as in a criminal ordinance of Philip II of Spain which acquired force of law in the Netherlands in 1570. Section 2 provided penalties for overweening ambition and corruption. It included the following passage: "We forbid one and all to offer, present, or give directly or indirectly any things to acquire whatsoever rank or office, to use any overweening ambition or intrigue." According to Hanlo this ordinance was also applied in the Dutch Republic as unwritten common law. Various edicts against the acceptance of gifts and presents followed in rapid succession and were recapitulated in an edict proclaimed by the States General on 1 July, 1651,[14] whilst the prohibitory enactments were confirmed anew in 1715. Hanlo consequently says that there was no lack of penalties against the offence during the Republic; but there were no accusers.[15]

The officials charged with tracking down corruption were especially guilty of this very crime.[16] On the other hand, we must bear in mind that as a consequence of this state of affairs the application of some intolerant laws, such as those relating to the public exercise of Roman Catholicism, was considerably relaxed.[17]

Very stringent provisions against accepting gifts are usually included not only in criminal law but also in official instructions. In my opinion the Dutch police are unrivalled on this point since

12 Salomonson, pp. 35, 47, and 60.

13 This oath of vindication even occurs in the Dutch Constitution: see Article 97 for the members of the Second Chamber. Before being permitted to take the oath (or promise) of fidelity to the Constitution, they take the following oath (make the following declaration and promise): "I swear (declare) that in order to be appointed a member of the States-General, I have not promised or given, directly or indirectly, any gifts or presents to any person under whatsoever name or pretext. I swear (promise) that in order to do or refrain from doing anything whatsoever in this office, I will not accept any promises or presents, directly or indirectly, from any person whomsoever." Amos J. Peaslee, ed., *Constitutions of Nations: The First Compilation in the English Language of the Texts of the Constitutions of the Various Nations of the World, Together with Summaries, Annotations, Bibliographies, and Comparative Tables*, Vol. II (second edition, The Hague, 1956), p. 767.

14 Athanasius M. A. Hanlo, *De leer der omkooping van ambtenaren* (The Theory of the Bribing of Officials; dissertation, University of Leiden, Leiden, 1867), pp. 28 f.

15 Hanlo.

16 Hanlo, pp. 34, especially in connection with the possibility of making a bargain whereby a prosecution could be bought off (known as "composition").

17 Hanlo, p. 33.

a policeman must refuse even a cigarette. Section 64 of the Dutch Regulations for Government Officials reads: "Officials are forbidden in the exercise of their duties to request or to accept payment, rewards, gifts, or promises from third parties, except with the approval of the competent authority. The taking of bribes is unconditionally and most strictly forbidden."

In the course of the Löffelholz trial in Bonn it emerged that buyers for the German Ministry of Defence may participate in the "übliche Werkspflegung" during negotiations with firms. They may therefore smoke and drink at the expense of the firms concerned during conferences. But here too a clear line was drawn: "Ergehen in diesem Zusammenhang Einladungen zum Essen oder zu einem anderen gesellschaftlichen Zusammensein, so sind sie höflich, aber bestimmt abzulehnen."[18]

However, the best guarantee against corruption seems to me to lie in the hierarchical structure of government and business organizations. The derived power can thus be contained in clearly-defined channels and subjected to strict supervision.

This may be observed in buses operated by the public transport authorities. The drivers have their fixed routes and time schedules and are, moreover, inspected. Although a bus-driver has certain freedom of movement within his time-table, he is not given much opportunity to endanger the objectives of his principal by means of corrupt acts. His opportunities cannot be compared, for instance, with those of the master of a sailing vessel in the seventeenth century who, under the influence of primage and far beyond the control of his owners, put the interests of the shipper above those of the owners of the ship.[19]

The public character of the proceedings at the top hierarchical levels helps prevent corrupt practices, instances of which are the legally prescribed public character of administration of justice, of the electoral process, of the sessions of representative bodies, and of the deposition of documents for public inspection before important decisions are taken or before such decisions go into effect (*e.g.* draft planning schemes and exemptions from military service.[20]

When, for any reason whatsoever, the hierarchy offers less protection on this score, management by more than one person usually provides some guarantee against corruption in any case (*e.g.* the Board of Government Arbitrators).

Finally reference should be made to the cultivation of an *esprit de corps,* by means of which the holders of derived power are closely associated with the values aimed at by their organization. This indirect form of internal social control has all the more significance since those whose posts expose them to the dangers of corruption can also be protected by it if the organizational measures fail.

STRUCTURALLY DANGEROUS POSITIONS

These structually dangerous posts can in my opinion be approximately localized in the Netherlands. They are to be found where, as a result of the great extent of state or business activities, derived power is exercised outside the immediate supervision of the most senior holders of power in the organization. They are to be found in government circles for instance among the officials in charge of a department or a section, in a limited company among the buyers, in municipal circles among mayors and the heads of municipal enterprises, and in the free professions among notaries public. They all hold key positions from the point of view

18 *Der Spiegel,* 2 September, 1959, p. 35.
19 Salomonson, p. 31.

20 But the answer to electoral corruption was the secret ballot.

of corruption, have opportunities which can be resisted only by good faith and in my opinion must be given the greatest credit for the Netherlands' good name in this respect. I seriously doubt whether the government always succeeds in making sufficient allowance for this important matter when fixing salaries. Pettiness by the principal towards officials whose integrity is exposed to such great temptations does not seem a wise policy to me.

I do not consider myself competent to give a provisional opinion on the structurally dangerous positions of those who are the occasion of corruption. People here tend to have a suspicious attitude towards business, which is seen in the light of international competitive methods (*e.g.* with regards to dumping).

In this context the fairness and the strictness of the formal regulations governing the performance of the function may also be mentioned as a factor. When children below a certain age are allowed to travel free of charge with their parents on international trains but are not allowed to have a sleeping berth unless the full child's fare is paid for the trip, too severe a norm is imposed on the travellers and the train staff which, when there is room to spare, cannot but lead to evasion.

THE PUBLIC IMAGE OF CORRUPTION

As a subject for further study I should like to point to the public image of the extent of corruption. A secret regarding corruption that has leaked out functions as a rumour, so that even corruption on a minor scale can easily suggest widespread decadence to the public.

Certain groups in the community have some reason to fan the flames of this rumour, such as a minority opposition group or—for purely economic reasons—the yellow press. Other groups, such as the government party or parties, may be inclined not to take the extent of the "scandal" too seriously: the leaders of these groups probably have better opportunities of verifying these rumours. It would seem that outside the Netherlands publicity is given above all to those corruption scandals which discredit certain political figures or parties. The secret is then leaked out at a strategic moment. For instance, in the Adams case the President of the United States was deprived of one of his most important assistants at a time when he could not really do without him. The German corruption trials, too, sometimes give the impression of having a political function. Certain scandals are deliberately allowed to leak out so as to make political capital out of them, in order to influence the behaviour of the electorate to the detriment of certain parties. This socio-psychological aspect, however, further enhances my uncertainty regarding the true extent of the phenomenon of corruption. Can the corruption that has been revealed be explained in part by the function that the scandal may have in the struggle for power against certain uncongenial persons or groups?

24. The British Method of Dealing with Political Corruption

MADELINE R. ROBINTON

In the winter of 1948, a sensational investigation of governmental corruption took place in England. Rumors of corruption in high places had for some time been rife. On the 27th of October, when Prime Minister Attlee moved in the House of Commons that a tribunal be set up to inquire whether there was any justification for allegations reflecting on the official conduct of Ministers of the Crown and other public servants, England was all agog. During the sittings of the Tribunal, public interest was widespread and press coverage extensive. Even though space was at a premium, because of the newsprint shortage, the London *Times* devoted column upon column to an almost verbatim report of the proceedings; the less dignified papers went in for "sob story" coverage and lurid headlines. To Americans, accustomed to the hullabaloo attendant on frequent sensational trials and Congressional committee hearings, the clamor and outcry in England may seem to be of no special significance. It may, however, be not without interest to note how the English reacted to indications of corruption, what procedures they used to establish the facts without sacrificing the basic common-law rights of individuals, and what actions were taken once the facts were established. The government acted swiftly, both in instituting proceedings and in bringing them to a conclusion. No attempt was made to derive partisan political advantage. Rather, all parties closed ranks in defense of the principle that "public administration in this country and public life in this country stand unrivaled in their high standards of service and incorruptibility."[1] As Winston Churchill put it, quoting from a speech by Clement Attlee in 1936, "any action of the nature of utilisation of a public position for a private gain cuts at the root of democratic government."[2]

On the motion of Mr. Attlee in the Commons and of Viscount Jowitt, the Lord Chancellor, in the Lords it was resolved by both Houses of Parliament:

> that it is expedient that a Tribunal be established for inquiring into a definite matter of urgent public importance, that is to say, whether there is any justification of allegations that payments, rewards or other considerations have been sought, offered, promised, made or received by or to Ministers of the Crown or other public servants in connection with licenses or permissions required under any enactment, regulation or order or in connection with the withdrawal of any prosecution and, if

SOURCE: M. R. Robinton, "The Lynsky Tribunal: The British Method of Dealing with Political Corruption," *Political Science Quarterly*, 68:1 (March 1953), pp. 109–124. Reprinted with permission from the *Political Science Quarterly*.

1 Speech by Clement Attlee, Feb. 3, 1949, in House of Commons, *H. C. Deb.*, Vol. 460, col. 1852.

2 Feb. 3, 1949, Clement Attlee, *H. C. Deb.*, col. 1859.

so, in what circumstances the transactions took place and what persons were involved therein.[3]

The Home Secretary appointed Sir George Justin Lynskey, one of His Majesty's Judges of the High Court of Justice, Godfrey Russell Vick and Gerald Ritchie Upjohn, two of His Majesty's Counsel, to constitute the Tribunal. The Lynskey Tribunal, as it was known popularly because Sir George Lynskey had been appointed chairman, set up under the Tribunals of Inquiry (Evidence) Act of 1921 was "itself responsible for the collection of evidence, taking statements from witnesses, presenting their evidence, then testing its accuracy and finally finding the facts."[4] In view of the physical impossibility of doing the job themselves within a reasonable time, both the Treasury Solicitor and his staff, as well as that of the Metropolitan Police, were assigned to assist in the interviewing and the taking of statements from all persons who seemed to have useful information. Decision as to what further inquiries were needed, and which witnesses were to be called to give public testimony, remained the responsibility of the Tribunal, which also determined the procedures to be observed.

The speed with which the Tribunal acted may be seen by reference to the timetable of events. The accusations had been first brought to the attention of an official of the department concerned on the 26th of August, 1948. On the 24th of September, the Lord Chancellor wrote to the Minister accused for an explanation. A month later, the 27th of October, the original motion to set up the Tribunal was introduced and passed by Parliament. Two days later, on the 29th, J. Chuter Ede, the Home Secretary, appointed the members of the Tribunal, and on November 1 the Tribunal sat in public to discuss and decide questions of procedure. The actual hearings began two weeks later, on the 15th of November; they continued for twenty-five days, ending on December 21, 1948. The report of the Tribunal was published January 21, 1949, and accepted by the House of Commons February 3, 1949.

Although the Tribunal did not act as a court, in accordance with normal English judicial procedure the duties of legal assistance to the Tribunal were divided between counsel and solicitor. The Attorney General, Sir Hartley Shawcross, with three other barristers, acted as counsel; they were instructed by the Treasury Solicitor. Witnesses, also, were allowed to be represented by their own counsel and solicitor, provided the Tribunal thought they had a sufficient intest in matters under investigation to justify it. Of the sixty witnesses who testified (fifty-eight orally and two, for reasons of ill health, by affidavit) nineteen were thus represented. The right of witnesses to be examined by their own counsel after cross-examination by the Tribunal's counsel and the right of their counsel to cross-examine hostile witnesses are very significant differences from the procedure of our Congressional committees.

At the first sitting for the hearing of witnesses, the Attorney General outlined the procedure proposed by the Tribunal. The Attorney General was to open the facts. Witnesses were to be called and examined in chief on the statements they had made in preliminary interviews. Each witness was then to be cross-examined by the counsel who had examined him in chief; and counsel appearing for witnesses were to be given the opportunity of cross-examining. Any witness represented by counsel was then to be examined by his own counsel. The concluding stage was to be a final examination by a counsel for the Tribunal. Counsel for witnesses were asked to

3 *Report of the Tribunal appointed to inquire into allegations reflecting on the official conduct of Ministers of the Crown and other Public Servants,* Cmd. 7616, p. iv.

4 *Report of the Tribunal,* p. 1.

comment on this procedure, and it met with their approval.

The procedure of the Lynskey Tribunal, with its careful regard for the rights of individuals appearing before it, was in consonance with the principles expressed at the time the Act of 1921 was originally drafted, and repeated on subsequent occasions. As Mr. Neville Chamberlain stated at the time the tribunal form was used to investigate the budget leak (1936), "in a matter of this kind it was desirable that the inquiry should be undertaken by a body of a judicial character accustomed to weighing evidence, with a knowledge of the rules of evidence and free from any possible suspicion of partiality."[5]

The original bill for setting up a tribunal of inquiry had been introduced on March 4, 1921, by the then Attorney General, Sir Gordon Hewart, and had been supported by Mr. James Hope, Parliamentary Secretary of the Ministry of Munitions. It was offered in response to a request made in the House of Commons for an investigation of the Ministry of Munitions because of allegations that an official of the department had ordered the destruction of "working papers" and concealment of material documents from the Exchequer and Audit Department. At that time a large proportion of outstanding accounts with contractors were being dealt with, and rumors had been current that there had been corruption in certain government departments in the handling of great sums of money; it had even been suggested "that under the stress of war the old traditions of the Civil Service had been destroyed."[6] Existing methods of investigation were deemed unsatisfactory. For obvious reasons a departmental committee might be suspected of whitewashing if it found no support for the allegations. On the other hand, the subject under investigation was of too narrow a scope for the creation of a royal commission. Nor did a select committee of the Commons offer the answer. Apart from the need for special authority to compel the attendance of witnesses and the submission of documents (which the House undoubtedly would have granted), there was the question of the partisan character of committee membership which might lead to voting along party lines as has frequently been alleged was true of the Marconi case (1913). The government, therefore, had decided to set up a special Tribunal of Inquiry, but, instead of preparing a bill to deal with this one instance, it had brought in a general bill establishing a new procedure of investigation.

The bill was brought in by the government and its second reading moved after 11 P.M., March 7, 1921, with the understanding that it would go through all the stages that night. However, criticism was immediately directed against some of its provisions: it was objected that a tribunal could be set up without a resolution of the House, merely on the undertaking of a Minister of the Crown, and further that the rights of the witnesses summoned to appear before it were not sufficiently protected. To be sure, Sir Gordon Hewart had stated in his remarks on his motion for a second reading: "It is expressly provided that a witness before any such tribunal shall be entitled to protection as if he were a witness before a Superior Court of Justice. In other words, a witness is entitled to absolute privilege."[7] It was pointed out, however, that the bill allowed the tribunal to exclude the public from its hearings, to deny a witness the right to being represented by counsel, and to punish by imprisonment up to three months a witness who refused to appear or answer questions. Bonar Law, Leader of the House, was impatient of the criticism and stated that if there were opposi-

5 *H.C. Deb.*, Vol. 311, col. 1346.
6 *H.C. Deb.*, Vol. 138, col. 883.
7 *H.C. Deb.*, Vol. 139, col. 189.

tion the government would withdraw the bill, because it was pressed for time and had only introduced it in response to the wishes expressed on all sides of the House. A compromise was arranged to allow a day for conference with the Attorney General on behalf of the objectors. On March 8 the bill was passed, with one amendment accepted by the government. A tribunal could not be set up without a resolution of one of the Houses and required the statement that the inquiry was a matter of urgent public importance. Introduced in the Lords on March 9, the bill met similar criticism with respect to the protection of the rights of individuals summoned to appear before the tribunal. The debate was longer, and the amendments were more drastic. For one thing, a resolution of both Houses was required to set up a tribunal. Secondly, if witnesses refused to appear, the tribunal could not punish them directly but had to apply to the High Court, which would hold a hearing on the question. Finally, the tribunal was not allowed to exclude the public from its sessions unless it decided it was in the public interest so to do. From the tenor of the discussion it was clear that this would be done only in a matter of the gravest importance in which secrecy were demanded for the public good. It was also clearly understood that, although the tribunal had the right to refuse representation by counsel to witnesses, it was the intent of the law to allow it except for unusual circumstances; as Sir Gordon Hewart said, "one can not conceive that the Tribunal would withhold such permission in a proper case. . . ."[8] These amendments of the Lords were in line with what the Commons had wanted and were therefore accepted by the House after several members arose to state that they were glad these matters had been discussed in the Second Chamber although "the House of Commons was supposed to look after the liberty of the subject."[9]

Anticlimactically, the first Tribunal, appointed to report on the alleged concealment of papers from the Exchequer and Audit Department by officials of the Ministry of Munitions, cleared these officials of the charges completely, to the satisfaction even of the original complainant. However, Britain now had a new procedure of investigation. A matter deemed of urgent public importance by both Houses could be investigated by a tribunal appointed by His Majesty or by a Secretary of State. The tribunal was to have "all such powers, rights, and privileges as are vested in the High Court, or, in Scotland the Court of Sessions" in respect to examining witnesses and compelling production of documents and a witness was entitled to the same immunities and privileges as if he were a witness before the High Court.[10] The judicial character of the tribunal tended to place it above the struggle of party politics so that its findings could be held to be nonpartisan. The careful regard for the rights of the individual expressed in both the Commons and the Lords and implemented by the Lord's amendments went far toward building up respect for the procedure and for the findings of the tribunals.

In all, between 1921 and 1948, the date of the Lynskey Tribunal, the tribunal of inquiry was invoked eleven times—the Lynskey Tribunal making the twelfth instance.[11] In every case the subject of the inquiry was a matter affecting some phase of government activity. The first was the investigation of charges against an official of the Ministry of Munitions;[12] the second, an inquiry into

8 *H.C. Deb.*, Vol. 139, col. 2827.

9 *H.C. Deb.*, Vol. 139, col. 2817.

10 11 & 12 Geo. 5, c. 7.

11 Peter G. Richards mentions four instances of the use of the tribunal procedure in "Tribunals of Inquiry (Evidence) Act, 1921," *Public Administration*, Vol. XXVII (1949), pp. 123–128.

12 *Journals of the House of Commons*, 1921, p. 55 [hereafter referred to as *C.J.*].

the actions of the Special Constabulary at Clones Junction when fired on by a unit of the Irish Republican Army.[13] In four other cases the police were concerned, whether the Metropolitan Police or the local constabulary.[14] One case involved the investigation of the loss of a submarine, the *Thetis*;[15] one, the question of drainage in Roncaster.[16] Four dealt with allegations of corruption, two on the local level,[17] and two on the national level; the latter were the budget leak in 1936[18] and the Lynskey Tribunal.

On the whole the judicial character of the tribunal inspired public confidence. In two cases, however, further investigation was considered necessary. In one, in connection with the activities of the Metropolitan Police in their methods of interrogation of a woman, the famous Miss Savidge case, the Tribunal itself was not unanimous, turning in majority and minority reports. The chairman of the Tribunal had been a judge of the High Court. He was assisted by two members of Parliament drawn from the Government and the Opposition; the minority report was drawn up by the Opposition member.[19] In the sequel, a royal commission was appointed to inquire into police methods, a more general question. In the second instance also, a royal commission was set up to inquire into the broader aspects of the original point at issue.[20]

Interesting as a sidelight to the question of the validity of the tribunal procedure was the debate in the Commons in 1936 when the government proposed to investigate the budget leak. The Opposition was violently against its use. At that time Clement Attlee and Sir Stafford Cripps fought bitterly for the use of a select committee of the Commons. Member after member who had been in the House before World War I arose to recall the dissatisfaction produced by the Select Committee on the Marconi case, in which the findings were held to be determined by party lines.[21] Sir Francis Acland, in supporting the tribunal procedure, stated that the proposed inquiry ought to rest on five principles, namely, speed of getting to work, freedom from any sort of partiality, certainty that every material matter will be thoroughly and skillfully investigated, the greatest amount of publicity, and, lastly, the absence of any opportunity for anyone to make political capital out of the conduct of the investigation. Evidently the Tribunal on the budget leak satisfied these conditions; for, in the debate on the acceptance of its report, Attlee admitted handsomely that his opposition had been wrong, stating: "I should like frankly to acknowledge that the Inquiry could not, in my judgement, have been done better."[22]

Although the Tribunal had satisfied the objectives laid down by Sir Francis Acland and generally accepted by the House, there had been procedural difficulties that disturbed those who had participated. Again, the difficulties reflected

---

13 *Journals of the House of Commons*, 1922, p. 27.

14 1. Inquiry into allegations made against certain officers of Metropolitan Police in connection with recent arrest of Major R. O. Sheppard, *C.J.*, 1924–1925, p. 341.

2. Inquiry into allegations made against Chief Constable of Kilmarnock in connection with dismissals from Burgh Police, *C.J.*, 1924–1925, p. 415.

3. Inquiry into complaints that have arisen between the Watch Committee of St. Helena and the Chief Constable of the Borough Police, *C.J.*, 1928, p. 30.

4. Inquiry into the actions of the police in connection with their interrogation of Miss Savidge, *C.J.*, 1928, p. 181.

15 *C.J.*, 1938–1939, p. 273.

16 *C.J.*, 1926, p. 194.

17 1. Inquiry into the letting and allocation of stands in the markets under the control of the Corporation of Glasgow, *C.J.*, 1932–1933, p. 139.

2. Inquiry into the administration by the Council of the City and County of Newcastle-upon-Tyne with respect to use of personnel, food, stores, for Fire, Police and Civil Defense Services, *C.J.*, 1944, p. 39.

18 *C.J.*, 1935–1936, p. 207.

19 Cmd. 3147; *H.C. Deb.*, Vol. 217, cols. 1921 and the following one.

20 Inquiry into effect of the working of minerals on the existing system of land drainage in the Doncaster area, *H.C. Deb.*, July 2, 1926; f. n. 16, earlier in this selection.

21 *H. C. Deb.*, Vol. 311, cols. 1561 and the following one.

22 *H.C. Deb.*, Vol. 313, col. 420.

concern for the rights of witnesses. In its report the Tribunal stated: "But the testing of the witnesses' stories by way of cross-examination or otherwise has necessarily been undertaken by members of the Tribunal themselves, with the resultant possibility of creating the impression that they were from the start hostile to some of the witnesses who appeared before them."[23] This was due to the fact that there was no prosecutor. Also, because there were no definite charges, the Tribunal reported that persons whose conduct was subject to the closest scrutiny were not represented by counsel before the Tribunal until some time had elapsed.

It was with these considerations in mind, that the Lynskey Tribunal devised its procedure and called upon the services of the Attorney General. Sir Hartley Shawcross declared "that although the Attorney General is a member of the Government he has certain duties which he cannot abdicate in connection with the administration of the law, especially the Criminal Law, and more particularly that branch of it which is concerned with the prevention of corruption"[24] and consented to serve as prosecutor to the Tribunal. A third criticism had been raised in regard to the inquiry into the budget leak. The Tribunal felt that witnesses' counsel had been hampered by their inability to object to reception of evidence in the form of hearsay evidence. The Lynskey Tribunal took this into account also. Recognizing that their first responsibility was to get at the facts, they did hear much evidence which "would not be admissible in the case of an individual witness in proceedings against him or in litigation in which he was concerned." They stated, however, "in coming to a conclusion as to the conduct of any individual witness and in particular whether any allegation made in reference to him has been justified, we have had regard only to such evidence as would properly be admitted in a case in which he was a party and his conduct was in question."[25] In this way they were carrying out the intent of both the Government and the Opposition as expressed in the debate in the Commons. As Mr. Attlee said: "His Majesty's Government are, and always have been, most anxious that the fullest public investigation should be made at the earliest possible moment into any allegations reflecting on the purity of public administration. Democracy can not thrive in an atmosphere of suspicion and distrust."[26] At the same time he went on to say that the Act of 1921 expressly provided for the witness the same immunities and privileges as if he were a witness before the High Court and that he need not answer questions on grounds of self-incrimination. To this both Winston Churchill and Clement Davies acceded.

To what extent did the Lynskey Tribunal achieve its purposes: first, as to the investigation of the facts; secondly, as to the satisfactoriness of its procedures?

To an American who is merely familiar with the newspaper accounts of investigations into the affairs of corrupt American public officials and of some of the criminal trials that have followed, it seems surprising that so much excitement was aroused in England about so little. One is struck by the difference in the scale—in America mink coats have become symbolic, whereas in England it was the man's suit of clothes, a clue perhaps to the difference in emphasis in the two societies. But more important than the quantitative difference in the size of what euphemistically might be called gifts, is the difference in the reaction in the two countries to these revelations —perhaps a true index to the different

[23] Cmd. 5184, p. 4.

[24] *Minutes of Evidence of the Lynskey Tribunal*, p. viii.

[25] Cmd. 7616, p. 3.

[26] *H.C. Deb.*, Vol. 457, cols. 89–90.

standards of political morality in these countries.

The Lynskey Tribunal concluded that two public officials had accepted gifts and hospitality knowing full well the purposes for which they had been given and had used their public position to further the interests of the donors. The Parliamentary Secretary for the Board of Trade, John Belcher, it was disclosed, had received three dozen bottles of wine and a little over a dozen bottles of whisky from a whisky distiller with whom he had become friendly. The distiller, Sir Maurice Bloch, was at that time trying to secure import licenses for sherry casks, hogsheads, and butts which were used for the storage and maturing of whisky. He had been having great difficulty in procuring these, and the Tribunal concluded that the gifts of sherry and whisky to Mr. Belcher were given with the hope of expediting these licenses. Mr. Belcher did get in touch, through his secretary, with the official in charge of granting such licenses, urging favorable action if it were proper to do so, and the licenses were issued. Mr. Belcher admitted that he had been indiscreet, and the Tribunal felt that he had accepted the liquor knowing the purpose for which it was intended and had intervened to expedite issue of the licenses.

More dramatic were the details disclosed of the relationship between Mr. Belcher and a Mr. Stanley. Sydney Stanley, an alien and an undischarged bankrupt, who had escaped deportation proceedings in 1933 by changing his name, appeared to be the evil genius of the whole affair. Rebecca West, who has done such distinguished reportorial work on the treason trials in recent years, used her powers of analysis and description to portray the dramatis personae at Church House and particularly the personality of Stanley.[27] He knew what he was doing, he was the personification of the contact man. With an elaborate apartment at Park Lane, which he had difficulty in paying for, he set out to meet members of the government, and was successful in impressing them with his importance. He entertained lavishly, and built up close personal relations with Belcher and others whom he then proceeded to exploit. Using his friendship or association with Belcher to convince his business associates he had influence with the government, he sought to sell his services as best he could. The details are fantastic but, as Sir Hartley Shawcross pointed out in his opening remarks, the pattern of his activities is somewhat characteristic of the ethos of modern business with its lavish expense accounts.

When Stanley could not "deliver" to one of his associates, he claimed he could not return large sums of money he had borrowed because he had used the money to pay off some government officials, including Belcher. That touched off the explosion. The persistent associate sought to bring pressure upon Belcher with the threat of possible publicity, and Belcher's secretary, being informed through another source that he, too, had been accused of being bribed by Stanley, reported the matter to an official of the department, and it was brought to the attention of the President of the Board of Trade. In the subsequent hearings, the secretary was completely cleared of any such imputation.

In the investigation, however, Stanley's associations with other government officials became known, and a second public official was tarred, Mr. George Gibson, a man who had been active in trade-union and Labor party circles for many years. He had served as general secretary of the Confederation of Health Service Employees, had been a member of the General Council of the Trade Union Congress and was chairman of the Trade Union Congress, 1940–1941. In 1946, he had been made a Companion of Honour and appointed a director of

27 *Harper's Magazine,* June and July 1949.

the Bank of England. Stanley having made his acquaintance offered him the chairmanship of a proposed new company in order to get his assistance in obtaining permission from the Capital Issues Committee for a public issue of the shares of the new company. Gibson turned down the offer when he was appointed chairman of the North Western Electricity Board by the government. However, he did approach other government officials on Stanley's behalf. The Tribunal's finding was: "We are satisfied that Mr. Gibson did this in the hope of material advantage to himself although in fact all that he received apart from some trivial gifts [a dozen cigars, some three lbs. of sausage at Christmas and half a bottle of whisky] was the present of a suit of clothes."[28]

In Belcher's case, too, all he had received from Stanley, apart from wining and dining, was a suit of clothes, a gold cigarette case, and the payment of his expenses for one week out of the two he had stayed with his family at a hotel in Margate during a Labour Party Conference. Mr. Stanley had invited Mr. and Mrs. Belcher to stay at his house, but when Belcher indicated they would have to bring the children because they had no one to stay with them, Stanley had arranged to put them up at a hotel instead.

Thus the Lynskey Tribunal after a searching investigation and exhaustive hearings had disclosed that two government officials had accepted gifts and used their official positions to secure help from government departments in expediting business for the donors. All other officials named were cleared.

What was the reaction to these revelations? What were the consequences?

A week before the adoption of the resolution by the House of Commons setting up the Lynskey Tribunal, Mr. Belcher had asked for a leave from his position as Parliamentary Secretary for the Board of Trade, and on the 15th of December, while the hearings were still being held, he sent in his resignation. On the 23rd of December, two days after the close of the hearings, George Gibson resigned his directorship in the Bank of England, retaining his chairmanship of the North Western Electricity Board; this, too, he gave up on the 26th of January.

The debate in the Commons on the acceptance of the Report of the Tribunal took place on February 3, 1949. It was prefaced by Belcher's request for the stewardship of the Chiltern Hundreds, a method of resigning from the House of Commons. He began his speech with an apology for his injudicious actions and indiscretions which, he acknowledged, reflected on the House. He ended on the note that he was not conscious of deviation from the paths of morality and rectitude. Yet the climate of opinion in the House was such that, although individual members expressed sympathy for the ordeal to which he had been put, there was an uncompromising insistence on the acceptance of the highest standards of political morality. As Mr. Attlee put it: "where any individual is highly placed, a finding that he has in any way departed from the highest standards involves a very heavy penalty . . . public administration in this country and public life in this country stand unrivalled in their high standards of service and incorruptibility."[29] This attitude was supported just as uncompromisingly by Churchill and other members of the House. No division along party lines took place. There was no attempt to make political capital out of the affair. Churchill fairly summarized the situation:

Whatever differences we may have, there is no doubt that this House of Commons has

[28] Cmd. 7616, p. 81.

[29] *H.C. Deb.*, Vol. 460, cols. 1850–1852; the Lord Chancellor removed the name of Sir Maurice Bloch from the list of Justices of the Peace.

shown itself most vigilant in matters affecting the honour of Members or Ministers in questions of breach of confidence or questions of breach of privilege, or in questions of the character which are now brought to our notice.[30]

This attitude was reflected throughout the country. As one Member of Parliament put it: "the majority of the British people were shocked to hear that these things could happen in connection with our Parliament and our Government. It is splendid to know they were shocked. I happen to know of other countries in which these things would not shock the public at all."[31]

The debate on the motion to accept the Report of the Lynskey Tribunal brought to the fore certain other questions. A constitutional question as to the relationship between the parliamentary secretary and the permanent secretary of a given department was clarified to the satisfaction of both sides of the House. Less easily solved was the problem whether increased controls over business by the government did not lead to the growth of contact men, who because of their greater knowledge of the regulations and acquaintanceship with government personnel sought to sell their services to business men and exert influence on officials. The Prime Minister promised further study of this aspect.[32] There remained, however, certain questions, also somewhat difficult of solution, as to the Tribunal procedure itself.

Belcher in his statement to the House had criticized the procedure of the Tribunal on several counts. One was that it was not possible to know in advance the nature of the allegations and that much irrelevant material was brought in that was damaging to the reputations of the people involved because of the widespread and pitiless publicity given to the Tribunal by the press. He also bitterly resented the questions on domestic matters (mainly financial) put to his wife. On the other hand, some criticism was expressed in the House, after the Attorney General had stated that criminal action should not be taken because of the wide publicity the Tribunal had received and the nature of the evidence before it, that the whole question should have been turned over to the Public Prosecutor as a criminal case in the beginning.

It is true, as Mr. Attlee conceded, that exceptional publicity was given the Tribunal, and that unjustified slurs might have been cast on innocent, or not so innocent, persons by witnesses who appeared before it. Yet it was essential to get at the facts publicly, because of the widespread whispering and allegations of corruption in the public service. No alternative method seemed able to dispose of the question as efficiently. Witnesses were given the same absolute protection of their rights that they would have been assured of in a court of law, save that there was no appeal from the findings except to the House. It was true that it might be a nice question whether the officials might be considered guilty of a crime in the legal sense. It was also true that the public did not understand the difference between a trial and an inquiry. But on the other hand the rigorous code that demanded resignations from the two public officials against whom the Tribunal had found is the basis of the whole English code of public morality. It is toward this goal that the Douglas subcommittee on improvement of ethical standards in the American federal government was moving when it stated:

It is argued that the leadership and prestige of the Congress depends upon its standards which it sets and maintains for its Members both on and off the floor. Some of the tes-

30 *H.C. Deb.*, Vol 457, col. 91.
31 *H.C. Deb.*, Vol. 460, col. 1881.
32 A Committee on Intermediaries, or contact men, was set up, Feb. 15, 1949; it reported in 1950, Cmd. 7904.

timony has urged the two Houses to take their disciplinary function seriously, and not to be content merely to allow any Member to sit, who, despite improper conduct, is not yet in jail.[33]

Significant, too, is this Committee's criticism of unfair and improper action of Congressional committees, and its urging that a form of procedure be adopted similar to the practices used by the tribunal of inquiry, in which individuals who may be under attack in a public hearing are given advance notice, so that they may be present and have the opportunity to cross-examine the witness. It concludes: "Experience has shown that such standards of fairness do not interfere with effective committee investigations, and it is particularly important that Congress, which is the popular branch of the government, should take the lead in respecting the rights of individuals and in securing the validity of its findings."[34]

[33] Report of the Subcommittee of the Committee on Labor and Public Welfare of the United States Senate, 82nd Cong., 1st Sess. 1951, p. 57.

The experience of the Lynskey Tribunal gives conclusive proof of the rightness of this position. No question of its impartiality or of the validity of its findings was raised in any quarter. It had conducted itself in a way that sought to give every witness seriously charged the fullest protection that a defendant would have under English law, the right of refusal to answer questions that would incriminate him,[35] the right to be represented by counsel which meant that his position could be skillfully clarified and that hostile witnesses could be cross-examined. Both Parliament and the press were convinced that a complete investigation had been made into the allegations and rumors that had been so widely whispered. The total result was a reaffirmation of the integrity of the British Civil Service and of the political morality of the members of Parliament.

[34] Subcommittee on Labor and Public Welfare, p. 56.

[35] Sir Hartley Shawcross revealed in the debate in the Commons on the acceptance of the Lynskey Report that no witness availed himself of this right before the Tribunal.

25. The Decline of the Bureaucratic Ethos in the Federal Republic

THEODOR ESCHENBURG

The Germans, spoiled by an extremely honest public administration for more than a century and a half, are very sensitive to the charge of corruption even today. Formerly, the integrity of the civil servants rested on their consciousness of being members of a special class which was distinct from all other classes. The civil servants were above the other classes and disdained their favors. Hence, other classes did not even dare offer any favors. The gap separating the civil service from other classes protected it from corruption.

This status consciousness does not correspond to modern ideas. Its shielding effect has vanished as well, so that, in fact, considerably higher demands are made on the present-day civil servant.

Now there is not only economic corruption but also political corruption. For example, a civil servant might not have a good conscience about doing a favor for his minister's political friend, but he does not want to spoil his relations with the minister. This lack of steadfastness in the politically corrupted also weakens the resolution of those who are exposed to materialistic enticements, which include the prospect of promotion as well.

Some ministers, who may be good politicians, are simply not very aware of their duties as department heads. According to German tradition, these duties include setting an example both officially and unofficially. These ministers do not realize that biased administrative favors to political friends must have a demoralizing effect on their civil servants. Quite often they lack the resolution to reject demands for administrative favors on the grounds that they cannot expect their civil servants to fulfill such demands. Exemplary behavior on the part of superiors and a strict code of supervision are more effective than all legal rules. Strict supervision cannot be exercised if superiors themselves do not set an example: permissive supervision leads to the corruption of a socially unprotected civil service.

At any rate, no one is forced to become a minister. Whoever takes such an office must renounce some things—*noblesse oblige*. If a manufacturer becomes a minister, his products should no longer be considered an object for state purchases, at least in his own department and during his tenure in office. Otherwise he will stimulate his competitors to corrupt practices.

However, ministers as representa-

SOURCE: Theodor Eschenburg, *Zur politischen Praxis in der Bundesrepublik,* 2d ed. Munich: Piper, 1964, pp. 110–128, 139–141, 204–207, 243–245. By permission of the publisher. Translation by Peggy Hofmann and Michael Libal.

tives of the government, and therefore of the state, must be judged differently from civil servants and according to different standards.

During the Weimar Republic it was common practice for large automobile firms to place cars at the disposal of the President of the Reich or of prominent cabinet members while they were staying away from Berlin. This caused no problem. It was regarded as an aid to democracy and not as some kind of obliging favor to the minister, who would have obtained a car from the administration in any case. At the same time, the use of the car could provide publicity for the firm: photographs of prominent people using their cars were published in magazines and newsreels and had a much higher publicity value than far more expensive advertisements.

However, when the same automobile companies loaned their cars to Prussian police officers for testing purposes, the administration intervened and forbade the practice because loaning cars to civil servants for their personal use was regarded as an unpermittable influence on the contract-awarding practices of the administration. In this case there seemed to be at least a suspicion of corruption.

Recent events have made the lending of cars a questionable practice. Thus, it is doubtful whether the lending of cars to ministers, by itself an unobjectionable practice, can be maintained, precisely because the industry has shown an inability to discriminate.

The fact that the provision of the civil service code that says that a civil servant may accept privileges of a certain value "in connection with his office" only with the consent of his highest ranking superior is often forgotten is part of the weakening of public morality. As a corollary to this, the business community has shown less and less self-restraint.

If a minister permits his wife to accept the gift of a piece of jewelry from a shipowner at the launching of his ship, then he does not formally do anything illegal, as the ministers' code (*Ministergesetz*) does not cover gifts in the way that the civil service code does. Furthermore, the minister does not have a superior whom he can ask for approval. This minister, however, sets a bad example for his subordinates. They think that they should be entitled to accept similar presents without further questioning. Even if they should ask their minister, he ought to give his permission, remembering his own behavior.

If a representative of the Federal Republic gives an official gift to another state, any gift which he receives in return belongs to the Federal Republic, not to him. Within the Federal Republic the nuisance of making gifts to government officials has increased to a considerable degree. It is superfluous and can too easily lead to a reciprocal relationship at the expense of a third person. One can speak of a "gift inflation" as an unwanted by-product of the *Wirtschaftswunder* ("economic miracle"). It is very doubtful whether most of the gifts, and especially the more expensive ones, have the public relations effect on the basis of which they are claimed as deductible to the tax authorities. A large department store is said to have required its employees to turn in all gifts received from other firms. Recently this store is supposed to have exhibited all these gifts in order to demonstrate to the companies they came from how senseless the whole thing was. In the long run no one is able to maintain his advantage in the distribution of gifts. One company is outdone by another which causes it to redouble its efforts in turn—one constantly tries to outdo the other. This is all basically true of favors to public officials, with the important difference that bureaucratic ethics, and thereby public life, suffer from it.

The time has come for the large

corporations to consider whether they might best serve their own interests by making a concerted effort to halt the present practices, as Mercedes director Konecke has advised. Of course, one will not be able to do without the public, legal, and, most of all, administrative acts that might counteract the present relaxation of public morals. But the manufacturers' associations do not have to wait for these laws; they could create their own regulations.

In doing this they would not have to deal with trivia and adhere to strict rules of correctness *ad absurdum*. They should not start on the level of pocket calendars and mailmen but rather at the top. If business associations agree that members of the government and the civil service should no longer receive any gifts, regardless of the occasion, then every firm could refer to this agreement and need not be ashamed about not sending any.

At this point we seem more and more often to be losing sight of the strict rules of morality in public life. However, public reaction (at least insofar as it is not just enjoying sensationalism) shows that we have not yet entirely lost these standards. There is still time to support them once more. On the whole the extent of corruption should not be overestimated. Considering all of the experiences of the war and its aftermath, it is rather surprising that we are not more corrupt than we are. The odds for a new attempt to live up to these standards are not bad, and it is precisely the actions referred to above which might help.

THE KILB CORRUPTION TRIAL

While he was still a personal assistant to Chancellor [Adenauer], *Ministerialrat* Kilb used cars that were lent to him by a large automobile firm without any charge. According to the civil service code, doing so required the approval of his superior, the Chancellor. From the decision of the Seventh Criminal Court of the Bonn District Court, explaining why the final proceedings against Kilb were suspended, it can be gathered that he did not request permission in the normally prescribed way. The Chancellor, however, according to his own admission, knew about the borrowing of the cars and "openly tolerated" it.

That the thought of accepting such a privilege would even occur to a civil servant in Kilb's position, even with the agreement of the Chancellor, is highly questionable, although it is unimportant from the point of view of criminal law. The fact that Kilb evaded his legal duty to obtain the approval of his superior speaks even more against his qualifications as a civil servant, although this may also be insignificant before the law. However, since the Chancellor knew about Kilb's use of the car and tolerated it, the responsibility is his and he certainly is willing to accept its full measure. He testified that Kilb could have acted on his tacit consent as if his official approval had actually been given.

The Chancellor's argument was as follows: his personal assistant was at his disposal not only in his official capacity as head of the government but also in his position as party politician. For example, his personal assistant was required to take care of the preparations for campaign speeches and in general had to handle matters that included "no objective policy decisions, no voicing of personal opinions, and very few duties typically performed by civil servants."

It must be recognized that it is impossible to restrict to official affairs only the activities of a personal assistant to a parliamentary minister, let alone to a head of government, who is a member of the legislative party and who ordinarily occupies a high position in the party. Quite often questions of government politics and party politics are so closely linked that they cannot be separated at all. Already during the Weimar Republic it was customary for the personal assistant of a minister to carry out partisan political tasks for his boss. In addition, it may very well be the case that personal assistants do not decide on policy matters and do not voice their opinions as other civil servants of the high ministerial bureaucracy do. Personal assistants wield far greater influence, and they wield it in a different manner.

They continuously gather information for their minister and transmit his instructions either in person or by telephone, so that there is no way to control these activities. For example, by carefully choosing their words and emphasis they can bias their reports for or against certain interests. It is at least theoretically possible—and it is said to have actually occurred—for personal assistants to insert their own subjective opinions in their verbal reports and to appear to be representatives of their bosses during inquiries and briefings without actually being so.

Whatever Kilb might have done in this one case, Adenauer's notion of the scope of activity and the position of a personal assistant is wrong. A personal assistant is not just a high-class errand boy who only executes his superior's orders and who could not possibly be influenced in his official activities by private favors. The fact that the Chancellor tolerated the usage of a car by his personal assistant and that he remained convinced of its legality implied a seriously mistaken conception of his official duties.

Adenauer argued further, according to the records of the Seventh Criminal Court, that, if the personal assistant "serves the head of the government," any aid that comes to him should also be regarded as promoting the policies of the head of the government. There was nothing illegal about such aid. If no objections were raised to a company's placing cars at the disposal of the Chancellor, and thereby easing his tasks, then nothing could be said about placing cars at the disposal of his assistants.

In point of fact, up until now the use of borrowed automobiles by members of the administration was not challenged because it provided publicity for the automobile manufacturers, and there was no concern about one-sided favors. This argument, however, is not valid when the civil servant who uses the car is not publicly known.

Up until now it has been an indisputable principle that, for the sake of the integrity of the government, all personal and business expenditures on governmental activities should be covered exclusively by the state, that is, by the budget approved by parliament. If the idea spread that private firms were permitted to promote and support the duties of members of the government by providing supplies and services, it might lead to an unforeseen change in our governmental and administrative order.

The Chancellor's testimony implying that support for his personal assistant from a private firm is equivalent to support for his own policy places the Kilb incident in an entirely new light. This affair could set an extremely important political precedent. If an unequivocal correction is not made here, then others could refer to the reasoning of the Seventh Criminal Court later.

It seems as if the Chancellor is excusing his personal assistant by accusing himself, according to the configuration of political ethics that have been followed up until now. But precisely because of this testimony the Chancellor has become the main character in the "Kilb incident," not in a criminal but in a politicial sense.

With or without approval, a civil servant in Kilb's position simply cannot afford to do anything that is not permitted to other civil servants. His bad example can undermine the good morals of the others. Even if the Chancellor had not just tolerated the use of a borrowed car (apparently Kilb did not obtain the ordinary permission, for otherwise a notice of approval would have been found in his personal file) but had given him outright permission, Kilb should have refused such an offer for the sake of the civil servants' moral discipline. He did not commit a punishable crime, but even the decision of the Court of Appeals (*Oberlandesgericht*) at Cologne cannot free him from the moral guilt.

The Kilb incident has shown again that there is and must be an inalienable nucleus of self-responsibility in the mind of civil servants. This nucleus remains even if the civil servant's superior takes responsibility for his behavior. The old, overburdened Chancellor, working in such a concentrated manner, may have committed an oversight under the pressure of other duties. However, the Chancellor does have experienced civil servants with expert knowledge in his administration to whom he could have referred the matter. Apparently he did not ask them. He certainly was not concerned about doing a special favor to a personal assistant who had already quit the job before the case became public. Instead Adenauer wanted to enable his assistant to fulfill certain predominantly partisan political duties much more quickly than he could have done without a car. Perhaps the Chancellor's car pool was too small. If the personal assistant was to serve the person of the Chancellor, Adenauer argued, then aid for his assistant had to be regarded as a promotion of the policy of the Chancellor as well. There was nothing illegal about such aid.

Deputy Arndt (SPD), who is highly regarded for his legal skill by all parties, considers it a violation of pariamentary budget rights if cars are loaned to the Chancellor's office by private companies. Government expenditures for personnel and supplies must be met exclusively by appropriations made by pariament. Parliament decides on the use of the budget not only by controlling its size but also by determining the scope and manner of the operation of public institutions.

If the violation of this principle were to become common, then Mr. Strauss could employ a private body guard with the aid of private donations, or Mr. Schröder could start a private detective agency. Regardless, no clear borderline could be drawn between purely governmental activities and those official activities primarily serving party and party interest if privately financed institutions worked together with, and under the protection of, official institutions, maybe even under the same roof.

In itself the Kilb incident may be regarded as more or less unimportant. The frightening thing is the precedent it may set. To the extent that Adenauer tries to excuse Kilb, he accuses himself.

It is probably not possible to prevent the personal assistant of a parliamentary minister from carrying out partisan political activities connected with the minister's duties as a member of the legislative party. Therefore it would be better if the personal assistants were not civil servants but employees who left public service as soon as their minister resigned, because their partisan political activities prevent them from being ordinary civil servants. It is even conceivable that a certain portion of the budget could be assigned to ministers so that their personal assistants could be their personal employees rather than employees of the state. The personal assistant who is a civil servant is legally and morally bound to the rights and duties of all civil servants; also, in carrying out his duties he may only use those means that are officially appropriated and explicitly placed at his disposal. Therefore, he can demand neither privileges for himself nor favors for his minister just because of his position.

In any case the partisan political activities must be restricted to the personal assistant and must not be transferred to other civil servants. The press-secretary might be an exception. But his relationship to his employer should be the same as that of the personal assistant.

This is not the only instance where the blurring of the borderline between governmental and party service does occur. It is simply not permissible for civil servants in the ministerial bureaucracy all the way down to an *Oberregierungsrat* or to a *Regierungsrat* to participate in meetings of the government party caucus or its committees for the purpose of providing information about either cabinet or ministry policy. Such contacts with members of the government party caucus are particularly objectionable since the opposition party cannot demand the same. Even if the opposition could do so, it would not be acceptable for civil servants to discuss government policy with deputies in this manner. This abuse of their office by the members of the federal government is probably not entirely unknown to the SPD and it should have opposed it. One must conclude that the institutional borderlines must be redrawn more sharply.

The Kilb incident also demonstrates that federal ministers are not allowed to grant extraordinary permission without having first consulted the competent adviser—either the undersecretary or the head of the personnel department. Some time ago in Bavaria two state ministers, presumably out of ignorance, gave a civil servant a special permission that was illegal. The civil servant who took advantage of this was then punished for it, which does not diminish the shame of the legally unimpeachable ministers. According to the criminal records the Kilb case is closed. Now it is the task of the federal government or even of the *Bundestag* or of the *Bundesrat* to evaluate the lessons learned from this case in order to solve institutional problems, which are obvious.

A REMINDER OF THE CIVIL SERVICE CODE

Besides the "big" corruption suits like the one against civil servants of the Army's supply office in Koblenz and the one against *Ministerialdirektor* Kunde of the federal Ministry of Transportation, there were a number of suits in recent years in which less was at stake but which, for precisely that reason, were more important with regard to drawing the line between legal and illegal behavior. Among these cases is the suit against Colonel Löffelholz of the Federal Defense Department. He had received relatively few favors from large companies. The District Court in Bonn had sentenced Löffelholz to imprisonment with a probationary suspension of the sentence. The review of the High Federal Court (*Bundesgerichtshof*) brought an acquittal.

Whichever side one chooses to take with regard to the latest corruption suits in the federal republic, one factor has become obvious: in most of the cases the provision of the civil service code which states that the civil servant may accept donations in connection with his office only with the approval of the highest authority has been neglected. The defendants could have saved themselves and their superiors the embarrassment of an inquiry—and a suit—had they carefully and in time followed this provision.

It is highly unlikely that the former personal assistant of the Chancellor, Kilb, would have had to expose himself to the inconveniences of detention had he been able to show the written approval of the Chancellor for the use of a borrowed car. In the case of the Lord Mayor of Stuttgart, Klett, it seems equally clear that he received part of the controversial birthday presents in connection with his office as Lord Mayor—not necessarily bribery in itself—and that according to the law he was required to obtain permission, which he did not even try to obtain, in order to accept these gifts. Similarly, those civil servants who got away without an indictment will have to reckon with disciplinary measures because they neglected to ask for permission.

However, it is hard to get rid of the impression that the corruption suits so far have had no lasting effect on large sections of the civil service. It seems it is precisely the consent requirement, which was forgotten during the war and postwar years, that has frequently not been observed and is not taken seriously any longer. There are even some civil servants who admit that they hesitate to obtain the required authorization because they are afraid they will look ridiculous in doing so. Actually the lessons from the corruption suits should have been obvious to the ministries and local administrations and should have strongly reminded their civil servants of this old provision and of the fact that it would be strictly enforced in the future. Nothing has been heard of any such reminders.

The authorization provision, which is to be found as early as 1873 in the Reich's Civil Service Code, has been issued to preserve the respectability and integrity of the civil service, but, at this time, it serves as protection for the civil servant: he can refer to it whenever favors are offered to him and thereby also avoid appearing rude. In its recently revealed Löffelholz decision, the High Federal Court stated that it was only natural that representatives of an administrative department that had a considerable number of government purchases to make should be treated by companies in question with the requisite courtesies. A civil servant who does not want to violate the social norms and by doing this endanger the reputation of his department can hardly turn his back on such courtesies. This is a correct view, but by itself and without the requirement to get authorization for accepting any emoluments, it would be dangerous. The civil servant is far safer if he is required to obtain authorization for accepting any privileges or gifts or, if that is impossible, if he renders an account at a later date. It cannot be argued that such a provision can no longer be put into practice. There are private firms and large independent organizations that require all of their employees without exception to ask for permission to accept any favors or privileges or at least to render an account of them. They also see to it that these rules are observed.

In an editorial on the Löffelholz decision, the *Süddeutsche Zeitung* speaks of the "enormous difficulty . . . of finding the reasonable middle ground in corruption cases between petty moral narrow-mindedness and demoralizing generosity." This may be true for the individual and often for the judges who have to decide on each individual case, but it is not true for the administration. The administration is faced with a wide variety of cases, so it has opportunities to draw comparisons and can set standards for its decisions. As things are in the bureaucracy there will probably be no lack of attempts to torpedo effective reenforcement of these regulations through numerous trifling requests. A skilled administration should have no difficulty in counteracting these attempts.

CHAPTER SIX

The United States

26. Corruption: The Special Case of the United States

JACOB VAN KLAVEREN

. . . The Northwest European development [of political corruption] is a unique, historically based phenomenon. We know that the political systems of the so-called underdeveloped regions still remain in the stage of systematic corruption, and there are good reasons for this which we cannot go into here. For simplicity's sake, let us say that the Age of Enlightenment has not yet, in a relative sense, occurred there, which is not too surprising considering the low educational level.[1] But the more difficult question is why in the United States, despite its independence due in part to the enlightened ideas of the colonists, corruption is systematically practiced even today.[2]

This is a well-known fact among those studying American history, yet it is difficult to obtain more specific explanations and information from American scholars. Particularly the present conditions are left unstudied.

Corruption is a delicate subject, and the dependent position of the American professor[3] is not conducive to the systematic study of this subject. However, during my stay in Siam, it was an American guest, strangely enough, who made an open statement on corruption in the United States today. Yet, this was meant to comfort the Siamese, who are accustomed to be treated scathingly by the Europeans because of the state of corruption in their country.[4] Yet in the past many American authors and journalists have discussed corruption in their coun-

1 A warning is in order here. An opposition is bound to arise as soon as the number of intellectuals and semiintellectuals (e.g. students) considerably exceeds the number of positions of profit with which they could be accommodated. Thus, in Southeast Asia I was able to observe that the lower civil servants, who were largely excluded from the benefits of corruption, took a hostile position toward corruption, as did the businessmen. Also compare the hostile attitude taken by the late President of the Philippines, Ramón Magsaysay, who had been victimized by corruption as a bus company owner in Manila before the war. Strong resistance is to be found in Indonesia, where the honest Dutch administration is not yet totally forgotten. Besides, it is hard to imagine that the purpose of "national" revolution could have been to enrich the revolutionary leaders at the expense of the people. Much agitation, however, is traceable to envy alone. As a rule, the influence of the few opponents of principle has been watered down by universal suffrage.

SOURCE: Jacob van Klaveren, "Die Historische Erscheinung der Korruption: Die Sonderentwicklung in den Vereinigten Staaten," *Vierteljahrsschrift für Sozial- und Wirtschaftsgeschichte,* 46:2 (1959), pp. 204–212. By permission of the publisher, Franz Steiner Verlag. Translated by Peggy Hofmann and Karl Kurtz.

2 Nothing needs to be said about the cities' administrations. Corruption on the federal level—shortly before new presidential elections—has become known to the public through the mutual accusations of the parties. Read the press report on Eisenhower's assistant, Sherman Adams. The President has not been saved either. See articles by Don Iddon in the Amsterdam newspaper *De Telegraaf* from June 18 and June 26, 1958. Iddon points out in several examples that the opponents are basically just the same. Therefore he regards the Adams scandal as a Washington scandal and not just a White House scandal.

3 It seems almost unnecessary to prove this observation. See, for example, N. F. Hofstee, *Organisatie en bestuur van de Universiteit,* Diss. Groningen, Assen n.d. (1949 or 1950), p. 77.

4 There Americans are also correctly considered as Europeans "since they have a white face as well."

try much more frankly than today. One can only infer from this that the United States became increasingly embarrassed about and correspondingly sensitive to this phenomenon. But even the nineteenth-century journalists rarely tried or were able to explore the specific basic causes. Considering all these reasons it may be plausible and acceptable for a European to concern himself with these truly American conditions. Perhaps this can be justified by the fact that the origins can only be explained by comparative observations beginning with the central European development.

Anyone who reviews American history must wonder why the corruption that was so common in the *ancien régime* and among English colonial officers never disappeared from the American scene in either the period of property requirements for suffrage or during the period of universal male suffrage. Occupants of countless offices, who are appointed by public authority in Europe, were selected in local elections in the United States, so that there were ideal guarantees for an honest administration. The key to understanding this lies in the fact that the majority of the population of the United States did not place any value on an honest administration, or at least they never collectively manifested this. This leads us again to the fact that the United States was not yet a "true" nation, as we will show later. It first had to become unified into a nation, a process that was frequently interrupted by the increasing number of immigrants, and which maybe has not yet reached its goal. Another factor may be that suffrage became universal too early. This seems like a contradiction within our system, but this is not the case, as we can prove by the European constitutional development. We shall refer to this later.

However, this does not say anything about corruption shortly after the Revolution, when immigration was still limited and suffrage was based on property rights in the majority of the original states. Proof that corruption existed is provided by the unsparing criticism [leveled at the United States] by the English in the early nineteenth century.[5] First we shall discuss the period when ownership of property was required for the suffrage.[6]

THE AGE OF THE COLONIAL ARISTOCRACY AND OF CENSUS SUFFRAGE

The Age of Enlightenment was decisively important in Europe for the development of an honest administration. But it was also important for the American revolt. England's strongest adversaries were the petite bourgeoisie and the artisans of New England, among whom the "Sons of Liberty" arose. These groups had been very heavily influenced by the Enlightenment. It is amazing to see the thirst for knowledge with which these common people sought out the theories of the Encyclopedists, how they worked to improve their education with evening courses . . . and all sorts of other subjects.[7] Benjamin Franklin was probably the most famous representative of these groups, although he emigrated to Philadelphia as a youth. The further south one went, the less important was this group. The colonial aristocracy, which was represented in the colonial assemblies, also toyed with enlightened, French ideas, but they became meaningful there only when they were related to the colonists' right of self-determination in relation to the mother country. Later it was discovered that many phrases in the Constitution had

---

5 See Merle Curti, *Das amerikanische Geistesleben* (translated). Stuttgart [1947 (1943)], p. 327 f.

6 I do not intend to prove in detail these well-known facts, which can be found in any good textbook on American history.

7 The detailed discussions in Carl Bridenbaugh, *The Colonial Craftsman*. New York: New York University Press (1950), are extremely interesting. For their activities as Freemasons and their courses in electricity, mathematics, and so on, see pp. 165, 166, 175.

never been thoroughly thought through. Thus, in 1857 the Supreme Court determined that Negroes could not be citizens of the United States according to its constitution.[8] Undoubtedly the majority of the framers of the Constitution were conservative representatives of the colonial aristocracy with little esteem for democracy.[9] In most of the original states only a minority, approximately one-eighth of the adult male population, had the right to vote.[10]

Thus it is understandable that the members of the colonial aristocracy, who usurped all power after the War of Independence, took over the positions of the former English civil servants and also demanded for themselves the revenues that belonged to those positions. These revenues derived to a high degree from the sale of public land.[11] The majority of the framers of the Constitution were interested in real estate speculation, and therein also lies an important reason for the rebellion. When the French had been driven out of the hinterland between the Mississippi and the Appalachians during the Seven Years' War and the big land business could get started, the English government forbade the distribution of land west of a so-called proclamation line generally coinciding with the western border of the Appalachians. This did not mean that no territories could no longer be distributed but that land concessions had to be secured from London instead of from the colonial administration. This inroad into the profits of the colonial administrators was eliminated by the rebellion, and, whereas corruption disappeared in England after 1784, it continued in the United States with double the strength.

Just a brief comparison of the different development of the United States and its former mother country will be provided here. In England the old upper classes had remained in office, but now they were controlled by the bourgeoisie. In the United States the old rulers had disappeared and the colonial aristocracy had stepped into the offices, but there was no bourgeois controlling group, particularly in the Southern states.[12] The colonial aristocracy gained primarily through the distribution of territories, but not all states were enlarged with parts of the hinterland. The representatives of the "have-not" states had no share in these benefits, so they wanted to make the land distribution a job for the federal government in which they were represented. When Georgia, in 1802, became the last state to agree to this, a considerable part of the land had already been sold, but from then on the big land business was done on the federal level,

8 This refers to the case of the emancipated Negro slave Dred Scott. See Ray Allen Billington, *Westward Expansion: a History of the American Frontier*. New York [1954 (1949)], p. 604. Compare the text of the Declaration of Independence: "We hold these truths to be self-evident, that all men are created equal; that they are endowed by their creator with inalienable rights. . . ." Of course, the Declaration was mainly concerned with laying down principles, so the judges had to find information in the commentaries and proceedings.

9 On this point see the thorough treatment of Leonard Woolf, *After the Deluge; A Study of Communal Psychology*. London: Pelican Books [1947 (1931)], p. 168.

10 See Harold U. Faulkner, *American Political and Social History*. New York (1937), chap. VII.

11 The revenues began with the building of the Capitol, the symbol of national independence. According to the reports, the expenditures for the building were estimated at $12 million, but $27.2 million more were needed. See Mark Twain. *The Gilded Age: A Tale of Today*, 2 vols. New York (1873) 1:263 f.

12 The New England states differ from the Southern states on this. They had no hinterland available for land speculation, so they were not hurt by the proclamation line. Despite the fact that the tightening-up of the navigation laws bothered them, the Northern upper class, which was a merchant aristocracy, remained loyal to the mother country, whose gentry they regarded as an example to be followed. Therefore, most of them had to leave the country along with the English. Those left behind, however, replenished the ranks by admitting the descendants of the numerous new rich, who made good profits from the newly opened trade with China and, particularly, as neutrals during the French War. The rise of the merchant aristocracy has been described well by Bernard Baylin in *The New England Merchants in the Seventeenth Century*. Cambridge, Mass. (1955).

and the representatives of all the states got a part of the benefits gained through speculation based on the continuous westward settlement. This settlement led to the creation of additional states with equal rights whose representatives were opposed to the old colonial aristocracy. The continuous settlement, which benefited the colonial aristocracy, was eventually to tear away its power in the country.

THE WEST AND UNIVERSAL MALE SUFFRAGE

Universal suffrage was introduced in the United States much earlier than in Europe. It was an option of the individual states. The new Western states introduced universal male suffrage in principle at once, and the original states followed suit during Andrew Jackson's presidency (1829–1837). This action on the part of the West is understandable. Marked inequalities in the distribution of property, on which a property discrimination for suffrage might have been based, was still unknown in the West, so almost all of the settlers were qualified to vote. In addition, the free frontiersmen would not tolerate such an obvious discrimination. Thus, since all of them had the right to vote, they could have eliminated corruption if they had wanted to.

The people of the West were not only lovers of liberty, they were also uneducated and outspokenly individualistic. Everyone had his own best interests at heart and did not think about the wider societal implications. Almost all of them went west with the one thought of enriching themselves by means of the land rush, and basically the pioneers were no different from the big land speculators who snapped up the best land. With a slight variation on the technique known as "catch-as-catch-can,"[13] we can characterize this spirit with the expression "grab-as-grab-can." Everyone snapped up as much as he could,[14] and naturally the politicians did likewise. The Westerners understood this but did not consider the deeper consequences. They had little education, and the number of semiliterates or illiterates was frighteningly high. This was particularly true for those parts of the West settled by "native" Americans, which was the rule until approximately 1850. The Westerners were outspokenly hostile to intellectuals, and candidates who were identifiable as intellectuals did not have any chance to be elected in the West.[15] In particular the members of the old colonial aristocracy, who were naturally unable to hide their identity, could not take a leading role in the West. When the number of Western states increased, the influence of the West on the federal government rose too, and even the presidency had to go to the West. This jeopardized the employment of the colonial aristocracy in the federal offices. The introduction of universal male suffrage in the original states dates from the presidency of the Indian fighter from Tennessee, General Jackson (1829–1837); at the same time the old upper class disappeared from positions of political leadership in the country.[16]

13 The Westerners were very familiar with this way of fighting. See R. A. Billington. p. 481.

14 We deliberately overemphasized this. Ernest L. Bogart and Donald L. Kemmerer, *Economic History of the American People*. New York (1942), p. 549, say it in different words: The public was "too much absorbed in private affairs" to complain about it. F. W. Taussig, *Principles of Economics*, II. New York [1921 (1911) Revised 1938], p. 415, sees the cause in the mentality of the American people. Corruption was regarded as something natural, general morality was low, and the larger implications were unknown.

15 In the widely spread settlements illiteracy led to crass ignorance and the practical apostasy of the Christian faith. Therefore, numerous churches and sects tried to send their preachers to the West. There were illiterates among the preachers as well, but this was regarded favorably because it helped in establishing contact with the rough pioneers. Read · Curti's interesting discussion. By the way, one must consider that France had approximately 60 percent illiteracy in 1830; however, they had no influence because of the property requirements for voting.

16 See Merle Curti, p. 345, and E. Digby Baltzell, *Philadelphia Gentlemen*; *The Making of a National Upper Class*. New York (1958), p. 188.

This in itself was not so disastrous since, unlike the lords and gentry in England, the American upper class had not yet made an honest administration a part of their common life style. Therefore, there was no basic change with the influx of Westerners into federal offices. Only the preconditions for the distribution of land, and therefore for speculation and corruption, were changed. Of course, the Westerners forcefully demanded from their representative a land policy that limited the large-scale speculation by reducing the minimum size of lots, thus giving the settlers the possibility of purchasing such lots at low prices, and preferably, in installments direct from the local land offices. Under the pressure of these demands the Homestead Act, which stated that every settler could get a quarter section, or 160 acres, for free, was enacted in 1862. This applied only as long as there was land available, so the smart politicians had provided themselves with a loophole of which they made abundant use.

As early as 1851 the erection of railroads had been subsidized by grants of land. The grants of land lay on both sides of the projected railroad track and formed a band whose width was proportionate to the size of the subsidies. One must imagine the landscape divided along meridians and parallels in blocks of one square mile (= one section) alternately colored black and white, just like a chessboard. The railway was only able to obtain alternate sections of one color, either black or white. If several sections were granted in one mile, the grants just stretched farther into the land. The size of the subsidy, that is, the width of the band,[17] was decided by the politicians in Washington, where relations between railroad companies and senators or representatives were established by lobbyists, wives, nieces, and so on. In this manner half of what was the most valuable land because it was situated close to the railroad was given to the railroads themselves, that is, to the big speculators. The legislators in Washington were quite good at inventing new excuses for giving public land to the big speculators, since these transactions were very profitable, unlike the distribution of land to the settlers. Even to the extent that the land was distributed to the settlers it fell partly to the speculators with the help of dummy buyers since the politicians had made the homesteads salable. These manipulations gave the civil servants from the local land offices their chance, too, since the sale could not take place without their cooperation. It follows that the settlers received only a small portion of the available land. They were thoroughly misled by their own politicians even when the politicians gave the appearance in public of representing the people's interests.[18]

The railways and "big business" gave the politicians new chances for personal gain, which they preferred to representing the interests of the electorate. The monopolistic exploitation of the public by big business (by which the railroads were primarily meant at this time) is closely tied to the political exploitation of the public by means of dealings between corrupt politicians and big business. This connection thoroughly confused the farmers. They confused cause and effect and fought primarily against big business

At this time the difference between Washington "society" and that of the East coast developed and was interpreted by Mark Twain, in *The Gilded Age*, p. 220: "It doesn't need a crowbar to break your way into society there as it does in Philadelphia."

17 If a railway company obtained ten sections for each mile of the track, railway land reached 10 miles deep on each side of the track.

18 Other laws that made possible the distribution of land to speculators were the Timber Culture Act (1873), Desert Land Act (1877), and the Timber and Stone Act (1878). The result was that 80 million acres were distributed to farmers—part of whom were still dummy buyers—but 521 million acres went to speculators. See Billington, pp. 696–701. Bogart and Kemmerer, p. 496, call the land offices "centers for the distribution of the plunder." When Theodore Roosevelt (1901) cleaned out the land offices, the disaster had already occurred.

—particularly against railway and grain elevator companies—and regarded corruption of the civil servants and politicians almost entirely as a consequence of the domination of capital. For this reason, the fight of the farmers' associations against corruption was only secondary in nature and not of primary concern. Generally, the policy of the farmers' associations must be regarded as a result of the "Big Depression" of the period 1873–1896.

THE STRUGGLE AGAINST BIG BUSINESS AND CORRUPTION

. . .[Taussig] rejects the frequently held opinion that big business is the cause of corruption . . .[and] seeks the reason among the dishonest politicians, whereby the identity of the initiator is unimportant.[19] The question of initiative is unimportant, because politicians and civil servants had always been corrupt long before big business developed. . . . Corruption is always extortion of the public, even if it is initiated and perpetuated by the interposition of businessmen. Hence it is incorrect to identify the question of initiative with that of "extortion or bribery," as Taussig does.[20] The question of initiative is only relevant if the administration itself is honest; even then it is important only from the standpoint of criminal law. It is possible that the initiative for many dubious manipulations in the United States came from big business, but the success of these maneuvers is only due to the fact that corruption already existed. For the entrepreneurs always had to pay, even for the fulfillment of the normal formalities, even if only *one* company applied for the right of way to one particular railroad franchise. If several railroad companies were trying to outdo one another, they had to compete in the size of the "bribes." Yet these were not real bribes because from the beginning it was understood that a concession could not be obtained without such special payments. Only the size of the payments differed, depending on whether and how many entrepreneurs and civil servants were in competition with one another. In any case, civil servants, judges, and politicians regarded the economy as an object for extortion. This can be learned from the correspondence of famous railroad magnates, which has been edited by Thomas C. Cochran. In general, the politicians were regarded by the magnates as parasites who accepted and promised everything but never kept their word or who took money from all of the competitors and decided in favor of the highest bidder without returning the losers' money.[21] Others drafted antirailroad bills if they were not given any free rides or bribes.[22] The opinion of President Cass of the Northern Pacific Railroad, writing in 1873, is interesting: "Wise and good men get corrupt in Congress."[23] It is clear that the railroad companies would rather have kept their money than pay it to a judge or politician.

This is not to say, however, that railroad entrepreneurs handled their own offices in an unobjectionable manner. However, corruption was less widespread within the railroad companies than among civil servants and politicians, since it was not tolerated among the employees. The beneficiaries were primarily the boards of trustees ("directors"), who are less important in Europe but who, in America, made the entrepreneurial decisions. Besides, the "managers" were also allowed to share the

19 F. W. Taussig, II, p. 431 f.
20 F. W. Taussig, II, p. 432.

21 H. R. Smith, p. 316, provides a striking example. Once, the rivalry between Vanderbilt and Jay Gould led Vanderbilt to pay an important member of the New York legislature $75,000. The same politician accepted $100,000 from Gould later. When the issue came up, the politician voted for Gould but kept Vanderbilt's $75,000.
22 See H. R. Smith, p. 315, and Thomas C. Cochran, *Railroad Leaders 1845–1890*. Cambridge, Mass. (1953), p. 195.
23 T. C. Cochran, p. 190.

profits. Prior to the great railroad crisis in 1873 the profits were secured by diverting the company's capital into the pockets of the executives. The directors, a few influential stockholders, and some managers usually formed a "construction company" to build the railroad line at much too high a price.[24] After 1873 the European public, which had to provide the capital, became more alert. However, functionaries still obtained revenues out of a variety of so-called sidelines, this is, projects that they bought out along the railroad line, often after having forced the previous owner to sell by charging high freight rates.[25] Of particular importance, however, was the land speculation close to the railroads.

They tried to cut off the lower railway officials from all benefits. In this they were quite successful since they could control employment and dismissals.[26] This was impossible in the civil administration, where many offices were elective. Thus Taussig's argument that the direct election of the civil servants was one of the reasons for the corruption of the civil servants becomes understandable.[27] Precisely those provisions that could have guaranteed the honesty of the civil servants led to just the opposite effect in the United States, because, as Taussig put it, "a community of good character, intelligence and conduct was lacking." Hence, the responsibility belonged to the public itself: "A good electorate will choose honest and capable officials, a debased and indifferent one will tolerate demagogues and thieves."[28] Thus the question is shifted to the "low level" of the American public. However, this is neglected by Taussig and almost all other students.

[The author then elaborates this delicate aspect of the problem and reaches the opinion that an incipient improvement was followed by a setback by 1900.]

24 Prior to 1873 this was normal. See T. C. Cochran, p. 111. The first transcontinental line was built by a construction agency with the beautiful name Crédit Mobilier. But it probably had nothing to do with the bank of the same name of the Péreire brothers, which was liquidated in 1866. Out of its immense profits it also had to reward the politicians who had voted for the subsidies. See H. R. Smith, p. 316, and Franklin M. Reck, *The Romance of American Transportation*. New York, Crowell, 1938, p. 141.

25 These included wheat silos, wheat mills, hotels, and so on. Consider, though, that the standards for an honest administration in the business world had not yet been determined, whereas they were already laid out in great detail for the civil servants.

26 Thus, Vice-President Oakes of the North Pacific Railroad ordered some employees to nullify their purchases of land or else face being fired. See T. C. Cochran, p. 216. It was impossible to control the freight departments since the tariffs differed from day to day and from customer to customer. It was the age of secret freight rates.

27 F. W. Taussig, p. 431.

28 F. W. Taussig, p. 431.

27. Spoilsmen and Reformers: Civil Service Reform and Public Morality

ARI HOOGENBOOM

The reaction of an American historian to the phrase "Gilded Age" is nearly as predictable as that of a Pavlov dog to a bell. Thoroughly conditioned, the historian thinks of corruption. He will condemn (often while enjoying) Senator Roscoe Conkling's affair with Kate Chase Sprague that Senator Sprague abruptly terminated by running Conkling off his property with a shotgun; Reverend Henry Ward Beecher's success at seducing his lady parishioners that resulted in the most spectacular trial of the nineteenth century; or capitalist Jim Fisk's insane infatuation for Josie Mansfield that led to his murder on the steps of the Fifth Avenue Hotel. A notorious libertine, ravisher of railroads, and corrupter of governments, Fisk achieved immortality thanks largely to two reformers, Charles Francis Adams, Jr., and his brother Henry, who described in intimate detail Fisk's sordid relations with both the Erie Railroad and public officials.[1]

Ever since the Adams brothers wrote their essays the immorality, especially the political immorality, of the Gilded Age has attracted historians. Using Fisk as an example, they insist that public and business morals matched private ones. On the municipal level there was New York's spectacularly corrupt Tweed ring, overshadowing the more modest activities of Philadelphia's gas ring and Washington's Boss Shepherd. State governments were also corrupt. The *Nation* reported in the spring of 1867 that votes of New Year legislators were bought and sold like "meat in the market."[2] And corruption was not limited to the Northeast. Southern governments, badly tainted during Reconstruction, found the Bourbon restoration only a slight improvement. In the West, United States Senator Samuel Clark Pomeroy of Kansas failed of re-election in 1873 after allegedly attempting to buy a state senator's vote for $7000.[3] And in the federal government itself, Oakes Ames bribed fellow congressmen with Crédit Mobilier stock, the whisky ring of internal revenue agents

1 I am grateful to the University of Illinois Press for permission to reprint portions of my book, *Outlawing the Spoils* (Urbana, 1961). I am also grateful to the editor of *The Historian* for permission to reprint portions of my article: "An Analysis of Civil Service Reformers," *The Historian*, 23 (November 1960), pp. 54–78. *See* Charles Francis Adams, Jr., and Henry Adams, *Chapters of Erie and Other Essays* (Ithaca, 1960); Ishbel Ross, *Proud Kate* (New York, 1953), pp. 246–249; W. A. Swanberg, *Jim Fisk* (New York, 1959); Robert Shaplen, *Free Love and Heavenly Sinners* (New York, 1954).

2 *The Nation*, 4 (April 11, 1867), p. 286.

3 C. Vann Woodward, *Origins of the New South 1877–1913* (Baton Rouge, 1951), pp. 66–74; Albert R. Kitzhaber, "Götterdämmerung in Topeka: The Downfall of Senator Pomeroy," *Kansas Historical Quarterly*, 18 (August 1950), pp. 243–278.

SOURCE: Ari Hoogenboom, "Spoilsmen and Reformer," *The Gilded Age*. H. W. Morgan, ed. Syracuse University Press, 1963, pp. 69–79. By permission of the publisher.

and distillers defrauded the country of millions, and the Star Route frauds cost the Post Office Department millions. In textbooks and lectures the Gilded Age consistently outscandalizes any other age in our history.

These familiar misdoings, and others, account for the free association of corruption with the Gilded Age. But should the association be so free? Were these scandals typical? Are Jim Fisk and the Tweed ring full-blown symbols of an age or are they symptoms, traces of a disorder that was by no means general?[4] Was this age as corrupt as historians have implied, or was it a prim age whose scandals have been exaggerated by contrast? More basically, what is meant by corruption?

If political corruption is the violation of duty for a consideration, usually monetary, many frequently cited examples of Gilded Age corruption are of questionable validity. President Ulysses S. Grant's participation in Jay Gould's and Jim Fisk's scheme to corner the gold market, for instance was naïve, not corrupt; ignorant, not immoral. The Salary Grab Act of 1873, while perhaps greedy, was not illegal. Indeed, salaries of high federal officials needed to be increased. John D. Sanborn's contract to collect delinquent taxes for a 50 per cent fee was not an invention of Secretary of the Treasury William A. Richardson but a new application of the ancient moiety system. Far more significant than the collection of moeties during this period was the public reaction resulting in their elimination in 1874. The resentment aroused by the Sanborn contracts should be cited as an example of growing administrative efficiency.

And if, like George Washington Plunkitt, one differentiates between honest and dishonest graft, he further reduces the ranks of the corrupt. Honest graft, that estimable Tammany Hall politician said, was the profit that flowed from advance inside information on future government action. Why not make a little money on real estate, paving blocks, or what the occasion called for, if one could? Who was hurt by it?[5] And while one usually does not speak of George Washington Plunkitt, Andrew W. Mellon, and George C. Humphrey in one breath, they are perhaps spiritual brothers, with Plunkitt exceeding the other two in candor if not in profits. Before rejecting Plunkitt's distinction between honest and dishonest graft, one should observe that twentieth-century conflicts of interest more than match nineteenth-century honest graft. The Gilded Age has lost some of its dubious distinction.

The typical historian has been too loose in applying the term "corruption." Specifically, he labels a politically partisan civil service corrupt rather than inefficient; he equates the spoils system with corruption when honest spoilsmen far outnumber dishonest ones; he pronounces Gilded Age politicians guilty of corruption for associating with corruptionists even while attacking guilt by association in his own day.

One apparent reason why the historian has exaggerated the corruption of the Gilded Age is his desire to enliven lectures and writings. All the world loves a scandal, and the historian is loathe to abandon the pleasure of dispensing "vicarious sin." More basically, the historian dislikes the dominant forces in the Gilded Age. The historian is usually liberal, more often than not a Democrat. He is, typically, hostile to big business, an advocate of government regulation, of strong executive leadership, and of a civil service staffed by experts. The post-Civil War era stands for all the historian opposes.

4 *See* John W. Pratt, "Boss Tweed's Public Welfare Program," *New-York Historical Society Quarterly*, 45 (October 1961), pp. 396–411, for a more charitable view of Tweed.

5 William L. Riordan, *Plunkitt of Tammany Hall* (New York, 1948), pp. 3–8.

It was an era of Republicanism, of big business domination, of few and ineffectual attempts at government regulation, of weak executives, and of an essentially nonprofessional civil service. The historian naturally dwells upon the shortcomings of the period, particularly on the failures of Ulysses S. Grant, whose political career both personifies all the historian abhors and symbolizes Gilded Age politics.

Another reason the historian has exaggerated corruption in this period is the bias of his sources. The most articulate individuals in this age were its severest critics. Their enforced inactivity (foolishly imposed by business and political opponents) gave them both a cause and the time for writing, while their enemies managed conventions and built railroads. Reformers' letters and writings, their journals and newspapers dominate footnotes with good reason. Take, for example, the *Nation* under the editorship of reformer Edwin Lawrence Godkin. Outstanding contributors and particularly Godkin, hard-working, hardheaded, a trifle hardhearted, and very hard-hitting, made the *Nation*, to quote James Bryce, "the best weekly not only in America but in the world."[6] When not quoting the *Nation*, the historian turns to George William Curtis' graceful editorials in *Harper's Weekly*, America's leading illustrated paper. For a quarter of a century Curtis was the most conspicuous civil service reformer in America. Among monthly magazines, both *Harper's* and the *Atlantic* reflected reformism, while the venerable old quarterly the *North American Review* could at times be considered a reform organ. Reformers dominated newspaper sources such as the *New York Evening Post* and the younger *New York Times*—in fact opposition to civil service reform by distinguished papers was almost limited to Whitelaw Reid's *New York Tribune*.

Finally, the reformers are the most quotable men in the period. Even though Jim Fisk could coin a beautiful phrase, the area of his interests and the level of his perception limits application of his words. Contrast his broad humor with the acid wit of Henry Adams' superb and readily available letters and his autobiography, *The Education*. Readers enraptured with Adams' prose also become enraptured with Adams' prejudices.

Reformers exaggerated the inefficiency and corruption of the Gilded Age. A typical instance was the estimate in January, 1866, by President Johnson's Revenue Commission that $12,000,000 to $25,000,000 were lost annually in the New York Customhouse. Six years later the Grant Civil Service Commission under the leadership of George William Curtis projected the earlier figures and estimated that one-fourth of the annual federal revenue was lost in collection. In the ensuing presidential campaign, liberal Republican Senator Lyman Trumbull, citing the commission's report, calculated that the corrupt Grant regime annually lost $95,830,986.22 of the nation's revenue. When an enraged Grant supporter protested and demanded to know the origin of these figures, the commission explained that its estimate was designed to provide the "most forceable illustration of the mischief of the system" and actually dated from "the administration of Andrew Johnson when the evils of the 'spoils' system culminated." The loss was not money collected and then stolen but money due the government and never collected. The commission also claimed that during Grant's administration deficiencies and defalcations under the internal revenue law had been reduced to one-seventh of those suffered during Johnson's term of office. "We regret," the commissioners concluded, "that in our desire to divest our report of any partisan character whatever and to make it as con-

6 Rollo Ogden (ed.), *Life and Letters of Edwin Lawrence Godkin* (New York, 1907); William M. Armstrong, *E. L. Godkin and American Foreign Policy 1865–1900* (New York, 1957).

cise as possible, we failed to explain this statement, more in detail, & to show how ingenious and successful were the efforts of the administration to prevent the loss to which we alluded."[7] Quite obviously the commission had wished to paint the bleakest picture possible to demonstrate the need for reform. To accomplish this purpose the commission knowingly used an obsolete estimate since it testified that the internal revenue system was seven times more honest under Grant than under Johnson. The commission could hardly afford to have the spoils system reformed by spoilsmen.

Along with exaggerating corruption in the civil service, reformers embraced a devil theory respecting their enemies. Grossly overrating the organization of satanic spoilsmen, reformers' writings abound with reference to conspiracies and rings. In November, 1871, Charles Eliot Norton wrote Godkin from Dresden, Germany, "The whole country is, like New York, in the hands of the 'Ring', —willing to let things go, till they get so bad that it is a question whether they can be bettered without complete upturning of the very foundations of law & civil order." So great was Norton's revulsion against rapacious capitalists that he questioned the further validity of the "systems of individualism & competition. We have erected selfishness into a rule of conduct, & we applaud the man who 'gets on' no matter at what cost to other men." Norton even approved the recent attempt of the Paris Commune to redress its grievances by force, and although he shared the typical reformer's aversion to violence, especially violence that would overturn social order, he advocated "occasional violent revolutionary action to remove deepseated evils." Norton's radicalism, though a temporary romantic aberration rather than a permanent view, reveals nevertheless a man deeply distressed, or more accurately frustrated, by repulsive politicians and capitalists. Norton was so frustrated that he advocated violent revolution to make men "more conscious of their duties to society."[8]

Norton revealed a good deal more of himself than of his homeland. The whole country was not in the hands of the "Ring," Tweed, whisky, or otherwise. All capitalists were not buccaneers like Jim Fisk, and there was no revolution. American reformers, with Norton among them, were content to espouse civil service reform, revenue reform, and hard money, a program they hoped would recreate the golden age of the past. But men with a program to reform society are hardly unbiased observers of that society. Obviously reform is achieved through "knocking" not "boosting" which explains the hypercritical bent of civil service reformers. The historian, however, faithfully reflects the reformers' dim view of the Gilded Age.

The cause of the reformers' dim view and their espousal of civil service reform can be found in their careers. Their morality, their heritage of Puritan virtue cannot be denied, but reformers recognized the evils of the spoils system only after it thwarted their ambitions. The career of the temporary revolutionary, Charles Eliot Norton, serves as an example. Son of Andrews Norton, Harvard Divinity School professor, and cousin of Charles W. Eliot, future president of Harvard University, Charles Eliot Norton was

7 *See* U.S. Revenue Commission, "Revenue System of the United States," *House Executive Documents,* 39th Congress, 1st session, VII, No. 34, 44–51; Charles Eliot Norton (ed.), *Orations and Addresses of George William Curtis* (New York, 1894), II, 39; W. W. Belknap to John A. Logan, August 15, 1872, Logan papers, Library of Congress; "Senator Trumbull and the Revenue," *Harper's Weekly,* 16 (September 7, 1872), p. 690; Curtis to Belknap, August 25, 1872, and Curtis, Cattell, *et al.,* to Logan, September [?], 1872, Logan papers. For another exaggeration of statistics by reformers *see Congressional Globe,* 41st Congress, 3rd session, 400, 459–460, 666. In fairness to Johnson the improvement of the Internal Revenue Service, no doubt, resulted more from the drastic elimination and simplification of excise taxes than from Grant.

8 Norton to Godkin, November 3, 1871, Godkin papers, Harvard University.

born into the "best" Cambridge circles. After graduating from Harvard, he attempted a career in business but was not successful. Literature and the arts enthralled him; account books did not. Norton traveled widely abroad where he met George William Curtis, his life-long friend, and hobnobbed with the Brownings, Thackeray, Ruskin, Carlyle, and the Pre-Raphaelites. Before the Civil War Norton contributed to the *Atlantic*, sympathized with the antislavery cause although he personally did not care for abolitionists ("the most self righteous set of radicals"), and supported the Republican party. During the war he edited the Loyal Publication Society broadsides, which for three years helped shape northern public opinion by supplying editorials to local newspapers. With James Russell Lowell, Norton became co-editor of the *North American Review* in 1864, and in 1865 he joined with Godkin and others to found the *Nation*.[9]

The postwar world disenchanted Norton. He was suspicious of democracy, observing that it contributed to the unfortunate national "decline of manners." Norton had no use for Andrew Johnson but even less for radical Republican politicos. He opposed the impeachment of Johnson reasoning that "three months of Ben Wade are worse than two years of A. J." Johnson's acquittal encouraged Norton only because it enhanced reformers' opportunity to capture the Republican party. "I think," he wrote Godkin, "we have a better chance now than we had any right to expect so soon for reforming the party & freeing it from the burden of the sins of extremists who have tried to usurp the leadership." As the election of 1868 drew near, Norton, like everyone else, fell under Grant's spell. " 'Honesty & Grant,' 'good-faith & Grant' must succeed," he wrote from Manchester, England. "Grant grows daily in my respect & confidence," Norton wrote Curtis after the election and rapturously described the president-elect as "so simple, so sensible, so strong & so magnanimous." Assuming Grant would be especially generous to the reform element, Norton added, "If you see a perfectly fit and easy opportunity, I should be glad to have you use it to suggest my name as that of a suitable person for the mission to Holland or Belgium." Although Curtis wrote to the newly appointed Secretary of State Hamilton Fish in Norton's behalf, nothing happened. The reformers' hope to re-establish themselves in their old stronghold, the diplomatic service, proved futile. A few months later, bitterly disillusioned after his season of hope, Norton wrote Curtis: "Grant's surrender, partial though it may be, to the politicians was an unexpected disappointment, but a very instructive one. His other mistakes were what might have been expected,—what indeed we ought to have been prepared for. But some of his appointments are disgraceful, —personally discreditable to him. . . . The question seems to be now whether the politicians,—'the men inside politics,' —will ruin the country, or the country take summary vengeance, by means of Jenckes's [civil service reform] bill, upon them."[10]

Norton's disappointments paralleled those of his friends, particularly those of George William Curtis. Exposed early to transcendentalism at Concord and Brook Farm, Curtis never escaped its influence. After the grand tour abroad, he embarked on a literary career, becoming one of the most popular writers of the 1850's and associate editor of *Putnam's Monthly*. When this magazine collapsed, Curtis as-

9 *See* Kermit Vanderbilt, *Charles Eliot Norton* (Cambridge, 1959); and Sara Norton and M. A. DeWolfe Howe (eds.), *Letters of Charles Eliot Norton* (Boston, 1913); Norton to Godkin, July 20, 1866, Godkin papers.

10 Norton to Godkin, March 13, 1867, May 30, 1868, Godkin papers; Norton to Curtis, July 24, 1868, Norton papers, Harvard University; Norton to Curtis, January 29, 1869, Curtis to Norton, March 13, 1869, Curtis papers, Harvard University; Norton to Curtis, July 22, 1869, Norton papers.

sumed a debt he was not legally responsible for and paid it by lecturing on the lyceum circuit. An ardent Republican, Curtis supported the Lincoln administration from his editor's post on *Harper's Weekly*. He soon became a power in the New York Republican party, unsuccessfully ran for Congress in 1864, attempted to influence patronage distribution during Lincoln's administration, and was offered a diplomatic post in Egypt. Curtis was not opposed to the spoils system until it ceased to function satisfactorily for him and for his friends.[11]

Not only Johnson but politicians in general snubbed Curtis and his peers. In the fall of 1866 Charles Eliot Norton launched a campaign to elect Curtis United States senator. Although Curtis' sensitive nature was not a political asset, the *Nation* and several other journals strongly supported him. Success, however, did not follow. "Conkling is undoubtedly to be the man," Curtis wrote Norton in January, "but his friends and [Noah] Davis's and [Ira] Harris's—the three real contestants—have each declared for me as their second choice. Still even that would not bring it because I am not enough of a politician for the purposes of the men who make Senators." As if to prove his point, Curtis "declined absolutely" to unite with the weakest candidate against Roscoe Conkling, who was elected. A few weeks later Curtis, in answer either to public opinion or to personal frustration with politics, wrote in *Harper's Weekly* favoring the passage of the Jenckes civil service bill by the expiring 39th Congress. Although tardy, Curtis' espousal of civil service reform lasted until his death twenty-five years later. In his period he became its most conspicuous leader.[12]

Politicians continued to snub Curtis and each snub made him more of a reformer. In September, 1870, he played a prominent role in Conkling's behalf at the New York State Republican Convention. To give convention proceedings an air of respectability, Conkling men elected Curtis temporary chairman. Having won by a wide margin, Curtis delivered an impressive address, which he hoped would stampede the convention into nominating him for governor. When William Orton, head of Western Union and one of Conklin's chief allies, approached him about the nomination, Curtis, feigning disinterest, replied: "If it is evidently the wish of the Convention I will not decline. But I don't want the office and I entrust my name to your honorable care." Professional politicians made short work of the Curtis candidacy. He was nominated by an efficient Conkling lieutenant, Charles Spencer, who effectively confused Curtis supporters by later voting for another candidate. "In one word, my dear boy," Curtis wrote Norton, "I was the undoubted choice of the Convention and I had been disgracefully 'slaughtered' by my friends!" Curtis attempted to convince himself he was "glad" that he would not have to run. "The only real harm the affair can do me," he confided to Norton, "is that my influence will decline with those who think I want office!!"[13]

Politics held further disappointments for Curtis who remained loyal to the Republican party, headed Grant's Civil Service Commission, and supported Grant in the campaign of 1872. The president, however, snubbed Curtis after 1872. When the New York surveyor vacated his position, reformers considered the nomination of his successor a test case. Grant hesitated but, prodded by Curtis, nominated the deputy surveyor in accordance with the new civil service

11 *See* Gordon Milne, *George William Curtis and the Genteel Tradition* (Bloomington, 1956), and Hoogenboom, *Outlawing the Spoils, passim.*

12 *The Nation*, 3 (November 1, 1866), p. 341; (November 29, 1866), p. 422; Curtis to Norton, January 2, 1867, Curtis papers; "Reform of the Civil Service," *Harper's Weekly*, 11 (March 2, 1867), p. 130.

13 Curtis to Norton, September 17, 1870, Curtis papers.

commission rules. Although reformers tasted victory, they again grew apprehensive when members of the Conkling machine bragged that Grant would withdraw the nomination. Two weeks later the nomination was indeed withdrawn with the assurance that reform methods would be used in selecting the new surveyor. A committee of three, including Curtis and Collector Chester A. Arthur, was named to select the customhouse employee best fitted for the post. Once more reformers' suspicions were allayed. But spoilsmen were to be the final victors. Curtis' serious illness kept the committee from holding an examination or making a report. In mid-March, George H. Sharpe, an active politician and the local United States marshal, was appointed without the committee's knowledge. Sharpe's appointment goaded an ill and testy Curtis into action. Three days after it was announced, he published a letter in the *New York Tribune* emphasizing that Sharpe's appointment was made without his knowledge or consent and ominously adding that "men do not willingly consent to be thus publicly snubbed." On March 18, 1873, Curtis resigned as chairman of Grant's Civil Service Commission.[14]

Curtis was more aggressive when he returned to his editorial work after his illness and resignation. Ignored by the administration and unable to realize his political ambitions, he attacked Grant's civil service policy with special vigor. Curtis relished his new independence and was proud when the anti-administration *Springfield Republican* called one of his articles "another Bomb Shell." He acknowledged in an editorial that "public disbelief of the reality and thoroughness of the reform" was not surprising. "The President forbids political assessments upon subordinates, and issues an executive order virtually reproving the political officiousness of officers of the service. But, in total contempt of his orders, they levy assessments, desert their posts of duty, assume the management of all party assemblies, and continue to use patronage as a party lever." Grant could have inspired confidence in his administration, Curtis contended, if he had fired his corrupt brother-in-law who was collector of New Orleans, dismissed the postmaster at St. Louis for levying political assessments, filled New York Customhouse posts according to the rules, and required civil servants to attend to their duties instead of their party's needs. "Unless these things are done, constantly and consistently done," Curtis concluded, "the work of the Commission, faithful, able, and devoted as we know it to be, will be in vain, and the Republican party will have no right to claim that it has really reformed the civil service."[15]

Unlike Curtis, Henry Adams expected little from Grant and very quickly learned to expect nothing. "We here look," Adams wrote from Washington in February, 1869, "for a reign of western mediocrity, but one appreciates least the success of the steamer, when one lives in the engine-room." Two months later, Adams wrote with the satisfaction his family always seemed to feel when it had just suffered defeat: "My hopes of the new Administration have all been disappointed; it is far inferior to the last. My friends have almost all lost ground instead of gaining it as I hoped. My family is buried politically beyond recovery for years. I am becoming more and more isolated so far as allies go. I even doubt whether I can find an independent organ to publish my articles, so strong is the current against us." And a few days later Henry wrote his brother Charles Francis, Jr., the treasurer of the Social Science Association, which was agitating for civil service reform, "I can't get you an office. The only members of

14 *The Nation*, 16 (February 20, 1873), pp. 126–127; 16 (March 20, 1873), p. 189.

15 Curtis to Norton, September 19, 1873, Curtis papers; "The Prospects of Civil Service Reform," *Harper's Weekly*, 17 (October 25, 1873), p. 938.

this Government that I have met are mere acquaintances, not friends, and I fancy no request of mine would be likely to call out a gush of sympathy." Nor could Henry obtain anything for himself. The administration was presumptuous enough to ignore the Adams family.[16]

With their ambitions thwarted, the Adams brothers forsook the conventional methods of political advancement and espoused civil service reform. In February Henry had recognized that the struggle against "*political* corruption" was more basic than free trade and its eradication would be more difficult than the antislavery crusade. By June he was writing an article called "Civil Service Reform," which he described as "very bitter and abusive of the Administration." Although Adams expected it to get him into "hot water," he believed he had "nothing to lose." Henry and his brothers, Charles Francis, Jr., and John Quincy, were "up to the ears in politics and public affairs, and in time," Henry hoped, "we shall perhaps make our little mark."[17]

The *North American Review* published and the *Nation* applauded Adams' article. In it Adams revealed reformers' disdain for the new men of politics and their concern over the passing of a more compatible political age. Two members of Grant's Cabinet, Ebenezer Rockwood Hoar and George S. Boutwell, epitomized that change. Boutwell, Adams stated, was "the product of caucuses and party promotion," but Hoar was "by birth and by training a representative of the best New England school, holding his moral rules on the sole authority of his own conscience, indifferent to opposition whether in or out of his party, obstinate to excess, and keenly alive to the weaknesses in which he did not share. Judge Hoar belonged in fact to a class of men who had been gradually driven from politics, but whom it is the hope of reformers to restore. Mr. Boutwell belonged to the class which has excluded its rival, but which has failed to fill with equal dignity the place it has usurped."[18]

The careers of Norton, Curtis, and Henry Adams demonstrate that the civil service reform movement fits into a pattern of those out of power versus those in power.[19] Reformers invariably wished to curtail the appointing power after they thought it had been abused, and to them abuse occurred when men of their own social station or political faction were not appointed to office. The post-Civil War political world was not what the "outs" expected it to be. In their disappointment they turned to reform.

16 Henry Adams to Charles Francis Adams, Jr., February 23, and April 29, 1869, and Henry Adams to Charles M. Gaskell, April 19 and June 20, 1869, in Worthington Chauncey Ford (ed.), *Letters of Henry Adams 1858–1891* (Boston, 1930), pp. 152, 156–157, 161–162. (By permission, Houghton Mifflin Company.)

17 Henry Adams to Edward Atkinson, February 1, 1869, and Henry Adams to Gaskell, August 27, 1869, pp. 151, 165–166.

18 Henry Brooks Adams, "Civil Service Reform," *North American Review*, 109 (October 1869), pp. 443–475; *The Nation*, 9 (November 11, 1869), p. 415.

19 *See* Hoogenboom, *Outlawing the Spoils*, *passim*.

28. Municipal Corruption: A Comment on Lincoln Steffens[1]

HENRY JONES FORD

This is a work of a kind that was abundant in England during the eighteenth century but is now extinct there, while it flourishes in this country. Mental growths are no exception to the general laws of growth as regards distribution of species in time and space. Dying out in one region, a species may in another region find favoring conditions and perpetuate the type. In many respects the political ideas of our own times in this country reproduce species which belong to England's past. Mr. Steffens's work belongs to the same class as Burgh's *Political Disquisitions* published in 1774, Browne's *Estimate of the Manners and Principles of the Times* published in 1757, and innumerable tracts and essays now sunk into oblivion.

Mr. Steffens says of the articles collected in his book: "They were written for a purpose, they were published serially with a purpose, and they are reprinted now together to further the same purpose, which was—and is—to sound for the civic pride of an apparently shameless citizenship." Burgh said of his work that it was "calculated to draw the timely attention of government and people to a due consideration of the necessity and the means of reforming those errors, defects and abuses; of restoring the constitution and saving the state." Mr. Steffens puts the blame for misgovernment upon the apathy of American character. He says:

> We are responsible, not our leaders, since we follow them. We let them divert our loyalty from the United States to some "party"; we let them boss the party and turn our municipal democracies into autocracies and our republican nation into a plutocracy. We cheat our government and we let our leaders loot it, and we let them bribe and wheedle our sovereignty from us. . . . We break our own laws and rob our own government, the lady at the custom house, the lyncher with his rope, and the captain of industry with his bribe and his rebate. The spirit of graft and of lawlessness is the American spirit.

In the same style Browne argued that virtue was rotting out of the English stock from the development of a sordid commercialism which was corroding all the moral elements which are the true foundations of national greatness. The thought flows in the same channels, the same ideas preside over opinion, and the resemblance extends even to details of suggestion.

> All we have to do [says Mr. Steffens] is to establish a steady demand for good govern-

1 Lincoln Steffens, *The Shame of the Cities.* New York: McClure, Phillips & Co., 1904. 306 pp.

SOURCE: Henry Jones Ford, "Municipal Corruption," *Political Science Quarterly,* 19 (1904), pp. 673–686.

ment. The bosses have us split up into parties. . . . If we should leave parties to the politicians, and would vote not for the party, not even for men, but for the city and state and the nation, we should rule parties and cities and states and nation.

All this goes back to the time of Addison. In the *Spectator,* Number 125, Tuesday, July 24, 1711, he recommended that honest men should

> enter into an association for the support of one another against the endeavors of those whom they ought to look upon as their common enemies, whatsoever side they may belong to. Were there such an honest body of neutral forces, we should never see the worst of men in the great figures of life because they are useful to a party; nor the best unregarded because they are above practising those methods which would be grateful to their factions. We should then single every criminal out of the herd and hunt him down, however formidable and overgrown he might appear.

One difference should be noted. It relates to temperament. American self-confidence and optimism make a distinctive mark lacking in the extinct English literature of this species. Mr. Steffens ends his sermon by saying:

> We Americans may have failed. We may be mercenary and selfish. Democracy with us may be impossible and corruption inevitable; but these articles, if they have proved nothing else, have demonstrated without doubt that we can stand the truth; that there is pride in the character of American citizenship; and that this pride may be a power in the land.

This is a small set-off for such tremendous defects, but the tone of sentiment is hopeful and buoyant as compared with the gloomy forebodings which Burgh expressed in his closing reflections. He said:

> I see the once rich and populous cities of England in the same condition as those of Spain; whole streets lying in rubbish, and the grass peeping up between the stones in those which continue still inhabited. I see the harbors empty, the warehouses shut up, and the shopkeepers playing draughts, for want of customers. I see our noble and spacious turnpike roads covered with thistles and other weeds, and scarce to be traced out. I see the studious men reading the "State of Britain," the magazines, the "Political Disquisitions," and the histories of the eighteenth century, and execrating the stupidity of their fathers, who, in spite of many faithful warnings given them, sat still, and suffered their country to be ruined by a set of wretches whom they could have crushed.

Such were the opinions of English reformers on the eve of the wonderful outburst of national energy which created the British empire and brought to England wealth and prosperity beyond the imagination of the wildest dreamer. And yet the forecast was not wholly mistaken, for corruption and mismanagement lost England the American colonies and brought her to deep abasement before the evil generated its cure and the constitution was brought into accord with the needs of the state. But historians of English political development point out that the transformation was accomplished by the politicians themselves, without the adoption of the nostrums prescribed by the reformers and by the very means which the reformers denounced as the essence of corruption. The reformers sought means of administration by the people; the politicians denied them that, but unwittingly provided means of control by the people through the formation of an agency of legislative direction and management possessing plenary authority and hence complete responsibility. This went to the root of the trouble; for in retrospect it is plain enough that the systematic political corruption was the result of political confusion. The doctrine of the separation of the powers of government had obstructed the development of any such agency or organ of sovereignty, clothed with power to provide a proper division of the functions of government and to correlate the exercise of those functions. The actual embodiment of sovereignty which gradually took shape came not by deliberate intention but through the constraint of hard necessity.[2] The formation of the English pariamentary type of government may be described, in the terms of American politics, by saying that boss rule grew up inside the government until it acquired complete authority, thus bringing within reach of public opinion, through the suffrage, competent apparatus of control over the behavior of the government and creating conditions of political activity which gradually substituted the leader for the boss. The forces which sustained constitutional development did not proceed from reform agitation but from the phlegmatic common sense of the British people, more interested in results than solicitous about means and not prone to extravagant expectations from the every-day human nature which forms the stuff of politics. To take things as they are and make the best of them, to deal with situations as they arise by the means that are available, to endure what cannot be cured, to look upon the bright side and to cultivate a habit of cheerfulness—these are the traits of which sound politics are compounded and by which constitutional progress is sustained. National hypochondria is a worse evil than national corruption. Happily the American people are free from that at any rate; they are disgusted but not dismayed by the situation, and they have a deep conviction that they will eventually find ways and means of dealing with it.

Meanwhile it must be admitted that Mr. Steffens' book does not exaggerate the facts of the case. What he says about the condition of affairs in our cities is true, and much more might be said to the same purport. In this book he confines himself to municipal graft. The graft system extends to state administration also. The "organization" judge who "takes orders" is another feature of the graft system, the more dangerous since its virus penetrates the very marrow of our institutions. The facts with which Mr. Steffens deals are superficial symptoms. Hardly any disguise of them is attempted in the ordinary talk of local politicians. One of the first things which practical experience teaches is that the political ideals which receive literary expression have a closely limited range. One soon reaches strata of population in which they disappear and the relation of boss and client appears to be proper and natural. The connection between grafting politicians and their adherents is such that ability to levy blackmail inspires the same sort of respect and admiration which Rob Roy's followers felt for him in the times that provided a career for his peculiar talents. And as in Rob Roy's day, intimate knowledge finds in the type some hardy virtues. For one thing, politicians of this type do not indulge in cant. They are no more shamefaced in talking about their grafting exploits to an appreciative audience than a mediæval baron would have been in discussing the produce of his feudal fees and imposts. Mr. Steffens has really done no more than to put together material lying about loose upon the surface of municipal politics and give it effective presentation. The general truth of this statement of the case is indisputable. But the same might have been said of the exhibits of the eighteenth century English reformers; and yet the impression made by them of decay and disease in the body politic has since been shown to be erroneous. The three stout volumes of Burgh's *Disquisitions* are crammed with accounts of bribery and corruption, making a more startling showing than that made by Mr.

[2] Sir Leslie Stephen, in his Hobbes (The Macmillan Co., 1904), makes some acute remarks upon the unforseen character of English constitutional development. See particularly pp. 180, 181, 199 and 200.

Steffens because more inveterate and extensive. Every part of the structure of government was involved, so that there appeared to be no spot of soundness where reform might find a lodgement and a starting point. Probably in every period of political transition, when an old order is giving place to a new, evidence of corruption has confronted the scrutiny of moralists. The formation of modern nationality itself originally wore the appearance of corruption to observers prepossessed by the ideals of the past. History has vindicated feudalism as a reparative process in the organization of society after the collapse of imperial rule. May it not be that the new feudalism which has developed in American politics, despite all its gross exactions of tribute, is also a natural development from constitutional conditions? When the English reform excitement was at its height, Hume acutely remarked that "those who complain of corrupt and wicked ministers, and of the mischiefs they produce, do in fact most severely satirize the constitution of the state, for a good constitution would exclude or defeat the bad effects of a corrupt administration." This is no more than saying that if a business is well organized, employees cannot steal without being found out and dismissed; but propositions which are obvious as applied to ordinary business affairs do not appear to be readily apprehended in relation to the public business, although there is no essential difference. Hume's opinion that the corruption of his times was due to bad conditions rather than to bad men turned out to be correct. It may be worth while to examine our own situation from this point of view.

Mr. Steffens gives blunt expression to the opinion that the typical American business man is the great source of municipal corruption. "He is a self-righteous fraud, this big business man. He is the chief source of corruption, and it were a boon if he would neglect politics." In his article upon "Tweed Days in St. Louis," Mr. Steffens says that "when the leading men began to devour their own city, the herd rushed into the trough and fed also." But in the same article, referring to the traffic in franchises, he remarks: "Several companies which refused to pay blackmail had to leave." In other words, conditions existed to which business interests had to submit or perish. The case does not suggest business initative of corruption, but rather compliance with it upon the universal principle that if you want to do business you must meet the established conditions.

The nature of those conditions is not difficult to understand if one is able to separate fact from fiction with regard to the suffrage. From the psychological principle of association of ideas it is difficult to separate anything in thought from the use it has served, and such has been the instrumental value of the suffrage that intrinsic qualities are habitually attributed to it of the most absurd character. The increase of literacy and the spread of agencies for diffusing information have imparted to the body politic in modern times a nervous organization unknown before, developing a public consciousness which is the true source of what is known as the democratic movement. The suffrage has played a wonderful part in serving the activities of this public consciousness, but it is merely a vehicle of impulse and its utility is strictly regulated by conditions. Want or desire does not alter in moral quality nor gain in real authority because it happens to be expressed through the suffrage. The right of the majority is a useful fiction as a rule of practical convenience, but if it is manipulated so that it is a pernicious humbug the appearance of corruption may be a healthy manifestation. Instead of being the betrayal of democracy it may be diplomatic treatment of ochlocracy, restraining its dangerous tendencies and minimizing its mischiefs. If any of our large cities should be preserved like Pompeii to remote ages, the archaeologists of that period, even without any historic record, would be bound to conclude that the society which evolved such structure was not deficient in great qualities of character; and if some of the lamentations of our reformers should be disinterred, telling how the men of affairs in our times corrupted the government in securing opportunities of enterprise, most assuredly those archaeologists would rejoice that they had done so. It is better that government and social activity should go on in any way than that they should not go on at all. Slackness and decay are more dangerous to a nation than corruption.

In order to appreciate the functional office of the suffrage, a clear distinction must be drawn between administration and control. As an instrument of administration the suffrage, from the nature of things, is of very limited value. What can be more absurd than to think that the average citizen, who finds it hard to judge of the qualifications of a clerk or a salesman or to pick out a competent servant for his household, can by any sort of political hocus-pocus be invested with the ability to make a real choice of governors, mayors, judges, clerks of court, district attorneys, sheriffs, constables, tax-collectors, assessors and school commissioners? It is obvious, when one discards cant and exercises common sense, that government by direct administration of the people cannot really be carried on except in small communities, having common and well understood needs quite level with the ordinary capacity of citizenship. Communities in such a situation might just as well choose their officers by lot as by election, as was demonstrated in ancient Greek communities. But in any growing and progressive community diversity of needs and interest is inevitable and specialization of functions becomes necessary. Administration of the government by election then collapses, and the pretence that it is retained is constantly contradicted by actual facts. To assign to the people a power which they are naturally incapable of wielding is in effect to take it away from them. And this is the concise philosophy of boss rule. Genuine democratic government becomes impossible when the suffrage is applied to uses of which it is not capable; the practical result of the system of filling administrative posts by popular election is ochlocracy; and boss-rule is an expensive antidote for ochlocracy provided by the instinctive good sense of the American people. The system is as firmly based upon social necessities under existing conditions as the old feudalism which it resembles in its essential character. So long as those conditions, now inherent in our constitutional arrangements, continue to exist, so long will the boss system endure; and it will secure its revenues and emoluments, no matter how greatly they may be reprobated under the name of graft.

The general tendency of attacks made upon the system is to confirm it by aggravating the conditions which produce it. There are lower depths of corruption than those so far reached; and the movement for what is known as the direct nomination system is likely to sound those lower depths. That movement proposes to parallel the present system of filling a long list of administrative posts by popular election, by choosing party nominees also by popular election. It is seriously preached as a moral duty that the average citizen shall take the time to inform himself upon the personal qualifications of the various candidates, sometimes numbering fifty or more at a time. How does the obligation arise? If sociologists are not mistaken, the paramount duties of the individual man are grouped about the functions of subsistence and reproduction. Or, in every day speech, the chief duty of every man, as a member of society, is to earn his living and provide for his family. What political obligation can contravene this fundamental obligation? Are institutions made for the people or are the people made for the institutions? The latter appears to be the view of those laboring for direct administration, but no such palpable humbug can be foisted upon the people. The mass of the people will quite properly hold that they have more important things to attend to than electioneering. They will leave that to those to whom it offers rewards. In practice the system will mean the legal establishment of gang rule. The law may provide equal terms but cannot provide equal conditions. It is obvious that if there were rewards for all comers two miles up in the air, only those able to get balloons would share in the distribution. Any free-for-all terms which election laws may make as regards nomination to office will be just as closely restricted to class opportunity. The crowning touch of absurdity and immorality is put upon the whole scheme by the assertion, sometimes made, that after the selection of candidates has been put in the hands of the people there will be nobody to blame if results are bad, since the people are entitled to bad government if they want it. Here is, indeed, a doctrine such as Burke would have called "a digest and an institute of anarchy." What is government for but the maintenance of justice? No more besotted claim of prerogative was ever advanced than that any body of men, however high they may heap voting papers in ballot boxes, have a right to perpetrate iniquity. A constitution which produces bad government is a bad constitution, and nothing can give it moral sanction. The extent to which such anarchic ideas prevail among reformers is a far more serious symptom of moral degeneracy than grafting. It is an aphorism of practical politics, for which a biologic explanation might be given, that the offices must bear the cost of filling them. The more elective offices the greater the cost of the government. So long as the people tolerate the system they will have to bear the expense, call it graft or what you will.

These views may appear cynical since they antagonize the political mythology now in vogue. The thought of the day is indoctrinated with the idea that, back of the real people one sees in the shop, the factory or the office, there is an ideal citizenship of great purity and intelligence which if brought into political activity would establish the integrity of our institutions. This hallucination energizes the direct nomination movement. The underlying purpose is to open free channels for the activity of that ideal citizenship. It is also traceable in the absurd importance attached to studies in the technique of government. The assumed existence of that ideal citizenship implies the need of educating it in its duties. Hence great effort is being made to spread the study of civics. Even lads whose chief interest in life is centered in their tops and marbles are considered fit subjects for cramming with civics. In this direction, the great supersitition that education can create character as well as train faculties goes to its most extravagant length. But if we regard statecraft as an activity analogous to other social activities, we shall not consider it an imputation upon the competency of the people to say that they are unfit to select their administrative officers, any more than it disparages the business capacity of the shareholders in a stock company to say that as a body they are unfit to appoint the clerks, book-keepers, salesmen and other administrative agents of the company. No sensible man will dispute the latter proposition. The essential principle of business control is universally recognized to be the delegation of administrative duties to a responsible management which, having full power, is subject to full responsibility for results. The notion that people should fit themselves for government by the study of civics is as if shareholders should qualify themselves in the practical management of the business of the corporation in order to secure proper administration of their interests. All that is necessary is an intelligent standard of requirement with a proper organization of responsibility, and the conduct of public business involves no different principles. Instead of the people themselves assuming the impossible task of looking after their servants and being continually fooled and bamboozled, they can turn that business over to a head servant and let him hire the rest and be responsible for them. We do this in the federal government but not in state or municipal government, and here the situation beautifully illustrates the Spanish proverb that the more you grasp the less you hold.

While the suffrage is incapable of serving as an organ of administration, it is capable of serving as an agency of control; but to be an efficient instrument of control, it must act upon some organ of government possessing administrative authority so complete that it may be held to full accountability for results. It is just because such an authority exists in Switzerland that that country is able to maintain such an advanced type of democratic government. Executive authority is so concentrated, and the connection between the executive and legislative departments is so simple, direct and immediate, that not even the mediation of party organization is needful to secure popular control over the conduct of the government. It is the principle of concentrated responsibility with which we are familiar as the basic principle of all business organization. In our governmental arrangements we have deviated from that principle by using the suffrage for administration. We have split up executive authority among a number of independent and coördinate administrative servants, who are practically irresponsible during their term of office if they are shrewd enough to keep out of the clutches of the criminal law. Thus they are put in a position to control the people instead of being controlled by the people. And in employing the suffrage in its proper use for representation, we make it ineffective by disconnecting legislation from administration. We elect a mayor to represent the community as a whole, but we do not give him the right nor do we make it his duty to present the public business by the legislative branch or to bring it to decision. That is left to the good-will and favor of the representatives of localities. Why should we wonder if they turn such irresponsible power to lucrative advantage?

The growth of an extra-legal system of connecting the disconnected functions of government for administrative purposes certainly entails corruption, but it does not follow that under such circumstances it is disadvantageous although founded upon venality. Our ordinary system of municipal government is so opposed to all sound principles of business organization that it is highly creditable to our practical capacity for government that we are able to work it at all. The graft system is bad, but it is better than the constitutional system as established by law. Mr. Steffens himself supplies evidence upon this point. In Chicago, after a reform movement had triumphed, he says:

> I found there was something the matter with the political machinery. There was the normal plan of government for a city, rings with bosses, and grafting interests behind. Philadelphia, Pittsburgh, St. Louis, are all governed on such a plan. But in Chicago it didn't work. "Business" was at a standstill and business was suffering. What was the matter?

Mr. Steffens goes on to say:

> I spent one whole forenoon calling on the presidents of banks, great business men, and financiers interested in public utility

companies. . . . Those financial leaders of Chicago were "mad." All but one of them became so enraged as they talked that they could not behave decently. They rose up, purple in the face, and cursed reform. They said it hurt business; it had hurt the town. "Anarchy" they called it; "socialism." They named corporations that had left the city; they named others that had planned to come there and had gone elsewhere. They offered me facts and figures to prove that the city was damaged.

It is possible that these business and financial magnates knew what they were talking about, and that it is better for a city government to lend itself to the operation of the forces of progress even through corrupt inducements than to toss the management of affairs out upon the goose-common of ignorance and incompetency, however honest. Reform which arrests the progress of the community will not be tolerated long by an American city. On the other hand, it is quite possible that public men who have done great things by methods which have brought obloquy upon them may be esteemed when the results of their activity are appreciated. The people of Washington city now regard as a public benefactor a boss of this type and have recently erected a statue to his memory. Historians speak respectfully of one Julius Cæsar, who rose to emminence not upon the recognized lines of the constitution but as a popular boss. He is now credited with having done a great deal for his city and its dependent territories.

If these considerations are sound it may be fairly argued that they raise a greater mystery than they explain away. How is it possible to reconcile with the good sense and business capacity of the American people the growth of governmental arrangements so antagonistic to rational principles of organization? I confess that this phase of the problem has often puzzled me. Ordinary political theory is certainly oblivious of political fact to an astonishing degree. For instance, popular election of public treasurers is ordinarily justified upon the ground that it is necessary for the safety of the public funds to put them in the custody of an independent official not subject to removal by any other authority save the people themselves. The facts are all the other way. The public is not exposed to loss by the appointed treasurers of the United States, but it has lost millions through the elected treasurers of state and municipal governments. Although the growth of suretyship as a systematic branch of business enterprise is reducing risks of loss through absolute defalcation, yet those on the inside of affairs know that the manipulation of public funds in connection with elective fiduciary offices is an extensive department of the graft system, while this particular development of graft is unknown under the federal government. And yet these notorious facts do not perceptibly affect public adherence to the theory. At this very time the appointment of federal postmasters by popular election is receiving organized and influential support as a reform measure, despite every day experience of the fact that in practice this would mean irresponsible appointment by local bosses. A satirist might extract from American politics many fresh instances in confirmation of Robert South's opinion expressed nearly three centuries ago: "The generality of mankind is wholly and absolutely governed by words and names, without—nay, for for the most part, even against—the knowledge men have of things. The multitude or common rout, like a drove of sheep or an herd of oxen, may be managed by any noise or cry which their drivers shall accustom them to."

But satire loses in comprehension what it gains in point. The persistence of ideas is an essential feature of the princial of social continuity which gives stability to political conditions. The ideas which have shaped our governmental arrangements are of the same class as those which were at the bottom of the past corruption of English politics. The derivation is distinctly traceable in our political origins. The check and balance theory of government which still controls our political thought was a colonial importation. Some perception of the true principles upon which democratic authority may be founded is shown in the Federalist;[3] but at that stage of constitutional development exact appreciation of those principles was impossible. Popular government was still undeveloped, and the principle of the separation of powers was not construed in its true significance as relating to the functions of government, but as an apportionment of power among classes and interests so as to confine prerogative upon the one hand and popular influence upon the other. The chief concern of the framers of the constitution was to erect barriers against democratic tendencies, and they used the check and balance theory for that purpose. As democratic tendencies gathered strength, they also settled upon the check and balance theory by natural momentum of thought, applying it to their own advantage. The class control which the gentry enjoyed under the closely restricted suffrage of the first period of the Republic was broken down by the extension of the suffrage and by the conversion of appointive posts into elective offices. The precautions taken by the framers of the constitution to secure executive unity proved so effectual that the latter movement was frustrated so far as the national government is concerned, but it has swept through state and municipal constitutions with increasing vigor until all the functions of government have been both disconnected and disintegrated in a way which leaves public opinion with no embodiment of authority capable of giving it complete representation or of assuming full responsibility for results. The stages of the process were not wholly disadvantageous so long as they were steps in the acquisition of power by the exponents of democratic tendencies, through partition of authority originally aristocratic in its tenure. But with the triumph of democratic principles of government, the partitions of power now useless as shelters from the class oppression against which they were reared, became obstructions which defeat democratic control by preventing its efficient exercise. No one now disputes popular sovereignty, but the people are in the position of the Grand Turk, who can cut off the head of an offender but whose affairs are so out of control that he is robbed right and left by his servants. What makes the situation more exasperating is that it is becoming a matter of common knowledge that democratic control is more complete and effective in some other countries than in our own; but the usual inference that we have somehow lost what our institutions were intended to secure is a fallacy. Our institutions have not lapsed from democracy into plutocracy; they never were democratic, and their present plutocratic character arises from the substitution of money power for the original aristocratic control. In other countries where democracy has arrived, it has not had to devise its constitutional apparatus but has had the far simpler and easier task of attaining control over that already in existence, whereas American democracy has never had a competent organ of authority. In developing such an organ we shall have to work out a constitutional application of the principle that division of the functions of government must be associated with administrative efficiency. The final result may be the formation of a new type of government. The exact form which it will assume it is now impossible to anti-

[3] See particularly No. 70, a masterly argument on the thesis that "the executive power is more easily confined when it is one"; also, Nos. 47 and 48, wherein it is argued that separation of the powers of government does not mean their disconnection.

cipate, but we can at least be certain from the very nature of sovereignty that there will be an organic connection of the executive and legislative functions. So long as the legal frame of government does not provide for that connection, it will take place outside of the legal frame; in which case we are in the habit of calling it the "machine" or the "ring" and of regarding it as a malignant excrescence upon constitutional government, whereas it is in fact the really constituted government, and the formal constitution is but a pretence and a sham.

The municipal situation is not really so desperate as one might think from a perusal of works like that of Mr. Steffens. Genuine improvement is going on through the undermining of our traditional constitutional principles under stress of practical necessity. In such charters as those of New York and Baltimore, the disconnection of the executive and legislative functions which is the root of ring rule is being practically overcome by the creation of boards of estimates and apportionment, which really unite executive and legislative powers in the same organ of government. Such appliances of government will gradually spread to other cities from the effect of example. In most cities, however, matters are likely to be worse before they are better; but even at the worst there are mitigating circumstances. Just as mediæval feudalism was a powerful agency in binding together the masses of the people into the organic union from which the modern state was evolved, so too our party feudalism performs a valuable office by the way it establishes connections of interest among the masses of the people. To view the case as a whole, we should contrast the marked European tendency towards disintegration of government through strife of classes and nationalities with the strong tendency shown in this country towards national integration of all elements of the population. Our despised politicians are probably to be credited with what we call the wonderful assimilating capacity of American institutions. They are perhaps managing our affairs better than we are able to judge. We certainly do not know how to manage the politicians, but that is a branch of knowledge which no people acquires save as the result of a long course of education in the school of experience. There is no royal road to learning even for the sovereign people of the United States.

29. A Theory about Corruption

WALTER LIPPMANN

It would be impossible for an historian to write a history of political corruption in America. What he could write is the history of the exposure of corruption. Such a history would show, I think, that almost every American community governs itself by fits and starts of unsuspecting complacency and violent suspicion. There will be long periods when practically nobody except the professional reformers can be induced to pay attention to the business of government; then rather suddenly there will come a period when every act of the administration in power is suspect, when every agency of investigation is prodded into activity, and the civic conscience begins to boil.

It is a nice question whether a period of exposure signifies that politics has recently become unusually scandalous or that an unusually efficient prosecutor has appeared on the scene. The current revelations about the Walker-Tammany régime in New York City, for example, relate to events that took place two, three, and four years ago. That they have come at this particular time is due largely to the ingenuity of United States Attorney Tuttle who within the last few months has discovered that a comparison of federal income tax returns with transcripts of bank accounts may provide useful clues to the hidden transactions of politicians. Mr. Tuttle's success in cracking the polished surface of the Walker Administration was due to the invention of a new political weapon. He may not be the original inventor, but he has certainly developed the invention remarkably. As a result, he is the first man in a long time who has penetrated the defenses of Tammany.

The contest against political corruption in America is very much like the competition among designers of naval armaments. At one time the reformers have a gun which can pierce any armor plate; then a defense against that gun is developed. I do not think it is a too cynical view of the facts to say that the traffic in privileges, which is what corruption is, has never long lacked men smart enough to find ways of defeating the ingenuity of the reformers. I do not mean to say that American cities are not better governed today than when Bryce said nearly forty years ago that they were the one conspicuous failure of the United States. They are much better governed. They are governed by men who often take a considerable pride in doing a good job. That is true today in New York City under Tammany.

Nevertheless, the fact remains, I think, that the ultimate power over appointments, nominations and policies is in the hands of professional politicians who in one way or another make the public business more profitable to themselves than any private business in which,

---

SOURCE: Walter Lippmann, "A Theory about Corruption," *Vanity Fair*, 35:3 (November 1930), pp. 61, 90. By permission of the author and publisher. Reprinted from *Vanity Fair* (now *Vogue* incorporating *Vanity Fair*);

with their abilities and opportunities, they might engage. I have heard, here and there, of a district leader or even of a boss who remains a poor man, and I am not forgetting men like the late Chief Magistrate McAdoo who, after a lifetime in politics, died in poverty. I am not forgetting rather high officials in Tammany about whose integrity there cannot be the slightest doubt. Yet it cannot be denied, I think, that the mainspring which moves the whole complex human organization behind the public government of New York is private advantage.

It certainly is not undiluted patriotism. District leaders are not primarily interested in the administration of justice when they insist on naming magistrates. They insist on naming the magistrates, in some and perhaps in many cases, because the candidate pays for the appointment; in all cases they insist because they wish to control the favors that a magistrate can dispense. The power of the district leader over the voters depends upon his ability to dispense favors. He is recognized as a political leader, not because of his views on public questions, but because he is able concretely to demonstrate day after day that his word is law. Because he controls government, he controls votes and because he controls votes he controls government: because he has power he is cultivated by those who have favors to give, and leaving out all items of bribery, he occupies a place where he has, so to speak, a multitude of business opportunities. If he is a lawyer, he has law cases which require his political influence rather than his legal ability. He is remembered by real estate syndicates and by corporations that are affected by government. In short he capitalizes, most often nowadays, I think, in accordance with the strict letter of the law, the political power he possesses.

The prosecuting agencies, when spasmodically they set to work, can deal only with the crudely overt features of political corruption. Anyone who has observed closely a prosecutor's office on the trail of a political ring knows how enormous is the gap between scandalous political conduct and specifically indictable offenses; in my time I have seen case after case of politicians who could not be indicted, or, if indicted, convicted, though they were guilty as Satan, because the development of conclusive legal proof was lacking. The truth of the matter, I think, is that an entirely objective view of political life at its base where political organization is in direct contact with the population, would show that corruption in some form is endemic. I do not mean that everybody is bribed. I do mean that the exchange of favors is the elemental and essential motive power which operates the semi-private machinery inside the political parties which in their turn operate the official machinery of government. It is, I think, literally true that if the exchange of favors were suddenly and miraculously abolished, there would be a wholesale voluntary retirement of petty politicians to private life, for they would lack then the incentive to stay in politics and the very means by which they maintain their political influence. The best proof of this is that the reformers who operate only with ideals and indignation never really make a party which lasts; they soon discover, when they deign to get down to the base of politics, that the motives they appeal to are unsubstantial.

If it is true that the exchange of favors is an essential element of politics, then the common American assumption about political corruption is naïve and misleading. The assumption, inculcated through patriotic text books, is that in the year 1789 a body of wise men founded a new government in a new world, and that corruption is a lapse from this contract to which all their decendants automatically subscribe. Almost all of us feel, I think, that Tammany, for example, is a kind of disease which has affected the body politic. There it is, to be sure; it has been there a long time, and the counterpart of it is to be found in virtually every American community. Nevertheless, we feel that it is not supposed to be there, and that if only we had a little more courage or sense or something we could cut away the diseased tissue and live happily ever after. The implications of this notion seem to me to be false, and I believe that our political thinking would be immensely more effective if we adopted an entirely opposite theory.

That theory would hold that organizations like Tammany, which bind together masses of people in a complex of favors and coercions, are the ancient form of human association. They might be called natural governments. Our modern, artificial constitutions were superimposed upon them partly by coalitions of the stronger factions and partly by compromises of interest. The natural governments are not abolished when this happens. They continue to a decisive degree to operate through the artificial government. When the conflicts between these natural associations become to momentous the constitutional goverment breaks down in civil war or it is swept aside, as it has been in all of Eastern Europe, by a dictatorship of one of these associations. In many countries it is only too plain that the constitutional system is a mere façade behind which the real exercise of power depends upon the barter of privileges and the use of violence.

My point is that Tammany is not a disease, but simply the old body politic in its more or less natural state, and that the American ideal of goverment as a public trust to be carried on by disinterested men represents not the actuality but a long step ahead in the evolution of man. The very conception of a public trust has not yet been heard of by the mass of mankind. It has been a recognized public ideal in Europe even among the most advanced thinkers for not much more than a few hundred years. It is a very difficult ideal to attain, and I know of no public man even in America and even in our time who has felt able to be completely loyal to it. The best test is the appointment of judges, for surely if there is a public trust more imperative than any other it is the task of the President or the Governor to insure the highest possible quality in the courts. Does anybody know a President who has been guided solely by merit in his selection of judges? I doubt it. The best of Presidents is as virtuous as he dares to be, but at some point or other he must for political reasons knowingly violate his conscience.

The difficulties increase as one descends in the political scale. Presidents, governors, perhaps even mayors, move in a realm where ideal motives may be effective, for their acts are subject to the verdict of the more sensitive minority and to the judgment of history. They are likely, moreover, to be exceptional men who have passed beyond the struggle for existence, to be educated men, and to appreciate the immaterial glories of the state. But down among district leaders, and second deputy commissioners, and clerks of court, the larger rewards, the larger issues, the intrinsic obligations of power, simply do not exist. These office holders are recruited from men who have to struggle to exist, who must hold on grimly to what they can get, who never have any feeling that they are public men making the history of their time. Men of genius have risen now and then from such political beginnings, but for the few who rise there is a multitude who know they never will. What can public office give to them except a job at a meagre salary, an opportunity to prosper a little on the side, a sense of importance in their neighborhood, and the excitement of working for the winning team? At the base of the political structure there are no adequate motives to give meaning to the conception of public office as a public trust. It is not surprising that this relatively new and high conception, which has so little ground in the instinctive life of man, should take hold slowly.

As a matter of historical fact we are justified in going a step farther to say not only that what we call political corruption is the ancient and natural political process, but that corruption in the form of jobbery represents a decisive step upward in political life. I think it could be shown from the history of the Mother of Parliaments itself and demonstrated today in certain politically backward countries that corruption is the practical substitute for factional wars. In the Eighteenth Century the civil wars in England came to an end and the habit of political violence dissolved finally in the organization of a thoroughly corrupt but peaceable parliament. There are places in the world today where corruption is progress. I once heard the President of a Latin-American Republic explain that he was consolidating his régime at home by making ambassadors, with extra large grants for expenses, out of his most dangerous political enemies. It had been the custom to shoot them.

I fear that my theory of corruption will seem fantastic to many and a justification for a lazy tolerance to others. It seems to me the serious truth, and conceivably a useful truth. For if it is true that corruption is not a disease, but on the contrary a natural condition which civilized modern man is seeking to surmount, the knowledge that this is so might very well provide us with a clearer idea of what our periodic scandal-chasing is all about, a better appreciation of the realities with which we are dealing, and even a stronger resolve to keep slogging at it. For we should then know that the campaign against corruption on behalf of the ideal of trust is no mere repairing of something perfect that has broken down, but the implanting of a new habit of acting in the ancient consciousness of man.

30. Corruption: The Shame of the States

JAMES Q. WILSON

The best state legislatures, observed Lord Bryce over half a century ago, are those of the New England states, "particularly Massachusetts." Because of the "venerable traditions surrounding [this] ancient commonwealth" which "sustain the dignity" of its legislature and "induce good men to enter it," this body—called the General Court—is "according to the best authorities, substantially pure." About the time that Bryce was congratulating the representatives in the Massachusetts State House, these men were engaged in a partially successful effort to regulate the government of the city of Boston on the grounds that City Hall was becoming a cesspool of corruption owing, in no small part, to the fact that the Irish, led by Mayor John "Honey Fitz" Fitzgerald, had taken over. The chief instrument of state supervision over the suspect affairs of the city was to be the Boston Finance Commission, appointed by the Governor to investigate any and all aspects of municipal affairs in the capital.

Now, a half century later, the tables have been, if not turned, then at least rearranged. While no one would claim that the Boston City Hall is "pure," the mayoralty of John Collins (an Irishman) has aroused the enthusiastic backing of the city's financial and commercial elite. Many leading Brahmins work closely with the mayor, support him politically, and—most importantly—stand behind him in many of his often bitter fights with the governor and the state legislature. In contrast, the legislature has been plagued with endless charges of corruption and incompetence, the most recent of which have emerged from the work of the Massachusetts Crime Commission.

This Commission, created by the (reluctant) legislature in July, 1962 and appointed by Republican Governor John Volpe, (who had recommended its formation in the first place), was composed largely of the sort of men who used to be *in* the legislature rather than critics of it. In a state where the principal politicians are Irish and Italian graduates of (if anything) Boston College or the Suffolk Law School, the Commission was woven out of Ivy. The Chairman was Alfred Gardner (Harvard '18), senior partner in the austerely respectable law firm of Palmer, Dodge, Gardner and Bradford. Of the other six members, three were graduates of Harvard, two of Princeton, and another of the Harvard Law School. (Although at least one Irishman got onto the Commission, he was an investment consultant and retired brigadier general, and is probably more Yankee than the Yankees.) The American melting pot has obviously not

---

SOURCE: James Q. Wilson, "Corruption: The Shame of the States," *The Public Interest*, 2 (1966), pp. 28–38. By permission of the author and the publisher.

changed the popular belief that, while the Irish are experts on politics, and the Jews experts on money, the Yankees are experts on morality.

The bad repute of Massachusetts government might seem an exaggeration to the casual reader of the recently published Comprehensive Report of the Commission. Except for a brief section on the Massachusetts Turnpike Authority, there are no juicy stories of boodle and skulduggery, nor any inciting accounts of the testimony. The legislature had taken pains to insure that it would not make the same mistake the United States Senate did when it created the Kefauver Committee. Public hearings were explicity forbidden. All testimony was taken in secret sessions; as interpreted by the Commission, this restriction also forbade it from publishing the names of witnesses, direct accounts of their evidence, or details of allegations. If it suspected wrongdoing, the Commission was to turn its information over to regular law-enforcement agencies. And when the life of the Commission expired this year, the legislature made certain that its files were locked away in a vault, secure against further scrutiny.

But if the report is dull, the results were not. Attorney General Edward Brooke, on the basis of information furnished by the Commission, brought indictments against fifty-three individuals and fifteen corporations. About two dozen of the individuals were (or had been) state officials, and they included the former Speaker of the House, a former governor, the public safety director, two present and two former members of the Governor's Council, the chairman of the state housing board, and several former state representatives. One can be reasonably confident that much the same results could be produced by similar commissions in many other states, particularly industrial states of the Northeast such as Pennsylvania, Ohio, and the like. Many of these states would never have been described as "pure" by Lord Bryce at any stage of their history (he singled out New York and Pennsylvania as having legislatures that were "confessedly among the worst"); about all that seems to have happened in the last fifty years is that, on the whole, their governors have become more respectable and their political parties more disorganized, thereby transforming what once was well-organized, machine-like corruption into disorganized, free-lance corruption.

THREE THEORIES OF CORRUPTION

Why should so many state governments seem so bad? The Massachusetts Crime Commission did not try to answer that question (if said it did not know whether corruption was worse in its state than in others), nor did it address itself to the more fundamental questions, "What is corruption?" "Why does it occur?" In short, the Commission did not develop a theory of corruption. This is not simply an academic deficiency (I am not trying to grade the Commission's report as if it were a term paper in a political science seminar); rather, it is a practical problem of the greatest importance, for without a theory of corruption there cannot be a remedy for corruption unless by happy accident.

There are at least three major theories of government corruption. The first holds that there is a particular political ethos or style which attaches a relatively low value to probity and impersonal efficiency and relatively high value to favors, personal loyalty, and private gain. Lower-class immigrant voters, faced with the problems of accommodation to an unfamiliar and perhaps hostile environment, are likely to want, in the words of Martin Lomasney, "help, not justice." If such groups come—as have the Irish and the Sicilians—from a culture in which they experienced a long period of domination by foreign rulers the immigrant will already be experienced in the ways of creating an informal and illegal (and therefore "corrupt") covert government as a way of dealing with the—to them—illegitimate formal government. The values of such groups are radically incompatible with the values of (for example) old-stock Anglo-Saxon Protestant Americans, and particularly with those members of the latter culture who serve on crime commissions. Whatever the formal arrangements, the needs and values of those citizens sharing the immigrant ethos will produce irresistible demands for favoritism and thus for corruption.

The second theory is that corruption is the result of ordinary men facing extraordinary temptations. Lincoln Steffens argued that corruption was not the result of any defect in character (or, by implication, in cultural values); rather, it was the inevitable consequence of a social system which holds out to men great prizes—power, wealth, status—if only they are bold enough to seize them. Politicians are corrupt because businessmen bribe them; this, in turn, occurs because businessmen are judged solely in terms of worldly success. The form of government makes little difference; the only way to abolish corruption is to change the economic and social system which rewards it. (Steffens admired Soviet communism because it was a system without privilege: "There was none but petty political corruption in Russia," he wrote after visiting there. "The dictator was never asked to do wrong.") A less Marxist variation of this theory is more familiar: men steal when there is a lot of money lying around loose and no one is watching. Public officials are only human. They will resist minor temptation, particularly if everyone else does and someone is checking up. They are not angels, however, and cannot be expected to be honest when others are stealing (no one wants to be thought a fink) and superiors are indifferent. The Catholic Church, having known this for several centuries, counsels the young in its catechisms to "avoid the occasion of sin." The solution to this sort of corruption is, obviously, to inspect, audit, check, and double-check.

The third theory is more explicitly political and has the advantage of seeking to explain why governmental corruption appears to be more common in America than in Europe. Henry Jones Ford, writing in 1904, observed that in this country, unlike in those whose institutions follow the British or French models, the executive and legislative branches are separated by constitutional checks and balances. What the Founders have put asunder, the politicians must join together if anything is to be accomplished. Because each branch can—and sometimes does—paralyze the other, American government "is so constituted that it cannot be carried on without corruption." The boss, the machine, the political party, the bagmen—all these operate, in Ford's view, to concert the action of legally independent branches of government through the exchange of favors. The solution to corruption, if this is its cause, is to bring these various departments together formally and constitutionally. This, of course, is precisely what the National Civic League and other reform groups have attempted by their espousal of the council manager plan for municipal government, and what advocates of strong and responsible political parties have sought with respect to state and national government. If the chief executive, by virtue of either his constitutional position or his control of a disciplined majority party, is strong enough to rule without the consent of subordinates or the intervention of legislators, then no one will bribe subordinates or legislators—they will have nothing to sell. The leader himself will rarely be bribed, because his power will be sufficiently great that few, if any, groups can afford his price. (This is how Ford explained the lesser incidence of corruption in American national government: the president is strong enough to get his way and visible enough to make bribe-taking too hazardous.)

Crime commissions and reform groups in this country have at one time or another adopted all these theories, but at least one has now become unfashionable. Fifty years ago the Brahmins were quite candid about the defects they found in the Boston Irish politicians. These "newer races," as James Michael Curley called them, were considered to be the carriers of corruption. In 1965, the Massachusetts Crime Commission—perhaps out of politeness as much as conviction—begins its report by finding "no basis for saying that corruption in Massachusetts is the peculiar attribute of any one party or racial or religious group." This commendable tolerance is perhaps a bit premature: it is at least arguable that the various ethnic groups which make up our big cities and industrial states differ with respect to their conceptions of the public interest as much as they continue to differ with respect to style of life, party affiliation, and place of residence. The structure of government in many states of the Northeast is quite similar to that found in the Far West, yet the incidence of corruption appears to be significantly greater in the East. The historical reasons for this may include the differing values of the populations involved. While one can understand the reasons a public body might wish to avoid commenting on this, the result is that one theory of corruption is discarded *a priori* and all reforms are based on the other theories.

WHAT HAPPENED TO THE CITIES?

The curious fact about all theories of corruption, however, is that they could apply equally to American cities as to American states, and yet it is the states (and to a considerable extent the counties) rather than the cities which are notorious for corruption. Although some corruption probably is to be found in almost all cities, and a great deal in a few, the most important fact about American municipal government over the last twenty years has been the dramatic improvement in the standards and honesty of public service. In no large city today is it likely that a known thief could be elected mayor (how many unknown thieves are elected must be a matter of speculation); a few decades ago, it would have been surprising if the mayor were *not* a boodler.

The reasons for this change are thought to be well-known—the reduction in the demand for and tolerance of corruption, owing to the massive entry of voters into the middle class; the nationalization and bureaucratization of welfare programs that once were the province of the machine; the greater scrutiny of local affairs by the press and civic associations; and the rise of forms of government—the council-manager plan and nonpartisanship—which make party domination difficult.

But if these changes in American society have had profound consequences for city politics, why did they appear to have so little effect on state politics? To be sure, known thieves are probably not often elected governor, but few people outside the states of the Far West are under much illusion as to the standards of public morality which prevail in and around state legislatures and cabinets.

There are at least two reasons for the difference. The first is that the degree of public scrutiny of government is not the same at the state as at the city level. Big cities have big newspapers, big civic associations, and big blocs of newspaper-reading, civic-minded voters. State capitals, by contrast, are usually located outside the major metropolitan centers of the state in smaller cities with small-city newspapers, few (and weak) civic associations, and relatively few attentive citizens with high and vocal standards of public morality. The cosmopolitan, in Robert Merton's language, seeks to escape the small city and get to the big city; the locals who remain behind typically place a higher value on personal friendships and good fellowship than on insisting that government be subject to general and impersonal rules. (The Massachusetts state capitol is an obvious and embarrassing exception: it is located in Boston but seems unaffected by that fact. Perhaps this is because Boston newspapers are so poor and its civic life is so weakly organized.)

The other reason is that anyone interested in obtaining favors from government finds the stakes considerably higher at the state level. With the exception of urban renewal and public housing programs, the city government administers services rather than makes investments. These services are often controversial but the controversy is more about who is to manage them, how they are to be financed, and whether they are fairly and adequately administered. Education, public welfare, street cleaning, and police protection are important services but (with the exception of police tolerance of gambling) they are not likely to make many people very rich. States, on the other hand, disburse or regulate big money. They build roads and in so doing spend billions on contractors, land owners, engineers, and "consultants." They regulate truckers, public utilities, insurance companies, banks, small loan firms, and pawnbrokers; they issue paroles and pardons, license drivers, doctors, dentists, liquor stores, barbers, beauticians, teachers, chiropractors, real estate brokers, and scores of other occupations and professions; they control access to natural resources, and supervise industrial safety and workmen's compensation programs. The stakes are enormous.

At one time, the stakes in city politics were also high. In the late nineteenth and early twentieth centuries, big cities were making their major capital improvements—in the form of subways, traction lines, utility systems—and the value of the contracts and franchises was huge. Local government was formally weak—it had been made so deliberately, in order to insure that it would be "democratic"—and thus it was possible (indeed, almost necessary) for a boss or a machine to control it in order to exchange privileges for boodle.

Prohibition, and later organized gambling, extended the rewards of municipal corruption beyond the time when rapid capital formation was at an end. Organized crime remains a legacy of Prohibition which is still very much with us, but on different terms. There are no longer any Al Capones. The gamblers continue to corrupt the police but, except in the smaller towns—Cicero and Calumet City near Chicago, Newport and Covington near Cincinnati—they rarely manage (or even try) to take over the entire political structure of a city. And even these famous "sin towns" are rapidly being closed down. By the time urban renewal came along—a program of capital improvements potentially ripe for corruption—the coalitions of businessmen and mayors which governed most big cities and which were most interested in renewal as a "progressive" program to "save the city" were not inclined to allow the success of the program to be threatened by stealing. More importantly, urban renewal is far smaller in scale than the highway program; the opportunities for "windfall profits" are not vast; the program is surrounded by sufficient public controversy to make it very difficult to transact many deals under the table; and the federal government supervises local renewal much more closely than it supervises highway construction.

UNRECONSTRUCTED STATE GOVERNMENT

Ironically, the very things which made matters better in the big cities may have made them worse in the states. The preoccupation with urban affairs and the attendant close scrutiny of the conduct of those affairs has diverted public attention from state affairs. If it was true that state capitols were ignored in the past, it is doubly true today. The civic-minded businessman wants to save the central city; the liberal cosmopolitan wants to improve urban race relations and end urban poverty; the federal government, especially the White House, seeks closer and closer ties with the big cities—in part because that is were the voters are and in part because federal officials are increasingly desirous of establishing direct relations with their city counterparts in order to bypass what they often consider to be the obstructionism of the state bureaucracy.

The various governmental innovations—at-large elections, nonpartisanship, the council-manager form—which have made entry into municipal politics attractive to, and possible, for the nonparty civic "statesman" have meant that increasingly the more traditional politician has felt uncomfortable in and disadvantaged by city politics. Elections for state office, which continue to be conducted under party labels in relatively small districts, are a more familiar and congenial experience. Success here can still come to the man with strong neighborhood ties, clubhouse connections, a proven record of party loyalty, and a flair for tuning the ear of his ethnic compatriots to the ancestral voices.

In short, if government is more corrupt in the states than in the cities, it is because all three theories of corruption (and perhaps others) apply with greater force to the states. The ethnic style of politics is weakening in the cities but not in the states; more boodle is lying around with no one watching in state capitols than in city halls; and state governments continue to be badly decentralized, with formal authority divided among a host of semi-autonomous boards, commissions, and departments. The states have rarely been subjected to the kinds of reforms which over the years have gradually centralized formal authority in the hands of a professional city manager or a single strong mayor.

The last point deserves emphasis. Governors are not "little Presidents." Their power of appointment and removal is sharply circumscribed. Duane Lockard estimates that only slightly more than half the 730 major administrative posts in state government are filled by gubernatorial appointments; the remainder are filled by election or by appointments made by the legislature or special boards and commissions. Nor does the governor generally have the full power of removal normally assumed to be the prerogative of the President. Only five governors can appoint their own superintendents of education; only half can choose their own men to run state departments of agriculture. Of equal or greater importance is the typical governor's weak position within the party and the interest groups which elect him. A governor who is the principal leader of his party and who has in addition a strong and popular personality may do well with little formal authority; lacking these, all the formal executive authority in the world may not suffice, if for no other reason than that the governor must still deal with an independent legislature.

The Massachusetts Crime Commission was not unaware of such problems but—perhaps because it was a crime commission rather than an "effective government" commission—it did not really come to grips with these issues. It was preoccupied with corruption that, in its view, could be attributed largely to the "occasion of sin" theory of wrongdoing. Dealing with such forms of larceny is relatively easy: employ well-qualified administrators selected on their merits to implement high professional standards. This, supplemented by careful inspection and audit procedures, will reduce or eliminate corruption in the letting of contracts, hiring of consultants, issuance of licenses, and regulation of conduct by such agencies as the Registry of Motor Vehicles, the Department of Public Works; the Massachusetts Turnpike Authority, and the Department of Banking and Insurance.

Recognizing that bookkeeper reforms alone are insufficient because they provide no ultimate checks on the behavior of the bookkeepers, the Commission sought to give elective officials clear authority over the behavior of their subordinates and clear responsibility to the electorate. Thus, many of the Commission's recommendations are designed to strengthen the formal powers of the chief executive—the governor and his principal subordinates—so that someone has the power and responsibility for weeding out corrupt underlings. The Commission follows a well-marked tradition: reformers, at least during this century, have favored strong executive authority. In this, of course, they have sometimes undone themselves: reformers correctly believe that a strong executive is less likely to tolerate or encourage corruption than a weak one, but they often forget that in the United States a strong executive is also likely to pay close attention to the demands of the masses. Legislatures, though more likely to be corrupt, are also more likely to be conservative. Reformers often secure cleanliness at the price of conservatism.

But because no attention is paid to the third cause of corruption—the need to exchange favors to overcome decentralized authority—the sort of executive-strengthening recommended by the Massachusetts Commission, while admirably suited to eliminating the occasion of sin, is not so well suited to dealing with legislatures or other independent bodies. The governor must not only be strong in his own house, but in the legislature's house as well. Otherwise, the executive branch may be pure, but only out of impotence.

THE USES OF PATRONAGE

Unless we are willing to adopt a parliamentary form of state government (and I take it we are not), then the way in which a governor can get important things done (at least in a state like Massachusetts) is by having something to bargain with that both the legislature and the party value. There are several such resources: for one, his own popularity with the voters; and for another, favors and patronage. The latter the Commission rejects and, I suspect, ill-advisedly. Certainly, patronage abuses should be curtailed (in large part because, as the Commission notes, such abuses lower the morale of public employees). Furthermore, the cumbersome Massachusetts civil service system in its present form probably serves the interests of neither the reformers nor the politicians. (For example, the legislature frequently passes statutes "freezing" certain employees into their jobs. This not only protects some incompetents, it also makes it impossible for the governor to use these positions for patronage purposes of his own.) But I believe that patronage itself should not be eliminated entirely.

The Commission was of course aware of the fact that patronage is often used to induce legally independent officials to act toward some desirable goal. The Massachusetts Turnpike Authority under the leadership of the late William Callahan raised to a fine art the use of jobs, contracts, and insurance premiums for political purposes—but the Massachusetts Turnpike got built, and on time. The Commission faces the issue squarely:

> The methods [the chairman of the Authority] used to get results have had no small part in bringing about the deterioration in the moral climate of our state government. This

deterioration in moral climate is of far greater importance to every man, woman and child in Massachusetts than the ease and comfort with which it is now possible to drive the length of the state on a multi-lane highway.

Perhaps. I suspect, however, that this is a question on which the people of Massachusetts might have some differences of opinion. It may well be that a deterioration in the moral climate of government and a concomitant weakening of the respect in which citizens hold their government are serious costs of corruption. But these costs, like all others, are matters of degree; hopefully, ways can be found to reduce them without a more than equivalent reduction in benefits.

What is clear is that the strengthening of the governor cannot be achieved by formal means alone, particularly if Massachusetts, like most states, needs two strong and highly competitive political parties.

It the Commission goes too far in some directions, it does not go far enough in others. The most serious cause of the corruption of law enforcement officials is organized crime; recognizing this, the Commission calls only for stronger laws, stiffer penalties, and a "reorganized" state police. "Bookmakers are not entitled to lenience." But raising the penalties against betting will not necessarily eliminate organized crime; it may only raise the price. Because more will be at stake, the police and the politicians are likely to demand bigger bribes and the criminals will be more disposed to use violence to protect their monopoly profits. At a time when the mayor of New York City is advocating offtrack betting, it would seem that some attention might be given in Massachusetts to lowering, rather than increasing, the incentives gamblers have to corrupt the government. (To be sure, in some states and cities vigorous police action has reduced gambling to a bare minimum, but these are states—like California—with very different histories and populations; unless one is prepared to reject entirely the "ethos" theory of corruption, one should not be too quick to conclude that equally good results can be obtained in any state.)

With respect to campaign contributions, the Commission confesses the limitations of its recommendations, which by and large follow a familiar pattern: better reporting systems, the removal of unrealistic and unenforceable limits on dollar amounts, and so forth. Such methods are not likely to deter the favor-seeking contributor, though they are likely to deter perfectly respectable contributors who feel that reports, inspections, and publicity involve too much trouble and possible embarrassment to justify giving anything at all. The Commission "leaves to others" a study of fundamental changes in methods of campaign finance. Unfortunately, calls for "more research" are likely to go unheeded.

It is, of course, easy to criticize crime commissions and to adopt a faintly patronizing tone toward reformers. This would be a mistake. The Commission has turned a number of highly-placed rascals over to the attorney general and the courts; and other, lesser rascals are likely to take heed—for the moment. But it would also be a mistake to make corruption (defined so broadly as to include "good" as well as "bad" patronage) the central issue. The central issue is that many states—Massachusetts is one—are badly governed in the sense that certain goals that should be sought are not, and others that should not be, are. The central problem is the problem of power—how can it be used responsibly but effectively for socially desirable ends? Power is hard to find and harder to use wisely, in great part because in many states we are destroying its informal bases (favors, patronage, party discipline) faster than we are building up its formal bases (legal authority). The result increasingly is that, with the states unable to act, they are being bypassed by cities (where the most visible problems are to be found) seeking the assistance of the federal government (where the power is). To the extent that the recommendations of the Massachusetts Crime Commission and its counterparts elsewhere can strengthen the legal capacity of a state to govern, they will have been worthwhile. To the extent they are used only for piecemeal attacks on the more titillating and exotic forms of public corruption, they may do more harm than good.

31. The Purity Potlatch: Conflict of Interests and Moral Escalation

BAYLESS MANNING

MORAL INFLATION IN OUR POLITICS—THE POTLATCH

As a nation, we like our politics neat. The heroes still wear white hats, and the villains black ones; we do not like to get them mixed up, and we decidedly do not like the players to wear gray hats. A foreign observer noting this might conclude that the American must be a stupid fellow. How can he not know that men are complex, fail to understand that good and evil dwell in all men, and be incapable of summoning the maturity required to accept a world of grays for what it is? But the American is decidedly not a stupid fellow. He is perfectly aware that the fellowman whom he knows in his neighborhood, his office, his church, and his club is neither a distillate of perfidy unalloyed nor a crystal of virtue unblemished. It is not here that the American and the foreign observer differ. The difference lies rather in the American's unusual, perhaps unique, conception of what his political process is about.

We look to our political process not only to run the government, but also to perform other vitally important social and spiritual functions for us. In our Democracy we look to the political process to identify, produce, and articulate many of our ideals, our goals, our standards, our heroes, our examples for our society, for ourselves, and for our young. In substantial measure, the American looks upon his politics as a Morality Play. Our national political conventions every four years are massive comings together for spiritual mutual support and communion, revival meetings for endless reassertions of our national moral symbols and rededication to those elevating ideals. For just this reason, the Democratic and Republican conventions are almost identically devoid of programmatic content while new parties are soon rejected by the body electorate as redundant or, if organized around a program or position, as an incompatible foreign engraftment.

To the extent that our politics partake of the nature of a Morality Play, they have inevitably required, and generated, a set of theatrical conventions as arbitrary, and as acceptable, as those of any dramatic form. The vocabularly of our politics conforms to its role as a national Morality drama. That vocabulary is formal, dogmatic, simplified, symbolic, repetitive, and goal-setting; it is not descriptive and must not be thought of as being descriptive. And the actors in the political drama must, as in epic

SOURCE: Bayless Manning, "The Purity Potlatch: An Essay on Conflict of Interests, American Government, and Moral Escalation," *Federal Bar Journal*, 24:3 (Summer 1964), pp. 243–249. By permission of the author and the publisher, the Federal Bar Association.

drama, appear as more than life-size, establishing, declaring, and appearing to live in accordance with, standards that are not of this world. We therefore demand ultimate moral pronouncements from our parties and our officials. We beatify or apotheosize our former Presidents, feeling the need for unifying national moral norms and having no national established church to do the job or to produce national saints. We are terribly concerned at a candidate's divorce because we are worried about our own divorce rate, and because in our Democracy we cannot be concerned about a king's divorce.[1]

The foreign observer encountering our politics for the first time deserves some sympathy; he cannot be expected to know that he is at the theatre. At the *bunrakuza* he would not think it peculiar that the audience seems not to detect the black-clad puppeteers. At Epidauros, he would not complain at the watchers for not protesting that the masks are wood, that the tall gods are men on clogs, and that Iphegenia is male. But at San Francisco and Atlantic City this summer, not knowing what he is observing, he is apt to perceive, and perceiving announce as discovery, that the party positions are more platitude than platform, that the non-stop speeches mainly rehearse the virtues of the national saints, the flag, freedom, and purity and denounce the unprincipled character of the opposition party.

Thus we look to our elected officials for moral affirmations. This does not mean, however, that the American voter thinks his Congressman a moral giant. Indeed, he often thinks of him not as a "government official"—a term of respect —but as a "politician"—a pejorative. We are bewilderingly ambivalent in our split vision of our officials—as religionists are apt to be about their priests. But when it comes to official public pronouncements, this double image makes no difference. When we are thinking of our officials in their role as public agents of governance, respect and authority, we demand that they speak with sobriety and uncompromising morality; when we suspect them of the worst, we demand that they constantly reassure us that they know where morality lies, and are dedicated to it. In either view of the matter, the public official in the United States must in his public dialogue take his stand foresquare and often for Absolute Rectitude. If presidents, senators, congressmen, and governors suspect that this world cannot be operated on such a simplified basis, they are expected to keep their suspicions to themselves—and they generally do.

Some would remark that this is a strange way to run a government. Perhaps it is. But the United States has turned in a record of governmental accomplishment over the past 175 years that is unapproached in world history, and in some measure, at least, its achievements are attributable to its insistence upon an elevated moral vision of itself and its officials—an insistence upon a moral reach that exceeds the practical grasp. Central to our political history has been the conviction that political man can be good, or made good, that reform is worthwhile, and that problems can be solved if addressed with faith and energy. To the observer from many other cultures, all this seems Americanly naive, amusing and, if not downright juvenile, at least unrealistic; and he has sometimes been moved to leap to his feet to declare his low opinion of simplistic success and his preference for sophisticated failure. But whatever the merits or demerits of the American way of doing politics, the present point is simply to note that this is the character of American politics, and that it substantially affects the problem at hand—conflicts of interest.

---

1 It may be that all men are monarchists and that they differ only in the method for choosing their monarchs.

For a major consequence of this special character of our politics is that in matters touching public morality we are inflation-prone.

So long as our extraordinary Two-Party Non-System blesses us with a massive majority committed to an ideological center, American elections are won and lost in a very few ways only. The main avenues to success are two—public dissatisfaction with a major irritant, such as a depression or unpopular war (these sorespots are always called "issues" in our political parlance) is one, and personal charisma is the other. When a candidate and a party have both, as Roosevelt did in 1932 and Eisenhower did in 1952, they win overwhelmingly. When these are not present—and they seldom are for the local candidate, and cannot be manufactured—the next most effective approach in the American political environment is to interpret the contest in terms of the great Morality Play. The opposition, and especially the Ins, must be made to be personal scoundrels and dishonest men; that they might be proven to be incompetent or inert is not enough; they must be shown to have been morally delinquent—deficient in patriotism, domestic habits, or fiscal responsibility. One may not always win with this argument, even when there are some supporting facts for the charges, but it offers the most promising strategy and is therefore regularly tried. Conversely, of course, the political spokesman must himself project a spotless purity, dazzling to the eye. What follows is something like a duel in public—a purity duel between the political contestants.

All public duels are substantially of the same character in every society. The theme of the duel is some personal attribute or skill highly prized by the society. It may be physical courage and personal honor-pride as in Scott and Dumas; it may be one's command over magic as in Southwestern Indian medicine-man duels; or it may be, as in the calypso singing duels, the divine gift of lyric creativity. In the Alaskan Tlingit potlatch, the virtue at stake is spirituality and generosity coupled with bravado and display. The duelists in the potlatch take alternate turns in destroying those things that are of most value the them, the winner gaining great community prestige by reducing himself to material ruin.

All such duel systems are inflation-prone. They tend to escalate. It is difficult for any participant to stop when he is a notch below his opponent; it is difficult for both participants to recognize a standoff; and it is difficult to get either participant to begin to climb down. If the participants were not playing in public, they would often find it possible to limit their engagement with each other. In the case of the potlatch, they could maintain their self-respect and their property as well. But when the duel is fought out in public view, and when the prize of power and position hinges on the public's estimate of who won the contest, escalation and rigidity are inevitable.

And thus it is with morality duels in American politics. Like bomb-rattling, virtue-rattling escalates. To permit a moral march to be stolen on you is exceedingly dangerous. When in the 1952 controversy over the Nixon campaign fund, candidate Eisenhower prescribed the "hound's tooth" standard, Nixon produced his "Checkers" performance. The next move was up to Stevenson. He responded with objective irrelevance but symbolic political relevance by publishing a list of his personal assets.[2] Since

2 *New York Times*, Sept. 29, 1952, p. 1, col. 8. A skilled practitioner recently provided us an instructive example of this kind of symbolic communication in his campaign to turn out unnecessary lights in the house where he lives—the White House. The money saved is insignificant, of course, and the rationalist is therefore tempted to dismiss or condemn the affair as cynical or hypocritical. I believe this reaction to be quite wrong. No one was misled to meant to be misled. "Lights Out" was

then, the practice has slowly begun to spread, and if one political candidate publicly lists his personal holdings it is very difficult for his opponent not to do the same. If there ever was a rational reason why this should be done, that reason is soon overtaken by the better reason that one must do it to stay in the purity potlatch. When the ante goes up, one must at least match it.

In a somewhat different form, the same process may be seen typically at work in the practice of the Senate Armed Services Committee to require Defense Department appointees coming before it to dispose of their stockholdings in companies doing business with the Pentagon. The rule is announced as an Absolute Principle. The Committee is fond of expressing its concern not only with actual conflicts of interest between the public duties of Defense Department officials and their personal stockholdings, but with the appearances in the matter; "Caesar's wife" appears often in the transcripts of the hearings. And, nearly always, a small shareholding is treated as being as offensive as a large one; a minor Defense Department contractor as being as dangerous as a major one.[3] No senator is anxious to take a public stand in favor of anything less than Absolute Purity—however small the practical risks involved might be. Further, there is the matter of precedent. Interrogations on stockholdings by government officials were almost unknown before the Wilson controversy in 1953. But once the issue was brought out, it became difficult for any committee member to retire it again. As a consequence, every Defense Department nominee since 1953 has had to run the gauntlet of the Committee's enquiry and suffer its Draconian divestment rule. There is considerable evidence that no one on the Committee likes the situation, but no one knows how to change it. This political susceptibility to moral escalation explains in part our present national fascination with conflicts of interest.

This is not the whole explanation, however. Throughout American history it has often been possible to fetch up evidence of casual, if not fraudulent, standards of public trust on the part of government officials. In the last century, a Vanderbilt could refuse to contribute to campaign funds on the ground that it was cheaper to buy the legislator after he was elected. Overt bribery was, if not common, at least not uncommon. And it was generally assumed and understood (as it still is in many countries and a few places in the United States) that men who live the political life somehow line their bank accounts in the process. The situation in the United States today is quite different. Though some may find it surprising, the fact is that in this country we are currently living in an era of unexampled honesty in public administration. Evolution of modern administrative techniques for fiscal control, development of a professional sense in the civil service, virtual elimination of the spoils system, spread of competitive bidding, increase in public education, enrichment of the economy, and other basic shifts in the national political organism have reduced blatant peculation of federal funds almost to the vanishing point. By now the governmental record is much better than that of private business in coping with the problem of the

a form of direct political communication, a formalized and readily graspable goal-setting statement by a protagonist in a stylized dramatic setting. It was a means of saying "I, too, am worried about the cost of government, and shall try to do something about it," and, as such, is no more and no less to be criticized than the same sentence delivered in a speech. ("Actions speak louder than words" is true in two quite different senses.) Of course the proposition asserted could itself be true or false, sincere, or hypocritical; but that is so regardless of the technique of communication chosen.

3 See, for example, the failure of the *de minimis* argument in the confirmation hearings on the appointment of Mr. Dudley Sharp discussed at *Conflict of Interest and Federal Service* 105.

dishonest employee.[4] World War II and the Korean War saw no great procurement rackets of the kind that were spawned by the Civil War, the Spanish-American War, and, to a lesser degree, World War I. When it is considered that the Department of Defense alone has dispensed some 686 billion dollars since the end of World War II, the federal, state, and municipal budgets currently aggregate over 200 billion dollars per year, and that there are over 9,000,000 people on government payrolls, excluding the uniformed military, the record for administrative integrity achieved by modern American governments almost passes belief.

The general improvement in governmental fiscal responsibility poses something of a problem to American political practitioners. How can the Outs convincingly demonstrate the perfidy of the Ins when thieves, grafters, and suborners stubbornly refuse to reveal themselves to be actively at work in the In-administration? There are only two avenues open. One is to blow up isolated instances of impropriety so that they appear as illustrations of massive, pervasive hidden corruption. This is attempted regularly. The other avenue is more subtle. If the facts will not make out a case of moral deficiency by accepted standards, the standards must be escalated to a point where facts can be found that *will* make out a deficiency; and the public must be educated to be horrified by the resulting new sins in substantially the same degree that they were horrified by the old. This process is constantly going on about us.

4 Compare, for example, the rate of occurrence of embezzlement by employees of private banks with that of government employees holding fiscal responsibilities. Though it is difficult to be statistical, most observers would agree that fraud, kickbacks, and inside deals are more common features of the corporate, union, and business world than they are of modern government in the United States—not because standards in the former are so low, but because they are so high in the latter.

As the old government briber-contact man—the fixer—has faded into history, the operator who for pay steers an outsider around the bureaucratic labyrinth of Washington comes to be called by the vaguely invidious tag "Five Per Center," and soon earns a place in the public mind close alongside Albert Fall. The public understands the fixer, but how many know what it is that makes the Five Per Center such a menace? When it proves difficult to find a suborned Commissioner, it may be discovered that one has received "*ex parte* communications" and should therefore be put in the stocks. What part of the public understands what this new sin is? If bribery cannot be shown, perhaps the public can be persuaded that it is as bad for the government employee to receive Christmas presents. If government officials are fired in disgrace at once *either* for taking a bribe *or* for accepting a gift, how long can the public be expected to distinguish between the two transactions? And if instances cannot be found where an official has diverted public moneys to his own pocket, coals can be heaped on the head of the official who *might* someday be tempted to divert public moneys to his pocket because his personal economic interests and those of the government *might* someday conflict.

In the public mind, to receive a gift or to have a conflict of interest has by now been equated with venality; a government official in a position of conflicting interests is a kind of a crook. What else is the public to conclude when Senate committees in confirmation proceedings, the Congress through legislation, the executive by regulations, and the Supreme Court[5] in chorus denounce in the most absolute terms the public vice of conflicting interests? And when no modulating or qualifying voice can be heard in our ethotropic political environment?

5 United States v. Mississippi Valley Generating Co., 364 U.S. 520 (1961).

The process by which yesterday's peccadillo becomes today's enormity has been sketched here metaphorically. Such transitions in public attitudes are not consciously brought on by master manipulators of American political psychology. The change comes about unconsciously, over time, and as a result of millions of signal impulses and receptions in the political interplay. And the change is fully as attributable to shifts in what the populace will listen to as to what new broadcasts are beamed to them. Moreover, those who are broadcasting political communications—officials, candidates, commentators, courts, scholars—are themselves among the listeners and indeed are apt to be ineffective politically if they are not. This blurring between the communicator and the receptor means that the political communicator does not need consciously to plan and manipulate his output; as a member of his own audience, he almost automatically transmits what they are willing, or want, to listen to. A more formal description of the change that has brought conflicts of interest to the front page of the newspapers would give greater emphasis to the role of audience reaction and dilute the implication that those in active political life have consciously arranged the evolution.

But the substance remains the same. Conflicts of interest have become a modern political obsession in this country, first, because American politics is highly susceptible to morality escalation and, second, because we are living in an era of unparalleled honesty in public administration when we can afford the luxury of worrying about public harms before they happen.

THE MORAL ESCALATOR—ANTICIPATORY RESTRAINTS

Is not this general rise in the governmental morality table a fine thing? Is it not symptomatic of progress that our society has brought under control the most flagrant forms of public fiscal abuse, such as bribery, and is moving on with increasingly sensitized moral nerve-ends to become aware of and deal with less blatant improprieties such as conflicts of interest? Whatever objective forces may have brought about this result, is not the result a matter for rejoicing?

If this were the whole story, the answer would be an easy affirmative. But there is more to the story. Before we push ahead farther in our ride up the moral escalator, we should ask what the fare is. My own estimate is that as we continue to elevate our conflict of interest standards, the costs are mounting and the marginal gains are dropping.

Under the conditions of modern government and technology, the numbers of responsible government officials are being steadily increased; their responsibilities are being added to; the standards and qualifications for their appointment grow continuously more exacting; the dependence of the society upon the judgment and skill of these officials mounts constantly; the government is engaged in a bitter, continuous competition in the market place for trained manpower, and is not doing too well in that competition; and the entire process by which the government gets its work done is under tidal pressures of change arising from our new international leadership, the Cold War, increasing governmental involvement in the economy, the explosion of government-financed technology, and the revolution in the way we staff the government—a revolution embodying both the maturation of a great civil service, and the emergence of new techniques for contracting-out performance of services on a vast scale.

Recruitment of political leadership and executive manpower for the government of in the United States is in a state of deep-seated and chronic crisis. And the society seems to generate one force after another tending to inhibit able men from embarking upon the hazardous seas of government service. The economic disadvantages of public service are a real, but only a minor, source of the problem. We do not adequately recognize an obligation to devote part of our careers to political service. The prestige and esteem we accord those who do enter upon it is disgracefully short of what it should be. The rising cost of election campaigns and our complete failure to solve the problem of how to finance them tend to restrict elective candidacy to those who can pick up the tab themselves, or those who are willing to accept the conditions that go with financial support by particular interest groups. Our steady move toward large group collective organization is muffling the political voices and participation of many of those who in the past provided much of our educated leadership; the company executive, the lawyer in the large law firm, the university president or dean, the news commentator, the foundation head, is increasingly forced—or thinks he is forced—to stay out of controversial political situations for fear that customers, clients, alumni, advertisers, or opposition forces within the government may be offended and retaliate against or withhold support from his institution. Our institutional welfare plans for retirement and insurance, seniority promotion, stock options, and the like all work to impede mobility into and out of public service. Most men have always tended to say what they think the group thinks, rather than what they themselves think—to be passive in civic responsibilities rather than active. Our modern society seems almost designed to reinforce this natural timidity and to give new excuses for inertia. And it is happening, as I have said, at the time when the demand for quality and quantity in appointive and elective public office grows daily more urgent. Under these circumstances, any additional hurdle thrown before the government in its efforts to attract men of ability to public office is costly and even dangerous. But we are setting up just such a hurdle with every new restraint on public officials imposed in the name of preventing conflicts of interest.

There is no satisfactory way of measuring just how much of a deterrent to federal recruitment is generated by the present system of conflict of interest restraints. But the general effect is undeniably negative. In 1960, *Conflict of Interest and Federal Service* reviewed the subject with some care, based on more than two hundred interviews, and concluded that restraints in the 1950s had little effect on employees in the civil service, but substantially contributed to the difficulty of recruiting executives, especially top executives for the Defense Department, middle executives from the business community, and, as intermittent employees, lawyers.[6] The study further pointed out the deterrent effect of the vagueness of the restraints, the incentive they provide for men in government service to leave it, and certain other undesirable side effects. Since then, the statutes in the field have been modernized, and experience under the new law will hopefully be somewhat better. The practice of the Senate Armed Services Committee remains unaltered and forbidding. The present point is not, however, to assail the existing structure of restraints as ill-conceived. It is rather to point out that they already embarrass the government in one of its most critical activities—the recruitment of leadership—that every further extension of restraints will add to that embarrassment—and that it will do so at the very moment in our history when we can least afford it.

---

6 *Conflict of Interest and Federal Service*, ch. 7. The methodology for the study made by the Special Committee on Conflict of Interest of the Association of the Bar of the City of New York, and its staff, is briefly described at *id.* Appendix C.

CHAPTER SEVEN

Africa

32. Corruption in the Public Services of British Colonies and Ex-Colonies in West Africa

M. McMULLAN

There is some corruption in all governments and in the public services of all countries. Some countries, however, suffer from a greater degree of corruption than others. Only very recently and in only a handful of countries has such corruption been so far reduced as to be practically negligible, that is to say so far reduced that it does not normally enter into a citizen's relations with his government. In most countries throughout most of their known history such corruption has been an accepted feature of life. In extreme cases today it can be a major obstacle to economic development and a major cause of political instability. It deserves attention for its intrinsic interest as part of the "pathology" of bureaucracy, for its practical importance for the political and economic development of the poorer nations of the world, and for the contribution that an analysis can make to sympathetic understanding of what may otherwise be a repulsive feature of some societies. In this paper I try to relate the corruption observed in the British Colonies and ex-colonies of West Africa to the social conditions and histories of those countries and to make some tentative generalisations from a comparison of conditions there and in other parts of the world.

I am not asserting that these West African territories are peculiarly given to corruption; there are many countries in the world where the governments are more corrupt and many more where they were equally corrupt in the recent past; the choice of these countries is dictated only by the accident of the writer's own experience.

THE EFFECTS OF CORRUPTION

Understanding is desirable, but it is wrong to underrate the evil consequences of widespread corruption. People sympathetic to African and other nationalist movements are sometimes tempted to brush aside corruption as being a "passing phase" of no real political or social importance. Whether it is a "passing phase" or not in West Africa I do not know, though I shall give reasons for thinking that it is at least not a phase that will pass quickly; but I am certain that it is of real political and social importance. Some of the evils which widespread corruption may be expected to bring are:—

1. Injustice. This needs no explanation.

2. Inefficiency. In countries where the general standard of technology is

SOURCE: M. McMullan, "A Theory of Corruption," *Sociological Review*, 9:2 (June 1961), pp. 181–200. By permission of the publisher.

low this is a serious matter. Railway accidents are caused by Station Masters corruptly agreeing to load logs that are too heavy for the wagons. Patients in hospitals may be denied treatment they require or bribe nurses to give them treatment they want (in West Africa usually injections), but which may be unsuitable for their condition. Corruption in making appointments may be relatively unimportant in a country where the general standard of competence is high, but in West Africa, where professional and technical competence is still rare, corruption results in the appointment of unsuitable people and the waste and frustration of the right man.

3. Mistrust of the government by the citizen. This is peculiarly serious where the government is anxious to carry out a programme of economic development for which the enthusiasm of the population needs to be enlisted. It also increases the difficulties of enforcing criminal, revenue, and other laws.

4. Waste of public resources. Corruption in the government involves the ultimate transfer of public funds to the pockets of politicians or officials. The businessman who has to bribe to get a government contract ultimately charges the bribe to public funds.

5. Discouragement of enterprise, particularly foreign enterprise. Corruption adds an incalculable hazard to the normal thickets of bureaucratic procedure. The final bribe is never paid. Investors and entrepreneurs are dismayed and frustrated, and may find that the unofficial cost of starting an enterprise is too great for it to be profitable.

6. Political instability. In a country where there is a great deal of corruption, political attacks on people in positions of power are easy to mount and easy to get popular support for. Much of the political history of some unfortunate countries could be told as the "ins" being accused, correctly, by the "outs" of corruption; popular indignation at the corruption causing the replacement of the "ins" by the "outs," who in turn become corrupt and are attacked by a new group of "outs." This process could be demonstrated in detail from the history of some local government bodies in West Africa during the past ten years. At the national level it can lead either to political chaos, or

7. Repressive measures. It may be easier to deal with the accusations of corruption than with the corruption itself.

8. Restrictions on government policy. I recall a conversation with an American doctor who was an admirer of the British National Health Service. "No such service would at the moment be possible in my home State," he said, naming the State, "the civil service is too inefficient and corrupt to be capable of running it." A corrupt civil service and police force restricts the range of policies available to a government.

EVIDENCE

There is one preliminary problem which must be faced but cannot be solved; the problem of evidence. Arguments and statements about corruption cannot be demonstrated by factual or statistical evidence of the type normally acceptable as a basis for political or sociological generalisation. There are plenty of reports, histories and trial records[1] ex-

[1] In West Africa, the Nigerian Governments have published some very useful reports of Enquiries into allegations of corruption, for example *The Report of the Commission of Enquiry into Port Harcourt Town Council*, Government Printer Enugu 1953; *The Report of the Enquiry into the Allocation of Market Stalls at Aba by P. F. Grant*, G.P. Enugu 1955; dealing with activities at a higher level there is the *Report of the Tribunal Appointed to Enquire into Allegations of Improper Conduct by the Premier of Eastern Nigeria in Connection with the Affairs of the African Continental Bank Ltd.*, G.P. Lagos 1957. From Ghana there is the *Report of the Commission of Enquiry into Mr. Braimah's resignation and the Allegations Arising therefrom*, G.P. Accra 1954. For similar phenomena in another colonial territory, see *Commission of Enquiry into Matters Affecting the Public Service*, G.P. Kuala Lumpur 1955.

emplifying corruption in different countries, but corruption is not a subject which can be investigated openly by means of questionnaires and interviews. Even if it were, in principle, possible to quantify the phenomenon, there would be no practical possibility of doing so. The reader is asked to accept as a premise of the argument of this paper that there is more corruption in these West African countries than in, for instance, the United Kingdom. This is a view based on my own observations over a decade, broadly shared by other well placed observers and supported by publice expressions of concern by indigenous political and religious leaders in West Africa.[2] But it cannot, nor can many of the other statements in this paper be proved in the ways in which statements about less disreputable aspects of society can be proved. Corruption still awaits its Kinsey report. This difficulty must be recognised but we cannot refuse to discuss important topics simply because the best type of evidence is not available.

DEFINITION

I shall not attempt a comprehensive or legally precise definition of corruption,[3] and will content myself with the common understanding that a public official is corrupt if he accepts money or money's worth for doing something that he is under a duty to do anyway, that he is under a duty not to do, or to exercise a legitimate discretion for improper reasons. Institutions have official aims, the human beings that work them have personal aims. The ideal relation between the individual and the institution is that the individual should be able to satisfy his personal aims in harmony with, and while forwarding, the official aims of the institution. It is nothing to the Home Office that the prison warder has six children to feed, but the prison warder is acting legitimately in working as a prison warder so that he can feed his six children with his salary. Should he find his salary insufficient, however, and take money from the prisoners for doing them favours, he will be described as corrupt. He will be using his position in the prison to forward his personal aims in a way which conflicts with the official aim of the institution. There is a conflict between the attitudes and aims of a corrupt official and those of the service, and an equally important divergence between the attitudes and aims of the member of the public who induces the corruption of the official, and the aims and attitudes of the society as a whole. These divergencies may be defined by reference to the laws and regulations in which the official aims and attitudes are set out.

THE ARGUMENT

The corruption discussed here is, by definition, illegal. People break laws because they do not accept them, or because they have other interests or desires which they prefer or are impelled to follow. Some laws in a society find almost universal acceptance, other laws are broken by large numbers of people. Head-hunting, for instance, is illegal in New Guinea and in France, but the laws against it are more often broken in New Guinea than in France. Obviously the law against head-hunting in New Guinea is further from the popular attitude towards that activity in New Guinea than is the similar law in France from the

2 E.g. President Nkrumah's announcement that the Ghana Government would set up a permanent Commission to investigate all forms of corruption and to receive complaints about it (*Ghana Today*, 22 June, 1960).

3 In England there are a large number of laws against corruption. The most comprehensive definition is that in Section I(I) of the Prevention of Corruption Act 1906, which includes not only corruption by public officials, but also similar behaviour by any agent or employee. Of course the type of behaviour which is the subject of this paper is not in West Africa or anywhere else confined to public officials. Similar behaviour is common among the employees of private companies, educational institutions, etc.

popular attitude there. If there is greater corruption in West Africa than in Denmark the popular attitude towards corruption in West Africa must be different from that in Denmark.

Thus far is tautology. The problem is to identify the reasons for the popular attitude. The argument of this paper is that a high level of corruption is the result of a wide divergence between the attitudes, aims and methods of the government of a country and those of the society in which they operate, in particular of the procedures and aims of the government which put particular groups of the population at a special disadvantage: that therefore the different levels of corruption in different countries depend on the extent to which government and society are homogeneous.

PRE-COLONIAL SOCIETY

The question of how far corruption can be said to have existed in pre-colonial times in West Africa, and how far present corruption is the result of the persistence of attitudes from that time, is an extremely difficult one. To discuss it adequately would require far greater knowledge of those societies than I can pretend to, and a great deal of space if due regard was to be had to the variety of social and political structures which existed. I shall, therefore, make only three points about pre-colonial society: points which are possibly obvious, but which are too important to be taken for granted.

1. Pre-colonial West African societies were familiar with conflicts between personal aims and official or social aims, hence their laws and customs and the punishments and other sanctions by which they were enforced, *but* although men wielded political power, judged causes, led armies, and collected taxes, their functions were less precisely defined in relation to those activities than they are in the bureaucratic governments of colonial and post-colonial times. The judicial functions of a chief were not sharply distinguished from his familial function as arbitrator and peacemaker, or his political function as a leader concerned with the manipulation of power, so that impropriety in the exercise of his judicial function, such as favouritism, could less easily be attributed to him as corruption than in the case of a modern magistrate whose sole function is to judge. To say this is to come near to saying that, as there was no public service in pre-colonial West Africa, there could be no corruption of it, but this is not quite accurate. In fact, examples could be given of behaviour clearly recognisable as corrupt (and recognised as such in the pre-colonial society) from the histories and legends of the peoples concerned. Such examples might be expected to be most common among the larger and more articulated political systems such as those of Northern Nigeria,[4] which had evolved many bureaucratic features long before the advent of the colonial bureaucracy.

2. A man may, of course, be bribed with a horse, a woman, or a gun as effectively as with a roll of notes, but the possibilities and utility of bribery obviously increases with the growth of a money economy. In pre-colonial West Africa, money played a relatively minor part, though its importance varied from place to place. To take an extreme instance: in an area where the people lived at subsistence level and, as would be likely, had a political structure almost without full-time professionals, there would be neither the need for, nor the means of, bribery. Even more important

[4] I can claim no direct acquaintance with Hausa Histories of folk-tales but Hausa friends assure me that bribery is a not uncommon theme or incident in them. It seems to figure much less in Akan legends and tales.

perhaps, is the availability of the sort of goods and opportunities on which to spend money, that makes money of greater value than any other single commodity. This is relevant to the claim that the Communist Government of China has greatly reduced corruption in that country, once notorious for it. Obviously, corruption must lose much of its attraction if there is little on which to spend the proceeds, and the acquisition of wealth is in itself (quite apart from the question of punishment for law-breaking) looked on with disfavour. Only in a money economy and a society which allows a good deal of freedom to individuals in disposing of their property, loosely speaking a capitalist economy, will the types of corruption we are dealing with be widespread.

3. In considering the relationship between corruption and traditional society in West Africa, observers often isolate the customary exchanges of gifts as the element in traditional life which has led to the growth of corruption in modern times. While not denying the relevance of customary gift exchange to bribery, the facility with which a bribe may be disguised as a customary gift, and, indeed, the genuine ambiguity of customary gifts in some traditional contexts, it is, in my opinion, wrong to isolate one feature of traditional life in this way. There were and are many features of the traditional way of life which, in the context of colonial and post-colonial society, contribute to the prevalence of corruption. My argument is that it is this clash of old customs, attitudes, etc., with the new forms of government that gives rise to corruption. The customary gifts are just one example. Other examples are easily found; the extended family system which leads to the overburdening of an official with family responsibilities so that his pay is insufficient, his family and tribal loyalties which obscure his devotion to the national community, the absence of an established class system which makes it hard for the official to cultivate the aloofness which perhaps must, for most people, be the accompaniment of official integrity.

CORRUPTION IN COLONIAL AND POST-COLONIAL TIMES

In modern times my thesis concerns the disharmony between the government and the traditional society on which it is imposed and which it seeks to change. Specifically, of course, this modern government was in West Africa the colonial bureaucratic government. It was alien to West Africa in obvious ways: it was controlled from a distant land, and the controllers were subject to pressures and had aims often quite unrelated to the situation in West Africa; its key men were foreigners, often with little understanding of West African society, usually with no understanding of the indigenous languages, while its junior officials recruited from the indigenous peoples struggled to find a balance between their alien masters and the demands of their own people. The disharmonies were innumerable, and I shall consider only two of the most important; the first typical of an economically underdeveloped country, second of a type found universally but which can be seen particularly clearly in West Africa. Before dealing with these, however, there is one important general topic.

THE CLIMATE OF CORRUPTION

Some years ago, I was escorting an African judge from the court in which he had just sentenced a murderer to death, to his car. The large crowd which had assembled to hear the case lined the path, cheering and dancing to express their pleasure at the verdict. One phrase was shouted over and over again, and was eventually taken up by the whole crowd and chanted in chorus. The judge asked me if I understood what it meant, and I said that I could catch the first words, "You're a good judge . . ." but could not understand the rest. "What they are shouting," said the judge, "is 'You're a good judge, we thought you had been bribed, but you haven't.' " With that he got into his car and was driven away.

No one there was surprised. A wryness of tone was the judge's only comment on the compliment that he was being offered. No one in the crowd saw any reason to disguise the implication that there would have been nothing surprising if the judge had been bribed. We were all living in a country where corruption was a very normal part of the scene and the assumption of corruption was part of everyone's equipment for his daily business.

Such a climate of corruption is in itself an important factor. There is a continuous interaction between the willingness of people to pay bribes and the willingness of officials to receive them. People normally behave in the way that the people they live with behave. In a society with a high level of corruption, hardly any citizen can carry out his business, avoid trouble with the government, and generally get through life comfortably, without acquiescing to some extent at least in the prevailing corruption. There are not a few such societies in the world, and persons from more fortunate countries must, when visiting them or doing business with them, conform (or at least acquiesce), unless they perfer empty gestures which will inconvenience themselves to no useful purpose. At the other extreme, in an ideally uncorrupt society, the single corrupt man would offer to give or receive bribes in vain.

DIVERGENCIES BETWEEN GOVERNMENT AND SOCIETY

The two examples of divergence between governments and West African society in Colonial and post-colonial times which I shall discuss are:—

a. that between a literate government and an illiterate society, and

b. that arising from laws in conflict with popular attitudes.

Literate Government in an Illiterate Society

Colonial rule in West Africa was and is the rule of an illiterate society by a literate government. The government operates in accordance with and by means of written rules and regulations. No one who cannot read and write can hope to occupy effectively any position in the public service. Entry into even the lowest grades is only for those who can read and write. Not only is reading and writing essential, but reading and writing *in English*, a foreign tongue. The majority of the population is illiterate and has little or no understanding of English. (Literacy and understanding English, are in these countries, almost synonymous). Friction between the literate public servant and the illiterate population is inevitable, and is, of course, greatest at the base of the public service pyramid, where functionaries and contacts with the public are most numerous, and it is at this level that the greatest *volume* of corruption occurs (the amount of damage done and money involved may well be greater at higher levels). Between the public and the functionaries with whom they most often deal, there is a constant flow of presents and bribes, given willingly or unwillingly, pressed on the official or extorted from the public.

Many examples of this process could be given (and it should be borne in mind that the public service in economically underdeveloped and colonial territories is of infinitely greater importance as the main channel of social initiative and the main route of personal advancement than it is in countries like Britain), but as an example of literate government operating in an illiterate society and how it differs from the same situation in an almost wholly literate society like our own, consider the confrontation of a police constable and a farmer. The farmer is barefoot, and the policeman is wearing a pair of large, shiny boots, and this difference may stand as a symbol of their relative ability to protect themselves in modern West Africa. The police constable is literate, he has learnt (at some pain perhaps) not only to adapt himself to a specific set of rules and regulations, but to wield them against others; he is an authority on the law, at least at his own level; he can arrest the farmer, or report him, and he has, again at his own level, innumerable official and semi-official contacts with officers of other branches of government service. The farmer is relatively a child. He is uncertain of the exact contents of the various laws that affect him, and uncertain how he stands in relation to them. He knows he should have a licence for his shotgun but cannot be sure that the one he has is still valid, or if the clerk who issued it cheated him with a worthless piece of paper. He knows he should have paid his taxes, but he has lost his receipt, and anyway there is something called a tax year, different from a calendar year, which "they" keep on changing, so perhaps he should have paid some more anyway. Even if he feels sure that he has committed no crime, he cannot defend himself against the policeman. To complain to the constable's superior would not be much good in the face of the *espirt de corps* of the police. He can defend himself only by going to some other member of the literate class, a letter writer perhaps, or if the case is really serious, a lawyer, but has none of the skills necessary to choose a competent practitioner, and he may be so misunderstood that his real case is never put. Even if he has a good case and wins, it may not do him much good. All the policeman's colleagues will know about it and sooner or later, of course, he *will* break a law. Much better give the policeman what he is asking for, or if he is not asking for anything, better give him something anyway so that when something does go wrong, he will be more likely to be nice about it. *A man does not,* says the Ashanti proverb, *rub bottoms with a porcupine.*

Consider for a moment a similar scene in, say, the prosperous county of Sussex. In Sussex the farmer would be as well if not better educated than the policeman, and will know those parts of the law which affect him better than does the policeman. The farmer may be himself a magistrate or a local government councillor, or know magistrates and councillors and perhaps the Chief Constable socially. For *this* policeman to demand money from *this* farmer for doing him a favour or not doing him a disfavour would be a laughable miscalculation.

This contrast may be overdrawn, but serves to make the point. The illiterate man entangled in the toils of a literate government is under a disadvantage for which practically nothing can compensate him, but wealth can help.[5] Sometimes the West African farmer, in addition to his other disabilities, would be poorer than the policeman, though the pay of a police constable in West Africa is not high; but if he were a cocoa farmer, a rubber farmer, a coffee farmer, or not a farmer at all, but one of the large number of persons who, although illiterate, make more money than a police constable, then the temptation for the farmer to compensate himself for his lack of power and knowledge by use of his money becomes clear. Equally clear are the opportunities for an ill-paid policeman to turn his power over wealthy illiterates into a supplement to his pay. This exchange of wealth for power, and

5 It is worth mentioning here that in many countries with a largely illiterate population the defence of the unlettered man against government officials is often an important function of political parties. Here the illiterate is buying protection in exchange for his vote or his general support for the party.

power for wealth, is, of course, the typical pattern of corruption.

The phenomenon of a literate government in an illiterate society arose in West Africa with the imposition of colonial rule, but it does not, of course, pass with the coming of independence. The independent governments in Nigeria and Ghana are quite as much committed to literate government as was the colonial regime, indeed, since independence, departments, officials, laws and regulations have multiplied at a great rate. The removal of this particular disharmony cannot be achieved by the abolition of literate government, but only by the abolition of illiteracy in the society.

The Operation of the Law

My second example of persons and groups put under a disadvantage by official policy and thereby becoming a source of corruption is the operation of cetain laws. All laws put certain persons under a disadvantage, i.e., those who do or wish to do what the laws forbid. Such persons are a source of corruption in every country.

But laws differ:

i. In the extent to which public opinion supports them;

ii. in the ease with which their breach can be detected;

iii. in the profits to be made by breaking them.

(ii) and (iii), of course, stem to some extent from (i).

If a man tries to land an aeroplane in a suburban garden he will find:

i. that all the neighbours are anxious to assist the police;

ii. that his transgression has become instantly notorious;

iii. that the financial rewards are not impressive.

If he tries to sell alcoholic drinks after hours he will find:

i. that many members of the public will be very pleased;

ii. that it can often be done without the police getting to hear of it;

iii. that it is a source of financial profit.

Obviously, it is breaches of the law of the second sort which are most likely to be a source of corruption. Laws regulating gambling and drinking, for instance, usually have little general support from the population, will be broken by otherwise law-abiding citizens, are difficult to enforce, and frequently broken. They tend to bring all laws into disrepute, and, by the creation of a large class of persons vulnerable to legal action at the hands of the petty officers of the law, they encourage corruption. An extreme example of this type of law was, of course, prohibition in the United States. Post-war rationing in the United Kingdom had similar consequences, fortunately on a smaller scale, but will remind us that such laws are occasionally necessary whatever the price that must be paid for them.

Let us return for a moment to our Sussex policeman. Is there any group of people with whom his relations are similar to the relations of his West African confrere with the West African farmer? The answer is Yes. There are, first of all, the professional criminals, those who habitually break the law. Such people he can harass, and they find it very hard to strike back at him, however unjustly he may beset them. Criminals are a notorious source of corruption in any police force. Next, and perhaps more important, as they usually have more money than the criminal classes proper, are people who engage in trade and activities where the line between legality and illegality is so fine, and the regulations so complex, that they are always in danger of unwittingly committing an offence, nearly always being tempted to commit one, and can therefore plausibly be accused of an offence at almost any time. Notable examples are public-house keepers, bookmakers and motorists.[6] Any government must, and does, put some activities out of bounds; each time it does so, however, it puts some of the population at a disadvantage and anxious to defend themselves by corrupting those whose duty it is to enforce the laws.

For obvious historical reasons, these West African territories have an unusually large number of laws which, by the criteria I have suggested, are likely to give rise to corruption. A colonial regime, especially one like the British, responsible to a representative government in the metropolitan country, is bound, and indeed most people in the metropolitan country regard it as duty bound, to frame its laws with more regard to British than West African standards of desirable behaviour. Particularly during the early years of colonial rule, the colonial governments were more responsive to British than to West African pressure groups. For instance, the abolition of slavery was brought about by a popular agitation in Britain, but brought the British Government's representatives in West Africa into conflict with powerful and traditionally respectable elements of African society. Another example is the rules which arose from the British Government's adherence to the Geneva Convention restricting the sale of spirits to the inhabitants of protectorates. These may have been excellent, but did not spring from West African conditions or West African demands, and were consequently a source of conflict and alienation between rulers and ruled. The enforcement of these laws was, of course, sporadic and uncertain, so lightly were the territories administered and policed. Many of the difficulties that might have arisen from the imposition of alien laws were avoided by the sheer impossibility of enforcing them, and the wide discretion given to District Officers to adjust the intentions of the Statute Book to the realities of the local situation. But not all conflict could be avoided. The Second World War, for instance, produced a great many laws intended to regulate economic activity. Without adequate means to enforce such regulation, and without any understanding by the population of why such regulation was desirable, laws of this sort served mainly to corrupt the officers charged with their enforcement. An excellent example is the Exchange Control laws. Introduced during the war, when the Imperial Government understandably required all sterling territories to have approximately similar laws concerning the import and export of currency, etc., they were practically unenforceable against the indigenous merchants who crossed and recrossed the unpatrolled and often undefined land frontiers of West Africa. At the same time, "smuggling" of currency was, and still is, profitable and completely devoid of any "criminal" stigma; after all, the evasion of currency regulations was widely practised in the United Kingdom, where the population had much more reason to appreciate the need for them. Still, the law was there, and was, through honest zeal, malice, or with intent to extort, spasmodically enforced, so that many who regarded themselves as honest merchants were vulnerable to attacks from officers of the law, and under the necessity of buying them off. Trade across the frontier in West Africa is often extremely profitable, and these laws became a serious focus of corruption for enforcement officers. At some customs stations a *pro rata* tariff was extracted by the officials from those travellers who wished to import foreign currency, but were too lazy to walk through the bush with it.

6 In West Africa lorry drivers are always complaining about extortion by the police. It is often alleged that the police on road patrol simply collect a toll from all passing lorry drivers. If the driver refuses to pay it is, of course, never difficult for the police to accuse them of some driving offence or to find some detail of their lorry that does not conform to the, inevitably, complex regulations.

Once again, this type of confiict between the government and society first arose with colonialism, but it does not disappear with the coming of independence. President Nkrumah's government, for instance, is more strongly committed to the transformation of Ghanaian society than the colonial regime ever was, and this transformation is bound to involve acute strains between the laws and the behaviour of the ordinary Ghanaians. This is particularly true, of course, of laws controlling economic behaviour in one way or another, inevitable when a government is committed to developing the country as rapidly as possible. High taxation, for instance, will enrol many normally honest people into the semi-criminal ranks of the tax evaders. Any form of direct control of rare resources has the same effect.[7] No society can be transformed without laws that go against the interests and accepted behaviour of some people in it; these laws will set up the sort of conflicts which give rise to corruption. A wise government might be expected, while recognising this regrettable fact, to limit such laws to what it regards as absolute essentials. Such attractive possibilities as the prohibition of nudity, polygamy, or football pools might be thought to be unnecessary additions to the strains and frictions which will be imposed by a nationalist government's essential programme.

THE SUBJECTIVE ELEMENT

As I said earlier, there is a constant interaction between the willingness of officials to receive bribes and the willingness of the public to give them. It is part of the general conflict between the aims and methods of the government and the society which is being governed that the subjective attitude of many officials in these countries should not be in harmony with their objective rôles. The official rôle is not one indigenous to West Africa, but an import from another society where it has grown up flanked and buttressed by many attitudes and social forces missing in its new environment. Many West African officials have successfully adopted and internalised the qualities required for their rôle, but it is not surprising that many have not been completely successful. The West African official, subject to pressures of which his British colleague knows nothing,[8] is caught and squeezed precisely at the point of conflict between the colonial (or post-colonial) government and the indigenous society. The British official in West Africa is an overseas projection of a well established and understood mode of metropolitan behaviour, protected by traditions of aloofness and difference, and the approval of those that matter most to him (other British officials) from the alien pressures of West African society. This subjective aspect of the question, the question of the individual morality, is of great importance, and I shall touch on it again when I discuss possible remedies for corruption.

HIGH LEVEL CORRUPTION

I have so far been dealing mainly with corruption at the lower levels of the government, the level at which hundreds of petty officials enforce the laws on the general public. Corruption at a high level, corrupt behaviour by Cabinet Ministers, Judges, Ambassadors, presents different though related problems. A Cabinet Minister who accepts bribes is trading his power for money just as surely as is the police constable, but we are

7 The allocation of Market Stalls by Local Government Councils in West Africa is a regular cause of scandals. The trouble is that these exceedingly valuable properties are usually let at rents greatly below what they are worth. The difference inevitably transforms itself into bribes. The simple device of charging as much rent as the traders would be prepared to pay does not, perhaps understandably, commend itself to the Councillors and officials.

8 See Chinua Achebe's novel *No Longer at Ease*, William Heinemann Ltd. 1960, for an excellent description of these problems.

here moving out of the realm where sociological generalisation is *necessarily* useful. A Cabinet Minister may be corrupt in any society, but this may have much more to do with his individual circumstances than any generalisation that can be made about the society. Yet most informed people would agree that these West African territories are more troubled by corruption among Cabinet Ministers of their like than is, say, Denmark. This fact can be related to certain features of these societies.

a. A climate of corruption in a society will affect Ministers as well as policemen, and, perhaps more important, will lead to public condonation of corruption by Cabinet Ministers. It is a most disconcerting feature of these societies that ordinary citizens will believe, and recount, the most fantastic stories, some of them palpably untrue, of corruption among their leaders, with no or very little sense of indignation. Even when official enquiries have disclosed instances of undoubted corruption, this has often had no effect on the political careers of the persons involved.

b. Politicians in West Africa do not come from an established patrician class. Most of them are "new men" and have therefore had no opportunity to develop standards different from the rest of society, such as can develop in a particular class or group, and are not personally wealthy (at the beginning of their careers at least). Elevation to Cabinet rank therefore presents them at once with new needs for money (see (c) below), and new opportunities for acquiring it by trading their power for the wealth of others.

c. As Ministers in a British-type parliamentary regime, they are playing rôles not well suited to their own education or to the society in which they are expected to play them. I will give two examples:—

i. The sharp distinction that has grown up in Britain between the purposes for which public funds can and cannot be used creates special difficulties in a West African context. In England in Henry VII's day the King's money was the King's money, and was used for forwarding the interest of his government in every way. Subsequently there grew up a constitutionally important but by no means wholly logical distinction between those functions of the government on which public money could be spent, and those functions (e.g., the organisation of public support) for which politicians organising themselves in parties were expected to find finance elsewhere. In England, money for political parties is available from the large funds accumulated by businesses or Trade Unions, but in West Africa such sources are not available. As in most other parts of the world, standard subscriptions from ordinary party members are not sufficient to finance this important aspect of government. Governmental corruption, "kickbacks" on profitable contracts, the sale of profitable or prestige-giving appointments, are an obvious source of party funds. A great deal of the corruption at ministerial level in West Africa is to be explained along these lines, and in these cases really amounts to a transfer of public funds from one type of political expenditure (i.e., legitimate by British criteria), to the other type, i.e., party political expenditure.

ii. In Britain, the distinction between the official and private capacities of the holders of high office is widely understood and accepted. As a private person, a Minister of the Crown is not expected to be particularly hospitable or lavish in his hospitality. In West Africa, if a man holds high office, he is often expected to entertain his relations, tribesmen, political supporters, for such generosity may be a condition of continued political eminence.

d. The desire for wealth, for whatever purpose, is reinforced in many cases by a sense of the impermanence of the new status. It is not easy for a man who has risen from poverty to eminence and riches in a few years, as many African leaders have done, to feel confident that the present affluence will continue. The widespread stories of secret bank accounts in Switzerland and other foreign countries are, if true, to be accounted for by the desire to hoard against possible lean years ahead.

THE FUNCTION OF CORRUPTION

What is the social function of corruption in West Africa? Although damaging to official ideals and aims, it is clearly not a subversive or revolutionary phenomenon. It is rather an emollient, softening conflict and reducing friction. At a high level it throws a bridge between those who hold political power and those who control wealth, enabling the two classes, markedly apart during the initial stages of African nationalist governments, to assimilate each other. At the lower level it is not an attack on the government or its instruments by the groups discriminated against, but an attempt by them to reach an accommodation by which they accept their inferior status but avoid some of its consequences. In spite of the damage it does to a government and its policies, it may be of assistance in reducing resentments which might otherwise cause political difficulties. This useful role can be demonstrated by the semi-official recognition given by the British colonial regime to a practice which in the United Kingdom would be classified as corrupt—the acceptance of gifts from local chiefs by District Officers. This well-established, well-known, but never, for obvious reasons, officially recognised practice, grew from the traditional custom of presenting gifts to chiefs when approaching them with requests for favours. It was tolerated by the colonial regime, albeit in a limited form, because of its value for that regime. The colonial District Officer was, to most of the chiefs of his district, an unpredictable alien, wielding wide, undefined, powers according to incomprehensible criteria, whose arrival in the local rest house was often a cause of alarm. The courtesies of the offer and acceptance of gifts of eggs and chickens brought this alarming official some way into the chief's familiar world, threw some bridge across the gulf which separated the two men, and created a relationship in which the inevitable frictions were softened by a personal familiarity and a traditional context. This was, of course, of great value to the District Officer in doing his job, and was therefore tolerated by the colonial authorities. A similar softening of what might otherwise be an intolerable relationship between the official and the people he deals with can result from more heinous dealings. Indeed, the greater the corruption the greater the harmony between corruptor and corruptee.

APPLICATION AND DEVELOPMENT OF THE ARGUMENT

I cannot attempt a detailed application of my tentative thesis to other societies, but on a superficial view it seems to have much to recommend it. Countries such as the Scandinavian States, with a marked homogeneity of society, are, it is generally agreed, fairly free from corruption. The shortcomings in this respect of the USA can be related to its large immigrant populations and its second class races. The rôle of immigrants in the corruption of big city politics is a commonplace of American political science.[9] The corruption in Spain, Portugal and some Middle Eastern countries might be explicable in terms of the wide divergence between the very wealthy classes, who have a considerable voice in government, and the general poor. Despotic and dictatorial government might be found to be more likely to produce and indeed to protect corruption

[9] The classic statement is, of course, in Lincoln Steffen's *The Shame of the Cities* and his autobiography.

than forms of government more responsible to the views of the ruled. A theoretically interesting limiting case is that of slavery. Slaves are a group under an extreme disability, with an obvious need to protect themselves. Under many forms of slavery, however, they have no money or other means to corrupt their overseers. The extreme degrees of disability therefore may not result in corruption, as they remove the means of protection. The optimum conditions for corruption, according to this theory, surround a group under a harsh disability but still possessed of considerable wealth—a Jewish money-lender in a 19th century Polish ghetto, for instance—a Negro bookmaker in an Arkansas town—a wealthy brothel-owner in London. These conclusions do not seem to be contradicted by what we know of the facts.

REMEDIES FOR CORRUPTION

Responsible leaders in West Africa often make statements denouncing the prevalence and the dangers of corruption and not infrequently launch campaigns to "root it out."[10] I am unaware of any such campaign which has had any lasting effect, or indeed has even led to many prosecutions. Various remedies from prayer to flogging have been suggested, but none has been seriously tried.

Draconian programmes for combating corruption are sometimes elaborated. These involve extremely heavy punishments together with a highly-trained, well-paid corps of *agents provocateurs*. The combination of the two is supposed to alarm all potential corruptors or corruptees so much that they are frightened ever to offer or accept a bribe for fear of being denounced. Unfortunately, such violent police pressure unsupported by public opinion would be quite likely to result in an *increase* of corruption and of blackmail. The *agents provocateurs* themselves would have to be members of the society in which they were operating and it is hard to imagine that such a job would attract persons whose integrity would be beyond doubt. Frequent change of personnel would be required so that large numbers of such *agents* would be needed, making it even more difficult to ensure a high standard. Their opportunities for blackmail would be immense, and it is easy to see that such a campaign could only lead to unpleasantness far outweighing any possible beneficial result.

Given the continued desire by the governments of the West African countries for rapid economic development and general modernisation, conflicts fruitful of corruption will continue and are indeed almost certain to increase so that no immediate improvement is at all likely. It will be a long time before the societies are remoulded and homogeneous with the government; even total literacy will take considerably more than a generation. Does this mean that there is nothing useful that can be done except to wait for the slow evolution of the society?

The answer is, I think, that a great many useful things can be done, but none which will have dramatically rapid results. To achieve anything at all, of course, the leadership of the country concerned must regard the problem as really important, and be prepared on occasion to sacrifice political advantage by, for instance, making an example of a corrupt Minister even though he has a politically useful following in the country. Given such leadership, and it cannot be taken for granted that it is always available, the following measures suggest themselves:—

a. Exemplary proceedings against Ministers or other important functionaries to publicise the government's determination;

b. A slight increase of police pressure against corruption at all levels;

[10] After this paper was written, President Nkrumah announced (see *Sunday Times* of April 19th, 1961, for a report by Mary Dorkenoo) new measures directed particularly against corruption among M.P.s and party officials. The tone of the announcement would seem to indicate that this new campaign will be conducted with some vigour.

c. A fairly low-pitched but steady and continuous educational effort in schools, colleges, and in the newspapers, and by other means of publicity. Not just a short and violent campaign, but one continuing over years and becoming a normal part of all educational processes.

d. Most important of all, a special effort with the public service. This is the most hopeful line of approach and might produce relatively quick results. If I am right about the effect that development and modernisation will have on these societies, there is no hope of removing the public servant's opportunities for corruption. It may, however, be possible to train him not to take advantage of his opportunities. Small groups of people can be trained to have different standards in some respects from those of the generality of people, and in any society this is a normal feature of specialisation; each specialised group has special standards in respect of its own work. By educational pressure and disciplinary measures it should be possible to raise the standard of the public service. Such a policy could only succeed, however, if service conditions and salaries were good and the status of the service high.

e. Careful scrutiny of existing and projected laws to eliminate those that tend to increase the opportunities for corruption unnecessarily.

It will be seen that I have not included in this programme any reference to religious or social emotions sweeping through the population. Such events are, however efficacious, not usually to be invoked by statesmen.

CONCLUSION

In conclusion, I should like to emphasise two points.

1. In the West African countries under consideration, the colonial regime is the obvious historical source of the conflict between the government and the society. It is not suggested that similar conflicts cannot arise without colonialism, or that colonialism is exceptionally potent as a cause of corruption. There are countries which have never been colonies in the sense in which the word is used of West Africa, where corruption is much greater than it is in these countries. Moreover, as I have indicated, the succession regimes there are committed to a far more thoroughgoing programme of change than their colonial predecessors, so that the conflicts productive of corruption may be intensified after independence. Moreover, corruption under the colonial regime was limited by the presence of colonial service officials whose standards were those of the British public service. It is not yet certain how far an indigeneous civil service can have the same effect.

2. Corruption is an evil, but the avoidance of corruption cannot be more than a subsidiary aim of government policy. If my thesis is correct, colonialism and the modernising westernising policy of succession governments give rise to corruption—but this, in itself, is not a condemnation of colonialism or a modernising policy. Governments must frequently act in ways which result in conflicts fruitful of corruption. The means of control, forced purchase and rationing necessary to deal with a local famine, for instance, are always productive of corruption, but no one would hesitate to pay this inevitable price when people are threatened with starvation. What one may, however, hope, is that a consciousness among policy makers that corruption is a phenomenon with causes that can be understood, will lead to a choice of methods designed to minimise corruption, and to an understanding of the need to strengthen factors working against it—the most important of which is the subjective integrity of the public service.

33. Nepotism and Bribery in West Africa

RONALD WRAITH / EDGAR SIMPKINS

To judge the venality of bribery and corruption in West Africa by the standards of contemporary Britain would be neither intelligent nor just. A fair judgment must take account of the *mores* of the two societies, a comparison of which will explain a good deal that appears to be culpable; and also of certain pressures within West African society, which will mitigate some of the rest. There remains much that is inexcusable.

The point is perhaps more clearly illustrated by nepotism than by bribery or corruption. Little was said about nepotism, except in passing, in the last chapter. There is really very little to say, except that public life is riddled with it, and that everybody knows this. A book written for publication cannot mention names and cases.

The concept of impartiality, and of appointment by merit, is embodied throughout Africa by the appointment of Public Service Commissions, and these have in fact done excellent work, and at the time of writing are not, in the writer's experience, the subject of malicious gossip. In their first years their Chairmen were expatriates who, being free from family and local pressures, and in every sense disinterested, would, it was hoped, assist these vitally important bodies to win respect. They have been replaced by Africans without any loss of such respect and they are, to use a cliché which puts the point well, bulwarks of the constitution. It is almost impossible to overstate their importance in the coming years. But although they have introduced and maintained objective and honest standards into the appointment of the bulk of the civil service, there is a limit to what they can do in a society which accepts nepotism not as something reprehensible but as a man's first and unquestioned duty.

Britain has had a hundred years to get accustomed to the idea that it is anti-social to advance the claims of relatives for public posts. A manufacturer or a shopkeeper may leave his business to his son, or get his nephew a job in the firm, and no one will think it improper, since he is free to do what he likes with his own. If he has shareholders to consider he will think carefully before recruiting his relations, but except in large firms which have developed bureaucracies of their own he is free to follow his own judgment, and in any case for the sake of his shareholders and his profits he is unlikely to appoint someone who is incompetent simply because he is related to him. In her public life Britain has enjoyed her golden age of patronage and nepotism, but since the Civil Service reforms of 1854 a distinction has become

SOURCE: Reprinted from pp. 33–45 of *Corruption in Developing Countries* by Ronald Wraith and Edgar Simpkins. By permission of W. W. Norton & Company, Inc. Copyright © 1963 by George Allen and Unwin Ltd. First American edition 1964.

established between what a man may do with his own money and what he may properly do with the taxpayers' money; and though there have been interesting survivals of patronage into the present century it has become accepted by and large that in recruitment to the public service, including the service of local authorities, entry is by competition, or by merit impartially judged, and that the pulling of strings by influential friends and relations will not merely not help but will disqualify.

This distinction between private and public employment is only a mildly sophisticated one, but it is beyond the level of sophistication of a good deal of thinking in West Africa. There is much to excuse nepotism. Any man rising to a place of importance in politics will be surrounded by relatives and friends looking confidently to him for patronage; the tradition of centuries leaves them in no doubt that he will provide for them, and that if jobs do not exist they will be created. He may grasp the constitutional idea himself, but it is difficult for him to explain it to his kinsmen. Consequently the life of Ministers and other people of importance is made burdensome by nagging and unceasing demands, as they find themselves enmeshed in the familiar net of family obligation. The writer has been told, in weary and oppressed tones, by Ministers both in Nigeria and Ghana, that a Minister's life seems to consist as to about half in getting people jobs, even down to the grade of messengers and office cleaners, a circumstance which might well surprise a Minister in Whitehall.

In a nutshell, nepotism in the public service in Britain would by now go against the grain of public opinion, and would cause a sense of guilt in both giver and receiver. In Africa uninformed public opinion would be surprised if anything different happened, the sense of guilt on the part of the giver would be mingled with a sense of family duty done, and the recipient would take it for granted. For why should a man become big and powerful except to look after his relations?

The absence of any distinction which is in the least subtle between public and private, or public and party, responsibilities is shown by the constantly recurring problem of the electoral activities of members of Government, who towards election times repeatedly travel at the public expense, as though on public duty, on journeys which are quite openly electoral campaigns. Some of them undoubtedly know what they are doing, but this is not true of all, for some find the distinction genuinely difficult to comprehend. In the strict sense they are acting corruptly, but only in the context of the *mores* of Great Britain; and an act is presumably only corrupt if society condemns it as such, and if the doer is afflicted with a sense of guilt when he does it; neither of these apply to a great deal of African nepotism.

Public conscience and a sense of private guilt are however taking root in some aspects of public administration which are exceptionally well understood and where feelings run high, and notably in the award of scholarships. The machinery for awarding scholarships impartially is plain for all to see, but no one in Africa would seriously deny, not only that it has been one of the more fruitful fields for bribery, but also that it happens mysteriously that the young relations of the eminent gain scholarships in a manner which, if open and aboveboard, would destroy the beliefs of the behaviourists and prove the hereditary transmission of talent.

Even the Public Service Commissions cannot altogether swim against the tide of pressure from the highest quarters.

The point we wish to establish is that over wide areas of African society nepotism may be regarded as a virtue rather than as a fault; that in more sophisticated circles, where it is accepted as wrong, the pressures of society in general and of families in particular make resistance to it an almost superhuman feat; and that therefore we may regard it with some sympathy and indulgence. Similarly, there is a good deal to be said, not in defence of corruption as such, but in mitigation of the deed. It derives partly from anachronistic custom and partly from the exceptionally harsh economic pressures of a rapidly changing and developing society. It is perhaps unnecessary to say that it derives also from simple avarice.

Mr. Bernard Storey, in his Report on the Lagos Town Council, has this to say:

> It is a custom of West African life (I am informed by those who have spent many years in the country and by Africans themselves) that a person in authority is entitled to expect (and not merely demand) and to receive some form of consideration (formerly a gift in kind but now usually cash) for something done, in the course of exercising his authority, to the benefit of the giver. . . . (p. 49, para. 280).

He then goes on to cite, as illustrations of persons in authority doing something in the exercise of that authority, the dreary chronicle of nurses, clerks, police and produce inspectors. This was written in 1952. Ten years later it can be said with confidence that the custom of exchanging gifts, regarded as a courtesy of life between the high and the low, or between host and guest, is fast diminishing.

Ten years ago it was a familiar embarrassment to overseas visitors, travelling with one suitcase and moving on by air the next day, to be presented with a splendid bowl of eggs, a brace of live chickens, or as happened to the writer in Togoland on one occasion, a magnificent ram. The embarrassment used to be twofold—what to do with these indigestible gifts without causing offence, and how to return them, also in kind, but to a value appropriate to the presumed relative importance of host and guest, from the contents of a night-stop bag. This dilemma is largely over and done with, at any rate on the beaten track. This may be partly because visitors now come not as single spies but as battalions of spies, so that even African customary hospitality has had to bow beneath the weight of expense; but it is more probably because general sophistication has spread, and people have realized that this sort of thing is not customary, and indeed would be highly inconvenient, in the wider world.

That this is not just the narrow view of an expatriate visitor, but does genuinely represent a trend of opinion, is shown in a Report—of which more use will be made presently—the Report on the Exchange of Customary Presents in the Northern Region of Nigeria, written as long ago as 1954, which says at one point:

> There is no doubt that the scale of compulsory gifts . . . has decreased considerably in recent years with the growing enlightenment of the *talakawa*

and again

> The payments also appear to be decreasing in extent and it may, therefore, be assumed that the public are becoming more sophisticated in their attitude to gifts of this kind.

If a social trend has penetrated the consciousness of the *talakawa* of the Northern Region it is unlikely that the wide boys of Lagos will have been unaware of it, and a defence of their depredations based on custom and tradition cannot have much weight in 1962.

Furthermore it is difficult to accept the implication that a cash payment, in lieu of the customary gift, has the venerable sanction of native custom. The exchange of gifts, in its pristine innocence and in its traditional setting, took place between men who had hardly entered the competitive, literate, busy western world. At its best, it is difficult to imagine the £5 note being substituted for the ram, or five shillings for the bowl of eggs. It is at best a debasement of native custom.

The matter is admittedly debatable, and involves odd subtleties. If we may revert to the traveller from overseas, it is not so many years since there was no scale of overnight claims for official hospitality, and those who wandered round from one District Commissioner to another did so at their host's expense. Common courtesy demanded that one acknowledged this, and it was acceptable to native law and custom as between expatriates that a bottle of whisky should be presented on departure. To carry six bottles of whisky in one's baggage, apart from the fact that could be misinterpreted, is less convenient than to carry six pound notes (alas, the equivalent value at the time); yet to present one's hostess with a pound note on leaving her house would not have been easy. The difference between the pound note and the bottle of whisky, which probably had the price indelibly stamped upon it in any case, was subtle to a fantastic degree, yet it was important. There are many occasions in British social usage when the gift of flowers or fruit, or the present bought in a shop, would be acceptable, while the offer of their cash value would be offensive in the extreme. Similarly it is an odd circumstance that one may stay in a man's house and consume his food and drink to the value of several pounds with a clear social conscience, but should you require a threepenny stamp for him custom demands that you give him exactly threepence in exchange, stamps being too closely associated with cash to make the gift acceptable.

Only a professional anthropologist, and a fairly specialized one at that, could say what corresponding subtleties exist in African society. But it is straining credulity to compare the offering of eggs, chickens or a goat to a village personage whose office is hallowed by tradition with greasing the palm of the nurse, clerk, produce inspector or policeman. For one thing, the latter are not persons of inherent dignity but minor functionaries in a bureaucracy, and neither bureaucracies or their functionaries form part of indigenous tradition.

However, the existence of a bureaucracy, and the consequent growth of a large number of people who are in a position to bestow favours, has introduced one new subtlety, easy to comprehend if not to define, namely the difference between a customary gift and a bribe. To this problem the Government of the Northern Region addressed itself in 1954.

The Report on the Exchange of Customary Presents, published by the Nigerian Government Printer in that year, is an instructive and possibly unique document. It began with a resolution in the Northern House of Chiefs on February 26, 1952, moved by the Emir of Gwandu, in these terms:

> That this House, agreeing that bribery and corruption are widely prevalent in all walks of life, recommends that Native Authorities should make every effort to trace and punish offenders with strict impartiality and to educate public opinion against bribery and corruption.

The resolution, which was carried unanimously, resulted however in a somewhat different kind of inquiry—the study of the customary exchange of presents between "Chiefs and District and Villiage Heads and their people." The whole of the subsequent inquiry was of course conducted on the borderline of bribery and corruption; the reports from Residents which formed the basis of its conclusions dealt widely and deeply with these topics, and it is understood that some startling facts emerged, which are unfortunately classified as confidential and are not available to the student; but the actual Report was not about bribery and corruption as such, since these are already dealt with under the criminal law, but about the related topic of custom, its use and abuse, and its adaptation to the twentieth century. This makes it a more, not less, valuable source of information from the point of view of this chapter.

Two paragraphs identify the problem so succinctly that we quote them *verbatim*:

12. . . . the view was expressed in one quarter that it would not be possible to forbid the customary exchanges of gifts in any form on the ground that these exchanges were an integral part of social behaviour, that the gifts from the richer to the poorer were alms the giving of which was a religious duty and that many poor and aged people who at present lived in reasonable comfort would find themselves destitute if the giving of presents, which often in their case were return presents, was forbidden. This view, it should be emphasized, was an isolated one but it was one to which the Committee felt that it must give the most careful attention, if only because of the religious and charitable issues alleged to be involved.

13. After prolonged and detailed consideration of the material at its disposal the Committee felt bound to say that, even though it recognized that customary gifts were far from a simple problem and involved the whole social system, it could not fully subscribe to the opinion put forward above. The evidence showed that only a very few customary gifts had origin in religious observance or charitable motives. The remainder were purely secular and ceremonial and in far too many cases nowadays (whatever may have been the case in the past) merely served the ends of *Neman Girma,* prestige, ostentation or avarice.

What was required, therefore, was to distinguish between one kind of gift and another, and this could not easily be done since one category faded into the next, and there were no sharp edges. Nevertheless, the distinctions which the Committee made assist clear thinking.

The existence of "legitimate gifts" is naturally acknowledged; they include the presents brought by guests to the party on the occasion of recognized ceremonials, and of course alms given out of compassion to the old, infirm or helpless (though a severe reference to parasites and hangers-on suggests that this is no simple matter). But "legitimate gifts" fade into "disguised bribes," and the problem becomes involved because the folk about whom this Report was mostly written were not the city slickers but the humble peasants, who are drawn into an evil system with no consciousness of wrong-doing. The offering of the guest, or even the tribute to the traditional superior, becomes an exaction by an official who has no shred of traditional entitlement to it; in other words a racket.

But most people, including the victims, are not aware that it is a racket, and public opinion does not react against it. There were—

simple folk who genuinely believed that it was customary and legitimate for a labourer to make regular monthly contributions to those above him, or for a litigant to give a native court judge a thankoffering after a case was successfully over or for a candidate for clan headship to distribute money to every member of the clan. To the educated, however, these were obviously cases of bribery and extortion.

It is at about this point, however, that the Committee was able to say that, looking over the years, the scale and extent of these gifts was decreasing, and as the Report was written in 1954 there is hope that the diminution has continued.

There was a further distinction of gifts which were in origin traditional and therefore "legitimate," but which had grown to such ostentatious size as to constitute an abuse of tradition, and indeed to have become a burden on the community as a whole, including even the more enlightened recipients; but it seems that this problem, at any rate in its extreme form, may be local to the North of Nigeria—the Salla Festival being one of the great occasions for it—and it need not therefore be developed in this study.

The rest of the Report is concerned with proposals for reform, and specifically with propaganda and the education of public opinion. They are interesting, but as to whether they have been effective there is, according to recent inquiries by the writer, little evidence.

A factor which contributes to bribery and corruption among town dweller and peasant alike, and which increases its severity, is the ingrained and universal love of ostentation. On the whole the traditional education of the African—in extended family and age grade—was aimed at conformity; the individual only had meaning in as far as he fitted into a system of relationships, and independence of thought and action would have been discouraged, even if it had been comprehensible. But from time to time there would emerge the big man who surpassed his fellows in physical achievement and bravery in battle; to him excessive adulation would be paid, and songs of praise, embarrassingly sycophantic to modern ears, would be sung; retinues of admirers, or hangers-on, would surround him, and precede him on his journeys. The tradition of the "big man" persists, but wealth and possessions have replaced valour in war as the criterion of bigness, and these generally come by way of politics. The praise-singers, the cheer-leaders and the sycophants remain, however, and this explains the fuss, so strange to western observers, which still surrounds politicians, and which could hardly be explained in terms of their political achievements. To act humbly even if you are a great man requires sophistication. It may of course be that this kind of sophistication is irrelevant to West African society, that one should not seek to strive for it, and that the sociologist would be surprised that one should even consider doing so. On the other hand it may be something which inevitably follows education, the change of spiritual values which this engenders, and absorption into other cultures. Most political parties in West Africa, and their importance and representativeness can hardly be denied, are anxious to claim that they are "socialist," and though their interpretation of this word may legitimately differ from that of Keir Hardy or Professor Tawney, as indeed it does, it can hardly include extravagant living on the material plane, if it is to maintain any shred of its dictionary meaning.

That sophistication of this kind may eventually take root in Africa is also supported by the fact that it already exists. But those who have achieved it find themselves trapped in the curious dilemma that if they put their principles into practice they will lose face, and consequently lose money and career. The successful lawyer cannot afford to run a modest car or live in a modest house or he will cease to be successful. There is of course nothing new in this, as is seen from a glance at the habits of film stars or tycoons, or at the buildings of banks or insurance companies, in Europe or America, but the characteristic thing about ostentation in West Africa is its pervasiveness and degree.

The facts that the retinue of politician or District Head must resemble those of an oriental potentate; that the graduate on his first job must possess a motor car that his counterpart in Britain might aspire to on retirement; that the labourer must possess a wrist watch and a fountain pen—with every intermediate gradation among the classes—these represent financial burdens which were appropriate, *mutatis mutandis*, to a society which did not have to live on cash salaries, but which in modern West Africa lead many to corruption and some to the magistrate's court. Again, for an inside view of this, the reader is referred to Chinua Achebe's junior civil servant, whose final downfall was caused by the insurance on his unnecessary motor car and the replacement of its tyres. It may be answered that his motor car was not unnecessary, since the Government gave him an advance for it. The Government is wrong. There are far simpler ways of solving this problem, even in a country as lacking in public transport as Nigeria. But it is relevant to note that the Government assisted its servant on the downward path by perpetuating a colonial standard of life which had been fixed, for themselves, by an expatriate administration.[1]

Not that the average man appears to need assistance on this path. He plunges all too eagerly along it of his own accord, as is shown by the unfinished houses, built beyond the owners' means, and the fantastic imbroglio of debt in which so many live. A country which on any comparative world list is among the poorest has taken to itself a standard of living appropriate to the top bracket.

All this helps to explain and mitigate, if not to excuse, bribery and corruption.

Another mitigating factor is the carry-over into a wage-earning economy of a vast network of family obligation appropriate to a simpler age. This too is diminishing, but it tends to diminish at the top instead of at the bottom where men can least afford it.

The wide family obligations of Africans and the comparatively narrow ones of Europeans are sometimes contrasted as though human nature and family affection differed fundamentally between the two races. It seems more probable that one kind of obligation becomes gradually transformed into the other as a result of moving from a self-supporting and communal existence on the land to a wage-earning and individualistic way of life in towns.

Unfortunately in West Africa this has not happened gradually but suddenly. It has meant that a man living on an inelastic wage, in an inelastic house—in conditions that is to say in which his only reasonable family obligation would be to his children and his parents—is still having to assume the obligations appropriate to the village and the farm in the setting of the tribe; where food from the earth can be stretched a little further than a wage, and where the family is not hemmed in by walls and streets. There comes a point beyond which this quite literally cannot be done any longer.

In Britain a man has an absolute obligation to support his children and his parents; society would censure him if he failed in either duty—indeed the law would step in and compel him to fulfill his natural obligations. But his obligations would not necessarily go further than this. They may very well do so, as the strength of family ties varies from one family to another, but neither public opinion, nor the opinion of his friends, nor the law of the land would compel him to support his cousins or his nephews, or indeed his own brothers, in the same way that they would compel him to support his children or his parents.

By contrast in Africa most men—for only a very few are emancipated from this—have an unquestioned obligation to share money, food and house with a very wide circle; a young man,

[1] Cp. The Prime Minister of Nigeria—" 'I wish I had the courage to downgrade all salaries to the levels which we can afford to pay.' But with a deprecating smile he said that neither he nor his colleagues had or were likely to have such courage." (*West Africa*—September 15, 1962.)

almost a boy himself, must pay for the education of younger brothers, and if he has himself moved into the stratum of modern professional employment, he must carry the double burden; if a man prospers and makes money he will often find that he grows no richer because the more he earns the more people he must share it with.

Several generations must pass before these obligations begin to accord with the everyday facts, including the facts of housing; for those who continue to flock to the towns, where they seek, and find, shelter with a kinsman, cannot imagine what the pattern of life there is like until they experience it. They do not know that there is, literally, no land on which food may be grown, and that every item of food must therefore be paid for; that there is no employment; and that the familiar props of existence will be knocked away. He cannot, or will not, return, and his kinsman, who cannot by custom fail him, must take on new and finally crushing responsibilities.

On a short view, we must be thankful that the net of family or tribal obligation is so strong, since it is all that there is to hold up the thousands of unemployed young men in the towns of West Africa. If this net were to break under the strain the results could be very serious; and it cannot go on taking added weight indefinitely. On a longer view we must hope that Africans will not for ever have to live in two worlds, either of which imposes burdens sufficiently hard to bear. For family obligations of a proportion now unimaginable to an Englishman add to the other pressures which keep pushing the swimmer under water. From his earnings, and his equally meagre perquisites, the average townsman simply cannot do what his own custom imposes on him. It is impossible to keep out of debt, and corruption thrives on indebtedness.

Lastly, there is simple poverty. Ostentation and the support of numerous relatives could by themselves make anybody poor, but quite apart from this there are in West Africa, two worlds perhaps even more distinct than the two worlds of Disraeli's England. There is of course no evidence from any age or country that the rich are less corrupt than the poor, and it would therefore be misleading to imply that if people were not so poor they would be less corrupt. The evidence points in fact the other way, for the appetite grows by what it feeds on, and when one thinks of corruption in West Africa the mind does not naturally turn to the masses of poor people, whose resources are indeed so slender that there is little about which they could be corrupt, but to the glossy and well-fed.

But the mere fact of living in two worlds, or even worse of living with one foot uneasily in each but with the obligations of both, is in itself unsettling, and inimical to the growth of private conscience and public morality alike; while the poverty of the lower world is poverty indeed for the urban wage earner. It is an ironical though familiar fact that whereas the African of the village and the bush is contented, his wants being few and his joys simple, his sons are so intolerably bored and discontented that nothing will satisfy them but to exchange this frustration, which is at least well-fed frustration, for the frustration of the towns where it is not always easy to eat.

Nigeria is at the difficult stage through which all countries seem to pass, of suffering extremes of poverty and wealth, and of living in fact on two completely different levels. Even today, Edwardian England seems incomprehensible, though so many people are still living who saw it through adult eyes; the glaring contrast between the luxury and ostentation of, for example, the country house weekend of the upper classes, and the degradation of the slums; the fact that a family lived for a week on the price of one good lunch in a West End restaurant—these and a hundred other contrasts now seem extraordinary.

They exist, reproduced with remarkable exactitude, in Nigeria today. Young men from the universities start work at £1000 a year, professional men earn many thousands, a meal and a bed at a hotel costs five or six pounds, an indifferent meal in a restaurant fifteen shillings. The wage of a labourer or servant is £5 or £6 a month; the salaries of clerks are reckoned in such figures at £84, £96 or £104 per annum. £10 does not go very far, is certainly not extravagant, for a dinner party for a few friends; the steward who serves it has that amount, if he is more than averagely well-paid, to support his wife and family for a month. The same thing, one assumes, may be found in Asia and the Middle East, and in other parts of Africa itself. The following words, written by the present author of East Africa, are not altogether untrue of the West:

The most significant fact about urban East Africa is that no Government or employer can even make the assumption, that is taken for granted in most parts of the world, that a man's wage should be sufficient to feed, house, clothe and generally support himself and his family. One of the documents of major importance to East Africa is the Kenya Report of the Committee on African Wages (1954), usually known as the Carpenter Report, in which we read that "approximately one half of the urban workers in private industry, and approximately one quarter of those in the public service, are in receipt of wages insufficient to provide for their basic, essential needs." The Government of Uganda, in reviewing its own wages policy in 1955, laid down as a general principle that it should work towards a state of affairs when a man's wage would support himself and his family, while admitting that to do so immediately would be impracitcable without a significant increase in the revenue, which could only come from higher taxation. This is the most important fact about the urban situation, and one which is not paralleled today in "western" societies. As a result of the work of the Carpenter Committee there has grown up a new comprehension of what a wages policy should be, and some of the lowest wages have improved, but only to the point when existence on wages is possible, not to the point when it is enjoyable or even tolerable.

A wage policy of 7s 6d a day for the lowest paid workers in the public service has been advanced by West African political parties as an immediate step forward, though a figure as large as this is not by any means the rule at the moment. It is barely possible to support a family on this wage.

In Victorian and Edwardian England this does not seem to have been necessarily destructive of morality. The honesty, thrift and self-respect of the very poor was often striking, and the integrity and principle of the early working-class movements, trade unions, friendly societies and the like, seem more and not less impressive than those of the labour movement in the affluent 1960s. But the Nigerian urban proletariat today lives in a world of more expansive ideas about equality than did the Victorians, of less rigid sanctions in matters of personal behaviour, and in a society which has been more violently disturbed. The field of temptation is correspondingly stronger, and a word to which the Victorians gave a quasi-religious flavour —thrift—is seldom heard.

We have tried to put forward, so to speak, the case for the defence; the reasons why African bribery and corruption should not be judged by the standards of contemporary Britain. It is not pretended that it is a powerful case since the people whom it defends most strongly are those against whom least complaint is made.

The customary exchange of gifts has affected the general climate of behaviour, but is a declining force, and cannot be quoted as a defence against the more iniquitous practices of today; the love of ostentation is something which a nation with aspirations towards equality and welfare must control and overcome; family obligation is a heavy drain on the salary and wage earner, and forces many thousands into debt, and the existence side by side of two nations with two unrelated standards of living, with traditional pressures weighing more heavily on the poor than on the rich, makes corruption a matter for no surprise and only modified reproach.

The case, such as it is, is a defence of private corruption, which usually starts with debt, which in turn is caused by intolerable private pressures. It is not this kind of corruption which is lowering to national self-respect, which causes frustration and anger on the part of honest men, or which breeds cynicism and revolt. This is brought about by public corruption on the part of elected representatives or holders of well-paid responsible public office. For this, the case that has been made is no defence at all. The simple cause of corruption in public life has nothing to do with traditional values, with the African personality, or with the adaptation to western values; those responsible for it have no difficulty in adapting to western values if they want to. Its simple cause is avarice; the wrong that is done is done in the full knowledge that it is wrong, for the concept of theft does not vary as between Christian and Muslim, African and European, or primitive man and Minister of the Crown.

34. New States and the Concept of Corruption

COLIN LEYS

It is clear that new states are very likely to be the scene of a great deal of behaviour that will be called corrupt. Neither attitudes nor material conditions in these countries are focused on the support of a single concept of the national interest or of the official purposes of state and local officers and institutions which would promote that interest. We can consider this under the headings outlined above:

1. The idea of the national interest is weak because the idea of a nation is new. And the institutions and offices of the states are, for most people, remote and perplexing. Even to the civil servants and politicians directly involved in them they are new; they are aware of the "official purposes" which are attached to them by importation, but they scarcely regard them as "hallowed" and hence they do not necessarily regard them as sacrosant.[1] On the contrary their western origin makes them suspect. To many people the "state" and its organs were identified with alien rule and were proper objects of plunder,[2] and they have not yet been reidentified fully as instruments for the promotion of common interests. Meanwhile to the illiterate peasant the "state" and its organs continue to be the source of a web of largely unknowable and complicated regulations, and hence of a permanent threat of punishment; against this threat it is very reasonable to take any available precaution, such as offering bribes. Some official purposes of public office are challenged by strongly supported counter-conceptions, especially the strong obligations of family, tribe, and district in the matter of awarding jobs, scholarships, or other scarce commodities in the gift of the state. Neither politicians nor civil servants are usually drawn from a class brought up for public service from an early age, or insulated from corrupting pressures by the established aloofness of a mandarin class. And to the extent that the rules of public morality lean ultimately on the strength of the rules of private morality, they are weakened by the hammer blows delivered to all moral rules by rapid social and economic change.

[1] Dr. Lucy Mair has put this excellently: "they cast for a play in which the *dramatis personae* are enumerated but the lines are not written. The new African governments are recruited from new men . . . The relationship of the leader with his followers, of ministers with their colleagues, with bureaucrats, with the general public, are new relationships." *The New Nations* (London, 1963), p. 123.

SOURCE: Colin Leys, "What Is the Problem about Corruption?" *Journal of Modern African Studies*, 3:2 (1965), pp. 224–230. By permission of the publisher, Cambridge University Press.

[2] Cf. Senator Kefauver's comment on the attitude of Americans to colonial administration before the American Revolution: "In a sense the whole populace engaged in the profitable process of mulcting the government—which was after all a hated tyrant—of every possible penny"; *The Annuals of the American Academy of Political and Social Science,* March 1952, p. 2.

2. The incentive to corrupt whatever official purposes public institutions are agreed to have is especially great in conditions of extreme inequality and considerable absolute poverty. The benefits of holding an office—any office—are relatively enormous; by comparison the penalties for attempting to obtain one by bribery are fairly modest, in relation to the low standard of living of the would-be office holder, or in relation to the pressure of relatives' claims on his existing standard of living. Generally, corruption seems likely to be inseparable from great inequality.

3. Corruption is relatively easy to conceal in the new states. Partly this is because people are generally not too clear about what the official rules are, or what (*really*) constitutes breaking them; or if they are clear, it may be because they do not greatly resent their being broken, and so are not zealous to prevent corruption. Partly it is because the law is ineffectively enforced and the police themselves may not be immune from corruption. And while traditional gift-giving can be distinguished from a bribe of money, it is quite obvious that from the point of view of the giver the one has shaded into the other, so that although the practice has taken on a new significance, as the open gift of a chicken is replaced by a more furtive gift of a pound note, it is nevertheless an established fact of life, in which the precise nature of the rule-infringement is partially concealed by continuity with an older custom.[3]

To say all this is only to explain, however, why there is likely to be much behaviour in new states that will be called corrupt. It is not to say anything about the "level" of morality of the citizens of these countries. It is only to say that, poised as they are between the inherited public morality of the western nation-state and the disappearing public morality of the tribe, they are subject to very considerable cross-pressures which make it unlikely that the western state morality, at least in its refined and detailed forms, will emerge as the new public morality of these countries; meantime, however, the criteria of the west have sufficient standing in some quarters to ensure that the accusation of corruption is freely levelled against all behaviour which does not conform to them. To go much beyond this is, in the apt words of Lucy Mair, to ignore

> the kind of social pressure that is in fact responsible for the practice of the virtues that are cherished in any given society. Good men do not practise . . . industry in circumstances where this would lead to a reduction in piece-rates.[4]

WHAT IS THE PROBLEM IN NEW STATES?

Of course there are ample grounds for *concern*, if not for moralising, about corruption in new states. The most important of them can probably be best isolated by making the comparison with Britain again, but from a different point of view.

Wraith and Simpkins tend to present a picture of Britain, for instance, as having been—around 1800—the scene of great corruption, which was then quite remarkably eliminated. However, the prevalence and the robustness, so to speak, of the practices which they, following the Victorian reformers, regard as corrupt, suggests a rather different interpretation; namely that according to the previously obtaining moral code many of these practices were not corrupt, but either had no moral significance, or indeed were actually quite right and desirable. For instance, the average landlord thought it quite natural, and to that

3 See the interesting and detailed discussion of this in A. W. Southall and P. C. W. Gutkind, *Townsmen in the Making* (Kampala, 1957), p. 189–194.

4 Lucy Mair, pp. 124–125.

extent desirable, that his tenants should use their votes on behalf of his favoured candidate and did not hesitate to put pressure on them to this end. Jobbery, sinecures, rotten boroughs, treating, and other colourful political practices of the period were practised with an openness that shows that they were not regarded as improper by those whose opinions mattered.[5] What is really remarkable is the rapidity and completeness of the reformers' victory during the nineteenth century.

What seems to have happened is that the ruling classes were induced to accept an altered perception of the nature of the public interest and so to redefine the purposes of the public offices and state institutions which remained, during most of this period, still under their control. It was precisely because they already had a clear notion of the public interest that the assertion of the new notion was established with such completeness. What was involved was not the establishment for the first time of a set of ideas about how public offices and institutions were to serve the public interest, but the adaptation of an established set. Britain did not, in other words, pass from a corrupt condition to a very pure one; rather it passed from one set of standards to another, *through* a period in which behaviour patterns which were acceptable by the old standards came to be regarded as corrupt according to the new. It is arguable that, at the height of this experience, public life in Britain was not much less "pure" than it is today. Certainly the records of so-called corruption in the early nineteenth century have about them an air of innocence which is largely lacking in the literature on the same subject in the USA.

Such innocence is also absent from the portrait of corruption in modern Nigeria drawn in the novels of, for instance, Chinua Achebe and Cyprian Ekwensi, and no doubt this partly explains the compulsive moralism of so many commentators on it. In Britain the corruption of public office was by a ruling class who *had* had a clear conception, even if in the end it was rather tenuous, of the public interest and the duty they owed to it by their use of the public offices and institutions under their control, a conception which complemented their frank exploitation of those offices and institutions for personal gain. In the era of reform they eventually accepted a redefinition of the principles governing the use of those offices and institutions and this, together with the other adaptations on their part, in large measure ensured their survival as a ruling class.

By contrast the ruling classes of Africa are new classes, exercising a new rule. Only a minority have been brought up in ruling-class circles. The idea contained in the phrase, *noblesse oblige,* scarcely applies. There is no previous experience, and so no prior ideology, of the roles of public offices and institutions in relation to the public interest, in terms of which the private exploitation of public office could be rationalised. There *is* a prevailing conception of the national interest and dedication to popular welfare. But it is precisely this idea that may be called into question by the way in which public office is actually exploited by those who occupy it. They have publicly accepted, at least by implication, the official purposes officially attached to public offices and institutions by the colonial powers. If their practice

5 "In the latter half of the eighteenth century *it was taken for granted* that the purpose for going into Parliament or holding any public office was to make or repair a man's personal fortune." R. M. Jackson, *The Machinery of Local Government* (London, 1958), p. 345. (Italics mine.) It seems clear that during this period there was a tendency for this attitude to become more widespread and the consequences more extensive and expensive, and that this in turn aided the development of the reform movement. However, the use of public office for private gain was a recognised public practice going back to a period in English history when these distinctions were still imperfectly worked out.

is indefensible by any standards which they are publicly prepared to defend, it robs the whole business of any air of innocence, and this is what provoked Dumont's reluctant protest against the creation in Africa of "a bourgeoisie of a new type, which Karl Marx could scarcely have foreseen, a bourgeoisie of the public service."[6]

The contrast between this contemporary phenomenon and the English scene in the early nineteenth century can be exaggerated. But it would not be hard to sharpen it further. Before the era of reform there were, as well as sinecures worth thousands of pounds, exacting civil service jobs which were not paid enough to induce anyone competent to occupy them, and which consequently were made attractive only by perquisites. Government-provided services, too, tended to be needed primarily by the relatively affluent sections of the population. And the idea was broadly accepted that well-born young men had some sort of entitlement to be maintained in one capacity or another in the public service. By contrast, in contemporary Africa public service is not merely paid well, in relation to local income levels, but lavishly;[7] government services affect the ordinary citizen in numerous ways, not as a luxury but as a conventional (or even an actual) necessity; and there is no accepted "natural" ruling élite. In any case, these eighteenth-century ideas do not seem to have been invoked in defence of "corruption" by those engaged in it today.

This is, perhaps, the main reason for the automatic condemnation of these widespread behaviour patterns by most contemporary commentators, and it seems rather reasonable. For to the extent that the official public morality of a society is more or less systematically subverted, especially if the leadership is involved in it, it becomes useless as a tool for getting things done, and this is expensive in any society where other resources are scarce. What is involved here is the idea of a "corrupted society."

It seems impossible to declare that a society without an effective public morality *cannot* develop economically. On the other hand, there do seem to be reasons for doubting whether in African conditions this is likely to happen. In the first place, most African states are extremely dependent upon government action for their development. Their development prospects largely depend on attaining the targets chartered in development plans, and by very fine margins. This requires single-minded hard work from all holders of public office. If the top political élite of a country consumes its time and energy in trying to get rich by corrupt means, it is not likely that the development plans will be fulfilled.

Secondly, if this is the pattern of behaviour of the élite and if this is fairly well known, it is likely to rob them of much of their authority both with subordinates in the government and with political followers in the countryside. The country will be apt to forfeit whatever benefits can be derived by the output of effort not solely motivated by the hope of personal gain.

Thirdly, the wealth improperly accumulated by the top élite may be modest by world standards, but still large in relation to the level of investment on which the economic development of the country depends. In this case much will turn on how such wealth is redeployed. If political leaders try to buy security by depositing their wealth in numbered accounts in Swiss banks it represents a wholly negative drain on the economy.[8]

6 R. Dumont, *L'Afrique noire est mal partie* (Paris, 1962), p. 66.

7 Cf. Dumont's notorious comparison: "A deputy works (?) for three months a year, but receives from 120,000 to 165,000 CFA per month. In six months of salary—i.e. in one and a half months' work—he makes as much as the average African peasant in 36 years, in a whole life of hard labour."

8 See, e.g., Frantz Fanon, *Les Damnés de la terre*, quoted by Dumont, pp. 67–68.

(But perhaps they will buy farms and make them very productive.) Fourthly, if the top élite flout the public moral code which is cherished by "donor" nations the supply of foreign aid may diminish.

The likelihood of the last two developments seems remote. The possibility which seems most solid and even obvious is the first; there are perfectly plain differences to be seen between one developing nation and another in terms of the amount of public spirit and devotion to duty shown by their élites, and the idea of a society economically stagnating in the grip of a self-seeking and corrupt élite is not a pure fantasy. The line of escape from such a situation is also fairly clear. Typically, a nucleus of "puritans"—drawn from groups such as an independent business class, professional groups, or small farmers—begins to exercise effective pressure to apply the official but disregarded public code of ethics.

By and large this was the experience of the reform movement in the USA. The moral vulnerability of the ruling groups was very great, and so piecemeal advance was possible. Distinctions were gradually insisted upon which narrowed the area of operation of self-interest and widened that of the public interest; it came to be held, for instance, that "private profit by public servants at the expense of the public welfare was corrupt; but private profit by public servants obtained as a *concomitant* to service in the general welfare was quite proper."[9] (A similar distinction was drawn by Achebe's hero when he took to accepting bribes: "But Obi stoutly refused to countenance anyone who did not possess the minimum educational and other requirements. On that he was unshakeable.")[10] The result in the USA is a patchwork: the scope of political patronage has been greatly reduced and the cash bribery of higher public servants largely eliminated. At the same time, large areas of public life have so far remained more or less immune to reform, and practices that in one sphere would be regarded as corrupt are almost taken for granted in another.

The question is where the puritans are to come from in the new states, with their prevailing lack of economically independent professional and middle classes and the corresponding weakness of the puritan ethos; and whether the puritans in new states can succeed by gradualist means, rather than by revolution.

---

9 Kefauver, Ref. 2, p. 3.

10 Chinua Achebe, *No Longer at Ease* (London, 1910), p. 169.

35. Kleptocracy as a System of Government in Africa

STANISLAV ANDRESKI

As the word "corruption" implies a condemnation of the practices to which it refers, it indicates an outsider's view of African affairs because very few Africans have any deep feelings about the states to which they belong. The ideals of impersonal service are often voiced in deference to the higher prestige of the European countries, but they have not been (to use a psycho-analytical term) introjected. What is regarded as dishonesty in countries well indoctrinated with political ideals, may appear as morally in order in a society where the bonds of kinship are strong and the concept of nationhood remains something very recent and artificial. For these reasons it seems better to use the word "venality" rather than "corruption," as it does not imply a fall from a previously attained higher standard.

However, as the word "corruption" is most commonly used, I shall not attempt to avoid it completely, and shall use it to designate the practice of using the power of office for making private gain in breach of laws and regulations nominally in force. Where, for instance, a traditional judge is allowed by custom to receive a payment from a petitioner we cannot regard it as corruption. On the other hand, an official who bases his claim to be obeyed on the body of laws and regulations which forbid him to solicit payments, nevertheless does so, can be said to practise corruption, regardless of the fact that he may not feel he is doing anything wrong. The additional difficulty here is, of course, that compunction, shame or remorse is a matter of degree, often subject to alteration and ambivalence.

Although corruption is common in all parts of Africa north of the Zambesi, there are considerable local variations in its importance. Where there is less wealth to circulate, where trade is less intensive and detribalisation less advanced, where there are fewer officials and politicians, and a larger part of the population lives in remote, self-sufficient villages, it is natural that there will be fewer occasions for bribery and embezzlement, and that the amount involved will be smaller. It is not, therefore, surprising that corruption is more pervasive, and on a larger scale, on the West Coast than in the less developed countries of East and Central Africa like Tanzania or Uganda.

Everybody who has lived in any of the African states knows that venality is a common practice there. The interesting question is not so much how widespread it is, but rather why it is so common. Nevertheless, some description of the phenomenon must be given because the conspiracy of silence on the part of

SOURCE: Stanislav Andreski, "Kleptocracy or Corruption as a System of Government," in *The African Predicament*. New York: Atherton, 1968, pp. 92–109. By permission of the publishers.

the great majority of European intellectuals, due to inverted racialism, prevents the dissemination of knowledge about this phenomenon. However, in view of the danger of libel suits, the subject of legally illicit gains from public office is not one which can be amply illustrated by well-documented cases. In *Corruption in Developing Countries*[1] Ronald Wraith has given some facts obtained from the trials which took place in Nigeria shortly before independence, but these are merely tiny splinters of a vast iceberg. Anyway, no such trials have been held since independence although the gains from office have vastly multiplied.

It lies in the nature of graft that we cannot have statistics which indicate its extent but there can be no doubt that in all African states the wealth acquired through illegal use of public office looms large. Everywhere people fear the police and their exactions, of which the most common form is imposition of fines for fictitious offences, the fines naturally going into the pockets of the policemen. The police are regarded by the ordinary people as extortioners or even uniformed bandits. The clerks who deal with innumerable small formalities expect individual payment, and if they do not receive it they attend to the matter with deliberate delay or invent a pretext for shelving it for ever. Especially in Liberia, it is quite impossible to get through any official business without the services of special contact men who know how and to whom to pass a bribe, part of which they keep for themselves.

Licences of various kinds and exemptions from import duties on articles which can be sold at great profit are frequently given to the favourites of the government or in exchange for bribes. Fabulous sums were obtained for granting concessions to foreign companies, and fortunes were made from sales of lands belonging to the state. A relatively minor form of corruption is the misappropriation of movable objects.

The study of venality well illustrates the inescapable limitations of sociological inquiry: here we have an extremely important phenomenon which decisively affects politics, administration, business, education, relations between classes or even sexes, and a host of other crucial aspects of social life; yet it cannot be studied with the aid of interviews, questionnaires or statistics, and even the documentary evidence provided by trials vanishes when the phenomenon becomes all-pervading.

The use of public office for private enrichment is the normal and accepted practice in African states and the exceptions are few and inconclusive: a top politician who is not known to have acquired a vast fortune is singled out for praise as some kind of ascetic. To keep a sense of proportion, however, we must remember that the situation has been similar in most of the states recorded in history, and that the custom of refraining from using the power of public office for private gain constitutes one of the most recent and fragile conquests of civilisation, and that in no country in the world are bribery and embezzlement unknown. In Britain (which scores high in respect of probity) outright bribery is rare but its subtler forms are noticeable: when, for instance, a high ranking civil or military officer obtains a directorate in a firm with which he has been dealing on behalf of the government, expertise may not be the only ground. The members of elected bodies appear never to accept cash; nonetheless, the devotion of some of them to various financial interests or even foreign governments does not seem entirely selfless: after all, apart from such things as free trips and other perks, being on good terms with wealthy and influential people opens all kinds of doors to oneself as well as to one's friends

1 Ronald Wraith and Edgar Simpkins, G. Allen & Unwin, 1963.

and relatives. Scandinavia, Britain and Switzerland are the countries least afflicted by venality, which is much more common in the rest of the highly industrialised countries, such as France, Italy and the United States. The prevalence of bribery in southern Europe and Latin America is well known, but what merits notice is how common it is in eastern Europe: in communist Poland, for instance, the act of passing a bribe has been nicknamed "a socialist handshake." It is true, however, that under a communist system nobody can become a millionaire by accumulating the proceeds of graft which, in consequence, is practised commonly but only on a relatively small scale: whereas in Latin America and "free Asia" it is big business in which fabulous fortunes have been amassed.

Enough has been said to show that there is no justification to regard venality as something peculiarly African; and the immunity thereto as typically European. The mere fact that attitudes vary from one period to another shows that they cannot be genetically determined, and therefore have nothing to do with race. Cupidity arises easily in human souls, and in order to understand the variations in the incidence of graft, we must look into the moral restraints which a given society imposes upon uses to which power may be put. Obviously, I cannot embark here upon a systematic inquiry into this problem, but I must dispel the common preconception that it is all a matter of opulence and industrialisation. There is more graft in the USA than in poorer Britain; more in Britain of today than thirty years ago; and in Germany it appears to have been increasing step-by-step since before the First World War.

The foregoing considerations must be borne in mind if we are to see things in the right proportions, but they do not alter the fact that venality pervades through and through the fabrics of African states. After only a few years in office the top politicians have amassed fortunes worth a hundred times the sum of salaries received. Many of them have simply transferred big sums from the treasury to their private accounts, but the practice of getting cuts on government contracts constitutes the chief fount of illegal gains. In Nigeria the customary cut is 10 per cent and for this reason the expression "ten-percenter" is often used to designate anybody active in politics. Nonetheless, the small fry also take part in this business, though naturally on a scale corresponding to the power they wield. People like municipal councillors and district officers or provincial commissioners can make substantial gains on local contracts and awards of licences for market stalls. Scarcely a waste paper basket is bought for an office without somebody getting a tip from the seller, who then gets it back from the public funds by charging a higher price than he could get from a private buyer.

Collection of taxes, excise and custom duties offer ample opportunities for graft. With the aid of bribes people can have liabilities drastically reduced or may even avoid taxation altogether, whereas those who refuse to play will receive most stringent assessments—which in cases where the amount of income cannot be exactly proven, could become exorbitant and crushing. Thus cupidity and the desire to evade the legal liability, and on the other hand the fear of victimisation, enmesh everybody who runs a business (regardless of the size) in a network of bribery. Powerful politicians, however, do not have to pay for preferential treatment: their debts to the state are simply overlooked until they show a lack of party discipline or are dislodged by their opponents.

The forms of bribery and embezzlement are profusely variegate and many of them must appear incredible to people who have always lived in better ordered countries. I have known hospitals in West Africa where the patients had to pay nurses to bring them a chamber pot; where the doctors (who were receiving a salary from the state and were supposed to treat the sick free of charge) would look only at those patients who had given them money, and saw those first who had paid most, regardless whose condition was most urgent. Those in charge of the dispensary stole the medicaments and then sold them either to the patients on the premises or to the traders. The doctors did the same, taking the medicaments for use in their private consulting rooms. Patients unable to pay got injections of coloured water. Many who did pay were cheated and got exactly the same.

The picture painted above is unpleasant, but the reader should not imagine that all the people guilty of such deeds are monsters. The less well placed of the staff would find it very difficult to mend their ways because very often their salaries do not come—sometimes being delayed for months, sometimes vanishing altogether. Many owe substantial sums borrowed to pay for their training or as bribes for getting the appointment. Their tasks, moreover, are so utterly overwhelming that it makes little difference what they do. Even if they worked without sleep or rest, they could attend only to a small fraction of the crowds which are waiting and dying in the yards, corridors or staircases. The quantity of the medicaments is so small in relation to the number of the sick, that even if they were dispensed in accordance with the regulations, only a tiny fraction of the patients would get what they need. Such circumstances, as well as the bad example of the old hands, extinguish all dedication among the newcomers and breed callousness. Furthermore, as in many other walks of life, (and not only in Africa) a person whose probity and sense of duty shows his colleagues in a bad light will be slandered and pushed out.

As in so many other fields we have here a sad example of the senseless implantation of an institution unadapted to its environment. A free medical service which is quantitatively utterly inadequate must become a mockery which embitters the patients and corrupts the practitioners. What is the point in employing doctors and nurses when no money is left to pay the cleaners, and in consequence the hospitals become dangerous disseminators of disease? It would be much better to end this bitter joke and abolish the so-called free hospitals; at least people would not be teased with what they are not going to get, and would feel less wronged.

The hospitals run by the missionaries usually constitute islands of relative efficiency and honesty; and, viewed against the true background, the criticisms levelled against Albert Schweitzer on the ground of his paternalism can only be regarded as preposterous. The missionary clinics, however, function mostly in outlying areas where the tasks are a bit more manageable than in overcrowded and insalubrious towns; and in any case they are mere drops in the ocean.

It must be remarked, incidentally, that it is absurd to use the word "paternalism" in a pejorative sense because the world would be a much better place if the rulers felt as benevolent towards their subjects as an average father feels towards his children. What we normally get in politics is a pretence of paternalism; and the common relationship is analogous to that of a shepherd who keeps on fleecing his sheep and eventually goads them into a slaughterhouse. Schweitzer's attitude was that of true paternalism: he was convinced that he knew best, he expected to be obeyed by his staff and the patients, and did not want to be treated by them as an equal; but all the time he was performing all kinds of unpleasant tasks, giving unstintingly, and taking nothing in return—which is a bit harder than inviting a few educated and opulent Africans to tea and talking about equality while doing nothing for the suffering multitudes. Whatever the members of the African ruling classes may say, a sick peasant will always prefer Schweitzer's paternalism to the rapacity of his masters or their pink partners.

The schools suffer from venality too. Nobody can find out how many scholarships and certificates are obtained through bribery but people often talk about such practices and assume that this can be done—as far as driving licences are concerned it is generally accepted that one must give a bribe unless one is an important person. Teachers' salaries are sometimes embezzled by the headmasters or higher officials. Moreover in the same way as people in other public services, many teachers had to pay for getting appointed, and continue to pay ransom for being kept on the payroll. In some places the children have to pay fees although according to law they should not. I am personally acquainted with the case of a headmaster of a government secondary boarding school who has paid for a sizeable house for himself out of funds received from the treasury and the pupils for running the school. The pupils have on several occasions staged riots in protest against insufficient food but to no avail.

Officials in charge of public works use lorries and other equipment, materials and man-hours belonging to the state or the municipality to build houses for themselves or hire them to other people. Customs officers have, of course, plenty of scope for peculation: in exchange for bribes they pass goods without levying the duty or at least reducing it substantially, whereas people who give them nothing may have to face interminable delays with the added danger that their goods will be damaged or stolen. There are, however, limits to the customs officials' freedom of action imposed by the demand for income on the part of the treasury; and, as far as I can judge this elusive phenomenon, the situation is much better in this respect in the former British and French colonies than in many countries of Latin America.

The police are among the worst offenders against the law: they levy illegal tolls on vehicles, especially the so-called mammy-wagons (heavy lorries with benches and roofs) which usually carry many more passengers than they are allowed and transgress a variety of minor regulations. They are allowed to proceed regardless of the infractions of the law if they pay the policemen's private toll. There are innumerable cases of the police turning a blind eye to the activities of contrabandists, thieves and robbers in exchange for ransom. Sometimes they actively help the criminals. They guard effectively only the houses of important people or of those who pay them, while ordinary citizens have to rely on self-defence. Unless he has committed his deed before the eyes of numerous witnesses, or his victim has influential avengers, even a murderer may be left unmolested if he can afford an appropriate bribe. What is really astounding is that if he can pay a big sum, the police may even help him to erase the traces of his crime by framing up somebody quite innocent but helpless, and getting him hanged. This, however, can be done only in fairly big towns containing uprooted individuals, or among semi-detribalised rural populations. Where kin solidarity retains its full vigour (as in Somaliland) such an action would call forth a tribal uprising.

Verification of bicycle and car registration, trading licences and opening hours, enforcement of traffic regulations and hosts of other functions provide the policemen with the opportunities for squeezing out bribes. As they hardly bother to conceal these operations, and as everybody knows about them, it is clear that the highest officers must be conniving and participating in the gains. My most vivid experience of this kind of thing was in Liberia in 1964 when we were arrested in front of the presidential palace on a trumped-up charge of trying to obtain forbidden information about this building; and we were not released until my companion (a Pan-Africanist American Negro who has emigrated to Ghana) paid up. Liberia, however, is the most extreme case in West Africa, and such a thing could not happen in such a place in Ghana, Nigeria, Ivory Coast or Senegal.

There are limits to the disregard for qualifications in making appointments: to be engaged as a pilot one must be able to fly, and nobody without some special knowledge will be able to construct a building which will stand. Moreover, certain functions (such as those of a doctor or lawyer) have been effectively monopolised by the holders of appropriate diplomas, which restrict the number of candidates. Nevertheless, within these broad limitations and with very few exceptions, the allocation of posts in public services (including the most humble) is mostly determined by criteria which have nothing to do with fitness for the job. Apart from a flair for manipulation and intrigue which everywhere in the world always helps the main criteria of selection are kinship and the ability to offer either a bribe or some other service in return—often on the principle of "if you appoint my kinsman, I shall appoint yours." Almost needless to say, the new states of Africa are not the only places where criteria unrelated to the fitness for the job affect appointments: in England for instance, in addition to family influence, there are "the old boy networks," the members of which identify one another by their old school ties, apart from cliques of newer type. The contrast with Africa is a matter of degree and the limits within which connections are allowed to outweigh qualifications. As a rough and a very general guess (and excluding such bodies as the diplomatic service, the guards and the court) I would say that in Britain qualifications counted for 80 per cent and connections for 20 per cent; and in Nigeria it would be the other way round. In Spain it might be 50/50. In Britain, moreover, reciprocity practically never takes the form of outright bribes. Another important difference is that in industrial countries nepotism and the old boy network significantly affect only the top jobs and a fairly small number of minor sinecures, whereas in Africa obtaining employment as an office cleaner or a postman depends on personal ties or quasi-feudal tribute. Apart from the persistence of extended kinship in Africa, one reason for this difference is that there is more scope for nepotism and squeeze in apportioning jobs when candidates have no alternative opportunities.

Unless he receives a substantial bribe from a non-kinsman, an average African official will give all the appointments which he controls to his kinsmen, except in cases of more complicated arrangements based on bargaining between clans in consequence of which an official may appoint a kinsman of a man who has appointed or will appoint his kinsman in return. The relative importance of bribery as compared with kin-nepotism depends on the extent to which a given set has become detribalised, as detribalisation involves weakening of kin-solidarity and thereby gives more scope to unfettered cupidity.

An interesting point here is that bribery and nepotism are often combined; a man in the position to decide whom to employ will give preference to his kinsmen, but they will still have to hand over to him a part of their pay. The resulting network of social relations will somewhat resemble the old custom of giving presents to the heads of clans, and will be less ruthlessly mercenary than when strangers are involved. It will present a fascinating and intricate hybrid of kin-solidarity, commercialisation, quasi-feudalism and disordered bureaucracy. Unfortunately, such networks are difficult to study because they involve illegal actions about which people do not like to speak to strangers.

Our understanding of African venality might be improved by a distinction between solidaristic and egoistic graft—somewhat analogous to Durkheim's distinction between altruistic and egoistic suicide (the former being prompted by obedience to the norms of the society, as with Japanese harakiri, and the latter due to social isolation and moral disorientation). To designate a prevalence of the latter two features in a society Durkheim coined the term anomie (i.e. normlessness).

We shall classify a given case of graft as solidaristic when we have reasons to believe that it was prompted primarily by the desire to help the kinsmen; and as egoistic when the motives appear to be purely selfish or at most concerned with the welfare of the nuclear family. Almost needless to say, these types are ideal and their relatively pure exemplifications can seldom be found, the majority of the cases presenting a mixture of both. Nevertheless the variations in the proportions of the two ingredients are clearly perceptible, and they make a great difference to the functioning of a given society.

With the partial exceptions of Liberia and Sierra Leone, where the elites descend largely from detribalised slaves resettled in Africa, the African administrations are staffed mainly by people who have been brought up under still vigorous systems of extended kinship, and whose exposure to the ideal of impersonal public service has been brief and backed neither by the tradition nor by genuine sentiments of nationalism. They feel deeply about obligations to their kinsmen but have no sense of duty towards the state—an artificial creation of the foreign masters imposed upon them by force only a few decades ago. A typical African official has been educated at the expense of a large number of his kinsmen who were patiently making collections to pay for his schooling in the expectation that he will look after them when he reaches a high position. If he put his duty to the state above this debt of gratitude, they would regard his as a despicable traitor, ostracise him and perhaps demand an immediate repayment in cash of what they have spent on him. Disowned by his kin he would find himself unable to rely on anybody's backing or loyalty in an environment where the struggle for existence is very bitter, where it is not customary to have close friends who are not relatives, and where his competitors enjoy the support of numerous kinsmen. Under these circumstances the regard for his own interest as well as deeply ingrained sentiments prompt a man to break or twist a law which prevents him from helping his kin, which he regards as his foremost duty.

An African who has reached the top is expected to provide jobs for hundreds of his clansmen, to give decent presents to a vast array of relatives as well as to the clan elders when he visits his village, to make contributions befitting his station to the association of people from his village who reside in the same town as he, to provide in his house food and lodging for kinsmen who come to the town seeking jobs and not finding them for months or even years: to help to pay for the education of the children of his poorer relatives, and last but not least to provide feasts and to defer the costs of sacrifices or funerals (including his own) apart from making donations to the church. As he cannot meet such extensive obligations out of his salary, he is compelled to squeeze bridges, embezzle public funds, take rake-offs and so on. He feels no remorse about doing this because everybody else who can, does the same, and nobody feels that it is something wrong. Solidaristic graft, then, inevitably results from putting an administrative machine devised by foreigners into a society where solidarity of kin still provides the only effective basis of social ethics.

In a country like Somalia, where urbanisation and commercialisation remain embryonic and consequently have made little impact on the traditional tribal structure, graft retains mostly (if not entirely) a solidaristic character; which means that its proceeds are widely distributed. The situation is different in the big cities of West Africa which represent the opposite pole of African social structures, where detribalisation and the spread of European education and values have produced a sizeable mass of rootless or almost uprooted individuals. As it is easier to undermine existing ethical standards than to implant new ones, such people tend to have few scruples of any kind, and eagerly and ruthlessly seize every opportunity to make illegal gains while shirking their duties towards their kin. In Liberia and Sierra Leone most of the venality probably is of the egositic kind because their elites consist of descendants of slaves sent back to Africa who had been torn away from their blood affiliations.

Under the circumstances of far-reaching disregard for fitness for the job in selecting personnel, while many of the most crucial decisions are determined by bribery, the administration cannot fail to be utterly inefficient. Equally deleterious, however, is the sheer weight of parasitism.

On the whole the British colonial administrators did not indulge in graft but they have manifestly failed to inculcate probity into their successors. Perhaps it was impossible; perhaps it could have been done only if the process of Africanisation had been spread over thirty or forty years or even a century. As it happened, their precipitated departure opened the gates to the flood. Perhaps the only method of decolonialisation which could have left a sounder basis for the future would have been to Africanise gradually the civil and military service—allowing the Africans to compete on merit with European candidates for posts left vacant by normal retirement—and when the process had been completed, leaving the country to be governed by this well-selected and indoctrinated corps. As it happened, power was given to those who clamoured for it most, with the consequence that a few well trained administrators and officers, whose indoctrination with the impersonal bureaucratic virtues had made some progress, were surrounded by half-baked newcomers, and became subordinated to the politicians who had reached the top by demagoguery and huckstering, and who had nothing to lose but everything to gain.

As there is much less wealth in their countries, and as they have been functioning for a much shorter time, the African kleptocrats cannot rival the Latin American top stars like Batista or Peron in the size of the booty. Nonetheless, even a casual inquiry into the ownership of the more conspicuous buildings in any African town reveals that a large part of them are owned by ministers or presidents who a few years ago were simple clerks or teachers. The members of parliament, civil servants and party functionaries possess less sumptuous properties but which nonetheless must have cost many times more than what they had received as salary since they took up their appointments. Such premises are often let to foreign-owned companies for housing their expatriate staff at rents well above the market price. The companies are prepared to co-operate in order to ensure the good will of influential or at least useful persons.

It must not be imagined, however, that foreign corporations do not participate in this game. On the contrary: operating in an environment where such things are regarded as natural, they shed easily the scruples which they might have in their home countries, and do not hesitate to use their financial power to obtain illegal advantages. The only thing that could be said in their defence is that as the indigenous potentates want to have partners, they will favour those who will play and will penalise the spoil-sports. The smaller firms simply allocate to their managers funds for which they do not account in writing but only verbally, and from which they draw bribes for the officials on whom they depend. The big corporations have entire teams whose job it is to operate vast networks of corruption, dabbling in politics, subsidising newspapers, politicians and even judges. The official name for these activities is public relations, and it is the only aspect of business where the Africans can rise to top positions because of their usefulness as go-betweens who know best how to ensure the good will of the politicians by discreetly distributing largesse. These jobs usually go to well-connected people and are very lucrative as no receipts need be presented. More will be said about these activities in the chapter on neo-colonialism.

There was a great deal of corruption in tzarist Russia and pre-war Poland, as there is in present-day Spain or Chile. Nevertheless, as far as I could gather, bribery in these countries was confined to restricted areas connected with the use of official power; and outside this sphere many services were rendered without money changing hands. Furthermore, the rich exploited the poor but within each class there was a strong feeling of solidarity. In Africa, however, genuine solidarity is confined to the clan, and there are no restraints on cupidity beyond its confines.

In urban Africa, venality, far from being a monopoly of the top people pervades all strata and ties up with various old customs and the heritage of slave trade. Many traditional activities and ceremonies involve making payments. A man cannot obtain a wife without paying bride-price to her family (father, uncle or brother). Celebrations of achievements, returns or departures occasion payments to the central person. Even more relevant is the custom of making gifts to a person of higher rank when visiting or receiving him. Clearly, customs of this kind are not equivalent to modern bribery, but it is easy to see how they have provided a propitious ground for it.

In all human societies wealth tends to flow towards power: and until the rise of highly efficient administrative and military machines, only kinship bonds could temper the proclivity to use the power of office for the purpose of acquisition of wealth. So even in the urban environment in Africa, within the bounds of the clan wealth usually flows both towards and from the wielders of authority, even though the former current is normally stronger. In relations between non-kinsmen power normally occasions uninhibited spoliation. Moreover, as it is always easier to release anti-social proclivities than to contain them, the process of detribalisation liberates the people from the sense of duty towards their kinsmen before they have begun to feel under obligation to adhere to more universal norms. In consequence in the urban society almost everybody is trying to squeeze something out of almost everybody else over whom he has power or to whom he is rendering an indispensable service. Thus for instance, if one worker introduces another to his employer, he will claim the first month's wages.

One of the most unsavoury forms of exploitation arises from the handling of applications for jobs. The clerks who have access to them as well as their superiors who have some say in the matter, will reshuffle, remove or destroy the applications so as to favour their kinsmen or those who have paid them a bribe, giving topmost preference to those who satisfy both criteria. Sometimes the competition takes the form of a kind of auction in which the prize goes to the highest bidder while the rest forfeit their bids. Private African firms sometimes openly charge a fee for considering an application, even if it is turned down. Another sinister racket is to demand from the applicants considerable sums as a pledge of honesty sometimes long before they start to work; and when the prospective employer has collected a substantial amount from the applicants he often goes bankrupt or simply vanishes. So many applicants fall prey to such tricks because even respectable big stores and banks demand similar guarantees owing to inveterate stealing by their employees.

Most people who have the power to hire and fire will try to impose upon their subordinates a ransom for being allowed to stay in employment; and if the latter have subordinates of their own, they will try to recover their expenses and make a profit by applying the same technique. So a kind of quasi-feudal network of tribute levying goes right through the public services. Expatriate employees of African public authorities often participate in such rackets. It seems that a kind of negative selection has occurred among the expatriates, so that those who remained or joined since the independence seem to be on the whole less scrupulous than the colonials of the old type. Working under a much stricter control, the expatriate managers of foreign-owned companies do not normally engage in peculation on their own personal account; and the African employees and applicants do not expect them to and do not offer bribes. The common desire of the poorer candidates without kinsmen higher up is to get to the European manager, but African doorkeepers, clerks and foremen usually bar the way.

Being guided in a very much larger measure by the fitness for the job in selecting their employees, foreign companies inevitably surpass in efficiency the African; and this is one of the reasons why the economic power in Africa remains in expatriate hands. The inefficiency of the African publicly owned enterprises, and parasitism and venality of their managers are such that they condemn "African socialism" to being a pipe dream.

The newly independent African states provide some of the closest approximations to pure kleptocracy that have been recorded. This does not mean that the amount squeezed out of the ordinary people is absolutely or even relatively larger than elsewhere in the world. The slice of the country's wealth appropriated by the pink castes in Rhodesia and South Africa is a great deal larger than what the African elites manage to take. In the former countries, however, exploitation occurs in accordance with the laws debarring the brown subjects from more lucrative occupations, and without recourse to embezzlement or bribery. This contrast does not make the South African method better from the ethical point of view, but it makes it into a distinct phenomenon with different consequences. The same is true about many societies where the lower classes are of the same race as their masters but where exploitation is sanctioned by more or less generally accepted customs and laws, as is the case for instance in Saudi Arabia. The exploitation of the slaves in Rome or the West Indies, of the serfs in old Russia and of the forced labourers in Soviet times or of the nominally free tenants in present day Peru or India, exceeded or exceeds in intensity anything that goes on in tropical

Africa, but these forms of exploitation were based on the use of economic or political power within the law (no matter how unjust), and therefore were distinct from exploitation through extortion of bribes. With the exception of Communist Russia, the kleptocratic squeeze was quite widespread in the societies just mentioned but, in contrast to post-colonial Africa, it did not constitute the main fount of inequality and exploitation.

As shown in detail in my *Parasitism and Subversion,* graft is rampant throughout Latin America but it constitutes there a relatively less important channel of the flow of wealth than in Africa; although the sums are absolutely larger. The amount of corruption in administrative machines of Latin America is sufficient to make them utterly inefficient, but the proportion of wealth absorbed by bribes and embezzlement is limited by the political power of the old-established property-owning classes whose chief concern is to preserve their possessions rather than to multiply them quickly. Like their African counterparts, the upstart Latin American politicians usually try to make fortunes rapidly but they cannot squeeze very much out of the powerful hereditary rich. As the latter, moreover, in their capacity of landlords and financiers appropriate the greater part of what can be squeezed out of ordinary people—and as about half of the proceeds from taxes have to be handed over to the army—the proportion of wealth which remains available for embezzlement by the officials and politicians (or extorted as bribes) must be smaller in Latin America than in tropical Africa where (with the exception of Ethiopia) neither latifundia nor the armies constitute equally important agencies of parasitic suction although the importance of the latter in this respect is rapidly increasing.[2] In Latin America, moreover, the class solidarity among the rich as well as among the poor seems to deter people from applying the squeeze to the members of their own class, whereas in Africa such scruples operate only within the much narrower confines of the clan.

When the new African states came into existence the control over the chief sources of wealth came into the hands of politicians and officials who (with a few exceptions) had no fortunes to defend or lose but only to gain, who did not have to serve as watchdogs of an aristocracy or a monarchy and who did not have to reckon with the influence of any non-bureaucratic professions or business circles. Directly or indirectly, therefore, they were free to put a squeeze on all their subjects, with the exception of the powerful foreign companies.

Until the military coup of January 1966, Nigeria was providing the most perfect example of kleptocracy: not only because from the highest to lowest practically everybody was involved in the kleptocratic circulation of wealth; but also because the positions in the structure of power were bought, and power itself rested upon the ability to bribe. As the apparatus of coercion was relatively rudimentary—and as it was used relatively sparingly—we can say that the regime rested mainly on fraud. The history of military dictatorships in other parts of the world does not encourage one to expect that this form of government will eliminate fraud—but it will certainly add force as the second prop of the regime which will no longer remain a pure kleptocracy.

According to Ronald Wraith (who was the first to raise this matter in a book):

> What Britain did in 500 years Africans in particular are determined to do in fifty. This is legitimate; what is not legitimate is to be selective—to say that for certain purposes Africa will move at ten times the pace of her former guardians . . . but reserve

2 Written before the military coups.

the right to travel at a more convenient pace in public honesty. . . . The public men on whom wealth has descended in a sudden and unimaginable torrent are not heirs to a tradition of comfortable bank balances and public responsibility; they are nouveaux riches tycoons of public administration. Those who happened to be in the right place at the right time were not all of them cultivated, educated or upright men. . . . Above all, young men from secondary schools and universities who enter the public service do not see a clear road ahead, along which they will travel as far as their abilities will take them in the knowledge that merit will be rewarded and integrity will be their greatest asset. They see a jungle of nepotism and temptation through which they must hack their way unaided.

The losses caused by corruption exceed by far the sum of individual profits derived from it, because graft distorts the whole economy. Important decisions are determined by ulterior motives regardless of consequences to the wider community. When a useless factory is built in an impossible place simply because the former owner of the site bribed the officials into buying it for an exorbitant price, then the cost to the community must exceed by far the profits of the manipulators. An administrative machine permeated by graft does not respond to direction, so that even a most enlightened and personally honest leader can achieve nothing, his instructions are perverted in execution; and the network of collusion is so thick that he gropes as in a fog. Every bureaucratic machine suffers to some extent from aversion to initiative and originality, from sycophancy and the preferment of intriguers and yes-men. But when graft adjoins these normal diseases the administrative services become a mere machine of extortion, scarcely able to maintain a minimum of public order, let alone to engage in successful economic planning.

The essence of kleptocracy is that the functioning of the organs of authority is determined by the mechanisms of supply and demand rather than the laws and regulations; and a kleptocratic state constitutes a curiously generalised model of laisse-faire economics even if its economy is nominally socialist. However, like pure democracy or pure autocracy, pure kleptocracy is an "ideal type" which has never materialised because everywhere there are certain bonds of solidarity which interfere with the workings of supply and demand. Until the factor of coercion by the force of arms became decisive, Nigeria presented a very close approximation to this ideal type but only on the level of supra-clan politics, while relations inside the clan and family continued to be regulated by customary rights and duties. Normally kleptocracy is not "pure" but intertwined with coercion by armed force; so that strategy and tactics as well as price theory are needed to explain the functioning of a system consisting of a mixture of venality and gangsterism, of which the Caribbean republics and the Philippines offer the best examples at the moment.

PART 3

The Analysis of Electoral and Legislative Corruption

Because corrupt electoral actions can, by definition, occur only as isolated instances every two, four, or five years, they are more difficult to study, or more easy to ignore, than a persistent pattern of administrative corruption. This is especially so because campaign techniques and other "inputs" have usually drawn much less scholarly attention than have voting results and other election "outputs." Electoral corruption has also been more difficult to study analytically because so many of the variables affecting campaign competition—number and character of parties, prevailing electoral laws, legal regulation of persuasion techniques employed, and so on—have been so frequently changed, often from one election to another, in a great many political systems. The problem regarding the limited quantity of legislative corruption studies appears to be the great divergence of models and criteria rather than lack of data. In terms of legal codes and political theory the "office" of the legislator is less clearly safeguarded against self-regarding exploitation than is the "office" of the administrator. Thus, definitions of legislative corruption vary greatly in accordance with the strength of pluralist traditions, the "responsibility" of party systems, and other characteristics of political systems as a whole and of particular kinds of legislative settings.

PARTY SYSTEMS, ENFRANCHISEMENT, AND ELECTORAL CORRUPTION

If a researcher were to try to construct a historically oriented atlas of electoral corruption, he would find that the literature provides reasonably complete historical information about only the British system. Since he knows that bribery and treating were at times very prevalent in other countries with self-government traditions, such as the United States and Canada, he might wonder why earlier scholars never worked out the underlying patterns in these countries. He might also wonder why there is not a more ample literature on the incidence of nineteenth-century electoral corruption in France and Germany, especially since both countries lowered suffrage qualifications earlier and more quickly than did Britain.

By fitting together fragmentary information about the kinds of conditions under which significant amounts of electoral corruption prevailed in Western countries it is possible to develop a tentative checklist of factors that appear to have facilitated or inhibited the prevalence of corrupt election practices, such as bribery and treating. The following is a checklist of facilitating conditions:

1. Elected assemblies are powerful prior to development of a bureaucratized civil service

2. Bribery and treating are prevalent election practices prior to extension of mass suffrage and growth of mass parties

3. High degree of competitiveness of small number of candidates competing within decentralized party structures

4. Individual rather than corporative basis of representation and relatively nonideological election campaigns

5. Gradual and step by step, rather than massive and simultaneous, extension of suffrage

A checklist of inhibiting conditions could also be constructed, as follows:

1. Dominance within the political system of a rational and internally responsible bureaucracy

2. Prevalence of class, religion, or ethnic-based parties endowing campaigns with a highly ideological nature

3. Unchecked resort by bureaucrats or party leaders to techniques based on coercion, intimidation, or threat of violence

4. Electoral law provisions (proportional representation, indirect elections, secret ballot), which reduce the personalized relationship between candidate, party and voter

5. Nationalization of political attitudes and centralization of candidate-selection and campaigning functions within parties

"Hard state" Political Systems

Available evidence seems to show pretty clearly that the countries of central and northwestern continental Europe engendered a far lower incidence of electoral corruption in the course of developing their modern electoral mechanisms since the eighteenth century than did either Britain or the United States. The most widely applicable and general factor contributing to this difference would seem to lie in the fact that in the continental countries fully developed national bureaucracies antedated the emergence of political parties or other instruments of mass political mobilization. Having become firmly institutionalized as autonomous entities, the bureaucracies were in most instances in a good position to regulate campaign conduct as representative institutions were established or democratized in the course of the nineteenth century. Insofar as oligarchies sought to check the influence of lower-class voters through electoral laws based upon indirect election, separate electoral rolls, and, later, proportional representation, they succeeded in lessening the decision-affecting potential of the individual voter to the point where potential vote purchases were discouraged from the outset. Finally, the conventional forms of electoral corruption were also inhibited by the subculture, or class-based, pattern of political identification, since the social pressures operating on voters to support "their" sectoral party were often much stronger than in the Anglo-Saxon countries.

As a consequence, particularly of the entrenched position of the state bureaucracy and of other high-status groups, undue influences brought to bear on nineteenth-century continental voters tended most characteristically to fall under the categories of coercion or intimidation, rather than corruption in our sense of the term. Thus in mid- and late-nineteenth century elections German and French voters were much more frequently threatened with the withholding of some privilege or right if they did not vote for the party endorsed by officials or employers, than they were offered monetary or material inducements to vote for a particular party. Successive regimes endorsed "official" and progovernment candidates and particularly in small towns and rural areas, employed the full influence of the bureaucracy to browbeat voters into supporting them. It is this kind of situation that is described in Zeldin's article (Selection 36) on campaign intimidation under the French Second Empire. At the time the appointed mayor, who "could make life very difficult for any man who displeased him and could be very useful to his favorites," was expected to prove his fitness for office by corraling his community's vote for the government ticket. He was assisted by postmen and schoolmasters, as well as government-licensed innkeepers and tobacconists, who helped bring home the message that government financial aid might be withheld if the town did not vote right. Similar tactics were employed by Prussian officials in rural areas, and to some extent the practice prevailed also in countries like Belgium and Sweden. Coercion of workingmen by their employers was an equally frequent occurrence. A particularly flagrant example occurred in 1877 in the Saar region of Germany, where the mining companies issued a public proclamation announcing that they would fire any worker who subscribed to Social Democratic newspapers or participated in Socialist election meetings. Under conditions of such relative pro- and anti-regime polarization, the supporters both of the state and of oppositional political subcultures developed a high order of identification with ideologically legitimated collectivities that inhibited their ability to sell or trade their votes for self-regarding material rewards.

Britain

In contrast to the continental development pattern, political parties antedated the creation of a hierarchical bureaucracy in Britain. Tory and Whig parliamentary parties were quite well established in the eighteenth century, and in many constituencies there existed embryonic local party organizations, which employed bribery and treating on a scale largely determined by local custom and tradition. Even after the Electoral Reform of 1832 political leaders of the "low stateness" point of view felt that the enforcement of anticorruption legislation was not the responsibility of the government. Election contests were regarded as the private concern of the adversaries involved, and in 1842 Sir Robert Peel turned down a move to create state-paid election commissioners with the argument that one should not "throw upon the public the charge of investigating matters of personal rather than public concern." William Gwyn (Selection 38) believes that this "stubborn insistence upon excluding the State from taking the initiative in prosecuting violations of electoral law prevented many instances of corruption from being brought to light and punished."

Historians like Lewis Namier have emphasized that the conditions which made possible the smooth evolution of British political institutions were the very same ones which were conducive to the prevalence and persistence of corruption.[1] Thus, the strength of the eighteenth-century House of Commons as a representative institution was attested to by the fact that rich men were willing to pay voters handsomely in order to elect them to membership in it. The step-by-step enlargement of the franchise (first by inflation, which lowered the relative barrier of property requirements, than by the successive nineteenth-century reform acts) also encouraged the short-term persistence, or even the increase, of electoral corruption. For increasing the electorate from 478,000 to 814,000, as in 1832, or to 2.5 million, as in 1867, left opportunities for the bribing of selected portions of new and old voters in the way that the sudden creation of 8.75 million new French voters in 1848 or 7.7 million German Reich voters in 1867–1871 did not. Given the motivations of candidates and voters, bribery and treating remained technically feasible because until the latter part of the nineteenth century British party politics remained very decentralized, so that the parliamentary candidate and his agent retained great freedom in shaping the character of their campaigns.

The rather dramatic reduction and virtual elimination of corrupt electoral practices during the second half of the nineteenth century (a "happy ending," which may have helped attract scholarly attention) is largely attributable to reforms that proved effective because of the entire system's acceptance of obligations incumbent upon a higher level of "stateness." Thus, successive Corrupt Practices acts introduced not only more realistic penalties, but (in 1872) transferred the hearing of election petitions from the House of Commons to a panel of judges and (in 1883) invoked governmental initiative to reinforce expenditure limits through the Law of Agency. The latter doctrine, which never has become adopted in the United States, holds the agents of parliamentary candidates responsible for all expenditures made on behalf of their candidates' campaigns. The fixing of responsibility upon a particular individual in each constituency was paralleled by the development of really responsible political parties, which nationalized politics by developing techniques for enforcing party discipline on individual candidates. Political attitudes also became more uniform in this period, with the result that "the homogeneity of change across parliamentary constituencies" in British elections of the 1890s was already higher than "the homogeneity of change in American Congressional districts" in elections of the 1950s.[2] If outcomes in individual constituencies were largely contingent on national trends, it obviously no longer paid for party agents to risk stiff penalties in trying to bribe or treat strategic portions of an enlarged electorate. These were the conditions that permitted the author of the 1883 act to pronounce nine years later that it had achieved "a greater measure of success than even the most sanguine had anticipated."

---

[1] Sir Lewis B. Namier, *The Structure of Politics at the Accession of George III,* 2d ed. New York: St. Martin's, 1957.

[2] Donald Stokes, "Parties and the Nationalization of Electoral Processes," in W. N. Chambers and W. D. Burnham, eds., *The American Party System.* New York: Oxford, 1967, p. 191.

The United States

The development of American political parties has been "quite exceptional" and certainly very different from the British case because, in the words of Walter Dean Burnham, "every major upsurge of democratization has led to a dispersion rather than a concentration of political power in the policy-making arena."[3] Thus the development of American mass parties in the 1830s destroyed the preexistent consolidated party leadership and accentuated the distinctions between the executive and the legislature and the decentralizing influence of federalism. Later, after Reconstruction, parties played the role of "bulwarks of localist resistance to the forced-draft change initiated by "cosmopolitan elites." It was this setting that gave rise to the American city boss, who as a political entrepreneur supplied ingenuity and coordinating ability to tie together the immensely complex and decentralized machinery of local government. By subordinating the civil service to yet tighter party patronage control he developed resources for the recurring treating of voters as well as supplementary vote buying on Election Day. Insofar as they helped new groups up the American social ladder, these political entrepreneurs have been viewed by sociologists such as Merton as handmaidens of social integration, just as the vote-buying English election agents were perceived by Namier as instruments of democratization.

A contemporary political scientist aired a more conventional viewpoint in pinpointing the negative relationship between party growth and electoral corruption: "When parties began to rule in the United States little corruption had appeared. Now, under party rule it is conspicuous and is so bound up with party machinery that party itself is held to be its cause."[4] From Rogow and Lasswell's insightful study (Selection 42) of "game politicians" and "gain politicians" it would appear that the incidence of corruption was probably just as extensive in cities where bosses were of the former as of the latter type. They show that the term *corrupt boss* covered a "multitude of sinners," among whom gain politicians differed from the other category in extracting commissions on all machine transactions, through which they build up their personal wealth. The game politician, by contrast, had independent means and may not have derived personal gain from his political activity. However, he "regarded the uses and abuses of money in politics as legitimate, and he was always willing to arrange matters, if at all possible, to promote the financial interests of friends." Thus, for motives of self-aggrandizement the game politician may have engendered as widespread a network of corrupt practices as the gain politician did from motives of personal material gain.

A reasonably moderate and valid estimate of the kinds and volumes of manpower and money that were employed on Election Day to carry a turn-of-the-century contest in New York City are presented in Selection 41 by J. G. Speed.

---

[3] Walter Dean Burnham, "Party Systems and the Political Process," in Chambers and Burnham, eds., *The American Party System,* p. 280.

[4] Jesse Macy, "Corruption, Political," *Cyclopaedia of American Government,* Vol. I. A. C. McLaughlin and A. B. Hart, eds. New York, 1914, p. 479.

His estimate of 25,000 Election Day employees and some 150,000 vote sellers makes evident why, on the one hand, the phenomenon was not too glaring in a city of four million people, and why, on the other hand, it is not absurd to believe that corrupt voters might have decided this election or others like it. What we very badly lack, however, are corroborative estimates of this and other kinds of nineteenth- and early twentieth-century American electoral situations.

"MACHINES" IN DEVELOPING COUNTRIES

Selections 47 and 57, by David Greenstone and James C. Scott, examine party mobilization techniques in developing countries from the perspective of the American "machine." Greenstone and Scott find that the transitional sectors of developing countries in particular contain many nutrients similar to those that fostered the growth of machines in American urban settings. Utilizing a conceptual framework developed by the editor in an earlier publication,[5] Scott emphasizes the particular susceptibility of societies to corruption during "Phase B" of sociopolitical development. In this phase of modernization the traditional patterns of deference are weakened. More freewheeling competition among leaders, coupled with the predominance of parochial loyalties, encourages the widespread use of short-run material inducements to secure voting support. In the American settings corruption was—and in non-Western societies it still is—more prevalent during this phase than during either the preceding period of established authority and limited politicization or the succeeding era of stronger identification on the basis of class and occupational loyalties.

Is there a basic difference between the patronage relationships that anthropologists study in informal situations, in which "authority is dispersed and state activity limited," and the patronage systems that political scientists have conventionally studied? At least one anthropologist, Alex Weingrod, stated that "patronage for anthropologists is an enduring relationship while in the political science sense patronage is most clearly enunciated during election campaigns."[6] This discipline-centered distinction is largely wrong and dysfunctional. The patronage relationships in Asian and African settings examined by Scott are frequently very enduring, and the ability of "machines" to deliver on Election Day presumes complex relationships established and maintained over a considerable period.

Weingrod argues that "the anthropologist who studies patronage considers 'dyadic contracts,' while the political scientist studies a formal organization." But the very characteristic that permits our authors to relate "machines" in American and Afro-Asian settings is that they exhibit a peculiar mix falling between the two polar types. In both kinds of setting, the formal party organizations (as they are depicted in party statutes and rules) bear only the remotest

[5] Arnold J. Heidenheimer, "Comparative Party Finance: Notes on Practices and Toward a Theory," *Journal of Politics* 25:4 (November 1963), pp. 790–811.

[6] Alex Weingrod, "Patrons, Patronage and Political Parties," *Comparative Studies in Society and History,* X (July 1968), p. 380.

relationship to the actual social and economic exchange relationships that bring voters to the polls on Election Day. In the contemporary postmachine setting, American political parties are indeed complex formal organizations, but in many districts the candidates endorsed by the formal organization are defeated on Election Day by challengers who have cleverly put together alliances based upon a complex set of permanent and temporary dyadic contracts. It is only in the bureaucratized European mass parties that the clever manipulator of sets of dyadic contracts really have no chance against the organization and its disciplined membership.

THE INCIDENCE OF ELECTORAL CORRUPTION

The extreme localization of American politics, compounded by the overlapping jurisdictions of *elective* and *appointive* offices, the consequent vast variety of electoral contests, and the lack of uniformity in applicable regulations, helped create the situation in which Walter Lippmann (Selection 29) came to the conclusion that "it would be impossible for a historian to write a history of political corruption in America." To this day there has not appeared any reasonably comprehensive and empirically based analysis of electoral corruption in the United States. Therefore, what obscured the view of the trees for historians has also made the forest inaccessible for other social scientists. The particularly pronounced cyclical patterns of American politics have made it difficult to distinguish long-term trends from among nonsequential patterns of charges by the "ins" and the "outs," intermittent and largely nonrelated court decisions, one-shot investigations, and reports by congressional committees and reform groups. There is much indirect evidence to suggest that the amount of electoral corruption was greatly reduced between the 1870s and the 1930s; but how this reduction was affected or whether it was really a national rather than a series of localized phenomena remain largely unanswered questions.

Such amateur studies of American electoral corruption as we are able to include here serve more to raise interesting questions than to answer them. Thus J. G. Speed's assertion (Selection 41) that in 1905 the New York price for votes was "a dollar for a negro, a dollar and a half for a dago, and two dollars for Americans," raises some interesting questions about the relationship between political socialization and susceptibility to vote selling. J. J. McCook (Selection 40), whose somewhat premature attempt to employ survey methods is inherently interesting on methodological grounds, seeks to pursue such questions by utilizing the estimates of informed observers as to the identity of vote sellers in several small Connecticut towns and city wards of the 1890s. Since his background might have led him to try to substantiate the widely held hypothesis that vote sellers were largely of non-Anglo–Saxon or immigrant stock, it is interesting that his data does not do so. Thus in the rural towns the percentage of vote sellers was as high among native whites as it was among the Irish-born, and the former, particularly the intemperate drinkers, were believed to account for fully three quarters of the corrupt voters. The fact that the second-generation Irish were thought to be much more corrupt than the Irish-born suggests that observers believed that the former had been socialized into corrupt habits. In the city ward, however, this generational difference disappears, and the Irish subculture was believed to account for nearly half of the total of corrupt voters. In this case the first immigrant generation was thought to be somewhat more corruptible than the second one. The only groups that were believed to be totally corrupt were Negroes and French–Canadian-born.

Only one portion of J. J. McCook's data is at all comparable with that of J. P. King (Selection 37), who utilizes corrupt practices petitions as a measure of corrupt practices incidence in English boroughs between 1832 and 1884. Both find that corruption was probably much more extensive in relatively stagnant communities with declining or slowly growing populations. King's study tends to deflate further the previously accepted thesis that the main factor in the decline of corruption was the mere increase in the size of the electorate, for he shows that corruption changes did not have the inverse relationship to "number of eligible voters" that this hypothesis would suggest. His findings, which might be developed through the application of other statistical techniques, suggest that corruption was due more to the persistence of local traditions of vote selling from the pre-1832 period than to the willingness of newly enfranchised voters to sell their franchise rights. His suggestion that new entrants were purer than old practitioners is in understandable contrast to the pattern attributed to American cities, and for clear reasons: the English working-class entrants had become politically socialized to value the franchise for several decades before it was extended to them in a way that the immigrants who acquired voting rights in American ghettos clearly had not been.

LEGISLATIVE CORRUPTION AND CONFLICTS OF INTEREST

Although many of the most infamous and lurid cases of political corruption have involved the selling of influence by legislators, the development of generalized rules regarding legislators' conduct has proved exceedingly difficult for constitutional theorists, potential norm enforcers, and political analysts alike. The most important reason for this is that in genuinely democratic systems the concern to protect legislators against reprisals caused by their expression of unpopular opinions has caused them to be much less circumscribed by rules than other officeholders. Since the legislator does not fit into a formal authority hierarchy and has no superior, he holds an office whose duties and obligations are much more difficult to specify than that of a civil servant. Insofar as it is part of his duty to articulate the interests of his constituents, and insofar as the varieties of political and material support are difficult to categorize, it has been hard to establish rules that would serve as clear boundaries beyond which self-regarding behavior is inadmissible. The consequence, as Theodore Eschenburg and Robert S. Getz (Selections 39 and 43) bear out for systems with such different political and legal traditions as the United States and Germany, is that there remain many varieties of action that would be clearly illegal if engaged in by a civil servant but that are perfectly legal if the "culprit" is a legislator. Although in the English-speaking countries the legislator's virtually absolute immunity against civil suits does not protect him against a criminal prosecution for bribery, it has in actual practice been difficult to convict even those legislators whose corrupt acts were clearly proven.

The most important determinants of the prevalence of corruption in legislators would appear to be their social background, the nature of inducements offered by competitors for legislative favors, and the informal norms of the legislative peer group. Around 1900, when Theodore Roosevelt estimated that one third of the members of the New York legislature were corrupt, all three factors combined to make the favors of American legislators purchasable. Most legislators were of lower social status than their British equivalents, were unaffected by ideals of public service or *noblesse oblige,* and were more avidly pursued by seekers of franchise and other privileges that had been shared out in Britain at a much earlier point. Favors at that time were more easily purchased in America the more one descended from the national to the state to the municipal level, whereas in Britain centralization of power in the national leaders foreclosed favor selling at the lower levels. Centralization of power at the national level, however, will of itself not reduce corruption, as the Philippine example (Selection 48) clearly shows. In the Philippines the "financial rewards for a seat in Congress have long been high for those who were unscrupulous and quick-witted" precisely because the centralized nature of the political system required influence in Manila in order to get action on the local level. Salary levels also do not relate as directly to corruptibility as they do in the civil service. Paid Philippine legislators are obviously much more corruptible than were unpaid British MP's before 1910. The difference seems to be that Filipinos are poorer than were the British when they came to Parliament, and their salaries are woefully inadequate for the standard of living at which their peers expect them to live. René Dumont (Selection 46) shows how exceptional the African situation has been insofar as legislators in such states as Gabon draw as much salary in several months as a peasant does in a lifetime. Since the burden that these official salaries constitute for Gabon are heavier than were the relative costs of maintaining the French court in 1788, they constitute an unusually heavy drain on development resources and still do not prevent further corrupt earnings on the part of the power holders.

In view of the fact that many contemporary material exchange transactions are too indirect to be caught in the net of old-style antibribery legislation, more sophisticated so-called conflict-of-interest legislation has been adopted in the United States and elsewhere. The problem with applying these rules to legislators has related directly to the legislators' unwillingness to be subject to them and indirectly to the distinction of the deviant case from the going model in pluralist systems. If, as it held by dominant academic and practical schools of thought, the public interest develops pragmatically from the conflict among contending special interests, then it is very difficult to distinguish an individual instance of *conflict of interest* from the general play of *conflict of interests.* When even reformers like Senator Paul Douglas hold that it is quite proper for the legislator to intervene on behalf of the interests of his state or a section thereof, the question arises as to when it begins to be improper for him to intervene on behalf of a particular constituent who is economically powerful in a section of his state. In American politics "money changing hands" cannot be used as a criterion of improper conduct, since the legislator can in almost all cases claim that funds received were spent to cover legitimate campaign and other political expenses. Since the Progressive era, Americans have sought to control channels of political finance by relying on symbolic expenditure limitations (which have proved unenforceable because they were not backed up by a law of agency) and by resorting to the principle of disclosure. Disclosure statutes usually the result of publicized allegations of the use of covert means to achieve privileged access, have been built on the stable premise that publicity could be a useful weapon against corrupt and other improper practices. But, as Edgar Lane points out in Selection 44, American legislatures have been more inclined to use disclosure as a weapon against external targets than to develop it as an instrument of self-indictment against their own members who violate the avowed norms of the legislature itself.

CHAPTER EIGHT

Western Europe

36. How the Government Won Elections under Napoleon III

THEODORE ZELDIN

The overwhelming success of the government at the first two general elections of 1852 and 1857 was no doubt due in some measure to the state of public opinion, but public opinion is not a spontaneous and independent force in politics, which elections have the function of registering and converting into numerical terms. It has to be organised and created, and governments had sought to do this since the time of the restoration. Now at length the system, long developed, reached its zenith. It became rather like the system based on the management of influence and interest, which prevailed in eighteenth-century England. Though the methods of Newcastle and Walpole might smell of corruption, they did in fact enable the king's government to function with greater ease than in the reign of Anne, when the queen had failed to "make her parliament." So likewise did Napoleon III's system fulfil a function.

It was based, first of all, on official candidates. The government was simply a party in power; it must join in the election fight like any other party, and not abstain in the hope that M.P.s favourable to it might possibly be returned. There was nothing radically new in this system. The opposition claimed that formerly the government merely recommended candidates but did not electioneer in their favour, and the empire has therefore won a reputation for packing its parliaments.[1] In fact it was merely its extraordinary success which earned it its bad name for methods which, as every reader of Balzac knows, had started long before. Villèle had, in 1822, issued a circular recommending that "All those who are members of my ministry must, to keep their jobs, contribute within the limits of their right to the election of M.P.s sincerely attached" to the government.[2] Peyronnet, keeper of the seals, likewise proclaimed two years later that "whoever accepts a state job contracts at the same time the obligation to devote his efforts, his talents and his influence to the service of the government."[3] Nor was this active participation of the government a mere vice of cynical and corrupt régimes. The Minister of the Interior of the idealistic second republic wrote this to his subordinates: "Ought the government to participate in the elections or simply confine itself to ensuring their orderly conduct? I have no hesitation in replying that it would be guilty of abdication or even treason if it confined itself to making out the official returns and to counting the votes. It must enlighten France and work openly to foil the intrigues of the counter revolution."[4]

There were men who claimed that this

SOURCE: Theodore Zeldin, *The Political System of Napoleon III*. London: Macmillan & Co. Ltd., 1958, pp. 78–87. By permission of Macmillan & Co. Ltd., London, and Macmillan Company of Canada Ltd.

1 ACL 1863, I. 86–87. Plichon.
2 S. Charlety, *La Restauration,* 183.
3 S. Charlety, 195.
4 Circular of 8.4.1848 in Billault papers; and of 10.4.1848, F(1a*) 2097, No. 47.

system would inevitably produce M.P.s who would be mere tools in the hands of the government. Tocqueville in 1837 thus refused the status of official candidate on this ground. "I want to be in a position," he said, "to give intelligent and independent support to the government. . . . I know very well that there are people who forget how they got into the house once they are there, but I am not one of these. I wish to reach it in the same position as I wish to keep inside it, that is, one of independence." The prime minister of the day, Molé, replied to him and justified the system in these words: "In my opinion my first duty is to fight in the elections as elsewhere for the opinion which brought me into power. . . . I do not therefore admit that to be returned through our influence would mean accepting a yoke from which delicacy or pride could suffer, or that to separate yourself from us later on a question on which you could in all conscience and conviction support us, that this would be betraying us." Will you be freer if you are elected by legitimists, republicans or any other party? "You must choose; isolation is not independence and you will be dependent more or less on those who elected you. The ministry's army in the elections is not composed only of men employed by it and owing their existence to it, it is composed above all of men thinking as it does and believing it good for the country that it should remain in power and that it should defeat its opponents. It is among these men, my dear sir, that I would have been happy and proud to meet you."[5]

The first condition of success in elections was thus active participation and the principal instruments of this participation were the mayors. Through the mayors of France the government could speak to every man in the country. Each commune with one or two hundred electors had a mayor almost always invested with its confidence, but appointed by the state and having therefore all the weight of government authority behind his influence. As the state's representative he was the leader, the guide, and the indispensable aid to every man in his village. He could make life very difficult for any man who displeased him and could be very useful to his favourites. He could say to anyone who sought to go against his wishes: "You want a road laid down to your farm—well, you won't have it. . . . You want your card signed—well, you'll have to go and get hold of the curate. . . . You will have need of me, but you won't find me."[6]

"The mayor holds the electors in his hand," wrote a judge of the peace. ". . . He has daily contacts with them, it is to him that they run on the most petty business, he is their adviser and very often their conciliator; and from this is born the confidence and the deference which the electors in the communes have for their mayor, whom they look upon as a father."[7]

The mayor was in turn most anxious that his commune should elect the official candidate unanimously, that it might testify to the sound principles he had inculcated into it and the supremacy he enjoyed over it. "A mayor who has not enough influence over the people he administers to make them vote for the official candidate of the government," said a sub-prefect, "ought not to hold his post."[8] It was seldom fear of dismissal, however, which made the mayor work for the government. It was a natural desire to oblige men who could be obliging in return. Strong personal relations with the sub-prefect were frequent; the

5 *Œuvres complètes d'Alexis de Tocqueville publiées par Madame de Tocqueville* (1866), 6. 71–5.

6 C. 1367, I.-&-V., protest.

7 A. D. Haute-Garonne 2M/34, J. P., Grenade to prefect, 22.6.1857.

8 Quoted C. 1347, Anatole Lemercier's protest, Charente-Inf.

M.P. was often a very useful man to the mayor; and there were, of course, the noble mayors for whom the whole affair was a private arrangement based on almost purely personal considerations. Like Jane Austen's Mr. Dashwood, these men had a great respect for influential men and were glad to place them in their debt. One of them wrote thus to his prefect: "I accept with great pleasure your candidate M. de Chaumont-Quitry, not because he is a chamberlain but because he is related to the emperor whom I like and admire. I know his wife's family very well; she is the daughter of the comte d'Orglandes, a neighbour of my brother-in-law, the comte de Semalé-Cromeral, who knows them very well. You do not tell me whether you know M. de Quitry personally. Has he any ability or any merit? He is very rich and that is already something. I shall see to the business of his election straight away."[9]

Now under the second empire more than ever before, the prestige and power of the administration was at its zenith and the government was the concentrated source of all action; the standing of the mayor, as its representative, augmented accordingly and the government, by consciously backing him up and seeking to increase his authority, brought him, too, to the zenith of his power.[10] He had solid arguments to urge the electors to vote as he pleased. It was, first of all, in everybody's material interest to vote for the government. The essential basis of the centralisation of France is the poverty of the communes. Nominally, since they elect their own councils, they can do as they please; but in practice they cannot since they have not enough money. Their taxes go almost entirely to the state, and it is from the state, therefore, that they must beg back their money in order to carry out the thousand little improvements they most urgently need and of whose necessity they are most immediately aware.

It is essential for them to keep on good terms with the government in order to get the subsidies they require. These facts were put before the electors in plain language and were generally understood. One mayor was criticised for being too plain and thus justified himself, in a half literate style which this translation seeks to render faithfully. "I have the honour to reply to your letter dated 30 May ult. and to certify that when I invited the electors to come and vote for M. Segris [the official candidate] I did not say that if the commune voted for him it would get whatever it wanted from you, I only engaged them to come to vote that all had a duty to fulfil this obligation which the inhabitants of Soulaines owe to be grateful for the favours we have received from the government, until this day for all our undertaking, that we need to keep the good harmony in order that we may get still more aid to finish the road works which by ourselves are unable owing to lack of finance to be completed . . ."[11] Such motives were in fact frequently decisive. Here is how the judge of the peace of Seilhac reported on the prospects in his canton in the election of 1863. "The commune of Beaumont will be unanimous. This commune has just voted for the levying of an extraordinary rate to raise 500 francs to mend its church; the cost of the work is 800 francs. It awaits a subsidy of the remaining 300 francs from you." The vote was accordingly 133 for the government and only 2 against. "The commune of Pierrefitte will also be unanimous. Like the former it has voted an extraordinary rate of 4000 francs for a parsonage. The cost will be 6000 francs. It is asking you for a sub-

9 A. D. Sarthe, M61/16 bis, Baron de Gemasse to prefect.

10 F(1C) III, Ardèche 8, prefect, 12.11.1852.

11 A. D. Maine-et-Loire, 8M53, mayor of Soulaines to prefect, 4.6.1863.

sidy of 2000 francs." The result was 130 for, 1 against. "It is important, *M. le Préfet*, that the grant of these subsidies should be announced before the date of the election. . . . Before yesterday I visited the whole of the commune of Chamboulive and despite all that has been done, it will vote almost unanimously and with enthusiasm. The change in the direction of the [proposed] road has produced its effect." Result: 528 for, 71 against.[12]

The mayor was, of course, the man who understood forms and the technical paraphernalia of bureaucratic government, and many ignorant electors carried out the formalities of voting in the way he told them. The system of voting was different to that now used in England. The voter was not presented with a list of candidates and asked to place a cross against one of them. Instead he was required to put in the box a ballot paper which he had to produce himself, bearing the name of his favourite. These ballot papers were generally supplied by the candidates, and the practice was for them to print about three times as many ballot papers as there were electors and to distribute them widely. The government would send the ballot paper of its candidate, together with a card which entitled a man to vote, to all electors. Every elector thus inevitably received a government ballot paper. The ignorant among them, therefore, frequently came to vote with their electoral card and their government ballot paper, which they would put in the box as though it was the only ballot paper available.

Candidates who did not visit the communes were frequently mere names. So when some poor peasant came to the village hall with a ballot paper an opposition agent had given him, the mayor presiding over the box would at once spot it.

12 A. D. Corrèze, 62M, 25.5.1863.

"Ah! Haven't you got any other ballot paper apart from that one?"

"Why, yes, *M. le Maire.*"

"Show me."

The elector shows several. The mayor takes the official candidate's and says, "Here, my good man, this is the *good one*, put the others down——" Then the mayor puts it into the box. Or he would say, "Put the ballot paper you've got into your pocket and take this one; this is the *good one*."[13]

Such proceedings took place when the mayor was a paternal figure and the elector a submissive peasant. But sometimes a more arrogant man would march into the voting hall and demand a ballot paper. He is given the official candidate's. He asks for "another one." The mayor says there are no others. The man insists. The mayor gets angry. A row would start; and the man would probably end up by being evicted.[14] Of course, the mayor would receive great sympathy, for was not this desire to vote against his advice a challenge of his authority, a doubt cast upon his knowledge of how administrative business should be carried out? It was for personal reasons rather than because of political preferences that the mayors lost their tempers with organisers of opposition. They looked upon it as a personal insult. One mayor, no more pompous than most, thus writes to his prefect: "Yesterday three men travelled over my commune, putting up red posters everywhere in favour of M. Casimir-Périer; when I and a gendarme asked them by what right they were putting up notices on the wall of the town hall without my authorisation, they replied in an *impertinent* manner, that they had no need of my authorisation."[15] This was a slur on his dignity and his rage can be imagined.

13 C. 1367, I.-&-V., Rouxin's protest.
14 C. 1347. A. Lemercier's protest, Charente-Inf.
15 A. D. Isère 8M13, mayor of Valbonnais, 27.5.-1863.

The mayor was the key man in this system and it was to a great extent he who determined the results of elections. To assist him, however, he had a large body of men. "In each commune, the official candidate has the services of ten civil servants, ten free and disciplined agents who put up his posters and distribute his ballot papers and his circulars daily; one mayor, one deputy mayor, one schoolmaster, one constable, one roadman, one bill-sticker, one tax-collector, one postman, one licensed innkeeper, one tobacconist, appointed, approved and authorised by the prefect . . ."[16] The work of these men is best described in their own words. One schoolmaster rejoiced in "the influence which I have the good fortune to exercise over my friends and peaceful inhabitants of Bellecombe, who never go to vote without dropping in on me to collect their ballot papers. . . . I had recourse to a little stratagem to make my (fifty two) firemen vote. I had it announced, by the beat of the drum, on Saturday evening that an inspection of arms would be held on the morrow, Sunday, after vespers; and after this inspection I made a short speech which achieved its object very well, since they all cried, 'To the vote, Long live the Emperor,' etc. . . ."[17] Here is a report of another of these schoolmasters. "Now, *M. l'Inspecteur,* here is how I acted on this solemn occasion. As secretary of the town hall, entrusted in this capacity with the preparation of all the election documents, I was able to exercise far greater influence on the elections. In conjunction with the village constable, I distributed the ballot papers I received from *M. le Préfet* to the electors; I strongly supported the candidature of M. Arnaud, the government's candidate. I tried to make the electors understand that we must all without exception consolidate the plans of our august emperor by a unanimous vote. Despite this, I was compelled to redouble my zeal and energy owing to the fact that some agitators had led astray a large number of electors and particularly twenty electors at a village not far away who had been earnestly solicited to vote for M. Dupont-Delporte and were completely disposed to vote for the latter and in consequence to reject the government's candidate. Having heard this vexatious news, I went to make them see the error into which they had fallen. To prove to them that the government is good, I gave them knowledge of a letter which *M. le Maire* of the commune had received from *M. le Préfet,* in which it is said that a new subsidy of 220,000 francs had just been given to the department to be divided between the communes which had suffered in the floods of 1856. In the presence of this testimony of the solicitude of the government, will you be so ungrateful, I told them, as to refuse it your co-operation: and at once they all threw down the ballot papers that had been given to them and came at once to the town hall to vote for M. Arnaud."[18]

The zeal of some schoolmasters knew no bounds, and, that all might go well, the schoolmaster of La-Chapelle-du-Bard in Isère decorated the polling-booth with flags and exhortatory inscriptions. When the voters entered the room they saw a notice: "La-Chapelle-du-Bard: Long live the emperor." On the right was placed a bust of His Majesty inscribed, "Long live the emperor. Long live the empress. Long live the prince imperial." On the left, "Through the genius of its emperor, France is today the nation which teaches all others by precept and by example." And finally, in front, "Gratitude! Devotion!"[19]

16 *L'Avenir du Gers,* 5.11.1868, quoted in *La Révolution de 1848,* vol. 29, p. 171.
17 *Instituteur* of Bellecombe to the Inspector of the Academy of Isère, 23.6.1857, A. D. Isère 8M12.
18 *Instituteur* of Versoud to the inspector of the Academy of Grenoble, A. D. Isère 8M12, 23.6.1857.
19 A. D. Isère 8M13, mayor of La-Chapelle-du-Bard to prefect, 3.6.1863.

The postmen likewise played their part. The illiterate were frequently in the habit of asking them to read the letters they delivered; the postmen were accordingly briefed and were able to explain the meaning of the electoral propaganda they delivered on behalf of the government.[20] The bill-sticker was delegated not only to put up the election posters, but also to watch over their staying up and to replace them at once if they were torn down.[21]

The activities of all these men were co-ordinated by their superiors. The judges of the peace would tour their cantons, talks to the mayors and the notables of each village and report on them. The inspector of primary education, on the basis of information from the village schoolmasters, sent daily reports on the attitude of mayors, clergy and communes in general. The government thus knew where it was weak. An energetic prefect might accordingly write five hundred personal letters to inflame the zeal of influential men who might help in dangerous areas.[22] The prefect was responsible for the whole operation and would "answer for its success" to the minister. The sub-prefect likewise regarded it as a personal matter to win; and a victory in an election of exceptional difficulty would gain him promotion.

20 A. D. Aveyron, 1863 election file, mayor of Montbazens to prefect.

21 A. D. Isère 8M13, notes of expenditure, Morel, *afficheur à Grenoble*.

22 Chevreau to Billault, 2.6.1863, Billault papers. A. D. Maine-et-Loire 8M51.

37. Socioeconomic Development and the Incidence of English Corrupt Campaign Practices

JOHN P. KING

Some English historians dispute Disraeli's contention that England in the nineteenth century was two nations. It cannot, however, be denied that certain parts of England developed more rapidly than others. Some towns expanded by over 300 percent in population while others stagnated or even declined. In the North and Midlands eighteenth-century villages became towns. Indeed one of the themes of Hanham's study of nineteenth-century politics is the contrast between "the old political world of the counties and small towns which looked back to the years before 1832, and the new world of the big industrial towns."[1] It was in these developing towns that the Anti-Corn Law League, trade unions, and political associations were most active. It was in these developing areas that the rising industrial and commercial classes were most apparent. The purpose of this article is to suggest a relationship between development and corruption.

Development is a concept with many aspects. Of course it suggests rapid population increase. More importantly it implies a social and cultural transformation of a town or an area. It is possible to measure the degree of development within a town not only by looking at the size of its population or even merely by examining its growth rate, but also by scrutinizing its class structure. To the extent that attitudes, values, and norms are a product of environment, development has a cultural aspect as well. Almond has defined political culture as a "set of attitude-cognitions, value standards and feelings towards the political system, its various roles, and role incumbents. It also includes knowledge of, values affecting, and feeling towards the inputs of demands and claims into the system and its authoritative outputs."[2]

It is contended in this article that within nineteenth-century England there were two political subcultures—preindustrial and industrial.[3] The existence of the two political subcultures was a product of the rapid but spasmodic urban, industrial, and intellectual development of the country. It is not argued that these two political subcultures were diametrically opposed. Nor is it argued that the degree of difference between them was as great

1 H. J. Hanham, *Elections and Party Management: Politics in the Time of Disraeli and Gladstone.* London: Longmans, 1959.

SOURCE: This article was written especially for publication in this volume. It is based upon the author's master's thesis, "An Analysis of Corrupt Campaign Practices in English Boroughs, 1832–1884," University of Florida, 1964.

2 G. A. Almond and J. S. Coleman, *Politics of the Developing Areas,* Princeton, N.J.: Princeton University Press, 1960, pp. 27–28.

3 Within these two subcultures, there were a variety of attitudes, many of them peculiar to a particular town—London, Liverpool, or Leicester. Hence the existence of borough cultures.

as that between the three continental political subcultures. Indeed, it may be that one was the logical development from the other. Colin Leys has argued that in nineteenth-century England no new set of ideas or political conduct was introduced, rather an established set was adapted.[4] Nonetheless, it is contended here that there were two different, if related, subcultures, with distinctive attitude differences toward the political system and the actors within it.

The older preindustrial, political subculture encouraged the continuation of certain predemocratic forms of political persuasion. Little emphasis was placed on the need for a dynamic state. There was little point within this subculture, therefore, for the development of the mandate, for the political party possessing a platform, or for program-oriented campaigns. The franchise was a piece of property. The purpose in voting was to satisfy a social better or to acquire a material reward. "According to the previously obtaining moral code many of these practices were not corrupt. Either they had no moral significance or indeed they were actually right and desirable. For instance the average landlord thought it quite natural, and to that extent desirable, that his tenants should use their votes on behalf of his favoured candidate, and did not hesitate to put pressure on them to this end. Treating and other colourful political practices of the period were practiced with an openness that shows that they were not regarded as improper by those whose opinions mattered."[5] It encouraged the continuation of an old style of political persuasion.

On the other hand, the new emerging political subculture, a product in part of the Enlightenment and urbanization, emphasized the creativity of the state. It encouraged the formulation of arguments; it encouraged the discussion of ideas. It implied that elections were occasions during which rational and informed citizens decided between competing programs. The voters' preference was dependent not upon the exertion of pressure or upon the offer of a bribe, but upon an appraisal of party platforms at public meetings or in the seclusion of one's house. It led, therefore, to the emergence of a new style of political persuasion.

During the nineteenth century the socialization of voters into the new political subculture rapidly increased. The process was still not completed, however, at the end of the century. Trade unions, chapels, friendly societies all instilled into their members the virtues of listening, discussing, and voting. Gladstone himself was most impressed by the behavior of the Amalgamated Society of Engineers and the Lancashire Cooperative Society.[6] This period saw, too, a significant increase in the literacy rate. Popular radical newspapers emphasized the use of the vote as a means of gaining social and economic reforms, not as the method of acquiring beer or a £1 note. Many of the newly enfranchised voters in 1832 as well as 1868 had thus already obtained the norms and values of a commercial and industrial century. Wraith and Simpkins argue that this is of considerable importance in explaining the change in the style of political campaigning.[7] Old voters, who voted before 1832 and who lived for the most part in the stagnant areas where the new political subculture had not really penetrated, were only partly socialized into its norms and techniques. They remained familiar with the older political subculture. They had played their parts in the old style of campaigning for many years—as spectators if not participants. They were unlearning the old as well as

[4] C. Leys. "What Is the Problem about Corruption?" *The Journal of Modern African Studies*, 3, 2 (1965), p. 227.

[5] C. Leys, p. 226.

[6] G. M. Young and W. D. Handcock, eds., *English Historical Documents*, XII. London: Eyre and Spottiswoode, 1956, p. 168.

[7] R. Wraith and E. Simpkins, *Corruption in Developing Countries: Including Britain until the 1880s.* London: George Allen and Unwin, 1963, p. 168.

learning the new. Thus corruption can be expected more frequently in those areas with a high percentage of old voters.

This article argues that it was in the most rapidly developing constituencies that elections became the rational choice between competing programs. It is suggested that corruption occurred most frequently in the small stagnating boroughs "uncleansed" by population increase or by the influx of new voters, representative of the emerging industrial and commercial classes.

SOURCE OF DATA

The statistical analysis is based on the alleged cases of corruption presented in election petitions arising from English borough constituencies, with the exception of London, between 1832 and 1885. All forms of corruption have been included in the general tables. There were, however, insufficient occurrences of the exertion of "undue influence" or the use "of intimidation" to permit individual analysis. Petitions were presented by a losing candidate, either to claim the seat or to force a new election. Sometimes, if both sides had been guilty, no petition was made. Occasionally in mid-century, because of the high cost involved, agreements were made between the parties to withdraw a certain number of petitions. On a few occasions petitions were presented with little evidence, in the hope of persuading the victors to come to a more acceptable arrangement, such as sharing the membership of a two-member borough. Such practices, however, became less frequent as the costs of the petitions became the responsibility of the petitioners. Sometimes the existence of corruption did not lead to a petition since both sides were equally "guilty," and neither could afford the cost of the hearing.

Until 1868, petitions were heard by a five-man committee of the House of Commons. Thus, frequently in giving judgment they split on party lines and were motivated by party considerations. After 1868, petitions were heard by a specially constituted court before an appointed High Court Judge. Even then, the failure of a petition did not necessarily imply that corruption had not occurred. Often it had, but the corrupt influence could not be associated with the candidate. Agency had not been proved. It is probable, therefore, that during the period from 1832 to 1885 the presentation of a petition, rather than its result, indicated the existence of corruption. Petitions as used in this article do not differentiate between extensive and limited corruption.

Despite these reservations, however, and bearing such modifications in mind, election petitions are a suitable corpus of material for an analysis in depth of electoral practices in England. Indeed, if a statistical analysis is to be attempted, petitions are the only suitable material. They do provide, if not a systematic measure of corruption, at least a barometer of the incidence of corrupt practices. They illustrate where such practices were rife and the type of constituency most liable to be affected. Hanham accepts them as the best index of corruption in England.[8] Petitions were a mirror through which was reflected an image of the electoral scene. The absence of corruption reflected the adoption of a more modern style of political persuasion—one in which the vote preference was the result of an association between voter and party and in which the target of the campaign was the group rather than the individual.

SIZE OF ELECTORATE

Although size of the electorate is an indication of development, it is the least satisfactory of those used in this article. Some old, well-established cities were

[8] H. J. Hanham, p. 262.

very large, such as Bristol and Liverpool; whereas some growing industrial towns, recently merely villages, were as yet of moderate size. Bolton and Blackburn are two examples. However, it has been argued that size was the most important determining factor in the adoption of a style of political campaigning.[9] (See Table 37.1.)

For the earlier period, it is apparent that size had little systematic effect upon the style of persuasion adopted. This conclusion was also reached by Young.[10] Although in part no doubt due to the existence of proprietary boroughs, the tabulated figures indicate nonetheless that factors other than mere size were of more importance in the determination of a constituency's electoral style.[11] Although the revealed pattern is more predictable, such a conclusion is valid for the later period as well. (See Table 37.2.)

POPULATION GROWTH

During the period from 1832 to 1867, the English borough population increased by 150 percent.[12] However, the increase was by no means consistent throughout the nation. Some towns expanded by as much as 400 percent, others even declined. Obviously, population growth has some merit as an index of development. Industrialization is usually accompanied by an increase in the birthrate as well as by migration to the industrializing areas.[13] A rapidly expanding town was more likely

9 H. Pelling, *Social Geography of British Elections*. New York: St. Martin's, 1967, p. 428.
10 G. M. Young and W. D. Handcock, eds., p. 114a.
11 For an examination of proprietary boroughs, see H. J. Hanham, p. 411.

12 J. B. Martin, "A Review of our Representative System." *The Journal of the Royal Statistical Society*, 47 (1884), p. 113.
13 A. Redford, *Labour Migration in England 1800–1850*. Manchester: Manchester University Press, 1926, p. 165.

TABLE 37.1
SIZE OF ELECTORATE AND THE INCIDENCE OF BRIBERY AND TREATING, 1832–1867

Size of Electorate	Percentage of All Constituencies	Percentage of Constituencies Where Bribery Was Alleged	Difference in Proportion	Percentage of Constituencies Where Alleged Treating Was	Difference in Proportion
3000+	13	6	− 7	15	+ 2
1500+	19	28	+ 9	30	+11
550+	33	41	+ 8	25	− 8
0–549	35	25	−10	30	− 5
N		88		39	

SOURCE: The returns in Great Britain, Parliamentary Papers, Vol. 1, LVII (1866).

TABLE 37.2
SIZE OF THE ELECTORATE AND CORRUPTION, 1868–1884

Size of Electorate	Percentage of All Constituencies	Percentage of Alleged Corrupt Cases	Difference in Proportion	Percentage of Alleged Corrupt Constituencies	Difference in Proportion
5000+	30	26	−4	24	−6
4000+	24	28.5	+4.5	31	+7
0–3999	46	45.5	−0.5	45	−1
N		136		58	

SOURCE: Compiled from Martin, "A Review of the Working of the Representative System," *The Journal of the Royal Statistical Society*, XLVII (1884), pp. 95–103.

to be indicative of developing England than a stagnating one. Such growing towns were not merely industrial boroughs. Some were dormitory areas serving the new middle classes; others were coastal resorts, such as Brighton and Hastings. Consequently, industrialization led not merely to the development of gloomy and dirty towns, but also to the growth of suburbia and coastal resorts. All such towns were part of the developing England. Most had grown from mere villages, others from out of the plains and valleys. They owed their growth to the new forces that inspired the Industrial Revolution. Rapidly growing boroughs were not representative of the rest of stable, stagnant England. Even towns that had an existence in the eighteenth century, were liable if growing fast to be transformed by the influx of migrants and the emergence of the industrial and social classes. It is in towns, therefore, that the newer style of political persuasion should have taken root. Hence in them the incidence of corruption should have been minimal. (See Table 37.3.)

To some extent the hypothesis is supported. The least corrupt constituencies were those expanding most rapidly. Therefore, it is probable that a relationship between this aspect of development and corruption did exist.

Turning to the later period, the results are extremely interesting, and at first sight a little perplexing. (See Table 37.4.)

The least rapidly expanding constituencies were those affected by corruption. The existence of proprietary boroughs is no doubt in part the explanation. It has been shown that such boroughs were for the most part stagnating or even declining as far as population growth was concerned.[14] Bearing in mind such important

[14] See John P. King, "An Analysis of Corrupt Campaign Practices in English Boroughs, 1832–1884" (Unpublished Master's thesis, University of Florida, 1964), pp. 61–63.

TABLE 37.3
POPULATION GROWTH AND CORRUPTION, 1832–1867

Percentage of Population Growth	Percentage of All Constituencies	Percentage of Alleged Corrupt Cases	Difference in Proportion	Percentage of Alleged Corrupt Constituencies	Difference in Proportion
85+	19	12	− 7	12.5	−6.5
20–84	38.5	51	+12.5	56.25	+7.75
0–19	42.5	37	− 5.5	41.25	−1.25
N		145		80	

SOURCE: Compiled from Martin, and Great Britain, Parliamentary Papers, Vol. LVII (1866).

TABLE 37.4
POPULATION GROWTH AND CORRUPTION, 1868–1884

Percentage of Population Growth	Percentage of All Constituencies	Percentage of Alleged Corrupt Cases	Difference in Proportion	Percentage of Alleged Corrupt Constituencies	Difference in Proportion
41+	27	32	− 5	29	+2
11–40	43	48.5	+ 5.5	47	+4
0–11	30	19.5	−10.5	24	−6
N		135		58	

SOURCE: Compiled from Martin.

reservations, it is possible to conclude that there was in all probability throughout the years from 1832 to 1885 a causal relationship between corruption and development as measured by the rate of population growth. However, it is also probable that population growth was not the aspect of development most significant in the determination of the style of political persuasion adopted.

CLASS STRUCTURE

From a study of the 1861 census it is possible to compute the class structure for most constituencies. Part of this census outlined the class structure of all the Poor Law districts in England, dividing the population into six classes.[15] They were: professional, domestic, commercial, agricultural, industrial, indefinite, and nonproductive. The domestic class included not only domestic servants, but also artisans such as engine drivers. By adding the domestic and industrial categories, it is possible to obtain a percentage of the male population aged twenty and above in the working class. This can be computed for all Poor Law districts. While there is not a complete correlation between Poor Law districts and borough constituencies, the similarity in the boundaries is sufficient to give a reasonably accurate picture of the class composition within each borough. Where the constituencies were predominantly working class, the incidence of corruption should have been less than the normal in other boroughs. A vast majority of the population should have possessed a political subculture that tended to see the state as a vehicle for the transformation of society. Hence, elections should not have been occasions to make a little money out of voting the right way, but opportunities for placing into Parliament members committed to a particular program.

Table 37.5 indicates a trend in the direction expected. It confirms the hypothesis that a particular type of class structure in a constituency facilitated the adoption of the more modern style of electoral persuasion. However, its significance is not such as to warrant the assertion that class determined the style of persuasion used.

PROPORTION OF NEW VOTERS

Possibly the most suitable indication of development is the proportion of new voters within a constituency after the 1832 Reform Act and the 1867 Reform Act. Not only is this a socioeconomic measure insofar as it is related to population increase and the class structure, it also has cultural significance. Most of the voters enfranchised in 1832 were from the commercial and industrial middle classes; a few were artisans. The 1867 bill granted the franchise to the majority of the urban working class, certainly to most of the artisans. Socially, as indicated above, these classes were undeniably part of the developing England. They wanted program-focused, issue-orientated elections. Many of the artisan class and

[15] Great Britain, "Appendix," *Census Report 1861*, pp. 128–135.

TABLE 37.5
CLASS STRUCTURE AND CORRUPTION, 1832–1885

	Size 5000+			Size 4999—		
Percentage of Working Class	Percentage of All Constituencies	Percentage of Corrupt Constituencies	Difference	Percentage of All Constituencies	Percentage of Corrupt Constituencies	Difference
76 +	22	14	—8	10	12	+2
75.9—	5.5	6	+0.5	62.5	68	+5.5

"shopocracy" were members of trade unions, cooperative societies, friendly societies, and chapels. Some had read radical newspapers. Some had even participated in, or been influenced by the Chartist movement. Gwyn suggests that, "as this political awakening of the masses took place, and the voter began to value his suffrage as a lever of political power rather than as a privilege for picking the candidate's pocket, corruption became outmoded and gave way to democracy."[16] Most importantly, few of the new voters had gained experience of the old style of political persuasion through participation in elections. Therefore, few had gained direct familiarity with the norms and mores of the old political subculture. Hence, such voters were not torn between the attitudes and values of the developing England, of which they were a part, and those of the older England, to which many old voters irrespective of class or location had become addicted. A large percentage of new electors should have facilitated, then, the adoption of the modern style of electoral persuasion. Those constituencies—still with a large proportion of old voters aware of the monetary gains derived from elections—should have remained affected by the techniques of persuasion associated with the old style.

16 W. B. Gwyn, *Democracy and the Cost of Politics.* London: The Athlone Press, 1962, p. 92.

It is apparent from Table 37.6 that there was a significant relationship between the decline of corruption and the proportion of new voters. The table strongly suggests that in those boroughs in which the old electorate was reinforced by a group of new voters possessing different experiences and attitudes, the old political style was replaced to some considerable extent by the new.

Table 37.7 confirms the impression gained from a study of Table 37.6. An influx of new voters unfamiliar with the practices and unaffected by the attitudes and mores of the old political subculture paved the way for the emergence of the new style and for the end of corruption.

The conclusions of these two tables can be reinforced by studying the behavior of those constituencies enfranchised in 1832. (See Table 37.8.) None of these constituencies had been participants in the old political style, although a few of their electors might have voted in the county elections.

Corruption, then, declined partly as a result of the expanding size of the electorate, partly as a result of population growth, and, most importantly, in proportion to the percentage of new voters in each constituency. However, even in some of the most rapidly developing parts of England corruption tended to linger. Gloucester was a developing city. It was both a port and a railway center. It possessed industry as well, and noncon-

TABLE 37.6
PERCENT OF OLD VOTERS AND CORRUPTION, 1832–1867

Percentage of Old Voters	Percentage of All Constituencies	Percentage of Alleged Corrupt Cases	Difference in Proportion	Percentage of Alleged Corrupt Constituencies	Difference in Proportion
A (50+)	34	54	+20	46	+12
B (25–49)	16	16	0	17	+ 1
C (0–24)	50	30	−20	37	−13
N		149		82	

SOURCE: Great Britain, Parliamentary Papers, Vol. XLIV (1837), as checked against Great Britain, Parliamentary Papers, Vol. XXVII (1833).

TABLE 37.7
PERCENT OF OLD VOTERS AND CORRUPTION, 1868–1884

Percentage of Old Voters	Percentage of All Constituencies	Percentage of Alleged Corrupt Cases	Difference in Proportion	Percentage of Alleged Corrupt Constituencies	Difference in Proportion
51+	20	27	+ 7	27	+7
31–50	50	56	+ 6	51	+1
30	30	17	−13	22	−8
N		136		58	

SOURCE: Compiled by comparing the electorate in 1865 as found in Great Britain, Parliamentary Papers, Vol. LVII (1866) with the Electorate in 1871 as reported in A. Ellis, "The Parliamentary Representation of the Metropolitan, Agricultural, and Manufacturing Division of the United Kingdom with Suggestions for Redistribution," *The Journal of the Royal Statistical Society,* Vol. XLVI (1883), pp. 84–89.

TABLE 37.8
DATE OF ENFRANCHISEMENT AND BRIBERY, 1832–1867

Date of Enfran-chisement	Percentage of All Constituencies	Percentage of Alleged Cases of Bribery	Difference in Proportion	Percentage of Alleged Corrupt Constituencies	Difference in Proportion
1832	20	8	−12	10	−10
Prior to 1832	80	92	+12	90	+10
N		88		60	

formity was strong. In many ways it was representative of the developing England. It had long been a city, however, and for many centuries it had been a parliamentary borough. Tradition and growth were combined. Over the years a style of political persuasion had developed in conformity to the norms and values of the old political subculture. So strong was this tradition that, despite nineteenth-century development, corruption remained a feature of Gloucester's elections throughout the century.[17]

Carlisle also was an expanding town and was also predominantly industrial. For many centuries it had been a city of considerable importance. The old and new, therefore, coexisted in Carlisle. Petitions were regularly presented alleging corruption. The coming of the Midland Railway Company merely intensified endemic corruption.[18]

PARTY ORGANIZATION

The growth of the political party was itself a factor in the decline of corruption, but not of supreme importance. Indeed, it was both a cause and an effect of the adoption of the new style of political persuasion. The post of party manager became increasingly important in the early years of the Victorian era. During this period, however, the party managers' influence was not exerted against corrupt practices. Their task was to find suitable candidates for each constituency. They were as much concerned with introducing rich men to constituen-

[17] Great Britain, Parliamentary Papers, 58 (1880).

[18] Great Britain, Parliamentary Papers, 8 (1847–1848).

cies of dubious tradition as with finding suitable men for the new industrial boroughs.[19] Moreover, they were not averse to becoming involved in corrupt practices themselves. At Sudbury and Ludlow the Liberal manager was proved to have personally bribed voters.[20] In the early period party headquarters did little toward replacing the old style of political persuasion in those areas dominated by the old political subculture. In the larger towns, where registration was so important, it did encourage the local parties to become organized and efficient.

Thirty years later, in 1867, party organizations began again to expand rapidly. With the increase in the electorate, organization both at the center and in the constituencies became more important. Nonetheless, the control of the central office was limited. Feuchtwanger summed up its influence as follows: "The chief scope of the central organization after 1870 lay chiefly in the large towns, while there was little it could do in the counties and smaller boroughs, where the methods of an earlier stage of electioneering still prevailed."[21] However, the 1833 Corrupt Practices Act, with its increased penalties for corruption, led to a more active assertion of central control against corruption. O'Leary suggests that the 1885 election was the first to be dominated by the national and local party organizations.[22] Nonetheless, even in the elections of that year, the effectiveness of the central offices was restricted. In certain areas they could not prevent the continued dominance of local families or industries. Nor could they, therefore, control the style of political persuasion adopted. Pelling has shown that during the last years of the century, corruption continued to dominate political life in at least ten boroughs.[23] Party organization was, then, not so much a vital factor in the elimination of corruption in the old system as a means of facilitating the adoption of the new style in the developing areas.

Candidates, too, exerted some pressure for the elimination of bribery and treating. One estimate of the cost of the 1880 election was that it was twice as expensive as any previous contest.[24] Hence, in Parliament many members were enthusiastically behind suggestions for the reform of electoral practices. The Ballot Act of 1872 introduced the secret vote. Henceforward the briber was less certain of a return on his money. The Corrupt Practices Act of 1883 also contributed to the decline of bribery. By limiting election expenses and increasing the penalties hitherto outlined in the Corrupt Practices Act of 1854 it made bribery less attractive than before. By making the central party organizations responsible for the conduct of elections in the constituencies, it placed the whole weight of the party machines against corruption.

OVERALL DEVELOPMENT AND CORRUPTION

Perhaps the best way of further validating the central argument of this article is to compare the incidence of corruption in a constituency with its score on a composite index of development. The three variables—size of electorate, proportion of new voters, and population growth—measure different but nonetheless important and complementary aspects of development. Of the three it was suggested that the sociocultural variable—the proportion of new voters—was the most

19 N. Nash, "F. R. Bonham: Conservative Political Secretary 1832–1847," *The English Historical Review,* 42 (October 1949), pp. 511–514.

20 C. O'Leary, *The Elimination of Corrupt Practices in British Elections 1868–1911.* New York: Oxford, 1962, p. 18.

21 E. J. Feuchtwanger, "J. E. Gorst and the Central Organization of the Conservative Party, 1870–1882," *Bulletin of the Institute of Historical Research,* 33 (November 1959), p. 199.

22 O'Leary, p. 18.

23 H. Pelling, p. 49.

24 T. Lloyd, *The General Election of 1880.* New York: Oxford, p. 128.

important. It measured class to some extent and was based on the behavioral or participant pattern of the electors. Hence, in compiling the combined index of development it has been weighted slightly heavier than the other two aspects. Constituencies with the highest proportion of new voters have been awarded four points; those in the middle category, three; and those in the lowest, two. Thus, in the earlier period, Manchester, with almost 100 percent new voters, scored four; Liverpool, with under half the electorate new voters, obtained three; and Bristol, with less than a quarter of its voters newly enfranchised, scored two. In the other two variables the most developed constituencies scored three; the middle group, two; and the least developed, one. The proportion of the electorate in the working class as measured by the 1861 census had not been used in the compilation of the index. It is felt that as class is somewhat involved in the proportion of new voters, to include it as an extra component of the index would be to overweight the class aspect. Thus the index ranges from four to ten. From this it can be seen that the most highly developed constituencies would total nine or ten. In the earlier period, for example, Manchester, Birmingham, and Bradford obtained ten; Leeds and Liverpool scored nine. At the other extreme, Lichfield scored five, and Bridgenorth obtained four. The constituencies scoring the highest totals should be those in which the new style of political persuasion had developed and corruption had declined.

It is apparent from Table 37.9 that for the period from 1832 to 1867 the hypothesis is valid. There is a relationship between the scores on the index of development and corruption. Indeed, a perfect step pattern emerges. This illustrates that the more highly developed the constituency, the less likely it was to be still dominated by the old political subculture and thus addicted to the old style of political persuasion. However, no clear step pattern emerges for the 1868–1884 period.

TYPES OF CORRUPT ACTS

So far, corruption has been considered in general terms. However, corruption took many forms. A necessary refinement in the analysis is to compare the incidence of different types of corruption with the stage of development reached by the constituencies. This is especially valuable because it can be shown that certain categories of corruption are more compatible with modern democratic practice than others.

Under the Corrupt Practices Act of 1854 bribery was defined as any form of persuasion in which financial gain was suggested by one person to another with the intention of influencing a person's vote.[25] Thus it included not only the payment of a simple bribe, but also the payment of excessive traveling expenses

[25] G. M. Young and W. D. Handcock, p. 145.

TABLE 37.9
THE INDEX OF DEVELOPMENT AND CORRUPTION, 1832–1867

Category Score on Index	Percentage of All Constituencies	Percentage of Alleged Corrupt Constituencies	Difference in Proportion
(9 and 10)	10	5	−5
(7 and 8)	32	30	−2
(6)	29.5	30	+0.5
(4 and 5)	28.5	35	+6.5
N	176	80	

and the payments to excessive election workers. Such cases as these have been excluded from the analysis of bribery in this article but included of course in the overall total of corrupt instances. Payment of excessive traveling expenses was more often than not an action that reinforced an apathetic's supporter's intention to vote. Therefore, it was not usually an inducement aimed at changing the voter's vote preference. The same could be argued about the employment of excessive messengers by the parties. The omission of such cases as fall into these categories permits bribery to be accepted as a practice typical only of the old style. In the case of bribery, not only is persuasion income channeled, but the attitude of the voter to his vote preference is commercial. Bribery usually was made possible by the entry of strangers into the borough. Voters would be approached in public houses and at home. They would be offered financial rewards if they voted for the right candidate. Such work was undertaken by strangers to make it more difficult to prove agency. Bribery, too, usually occurred under cover: it was known to be illegal and was considered undesirable. Bribery was considerably facilitated by the open voting system and by the extended duration of the poll. Bribers could see the voter's choice made; and the voter could delay voting until the last desperate hours. Sir Lewis Namier has argued that the existence of bribery, as distinct from the exertion of undue influence or intimidation, illustrated the independence of the British elector.[26] It might do this, but it was an independence within the old style. Within the new style, independence is revealed by the ability of the voter to make a rational choice between competing programs.

Treating was defined as "the indirect or direct offer, or promise of an offer of any meat, drink or entertainment."[27] It included both the provision of drinks and excessive or delayed contributions to charity. It included, too, the provision of facilities such as slipper baths or clock towers for the constituency as a whole. Much difficulty centered around defining the time prior to an election at which such marginal activities as supporting the local hospital should cease. Hence, some types of treating do not need a small electorate and an open ballot to be effective. Not all forms of treating were aimed at an individual. However, treating does not conform to the norms of the modern style of political persuasion. On the other hand, many members of Parliament found treating of a communal nature absolutely essential if they were to retain their seats. Many members, especially from locally well-connected families, believed that contributions to local charities, the poor, and organizations in the locality were gifts expected from men of their station and not inducements to vote. Thus Parliament was not so hostile to treating during the 1870s as to bribery.

O'Leary noted that election petitions after 1867 increasingly cited treating rather than bribery.[28] From the figures below, taken from petitions arising from English borough constituencies outside London, O'Leary's point is quite clearly substantiated.

	No. of Petitions	Bribery	Treating
1832–1867	125	86	39
1868–1885	99	49	50

These figures definitely indicate a move in the direction expected. It is apparent that treating was replacing bribery as the more common form of corruption,

26 Sir Lewis Namier, *The Structure of Politics at the Accession of George III,* 2d ed. New York: St. Martin's, 1957.

27 G. M. Young and W. D. Handcock, p. 146.

28 C. O'Leary, p. 202.

especially in the more developing parts of the country—the boroughs.

Such a conclusion is reinforced and refined by a comparative analysis of bribery and treating with the Index of Development. (See Table 37.10.)

It is noticeable that the most highly developed constituencies in the early period (1832–1867) were more afflicted by treating than by bribery. Also, the least developed constituencies were more likely to be affected by bribery than by treating.

CONCLUSION

From the analysis of election petitions arising from English boroughs (except London) it is noticeable that a relationship between development and corruption does exist. In particular, the analysis has shown that the most highly developed constituencies refrained more from corrupt techniques of political persuasion. Electoral campaigns in these constituencies approximated more closely to the norms and values of modern democratic practice. Beneath the highest level of development the pattern is not as clear-cut. Except in the most developed areas, the correlation between the campaign practices adopted and development was not so apparent. It must therefore be concluded that other intervening factors were of importance. Of these the participation experience, or past behavior of electors, was of most significance.

At first, the new style of political persuasion was limited to those areas conducive to its growth. Legislation and party could do little to speed its influence into hostile territory. In the last quarter of the nineteenth century, however, the new style increasingly influenced elections, even in the areas least suitable for its adoption. The development of a concerted move to wipe out corruption started after the 1867 Reform Act. Deriving partly from the new political subculture, and partly from the new circumstances created by "development," this movement was responsible for the legislation attacking corruption. More importantly, it was responsible for its vigorous enforcement. By the turn of the century, then, the new political style had become the normative one used in English elections. Corruption was almost extinguished. The new political style had become not merely a part of the developing England, but had increasingly become the style adopted throughout the country. The speed at which it spread, especially after 1868, was quite outstanding.

TABLE 37.10
THE INDEX OF DEVELOPMENT, BRIBERY AND TREATING, 1832–1867

Category Score on Index	Percentage of All Constituencies	Percentage of Corrupt Constituencies	Difference in Proportion
	Bribery[a]		
(9 and 10)	10	3	−7
(7 and 8)	32	33	+1
(6)	29.5	28	−1.5
(4 and 5)	28.5	36	+7.5
	Treating[b]		
(9 and 10)	10	5	−5
(7 and 8)	32	28	−4
(6)	29.5	33	+3.5
(4 and 5)	28.5	33	+4.5

[a] N = 88 [b] N = 40

38. The Nature and Decline of Corrupt Election Expenditures in Nineteenth-Century Britain

William B. Gwyn

To generalize from available information, the pattern taken by corrupt expenditure in nineteenth-century elections was as follows. In nearly every constituency there was the possibility of some bribery and treating, a possibility actualized whenever the balance of power within the constituency was nearly equal. In the counties, the principal means of corruption remained treating; in the boroughs this means was sometimes supplemented by outright money bribes, which when the bribable class was small might amount to £5 or £10 a voter but more usually did not exceed a pound, and often in large constituencies came to no more than a half-crown. To evade the bribery laws, less direct methods were frequently used. The friends and relations of voters, and often, despite the law which forbade it during part of the century, the voters themselves, were sometimes employed in large numbers during a campaign ostensibly as messengers, chair-men, flag-bearers, watchers, or something of the sort but in reality only to influence votes. Until the law hindered the practice, it was easy under the guise of paying elector's travelling expenses to give them bribes. Such devious modes of bribery tended to take the place of the more open variety as the century progressed. Actual expenditure on corruption varied tremendously from place to place and from time to time. At mid-century, in probably not more than fifty English boroughs was it carried on continually and extensively.[1] Although the general opinion of the time was that the small pre-Reform boroughs were the most corrupt, the facts now available indicate that the larger ones were just as often at fault.[2] What has been said of England may also be said of Ireland until the rise of the Nationalist Party, which neither had the money nor needed to appeal to the electors' venal instincts. In Scotland, where populous constituencies were all newly

Source: William B. Gwyn, *Democracy and the Cost of Politics in Britain*. London: The Athlone Press. 1962, pp. 64–75, 83–92. By permission of the publisher and author.

1 Dr. Hanham has found that "undoubted cases of corruption occurred in at least sixty-four English boroughs at parliamentary elections between 1865 and 1884." He maintains, "It is certain that corrupt practices occurred in between one-third and one-half of the English boroughs on a sufficient scale for them to be noticed." H. J. Hanham, *Elections and Party Management* (London, 1959), p. 263. His estimates do not necessarily conflict with mine.

2 Seymour pointed out that "of the 77 voided elections between 1832 and 1854, 12 were in towns of less than 500 voters and 22 in towns of more than 1,000, while the remainder, or more than half, occurred in towns of between 500 and 1,000." Charles Seymour, *Electoral Reform in England and Wales* (New Haven, Conn.: Yale University Press, 1915), p. 192. Of course not all these boroughs were extensively corrupt, but that should not affect the pattern which is illustrated.

created and consequently untainted by the existence of a corrupt class of voters and a tradition of bribery, corruption was almost unknown.[3]

What characteristics distinguished the venal portion of the British electorate from the pure? The opinion widely prevailed during the last century that those who voted under pre-Reform suffrages, and especially the remaining freemen, were the most corrupt part of the post-Reform electorate. Although this was the case in some boroughs such as Sudbury and Barnstaple, it was not universally true. In 1850, St. Albans contained 483 electors of whom 308 habitually took money. The table on this page shows the distribution of venal electors.[4]

	Number on Register	Number who usually took money
£10 Householders	354	212
Scot and Lot	66	65
Freemen	63	31
Total	483	308

Two-thirds of the Bridgwater voters newly enfranchised by the Reform Act of 1867 were considered by well-qualified opinion to be corrupt.[5] At Reigate in 1865, 346 of its 912 registered electors received bribes, yet not a single individual in the borough voted under a pre-Reform franchise.[6] The truth of the matter appears to be that, while the corrupt element in the pre-Reform electorate retained its character after Reform, in several constituencies many of the new voters eagerly grasped the spoils of election contests for which they had long hungered.

Other opinions attributed the electors' venality to their ignorance, a view fostered readily by the Victorian fear of rule by the masses. The fact that many bribed voters who came before election committees could neither read nor write gives plausibility to this opinion; however, a closer examination of the evidence indicates the difficulty of establishing a causal relationship between illiteracy and corruptibility. It is evident that many of the persons investigated for taking bribes had some education. In 1880, the voters unable to read in England and Wales composed about 1 per cent of the electorate, a figure well below the most conservative estimate of the number of corrupt voters. Of the borough electorates found guilty of extensive bribery in that election, none possessed a high degree of illiteracy.[7]

More convincing than the arguments respecting the type of qualification and the literacy of voters is that which attributes their venality to their economic condition. To poor agricultural workers earning two shillings a day, the offer of even a half-crown might be an irresistible temptation. Typical of many voters at mid-century was James Bridle of Lyme Regis, a hard-working man who just managed to support himself by growing a few potatoes and turnips on a small plot of rented land and by occasionally hiring out his horse and cart for six shillings a day. Though inclined to vote Conservative, he was seduced from his political convictions by a Liberal bribe which allowed him not only to pay off his debts but to buy a new horse and cart.[8] Small tradesmen were equally susceptible to bribes. In the words of one of the Gloucester commissioners, "Many of the persons who take bribes are men not much given to hard work; they are men

[3] B.P.P. (1870), vi, 5.
[4] B.P.P. (1852), xxvii, p. x.
[5] B.P.P. (1870), xxx, p. xxxiv.
[6] B.P.P. (1867), xxviii, p. viii.

[7] B.P.P. (1883), liv. Gloucester in 1906 was described by a Royal Commission as having a corrupt class of voters numbering 500, yet in 1910 only six illiterate voters were found in the borough. B.P.P. (1910), lxxii.
[8] B.P.P. (1842), vi, 250–1.

in small trades, men in failing businesses; some of them are no doubt working men."[9] On the other hand, in Southampton in the 1840s the most corrupt part of the electorate was described as "labouring men with wages under a guinea a week," while bribes were usually not taken by "the respectable mechanics, men working at tolerably decent wages, from 25*s*. to 30*s*. a week."[10] The corrupt voters in Boston in 1880 consisted of 600 persons who were "either indigent or gain their living by means of poorly paid or precarious trades or employments."[11] However, although poverty often led people to accept bribes, it was not a necessary cause of corruption. Poor men did reject bribes and well-to-do tradesmen and professional men in constituencies such as St. Albans[12] were not adverse to receiving them. Indeed, there is only a thin line between the acceptance of money bribes and the over-charging of candidates which was practised by tradesmen in every constituency. All too often the attitude of local tradesmen was that encountered by G. W. E. Russell at Aylesbury in 1880. "Our three candidates," a tradesman remarked, "are Mr. S. G. Smith, head of Smith, Payne, and Company; Sir Nathaniel de Rothschild, head of N. M. Rothschild and Sons; and Mr. George Russell, who, we understand, has the Duke of Bedford behind him. So we are looking forward to a very interesting contest."[13] The tradesmen most notorious for bleeding candidates were the publicans who often gave their votes only to the candidate who "opened" their houses at election time. The publicans frequently composed a large section of the electorate, amounting to one-tenth in Southampton and one-eighth in Tynemouth.[14] Professional men also looked to elections as a time for augmenting their income. For solicitors there was money to be made as election agents. Respectable newspaper owners saw nothing wrong in charging candidates double the normal rate for election advertisements. In short, as was observed in the House of Commons, "Tradition had created a vested interest in the expenditure of money at elections."[15]

As men of any economic class are normally quite willing to receive a present of money, they are deterred from doing so only if they believe their acceptance to be morally wrong or eventually against their self-interest. In the pre-Reform era, the moral and egoistical awareness of the British electorate concerning the sale of their votes was very under-developed. In the course of the nineteenth century, although progress occurred in both types of awareness, it was gradual and unsymmetrical, with the result that throughout the period, and especially near the beginning, many voters could be found who were indistinguishable from their venal eighteenth-century ancestors. One election committee or commission after another discovered that voters who accepted bribes felt no shame about their actions. It was not that they were less law-abiding or God-fearing than the uncorrupt part of the electorate but simply that they could not see anything very wrong about selling their votes. As a Yarmouth elector put it, while he was ready to lay down his life for Jesus Christ, he did not consider it a sin to take money for his vote.[16] Self-interest might have been expected to succeed where morality had failed, but corrupt voters continued to look upon their suffrages merely as means of making a little money or receiving free food and drink. According to reliable testimony, during the first decade following the first Reform Act, the majority of Sudbury electors, about two-thirds of whom ac-

9 B.P.P. (1854), x, 14.
10 B.P.P. (1842), viii, 189.
11 B.P.P. (1881), xxxviii, p. viii.
12 B.P.P. (1852), xxvii, p. xxvii.
13 G. W. E. Russell, *One Look Back* (New York, 1912), p. 182.
14 B.P.P. (1842), viii, p. v; B.P.P. (1860), x, 23.
15 279 Hansard, 3 s., 1672.
16 B.P.P. (1867), xxx, 159.

cepted bribes before taking the bribery oath, had no knowledge or concern to know about the platforms of the political parties but troubled themselves only to discover which side would pay the most.[17] In places like Bridgwater where corruption had existed for many generations, voters actually came to claim their bribes as a right founded upon prescription. In such a political and moral climate, it is not surprising to find as late as 1880 a Nonconformist minister in Mid-Surrey writing to the Conservative Members for the division to warn them that if they did not increase their contributions to the church's debt extinction fund so as to surpass that of the Liberal candidates the two hundred voters in the congregation would throw their influence against them. In explaining the attitude of his flock the minister wrote that the largest portion of them reasoned in the following manner:

> We don't take any interest in politics. It seems to us that there is not much difference between Conservatives and Liberals. But we do take a deep interest in our place of worship, and we are anxious to get it out of debt—so that our consciences may not trouble us when we worship God, in the remembrance that we worship Him in a house that is burdened with debt. Those who help us most in our struggle to meet our liabilities are our best friends, and will get our votes, be they Liberal or Conservative.[18]

If numerous electors continued throughout most of the nineteenth century to find that neither their interest nor their consciences forbade them to solicit and accept bribes, the persons distributing these prerequisites were of much the same mind. In only rare instances was the candidate himself directly involved in the unsavoury side of elections; indeed, in order to circumvent the law everything possible was done to keep separate the legal and illegal aspects of electioneering. This was accomplished through what in modern parlance is called the local party. Although it was not until the nineteenth century that these groups evolved a complexity of structure, they had existed embryonically in many boroughs throughout the eighteenth century. Election to Parliament was impossible without their assistance, which often proved very costly to the candidate, as is revealed in a letter written by George Selwyn relating to his approaching Gloucester election of 1774:

> I am not personally menaced with any opposition, but have a great dread of one, because the contentions among those who live in the country and have nothing to do but quarrel, are so great, that without intending to hurt me, they will stir up trouble and opposition, which will be both hazardous and expensive. I am tormented to take part in I know not what, and with I know not whom, and my difficulty is to keep off the solicitations of my friends, as they call themselves, who want a bustle, the expense of which is not to be defrayed by themselves.[19]

Similar complaints could be heard throughout England during the ensuing century from candidates so unfortunate as to represent the remaining corrupt boroughs where the local politicians resembled Trollope's Mr. Pile, who "loved bribery in his very heart" and thought it was a privilege of a poor man to receive some small consideration for his vote. Thus, writing about his Hertford contest of 1832, Lord Mahon complained, "Much as I have preached economy to my committee at Hertford, I fear that they are running riot and going to considerable expense, however, I shall do all I possibly can to keep them within bounds."[20] After the first Reform Bill, candidates

17 B.P.P. (1842), vii, 1–3.

18 280 Hansard, 3 s., 581–582.

19 Roscoe and Clergue, *George Selwyn: His Letters and His Life* (London, 1889), p. 85.

20 A. Aspinall, *Correspondence of Arbuthnot,* p. 164. Mahon's efforts were in vain, for he was subsequently unseated for bribery and treating, an event which he found particularly disagreeable after having spent so much money, p. 168. The election was said to have cost the two Tory candidates £14,000. T. H. Duncombe, *The Life and Correspondence of Thomas Slingsby Duncombe* (London, 1868), i, 128.

were even more at the mercy of their local supporters. The number of small boroughs which could be directly controlled by a patron was considerably reduced, while the number of large boroughs where control was lodged in a committee of local inhabitants was proportionally increased. In 1835, the Municipal Reform Act was passed, abolishing in the large towns the closed corporations which hitherto had been the prevalent form of local government and providing for popular elections in 179 municipalities.[21] The reform had the effect of quickening the pace of local political activity. Henceforth, every year the principal professional and trades men in many constituencies were obliged to engage in electoral contests if they hoped to maintain the governmental power which it pleased them to exercise over their fellow townsmen. To finance these contests Parliamentary candidates were frequently called upon for liberal donations after being told that a small amount spent at a municipal contest would prove more advantageous than a large amount spent on their own elections.[22] The practice in the ninety English boroughs with identical Parliamentary and municipal boundaries[23] seems to have been from the start to employ the same electoral machinery in national and local elections. In order to return a majority of members to the town council, it was necessary to have a permanent organization in each of the town's wards. For Parliamentary contests these ward organizations were coordinated by a central association composed of the most important citizens who were usually also the holders of municipal office. The central association was usually little more than a formal body, the real direction of the contest being in the hands of a much smaller group of party leaders who were normally called the finance committee and met secretly to plot electoral strategy and to allocate the funds provided by the candidates. In smaller boroughs the machinery was far less complicated but the decision concerning the methods of spending the candidates' money remained with the same type of persons.

A good many of the local politicians were honest enough in most respects, and several testified to losing money in the pursuit of their vocations, which they seem to have followed primarily to satisfy a desire for power and eminence. On the other hand, those workers further down the social and economic scale employed in the distribution of bribes normally undertook the task simply to earn a bit of extra money. Such was the "stranger" or "man in the moon," an outsider brought into some boroughs at election time to make the actual distribution of money. The man who was employed in this capacity by the Bridgwater Conservatives in 1837 was described by the Royal Commissioners as "a low fellow from London," devoid of political principles, who hired "himself out from borough to borough as "Man in the Moon," at one time to this party and at another to that."[24] Often local men were just as unscrupulous. James Bussell of Bridgwater, after accumulating over a half-dozen local public offices for his political services to the Whigs, deserted to the Tories for a bribe of £500.[25] In St. Albans, besides the Whigs and

21 The Act provided for an elected council, three-fourths of which was chosen by the rate-payers and the other fourth, known as aldermen, by the council itself. For a convenient summary of the Act and its effects, see Laski, Jennings, and Robson (eds.), *A Century of Municipal Progress: 1835–1935* (London, 1935), chaps. 1–3; and K. B. Smellie, *A History of Local Government* (London, 1946).

22 After the Election of 1880, Commissioners at Canterbury, Boston, Gloucester, Macclesfield, and Oxford found that corruption had also prevailed in municipal contests. With an annual bribery of the electorate, venal habits could not be expected to die out. To eradicate these habits, in Canterbury during the 1870s the two political parties in the city decided to eliminate municipal contests by apportioning council seats according to an arrangement worked out by their leaders. B.P.P. (1881), xxxix, p. x.

23 B.P.P. (1867), lvi.

24 B.P.P. (1870), xxx, p. xii.

25 B.P.P. (1870), pp. x–xi.

Tories there existed the "third," or "contest," party, a group of unprincipled individuals who introduced candidates into the borough simply to provoke a contest in which they might enrich themselves.[26] Whether local politicians supported a Parliamentary candidate from party zeal, for the enhancement of their own prestige and authority, or from a desire for money, they all were under a powerful temptation to spend a great deal for success, for not only did they share in the general moral blindness to corruption but also they were not hampered by the thought of depleting their own fortunes.

In some instances, candidates were as corrupt as their agents. For most of the century, a man was not considered immoral for making a travesty of the electoral process by buying his way in to the House of Commons. To persons of aristocratic inclination, the purchase of a seat in the Commons was a legitimate method of circumventing the democratic evils that had been thrust upon the nation. The attitude of the majority of the House of Commons was summed up by the *Westminster Review* in the following terms:

> It is a painful truth that a wealthy man, known to have bribed, nay, actually convicted of bribery, is not the whit less respected by the majority of the House. . . . That a candidate spent £10,000 in the corruption of a borough will no more exclude him from the general society of the House of Commons, than a man of fashion would have been tabood, in the age of Congreve, because he had laid out a similar sum to corrupt a friend's wife.[27]

Like duelling during the previous century electoral corruption during the nineteenth century was a practice deplored by the moralist but countenanced and often encouraged by the greater part of society. As late as 1883, a Liberal M.P., asserted that it was useless to rely upon public opinion to remedy corruption, "for a sharp practice on the one side or the other only elicited admiration or amusement."[28] In such a moral climate only self-interest could limit corruption. Some wealthy men, such as the rich ironmaster Alexander Brogden and the London merchant and banker Alexander Vanderbyl, both of whom contested Yarmouth in the Liberal interest in 1865, appear to have worried very little over squandering thousands of pounds to round off their business careers with a seat in Parliament. Other candidates who would have preferred not to part with so much money were deterred from limiting expenditure by the fear that their opponents would not follow their example. Once a candidate had spent several hundred pounds on his election, it seemed more practical to pour out several hundred more than to risk the loss of the initial investment. Economy simply was not good business in electoral matters. Probably by mid-century, the large majority of candidates did not enter upon an electoral campaign with the deliberate intention of bribing. This, at any rate, was the opinion of a number of well-informed persons. According to Philip Rose, the principal Conservative election agent between 1853 and 1859, premeditated bribery by candidates was exceptional. "The vast majority of cases are those in which a candidate has been drawn either involuntarily into the sanction of illegal expenses, or into the subsequent adoption of them." He knew of many instances when Members had conscientiously striven to prevent illegal practices, but once they had been perpetrated by their supporters, had felt obliged to reimburse them for their corrupt financial assistance.[29] For an example of how a

26 B.P.P. (1852), xxvii, pp. x, 168, 220.
27 *Westminster Review,* 78 (1862), 36.

28 279 Hansard, 3 s., 1672.
29 B.P.P. (1860), x, 89. See also the speech of Lord Fitzroy Kelly on his Corrupt Practices Bill of 1854, which was based upon the assumption of the honesty of candidates and the dishonesty of their agents. 130 Hansard, 3 s., 736–753.

candidate might easily fall into this predicament, let us trace for a moment the unhappy experience of Walter Bagehot in his first and only parliamentary contest.

It was Bagehot's misfortune to be sought out as a candidate by the Liberal solicitors of Bridgwater, who controlled the party in that sink of electoral corruption. Some time before this event, desiring to enter Parliament, he had let his intentions be known to Mr. Travers Smith, one of the two legal advisers to the central Liberal Party and an active hand in establishing contact between parliamentary aspirants and constituencies requiring candidates. On the eve of the general election of 1865, Smith gave to Benjamin Lovibund, the leader of the Bridgwater Liberals who had made a journey to London in search of a candidate, the names of four persons, all of whom were described as "men of wealth and position." Among the names on the list was Bagehot's, who had succeeded his father as vice-chairman of a bank in the neighbouring town of Langport and had a family connexion of seventy years with Bridgwater. At that time, however, the Bridgwater lawyers preferred Sir John Shelley, a wealthy country gentleman, who stood along with the existing Member, Alexander Kinglake, author of the popular travel book, *Eothen,* against a single Conservative candidate, Henry Westropp. For the first time in many elections the Liberals did not resort to bribery, with the result that they were able by petition to unseat Westropp, who had topped the poll after spending £3000. Bagehot was asked by the Liberals to stand as their candidate in the bye-election which followed. He had naturally heard of Bridgwater's reputation for venality and was induced to accept the offer only upon the promise of the lawyers to conduct the election on purity principles. The fact that in the previous contest the Liberals had not bribed led him to accept their word more readily than prudence should have allowed. Also, in talking electioneering matters over with his friend Kinglake he had been misled, for the latter, according to his later testimony, had no idea of the money spent corruptly for him by his brother, Dr. Hamilton Kinglake, who always acted as his money agent. The day after his acceptance of the candidature Bagehot travelled to Bridgwater where amid the loud cheers of his supporters he made a speech in which he strongly denounced electoral corruption. Throughout the campaign he remained in constant communication with his local agents, who also accompanied him during his canvass; however, it was not until the poll, when he found himself doing extraordinarily well during the first part of the day that he began to suspect that corruption was being employed on his behalf. He became certain of it when, after he had been defeated by only seven votes, his local agents said nothing about a petition. Exactly what transpired during the contest was made known to him a few days later. Lovibund in an interview with Bagehot's solicitor informed him that in addition to the £200 spent legally, £1100 had been spent in purchasing votes, £1000 of which he and three other lawyers had made themselves responsible for. Upon learning of this, Bagehot, disgusted with the manner in which his campaign had been conducted, was at first inclined not to reimburse his faithless agents. However, under the advice of his solicitor and motivated chiefly by the desire not to acquire a reputation for meanness, he gave way and paid the entire amount. One is not surprised to hear that he refused to stand a second time for the borough.[30] . . .

The first comprehensive act to deal with corrupt practices was not passed until 1854, when Lord John Russell

[30] B.P.P. (1870), xxx, pp. xxiv–xxvi, 975–980, 1044–1099; Mrs. Russell Barrington, *Life of Walter Bagehot* (London, 1918), x, 390–395. His experience at Bridgwater left Bagehot a bitter enemy of electoral corruption, which he inveighed against in the pages of the *Economist.*

finally succeeded in redeeming his promise of two decades before. Bribery, treating, and undue influence were all carefully defined. The old £500 fine for bribery, long a dead letter, was abolished, as it was unpractical to inflict a penalty of such proportions upon persons who could not possibly pay it. Bribery remained, however, a misdemeanour and punishable as such. Persons guilty of treating were to forfeit a sum of £50 to any person suing for the same, and any elector accepting a treat was incapacitated from voting in the election and if he voted was not to be counted. Candidates guilty of bribery and treating by themselves or by their agents were incapable of being elected for the constituency during the existing Parliament. Because it had been so frequently ignored, the provision in 7 & 8 Geo. IV, c. 37 disqualifying voters employed during a contest for electoral purposes was repealed. None of these provisions made any extensive alteration in electoral law. The one important innovation was the creation of an election auditor to be appointed once a year in every constituency by the returning officer. His function was to keep a record of all money spent by candidates in order that any funds used to defray the expense of illegal activities would not escape notice. All charges on the candidate were to be sent to the auditor within one month of the election, after which time the right to recover payment was barred. Also an account of the candidate's personal expenses and the payments made by him or his agent before nomination day was to be submitted to the auditor.[31] The effect of the statute upon bribery and treating was very slight. Agreement was unanimous that the system of auditors failed completely to prevent corruption when a candidate or his agents were intent upon using such means. The provision was constantly evaded by the simple device of sending to the auditor an account which appeared to be reasonable and not mentioning the money spent on illegal activities. Since the auditors had no power of investigation, they were unable to check the accuracy of the returns. Only in the instance of candidates who were determined not to employ corruption did the Act prove at all useful. The fact that their bills had to be paid through an auditor gave them an excellent excuse for not bribing, treating, hiring bands, distributing flags, or spending excessively on legal activities. Opinion was also unanimous that the repeal of the Act disqualifying electors employed in electioneering had led to a considerable increase in corrupt employment; an inefficient measure was better than none at all.[32]

The next attempt to curb electoral corruption did not occur until the year following the passage of the second Reform Act. At that time an effort was made to improve the expensive and overlenient method of trying election petitions. In spite of the remonstrance of the judges that the change would degrade and overburden them, the House of Commons relinquished its ancient right of deciding petitions and put it into the hands of the High Court of Justice.[33] An election trial was to be conducted by a judge selected from a rota composed of one judge from each of the courts of Queen's Bench, Common Pleas, and the Exchequer of England and Ireland. Unlike in the past when petitions had been

31 17 & 18 Vict., c. 102.

32 B.P.P. (1860), x, the evidence of Kinglake, Phinn, Edwin, Parkes, Rose, Phillpotts, Slade, Clabon, Cooper, and Clerk. In 1863, the auditors, who had gained a reputation for nearly complete worthlessness, were abolished and the functions given to the returning officers. The change seems to have done little to improve the audit. 26 Vict., c. 29.

33 In the years following 1604, when the House of Commons took to itself the right of deciding disputed elections, a number of procedures were tried, all of which were lengthy, expensive, and, particularly before the Grenville reform of 1770, partial. So costly was the procedure that the Tory philanthropist Lord Ashley was obliged to announce to the House in 1831 that, although he could swear that his election had been pure, he had to give up his seat for Dorchester since he was unable to afford opposition to the petition lodged against him. 9 H.C. Deb. 3 s., 560–561.

tried in London, the trial was henceforth to take place in the constituency involved. The judges were instructed to report to the Speaker whether or not extensive corrupt practices had prevailed, and, if petitions were withdrawn, whether or not they thought it was as the result of a corrupt compromise. The Act also stiffened the punishment for bribery. Anyone found guilty of the offence was not allowed for the next seven years to be an M.P. or to hold any other national or local public office. If a candidate knowingly engaged for his campaign an agent or canvasser who within the past seven years had been guilty of corrupt practices, his election was void. This was probably the most effective measure which had yet been passed to prevent electoral corruption. On the one hand, it increased the severity of the penalty for bribery, and on the other, it instituted a body to try petitions which was more likely to convict guilty persons of the offence. Since the Act of 1854, election committees had tended to construe narrowly the law of agency in electoral matters so as to make it difficult to connect a candidate with bribery and treating and consequently to unseat him. As a result, convictions for corrupt practices had dropped off considerably. In 1869, however, the new election courts established a rule in the Guildford, Bridgwater, and Lichfield cases whereby an election was void if, apart from the actions of candidates and their agents, such general corruption had prevailed as to prevent a "pure and free choice" from being made. This common law doctrine, while perhaps unfair to Members, who, indeed, were quite alarmed by it, was found to make them more careful in overseeing their campaign expenditure.[34]

The greatest weakness of the Act of 1868 was its failure to reduce the tremendous cost of election petitions. It was estimated in 1860 that the average cost of a petition was £2500, although the price might go twice as high. After 1868, when the trial of petitions was held in the constituencies, although a saving was made in not having to transport witnesses up to London and to pay their keep while there, this was more than offset by increased counsel's fees, which aside from the effect of the Act had steadily risen during the second half of the century. When they found they would have to travel down to the constituencies, leading counsel agreed among themselves not to offer their services for less than £200 for the brief and fifty guineas a day; junior counsel charged £75 to £100 for their briefs and twenty-five guineas a day. The exception to these rates was those asked by Henry Hawkins, Q.C., the "great gun," as he was called by one M.P. Hawkins was called upon in so many petitions that he began to charge the prohibitive fee of £500 for his brief and 200 guineas a day. Rather than lose business, his high charge seemed to increase its volume. After spending a great deal of money and trouble winning a seat in Parliament, Members were willing to pay the most extravagant sums to secure the best legal talent to prevent themselves from being turned out because of a point of law or want of knowledge in a junior counsel. The Beverley petition of 1868 cost the two Members £3000 and the Taunton petition, the trial of which lasted thirteen days, cost a single Member £4335, £2418 of this huge sum going for counsel's fees. With the cost of petitions as high as this, it is little wonder they were rarely pressed.[35]

Looking back upon the century, one is apt to conclude from the inadequate measures they passed that the Commons were not seriously concerned with eliminating corrupt election expenditures. To

34 31 & 32 Vict., c. 125; B.P.P. (1860), x, 222; 279 Hansard, 3 s., 1677, 1690–1691, 1702. The doctrine of General Corruption remained a part of the Common Law until 1949 when it was superseded by a similar statutory provision. 12, 13 & 14 Geo. VI, c. 68, Sec. 142 (1); A. N. Schofield, *Parliamentary Elections* (London, 1955), p. 401.

35 B.P.P. (1860), x, 271; B.P.P. (1875), viii, *passim;* Baron Brampton, *The Reminiscences of Sir Henry Hawkins* (London, 1906), p. 170.

do so, however, is to ignore the climate of opinion in which they worked. In the first place, politicians could not, and still have not, rid themselves of the belief that election controversies are private matters to be settled at law by the parties concerned. This stubborn insistence upon excluding the State from taking the initiative in prosecuting violations of electoral law, prevented many instances of corruption from being brought to light and punished. No-one can doubt that Sir Robert Peel was anxious to prevent corruption, yet when Russell in 1842 first proposed to him the creation of electoral commissioners paid by the State, Peel emphasized to him, "We must take care that we do not throw upon the public the charge of investigating matters of personal rather than public concern. There will be a prevalent desire to shift the whole burden of mere election trials for the public purse."[36] A second reason for the inadequacy of corrupt practices legislation is also clearly illustrated by Peel's attitude towards Russell's proposed bill. Many politicians would gladly have seen the end of corruption but they were reluctant to support too stern a measure for fear that through no fault of their own they would be unseated or at least be forced to spend a great deal of money because of the illegal activities of their supporters or the machinations of their enemies. Every member knew of innocent colleagues who had suffered in this way. Peel, along with most Members, believed that persons bringing suits against Members should continue to pay for recognizances, for otherwise the Bill would be a "constant menace to the sitting Member returned by perfectly honest means. . . . Party feeling, inseparable from an Election contest, and not the hatred of corruption, may lead to a very general system of vexatious petitioning if there be no risk of expense in conducting the Inquiry."[37] Peel's fear was not without foundation, as was demonstrated a few years before by the unscrupulous activities of the "Spottiswoode gang." On 6 December 1837, William Smith O'Brien presented a petition to the House of Commons protesting against a subscription that had been raised in England for the purpose of encouraging and financing election petitions against the Irish Repealers. The fund, he maintained, was part of a plot to overcome the resistance of sitting Irish Members to petitions lodged against them. Also by presenting petitions against a large number of Irish Members, the latter would be excluded from one another's election committees. This allegation was substantiated in the debate which followed. Spottiswoode and his friends had met before they could possibly have known whether an election was faulty and decided to oppose by petition the elections of a number of Irish Members. For this purpose they had advertised in the newspapers for subscriptions. Among the subscribers was the once radical but now reactionary Sir Francis Burdett. An Oxford subscription list contained the names of 700 graduates and undergraduates donating 10*s*. each, besides several anonymous contributions of £25 and £20 each. Such a fund, according to the Attorney-General, was illegal, since English law to secure the pure and impartial administration of justice embodied the rule "that if any person should assist with money, or even advice, unless professional, a suitor in any court, he should be deemed guilty of maintenance, and punishable accordingly."[38]

In 1872, two laws were enacted which tended towards the prevention of treating and bribery. The first provided for the secret ballot, an important item in the Radical program since the 1830s when Grote was its chief exponent. The reform was expected to attain two objects: the prevention of electoral intimidation and the lessening of bribery. The

36 Add. MS. 40508, ff. 299–300.
37 Add. MS. 40508, ff. 297–298.
38 39 Hansard, 3 s., 687–844.

latter object was to be achieved by making the briber uncertain of a return on his money. Besides, as the state of the poll would not be known until an election was over, it would be impossible to judge whether a contest was close and consequently whether it was necessary to bribe. As the record of bribery in the elections of 1874 and 1880 showed, the ballot enthusiasts were to be disappointed in their expectations. It is impossible, however, to say, as some writers have done, that the Ballot Act had no effect upon the decline of electoral corruption. If it did have an effect it probably would not have been immediate and this would account for the amount of bribery in the following decade. The second reform was a statute assimilating the corrupt practice laws for municipal elections with those for parliamentary elections. This was done partly because of the realization that it was impossible to secure purity in national contests when those for local offices were carried on by corrupt means.[39]

As mentioned in the preceding chapter, the reports of the Royal Commissioners investigating corrupt practices in the General Election of 1880 raised a loud cry for a more drastic solution of a problem which was considered more important than formerly. The Corrupt and Illegal Practices Act of 1883 incorporated and considerably amended all foregoing legislation on the subject. By setting a limit upon expenditure, Parliament hoped to make bribery and treating impossible. Should persons disregard the law, they were subjected to much severer penalties than formerly. Anyone committing bribery or treating was guilty of a misdemeanour and liable to imprisonment with or without hard labour for a term not exceeding one year, or to be fined any sum not exceeding £200. After the fiasco of the election auditors created in 1854, to ensure the success of the new system, the Act provided that election agents guilty of making a false declaration of expenses were liable for seven years' imprisonment, the penalty for wilful and corrupt perjury. Besides these stern penalties, certain important disqualifications followed upon conviction for corrupt practices. The guilty party was incapable during a seven year period of voting in any parliamentary or municipal election, nor might he during that time hold any public office. Candidates guilty of corrupt practices were subjected to even more far-reaching incapacities. If an election court reported that bribery had been committed by or with the consent and knowledge of a candidate, or that treating had been committed by him, he would no longer be capable of being elected to the House of Commons for the constituency. Even if the candidate was not personally guilty of corrupt practices but was guilty only through the acts of his agents, he was incapable of being elected for the constituency for a period of seven years.

Nine years after the passage of his Act, Sir Henry James wrote that it had had a greater measure of success than even the most sanguine had anticipated. "Corrupt practices," he said, "have in most localities ceased to exist; everywhere they have vastly diminished."[40] Perhaps the best proof of the efficacy of the statute is that when Ostrogorski, no friend of the British electoral system, was carrying out his investigations at the turn of the century, he was unable to discover

39 35 & 36 Vict., c. 33; 35 & 36 Vict., c. 60.

40 Sir Henry James, "The British Corrupt Practices Act," *The Forum*, 15 (1893), p. 141. The last case of extensive bribery was in 1906 at Worcester, which had a long tradition of corruption. Five hundred voters were discovered to have been involved in bribery and treating. None of the bribes amounted to more than a half-crown. B.P.P. (1906), xcv. Naturally, habits of corruption died slowly. As late as 1920, Herbert Williams, Conservative candidate for Wednesbury, discovered that his supporters had made him financially responsible for treating a number of them with beer, wine, and whisky. Sir Herbert Williams, *Politics—Grave and Gay* (London, 1949), pp. 65–66. The last instance of a Member being unseated for an election offence occurred at Oxford in 1823, after his agent had exceeded the expense limit and made a false return. There was no evidence of extensive bribery. D. E. Butler, *The Electoral Systems in Britain: 1918–1951* (Oxford, 1953), p. 57.

any extensive direct bribery or treating.[41] However, while James could justly be proud of his Act, it is highly doubtful whether one can attribute entirely to it the very rapid decline in corruption which marked the last two decades of the century. Certainly it made bribery and treating more difficult and its punishment more severe, but had there continued a determination on the part of the candidates or their agents to offer money and refreshments and of the electors to accept and solicit them, it is probable that, as in the past, some way would have been found to evade the law. If a candidate and his agent were careful to display ignorance of corruption, it was difficult to trace it to them. We must conclude that the success of the statute was founded upon the course events had taken in Britain during the second half of the century. The new penalties could be very useful in checking bribery and crystallizing public opinion against it, but only if they were enforced. When the Act of 1854 had been passed, an opinion existed throughout the country that it was intended as a strong measure to punish bribery. As Charles Lewes testified in 1860, "Both parties set to work to get rid of it, and they did effectually get rid of it in 1857; but as the punishment proved a dead letter, things got worse in 1859."[42] The electors themselves could see little reason to fear prosecution for accepting bribes. Between the years 1847–1859, election committees reported 315 voters for the offence, but in only one instance, that of the Beverley Committee of 1859 involving two voters, was prosecution recommended.[43] By 1880, although prosecutions remained infrequent, there was indication of a trend towards harsher treatment of offenders. Of those charged with misdemeanour at the summer assizes of that year, the larger portion were acquitted. At Sandwich, of the more than a thousand electors involved in corruption, ten were tried, found guilty, and sentenced to penalties ranging from six to eighteen months' hard labour. A shout of protest immediately went up against what was considered by many to be a much too severe penalty for a crime so long condoned. Memorials calling for the remission of the sentences were sent to the Home Secretary signed by 43,841 persons including 32 peers, 75 Members of the House of Commons, 313 bankers, 1113 clergymen, and 3597 solicitors. Harcourt, to his honour, stood fast and declined to interfere with the sentence.[44] From that moment, many persons who would have considered giving or taking bribes must have thought a second time.

As for the candidates, who had long groaned under the weight of corrupt expenditure, and their supporters, who had so often encouraged it, by 1885 they were becoming increasingly convinced of the inefficacy of corruption. In 1860, Joseph Parkes had expressed the opinion "that no possible legislation will be the means of putting down bribery, except by making the constituency too large for individual corruption."[45] There would appear to have been much wisdom in his observation, although it is doubtful whether mere size alone would have been sufficient to suppress bribery. Following the Reform and Redistribution Acts of 1884–1885, only twenty-five English constituencies remained with electorates less than 5000. In such large constituencies, voting with a secret ballot, corruption could be efficient only if carried on extensively. But extensive corruption could no longer avoid detection and when discovered, according to the doctrine of General Corruption accepted by the new election courts in 1869, would lead to the candidate's losing his seat whether he had condoned the action or not. Thus, even

41 M. Ostrogorski, *Democracy and the Organization of Political Parties* (London, 1902), ii, 468–482.
42 B.P.P. (1860), x, 142.
43 B.P.P. (1860), x, 140, 260.

44 *Annual Register* (1881), Part I, pp. 129–130.
45 B.P.P. (1860), x, 79.

had the 1883 Act not been passed, it is probable that bribery and treating would have declined anyway as the electorate grew ever larger and the smaller corrupt boroughs were disfranchised. What the Act did assuredly do was to accelerate this process by further improving the means of detecting bribery and increasing the punishment for those caught.

Moreover, in determining the causes of the disappearance of bribery and treating in Britain at the end of the nineteenth century, thought must also be given to a less tangible but no less important one. The rising democratic tide which so distressed the conservatives and delighted the radicals of the period was not simply a succession of legislative enactments concluding with the Representation of the People Act of 1918; on the contrary, none of the statutes would have been effective had there not also occurred a revolution in the outlook of the mass of the people—admittedly very much influenced and encouraged by legislative reform—which gradually transformed their role in the government of the nation from a relatively passive to a relatively active one. In this mental transformation, so significant for an understanding of all aspects of modern politics, lay a powerful force for bringing electoral corruption, and the huge expense it occasioned, to an end. As this political awakening of the masses took place and the voter began to value his suffrage as a lever of political power rather than as a privilege for picking the candidate's pocket, corruption became outmoded and gave way to demagogy. Men are now bribed by words rather than money, a system, which if less lucrative to the voter in the short run, appears on the whole to work to his advantage, and has the additional merit of sparing the finances of the candidate and his supporters.

39. German Attempts at the Legal Definition of Parliamentary Corruption

THEODOR ESCHENBURG

The German criminal code does not recognize the act of "bribery of members of parliament." For example, the defendants in the case of the Bavarian gambling casinos were convicted because—in the opinion of the judges—they had signed false affidavits to the effect that they had received no favors in connection with the distribution of gambling concessions. They were not convicted due to receiving favors per se. Various events, including the case of gambling casinos, again gave rise to public demands to introduce regulations for the bribing of members of parliament.

German law protects only the "unpurchasability of the bureaucratic act" and thereby the integrity of the officeholder performing his duties. A necessary characteristic of bribery as defined by the criminal code is that the bribed person must be a public official; the criminal code interprets the term "public official" broadly.

Ordinary bribery occurs when a public official receives gifts for an act "related to his office" but not necessarily in conflict with his duties. It is punishable by a fine or by imprisonment up to six months. Aggravated bribery, which is defined as an act that constitutes a violation of official duties, is punishable by a jail sentence of up to five years. These provisions of criminal law are supplemented by civil service regulations according to which a civil servant is allowed to accept gifts only with the consent of the highest authority of his department.

After the gambling case, the question was again raised as to whether the legal provisions against the bribery of civil servants could not be extended to members of parliament in some form that would recognize the peculiar position of the deputy. This question had already been dealt with in the Weimar Republic. But at that time, the extension of the civil service regulation to members of Parliament was not discussed, and for good reasons. The deputy, who is bound only by his own conscience and not by any explicit set of instructions, has no superior; hence, there is no one whom he can ask whether or not he may accept a reward or a gift.

However, the Anhalt state constitution of 1919 included an article which stated that members of Parliament could be tried for bribery by the state Supreme Court. The constitution of Mecklenburg-Schwerin contained a similar proviso. In 1925 in the Bavarian legislature, State Representative Schäffer of the Bavarian

SOURCE: Theodor Eschenburg, *Zur politischen Praxis in der Bundesrepublik*, 2d Ed. Munich: Piper, 1968, pp. 110–128, 139–141, 204–207, 243–245. By permission. Translation by Peggy Hofmann and Michael Libal.

Peoples' Party, now the Federal Minister of Finance, was induced by a series of corruption scandals in Berlin to introduce a bill which provided that deputies could lose their seats in the state legislature if, out of greediness, they abused their positions as deputies, particularly with regard to gifts or other advantages that they accepted, demanded, or were promised in connection with their position; or if, relatedly, they held a position as director, manager, or member of a board of directors of any profit-making private company.

Schäffer's motion was not passed in that form, but the state legislature did decide to amend the constitution so that any member of parliament "who, out of a profit-making motive, misused his influence as a member of parliament in a manner gravely impairing the honor and the reputation of the assembly" would be punished.

This provision was not carried over into the new Bavarian Constitution of 1946. According to the Bremen Constitution of 1946, however, a member of the city council who abused his position "to gain a personal advantage for himself and others" could be unseated by a three-fourths majority on a motion presented by one fourth of the council's members.

There is a similar article in the new constitution of Hamburg. In both the Bremen and Hamburg constitutions there is no provision for a judicial decision. The Lower Saxony Constitution of 1951 includes rules similar to those of the old Bavarian Constitution.

In 1951 the Bundestag also discussed this question. Stimulated by the discussion of the report of the so-called Spiegel Investigation Committee, which had discovered that several representatives of the Bavarian party had received financial contributions, the CDU moved that the bribery of members of parliament be declared an act punishable by law. The SPD also presented a motion that the federal government should draft a bill stating that whoever attempts to buy the vote of a deputy should be imprisoned; any member of parliament whose vote has been bought and who therefore is declared to have forfeited his seat by the Federal Constitutional Court should be punished in a like manner. Neither motion has gone beyond the introductory stage, and the Bundestag has yet to make up a code of ethics.

The assumption that the legislature has no interest at all in regulations regarding bribery of its members is not wholly justified. The Bavarian state legislature of 1925 and the postwar parliaments of Bremen, Hamburg, and Lower Saxony, which were seriously concerned about the problem, intentionally avoided the use of the term "bribery." There are various reasons for this.

First of all, it is much more difficult to define legally criteria relating to the bribery of legislators than to that of civil servants. The official and unofficial duties of a deputy are far more varied than those of a civil servant. In the case of a deputy, what would be the equivalent of such terms used in the criminal code covering civil servants as "actions pertaining to his official functions" and "administrative and official duties"? The civil servant has only one sphere of action, namely that controlled by the department he belongs to, with the possible exception of sideline jobs, which require special permission if they involve monetary compensation. The member of parliament, on the other hand, ordinarily has two jobs: the parliamentary job and a professional one. In addition, there are also abuses of the deputy's office that are not influenced by bribery. The SPD restricts its bill to bribery relating to votes cast in the legislature. A far more frequent abuse occurs when a deputy is bribed into abusing his position outside of parliament, for example, by intervening with the bureaucracy. Bribery is only one type of parliamentary corruption among many others. Thus the concept of bribery of members of parliament cannot easily be given a precise definition.

However, the interest in a precise definition is very great, for the deputy stands in the midst of the political battlefield and ought to be protected from unjustified, demagogic accusations. It is a fault, however, inevitable, of the constitutions of Bremen, Hamburg, and Lower Saxony that they lack method for indicting their representatives other than by a political decision.

In order to avoid the abuse of the power to impeach deputies, a three-fourths or two-thirds majority is required, unlike the former Bavarian regulation. This means, however, that action can be taken only in extremely severe cases. It is difficult to imagine the creation of a prosecutor for the legislature, a parliamentary prosecutor.

Nevertheless, the rules in the three Länder guarantee a certain amount of protection, and something would be gained if the other Länder followed suit.

Perhaps now the idea will be advocated to prohibit the deputies from accepting any favors and donations at all. This reasoning does not take into account the fact that, while the civil servant has a stable and secure income, the deputy ordinarily gains part of his income from his original profession. A law like the one mentioned above could lead to a situation where the private incomes of many deputies would be under strict control. One need only think of lawyers or tax advisers or specialists who provide expert evaluation. Admittedly, the linkage between an attorney's, a tax adviser's, or such specialist's profession and a deputy's mandate is a questionable one. But where should the boundary be drawn between illegal allowance and legal income?

Above all, a member of parliament may accept donations for his party, which he may place at the disposal of the national, state, or local party organization or which he may use for his own publicity, as he pleases. Declaring such practices illegal—aside from the fact that there might be ways to circumvent the rules—would further increase the deputy's dependence on his party. Thus, it will be very difficult, if at all possible, to reduce the danger of corruption through contributions for a party given directly to its deputies. On several occasions the proceedings of the Bavarian state legislature of 1925 referred to the "code of honor" that "had developed through a century of practical experience in parliamentary life concerning what a deputy could and could not do in carrying out his legal duties." This unwritten law should be the starting point.

Undoubtedly, many deputies still do uphold strict ethical standards. But it is equally clear that the "code of honor" has suffered considerably. Today it is not possible to rely only on this code. It has become more and more necessary to fight parliamentary corruption by legal means.

This requires thorough preparation. Neither the heavily preoccupied ministerial administration nor the excessively busy legislative committees are able to do this. The Bundestag or its president should create a commission of experienced, honest deputies and laymen who are familiar with the legal aspects of the problem. The task of this commission would be to seek some kind of a legal provision protecting against parliamentary corruption and dishonesty of deputies in general. An isolated treatment of the problem of bribery would be insufficient. A comprehensive regulation could be a very important, perhaps an indispensable supplement to the party law (*Parteiengesetz*).

Paragraph 404 of the draft of the penal code of October 1962 contains a provision against the buying of votes: "Anyone who attempts to buy or sell a vote on a roll call will be punished by punitive arrest or by imprisonment up to three years." According to Paragraph 409, these provisions are also valid for "elections and other voting acts in the national assemblies and other federal, state, or local institutions." Provisions against bribery in elections are included in the criminal law code (Paragraphs 108b and 108d). Now they will be extended to elections and roll calls in the legislatures. The following explanation is given: "The preconditions for the bribery of a vote are in some respects different from the ones for bribery of an administrative office. Within the civil service it is entirely illegal and reprehensible to accept or grant an emolument for an official act or in connection with one. . . . The same rules, however, cannot apply to the exercise of voting rights, even if the voting deals with 'public affairs.' "

It is quite possible that decisions on policy matters concerning public affairs, the regulation of which counts among the duties of representative bodies, at the same time imply the pursuit of partisan ends that correspond to the particular interests of those voting on these decisions. With regard to votes on political questions or on matters where political influences are foreseen or tolerated by the law, promises or expectations are not necessarily contrary to the rules of democracy nor need they be reprehensible, even if they contribute to the improvement of the living condition of the deputy casting his vote or of the political group he represents. This is something inherent in the interplay of political forces. Certainly campaign promises and pledges concerning the improvement of general living conditions provide no benefits as defined in the regulations concerning bribery.

On the other hand it is doubtful whether emoluments in the judicial sense do not already exist if, during an election campaign, specific promises that have a very narrow appeal to highly restricted groups are made in order to maintain the favor of certain voters. For example, a group may favor increases in social welfare benefits or a candidate may promise to see to it that the funds necessary for improving the roads in his constituency will be appropriated. In a mayoral election the prospect of converting municipal land into a soccer field may be held out. In legislatures or elsewhere in political life, agreements on votes may be made or offers and promises may be exchanged which, regarded by themselves, may even provide benefits for one individual only. These proceedings are not necessarily reprehensible; sometimes they are an important part of democratic politics. For instance, a minister's position may be promised to a deputy provided that he take the right stand on an issue. It is precisely those legislators who represent specific group interests and are supported by certain political factions who are in fact dependent on the support of these factions, even though, in principle, they are not bound by instructions in casting their ballot. Thus, numerous committees and corporations that were established for the purpose of executing administrative tasks are, according to law, composed either entirely or partly of representatives of specific interests. . . .

That the legislator receives or stands to receive some benefit from his vote is insufficient evidence of bribery. In addition, the fact must be obvious that the accepting or granting of this benefit is made in order to abuse the voting privilege, the vote being determined by nonobjective, selfish, or otherwise improper influences. This reprehensible linkage between casting a vote and gaining a personal advantage takes place if a legislator yields to someone else's demands for the sake of some personal gain, instead of casting his ballot as a free citizen to the best of his knowledge and according to his conscience for the sake of a good cause, or if he receives improper payments from a pressure group for his vote. . . . Hence the criterion of purchasability constitutes the essence of vote bribery. . . . Thus, only cases are included in which benefits are granted or accepted in an objectionable manner because the right to vote on public matters is abused for the purpose of some immoral deal, but not other cases in which common political ploys are brought to bear on the voter. According to the provisions of this bill dealing with the bribing of votes in general the corruption as well as the corruptibility of deputies and other representatives of the people are punishable only if a deal on future voting is involved. Of course, one can think of other cases in which emoluments are accepted in a punishable manner, not for the act of voting but for some other kind of action. However, the different types of duties a deputy has make it impossible to clearly define such different acts as possible objects of bribery; the deputies' activities stretch beyond specifically parliamentary work to general political affairs, where, although valid rules are recognized, precisely defined patterns of behavior do not exist. Therefore, it is impossible to equate the authorized activities of deputies related to their mandate with the official duties of officeholders, judges, or other public servants without some further considerations. . . . Thus, objective considerations justify the punishment of bribery of members of parliament only in the case of bribery of voting.

In answering a question by Bundestag Deputy Moersch on "the suspicion of corruption" in the purchase of the infantry tank HS-30, an occasion on which parties, politicians, and members of parliament were said to have received financial donations, Undersecretary Gumbel of the Defense Ministry stated:

> The suspicion that had been voiced could not be substantiated at all by investigations and inquiries. Further—Mr. Deputy, donations to deputies or to parties are in no way prohibited (Hear! Hear! from SPD Deputy Wehner: Try being a deputy, Mr. Gumbel!) —Mr. Deputy, in no way did I state that donations were given. According to our findings they were not given. But, in connection with the question raised here I must point out: Even if such donations were given—and they might have been given to your party as well—this would be no reason to send the case to the public prosecutor.

In March 1967 the Bundestag, on a motion of the FDP, decided to form an investigating committee to clarify the facts of the purchase of the infantry tank HS-30 according to the wishes of public opinion. Deputy Moersch stated on the floor: "The Bundestag has good reason to make it unmistakably clear that there is no overt or implied *quid pro quo* relationship between the awarding of government contracts and contributions to party funds."

CHAPTER NINE

The United States

40. The Alarming Proportion of Venal Voters in Connecticut

J. J. McCook

I am a voter and am interested in political questions. But I have never taken an active part in politics and have never held any civil office. My interest in the subject of venal voting is therefore less political than social. It is such an interest as any person might feel who loves his country, respects himself and his fellow man, and stops occasionally to think.

Moreover, such interest as I have is of recent date. The history of its birth is on this wise: In the fall of 1890 I was chosen, by Hartford town meeting, chairman of a committee on out-door alms, and it became my duty to study with considerable care the whole pauper question. This brought into view the tramp problem; and last summer the "Quill Club," of New York, asked me to write a paper for them on that theme. Thereupon I set to work to inform myself concerning the habits of these curious folk, and sent out blocks of question blanks to mayors of various cities, requesting attention to them from proper officers. These blanks included the inquiry, "When and where did you last vote?" Thirteen hundred and forty-nine of the blanks were returned filled, from fourteen different cities or institutions.

In most instances the information was gathered by the chief of police or his delegate, in all cases through direct questions to the tramp; and it has been assumed by me, in weighing the answers, that they were reliable, with but few exceptions, at least whenever the evidence was unfavorable to the witness. Of the one thousand and eighty-six who replied to the question on voting, five hundred and three had voted—one hundred and fifteen within a year; one hundred and fifty-two, one year ago; seventy, two years ago; fifty-eight, three years ago; twenty-three, four years ago; eighty-five, over four years ago. Many had spread themselves politically over several States. One at Worcester had voted in California within the year.

On reading these records, the question naturally arose, How would such persons vote? There are dark whisperings, with not a little newspaper talk, about corruption. Can there be something in it, after all? That there might be was more than hinted at by certain facts which had come to me incidentally not long before in the committee work already alluded to. It had been ascertained that the doors of the Hartford Almshouse were thrown wide open early in the morning of every election day, and that the inmates returned in the evening quite uniformly intoxicated, a mystery the mysteriousness of which was not diminished by the facts that such inmates were supposed to be impecunious and that drinking-places were all closed by the law on election days. Furthermore, from

SOURCE: J. J. McCook. "The Alarming Proportion of Venal Voters," *The Forum*, 14 (September 1892), pp. 1–13.

November 1, 1882, to January 19, 1891, an average of one hundred and thirty-seven persons was found to have been convicted before the police court twice or oftener; forty-nine, three times or oftener; fifteen, four times or oftener. And since each conviction was found to represent an average of three and nine-tenths arrests, these one hundred and thirty-seven were under arrest at least eight times apiece; while forty-nine of them must have been behind bars twelve times and fifteen about sixteen times.

Careful examination showed that the greater number of these persons appeared before the police court and in jail year after year until the usual processes of vagrancy, or death, removed them from the community. The history of some was traced back for twenty years. Many of them have repeated this last year the history of their previous life. Ninety-four of the one hundred and thirty-seven had averaged one hundred and sixty-one days in jail during the twelve months. Most of these were drunkards; all of the ninety-four were. And what kind of voters would such persons be? For most of them were also men and could vote. To any one who has had any intimate knowledge of drunkards the answer could not be doubtful. The average drunkard, however well educated and under whatever bonds from ancestry and station to behave like a decent man, when once he is possessed by the impulse to drink will sell anything he has to gratify it. Neither honor, nor pride, nor any other consideration counts. These men, chiefly without the restraints of respectable surroundings, the old vestiges of self-respect long since worn away by long familiarity with station-house and jail—how would they probably act in the presence of the three influences: chronic penury, consuming thirst, and proffered money? I have since learned, and I shall presently state, how a majority of them act.

These facts and the conclusions toward which they kept pointing induced me to lead the conversation toward the question of venality while in the company of a few friends known to be, or to have been, actively engaged in what is called politics. Their statements were specific, and they were good enough to permit me to make them public. This was done May 10 of the present year, on invitation of the Board of Trade of Hartford, at a largely attended meeting called for the purpose. The address at that time made was extensively clipped and commentated. Absolute exactness was sometimes sacrificed to brevity; the more striking facts were occasionally printed without giving all the limitations; here and there an unusually boyish scribe attempted to make merry and indulged in flippancy. Generally, however, the press was respectful as well as interested. And if it was often incredulous and demanded more proof, that was scarcely to be wondered at. People in Connecticut who knew most about the situation criticised chiefly the moderation of my estimates. But it was not a matter of surprise that strangers should have been skeptical as to the alleged prevalence of venality in a State with the history and the advantages, educational and other, of this. That from seventeen thousand to twenty-five thousand of our one hundred and sixty-six thousand voters were liable to be bought and sold at every election was hard to believe.

Nevertheless, it is true, or, if incorrect, it is rather below than beyond the mark. And this I hope to show, though I shall here again be debarred, from the very nature of the case, from giving names of persons or places. I will only state that my informants, who are almost equally from the two greater parties, are gentlemen who are considered by myself and by those who know them qualified in a very eminent degree to testify. They include professional and business men of excellent position in the community, and, so far as I know, of exemplary lives; they exclude under-strappers and go-betweens. They include no man who has enriched himself in politics by illegitimate means, to my knowledge. They are, however, men who have pulled the wires. In a word, they were neither the spies nor the private soldiers of the army. They were colonels, generals, officers of the general staff, paymasters, and the like. They knew what was done—they did it through others. As to general credibility, my statements must be taken like those of any witness. If the circumstantiality and detail of the allegations made do not carry conviction, there is nothing more to be done.

As I write I have before me four tables. Two of these were prepared from books which have been actually used in campaigns by town committeemen, and which bear all their original marks, together with others which have since been added by them for my present uses. These books too are before me. The third table is prepared from a check-list marked by me at the dictation of a committeeman. This list is also before me. The fourth is made up out of materials supplied from memory by an active politician. He vouches for its approximate accuracy, and I believe him. I do not, however, attach the importance to it which the other three receive, because I distrust memory and impressions. I believe in, and for the purposes of this paper have taken only formal cognizance of, particular statements treating of voters man by man, noted in black and white opposite each name, and reduced to tabular form by myself, with the employment of all possible means for detecting and correcting error. In two of the tables which will be given I feel as great confidence as in any that I have personal knowledge of. And I should be glad to believe that statistical statements are always as accurate as I think the third to be. Necessarily only percentages can be given.

One remark should be made here which applies equally to all the tables. Attention is given to the proportion of the venal: first, according to origin; secondly, to habit; thirdly, to police record. Thus in Rural Town I [Table 40.1], column 1 shows that seven and five-tenths out of every hundred, or seventy-five out

TABLE 40.1
RURAL TOWN I

Origin	Total Venal of Each Stock	Percentage of all Venal	Temperate	Intemperate	Drunkards	Total Intemperate and Drunkards	Shiftless	Arrested or Imprisoned
American stock	7.5	59.8	1.69	[1]70.0	[2]100.0	80.0	[3]100.0	100.0
English born	0.0	0.0	0.0	0.0	0.0	0.0	0.0	0.0
English, second generation	0.0	0.0	0.0	0.0	0.0	0.0	0.0	0.0
German born	11.8	5.5	6.25	100.0	0.0	100.0	0.0	0.0
German, second generation	33.3	5.5	11.1	100.0	0.0	100.0	100.0	0.0
Irish born	11.1	5.5	5.9	100.0	0.0	100.0	0.0	0.0
Irish, second generation	29.3	23.7	6.8	100.0	100.0	100.0	100.0	100.0
Scotch born	0.0	0.0	0.0	0.0	0.0	0.0	0.0	0.0
Scotch, second generation	0.0	0.0	0.0	0.0	0.0	0.0	0.0	0.0
Other foreign born	0.0	0.0	0.0	0.0	0.0	0.0	0.0	0.0
Other foreign, second generation	0.0	0.0	0.0	0.0	0.0	0.0	0.0	0.0
Totals	9.8	100.0	2.5	75.5	100.0	85.4	100.0	100.0

[1] Four are also shiftless. [2] One is also shiftless. [3] One is an idiot.

of every thousand, of the voters of American stock in this town are venal; column 2, that five hundred and ninety-eight out of every thousand of the venal are Americans; column 3, that seventeen out of the thousand temperate Americans are venal; column 4, that seven hundred in a thousand intemperate Americans are venal; column 5, that every American drunkard—and there are ten of them here—is venal; column 6, that eight hundred out of one thousand intemperate and drunkard Americans are venal; column 7, that all the shiftless Americans in the town are venal; column 8, that all the Americans who have been under arrest or imprisonment are venal. By American stock is meant those whose parents were born here. By "second-generation English" is meant those whose parents were born in England. Finally, by venal is meant any person who accepts or is known to have accepted money or other valuable consideration either to "turn out for his own side" or to vote for the other.

The prominence here given to race and habit should perhaps be also explained. From the first, and from every quarter, came the testimony that in the country the venal were largely of American, in the city of foreign origin; and that whereas persons of Irish extraction headed the list among foreigners, Irish of the second generation considerably surpassed those of the first in venality. Would the actual facts support this theory? In this case they do.

It was constantly affirmed that intemperance figured very largely in the annals of vote-buying. Now, I am not a total abstainer either theoretically or practically, and I have always voted in favor of license. It is needless to say that I do not belong to the Prohibition party. But anybody who can see must know that, considered merely as a question of social economy, of dollars and cents, of tax-bills and public convenience generally, the "drink question" is the question of the day. The tariff wrangle is a mere baby to it. If intelligent, steady-going people could be induced to spend upon the drink question a fraction of the time and money they employ upon the other, we might hope for some real improvement in its treatment. Prominence is given, therefore, to the temperance and intemperance in venality simply because the subject cannot be treated at all without giving that prominence. The table speaks positively as to the prevalence of intemperance among the venal. Negatively, or conversely, it may be stated that out of the whole population of the town there are, or rather were, but seven intemperate persons who were not purchaseable and not a single drunkard or shiftless person.

Next in order is a second rural town in a different county, and with quite different conditions as to soil, manner of life, etc. [Table 40.2]:

In this town twenty-one out of every hundred voters, nearly, or more than one in five, are venal, or "commercial" as they are sometimes called. Nearly four in five are "straight goods," to employ another term in use there. Of "American" voters 21 per cent are venal; Irish of the first and second generations maintain their relative position as above, though in far less striking proportions; but they are considerably outnumbered by French Canadians; and in the proportion of venal to non-venal of their own blood, these latter and also the Germans go far ahead of them. There is but 16.3 per cent of foreign population in this town. The make-up of the native population is pictured by the fact that ten family names represent more than a hundred voters—one of them not far from thirty. And it was to me a very impressive object-lesson to note how my informant sailed through that last family. Now and then he hesitated for a moment as Christian names repeated themselves. But in an instant he recovered himself as a second initial or some hint from neighborhood

TABLE 40.2
RURAL TOWN II

Origin	Total Venal of Each Stock	Percentage of Venal	Temperate	Total Abstainers	Total Temperate and Total Abstainers	Intemperate	Drunkards	Total Intemperate and Drunkards	Shiftless	Arrested or Imprisoned
American stock	21.0	84.5	12.0	0.0	11.5	65.5	100.0	66.1	100.0	100.0
Colored	100.0	1.0	0.0	0.0	0.0	100.0	0.0	100.0	0.0	0.0
English born	7.7	2.1	0.0	0.0	0.0	66.6	0.0	66.6	0.0	0.0
English, second generation	14.3	1.0	14.3	0.0	14.3	0.0	0.0	0.0	0.0	0.0
French Canadian born	100.0	3.2	100.0	0.0	100.0	100.0	0.0	100.0	0.0	0.0
French Canadian, second generation	66.6	2.1	66.6	0.0	66.6	0.0	0.0	0.0	0.0	0.0
German born	33.3	1.0	50.0	0.0	50.0	0.0	0.0	0.0	0.0	0.0
German, second generation	0.0	0.0	0.0	0.0	0.0	0.0	0.0	0.0	0.0	0.0
Irish born	14.3	1.0	25.0	0.0	25.0	0.0	0.0	0.0	0.0	0.0
Irish, second generation	27.3	3.1	12.5	0.0	12.5	66.6	0.0	66.6	0.0	0.0
Nova Scotian born	0.0	0.0	0.0	0.0	0.0	0.0	0.0	0.0	0.0	0.0
Nova Scotian, second generation	0.0	0.0	0.0	0.0	0.0	0.0	0.0	0.0	0.0	0.0
Scotch born	0.0	0.0	0.0	0.0	0.0	0.0	0.0	0.0	0.0	0.0
Scotch, second generation	100.0	1.0	100.0	0.0	100.0	0.0	0.0	0.0	0.0	0.0
Swede born	0.0	0.0	0.0	0.0	0.0	0.0	0.0	0.0	0.0	0.0
Swede, second generation	0.0	0.0	0.0	0.0	0.0	0.0	0.0	0.0	0.0	0.0
Totals	20.9	100.0	12.2	0.0	12.0	63.4	100.0	63.9	100.0	100.0

or relationship gave him the cue, and went swimmingly on to the end. He could made a census of that town at his desk at home. And not at all behind him, considering the greater populousness of his town, had been the other rural politician.

This town is somewhat unusually sober and orderly. But the nearest approach to the village drunkard is venal. Two-thirds of the intemperate and drunkard Americans, Irish of second generation, and English, and all of the colored and of the French Canadian intemperate are venal; and sixty-four out of every one hundred of this whole class are venal. The only "shiftless" voters are Americans: and they, together with the few arrested or imprisoned, are all venal.

The next table [Table 40.3] exhibits the condition of a single ward in one of our Connecticut cities:

This table is composite, the materials being drawn from three sources, not all of one party, and, party-wise, without consultation or conference. There were in consequence such uncertainties as are sure to arise from different standards as well as diverse minds. This appeared most of all in the matter of drinking-habits and that of origin. A reasonable degree of uniformity was secured as to the first by steady explanation of and insistence upon my own interpretation of the terms, which was that temperate means a man who drinks, if at all, only with strict moderation, being never known to get drunk; intemperate a steady drinker who now and then becomes the worse for liquor,

TABLE 40.3
CITY WARD I

Origin	Total Venal of Each Stock	Percentage of all Venal	Temperate	Total Abstainers	Total Temperate and Total Abstainers	Intemperate	Drunkards	Total Intemperate and Drunkards	Arrested or Imprisoned
American stock	5.9	35.9	2.3	34.8	3.2	25.5	66.6	39.4	5.8
Colored	100.0	0.7	0.0	0.0	0.0	100.0	0.0	100.0	100.0
English born	0.0	0.0	0.0	0.0	0.0	0.0	0.0	0.0	0.0
English, second generation	0.0	0.0	0.0	0.0	0.0	0.0	0.0	0.0	0.0
French born	0.0	0.0	0.0	0.0	0.0	0.0	0.0	0.0	0.0
French, second generation	0.0	0.0	0.0	0.0	0.0	0.0	0.0	0.0	0.0
German born	13.6	7.7	8.0	0.0	8.0	45.5	50.0	46.2	100.0
German, second generation	8.6	3.2	2.0	100.0	40.0	33.3	50.0	37.6	100.0
Irish born	17.8	24.9	6.0	100.0	7.1	68.8	78.9	74.3	25.0
Irish, second generation	13.8	23.0	3.6	100.0	4.5	63.0	75.0	66.6	100.0
Italian born	0.0	0.0	0.0	0.0	0.0	0.0	0.0	0.0	0.0
Italian, second generation	0.0	0.0	0.0	0.0	0.0	0.0	0.0	0.0	0.0
Scotch born	6.6	0.7	7.1	0.0	6.6	0.0	0.0	0.0	0.0
Scotch, second generation	10.0	0.7	0.0	0.0	0.0	0.0	100.0	100.0	0.0
Other foreign born	33.3	1.3	50.0	0.0	40.0	0.0	0.0	0.0	0.0
Other foreign, second generation	0.0	0.0	0.0	0.0	0.0	0.0	0.0	0.0	0.0
Unknown	11.1	1.9	0.0	0.0	0.0	0.0	0.0	0.0	0.0
Totals	9.3	100.0	3.4	43.3	4.2	42.9	71.7	52.9	72.7

and is on the straight road to the next stage, that of drunkard—the man who is hopelessly in the toils and is often and publicly drunk. But for the other there was no remedy. And in so large a community bounded by artificial lines and including not a few persons on the constant move, it was not possible to secure that intimate knowledge of parentage on which alone certainty could be based. In fact, on two separate occasions one of my informants, while deviating but one from the tally of "Irish," made a difference of over fifty per cent in the score of Irish of the second generation; in one instance figuring them at less than half those of the first generation; in the other marking them as they have been left in the table, a trifle below these.

Whereas in the country towns the total of venals showed 59.8 and 84.5 per cent respectively Americans, in this city precinct only 35.9 per cent are of American stock. The percentage of intemperate, or drunken, Americans who are venal drops here from 80 and 66.1 per cent to 39.4, and of the arrested or imprisoned from 100 in both rural communities to 5.8—a tremendous fall. The proportion of venal among American intemperate and drunkard is in excess of that of Germans of the second generation, but falls behind that of Germans of the first and Irish of both generations. In studying this table it need only be added that the district is said to include one of the best and richest parts of the city and none or but little of the slums. This will account for the fact that the percentage of venality is but 9.3, while

TABLE 40.4
CITY WARD II[1]

Origin	Drunkards and Hard Drinkers	Every-day Drinkers but not Drunkards	Not Drinkers and not Shiftless	Total Drunkards and Every-day Drinkers
American stock	7.7	15.3		23.0
Irish born	11.5	7.7		19.2
Irish, second generation	17.2	11.5	9.7	28.7
German	1.9	3.8		5.7
Colored	6.1	7.7		13.8
Totals	44.4	46.0	9.7	90.4

1 The percentages represent the proportion the class bears to the proportion of all venals.

that of some of the other wards ranges as high as 26.5 and 32.3, and that of the whole town is 13.5.

The next table [Table 40.4], representing City Ward II, is a reduction to systematic form of a statement made by an experienced practical politician concerning the number and distribution of venal voters in his ward. This, too, is a ward in a city. The statement was limited to the total of the venal according to origin. The data were therefore lacking for the other percentages. It must be remembered, consequently, that the figures represent the proportion between each class and the total of all venal, whereas in the other tables the proportion is between the number of venal in each class and the total of voters in that class. This last has been preferred as being fairer, though the other is the more usual. It seems to me more just and useful to know, for example, what proportion of American, or English, or Irish voters are venal than to know what proportion they bear respectively either to the total of venal or to the total of voters; though these, too, have been given under columns 1 and 2 in previous tables.

The consolidated table [Table 40.5], which has been made up from the first three tables, fairly represents the State, I think, so far as the rural factor is concerned, but not so fairly on the city side; because the single ward here included has less than ten per cent of venal, while the city has nearly fourteen. Moreover, the status of some of the classes would be materially changed if the whole city were included. There were all but no colored, French, Italian, and Swede voters in these precincts. And it happened that the few colored were all venal, while none of the others were. Now, it is certain that the colored voters are by no means all venal[1] and that some of the stocks mentioned are. And this would appear if a larger area were covered. But as to the more prevalent national stocks, it is probable that the rank here established would not be far from the general truth, though the intervals would almost undoubtedly be much altered. The specialist in sociology and politics will probably study the details. But the general reader will be chiefly interested in the totals. From these it appears that out of several thousand voters, taken not far from equally from city and country, one hundred and thirteen out of every thousand were venal. And of these venal, five hundred and fifty-six in every (assumed) thousand were of American stock; one hundred and seventy-three Irish of the second generation, one hundred and

1 Probably not far from three-fourths of them in this city are. They have distinct political preferences, but these need to be confirmed or can on occasion be overcome by the use of money. This is fully comprehended by both parties.

TABLE 40.5
THREE DISTRICTS, TWO RURAL AND ONE CITY, CONSOLIDATED[1]

Origin	Total Venal of Each Stock	Percentage of Venal	Temperate	Total Abstainers[4]	Total Temperate and Abstainers[5]	Intemperate	Drunkards	Total Intemperate and Drunkards	Shiftless[4]	Arrested or Imprisoned
American stock	9.5	55.6	4.1	27.6	4.3	51.2	77.1	56.9	100.0	69.2
Colored[2]	100.0	0.6	0.0	0.0	0.0	100.0	0.0	100.0	0.0	100.0
English born	3.6	0.6	0.0	0.0	0.0	33.3	0.0	33.3	0.0	0.0
English, second generation	5.9	0.3	5.9	0.0	5.9	0.0	0.0	0.0	0.0	0.0
French born[2]	0.0	0.0	0.0	0.0	0.0	0.0	0.0	0.0	0.0	0.0
French, second generation[3]	0.0	0.0	0.0	0.0	0.0	0.0	0.0	0.0	0.0	0.0
French Canadian born[3]	100.0	0.9	100.0	0.0	100.0	100.0	0.0	100.0	0.0	0.0
French Canadian, second generation[3]	66.6	0.6	66.6	0.0	66.6	0.0	0.0	0.0	0.0	0.0
German born	13.6	5.3	8.3	0.0	6.4	50.0	50.0	50.0	0.0	100.0
German, second generation	12.7	2.8	3.4	100.0	5.0	50.0	50.0	50.0	100.0	100.0
Irish born	16.8	13.6	6.4	100.0	7.2	60.0	78.9	69.2	0.0	71.4
Irish, second generation	17.0	17.3	4.4	100.0	5.1	67.7	86.4	74.1	100.0	100.0
Italian born[3]	0.0	0.0	0.0	0.0	0.0	0.0	0.0	0.0	0.0	0.0
Italian, second generation[3]	0.0	0.0	0.0	0.0	0.0	0.0	0.0	0.0	0.0	0.0
Nova Scotian born[3]	0.0	0.0	0.0	0.0	0.0	0.0	0.0	0.0	0.0	0.0
Nova Scotian, second generation[3]	0.0	0.0	0.0	0.0	0.0	0.0	0.0	0.0	0.0	0.0
Scotch born	4.8	0.3	5.0	0.0	5.0	0.0	0.0	0.0	0.0	0.0
Scotch, second generation	18.2	0.6	10.0	0.0	10.0	0.0	100.0	100.0	0.0	0.0
Swede born[3]	0.0	0.0	0.0	0.0	0.0	0.0	0.0	0.0	0.0	0.0
Swede, second generation[3]	0.0	0.0	0.0	0.0	0.0	0.0	0.0	0.0	0.0	0.0
Other foreign born[2]	22.2	0.6	33.3	0.0	28.6	0.0	0.0	0.0	0.0	0.0
Other foreign, second generation	0.0	0.0	0.0	0.0	0.0	0.0	0.0	0.0	0.0	0.0
Unknown[2]	11.1	0.9	0.0	0.0	0.0	0.0	0.0	0.0	0.0	0.0
Totals	11.3	100.0	4.5	34.2	4.9	54.0	79.0	61.0	100.0	77.8

1 The percentages represent the proportion the class bears to the total of all venals.
2 Two districts.
3 One district.
4 Two districts.
5 Temperate from three districts; total abstainers from two.

thirty-six Irish born; twenty-eight Germans second generation, fifty-three German born; three are English second generation, six English born; six Scotch second generation, three Scotch born; six colored; six French Canadian second generation, nine French Canadian first generation; and six of other foreign birth. It further appears that out of every (assumed) thousand of intemperate voters, five hundred and forty were venal; in every thousand drunkards, seven hundred and ninety were venal; in every thousand shiftless, all were venal; in every thousand total abstainers, three hundred and forty-two were venal; while in every thousand temperate voters, forty-five only were venal. This latter is again a case where the actual numbers represented on the side of the total abstainers may be so small as to give misleading percentages. The final fact is, however, liable to no such correction. Out of every thousand voters known to have been arrested or imprisoned—chiefly for drunkenness and its attendant crimes—seven hundred and seventy-eight were venal.

In the Board of Trade address percentages of venality and ranges of prices were given for fourteen towns. I have since obtained seven more towns, covering fifteen polling-districts. The entire twenty-one will now be given; and in order to illustrate a point of curious interest, they will be separated into two categories according as they have lost or gained in population during the decade 1880–1890 (Table 40.6):

This seems to show that the decaying towns have more venality than the others, and also that the prices range higher. There are wards in every city and districts in every growing town where there is as much or nearly as much corruption as in any of the country towns. But in general I think it will be found that where the soil is poorest, money most rare, the conditions of life least favorable to enterprise and mental activity, there is more bribery—and this in spite of the fact that there is more drunkenness, though perhaps not more intemperance, in the city. Still, we are here, as everywhere, reminded that the offence is individual and follows the laws of all disease in respect to contact and infection. The average health of a city or town may be high, while that of particular neighborhoods in it is low.

That this theory is true of venality the following will show. In one of the above towns there is a precinct in which

TABLE 40.6
TWENTY-ONE TOWNS

Losing Towns	Percentage	Range of Prices	Gaining Towns	Percentage	Range of Prices
1	35.0 to 50.0	$2.00 to $15.00	2	35.0 to 50.0	$2.00 to $15.00
3	35.0 to 50.0	2.00 to 15.00	6	12.0	2.00 to 20.00
4	35.0 to 50.0	2.00 to 15.00	7	15.0	2.00 to 20.00
5	7.0	2.00 to 15.00	8	3.0	5.00 to 10.00
9	10.0	2.00 to 15.00	11	20.0	2.00 to 15.00
10	5.0	5.00 to 10.00	12	3.0	5.00 to 10.00
13	70.0	2.00 to 15.00	15	21.0	5.00 to 20.00
14	4.0	5.00 to 10.00	17	14.0	1.50 to 15.00
16	29.0	Not given.			
18	25.0	2.00 to 50.00			
19	28.0	2.00 to 15.00			
20	35.0 to 50.0	2.00 to 20.00			
21	17.0	2.00 to 15.00			
Venal average[1]	20.5	$2.00 to $50.00	Venal average	12.7	$1.50 to $20.00

[1] Venal average for all the twenty-one towns, 15.9 per cent.

the venal percentage is only fourteen and two-tenths, while in the other it is thirty and nine-tenths. In the first of these there are only three groups of father and son and four of two brothers, representing but thirty-six per cent of the purchaseable element there. In the second there were five groups of father and son, one of father and two sons, nine of two brothers, one of four brothers, four of nephew and uncle, representing thus sixty-five per cent of all the venal. In another town the percentage of venality to the whole number of voters in the different school district ranges as follows: 11.3; 9.1; 6; 2.7; 2.9; 0.6; 3.3; 15.7; 0; 19.2. By families there were eleven groups of two and three of three.

In one city precinct above tabulated there were twenty-one groups with identical family names and suggestion of relationship; of these there were known to be four groups of father and one son, three of father and two sons, four of two brothers, one of three brothers, one of uncle and one nephew, one of uncle and two nephews. In the same house, or within two doors on the same side of the street, were twenty-nine groups representing sixty-three per cent of the whole number of cases. I call them cases: the parallelism is so manifest. There were eighteen streets where there was not a single case; there was one where forty per cent of the voters were marked purchasable, and the informant remarked sententiously, "I can get about all of them on that street."

The disease may have been first introduced by the direct action of the briber.[2] But in its present stage it is propagated, I am convinced, chiefly by contact with the infected. It first appeared, within the memory of men well advanced in years, thirty to forty years ago. "Old A—, one of the village good-for-nothings," so related one informant, "had always been hired by old man B— to 'fix up' his place on election day; and it was understood as a matter of course that 'voting straight' was to be among the day's chores. This went on for a long while, till presently they began to extend the thing, and I remember well how mad C—, of our town, was when he first heard of it. He raged around at a great rate and refused to vote on account of it. Within four years you couldn't get him to vote without paying him." A city informant relates:

> There's one fellow who would have knocked you down, ten years ago, if you had approached him; and now he comes regularly for his pay. It seems only to be necessary to have it go out that "there is money in it this time," and the tribe of the venal swarm toward it like bees to a sugar-barrel. One tells another and the news spreads like wildfire. It is the same law and instinct which make the procuring of undeserved alms and pensions so catching and so dangerous. "The money is there; it is contributed by rich people who won't feel it or by candidates who will get it all back, and more, out of their offices, and I may as well have it as anybody.

This last table also establishes the percentage of the venal for twenty-one towns, including one city, at 15.9. Since the proportion between the city and the country population included is as nearly as may be that of the whole State,[3] it follows that we have here a basis for an estimate of the aggregate of venality in the entire State. If this be so, there are twenty-six thousand three hundred and ninety-four purchasable voters in Con-

---

2 A veteran in politics has related to me circumstantially the first instance in which it appeared, within his memory, as a disturbing element within the limits of his own party. It was about thirty years ago. The offender was at once betrayed, confronted with his treason, and reduced to a suitable state of contrition. The thing is now one of the most formidable dangers in party experience.

3 Out of a total of 746,258 in population, 370,703 are in cities of 10,000 and over. Connecticut "Register and Manual," 1891, pp. 454, 455.

necticut. I am in no position to affirm the absolute accuracy of this estimate, simply because my facts are only from one-eighth of the towns in three of the eight counties. But if analysis of samples taken without selection from the whole is ever conclusive concerning the entire mass, I see not why this may not be called a fairly reliable estimate. And surely twenty thousand would allow a sufficiently wide margin for possible error. . . .

41. The Purchase of Votes in New York City

JOHN GILMER SPEED

Such a large proportion of voters in every closely contested section of the United States is corrupt that enough votes can be bought at elections to decide which side will win. *Moreover, these purchases are made.* They are made brutally, frankly, as a merchant would buy any commodity, as a huckster would buy potatoes or cabbages. It may be said at once that it is useless to try to get pure Executives, pure lawmakers, and pure judges if the people who control the selection of these officials are themselves corrupt in such numbers that the purchasable element can decide between the great parties whenever there is money enough to secure their votes.

Listen to the story of New York. The city in all of its boroughs has a population of 3,850,000. At the last November election 652,116 votes in the aggregate were cast in the greater city for all the candidates for President. Mr. Parker had 27,645 more votes than Mr. Roosevelt, but he only had 1638 votes over all. I estimate, and I shall be at pains to explain my method of estimating presently, that there are in excess of 170,000 venal voters in the city of New York—men who expect to be paid in one form or another for their votes, chiefly in ready cash. Moreover, they *are* paid when either party has the money to buy. When both parties have full treasuries they are paid handsomely, and are warranted in considering that their election-day "earnings" are well worth looking after.

The importance of this immense venal vote will be better understood when it is recalled that McClellan, when running for Mayor the year before (1903), had only 63,696 votes in excess of Low, his opponent, and it was considered a great and signal victory, while Low in 1901, in his race against Shepard, had an excess of only 31,638, though he carried every borough, and there was a strong revolt in Tammany Hall against Deveryism and all it stood for. Any one can see that in the city of New York at least there are times when the offices can be bought by the party which has the most money, provided that money is put in the hands of men who know how to use it and will use it. This is a most important proviso, as will be seen as I go on with my narrative.

It is not often that Tammany buys an election in New York City, or that the Republican purchases carry the city, though the latter purchases may often do much towards determining the election in the whole State of New York. The whole truth of the matter is that the expense of carrying the city of New York and of holding it is so great that the Republican practical men do not really want it. To hold it would require

SOURCE: J. G. Speed, "The Purchase of Votes," *Harper's Weekly,* 49:1 (1905), pp. 386–387.

them to be as the "wicked" Tammany men are, and their best argument with the up-State voters would be lacking. What the Republicans want is the State. They are satisfied with that. But when we consider the phalanx of venal voters—170,000 strong—it is evident that the men who have the money, in alliance with those who know how to spend it, *can* control the city at any time and every time, except on the rare occasions when the really good people of all parties get together to protest against excesses. A plurality of 60,000 in New York is high; 100,000 would be considered a landslide. So the 170,000 can control when properly enlisted; and the enlistment being merely a matter of money, there is no reason to feel safe that it will not happen when the time arrives to make it worth while to any band of plunderers with sufficient capital to enter on the venture.

But before proceeding further I wish to disclaim any intention of saying that the majority of voters in the city of New York are venal, or that anything like a majority are actively corrupt. I believe, and my investigations justify me in this belief, that more than seventy per cent of them are not only honest themselves, but genuinely desirous of the honesty of those to whom official affairs are entrusted. The difficulty is that this seventy two or three per cent is divided between two parties, and most of them vote with the one party or the other, as the saying is, first, last and all the time. Here is where the manipulators of the venal voters get their chance to make their work effective. And they make it so effective that our civic body, infected in the source of its life, is corrupt all through, from the bottom upwards, from extremity to extremity.

In the course of my investigations in New York City I found no man who confessed to having bought a vote. That is not what they call it. "Convey," the jolly *Falstaff's* ancient *Pistol* said it was when discussing stealing. And so, also, these wise politicians do not buy votes, they simply employ the voters. They employ them for the day. There are 1550 election districts in the city of New York, and each district has two captains—one Democratic and the other Republican. There is not a captain of either party in any district in New York who has not a list of men employed by him, varying from eight—that is the lowest—to two hundred. The conventional price for the eight on each side, who may be considered regulars, is \$5 a day. That foots up to a very pretty sum total, as follows: $2 \times 8 \times 5 \times 1550 = \$124{,}000$. But these 24,800 men do not constitute the great body of the venal voters. They consider that they give valuable services outside of their votes, and they do give some, though not much, certainly, in those few districts where practically no votes can be bought. And there are a few such. But there are many districts where the great majority expect to be bought. These, it may be said, are generally in those crowded districts where the population lives in tenement-houses. They fall easy victims to the corrupters, and their settling in New York in great numbers has complicated the electoral problem very seriously. They are distressingly poor, and the offer of two, three, four, or five dollars on election day is a temptation too sore for them to withstand. When all of these aliens have become naturalized citizens and, as such, voters, the sections in which they live will be even a more attractive field for the politicians than it is now. Be it said to the credit of these wretched folk that a very great many of them were attracted by Mr. Roosevelt in the last campaign, and nothing could dissuade them from voting for him. But even such were not averse to taking money to vote the Republican ticket.

In getting my facts together I found that in a Republican district I could not get the Republican to tell what he had done, but he was not averse to telling what his Democratic opponent had done and exactly what that opponent's resources were. I also gathered facts here and there all over the various boroughs from men who know and upon whom I place dependence. Adding up the totals, after a careful study of these facts, I found that the venal vote, besides the workers, was 155,000. To these add the workers, and we have a grand total of 179,800. Some few of these workers really do work, so I take off about one-third, and leave the net total at 170,000.

Who are these people? And how much are they paid? They belong to various classes, and they are paid amounts differing according to the heat of the contest and the available amount to spend. As one very practical man remarked: "It goes like this: A dollar for a negro, a dollar and a half for a dago, and two dollars for an American." At the last election money was plentiful. I am told, and it is safe to say, that $300,000 was spent in addition to the $124,000 for workers, or a total of $424,000. If that much was distributed among the voters, it is quite safe to say that $150,000 more was given out to the leaders and captains, and "knocked down" by them. Adding this in, the grand total spent on election day by the two parties amounts to $574,000.[1] And I have not the shadow of a doubt that these estimates are within rather than without the truth; that they undertake, rather than overrate, the facts.

As I have said, the venal voters belong to all classes of what we might term the "unclassed"—that is, people who lack position and definite "stake" in the community. It is very unlikely that many property-owners sell their votes in the city, as they not infrequently do in the country. Nor do proprietors of any kind—not even proprietors of liquor-saloons. The latter are buyers rather than sellers. The captains, whether Democratic or Republican, were agreed as to one class. They said that nine negroes out of ten wanted money. There are no exact data as to how many negro voters there are in New York. I estimate them at 14,000. If we give them the benefit of the doubt, and only agree that eight out of ten are venal, then from this class alone we have 11,200 purchasable voters. In a Presidential year a negro is indisposed to vote against the Republicans, but he will take a bribe not to vote at all. I was told that one method of disfranchising a negro who wanted to seem to vote was to have him mutilate his ballot by cutting out the "eagle," the emblem of the Republican party. This would serve two purposes: his ballot would be defective and therefore thrown out, and the eagle, turned over to the Democratic captain, would serve as a voucher, showing that the voter had "delivered the goods." I do not believe this expedient was resorted to very generally in November, as there were only some 4000 defective ballots in all and from every cause. In years other than Presidential, the negro voters of New York, as a general thing, have no preferences. They band into associations, and their leaders try to sell them *en bloc*. When they do this the leaders usually make a neat sum, but whether their followers fulfil the contract or not it is very hard if not impossible to say.

Among the paid voters are the men who some thirty days before election are colonized in various lodging-houses. These are the very "scum of the earth," miserable wretches who are glad enough to get free lodging each autumn when the cold weather comes. This is an expensive form of corruption, as the lodg-

[1] There are 1550 polling-places in New York. These cost at each election, for registration and polling, the sum of $394,075. This sum is divided among 12,400 men and 1550 landlords, from whom the polling-places are hired. These election officers are all practical politicians, and each place is secured by political favor. So if we add this to the grand total of corruption fund and money "knocked down" we get a total of $968,975, which is divided up each election day among those in the employ of either party.

ing of each man will cost something like $5 for the thirty days, and each one needs to be tipped off from time to time. Besides, they need, each group of them, to be kept under surveillance, so that they will not stray or be stolen. There are thousands of such at each hotly contested election. Few of them are ever convicted.

The lodging-house keepers who are in this business keep many of the same names on their registers from year to year. This is a great convenience for the professional repeaters, who are considered very valuable by the practical election manipulators. This is a hazardous business, and the men who do it are generally professional criminals, who look upon a term in prison as a matter of course, and merely an incident of the day's work. They register under the names kept by the lodging-house keepers, and then, if still out of jail, vote under the names assumed. An active and experienced repeater may get in thirty votes in a day. Then, again, these adventuresome criminals do another kind of work. The election captains study these registration lists very carefully, and get what they call "a line" on all the voters. Some are too sick to come to the polls, some move away between registration and polling days. The captains think it would be a pity to lose these votes, so enough repeaters are brought in to cast the votes. They are coached as to the living-places of John Doe and Richard Roe, and it is rare that the "wary" election inspectors reject any such votes. These repeaters do not, I believe, go so far in New York as in Philadelphia, where, I am told, they vote whatever name happens to be on the list, so that it not infrequently happens that a man, even of note, will go to the polls towards midday and be blandly told that he has already voted.

The men who work along the river-fronts are said to be almost universally purchasable; the tenement-house dwellers to a very great extent; and the rowdies who belong to the "gangs" sell themselves as a matter of course. But the Assembly leaders and the district captains know their men thoroughly. They are not in politics just at election-time only, but they are in it every day of the year. That is how they live. The Assembly leaders on the Democratic side are all office-holders or do public work as contractors. Nearly all the district captains are also in public employ. So it is natural that they should each and every one keep in touch with the voters of the district, for carrying the district means keeping the job, losing the district means losing the job. These men know long before election day which of the voters they are to employ. It is not merely left to chance. It is no bargain-counter affair. It is all carefully arranged and carried out with as much exactness as is possible considering the curious character of the personal equation that enters into the transaction. These office-holding leaders are also said to be much more trustworthy in handling the corruption money than non-office-holders. The former feel it incumbent upon them to produce results, or, to use their own expression, "to make good." If they cannot "make good" they are likely to lose place and salary, besides that rich but indefinite graft which goes along with pretty nearly every public office in this part of the country. But the leaders and captains of the minority have no such strong incentives to be honest in the handling of their corruption money. Few of them have place, and the great majority of them will tell you with simple frankness that they are not in the thing "for their health." For what it brings, then, of course; and it brings to them just what they can safely "knock down" from their own "boodle" and what they can secure from the majority leaders for being inactive. The price of votes on election day is regulated by the amount of money in hand and by the activity of the fight. If the majority leaders tell the hungry inquirers, "There's nothin' doin'," it will readily be seen that the market price of votes depreciates considerably. So it is a good business transaction to pay the minority leaders for their inactivity, and, therefore, have to pay much less *per capita* for the men on their lists. The Republican, or, for that matter, the fusionist, politican will use exactly the same methods as Tammany men employ, and they do use them when they have the means and find it to their advantage.

I trust these facts will assist in finding a remedy for evils which often make popular government a corrupt tyranny. Bribe-giving to voters and bribe-taking by voters cannot now be successfully prosecuted, for lack of evidence. In the first place, the men are not bought, but are employed. This is a mere pretence, a subterfuge. This flimsy device, it seems to me, ought not to defeat successful prosecution. But there is a provision of law which at present effectually prevents anything being done. These transactions are not made in the open with witnesses looking on. On the contrary, they are as privately conducted as possible. It is man to man. Now the law provides that that the uncorroborated testimony of one party to such a corrupt transaction is incompetent. The difficulty is to get the evidence of men who would confess corroborated. Can such a law be changed? Probably it would be dangerous to change it. But we might get a hint from Mr. Jerome's bill, which enabled him to get such accumulations of evidence against the New York gamblers that many of them have voluntarily gone out of business.

There is, apart from the difficulties in doing it, an indisposition to convict men criminally for what politicians have been doing time out of mind. This suggests that we might study with profit the English "Corrupt Practices Act," which provides, I believe, that a civil suit can be brought by any number of citizens, and if the court decides that the election has been won by bribery, or that any considerable bribery has been practised, the successful candidate shall vacate his office, and be ineligible for the same office for a certain length of time. In the country, where every one knows every one else, the remedy for venal voting may be in an awakened and aroused public sentiment. This would scarcely be effective in the cities, because the better people do not know those who sell themselves. They cannot exert either influence or sentiment. But I firmly believe that much can be done in our public schools by teaching, year in and year out, the necessity for patriotism and civic righteousness. Then, again, we have the courses of people's lectures. Here is a chance to talk truths to those who rarely hear them on such a subject. The difficulty with this plan of education is that the public schools are just as much under political control as any of the other public departments. The school boards would probably not only discourage, but forbid, such courses of teaching. But I am not pessimistic, even though at the moment there hardly seems to be at hand a wholly satisfactory remedy. One old Tammany leader told me, with considerable concern, that he could not hold his children and grandchildren and keep them loyal to the machine. They thought they saw more congenial and cleaner associations elsewhere, and were better pleased to be independent of machine control. This old man was fearful that in his decline he was passing through evil days. This may not be very significant; but his lament emphasizes somewhat the very well known fact that the very great majority of our new and young voters last year were uninfluenced by party ties, and voted for the candidate whose manliness appealed to their own love of strength, and whose outspoken candor was in tune with the ambitions of their own energy and youth.

42. The City Boss: Game Politician or Gain Politician

ARNOLD A. ROGOW / H. D. LASSWELL

We so far have established support for the hypotheses that power-seeking in and of itself does not engender corruption and that sudden increases and decreases of power are not invariably attended by corruption. But it may be argued that the careers of Arthur, Van Buren, and Burr are unique in American politics and constitute unique exceptions to the Acton rule. Certainly in the popular imagination the images conjured up by "power tends to corrupt . . ." have been typically those of the major political bosses who dominated local governments in the late nineteenth and early twentieth centuries. Men like Blaine, Tweed, Penrose, and Wood have long served as conventional objects of the Acton aphorism employed as epithet. There can be no question that many of these politicians were ruthless power-seekers and proven corruptionists. Were they also exemplars of the Acton principle?

Analysis of the careers of thirty of these politicians suggests that, broadly speaking, there have been two conspicuous types of political boss in the United States and that neither type lends itself to the Acton generality.[1] The typologies which follow are composite creations based on representative figures—the identifying characteristics of each type are not wholly those of any one individual—and we shall here distinguish them by the terms *game politician* and *gain politician*.

Our first type of boss, the *game politician*, was of early American stock and upper-class background. His father was important in business circles in the community and active in civic affairs. A Puritan in morals and a conservative in politics, the father had a strong sense of family position, and he impressed upon

SOURCE: Arnold A. Rogow and Harold D. Lasswell, *Power, Corruption, and Rectitude.* Englewood Cliffs, N.J.: Prentice-Hall, 1963, pp. 44–55. © 1963. And reprinted by permission of Prentice-Hall, Inc.

[1] The political bosses selected for analysis were: Albert A. Ames, Martin Behrman, James G. Blaine, Edward Butler, Roscoe Conkling, George B. Cox, Richard Croker, James M. Curley, Israel W. Durham, William Flynn, Frank Hague, John Kelly, Martin Lomasney, Frederick Lundin, Christopher Lyman Magee, Hugh McLaughlin, James McManes, Charles F. Murphy, George W. Olvany, Boies Penrose, Thomas C. Platt, George Washington Plunkitt, Matthew S. Quay, Abraham Reuf, Roger C. Sullivan, Timothy Sullivan, Samuel J. Tilden, William M. Tweed, Edwin H. Vare, and Fernando Wood. The standard work on the municipal bosses is Harold Zink, *City Bosses in the United States* (Durham, N.C.: Duke University Press, 1930). A large number of the individuals mentioned have never received detailed biographical treatment. Of those biographies and other books that deal at length with individual bosses the following are especially important. For Blaine: T. C. Crawford, *James G. Blaine* (Philadelphia: Edgewood Co., 1893); Mary A. Dodge, *Biography of James G. Blaine* (Norwich, Conn.: Henry Bill Publishing Co., 1895); David S. Muzzey, *James G. Blaine, A Political Idol of Other Days* (New York: Dodd, Mead & Co., 1934); Charles E. Russell, *Blaine of Maine* (New York: Holt, Rinehart & Winston, Inc., 1931). For Conkling: Alfred R. Conkling, *Life and Letters of Roscoe Conkling* (New York: C. L. Webster & Co., 1884); George C. Gorham, *Roscoe Conkling Vindicated.* Reprinted from *New York Herald,* June 4, 1888. Croker: Alfred H. Lewis, *Richard Croker* (New York: Life Publishing Co., 1901); Theodore L. Stoddard, *Master of Manhattan, The Life of Richard Croker* (New York:

his son at an early age his own conviction that the best traditions of America, which the family represented, were being engulfed by a rising tide of immigration and radicalism. The father was also convinced that discipline produced moral virtue, and he was firm and unyielding in meting out punishment for youthful infractions. Since the home rules were rather strict, the boy was never certain when he was called to his father's study whether his father was to administer a sermon, a scolding, or both.

Timid, frail, and ill a good part of the time, the boy's mother played a relatively minor role in his life. Although she loved the boy (who was an only child) and longed to comfort him after an especially painful session in the study, she rarely interfered, knowing that any intercession from her was apt to increase her husband's wrath rather than reduce it. She was not passive by nature, but her role as wife had always been passive in accordance with her husband's wishes. There were few expressions of affection in the family circle, and the boy's mother, espeically in her later years, became increasingly occupied with an intensely personal type of religion. It is probable that her various illnesses served as expressions of acute inner distress.

Looking back from a later vantage point, the *game politician* could not remember a time as a boy when he had been happy, and he often remarked that his life had really begun when he left home for college. He was a student leader and led an active campus life at college; he also earned sufficiently good grades to be admitted to an eminent law school. Following graduation he became attached to a well-known law firm in his home city, but the practice of law was never his foremost interest. His legal work brought him into close contact with local politicians, and within a short time he was one of them.

By the time he was thirty the *game politician* had held a variety of posts in the local government and majority party, and by the age of forty he was serving in the state legislature. During his middle years he was firmly in control of the state party organization with the power to appoint, or influence the appointment of, mayors, governors, United States senators, and other public officials; frequently he himself held one or the other of these offices. At the national level he was influential in nominating the presidential candidates of his party, and he was active, on occasion, in promoting his own chances. Frequent charges of corruption and the occasional success of reform movements threatened his career only intermittently. For most of his forty years of active political life he exercised effective control or was "the power behind the scenes."

In the course of after-dinner speeches at political banquets he was apt to make reference to "the great game of politics," and for him this expression was no more cliché. A man of independent means, he did not exploit politics primarily, if at all, for personal gain,

Longmans, Green & Co., Inc., 1949). For Curley: Wendell D. Howie, *The Reign of James the First* (Cambridge: Warren Publications, Inc., 1936); Joseph F. Dinneen, *The Purple Shamrock* (New York: W. W. Norton & Company, Inc., 1949). For Hague: Dayton McKean, *The Boss: The Hague Machine in Action* (Boston: Houghton Mifflin Company, 1940). For Penrose: Robert D. Bowden, *Boies Penrose: Symbol of An Era* (Philadelphia: Chilton Company, 1937). For Platt: his *Autobiography* (New York: McBride Books, 1910); Harold F. Gosnell, *Boss Platt and His New York Machine* (Chicago: University of Chicago Press, 1924). For Plunkitt: William L. Riordan, *Plunkitt of Tammany Hall* (New York: Alfred A. Knopf, Inc., 1948). For Reuf: Walton Bean, *Boss Reuf's San Francisco* (Berkeley: University of California Press, 1952). For Tilden: John Bigelow, *The Life of Samuel J. Tilden* (New York: Harper & Row, Publishers, 1893). For Tweed: Denis T. Lynch, *"Boss" Tweed, The Story of a Grim Generation* (New York: Liveright Publishing Corporation, 1927). For Wood: Samuel A. Pleasants, *Fernando Wood of New York* (New York: Columbia University Press, 1948). Timothy Sullivan and Tweed, among others, enjoy some prominence in Gustavus Myers, *The History of Tammany Hall* (New York: Liveright Publishing Corporation, 1917). Blaine receives extensive treatment in Matthew Josephson, *The Politicos* (New York: Harcourt, Brace & World, Inc., 1938).

although he was privy to innumerable "deals" which involved the buying and selling of political favors. He regarded the uses and abuses of money in politics as legitimate, and he was always willing to arrange matters, if at all possible, to promote the financial interests of friends.

For the *game politician* politics functioned as the principal mode of self-expression and self-realization. He enjoyed "the game" for the ego rewards it offered, which were chiefly power, prestige, adulation, and a sense of importance. The manipulation of men and events, in which he excelled, served less his convictions, which were few, than as an exercise in strategy, which he valued for its own sake. Viewing the outcome as always more important than the issue, he derived great satisfaction from political victories of large and small consequence, no matter how obtained.

It was often said of our *game politician* that "he had many acquaintances and few friends." In reality he had many associates—most of them political dependents—few acquaintances, and no friends. He permitted himself a number of physical pleasures, respectable or otherwise, and on these occasions several cronies were usually to be found in his company. But his confidences in them were confined to political topics, and his association with them was based on a reciprocal exchange of various services. His relations with his immediate family were not close; indeed his wife and children saw less of him during his active life than certain key individuals in his political organization. As a result he is remembered less by his family than by the state which he dominated for so many years. His grave in the family plot is unattended, but his statue stands in front of the state capitol building.

Between 1870 and 1920 the *game politician*—to whom we shall return shortly—shared the national stage with another type of political boss, whom we shall here style the *gain politician*. Unlike his confrere in politics the second composite figure was the eldest of six children of an impoverished Irish immigrant family. The boy's father, an amiable if ineffectual man, was a bricklayer, but his earnings were too meager to support the family. The boy left school and worked at a variety of low-paid industrial jobs even before his father's death; after his death, which occurred when the boy was twelve years of age, the full burden of the family fell on the boy and his mother.

The mother lavished on the family all the love and attention of which she was capable, and the boy was her special favorite. Long after the other children were in bed, she and the boy would sit at the kitchen table discussing family affairs and exchanging gossip of the neighborhood. She occasionally would reminisce about the Ireland of her youth, and she often expressed a desire to make a stylish return someday to the Irish village in which she had lived as a young girl (she was later to realize this dream several times over). The boy confided his own ambitions and plans, and it became his practice over the years never to make any important decision without consulting her.

He meanwhile was fighting his way to power in the neighborhood gang. In the process he became quite skilled in fighting with fist or club, and he later was to put these methods to practical use in the rough-and-tumble ward politics of his day. The gang specialized in disrupting the political rallies of the minority party in the area, and it eventually became the nucleus of his own political machine. His good looks, stature, and powerful physique—as a young man he was able to lift a barrel of beer to shoulder height—endowed him with a certain physical magnetism which was of benefit throughout his career.

While still an adolescent he was entrusted with various missions by the long-time political boss in his section of the city. He and the boss became rather friendly, and eventually, on his own authority, he was able to distribute minor political favors and small amounts of patronage. In a few years he had created a machine within a machine, and he was then capable of dealing with rivals for the boss's favor from a position of strength. When the boss died, he moved quickly to consolidate his power, and within a short period he established himself as the head of the organization.

By this time he was approaching thirty years of age and had married. He had long since learned to turn political favors to his own financial interest; and with the proceeds derived from politics he had become the owner of one retail store and part-owner of several others. He also invested in various services which the city government patronized, the operations of which he could influence in his own favor. Meanwhile his political advancement was rapid, although it was confined to local party posts and municipal offices. He served as councilman, city treasurer, and mayor, and for many years was especially popular in the role of the latter. As city treasurer he was able to extend his power in the party, and long before he was mayor, he had become the most powerful political boss in the city's history.

He had also become one of the wealthiest. His opponents believed—and correctly—that in the city no contract was let, no tax collected, no post filled, and no facility established without his extracting a commission. It was revealed after his death that he was worth considerably more than one million dollars and that he had lived in lavish circumstances for a number of years. While his children were still young, he moved his family to a large mansion in the most fashionable part of town, and he also established his mother in a comfortable home, which was staffed by several servants. All seven children, with the exception of one daughter, who became a nun, attended expensive colleges. It was his wife's custom, on shopping trips, to be accompanied by her liveried personal chauffeur.

The *gain politician,* unlike the first type of political boss we have considered, had only a minor interest in state and national politics. He twice declined to be nominated for any higher office than mayor, and while he insisted upon being consulted, especially with regard to patronage, by governors and senators, he was primarily concerned to maintain good relations with "higher-ups." He was consistently opposed to, as he put it, "rocking the boat," and he dealt wrathfully with occasional mavericks, bolters, and would-be reformers within the party. Placing enormous importance on loyalty to the organization, he prided himself on the fact that he had never deserted a party stalwart, no matter what his personal or political difficulties.

Although the *gain politician* was firmly attached to few principles, he thought of himself as a "friend of the people," and indeed in a sense he was. He put innumerable relatives and friends on the city payroll and befriended countless others with gifts or loans of money. Widows, orphans, derelicts, the sick, the unemployed, the aged, the struggling, and the fallen—all of them received a hearing from him or his lieutenants and almost all of them received some tangible help. He donated large amounts of money to churches and synagogues, schools, hospitals, and orphanages and found time to sit at sickbeds and attend funerals. Radiating warmth, fellowship, and generosity, he earned a citywide personal following that was sufficiently large and loyal to maintain him in power through several damaging investigations of his political machine.

His marriage was a happy one, and no breath of domestic scandal touched him during his entire career. He derived much satisfaction from the achievements of his children, almost all of whom were successfully established in a business or profession at the time of his death. He also had a number of close personal friends, in whom he was in the habit of confiding his innermost thoughts. Several of these friends have written eulogistic biographies of his life; others have named their children after him. And for many citizens in the city he remains, many years after his death, a vital, almost living figure.

It is common to treat the *game politician* and *gain politician* not as cousins and not even as brothers in corruption, but as identical twins. The case histories, however, suggest that the term "corrupt boss" covers a multitude of sinners whose relations to each other are limited to a common involvement in political *flagrante delicto.* The fact of corruption may constitute only the weakest link between personality types as distinct from political careers. Moreover in the cases examined here, of which the *game* and *gain* politicians serve as archetypes, the variety of motivations is as diverse as the variety of acts.

Although psychological detail in the relevant biographical materials is, on the whole, sparse, the available data indicate that severe deprivation in early life is a key factor in the background of the corrupt boss. But it is the character of the deprivation, rather than deprivation as such, which is crucial for future behavior. Our *game politician,* for example, was deprived of love and emotional security during his formative years. It is clear that the cold and withdrawn personality of his later years was essentially developed in childhood as a protective response to a punitive environment. His inability as an adult to initiate and sustain close relations with family or friends is another derivative of the early period.

But a hostile environment may be made friendly and safe through manipulation, and we may infer that manipulative skills of various types were brought into play during the frequent sessions in the father's study. The study "game"—his boast in later life was that he was often able to "get around" his father on such occasions—was the early form of the political "game," and the deviousness, evasiveness, and capacity for intrigue of the mature politician also described the behavior pattern of the boy. In other essentials of personality development, however, the boy did not succeed in "getting around" his father. His repressed hatred of his father generated in adult life an hostility to others which created unnecessary difficulties in his political relationships. It is also true that his convictions were dominated by the rigid and outmoded conservative views with which he had been indoctrinated as a child. Although he was careful to avoid taking positions, he was generally understood to favor principles rather similar to those which had been espoused by his father. His arrogance and superciliousness, which were also qualities shared with his father, were added handicaps to his ambition for political preferment beyond the state level.

Unlike his father, however, the *game politician* was never attached to moral virtue, family honor, or a conscious, if misdirected, sense of tradition. His principal attachment was to the political "game" as such, to which all other considerations related as mere expedients. Self-realization and political realization were simple equivalents; indeed the personality system did not function well outside the political arena. But the stakes of the "game" were not confined to power as such. The demands of the self upon the environment largely related to deference values, and as Table 42.1 indicates, the "game" indulged a number of demands which had been blocked or frustrated elsewhere.

TABLE 42.1
PERSONALITY SYSTEM

Deprivation	Demand	Indulgence
Parental acceptance	Power	Office, bossism
Parental recognition	Respect	Votes, elections
Parental approval	Rectitude	Self-righteousness, moral superiority
Parental love	Affection	Following, clique, cronies

The major point, however, is that politics afforded our *game politician* a control of environment which facilitated the indulgence of demands. Relative to other arenas (home, business, profession) the political world was more indulgent of demands of the self upon the environment, and it also was capable of providing a greater variety of indulgences.

Viewed from this perspective, corruption was less an indulgence than a method by which the *game politician* maintained the necessary control of environment. While corruption served the end of power, power itself mainly functioned as the means of enforcing demands generated throughout the entire personality system. Put another way, power *and* corruption were the agencies by which the personality system sought to establish and support itself. The political man represented by the *game politician* was merely an older and more successful version of the emotionally deprived and rejected child.

For the *gain politician*, on the other hand, power and corruption were also disposition and warm manner than to coercive tactics. Although he consistently exploited politics for gain, it was a fact of his long career that he had won over many political enemies and never lost a friend.

The character of early deprivation largely related to the welfare values of well-being, wealth, skill, and enlightenment. But the demands of the self upon the environment, which were generated by such deprivation, were of a different order from those which developed in the personality system of the *game politician.* To begin with, the "self" was an aggregate rather than a single entity, a "we" rather than an "I." It initially included his mother, brothers, and sisters, and it later incorporated his wife and children. In a sense the collective self also embraced distant relatives, friends, and associates, because they too were beneficiaries of corrupt acts. In the second place, the demands of the self upon the environment were mainly confined to the wealth value; although other welfare values were important, the control

TABLE 42.2
PERSONALITY SYSTEM

Deprivation	Demand	Indulgence
Comfort	Well-being	"Rich" living
Income	Wealth	"Pay-offs," graft, "commissions"
Opportunity	Skill	"Deals," manipulations, promotions, combinations
Education	Enlightenment	"Inside" information, foreknowledge, "tips"

functional, but functional in a different context of demands. The early environment, except in its material aspect, was largely indulgent, and throughout his life he was supported by various emotionally satisfying relationships. His ambitions for office never extended beyond the local level, despite opportunities afforded to play a major role in state and national politics. Although he could be ruthless in dealing with opponents, his personal success owed much more to a genial payers of their money, he was careful to avoid cheating them of their self-esteem.

It is also important that the *gain politician* was less cynical than indifferent to rectitude standards. Such standards had been absent in his early political training, and youthful experience had favored the view that politics essentially was a variety or form of commercial enterprise. In the context of prevailing political morality he would have considered it foolish *not* to exploit politics for gain and irresponsible to retire poor from office.

But the significant fact is that the *gain politician* employed corruption not in behalf of power, but in behalf of welfare values. As Table 42.2 illustrates, the political arena was indulgent of demands of the self upon the environment which related to early deprivation. Again, as in the case of the *game politician,* power *and* corruption were directed toward specific ends which were generated in the personality system.

The analysis of composite "boss" types, therefore, does not support the Acton formula that "power tends to corrupt. . . ." The biographical test in general suggests, on the contrary, that corruption is a function of the relations among a number of variables in the per-

of environment largely was exploited for material advantage. Finally the demands which were indulged, unlike demands related to deference values, rarely involved or affected interpersonal relations. Our *gain politician* did not need to dominate others; nor did he require their psychological submission. Indeed his success as a corruptionist owed much to the fact that he was never arrogant in his relations with peers or subordinates. In cheating the business leaders and taxsonality system. The propositional form of such relations may be stated as follows:

1. Corruption may ensue when the early environment of the personality system promotes severe deprivation.
2. A background of severe deprivation may encourage the use of power in corrupt forms as a means of acquiring and maintaining environmental control.
3. The character of the early deprivation affects the purposes for which power is employed.
4. If the deprivation has been experienced mainly with reference to deference values, power in corrupt form will be employed in behalf of self-aggrandizement (*game politician*).
5. If the deprivation has been experienced mainly with reference to welfare values, power in corrupt form will be employed in behalf of material advantage (*gain politician*).
6. Power in and of itself neither expresses nor promotes any tendency, whether to corrupt or to ennoble.

These propositions, however, do not relate to the institutional settings in which power and corruption function and by which they may be affected. We now turn to this context to determine its relevance to the major problem.

43. Congressional Ethics and the Conflict of Interest Issue

ROBERT S. GETZ

The acceptance of the broker theory of representation has a direct bearing on the application of the disqualification rule of both Houses of Congress. As a broker among competing interests, the legislator occupies a middle ground between trustee and delegate. He is more a free agent than the delegate, but is expected to be more responsive to his constituents' wishes than the trustee. Furthermore, the biographical sketches of the members of Congress reveal considerable overlap in many cases between the major economic interests of a constituency and the personal economic interests of its representative or senator. The broad sweep of modern present-day legislation also makes it extremely difficult for a legislator to avoid voting on proposals that have a bearing on his own material well-being.

Professor Norton E. Long has pointed out that our society has come to expect a conflict of interests in the struggle to control or reap the fruits of Government. It is accepted that these interests be represented by officials, including legislators, who will seek to further them. What is not accepted is a conflict of interest, the situation which exists when officials use their position to further their personal interests. Unfortunately, the distinction between conflict of interests and a conflict of interest is often not clear. "Conflict of interest at one edge shades off into corruption and theft, at the other into the representation of interests."[1]

The ambiguity described by Professor Long, coupled with the broker theory, has made enforcement and rigid adherence to Rule VIII impractical. As previously noted, this rule requires a member to vote on all questions unless he has a direct personal or pecuniary interest in the matter.

In 1874, Speaker of the House James G. Blaine interpreted Rule VIII and set the pattern for future Congresses. The votes of three members were challenged on a bill to create a national currency and to establish free banking. The Speaker attempted to avoid the issue, but persistent moves from the floor forced his hand. In not sustaining the point of order, Blaine couched the question in terms of whether the House had the right to say to any member that he shall not vote on any question. If 147 members each owned one share of national bank stock, said Blaine, the House would, by strict application of the rule, be unable to legislate on the subject. He ruled that a member may vote on legislation that affects a class as distinct from an indi-

SOURCE: Robert S. Getz, *Congressional Ethics: The Conflict of Interest Issue*. Van Nostrand, 1966, pp. 57–63, 67. By permission of the publisher.

[1] Norton E. Long, Conflict of Interest: A Political Scientist's View, Paper delivered at ASPA Annual Meeting, Washington, D.C., 1962, p. 6.

vidual. Thus, a man could not vote in a case contesting his own seat; but, where his interest is not distinguishable from the interest of the class of people affected by the bill, a member may vote. Blaine concluded that any other interpretation would disqualify members from voting on a whole spate of legislative enactments.[2]

The number of issues which can clearly be shown to affect a distinct class or individuals is small. The most frequent invocation of Rule VIII is made by members of Congress who stand to benefit by increases in compensation voted to veterans suffering from service-incurred disabilities.[3]

The late Senator Robert S. Kerr (D, Okla.) very frankly discussed the disqualification rule and conflict of interest. On the National Broadcasting Company's radio-television program "Meet the Press," of August 19, 1962, Senator Kerr described the community of interest that members of Congress share with the people they represent. Citing himself as an example, he said that if he voted against the things that the people of Oklahoma depend upon, he would establish a conflict of interest that would eliminate him from the Congress.

Turning to the issue of voting and disqualification, the Senator stated that no man in Congress can avoid voting on things that, in one way or another, affect him because they affect his people. He stated that he represented the farmers of Oklahoma and the oil interests of his state. At the same time, Senator Kerr readily acknowledged his extensive farm and oil holdings. He was elected to represent these interests, Kerr claimed. He added: "They don't want to send a man here who has no community of interest with them, because he wouldn't be worth a nickel to them."[4]

When interviewed for an article in the *Saturday Evening Post,* the Oklahoma legislator was even more blunt. He said that the voters can judge for themselves and that a man's opponents were quick to bring up any conflict of interest. He capped his argument with the following remarks:

> Now wouldn't it be a hell of a thing if the senator from Oklahoma couldn't vote for the things Oklahomans are most interested in? If everyone abstained on the grounds of personal interest, I doubt if you could get a quorum in the United States Senate on any subject.[5]

The legislator's community of interest with his constituents, the broad sweep of legislation, the role of broker, and the complex backgrounds and varying financial holdings which the legislators bring to the Congress, all have operated to relegate Rule VIII to the category of admonitions that are "honored in the breach."

The role of broker, particularly in its second aspect of constituent–executive-branch relations, appears to negate the practicality of extending the uncompensated appearances and self-dealing sections of the conflict of interest statutes to cover members of Congress. The legislator is expected by his constituents to act as go-between in their relations with the executive branch. Of course, the constituents' expectations run the gamut from simple advice to active championing of their cases. The inclusion of members of Congress under the scope of section 205, which prohibited even uncompensated appearances in a matter in which the United States is a party, would require a sweeping revision of our currently accepted theory of representation.

2 U.S., *Congressional Record,* 43rd Cong., 1st Sess., pp. 3015–3021.

3 Representatives Williams, Bennett, and Potter have disqualified themselves on this question. See U.S., *Congressional Record,* 81st Cong., 1st Sess., pp. 10591–10592; 82d Cong., 1st Sess., p. 13746; 83rd Cong., 2d Sess., p. 11262.

4 Text quoted in *U.S. News and World Report,* September 3, 1962, p. 86.

5 Bagdikian and Oberdorfer, *Saturday Evening Post,* November 17, 1962, p. 26.

Section 208, which barred administration officials from acting in an official capacity on a matter in which the individual has a pecuniary interest, presents an even more interesting problem. The inclusion of legislators under this section strictly interpreted, would prohibit a representative or senator from rendering advice or making recommendations to a constituent concerning a quasi-judicial or quasi-legislative matter, if the legislator had some financial interest in the decision. If there were a community of interest between the constituent and the legislator, any substantial advisory role played by the latter could amount to a violation of the statute. Senator Kerr, by virtue of his personal holdings, would have been precluded from constituent problems centering on oil or farm issues.

Whereas the nature of the representative function has made impractical the inclusion of members of Congress under certain conflict of interest statutes, it does not excuse the abuse of congressional power in the individual legislator's dealings with the executive departments and agencies. This problem has frequently been considered under the subject of *ex parte* communications.

EX PARTE COMMUNICATIONS

Legislative intervention in the operations of the Federal executive has become increasingly complex, subtle, and detailed. Members of Congress are expected by their constituents to intercede on their behalf with Federal agencies. The motivations are innumerable, running the gamut from the transfer of a soldier son to a favorable decision from a regulatory commission. The legislator increasingly is burdened with the role of broker for the community in its individual and collective dealings with the Federal Government.

Intervention appears to be greater in programs involving loans, subsidies, contracts, franchises, or permits. The scope of administrative discretion characteristically is very broad, since the criteria for action in the public interest is often only vaguely outlined in the statutes. Economic decisions made by the Federal Government, in the view of Senator Paul H. Douglas, are not made on a lofty and abstract plane. They are produced in an atmosphere of pressure, influence, and favoritism.[6]

Many members of Congress would be relieved of an awkward and time-consuming burden if they were forbidden to intervene in matters before an agency which involved formal adjudication. "But almost all of them regard such intervention as an honorable and necessary part of their representative function."[7] The legislator and his constituents adhere to a concept of the officeholder's responsibility to serve his people which overrides the normal objections to the back-door approach.

Another facet of the broker concept is that it provides the Congressman with the opportunity to create an illusion of power. Many decisions would be made and actions taken without legislative intervention. However, the politician benefits by creating the impression in the mind of his constituent that he has materially affected the outcome of a proceeding.[8]

An example of congressional intervention came to light as the result of the 1963 Senate probe of the TFX contract award. At least 12 members of Congress had made *ex parte* contacts with Secretary of the Air Force Eugene M. Zuckert.[9]

6 Paul H. Douglas, *Ethics in Government* (Cambridge, Mass.: Harvard University Press, 1952), p. 33.

7 Marver H. Bernstein, "Conflicts of Interest in Federal Employment," paper delivered at the Annual Meeting of the American Political Science Association, Washington, D.C., September 10–12, 1959, p. 15.

8 Marver H. Bernstein, *The Job of the Federal Executive* (Washington, D.C.: Brookings, 1958), p. 101.

9 *New York Times*, August 7, 1963, p. 14 and August 8, 1963, p. 32. The Senate conducted closed hearings; therefore, accounts of the proceedings must be drawn from the newspapers. The list appeared in the August 8, 1963 issue. The men

An *ex parte* communication is an undisclosed, extra-mural contact, oral or written, to an agency or a department official, concerning the merits of any matter upon which the agency member is exercising a quasi-judicial function. The contact may be made by, or on behalf of, an interested party. It is *ex parte* because it fails to appear as part of the public record of the proceeding. The attitude of all the parties involved toward these off-the-record visits and letters sheds light upon the difficulties which attend any efforts to prohibit or minimize the effects of *ex parte* communications.

In his testimony before the Senate Investigations Subcommittee, Mr. Zuckert denied that the legislators had made any attempts to influence his decisions. He characterized their efforts as an expression of their interest "in seeing that this thing got proper consideration." The lawmakers in question all represented states and districts having a vested economic stake in the allocation of the TFX contract and subcontracts.

A unanimous denial of unethical activity echoed from the respective congressional offices. Speaking in reference to the Kansas delegation's visit, Senator Frank Carlson said that, as members of Congress from the state where the airplane would be built if Boeing Aircraft received the contract, "we were not only justified, we should do it." Senator Monroney (D, Okla.) had spoken to Mr. Zuckert on behalf of a potential subcontractor in an effort "to remind him of the vast government-owned plant in Tulsa, Oklahoma, which the Douglas Aircraft Company operates, and its large unused machinery and manpower capabilities."

involved were: Senators Frank Carlson (R) and James B. Pearson (R), and Rep. Garner E. Shriver (R), all of Kansas; Sen. Stuart Symington (D) and Rep. Clarence Cannon (D) of Missouri; Senators Robert S. Kerr (D) and A. S. Mike Monroney (D), and Rep. Carl Albert (D) of Oklahoma; Rep. Joseph M. Kilgore (D) of Texas; and Senators Henry M. Jackson (D) and Warren G. Magnuson (D) of Washington.

The 1959 hearings on an *ex parte* bill provided the opportunity to compare the views of two prominent Illinois senators, Paul H. Douglas (D) and Everett M. Dirksen (R). Douglas was asked if he thought there were occasions when a Congressman might properly and openly present a brief in behalf of his constituents. He replied: "Oh, yes, absolutely, where it is a question of the interests of the state as a whole or of a particular region in the state, it is quite proper for a Senator or Congressman to intervene."[10]

Senator Douglas' attempt to draw a distinction between activity on behalf of his state or a subdivision thereof, and intervention for the benefit of a particular person or business entity, was very vague at best. Does not the award of a contract to a specific corporation usually benefit the state or congressional district in which it conducts its operations? Using Senator Douglas' yardstick, few significant economic decisions of the executive branch would be beyond legitimate legislative intervention.

Dirksen took no pains to draw the distinction made by his colleague. He cited a 1959 remark by Trowbridge Vom Bauer, general counsel to the Department of the Navy, to which he took exception. Vom Bauer, a critic of congressional intrusion, had said that "even the most general inquiry by a congressman carries a great deal of weight anywhere."[11] Dirksen labeled this remark an inference that every communication from a member of Congress is an effort to exert influence.

In defense of his right to contact administrators, the Illinois Republican

10 U.S., Congress, Senate, Subcommittee on Administrative Practice and Procedure of the Committee on the Judiciary, *Hearings: Administrative Procedure Legislation,* 86th Cong., 1st Sess., 1959, p. 29. Hereafter referred to as *Hearings: Administrative Procedure Legislation.*

11 U.S., Congress, House, Special Subcommittee on Legislative Oversight of the Committee on Interstate and Foreign Commerce, *Hearings: Major Administrative Process Problems,* 86th Cong., 1st Sess., 1959, p. 722.

contended that ever since 1933 he had been calling every agency in the Government in the interest of his constituents. He added that he intended to do so whether or not the bill became law. Dirksen insisted that such action was necessary to prevent people from getting lost in our baffling, bewildering, and labyrinthine Government. He strongly opposed S. 2374 and similar measures because no court would have any difficulty in finding that the element of intent to influence was present in most *ex parte* contacts. He summed up his disapproval in the following terms:

> First, I do not want to go to jail; secondly, I can't afford to pay a $10,000 fine. More important I do not want to be all over the front pages because I did what I thought was my representative duty in looking after the affairs of 10 million people in the sovereign state of Illinois.[12]

Concluding his remarks, Dirksen raised an interesting point by saying that administrators wished to create a one-way street for contacts. Dirksen pointed to the occasions on which they had come to him to discuss legislation that their departments wanted. Yet, he noted, some of these same individuals supported recommendations which would deny Congressmen the same privilege.

Dirksen's rejoinder reflects the complexities involved in the *ex parte* communications problem. Most lawmakers have accepted these extra-mural contacts as part of their representative function, but few of them would endorse the naked application of pressure to influence administrative decisions. However, as Dirksen pointed out, any communication may contain the element of intent to influence. If this is so, how may an enforcing agency draw the line between a legitimate exercise of the representative function and an attempt to tamper with the adjudicatory process? This question plagues any efforts to enact *ex parte* statutes. . . .

CAMPAIGN CONTRIBUTIONS

While it is beyond the scope of this study to dwell at any length on the effect of campaign contributions on legislative behavior, it would be an error of omission not to mention this topic in connection with *ex parte* communications.

Alexander Heard, in *The Costs of Democracy,* has noted that one motivation for political contributions is the desire for governmental privileges or access. The impact of campaign contributions on government can be measured only by the intentions motivating them, the use made of the money, and "the nature of the *quid pro quo* if any!" There is no consensus on just how many donors want something; nevertheless, a tenuous nexus frequently exists between contributors and recipients. Professor Heard pointed out that politicians obtain financial support, like votes, because of the views they hold. "That their contributors agree with them ought to surprise no one."[13]

The term most often used by politicians and modern political scientists to describe the objectives of the large contributors is "access," meaning the opportunity to make one's case at crucial times and places. The need for access has been accentuated since the Depression. The growth of Federal regulatory power has forced various affected interests to seek representation at every relevant point within the Government.

An enforced *ex parte* rule would choke off one avenue of access and influence. Of course, this is not the only channel of influence. The effect of an

[12] *Hearings: Administrative Procedure Legislation,* p. 94.

[13] Alexander Heard, *The Costs of Democracy* (Chapel Hill, N.C.: The University of North Carolina Press, 1960), pp. 72–88.

ex parte rule on the flow of money into political campaigns is only a matter of speculation. However, Heard believes that a legislator often creates an illusion of power. Many decisions could be made and actions taken without legislative intervention, but the politician benefits from giving the impression that he has materially affected the outcome of a proceeding.[14] The acceptance of this view adds another reason for congressional reluctance to initiate *ex parte* reform.

14 Heard, pp. 91–92.

44. Group Politics and the Disclosure Idea

EDGAR LANE

Although it has taken many forms, the belief that disclosure statutes are and should be concerned with questions of "propriety" and "impropriety" has long had considerable appeal. For Carr and Bernstein, disclosure could help legislators to evaluate the "propriety of the pressures" that converge upon them, and presumably reject those found tainted with impropriety. For the Douglas Subcommittee in 1951, it was

> . . . like an antibiotic which can deal with ethical sicknesses in the field of public affairs. There was perhaps more general agreement upon this principle of disclosing full information to the public and upon its general effectiveness than upon any other proposal. It is hardly a sanction and certainly not a penalty. It avoids difficult conclusions as to what may be right or wrong. In that sense it is not even diagnostic; yet there is confidence that it will be helpful in dealing with many questionable or improper practices. It would sharpen men's own judgments of right and wrong if they knew these acts would be challenged.[1]

The general notion that disclosure can be helpful in dealing with "questionable or improper practices" has not often been asserted with such thoughtful diffidence. Sixty years earlier, Governor Russell of Massachusetts said of his state's pioneer disclosure law: "The fear of publicity, and through it of defeat, may stop improper practices by making them worse than useless."[2] Within the past few months, a California legislative committee has declared that the fundamental purpose of that state's law is "to protect the legislative process from being influenced by improper or unethical lobbying practices."[3] While each generation must redefine "improper practices" in its own terms, the belief that publicity can be a useful weapon against them remains one of the staple premises underlying the continuing enthusiasm for the disclosure idea.

The difficulty is that the ordinary operation of a disclosure law cannot realistically be expected to provide evidence of "impropriety," unless this is rather strictly defined as group activities or expenditures deemed excessive after the fact by electoral consensus registered against candidates or proposals publicly associated with them, and this test would be exceedingly difficult to apply to most situations. To assume that disclosure requirements can serve as instruments of

1 U.S. Congress, Senate, Committee on Labor and Public Welfare, Subcommittee on the Establishment of a Commission on Ethics in Government, *Ethical Standards in Government,* 82nd Cong., 1st Sess. 37 (1951).

SOURCE: Edgar Lane, "Group Politics and the Disclosure Idea," *Western Political Quarterly,* 17:2 (June 1964), pp. 203–207. Reprinted by permission of the University of Utah, copyright owners.

2 *Address of His Excellency William E. Russell* (Boston: Wright and Potter, 1891), p. 23.

3 Assembly Interim Committee on Legislative Representation, *Final Report* (Sacramento, 1963), p. 16.

self-indictment for violations of less elusive juridicial standards (bribery, fraud, intimidation, deceit, and the like), is no less groundless. This at least is true of such laws as we have managed to enact, and the prospect of more demanding ones is unimaginably remote.[4]

We should indeed be entirely clear as to whose "improper practices" we think disclosure can "deal with" or "prevent." Governor Russell was talking about private interests which had, in effect, been caught with their hands in the till, and, while its strictures were more general, the California committee was speaking to a background of not dissimilar events. For the Douglas Committee, however, the men whose judgments needed sharpening were public officials unable to disengage their private preferences from their public responsibilities. No disclosure law alone will force such men to hone their ethical sensibilities to keener edge until they have turned it on themselves, and this they have been disinclined to do. American legislatures regard disclosure as, at most, a weapon to be used against selected external targets; legislative ethics, interests, or behavior have seldom been regarded as fit subjects for inquiry or candor.

For the "general effectiveness" of disclosure, the Douglas Committee adduced neither criteria nor evidence. The criteria could possibly have been devised, but of evidence there was—and is—none. (How does one measure a politics from which "pressure" and "involvement" have been withdrawn?) More in point was the Committee's observation that discolsure "can do no harm to the public, and the long-run effects may be helpful."[5] And even here there is room for doubt. Disclosure laws could do very great harm if they were widely accepted as final and effective solutions to such problems as give rise to them. That these laws were intended more as demonstrations than as remedies does not prevent well-meaning men from imputing to them more curative powers than they possess.

Among observers less concerned with clean living in high places, disclosure requirements are more commonly regarded as means of "improving the legislative process,"[6] or of preserving and maintaining its "integrity."[7] This view assigns the legislature a more creative function than that of merely serving as a battleground where the myriad interests of a free society can have it out; it is more the conscious manager of our survival by consensus, the social orchestrator charged with blending many voices into one. But it must hear the voices clearly. Since lobbyists' "conflicting claims and propaganda are confusing, annoying, and at times, no doubt, deceiving and corrupting,"[8] or "cryptic, deceptive, and obscure,"[9] the main purpose of disclosure is to keep political discourse civilized, open, and on the merits between identified protagonists of competing interests so that the legislature can "identify pressures and be guided thereby in making its decisions."[10] Thus Chief Justice Warren as, with inadvertent irony, he cut the Lobbying Act to ribbons in the Harriss Case:

> Yet full realization of the American ideal of government by elected representatives depends to no small extent on their ability

[4] As Truman puts it, disclosure statutes usually have emerged from "publicized allegations of privileged access or from charges of attempts to achieve such a favored position through covert means." David Truman, *The Governmental Process* (New York: Knopf, 1951), p. 527.

[5] *Ethical Standards in Government,* p. 38.

[6] "Improving the Legislative Process: Federal Regulation of Lobbying," 56 *Yale L.J.* 316 (January 1947).

[7] Belle Zeller, "The Regulation of Pressure Groups and Lobbyists," *Annals,* 319 (September 1958), 103. The language is from the preamble of S. 2191, introduced in the 85th Congress, 1957.

[8] Justice Jackson, dissenting in United States v. Harriss, 347 U.S. 615 (1954).

[9] Emanuel Celler, "Pressure Groups in Congress," *Annals,* 319 (September 1958), 3.

[10] George B. Galloway, "A Report on the Operation of Title III of the Legislative Reorganization Act of 1946," in U.S. Congress, Senate, Special Committee to Investigate Political Activities, Lobbying, and Campaign Contributions, *Final Report,* 85th Cong., 1st Sess. 200 (1957).

to properly evaluate pressures. Otherwise, the voice of the people may all too easily be drowned out by the voice of special interest groups seeking favored treatment while masquerading as proponents of the public weal. This is the evil which the Lobbying Act was designed to help prevent.[11]

Now for all the modish derogation of something like "the public interest" (here "the public weal") as the grail of democratic politics, it obviously figures prominently in any respectable majoritarian ethos.[12] That there is a "voice of the people" in every political situation, or that a disclosure law can give elected representatives the means or wish to hear it, is a good deal less obvious. What if the people's voice is a discordant babel, or legislators take affirmative action not to hear it? What if the voice of interests that cannot claim majority support is the voice of equity, logic, or high principle? Is not the central purpose of government, as Willard Hurst reminds us, "that men should come to it, all the more so because what they want may be against the general welfare"?[13] One need not choose between warring conceptions of "the general welfare"—or even concede that there is one—to erect as a fundamental article of faith that men have the right to assail apparent majority beliefs and seek preferment for their own.

Since our public life has from the beginning proceeded from the unstated premise that government is not a distant monolith, greater somehow than the sum of its human parts, but only an instrument for the achievement of such special ends as we have brought within our public competence to reach, it rings earnestly hollow to assert that the ideal of representative government has only to do with hearing the voice of all the people, or that throwing protective mantles of disclosure around legislatures that may not need and do not want them can much contribute to its realization. There was wisdom, candor, and humility in T. V. Smith's description of legislation as "a business in which you do something, then wait to see who hollers, and then relieve the hollering as best you can to see who else hollers."[14] In the end, the use of a disclosure law to enhance the legislature's ability to "properly evaluate pressures" cannot amplify the voice of all the people or maintain the "integrity" of the legislative process, but it might conceivably help to test the earnestness and need of him who hollers loudest. A close reading of the legislative history of the Federal Lobbying Act suggests that this was precisely what its sponsors were about; if they regarded the hollering as "evil," they kept the judgment to themselves.[15]

Another cluster of perspectives on disclosure stands in sharp contrast to those heretofore discussed. These views tend to be "group-oriented," "tough-minded," and "operational," with no room for any sentimental nonsense about the "voice of the people," or "the public interest," or the "creativity" or "integrity" of the legislative process. Truman caught most of it with his passing reference to disclosure statutes or proposals as "minor weapons in group politics and . . . reaffirmations of the 'rules of the game.' "[16] Writing later and from a closer vantage point, Gross observed in more extended form that the best answer to the question of what to do with a "complex pass" of disclosed information

11 *United States* v. *Harriss*. The "cutting to ribbons" had to do with the Court's validation of the Act as regards the conventional meaning of lobbying only, i.e., direct solicitation of members of Congress.

12 See Glendon Shubert's brilliant tour de force, *The Public Interest* (New York: Free Press, 1960), throughout.

13 J. Willard Hurst, *The Growth of American Law* (Boston: Little, Brown, 1950), p. 62.

14 T. V. Smith, *The Legislative Way of Life* (Chicago: University of Chicago Press, 1940).

15 See particularly 92 *Cong. Rec.* 6367–6368, 6456 (June 6 and 7, 1946); and Norman Futor, "An Analysis of the Federal Lobbying Act," 10 *Fed. B.J.* 384 (October 1949).

16 Truman, p. 528.

> . . . probably lies in the potential use to which the disclosed information can be put by various participants in the legislative process, including not only members on Congress and executive officials, but also the leaders of private organizations and the lobbyists themselves. The information would be of greatest use to those participants in the legislative process whose sources of information are meager and whose power might be buttressed by facts of this type concerning other participants. In short, the information could, to some extent, serve to deprive some participants, particularly the stronger ones, of the advantages achieved through more complete secrecy and add a minor increment to the power of the weaker participants.[17]

It may have been no accident that Gross chose to cast his argument in such persistently conditional terms, for while disclosure laws *should* provide disadvantaged groups with potent weapons against better situated competitors, there is little evidence that they often do. What appears to be the best example—the relatively intensive and imaginative use of disclosed data by "weaker participants," particularly those promoting public housing and medical insurance, during the 81st Congress—will not withstand much probing. These efforts were more encouraged by the parallel Buchanan investigation than they were by the data themselves, or by the normal operation of the law that made them available. With the Lobbying Act gutted by the courts and the Buchanan Committee no longer in the prompter's box, the data washed up by the law lost most of their wallop, and their tactical use has dwindled to the vanishing point. Apart from a scattered handful of temporary exceptions, the state experience points to the same conclusion: groups persist in their reluctance to use disclosure as logic argues that they should.[18]

---

17 Bertram Gross, *The Legislative Struggle* (New York: McGraw-Hill, 1953), p. 46. On the point of complexity, Blaisdell has observed that "Some opinion, both official and private, has held that federal and state lobby regulation laws have failed and have been ineffective because of the sheer mass of data filed." Donald Blaisdell, *American Democracy Under Pressure* (New York: Ronald, 1958), p. 90. No. There is not too much data but too little use made of it.

18 For a suggestive example, involving non-compliance rather than its converse, see the discussion of the events leading to the resignation of Wes Mitchell, Chairman of the Republican National Committee, in the *New York Times,* March 28, 1953. For other cases, see *Columbus* (Ohio) *Citizen,* January 26, 1949; *Raleigh News and Observer,* April 6, 1949; *Indianapolis Star,* March 2, 1949; *Cleveland Plain Dealer,* July 31, August 1, 14, 1959.

CHAPTER TEN

The Developing Nations

45. Bribery in the Election of Ashanti Chiefs

K. A. Busia

We have explained that the Ashanti system of electing chiefs combines kin-right with popular selection. The elders select a candidate from the royal lineage of the particular tribe. As each matrilineal lineage consists of several subordinate branches, there are always a number of candidates available.

In the account of the election of the Chief of Wenchi, we noted that after a candidate had been nominated and accepted, the royal lineage held a special meeting at which differences between the chief-elect and any members of his lineage were settled, after which they swore allegiance to him. The people realized that the smooth working of the system depended on harmony amongst the members of the royal lineage.

One of the characteristics of the Ashanti system to-day is that lineage solidarity is weakened, and royals compete jealousy for the stool. Whenever a stool falls vacant, the eligible candidates canvass for it by distributing presents and bribes to the electors. Moreover, the successful candidate always has rivals who are working against him openly or secretly. This not only adds to stool debts, but also contributes to the insecurity of the chief.

The chiefs have been very concerned about this matter, which they have discussed at several of the sessions of the Confederacy Council. The discussion they held in 1938 provides good evidence of the facts stated above. The men who have themselves been elected as chiefs are the best qualified to speak on the subject, and we may let them speak for themselves:

1938. Item 5. The offering and accepting of bribes in connexion with election and destoolment of Chiefs.

Asantehene This subject was discussed at the last session of the Council, but at that time the Council had no power to make by-laws, therefore our decision in the matter could not have legal effect. As the Council has now been granted powers to do so, the subject is introduced again so that the necessary by-laws may be made.

Mampong Representative The practice of offering and accepting bribes in connexion with election and destoolment of Chiefs is as bad as it is detrimental to the welfare of the country. It should, therefore, be prohibited and made a punishable offence. I suggest that by-laws be passed by the Council providing that any Chief found guilty of such offence shall be destooled and any youngman found guilty of the same offence shall be imprisoned for six months with hard labour.

Juabenhene I support the view of the Mampong representative. A trader always wants to gain on his investments; in the same way if a person is compelled to spend all his money and to borrow in

SOURCE: K. A. Busia, *The Position of the Chief in the Modern Political System of Ashanti*. London: Oxford (for the International African Institute), 1951, pp. 209–217. By permission of the publisher.

order to bribe the Elders of a Stool before he is elected to that Stool, he would naturally try to pay off his debt with Stool money and to have some profit whilst he is on the Stool. Moreover, as he is conscious of the fact that he might be destooled on the least pretence, he thinks more of his personal interest than the welfare of the Stool. Such a state of affairs is deplorable, and therefore its cause which forms the subject of our discussion should be removed. In the olden days affairs were not in such a deplorable state as they are to-day, and destoolments were of very rare occurrence.

Nsutahene Bribery in connexion with destoolments and enstoolments is bad and should be stopped. I therefore support the previous speakers.

Agonahene I support the views expressed by the previous speakers and would further suggest that royals should not be allowed to contest for a Stool. If and when a Stool becomes vacant the Elders should approach the Queen-Mother for a candidate and in consultation with the Gyase and Ankobea Chiefs and the members of the Stool family, she should nominate a candidate and the Elders may accept or reject her nominee without allowing any of the royals to influence them in any way in their decision.

Nkoranzahene In certain cases if a Stool becomes vacant, wealthy subjects of the Stool try to bribe the Elders concerned in order to gain election. Under these circumstances, the royals too start to give bribes in order to ensure election to the Stool. Whilst, therefore, agreeing with the previous speakers, I should like to suggest further that any subject of a Stool who tries to contest for that Stool should be banished from the Division concerned.

Oyoko Clan We agree with the previous speakers and would add that certain Chiefs instigate the subjects of another Chief to destool their Chief. By-laws should therefore be passed to the effect that any Chief who is found guilty of such an offence will be destooled.

Asantehene The matter under discussion is so important that I should like all present to listen attentively. It is a disgrace for any Chief to neglect to train his nephews who will succeed him in future. The practice of offering and accepting bribes in connexion with the enstoolment or destoolment of Chiefs is also very bad and should be stopped. . . . I request the Committee which was appointed yesterday to deal with the question of the payment of annual "sheep" in respect of cocoa-farms to deal with this subject also.[1]

The committee appointed later submitted its suggestions, which the Confederacy Council adopted. "After a lengthy discussion the Committee was of the opinion that the practice of people offering and accepting bribes to destool or enstool a chief has become very common and has been the source of political unrest in this country." It made the following recommendations:

1. It shall not be lawful for any member of a Royal Family to contest for a Stool whenever a Stool becomes vacant, and he shall not canvass for votes from any Elder of the Stool.

2. Any member of a Royal Family who contests, offers, or accepts any bribe in any form in any enstoolment case shall be guilty of an offence and shall be struck off the roll of the Royal Family and shall forfeit his right of succession to the Stool.

3. It shall not be lawful for any Elder or Elders to nominate, elect, or install any candidate on any Stool other than a member of the Royal Family of such Stool.

4. Any Elder or sub-chief who offers or accepts a bribe in an enstoolment case, or nominates, elects, or installs any candidate other than a member of the Royal Family of any such Stool, or breaks away from the Elders' meeting with the intent to prolong or delay the enstoolment of a Chief shall be guilty of an offence and shall on summary conviction thereof be removed from his office and destooled.

5. Any subject of a Stool who offers or accepts a bribe in an enstoolment case or interferes with or canvasses votes for any candidate shall be guilty of an offence, and shall on summary conviction thereof be

[1] Minutes of the Confederacy Council (1938).

liable to imprisonment for a term not exceeding six months with hard labour.

These regulations reveal the abuses which have been practised in connexion with stool elections, and give evidence of the tension already alluded to regarding the weakening of lineage solidarity and the competition amongst matrilineal kinsmen for the inheritance of offices and property. The rivalry is heightened as regards chiefship owing to the prestige attached to the office.

Quite apart from these abuses, the permitted customary donations in connexion with stool elections make it expensive for anyone to become a chief.

The chief-elect makes a donation (*aseda*: token of thanks) to the elders when he is offered the stool. The customary amounts donated range from £4. 13*s*. in the case of a village headman or an elder, to £93 in respect of the Golden Stool. The amounts paid vary between these two limits, according to the rank of the stool.

Then there is *abradie,* the customary sums or drinks a new chief distributes to his principal elders and other chiefs of his clan or wing to "inform them that he has come to sit in the place of his ancestors" (*wabɛtena ne nananom anam mu*). The amounts that different chiefs spend on this vary from £25 to £100.

Thirdly, there is the *nsuaaka* (allegiance oath debt), the amount a chief pays when he takes the oath of allegiance to the Asantehene. The sum depends on the chief's place in the following gradations:[2]

Grade I Chiefs pay £37.4*s*. These are: Mamponghene, Juabenhene, Nsutahene, Bekwaihene, Kokofuhene, Adansihene, Kumawuhene, Essumejahene, Adontenhene Kumasi, Nkoranzahene, Dormaahene, Techimanhene.

Grade II paying £27.18*s*. Offinsuhene, Ejisuhene, Agonahene, Kontihene Kumasi, Akwamuhene Kumasi, Denyasehene, Wenchihene, Berekumhene, Asokorihene, Kuntanasihene, Sumahene, Drobohene, Nkwantahene.

It is of interest to note that the chiefs of Mo, Abeasi, and Banda, who belong by prestige to this grade, asked the Confederacy Council to place them in Grade III, because the donation for Grade II is too high.

Grade III paying £18. 12*s*. Kyidomhene, Gyasehene, Oyokohene, Ankobeahene, Manwerehene of Kumasi, Abeasihene, Mohene, Amakomhene, Tafohene, Antoahene, Assamanghene, Bandahene.

Grade IV All other chiefs not included in the above grades. The amounts they pay vary from Division to Division and range from £2. 7*s*. to £9. 6*s*.

The fourth item of expenditure at elections is *nsanom* (drinking of wine), the amount spent on drinks and entertainment during the rites of election and installation. Again the actual amounts spent vary from chief to chief. The range is from £20 to £100.

The total cost of an election to a chief of Grade I or II is usually more than £150. Some chiefs are known to have spent more than £800, and one informant estimated that he had spent over £1000. Many of them borrow the money to meet these expenses and thus add to the financial burden of their office. It also affects their tenure of the office, for a chief known to be in debt is always in danger of destoolment.

INSECURITY OF THE CHIEF'S OFFICE

All these show the predominantly characteristic feature of chiefship in Ashanti to-day—its insecurity.

Before 1900 chiefs were mostly de-

2 See "The Ashanti Confederacy Council." The fees were standardized at its session in 1943.

stooled for failure to consult the elders or the breaking of custom, though there were other causes.

Nowadays the most common cause is that of "misappropriating stool funds." This has become a prominent charge against chiefs since the 1920s. We have referred to the series of constitutional disputes that occurred in 1920 at Offinsu, Kumawu, Bekwai, Agogo, and Agona. A common feature of all those destoolment cases was the charge of the maladministration of stool revenues. The charge now regularly appears in every destoolment case. Of recent cases that have been heard by the Confederacy Council one may cite the cases of Wenchi, Nkoranza, Agona (1942), Kumawu, and Techiman (1944), in all of which the chiefs were accused of misappropriating stool funds.

Some subsidiary charges also recur: that the chief has violated native custom; that he has broken the laws to which he assented on his enstoolment; that he does not add to stool property; and that he does not keep up appearances as befitting his rank. With native custom in its present confused state it is always possible to find a custom that the chief has violated. For example, a chief who owned private property (houses and cocoa-farms) was said to have violated custom.

The more fundamental causes of destoolment have been indicated in this and previous chapters; the rivalry among royals; the confused state of custom in a society in transition from a subsistence to an exchange economy; lack of definiteness about the chief's functions; his loss of economic resources; the emergence of the educated commoner or the successful cocoa-farmer; the presence of a superior authority. These and the other changes discussed have destroyed the old correlation between the chief's political power, religious authority, economic privilege, and military strength, with the consequent decline in his prestige and authority.

The chiefs have tried to stop the frequent destoolments. In 1938 the Confederacy Council adopted the following rules:

1. Any member of a stool family who attempts to undermine his chief or offers or accepts a bribe for the purpose of inciting the destoolment of a chief shall be guilty of an offence and shall on summary conviction thereof be struck off the role of the royal family, and shall forfeit all his rights of succession in the family.

2. Any subject of a stool who conspires with any member of a stool family, or offers or receives a bribe, or undermines or maliciously prosecutes a chief or sub-chief for the purpose of destooling such chief or subchief shall be guilty of an offence and shall on summary conviction thereof be liable to imprisonment for a term not exceeding six months with hard labour.

3. Any elder, sub-chief, or chief who conspires with any subject or royal of a stool, receives or offers a bribe, or undermines or maliciously prosecutes a chief or sub-chief for the purpose of destooling such chief or sub-chief shall be guilty of an offence and shall on summary conviction thereof be destooled.

The Confederacy Council has tried to enforce these rules, and has dealt severely with those who have attempted to destool their chiefs. For example, in two instances in 1942, when the council acquitted the chiefs of Wenchi and Nkoranza against whom charges had been brought, some of those who had preferred the charges "malcontents" were imprisoned, and the ringleaders were banished from their respective Divisions.

But the severe measures have not checked the deposition of chiefs. Formerly there were two ways in which a commoner could express criticism or dissatisfaction with the Government. One way was for him as an individual to lay his complaint before the elder, his lineage head, who represented him on the central authority. This channel was used for the expression of individual grievances. Secondly, the commoners could, as a body, express criticism of the chief and his council through their Nkwankwaahene, the commoners' leader. This position has been abolished by the Confederacy Council, and there is no established organ for the commoners to express jointly any criticism or dissatisfaction with the Government. They may as individuals complain to their respective elders; but the elders are themselves members of the central authority and they are unable to represent the views of the youngmen without incurring the chief's suspicion. They share a joint responsibility with him in the conduct of the affairs of the Division. The commoners now jointly express their dissatisfaction in attempts to destool the chief.

The frequency of destoolments may be seen from the following table. Vacancies caused by deaths are excluded, and account is taken only of destoolments or abdications among the twenty-one chiefs who are presidents of the twenty-one Native Authorities in the Ashanti Confederacy:

from the above analysis that a chief's tenure of office is very insecure. It is an index of the disequilibrium of the Ashanti political structure to-day.

Yet as an institution chiefship is honoured and respected, and, judging from the keen competition for stools and the amounts candidates are willing to pay for them, the office is very much sought after. The people still look to the chief as their ruler and guide, the symbol, too, of their unity, traditions, and values. It is about his position and functions in the changed situation, what he should be and should do, that there is conflict.

The community attempts to resolve the conflict by now and again deposing one chief in order to try another; but, alas, though there are faults in every man, the greater faults are with the times and the system. With the times it is fruitless to quarrel; with the faults in the system we may hopefully grapple. That requires the head, heart, and hand of all concerned.

Name of Chief	Native Authority	Year of Destoolment or Abdication
Akuamoa Boaten	Juaben	1942
Kwadwo Apawu	Agona	1942
Kwabena Kunadu	Suma	1943
Kwabena Kakari	Essumenja	1943
Kwaku Jarko II	Techiman	1944
Kwame Affram	Kumawu	1944
Kwaku Nkansa	Adansi	1944
Yaw Gyamfi	Bekwai	1945
Osei Akoto	Kuntanasi	1945
Asum Gyima III	Ejisu	1945
Yaw Boakye III	Bekwai	1946
Amoako Agyeman	Adansi	1946
Kwabena Wiafe II	Offinsu	1946
Kwabena Asubonteng	Dormaa	1946

Twelve Native Authorities out of twenty-one have changed their chiefs at least once during the five years, and two of them, Bekwai and Adansi, have had two changes within that time. On an average three out of the twenty-one chiefs have been destooled every year. Although there are some chiefs who have held their position for many years, it is evident

Our analysis has shown that there have been two major changes in the political structure of Ashanti during the period of British rule, both the results of government policy.

The first is the trend towards centralization of administration on a territorial basis. This, as we have shown, has become necessary owing to new social factors such as improvement in communications, the presence in tribal areas of permanent settlers who are not members of the tribe of their place of residence, and, above all, because of the new functions expected of a Native Authority.

This centralization on a territorial basis we have seen to be at variance with the decentralization which characterized the kinship political institutions of Ashanti:—the small, more or less autonomous units of lineage, village, sub-division, or Division.

In the second place, as we have emphasized throughout, Ashanti chiefship is sacral. An important political development during the period of British rule has been the progressive secularization of the chief's office. Government has increased his administrative functions. The conflict between chief and people has centered round this development. The insecurity of the chief is a consequence of the secularization of his office.

These two processes in association with the other social changes to which we have referred in the preceding pages have caused the disequilibrium of the political structure.

In concluding this contribution towards the task of grappling with the political system of Ashanti as it is to-day, the author is reminded of an Ashanti proverb:

> *ɔman te sɛ adesoa, wonhu mu dakoro:*
> The nation is like a load (with many things tied up)—one cannot perceive everything in it in a day.

What he has perceived and attempted to describe and interpret is but a small portion of the load.

46. Remuneration Levels and Corruption in French-Speaking Africa

RENÉ DUMONT

[A chapter from a critical study by a French author of postcolonial political development, the original title of which was "Independence Is Not Always Decolonization"]

"One cannot develop a country by doubling the employees in administrative services or by distributing sinecures to one's friends, but only by mobilizing men and enthusiasm to work for an ideal based on the common good," concludes R. Gendarme. The principal "industry" of these countries at the moment is administration. It is not productive and simply adds to general costs. Such costs should be reduced, but in fact are being swollen to the point where personnel expenses alone absorb 60 per cent of the internal income in Dahomey. As presently conceived, administration will be the ruin of these countries.

The balkanization of Africa is one of the principal causes of it. Until more progress had been made, it would have been preferable to retain the former federal structure, French West Africa with Togo and French Equatorial Africa with the Cameroons, and be satisfied to grant each "territory" a good deal of autonomy. By including Madagascar, three parliaments and three federal governments could have had only one diplomatic corps to represent their foreign interests.[1]

There should be a joint army, if forces other than the police are needed. At least African unity would not have made a step backward. But we encouraged Houphouet-Boigny to reject the Federation and keep Guinea out of the group. This unfortunate beginning intentionally complicates the task of the new governments, and evokes the dictum "divide and rule."

A general reconsolidation of West Africa could do worse than follow the lines of former French territories. Colonial frontiers, a result of the more or less hasty occupations of this or that

SOURCE: René Dumont, "Independence Is Not Always Decolonization," *False Start in Africa*. New York: Praeger and London: André Deutsch, Ltd., 1966, pp. 78–87. By permission of the publishers.

[1] Iwiyé Kala-Labe proposes a system of one African representation in *Communauté-France-Eurafrique*, June, 1961. "African diplomacies—why the plural? Because the young independent states of Africa have adopted a ruinous policy of diplomatic representation: ruinous for their fragile finances, which can never support, without immense and needless sacrifices, the enormous costs of installing and maintaining a diplomatic corps, whose direct importance to their countries is nebulous; ruinous also because the new states have other fish to fry, and more serious ones. They should concentrate on these, instead of joining the race for prestige which only serves to construct 'Potemkin villages' and cover over the abysses in their budgets for non-existent equipment . . ."

expeditionary force, did not take ethnic groups into account (e.g. Togo and Ghana) any more than so-called "natural" frontiers. However, colonial history has thrown up barriers to a new division, such as diversity of language, administrative methods and monetary systems. Thus Cameroon admits of two languages, two monetary systems and three parliaments, none of which helps cut down administrative expenses. Certainly, the entry of England into the Common Market would facilitate these regroupings.

M. Apithy envisages a Benin union[2] of Ghana, Nigeria, Dahomey and Togo. Another recently proposed frontier is that of the Casablanca group, comprising Guinea, Ghana and Mali, plus Egypt, Morocco and Algeria on the one hand, and the Brazzaville "twelve," together with Nigeria and Sierra Leone, on the other. The end of the Algerian war meant the diminution of many of the antagonisms that a union like the Benin would also have to surmount.

The former colonies confront one with fifteen governments, more than 150 ministers, several hundred cabinet members, and several thousand members of parliament. Yet as a unit, they have much less population and resources than France. Gabon alone, with 450,000 inhabitants, has sixty-five deputies, one for each 6000 people, as against one per 100,000 in France. These countries have not quite understood their poverty yet, because they can "touch" France so easily for money. In addition to providing the great majority of their investments (86 per cent in Upper Volta), France also balances their budgets, except for Senegal, the Ivory Coast, Mali and Togo.

Each cabinet member has an official car at his disposal, rarely a modest one, with chaffeur. The President of Dahomey cannot take a step without his motorcade, and many dream of equalling the ostentation of the Elysée Palace. This last costs us, for each reception given a visiting African head of state, a sum which could accomplish far more in African agriculture. President Youlou wants his little Versailles, and goes to Switzerland to borrow the money for it. Houphouet-Boigny has already built his, at a cost of four billion francs. Excellent buildings were demolished in order that his park might be enlarged. For its construction, hundreds of tons of malachite were imported from Russia . . . by air.

During the last phase of colonialism, the policy was to equalize salaries of Africans and Europeans in similar jobs, a defensible position only in the framework of "assimilation." The native civil servant, in addition to his regular salary, received a colonial supplement. This has been reduced in some cases, but not abolished. At independence, this pseudo-equality has led to flagrant disparity with the rest of the population, whose standard of living is often a fifteenth of the French.

Massive departure of the French resulted in a high rate of promotion of subordinate African civil servants, who thus earn even more now than before, for the same qualifications. The student returning from France is appointed director if he is the only African technician or graduate in his field. A labour leader who had been one of my students six months before at the *Institut des Hautes Études d'Outremer,*[3] was already returning for further training in France, by first-class aeroplane. He would no doubt have been astonished had I told him that the Cuban ministers cross the Atlantic in second. This tendency applies above all to the urban *élites,* and works to the detriment of the peasants. It could be postponed for a while.

The elements of the civil service, deputies and ministers constitute a highly privileged group whose members support each other. In England, a Member of Parliament draws the pay of a middle

2 *Jeune Afrique,* March 26, 1962.

3 A former colonial educational institution.

rank civil servant. In France he draws the salary of a top level civil servant. Because of the "assimilation" policy, whereby the colonies were to be put on the same footing as France, a Gabonese deputy earns more than the British MP: 165,000 CFA francs, compared to about 100,000 CFA francs a month in England (£1000 in salary and £750 for expenses per year). As for the cost of the Gabonese Presidency, Parliament and ministers, with all their supposedly useful trips, it probably represents, in relation to the national income of the country, more than the cost of the court of Louis XVI in 1788, relative to French national income of that period. Certainly the latter supported parasites, and Libreville has less of them—but it too has its "hangers-on," none of whom perform a useful function.[4]

LIFE'S WORK OF A PEASANT EQUALS 1½ MONTH'S WORK OF A DEPUTY

A deputy works (?) three months out of the year, and receives 120,000 to 165,000 francs a month all the year round. In six months of salary, or 1½ months of work, he earns as much as the average peasant in thirty-six years, a whole lifetime of hard labour. I brought out this fact in lectures in Porto Novo, Dakar, Tananarive, Douala and Yaounde. There were always many civil servants, deputies, sometimes ministers, and in the last cities, the President of the Republic and the President of the Council as well. That time I permitted myself to add that "This will not last thirty-six years." They would appreciate my meaning in the Cameroons, where efforts to subdue rebels are still carried on, more easily than elsewhere.

Far-sighted Presidents and ministers build up savings accounts "for their old age" in Swiss banks, and their wives buy villas on the Lake of Geneva. At that same gathering at Yaounde in 1961 at the *École Camerounaise d' Administration,* I asked the group of two hundred civil servants and students if anyone there, out of patriotism, would be willing to give back to the government a substantial portion of his salary. One hand, a courageous one, was raised. I then remarked that this fact would be duly noted in my book. Four other hands went up. I appealed to their patriotism, but not one of the students present, which included the entire school, raised his hand.

The situation is largely a hold-over from colonial times, and is encouraged by the fact that France helps balance the budget in these countries. This relieves the African governments from facing up to their real difficulties, and thus holds off their economic maturity. A new type of bourgeoisie is forming in Africa, that Karl Marx would hardly have foreseen, a bourgeoisie of the civil service. One day we may look back on the old bourgeoisie of Western Europe with nostalgia and affection, and it has had its share of criticism.

It often abused its privileges by exploiting peasants and workers, although they were the ones who built Europe. It often lived too luxuriously. But do not forget that in general it offered the two motivating forces of development, work and savings, and thus insured progress. Work was often pushed to excess. In order to save, Père Grandet imposed terrible privations on himself. In underdeveloped countries, laxity and profligacy are too often seen.

A typist for the Dakar government types an average of six to seven pages, double spaced, a day, less than a quarter of what an average French typist accomplishes, for a salary that is equal if not higher. At the Djebilor station in Casamance, the agricultural worker who is a *décisionnaire*[5] hoes an average of ten square metres a day, or scarcely 1 per

4 Reductions in salary are being made in most of these countries (Senegal, Mali, Guinea, Dahomey), but they are very insufficient.

5 One so designated by a *décision,* who is given a paper stamped with a miraculous seal, which permits him to work less and earn more.

cent of what his Californian counterpart accomplishes. As a *décisionnaire,* however, he earns almost 400 CFA francs a day, a sixth of the Californian's wages, which are about ten dollars. The hoed square metre ends up costing sixteen times more in Casamance than in California. Citrus plants cost twelve times more to raise than they do the Sicilian nurserymen. These *décisionnaires* consider themselves practically civil servants, and therefore do very little work, particularly as some of them are related to deputies.

Deputies, like the young students back from France and quickly promoted, can usually buy cars on hire-purchase with loans made available by the Treasury Department. In other words, public funds are being diverted for consumer loans. Even worse, the loans are used to pay for imported luxuries. The two or four horsepower Renaults are not considered good enough even for driving in town (the Mayor of Ouagadougou passed a law forbidding use of the small two horsepower cars as taxis). These loan concessions will make it more difficult to lower salaries, as too many civil servants are burdened with high monthly payments.

Any visit to a sub-prefect or prefect in the bush involves the inevitable glass of whisky, a solid colonial tradition. I have always refused it, asking instead for fruit juice or a local drink, adding that since I was going to propose that the government reduce my host's salary (among others) by 40 to 50 per cent, I didn't feel I should accept such an expensive drink from him! The governor at St. Louis, an excellent man, offered me fruits imported from France by air. That evening I brought him six mangoes from the neighbouring market. He had insisted that local fruits were unavailable.

After having written this, I read *Les Damnés de la Terre* by Franz Fanon, from which I take these quotations at random. They attack particularly the business bourgeoisie. "The national bourgeoisie, which takes power at the end of the colonial régime, is an underdeveloped bourgeoisie with practically no economic power . . . not oriented towards production, invention, construction, work . . . it enters, soul in peace, on the terrible anti-national path of a bourgeoisie flatly, stupidly, cynically bourgeois. Nationalization means the transfer to the peasants of injustices inherited from the colonial period . . . its enormous salaries are not reinvested, as it deposits them in foreign banks. Enormous sums are spent on displays of ostentation, cars, houses. . . . Despite declarations which are fine in form, but empty in content, it is proving its incapacity to make a minimum humanist ideal triumph."

EXPENSIVE TOWNS AND NEPOTISM

The villas recently constructed in Dakar for Senegalese officials are widely spaced, as in the old colonial quarters, and form a striking contrast, seen from the air, with the "native" town, which is extraordinarily densely populated. Aside from the high construction costs, there are enormous expenses for services: roads, water, gas, electricity and telephone. By spacing out the houses, the town is greatly enlarged, and transportation costs are raised accordingly. Highrise buildings, of twelve, fifteen or even more storeys, would be much more economical. Western aid favours this trend, both by helping to balance budgets, which make high salaries possible, and by financing investments in urban construction. If urbanization was dependent on local resources, Africans would be forced to build more modestly, mostly with local materials.

Africans rebel against the idea of a cut in their salaries, in inverse proportion to their degree of dedication and honesty. One Senegalese official told me that he could not possibly receive properly without his high salary. I have been received by Greek and Portuguese colleagues who earn far less than their African counterparts, and they live in countries where the general standard of living is much higher; their homes were extremely attractive.

Whether deputy or civil servant, the African who has "arrived" feels obligated to take his large family in charge, sometimes his friends and village. The African tradition of hospitality is very laudable when it means, say, that a man supports his penniless nephew until he finishes his studies. In the old days, a visitor received in a Sudanese village took up the *daba* with the others in the season of planting, and hoed the millet, sorghum or peanut crops. In the city, a guest no longer does anything, and becomes totally parasitic. Africans are proud when they can "maintain" young people in robust health, and enable them to be idle. This is a sad state of affairs for a developing country which needs all hands.

Agbessi, my Dahomean chauffeur at Bangui, had abandoned his wife and children in Porto Novo simply to get away from all his parasitic relations. One way of getting them off your hands is to find them a job, and too many positions are filled by nepotism, and not on the basis of competence. The top staff of a minister usually belongs to the same ethnic group as its chief. Officials, particularly ministers, lose precious time which could more usefully be spent studying their briefs or viewing problems on the spot, when they receive these parasites seeking favours.

Conditions in Cuba are in marked contrast. In August, 1960, the Hotel Habana Riviera, a luxury hotel built for rich American tourists, was suddenly invaded by ebullient *Maestros volontarios* and their families. These young men and women were mostly college graduates, and had come to teach literacy to peasants and agricultural workers, who came from the most distant parts of the country. They were highly indignant when several of them were offered jobs in Havana. Africa will be fortunate indeed if it can create a comparable spirit of service and dedication in its civil servants. When I talk about the "general interest" in Yaounde, people begin to laugh, much as they do in São Paulo.

TIE AND JACKET, THE NEW SYMBOLS

The Republic of the Congo (Brazzaville) had only eleven French-trained African doctors in May 1961. All of them were assigned to Brazzaville or Pointe Noire. "Jobs in the bush are all right for the whites." Too many young officials try to obtain a training period in France, often without caring whether or not it increases their usefulness. A stay in France is a mark of prestige, helpful to obtain positions in the capital. The Prefect of Education for the Northern Congo received just one such training period in France; now he no longer journeys into the bush, and never leaves his office, or takes off his jacket and tie.

Jackets and ties have become the new symbols of prestige. Ministers and cabinet members keep them on even when the heat makes them insufferable, which also justifies the expense of installing air-conditioning. Most of them require all officials, European or African, to wear jackets and ties when they appear for an appointment. People have been sent back to France for taking them off for a minute.

By insisting on these exterior forms of respect, Africans betray a fear of not being able to inspire it otherwise. As Bismarck said, every man has his own value, diminished by his vanity. I wonder by how much the construction of the Abidjan palace diminished the militant Houphouet-Boigny. Whoever dons a tie and jacket is eager to show his membership in the new *élite*. He does not realize or perhaps he does not care, that he is drawing further and further away from the tieless, coatless peasant. For that reason I arrived without these "attributes" to make my report to the Dahomey Council of Ministers, and to Presidents Ahidjo and Assalé.

At the Israeli Ministry of Agriculture

one can quickly distinguish between subordinate civil servants, all wearing ties, and the service chiefs, top officials, the minister and his staff, none of whom wear one. Many of these are members of a *kibbutz,* and turn over all of their salaries to it, keeping back an amount so small that the purchase of a tie would mean sacrifices. I may seem to be stressing an insignificant detail, but if Africans followed the Israeli example their future would be much more hopeful.

CORRUPTION

Too many African *élites* have interpreted independence as simply meaning that they could move into the jobs and enjoy the privileges of the Europeans. Along with high salaries often go beautiful houses, completely furnished, sometimes palaces for governors and a large domestic staff, on the expense account, and cars usually with chauffeurs. After independence, the "403" car was succeeded by Chevrolets in Abidjan and Mercedes in Yaounde. These are often traded in every six months, which of course enrages ordinary workers. When some of these "extras" were limited, some people were able to get them back without being too particular about how they managed it.

Sudden accession to power affected certain leaders adversely and corroded their moral sense. Corruption was certainly not unknown in the colonial *milieu,* viz. the Indo-Chinese customs. Since independence, however, the increase in corruption has taken on alarming proportions in certain countries, particularly the Central African Republic, the Republic of the Congo (Brazzaville),[6] Gabon, the Ivory Coast and Dahomey. Investigating committees were established in the Cameroons to ferret out corruption, and it has been asserted that the embezzlements thus detected amount to a tenth of the budget. This figure seems high, yet it is by no means certain that the investigations reached very far up in the hierarchy.

Cocoa Purchasing Associations are entitled to allot premiums to "superior" cocoas. During the 1960–1961 season, 25,000 tons were so designated, but at the inspection service in the port at Douala, only 9000 tons were found to merit the premium. Five or six thousand tons of coffee beans had been mixed in with very mediocre lots. Premiums on at least 1000 tons, worth more than 200 million CFA francs had been fraudulently allotted for lots which were either fictitious or did not merit the classification. Equally bad, one lot of high quality was sometimes given a premium two or three times.

A big effort to reduce salaries and promote honesty has been made by Guinea, which has had the courage at least to point the way towards complete political and economic independence. Mali has made great strides also. However, even there results have not always been satisfactory. The ardour for work among Guinean officials who accompanied me in 1959 was very moderate. I had hoped that independence would stimulate it; not at all. Corruption appears to be more developed along the African coast, perhaps because it has been longer in contact with the worst colonial influences, the exploiters, adventurers and prostitutes. Further inland, in the savannah, land is generally now owned individually. M. Mazoyer writes to me that "the relationship between the degree of corruption in men and ownership of the means of production cannot be underestimated. It is here that man began to exploit his neighbour, here is the first robbery, the original sin which brings all the others in its wake.[7]

[6] See the author's article in *France-Observateur,* June 15, 1961. After its appearance one of my namesakes was coolly received in Brazzaville.

[7] Conditions are worse in Liberia and Abyssinia than elsewhere. In Abyssinia the Civil Code provides that a landowner can claim up to three-quarters of the crop. This Code is the work of a French jurist, René David, and of a codification commission composed exclusively of landowners or representatives of the Church, a privileged and extensive landowner.

47. Corruption and Self-Interest in Kampala and Nairobi

J. DAVID GREENSTONE

[In this "Comment on Local Politics in East Africa," the author relates his own studies of Kampala (Uganda) to those of another writer, Professor Herbert Werlin, who had studied politics in Nairobi (Kenya) and found that a major goal for Kenyan politics was "to build up the basis for cooperation."]

Cooperation existed in Kenya under British colonialism; it exists in Britain today. Lack of cooperation at present makes it more difficult for Kenya and Nairobi to solve acute social and economic problems. For Werlin, cooperation requires an educated, public-spirited citizenry, a politically conscious, reform minded business class, and a corps of dedicated professional administrators (p. 197). Cooperation requires a modern social order which in American cities has functioned to encourage "good government." But this very modern concept of cooperation tells us more about where Kenya and Nairobi ought to go than how they should get there. Once cooperation is achieved, the government administration will be more efficient in combatting poverty and ignorance. But such cooperation by different social and political groups, all of whom are dedicated to the general interest, is as much an effect of economic and social development as a cause. In fact, the politics of many American cities was at first characterized not by disinterested cooperation but by vigorous individual self-interest and even the outright corruption which Werlin deplores in Nairobi.

As this comment will try to demonstrate, the American experience, Werlin's discussion of Nairobi, and my own investigations in another East African capital, Kampala, Uganda, all suggest that self interest is an appropriate motive in an underdeveloped political system. This critique will begin by attempting to state some of Werlin's theoretical and empirical arguments more explicitly and systematically.

I

In Section II Werlin refers to power, then to control and cooperation, and then again to power. These shifting terms, when analyzed in conjunction with his subsequent empirical discussion, actually refer to two distinct dimensions of political behavior which we will call *cooperation* and *total political capacity*. Cooperation concerns the micro-political relationships, including power, among individuals and groups; total political capacity concerns the macro-political "power" of the whole system to function effectively. Levels of cooperation depend on the attitudes of the parties to each other and the inducements they employ to implement these

SOURCE: J. David Greenstone, "Corruption and Self-Interest in Kampala and Nairobi," *Comparative Studies in Society and History,* 8:2 (January 1966), pp. 199–210. By permission of the publisher, The Society for the Comparative Study of Society and History.

attitudes. In command-obedience situations in which A orders B to do what A desires, inducements are often sanctions. In such situations, where B is effectively subordinate to A, possible sanctions vary from the American President using persuasion on his fellow citizens, to the Kenya central government legally "requiring" Mayor Rubia of Nairobi to divulge his business transactions, to "forceful forms of power" including imprisonment (Werlin, pp. 182, 185–186). The power to command does not exist where B is equal to A and is unlikely to exist where A's superiority to B is not clear to the participants. When A feels uncertain that he can command B, A tends to bargain rather than command or even urge. Although the Kenya Minister for Local Government officially supervises the Mayor of Nairobi, the Mayor's election by the council appears to give him some degree of real independence. In those situations where the power to command is not exercised, A will offer inducements through bargaining. If the bargaining process breaks down, A may try to employ legal authority or physical force.

The second element in cooperation, the attitudes of the parties toward each other, determines how closely and willingly A and B work together or collaborate. These attitudes range from hostility to indifference to mutual good will. Werlin observes that cooperation is poor between Kenya's racial groups, but it is close in Britain between city officials and the chairmen of city council committees (pp. 183, 187). Attitudes affect cooperation in command as well as bargaining situations. For example, A may decide to collaborate with B rather than command him, despite their inequality. Even where A commands B, their relationship may be friendly, indifferent or hostile. In terms of both attitudes and inducements, Werlin urges Africans to emulate the Western democracies. They should minimize force and hostility and maximize friendly collaboration and persuasion, both among political groups and among social groups such as races and tribes.

The other dimension, total political capacity, measures the effectiveness of all political units in coping with problems raised by their environment. The issue is not primarily the relationship between A and B but the effectiveness of their individual and joint efforts. Here Werlin persuasively rejects the notion that local and national governments must compete for a fixed pool of governmental functions ("powers" in the vocabulary of the American Constitution).[1] In the United States, total political capacity has grown dramtically at local, state and national levels in the last century as the political system responded to industrialization. By contrast, Werlin finds that capacity is clearly inadequate in Nairobi. This notion is developed in the systems analysis of David Easton which equates the "persistence of a [political] system" with "its *capacity* to continue the production of authoritative outputs."[2] Total political capacity varies between systems and over time in a single system. In Werlin's discussion, capacity as a dimension measures not only how easily threats to persistence are handled, but how adequately the system satisfies important demands of its citizens.

Werlin's most important, if only implicit, empirical proposition holds that the degree of cooperation, as a measure of individual and group relationships, affects total political capacity. This causal relationship, indeed, provides the connection between his theoretical reflections and his empirical analysis. Of course, political capacity is too general a factor to be affected only by cooperation. Sheer technical competence is another element. Werlin reports that political capacity fell

1 See Morton Grodzins, "Centralization and Decentralization in the American Federal System," in *A Nation of States*, Robert A. Goldwin, ed., pp. 1–23 (Skokie, Ill., Rand McNally, 1964), and Daniel J. Elazar, *The American Partnership* (Chicago, Ill., University of Chicago Press, 1962).

2 David Easton, *A Framework for Political Analysis* (Englewood Cliffs, N.J., Prentice-Hall, 1965), p. 132. Emphasis supplied.

after poorly trained African city officials and inexperienced African city councillors began to take over the government. But the loss of technical skill was compounded by a fall in cooperation. Werlin makes clear that the effectiveness of Nairobi's government suffered when hostile attitudes between city councillors and city officials replaced friendly ones, and when threats of coercive sanctions replaced persuasion and bargaining in national-local relations.

Even after admitting the force of Werlin's argument, it still can be asked if there are not also cases where the level of cooperation is affected by changes in capacity. Specifically, the exodus from Nairobi of technically skilled European city officials and politically sophisticated European city councillors, which directly reduced capacity, in turn indirectly reduced cooperation. This is not simply friction between new African city councillors and departing officials who are temporarily in office. Cooperation between councillors and officials was not based merely on the mutual affinity of men who shared common experiences and culture. Their cooperation grew out of respect for each others' competence and the political ability to provide each other with effective mutual support. At the same time, the loss of administrative expertise makes it more difficult to provide stable predictable relationships between government agencies (Werlin, pp. 193–194). The problem here is the predictable behavior Weber thought necessary for all modern bureaucracies. Local government officials cannot expect consistent cooperation from central officials who lack the ability to deal effectively with all the problems which come across their desks. Central officials face the same difficulty with local officials. As a result, each agency cannot fully anticipate which problems other agencies will happen to handle adequately. Relationships begin to deteriorate as mutual respect and confidence disappear.

The relative speed of the changeover from British to African control in Nairobi also appears significant, since cooperation appears to suffer most when capacity changes most rapidly. A slow decline in capacity permits adjustments among politicians which would preserve much of the former cooperation. Conversely, when new programs are rapidly being introduced, patterns of cooperation grow more slowly than the government's capacity to execute programs. This lag explains much of the short run inefficiency, chaos and seemingly arbitrary behavior which has distributed even sympathetic observers of the New Deal and, more recently, of the War on Poverty. In sum, any decrease or rapid increase in capacity functions to reduce cooperation. Thus the quadrants in . . . [Model 47.1] can be ranked: I (greatest cooperation), II, III, IV (least cooperation).

MODEL 47.1

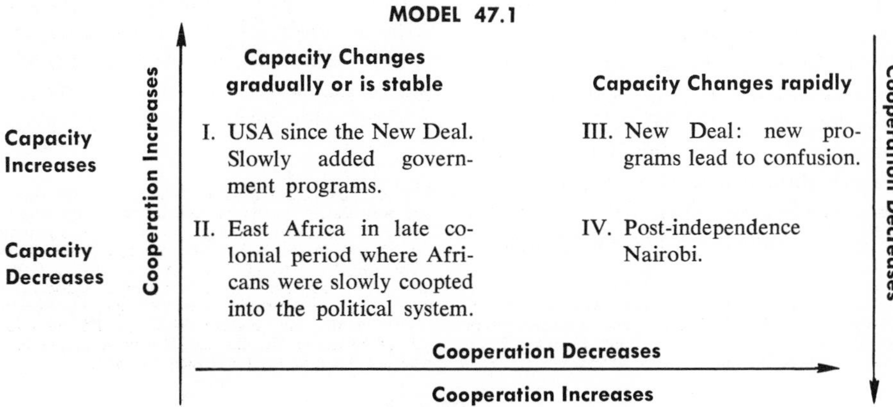

Public-spirited cooperation is a crucial independent causal factor for Werlin because it is valued for its own sake. As such it motivates officials, political leaders and others to work together for the public interest and thus increases capacity. Werlin points out that the social transformation necessary to bring about such elevated values in Nairobi "is by no means easy. . . . Basic reforms simply cannot far outpace economic and social development" (p. 197). Since the cooperation Werlin favors is unlikely to come soon, our analysis suggests that the entire approach could be reversed. A political system could try to offset at least some of the loss of public-spirited cooperation by introducing the incentive of individual self-interest. This was the procedure of the great American political machines. Members of the machine cooperated with each other and with their interest-group clients, but they were motivated by self-interest. When the machine weakened the interests of the individual members no longer led them to cooperate. Interestingly enough, a similar pattern of self-interest has emerged in the politics of Kampala.

II

Kampala is considerably smaller than Nairobi, and has many fewer whites and somewhat fewer racial tensions. Africans, for example, made up a third of the Kampala Council in 1961, the year before Independence, and a wealthy African businessman served as mayor for two terms in the colonial period. Militant nationalism was further inhibited by the parochialism of the largest, richest and most cohesive tribe, the Baganda.[3] This parochialism produced a three-party system which persisted in 1964 despite the growing strength of the ruling Uganda People's Congress. As a result, four of the six City Council seats contested in February 1964 were won by the opposition Democratic Party.

In many respects, however, Kampala closely resembles Nairobi. The Kampala Council has faced problems nearly as intractable as Nairobi's. With Independence, the Council assumed responsibility for primary education and housing, which presented almost insoluble problems given the city's limited resources. Nor did Kampala escape all of Nairobi's racial tensions. As in Nairobi, the policy of putting Africans in all top administrative posts as soon as possible created a crisis of morale among senior European city officials and considerable disquiet among Uganda Asians. Many of the African replacements in Kampala also lacked their European predecessors' educational qualifications and experience. As in Nairobi, the new African councillors had difficulty in understanding complex issues. The upshot has been a repetition of the Nairobi experience: highly confused council and committee meetings which last two or three times as long as before Independence.

Until recently the African majority in Kampala, as well as in Nairobi, was excluded from effective power. Even with a third of the whole membership in 1961, Africans were under-represented on the Council. More importantly, the colonial government carefully chose councillors from the African social and business elite, who usually acquiesced in the patterns established by the European councillors.[4] Only with the elections of 1962 did several lower income, more militant African nationalists become councillors.

3 See Donald Rothchild and Michael Rogin, "Uganda," in *National Unity and Regionalism in Eight African States,* ed. Gwendolyn Carter (Ithaca, N.Y., Cornell University Press, 1965).

4 Of the ten Africans among the thirty councillors, one was the *ex officio* representative of the British Resident, Buganda; another, the mayor, was among the richest Africans in the country. Two others were civil servants; one was an unaggressive Catholic priest; another was a substantial shopowner; two others were owners of small shops; one was a lawyer. Only one, Aggery Willis, could be considered anything like the anti-European nationalists who set the tone of the council by 1964.

Both Nairobi's and Kampala's European-dominated councils adhered in American terms to "good government" standards in the colonial period. In each city these standards have been severely attacked since the Africans took over the government. Some wealthy European and Asian councillors did benefit from the previous system despite their sincere commitment to "good government." Clients chose lawyers on the Council because they felt that they might somehow obtain more effective representation. The councillors associated with large companies could use their experience on the Council to estimate the bids or tenders most likely to win contracts from the city. These same councillors in the colonial period were also, perhaps inevitably, less sensitive to the wishes and feelings of the majority of lower class Africans, who have elected the new Council majority. On such issues as providing shops to inexperienced African merchants at less than economic rent or adjusting housing regulations in the African housing projects, the former Council shared the subtle upper class bias of many American cities with "good government" politics.[5]

It must also be conceded that in 1964 standards of efficiency and competence prevailed with the selection of an experienced district commissioner as the first African Town Clerk and the rejection of a much less qualified but politically influential candidate. In addition, African professionals in the city administration have begun to influence some politics. For example, they energetically protested the decision of several elected African councillors to permit substandard African housing which the officials felt was "ruining the city."

Yet the most striking similarity between Nairobi and Kampala politics since Independence is the rise of extensive corruption, that is, the violation of one's duty to the regime as a citizen or public official.[6] Widespread rumors in Kampala alleged the outright buying of votes to secure city approval for various commercial projects. In one case some councillors successfully vetoed a project by asserting that it would benefit wealthy Europeans and Asians at the expense of Africans. After the project was approved without dissent two months later, some council officials and councillors suspected that lavish bribes accounted for the complete reversal of attitudes.[7] Other allegations include political intimidation to prevent lawyers from suing powerful political leaders, and payments of up to £250 ($700) to arrange the citizenship status of Asians. Although cases of corruption are hard to document,[8] one case, which was described in the press and a parliamentary debate, involved the city's sale of a gasoline station site. Some of the major companies indicated they would pay the successful purchasers as much as £12,000 for the site, and the highest bidder, an African businessman, offered the city £11,000 ($30,800). This offer and several other intervening bids, however, were rejected in favor of a new African councillor's bid for £4000 ($11,200) the price set by the government appraiser. Charges flew in all directions. Several councillors reported that the fortunate bidder bribed other councillors and that national party leaders had applied pressure to have the £4000 bid accepted. These charges were officially denied, but no one denied that the fortunate bidder turned a handsome profit.

5 See for examples, Patricia Sexton, *Income and Education* (New York, Viking, 1961); Oliver P. Williams and Charles R. Adrian, *Four Cities* (Philadelphia, Penn., University of Pennsylvania Press, 1963), esp. pp. 255–256. Edward C. Banfield and James Q. Wilson, *City Politics* (Cambridge, Mass., Harvard University Press and the M.I.T. Press, 1963), chs. 11, 12, and 13; and Edward C. Banfield, ed., *Urban Government* (New York, The Free Press of Glencoe, 1961), Part IV.

6 Banfield and Wilson, p. 125, n. 7.

7 See the *Uganda Argus,* February 24, 1964 and March 24, 1964 for some further detail.

8 Ronald Wraith and Edgar Simpkins, *Corruption in Developing Countries* (London, G. Allen and Unwin, 1963), pp. 14, 52–53.

As one of his colleagues on the Council wryly remarked, "He certainly has begun wearing very nice suits recently." The last European mayor, Mrs. Barbara Saben, resigned as a councillor after a futile effort to reverse the sale. She explained ironically, "My own principles and ideals of public service for the public good may be outdated and outmoded."[9]

This incident was unusual both in its crudity and the resulting publicity. It symbolizes a less publicized and more complicated system in which money is regularly exchanged for political influence. This system affected the presentation of an application to build the city's first motel. An Asian councillor bitterly denounced the Uganda Town and Country Planning Board for delaying its approval after the Council had assented. As a result, he complained, the developers lost part of their promised capital, endangering the whole project. The embittered councillor attacked the "imperialist" methods and prejudices of the Board since the request for approval had been made by an African.[10] This attack was an unusually striking case of obfuscation by rhetoric. Another Asian councillor, a member of the Board, angrily retorted that eight of the ten Board members were Africans and that the UPC had recently reconstituted the Board to secure nationalist control. Even more to the point, the real promoters were Asian investors who hoped to secure a better government response by having an African act as the applicant of record. The Asian councillor was in fact accusing the African-dominated Town and Country Planning Board of anti-African prejudice against a project financed by Asians. Here in complex form are the central elements of Kampala politics: an anti-Asian political climate, a pro-African rhetoric with anti-imperialist and racial slogans, and a series of side payments from those with money to those with various kinds of political influence.

The politics of self-interest in Kampala extends beyond open corruption. Partly to increase their standing in the community, the first group of elected councillors called for special parking privileges, flags on their cars and, of more substance, the extensive medical services which the Council regularly provided at nominal cost to all its senior officials.[11] The national Minister for Regional Administration exercised his supervisory powers over the Council and vetoed the demand for medical services outright. The councillors then pressed for the less substantial privilege of receiving without the usual delay the ordinary government medical services available to any citizens willing to wait in line several hours. The evasive reply of the Council's medical office left the matter officially unsettled.

The councillors had more success in securing direct money payments. Until Independence the councillors had served without pay, according to the common British practice. The Africans first sought 600 shillings per month ($84.00) plus 60 shillings per meeting ($8.40). After first resisting any payment, the Minister of Regional Administration finally approved 200 shillings per month and 10 shillings per meeting ($28.00 and $1.40). The expatriate senior staff angrily cited the Council's governing ordinance which permitted reimbursement only for out-of-pocket expenses. These officials paid the money—and then reluctantly—only after directives from the minister which exempted them from liability. According to one European observer, well acquainted with the city administration,

> [The officials] felt that pressures were just too great. They had to yield. Anyway, there is no threat that they will be sued. The

9 See the *Uganda Argus,* July 26, July 31 and September 28, 1963 and *The Daily Nation,* August 27, 1963.

10 See the *Uganda Argus,* February 29, 1964.

11 That is, those officials with annual salaries above £687 (about $2000).

government would see to it that no lawyer brought an action. In this atmosphere you can't use the fine points of the law.[12]

African politicians unanimously respond that the former system only suited European councillors who could afford to attend the seven or eight Council meetings each month without pay. By comparison with the former Council, the new Council does indeed seem to speak for African aspirations on a number of issues, as the old Council did not. African shopkeepers have been encouraged by special rents; some streets have been renamed for African leaders in place of European explorers. Councillors please their non-Baganda African constituents with flights of anti-imperialist rhetoric. Moreover, direct voter pressure has had some effect. As in Nairobi, citizens have successfully pressured to relax housing regulations. In another instance, an Asian councillor in Kampala, responding to the wishes of some of his African constituents, persuaded the Council to open a footpath linking a major market area with groups of African homes and to cut elephant grass on its sides, making travel easier.[13] Significantly, party discipline was effective in 1964 on these matters of specific material incentives rather than on policy questions such as education, street maintenance, traffic and public health.[14] As one Council leader put it, "Parties aren't very important on the Council. Party members don't vote together." Meetings of the UPC caucus were abandoned soon after the first Council election in 1962 (although another attempt to hold them was made in late 1964) because many members simply ignored caucus decisions. African members who publicly attacked Kampala Asians were not willing to accept decisions which reflected considerable Asian influence. And some Asian and African councillors were unwilling to stop speaking freely on the floor. The remaining senior European officials would have opposed parties in the colonial period as blocking the disinterested consideration of public questions. But after 1962 they regretted the demise of the UPC caucus which they felt would have produced more consistent and "responsible" proposals.

The contrast between party weakness on policies and its predominance on perquisites and personnel was striking. In the style of the American Jacksonian Democrats 'spoils system in 1828, the UPC has successfully kept Kampala's Democratic Party councillors from the Administration Committee which passes on all council appointments, salaries and terms of service. According to one UPC councillor, "Anyone who wants to get an appointment must be in the party." A UPC African added, "We should give jobs to the people who are loyal to the party. It's silly to have opposition members. How can they implement policies if they don't support them?" The UPC councillors forced the deputy mayor, an appointee in the colonial period who had no party loyalties, to join the UPC in order to win election by the councillors as mayor. The party caucus also pressured the UPC Minister for Regional Administration to approve payments to the councillors. Later it successfully appealed to the Minister to reappoint a leading UPC Asian whom the European town clerk had succeeded in removing from the Council.

III

The rise of narrow self-interest and even corruption is so common in new states that its causes have been extensively examined.[15] As Werlin observes, the most

12 Personal interview.

13 The *Uganda Argus,* August 26, 1963.

14 Banfield and Wilson, p. 115 ff. See also Peter B. Clark and James Q. Wilson, "Incentive Systems, A Theory of Organizations," *Administrative Science Quarterly,* VI (September 1961), 129–166.

15 See Wraith and Simpkins, and M. G. Smith, "Historical Conditions of Political Corruption Among the Hausa," *CSSH,* VI (January 1964), 164–94.

important cause in East Africa may be the sharp disparity between the wealth of Asians and Europeans and the political power of the Africans (Werlin, p. 192). The many immigrant poor in nineteenth-century American cities were also divided by culture and income from the few usually native Protestant business leaders. The two groups were linked by the self-interest and corrupt politics of the machine. The machine took bribes from businessmen and in exchange arranged for favorable government policies. Most of the money was not distributed to the mass of voters despite such material benefits as Christmas gifts and emergency food baskets.[16] The largest payoffs to most voters were symbolic and non-material. Party tickets were ethically balanced; and ethnic feelings sometimes favorably influenced American foreign policy toward the countries from which the immigrants came. Most of the material incentives were retained by the members of the machine themselves, who emerged from the immigrant groups by virtue of political aptitude.

The American cities after the Civil War were far more economically developed than the present cities of East Africa and enjoyed a much wider consensus on political beliefs.[17] Yet the role of the uneducated, newly arrived European peasants in American cities may not have been so very different from the position today of the uneducated, newly arrived tribesmen in African cities. Certainly some parallels are striking. Given their sharply restricted economic resources, Kampala's political leaders can only appeal to the mass of voters with symbolic payoffs such as racialist and anti-imperialist rhetoric, changing the European names of city streets, and recognizing various tribal groups within the party. Material payoffs are necessarily concentrated on the few most capable political leaders who emerge from the rank and file. These leaders help manipulate the symbolic payoffs to attract the loyalty of their fellows.

By themselves, these considerations indicate the causes and conditions which foster a politics of self-interest rather than the effects or functions of this pattern within the political system. Banfield and Wilson note that urban American machines performed a number of positive functions, including services to the poor and to business concerns, and social mobility for ambitious politicians. But "of particular interest" was the machine's function in helping to overcome "the constitutional dispersal of authority" typical of the system of separation of powers.[18]

As Werlin shows, the difficulty in East Africa is not the constitutional dispersal of authority but the decline in political capacity. Political capacity is so general a variable that the causes for its decline are numerous and complex. If anything, the introduction of self-interest politics may hasten a decline in technical competence, one of the major elements in political capacity. The introduction of patronage practices may demoralize the most professionally competent administrators by keeping them from reaching key positions. But Werlin is concerned about the loss of motivation and cooperation as well as the loss of professional competence. The crucial function of self-interest politics is to replace a mutual dedication to the goals of "good government" with a mutual if more selfish loyalty to a system of specific material incentives. Some of the decline in political capacity is offset by a modified and politicized version of the invisible hand.[19] The members of the politically dominant group in both the city and national gov-

16 Banfield and Wilson, p. 117.

17 Louis Hartz, *The Liberal Tradition in America* (New York, Harcourt, 1955).

18 Banfield and Wilson, p. 126.

19 Edward C. Banfield, *Political Influence* (New York, The Free Press of Glencoe, 1961), p. 328.

ernments cooperate in order to maintain the strength of the party.

The UPC in Kampala only begins to approximate the typical American party machine. In particular, the current drift toward one-party government in Uganda is sharply reducing the influence of the individual voter. Still, the new regime must secure some popular support. It will have to find some way of coopting or controlling the politically able and ambitious.

A politics of self-interest is not the only alternative. Indeed, Werlin links corruption with physical force as two politically "dysfunctional" alternatives to "various forms of subtle persuasion," that is, cooperation for "good government" goals (p. 185). In a coercive system, cooperation among politicians and administrators is not the indirect result of self-interest but the direct response to the threat of physical force. This alternative in the African context is likely to be legitimated and molded by a radical or at least generally socialist ideology of the common good. Such an authoritarian, socialist alternative has real merits, particularly if it includes a quasi-puritan obligation to help build the country. It is likely to produce more egalitarian policies than will a politics of self-interest. Indeed an ethic of self-interest undeniably impairs devotion to the public good. A government utterly dominated by corruption—as Kampala's is not—would be an utter disaster. And these costs of corruption and self-interest are all the more severe in a society with few trained personnel and meagre economic resources.

Nevertheless, it seems reasonable to distinguish much more sharply than does Werlin between coercive and corrupt government. A coercive authoritarian system has obvious drawbacks. Wraith and Simpkins note that bribery and corruption in England after 1688 replaced the force and violence of the preceding 250 years.[20] A politics of self-interest and corruption was compatible—as violence is not—with Britain's constitutional government after the Glorious Revolution and with the vigorously democratic government of nineteenth-century America. The divisible character of material incentives allows a process of bargaining in which many parties and interests may obtain some rewards.

By emphasizing cooperation on behalf of "good government," Werlin seeks to replace externally applied sanctions and inducements such as corruption and coercion with, in Weber's terms, an internalized rational-legal system of authority. This pattern of authority did motivate most East African politicians and administrators in the colonial period, however much it was ultimately sanctioned by British military power. Since Independence, legal-rational authority has itself been replaced by self-interest, reversing the historical sequence in both England and America. Like socialism, unions, liberalism, parliamentary government and Western culture, the norms and practices of "good government" were imported in East Africa fully grown. They did not slowly develop as they did in the West. "Good government" preceded and succumbed to corruption in Kampala, rather than following and supplanting corruption as it has done in many but not all American cities.

Werlin concludes by urging reforms which would introduce honesty, efficiency and public dedication so that "progress, however defined, can take place." These procedures "need not be those *currently* used in the Western democracies" (p. 198, emphasis supplied). I have tried to argue that even this modified prescription is premature. Attention might be more profitably paid to the past experience of Western countries, such as the United

---

20 Wraith and Simpkins, p. 60.

States, rather than to their current practices. In a society with a sharp division between wealth and political power, self-interest may *for a time* play a paradoxical but decisive role in securing unity. Political regimes must first assemble enough strength through the distribution of material incentives to undertake the development which then makes "good government" possible. Many American cities followed this course during the last hundred years. The cities of East Africa may be following the same course today.[21]

---

[21] The author wishes to thank Michael Barkun of Syracuse University, Richard Flathman of the University of Chicago, and Ali A. Mazrui of Makerere College, Kampala, for helpful criticisms of an earlier draft.

48. The Peso Price of Politics in the Philippines

ALBERT RAVENHOLT

Each national political edifice has its own structure of inner authority and "silent" symbols for identifying the "pecking order of officials." Sometimes this is a matter of ideological skill or party rank or military connections. There are still countries in Asia where an accident of birth bestows on an official greater influence of sorts than his colleagues can hope to achieve on their own. In this young Republic the most potent "quiet tool of political influence" is money, as it is also to a degree in the United States. But the fast growing supremacy of the peso in politics has some particularly disturbing implications here. It is certainly a major inducement to, and result of, official corruption. More consequential is the extent to which it is diverting political efforts from national objectives to narrow concern for the advantage of well-heeled economic groups. Recent events raise the question of whether Filipinos in effect are losing, or perhaps squandering, the political franchise Americans brought them. Equally critical is the issue of what kind of political opposition can survive with prospects of effective use of legal methods. And ahead looms the problem of who will not only speak for but act on behalf of more than 90 per cent of all Filipinos who cannot afford to pay for a politician. It is within the Philippine Congress that these trends are most conspicuously on display. The 24 senators and 102 representatives share a many-columned, imposing, yellow masonry structure that overlooks the crumbling stone walls and shattered church skeletons of Intramuros, the ancient Spanish city wrecked during the liberation in 1945. Within, the corridors that ring the rectangular building on the four floors are flanked by the offices of the elected elite; before each congressman's door hangs a shingle with his name and below it lesser shingles, each one denoting a committee assignment. The session hall of the House lies directly before the main entrance where members of Congress and visitors alight under awnings that ward off the blistering sun. On the center door leading to the air-conditioned chamber a white-lettered sign warns: "No firearm is allowed inside the session hall—by order." It is a large hall with a level floor and the representatives' allotted desks nearly fill it leaving narrow balconies on the sides for guests and the press, and a special section for diplomats at the rear. Dominating the room is the raised dais of the Speaker with its leather-paneled front and array of microphones. Two floors up, the smaller, more intimate senate meets in a high-ceilinged hall, with Greek, Roman, and Malayan statues above the long windows that let in light over the more commodious visitors' gal-

---

SOURCE: Albert Ravenholt, "The Peso Price of Politics," *AUES Reports,* Southeast Asia Series. 6: 4 (May 1958), pp. 1–10. By permission of the American Universities Field Staff, Inc. Copyright 1958.

leries. Recently this chamber has also been air-conditioned, as Filipinos have taken avidly to this new and expensive device for shielding themselves from the heat and humidity. And the senators have traded their tall, Spanish-style, woven swivel chairs for tidy modernistically fashioned seats and small padded desks.

While Congress is in session this place exudes the air of an arena where competing ambitions and demands are compromised, fused, occasionally broken or permitted a rare triumph, while the business of legislating, appropriating and conducting hearings goes on. And yet, it is utterly casual. In the Senate, debate as a rule is leisurely in English or Spanish with an occasional speech in Tagalog. The President of the Senate, chosen from among the members, maintains an unhurried rule among these men and one woman who all have been elected at large throughout the Islands and are lionized relatively even more than their opposites in Washington, D.C. Down below in the House the tone of debate is more raucous. Spanish is rarely heard and the Speaker maintains a far firmer discipline. On days when Congress meets, the halls and offices as well as the balconies usually are crowded with folks from all walks of life. Delegations of weathered farmers come to the big city and, determined to see their congressman, may wait for hours for him to return from a hearing or a caucus—a device Filipinos love. He is then expected to feed these visitors and perhaps pay for a show or expedite a title at the Bureau of Lands. Job-seekers are omnipresent as are the so-called political "leaders" who really are the lieutenants and sometimes the bodyguards or relatives of politicians. Labor leaders, newspapermen, and representatives of potent financial groups all mix around the place with an easy familiarity that does not disguise the fact that this is where elected representatives do make decisions for the Republic.

The peculiarly centralized character of the Philippine Government affords the members of Congress extraordinary powers. The very nature of their colonial administration, since they functioned here on behalf of the viceroy of Mexico and the King of Spain, encouraged the Spanish governors to concentrate authority in Manila. And the American governors generally continued this tradition, reasoning that their first responsibility was to give the Islands an efficient administration which "would teach these people how to run a government." Since the election of the first National Assembly in 1907 Congress has been a forum for the expression of nationalism and an instrument for furthering the careers of Filipino leaders whose future was identified with this cause. Consequently, they wanted more rather than less political power at the center and argued with some justification that geographic, linguistic, and cultural fragmentation must be countered with vigorous rule from Manila. These patterns of government were incorporated in the Constitution adopted in 1935 and reinforced by a centralized system of taxation which provides that officials in Manila will determine the use of most funds collected throughout the land and gives little substance to local government in the provinces, municipalities, and *barrios*. Despite repeated promises of local autonomy Congress has backed away from it—its members clearly sense that if provincial folk no longer needed come hat in hand to Manila there might be an end to some lavish, golden rides on the political merry-go-round.

With rare exceptions the members of Congress maintain a standard of living—or consumption—that is far out of proportion to their annual salary of 7200 pesos. And the cost of living is variously calculated here to be 50 to 100 per cent higher than in New York City, depending upon family tastes. The average senator lives in a home that can fairly be described as "near-palatial," would rent for the equivalent of his salary or more, and is staffed usually with the multitude of servants that prominent Filipino families habitually accumulate. Formerly, many of them rode in chauffeured Cadillacs, but now they are switching to smaller European cars that consume less gasoline and appear more modest in the eyes of constituents. It is the unusual senator who does not accumulate wealth while in office. But reliable figures are elusive. Members of Congress are notorious for not paying their income taxes fully on time—again there are a few men who are outstanding exceptions and meticulously file honest returns as and when the law requires. The indicia to financial advantages of political power are land purchased—particularly urban real estate—businesses launched or acquired and special privileges granted relatives of members of Congress. The late President Ramon Magsaysay described one senator whom he said had made seven million pesos through political influence in two years, a figure that could be matched by very few of his colleagues.

Representatives, whose opportunities to garner riches are more limited, also are handicapped by the fact that, like some senators, most of them are gamblers and patrons of garish night spots along Dewey Boulevard. Americans taught them poker, and blackjack and today monte also is popular. Manuel Quezon, first president of the Commonwealth, institutionalized it politically with his regular card sessions where affairs of state also were threshed out. President Quezon maintained a "Union Club" for political followers who also had their own "Pasay Club" where some of them kept their girl friends. The last Liberal Party regime maintained its own "Congressional Club" where members of Congress could relax without being disturbed. A more modest illustration of the rewards that come with office is that of a former Malacañang Palace reporter elected to the House of Representatives last November. He had sold his house to pay for an earlier unsuccessful campaign. Last fall he took his terminal leave pay from the newspaper, the savings to which his wife had contributed as a teacher, contributions from friends and party totaling an estimated 40,000 pesos and invested them in a successful campaign. While his is still a middle-class style of living the family consumption scale measured in home furnishings, entertainment, and automobile has definitely risen since his political victory. And he has indulged in a not uncommon pattern of political vindictiveness, arranging in the House version of the national budget to abolish funds for two out of three heads of the Agricultural Tenancy Commission—they once dismissed his present staff assistant from the Commission.

The average congressman's chronic shortage of cash to maintain his style of living in Manila, plus a residence in his district, and meet the continuing demands of his followers puts him at the mercy of a pernicious system that has grown up in the House and Senate in recent years. While the prewar Speaker of the House of Representatives refused a discretionary fund of 30,000 pesos, the presiding officer this year has more than four and one-half million pesos that he can disperse. And the President of the Senate has 1,241,260 pesos to allocate among his colleagues. These are itemized in the budget under headings such as "Sundry expenses," "For supplementary force," "Secretarial and clerical service," "Travel expenses of members," etc. Actually, the funds are in addition to the line item appropriations for regular employees of the House and Senate; each member selects three assistants and such additional staff as are allowed the floor leaders and committee chairmen. This includes eight public relations officers for the President of the Senate and ten PROs at the service of the Speaker plus a considerable office force. In addition a number of the reporters covering Congress receive a monthly stipend from the discretionary funds. As Congress has allocated increasing sums for its own use it also has become bolder in ignoring accounting formalities. Two years ago the budget began stipulating that such items as the 1,362,000 pesos now allocated for "Sundry expenses" should be considered "expended upon issue thereof." And the two presiding officers have authority to transfer appropriations from one item to another and create new positions, provided not more than forty per cent is added to a specified category.

In practice this system means that the Speaker of the House and President of the Senate can and do add substantially to the income of their colleagues. A lowly ordinary member of the opposition in the House may receive 20,000 pesos, part of which he then disperses for his followers who may be hired as "emergency technical assistants" for the duration of the 100-day session and also to pay for essential telegrams and envelopes. But a member of the majority, and particularly the chairman of an important committee, can collect considerably more. And it appears that the extent to which members co-operate with the presiding officer determines just how much they do receive. Sometimes this discretionary account is employed for odd purposes. Last year just before the elections each congressman collected an additional 16,000 pesos from the discretionary fund, evidently to help him out with his political expenses. Funds from these sources have been known to find their way to the purchase of land for individuals and for travel abroad of family members of a presiding officer. Some politicians use it to support sons of their leaders attending school in Manila. A House member who needs to satisfy a political supporter can sometimes arrange for the Speaker to take him on as an emergency employee. Senators, each of whom on the average has twice as large a sum from the discretionary fund as a representative, are classed among their intimates according to whether or not they take care of their minor followers. Some senators spend all they collect to sustain their political subordinates while others appear to pocket most of the funds they receive from the discretionary fund. And there are several members of both the Senate and the House who meticulously collect only what they spend for legitimate official purposes. The clearly needed major increase in salaries for senators and representatives has been delayed by the constitutional prohibition against any member of Congress benefiting from a pay raise voted during his term. More consequential than the diversion of funds for odd uses is the compulsion toward a one-party Congress that the discretionary accounts encourage—a member of the opposition must be strong and rich or have ascetic habits to survive, and then he still has little opportunity to help his followers.

Any member of Congress who ventures too far or furiously into the opposition may find himself even more embarrassed politically—he may be denied the usual release of his "pork barrel" as it is candidly described in debate and the press. Each year Congress enacts an appropriation to be spent where and as each member designates by the Department of Public Works; this sum may be as high as 250,000 pesos for each representative and 300,000 for each senator. And it is a vital means whereby he can take care of his constituents. During the election campaign he may have promised supporters residing in certain *barrios* a road or a bridge and the "pork barrel" is the means to making good on this commitment. When traveling in the countryside with a congressman, I have on occasion been proudly told: "That's my irrigation system. I built it with my pork barrel last year." Also, there have been municipal water systems installed in districts where a senator or his family owned land and schools provided for communities where a congressman wanted to cultivate a following. While Congress appropriates the funds for "pork barrel" the release of them is not automatic. In the past senators and congressmen who had become overly vocal in their criticism sometimes found that "Malacañang"—the term politicians use in referring to the President and the executive authority—delayed interminably in releasing their particular sums for use by the Secretary of Public Works. During the present session the House tried to overcome this handicap by passing a public works bill stipulating that all projects in a representative's district must be approved first by him and that only such workers can be employed as have been personally recommended by the congressman. The Senate at first balked at the bill on the grounds that 159 million pesos appropriated over the past three years remained unspent and then pushed the entire budget aside to be taken up at a special session. Senators on the "Blue Ribbon" committee and impatient representatives may dig for and expose corruption in the administration. But like their American counterparts, Filipino members of Congress are most reluctant to be publicly critical of colleagues.

Almost every member of Congress heads or is a prominent partner in a law office. The Constitution prohibits the twelve senators and twelve representatives on the Commission on Appointments from practicing in the inferior courts. However, they are permitted to appear before the Supreme Court. Every member of Congress also is barred by law from taking a case where the government is involved, although in practice this was modified by a Supreme Court decision four years ago. Two of the abler senators who have a reputation for integrity and really do practice law net annually approximately 50,000 pesos each from their practice. Additional income is also available from lectures they give before classes of law colleges in which they may own stock. One of these senators explained to me the price of going into opposition; when he came out with serious charges against the administration several of his most prominent clients sought other legal counsel hinting that he could no longer help them at the Central Bank, the customs department, or the executive agencies where they wanted co-operation. And it is just within these entities, including the government credit institutions, the agencies that buy for official use, and the bureaus superintending natural resources, that a member of Congress must have influence in order to command the fees of high-paying clients. This is one of the considerations that leads Congress to insist upon a line-item budget despite repeated efforts to introduce the performance type budget—a congressman thereby can threaten to eliminate from the next budget the appropriation for the salary of a specific government official who has refused to co-operate. Facilitating a substantial import license for an appreciative Chinese client not uncommonly brings a member of Congress, or his firm, a 50,000-pesos fee. Some congressmen who were impoverished after the election-collected names of firms granted dollar licenses by the import control authorities and then contacted these firms in time to collect a fee before the allocation became public. A senator or congressman or a group of them may organize a special sphere of influence. Probably the most lucrative at the moment concerns Japanese reparations, under which more than 500 million dollars worth of goods is to reach the Philippines over a 20-year period. A recent congressional hearing made public the strange arrangement whereby companies with effective connections at Malacañang as well as in Congress obtained brand new ships from Japanese reparations without having signed a lease or purchase contract for them with the government. Using a vernacular expression one amazed senator inquired if the ships were acquired "simply with saliva?"

At present opposing groups in Congress are devoting much time to fighting about rights to reclaim some 3700 acres of Manila Bay foreshore that in time may be worth 750 million pesos. Most of the important bills are being left for the last day and night's rush session, when horse trading among members is at its most vigorous. As a rule, today's influence-peddling congressman is more discreet than he was during the previous Liberal Party administration. Then for a period each member of Congress was allotted a quota of Chinese he could admit into the country while virtually all other legal Chinese immigration was halted by law.

Although the financial rewards for a seat in Congress have long been high for those who were unscrupulous and quick-witted it was only with the election of last November that the cost of securing membership reached its present exorbitant level. In part this reflects the increasing difficulty of doing business without official influence. But it also results from a change in the nature of political action. The late President Ramon Magsaysay transformed election campaigning from a contest to capture the allegiance of provincial political bosses and cliques to a direct appeal to ordinary voters. While he lived they usually voted for him and his candidates without financial inducement. But now—perhaps it's a sixth sense that operates—Filipino voters often are determined to get as much as possible out of a candidate during the election, with little regard to what he does afterwards. Among the brazen evidence of this in the last election was a banner stretched across the main street of a town not far from Manila which read: "No Money, No Honey—No Votes." To a degree reflecting their cynicism about government, ordinary voters in large blocs traded their franchise for pesos. On the morning of election a priest in Quezon Province rose and admonished his parishioners that it was their duty to vote. He also said it was his responsibility to inform them what the various candidates had done for their community. On his first campaign visit President García had contributed 500 pesos toward building the new church and matched this sum on his next visit. José Yulo, the Liberal Party candidate, had contributed 2000 pesos. The other candidates, he said, had added nothing to the construction of the building where they now were worshipping. The present Nationalista Party administration of President Carlos P. García appears to have purchased a considerable portion of its votes with distribution of cash, relief goods, rice, and promises of more, which the Liberal Party despite lavish expenditure could not match. While the Liberals may have spent 21 million pesos all told through their national headquarters and through their provincial organizations, the Nacionalistas are estimated by those who have studied the problem to have spent four times that sum, including some government grain that was parceled out, and public works allocations. One important source of funds was the political contributions collected in return for foreign-exchange licenses which, according to an informed report, depressed the dollar reserves by 160 million during the campaign.

While the national campaigns have become vastly more expensive, it is in the congressional contests that the pesos really count, despite the legal provision limiting a candidate's expenditures to the equivalent of one year's salary for the post which he seeks. The unsuccessful campaign of a young friend who ran for the first time for office in Mindanao cost over 80,000 pesos and his is a family of modest resources. Expenses of another friend who sought office in Bataan were 70,000 pesos—he lost by 30 votes. Now he is engaged in a recount which so far has required the expenditure of 2000 pesos and will cost at least that much more before it is completed three months hence. In the Central Visayan Islands congressional seats are even more furiously contested and expenditures by a candidate of 250,000 to 400,000 pesos are not uncommon. One of the more intriguing examples is the province of Batanes composed of the typhoon-swept, rocky islands north of Luzon with 3185 registered voters. Here the successful congressman spent roughly 30,000 pesos and his opponent almost as much. A goodly portion of this was used to transport voters between islands, bring precinct leaders to Manila for the convention, and buy cloth and similar items. A run-down on a typical candidate's expenditure could be apportioned approximately as follows: printing of posters, sample ballots (so the voters can write in the candidate's name properly), pamphlets and personal histories—20 per cent; transport for candidate, lieutenants and fellow campaigners and bodyguards, and hire of jeepneys and buses to haul voters on election day—20 per cent; organization including payment to precinct leaders and watchers—10 per cent; cash donations to voters who are wavering or simply sell the votes of their families and followers—40 per cent; and, 10 per cent to pay for feeding voters before election. Throughout the lowland Christian areas *caldereta,* or goat stew, is the favorite, while among a few minority groups (such as some of the mountain people of Northern Luzon), dog, stewed or roasted, is preferred.

With large sums changing hands casually, congressional and presidential elections held every four years inevitably become a time of bounty for petty political chieftains who control a few dozen or even a few hundred votes. They have evolved ingenious devices, such as carbon paper pads that voters carry into the booth and place behind their ballots to prove whom they voted for, in order to collect accordingly. Voters who sold their votes explained to me that the candidates are all more or less alike and since they profit from the government the voter is entitled to collect from the candidate for whom he votes. This attitude, so generally accepted by ordinary citizens, has barred political parties from securing mass financial contributions. Instead, parties and individual candidates for congressional and other seats rely upon large contributions from special groups whom they favor.

A typical congressional candidate from North Luzon received about one-fourth his reported 50,000 campaign budget from the party, one-fourth came from his own family and the remaining portion was contributed by growers of Virginia tobacco (who have been enriched in the last few years by restrictions on imports from the United States and high support prices) and Chinese money-lenders. Since the Chinese control three-fourths of the retail trade, almost as much of the wholesale trade, most of the rice mills, and a large portion of the new processing and packaging industries that have appeared since import control was imposed eight years ago, they are a vital source of campaign funds. And the precarious legal position of the Chinese whose businesses can be closed for minor violations of laws make them vulnerable to political plucking. Other powerful interests also bargain with cash for campaigns. The Liberal Party relied heavily upon prominent families in control of some of the largest sugar centrals. During the last election a group of prominent rice-growing *hacenderos* in Central Luzon offered the new Progressive Party two million pesos in return for a promise to amend the Agricultural Tenancy Law in favor of the landowners. Since the Progressives spent only about one and one-half million pesos and were desperate for cash just before the election, considerable conviction was required to refuse this offer—the cash was then used against these political newcomers. And the Progressives, like the other two smaller "maverick" parties, failed to elect a single man to Congress. Their experience is perhaps the best index to what becomes of the lone candidate who is long on principles but lacks funds and friends in office.

In this land, where the aspiration to "be somebody" is nearly universal, politics is far more than a short cut to wealth. It is the pre-eminent yardstick by which a man's life is measured. And a young Filipino's dreams of reaching the top readily picture him as a senator, courted by the rich, feared by officials and with an entree everywhere that inevitably gives him a seat at the head table. It is one of the distinguishing marks of Philippine society that distinction in politics has yet to be commonly equated with genuine public service. The late President Ramon Magsaysay began to offer another measure of political performance. And his magical following was a product in part of popular instinctive grasp of his sincerity. He had planned to start remaking Congress by securing the election to the House and its speakership of former Senator Tomas Cabili, who died in the same plane crash that took Magsaysay's life.

Today the members of Congress are not afraid of the Malacañang incumbent, although he may prove firmer than they think. They do not fear that President Carlos P. García, the well-read, wily and quiet, lifelong professional politician will go directly to the people to vote them out of office. And the Philippine Government shares a trait with our own in Washington, D.C.; without firm executive leadership Congress tends to become preoccupied with the petty individual interests of its members. The corruption that nearly engulfed our Congress during the years following the American Civil War, when railroad promoters bought their franchises and bribed Congress to subsidize construction with cash and millions of acres of national domain, was ended in time as the electorate became educated and informed. No other remedy promises a permanent solution here if representative government is to be meaningful. The achievement of such a massive education of the simple *barrio* voters will require a kind of grass roots mobilization for understanding and action such as barely has been tested in these islands. The extent to which it is initiated will be a revealing indicator of the prospects for democratic progress.

PART 4

Corruption and Modernization

In 1957 the *Economist* found it "surprising" that political scientists have not done more to work out a general theory of the "toxic and tonic" effects of political corruption on the body politic, and challenged them and economists to fill "one of the most obvious gaps in general textbooks on economics and political science—the unwritten section on graft" (Selection 49). Since then, a considerable number of theoretically oriented contributions have been published during a period when general theorizing has been focused predominantly on the processes of modernization and development. Thus corruption has come to be perceived as a problem that most typically arises in the process of modernization, or in the careful formulation of Samuel Huntington (Selection 50): "Corruption may be more prevalent in some cultures than in others but in most cultures it seems to be most prevalent during the most intense phases of modernization." Although there is widespread agreement that there is a general link between modernization and corruption, there is vociferous disagreement as to the nature of the conjunction. Is corruption a necessary or an avoidable concomitant of modernization? Is it on balance more "toxic" or "tonic" from the perspective of economic growth and of political development? Some scholars argue that on balance corruption is toxic from the perspective of political development goals, although it may be tonic in terms of promoting economic growth. Others, such as José Abueva in Selection 54, a Philippine public administration scholar, argue that it is tonic even for the former:

> Not only are rampant nepotism, spoils and graft unavoidable, under the circumstances of most developing countries, but they may have positive, unanticipated consequences for political development. . . . In the early stages of politico-administrative development, particularly where a democratic political system is consciously desired, nepotism, spoils and graft may actually promote national unification and stability, nation-wide participation in public affairs, the formation of a viable party system, and bureaucratic accountability to political institutions.

At the other end of the social-scientific spectrum Gunnar Myrdal (Selection 55) believes with equal firmness that "the prevalence of corruption provides strong inhibitions and obstacles to development." He is scornful of "opportunistic rationalizations," believes that "unproved assumptions" about the usefulness of corruption in development are "totally wrong," and posits that "corrupt practices are highly detrimental from the point of view of the value premises of modernization ideals." Fortunately, other scholars have applied themselves to breaking up the analytical problem into its component parts and have supplied thoughtful subhypotheses that serve to make the somewhat polemical discussion more rewarding from a scientific point of view.

THE FUNCTIONS OF CORRUPTION

The revisionists who have more or less self-consciously challenged the earlier assumption that the public consequences of corruption were overwhelmingly negative share the concept that certain kinds of corruption may perform functions that are more or less beneficial from the perspective of the society at large as well as beneficial for the interests of those directly involved. Startling though this perspective would have been for the generation that derived its intellectual nurturance from Woodrow Wilson and Lord Bryce, it has since become so widely accepted as to give rise to something like a new orthodoxy, particularly within American social science. However, not all writers who attribute some positive functions to corruption should be considered "functionalists," and it is worthwhile to identify three rather distinguishable conceptual frameworks that have influenced the literature and been evolved in it.

1. Writers who have been inspired particularly by the structural-functional schools in sociology and anthropology perceive corruption as fulfilling positive functions, particularly with respect to social integration. Robert K. Merton's study, "Some Functions of the Political Machine" (in his *Social Theory and Social Structure,* New York: Free Press, 1957, pp. 72–82), stands out from the structural-functional literature because of the enormous influence it appears to have had on students of political corruption. Merton stresses that "in our prevailingly impersonal society, the machine, through its local agents, fulfills the important social function of humanizing and personalizing all manner of assistance to those in need." He argues that the persistence of the machine at the turn of the century "as an apparatus for satisfying other unfulfilled need of diverse groups" implied that the official structure had "functional deficiencies." He admonishes potential reformers who aim to "do away with" corruption that *"to seek social change, without due recognition of the manifest and latent functions performed by the social organization undergoing change, is to indulge in social ritual rather than social engineering"* (italics in original). Although turn-of-the-century social theory developed somewhat similar perspectives (see Selections 28 and 51), the persuasive theoretical presentation by Merton inspired many of the more tough-minded recent writers. This variety of functionalist approach has proved very appealing to students of political development like David Bayley, José Abueva, and James C. Scott (Selections 53, 54, and 56), especially because the social and political integration problems of American cities and developing countries appeared to be somewhat similar.

2. Another group of writers, who relate more directly to the market-based definitions of corruption, ascribes positive functions to corruption as a regulatory instrument for the informal allocation of scarce licenses and services. Thus, for V. O. Key corruption serves to regulate, control, "license," and keep within bounds such practices like prostitution and gambling, which, because they are illegal, are not adequately controlled through legitimate political authority or the market mechanism. Robert Tilman (Selection 7) bureaucratic black marketeering in the developing countries serves the function of maintaining an equilibrium between the limited supply of governmental services and the increas-

ing demand due to rising expectations. For economists like W. H. Leff (Selection 52) the most important functions of corruption in developing countries lies in its utility as a tool permitting entrepreneurs to get around a sluggish bureaucracy and in the role it may play in diverting resources from consumption to investment.

3. Still other writers, who are basically institutionalists and relate to the public-interest definition of corruption, perceive corruption as fulfilling a useful function as the least of the evils that may become prevalent in political systems during periods characterized by political degeneration and the decay of political institutions. Their outstanding theorist, Samuel Huntington (Selection 50), who believes in calling a "spade a spade," posits that most modernizing countries are buying rapid social modernization at the price of political degeneration. In such situations corruption and violence are seen as alternative means of making demands upon the system, with the latter posing the greater and more direct threat, while the former may simultaneously satisfy demands in a way that violence does not. ("He who corrupts a system's police officers is more likely to identify with the system than he who storms the system's police stations.") Huntington's theses are bold and provocative, and for that reason many of his generalizations may be open to challenge.

Corruption as an Aid to Economic Growth

A number of economists and political scientists have launched a vigorous frontal assault against what one of their number, Nathaniel H. Leff (Selection 52), has labeled the "development-bureaucracy-efficiency" probability logic of the previously conventional view that political corruption was harmful to economic growth. In essence they challenge the assumption that government planners and economic policymakers in developing countries, even if honest and efficient, are the best possible instruments for defining the public interest and for seeking to implement goals based on such definitions. Thus Bayley (Selection 53) bases his guess that corruption might systematically serve to impel better choices in certain economic arenas on the assumption that government-established criteria for choice may be not only imperfect but at times actually stupid. Scott has suggested elsewhere that those Southeast Asian economic systems in which the private sector is predominant have performed better than state-run economies, due in part to the ease with which corruption can vitiate government restrictions. He goes on to speculate that, "Other things being equal, corruption which secures greater freedom of operation for the private sector will generally promote economic growth."[1] Leff is even more forthright in suggesting that, "rather than leading the development process, the governments and bureaucracies may be the lagging sectors," who tend to be in league with vested *status quo* economic interests. In this kind of situation, he believes, corruption will help economic growth because it will "enable an economic innovator to introduce his innovations before he has had time to establish himself politically." Thus, those who hold a relatively low opinion of

---

[1] James C. Scott, "An Essay on the Political Functions of Corruption," *Asian Studies,* V:3 (Dec. 1967), p. 518.

the development potential of bureaucratic allocation vis-à-vis market mechanisms tend to believe that the cost of corruption in terms of lack of achievement of governmental aims may as often as not redound to the benefit of the development goals of the economy.

Contrary to the assumption that the corrupt diversion of public funds constitutes economic waste, writers like Bayley believe that corruption may actually constitute a supplemental allocative mechanism that drains resources away from consumption and toward investment purposes. Thus the corrupt official who diverts funds from famine relief or village economic aid, investing his gains in firms manufacturing tires or machine tools, is seen as benefitting economic growth. In a country where private capital is scarce and tax-gathering agencies inadequate, the official who squeezes a bribe out of a poor peasant and diverts that money to investment is likewise seen as a potential benefactor to economic growth. Of course, the process can work the other way if the bribe giver is an investment-prone well-to-do peasant and the bribe taker a big spender in night clubs; the key elements in the equation are the marginal consumption and investment propensities of the bribe extractor and extractee. J. S. Nye in Selection 57 does some inspired theorizing about what consequences may probably develop out of these kinds of situations. He sees little growth advantage occurring if "squeeze money" is extracted primarily by lower-level civil servants whose tendency to spend it for consumption purposes will be just as high as that of the extractees. If pay-off money flows primarily to upper-level civil servants, it may be channeled into growth-promoting investments, but only if a tolerant environment makes the corrupter feel secure that the ill-gotten gains are firmly his. If he does not feel that way, the corruption income will be transferred to Swiss bank accounts and be of no assistance whatsoever to that economy's development.

Another way in which the prevalence of corruption may possibly contribute to economic growth is by providing informal techniques for reducing delays due to bureaucratic red tape and excessive regulation. Thus "speed money" paid as *baksheesh,* or tips, to government clerks may contribute to economic growth even if the latter spend it on baubles and incense. Leff believes that "graft can provide the direct incentive necessary to mobilize the bureaucracy for more energetic action on behalf of the entrepreneurs." He is directly challenged by Myrdal (in Selection 55), who believes that the "popular notion that corruption is a means of speeding up cumbersome procedures is palpably wrong." Myrdal cites the findings of the Santhanam Committee, which reported that the "speed money" practice was actually the direct *cause* of administrative delays because lower-level officials got into the practice of holding back all papers from the public until payment was forthcoming.

The theoretical projections of Nye tend to suggest that those who seek to argue that corruption has the predominant effect of liberating market mechanisms to produce beneficial effects for the economy as a whole have often, in their zeal, overstated the case. At times these writers allow their empathy and sympathy with the entrepreneur to carry them out on the limb, as when Leff and Bayley argue that the entrepreneur's ability to outbribe competitors might be accepted as a criterion of his efficiency as a producer. Such theoretical hand-me-downs from turn-of-the-century Social Darwinism can scarcely help develop remedies that conscientious analysts would prescribe for the problems of developing countries today.

Corruption and Sociopolitical Integration

Writers who perceive political corruption as playing a useful function with respect to the processes of social and political integration have sought to make their point by borrowing extensively from the vocabulary of lubrication mechanics. Functions and effects normally associated with an emolient (M. McMullan in Selection 32), a solvent (Bayley), or a lubricant (Huntington) have been attributed to corruption. Corrupt practices are believed capable of reducing friction, bridging cleavages based on tradition and ideology, creating bonds of mutual interest between groups with initially antagonistic interests, and providing links between the socially privileged and the marginal outsiders. Although sometimes a concomitant cause of revolution, it may also serve as a substitute for either reform or revolution in bringing concrete benefits to groups that might otherwise be alienated from society, the political regime or both. Whether corruption will have some or all of these effects in a developing society is determined in part by whether its incidence conforms to a pattern of "top-heavy corruption," where most of the corrupt revenue is paid to a small political elite, or to a "pyramid" pattern, where corruption incidence is more characteristic of lower echelon and strata. This "pyramid" pattern serves to distribute rewards more widely within the system, more so in systems with competitive party politics than in one-party or bureaucratically dominated systems.

Patterns of "top-heavy" corruption may serve limited, but from the perspective of regime survival, important, functions of integration by reconciling hostile wealthy elites to the political elites who sell them favors. In this setting corrupt payoffs provide no benefit whatsoever for the mass of the population, but they may serve to provide a stake in the system to groups disaffected as the result of exclusion from political power. Patterns of top-heavy corruption under which the heads of government siphoned tens and even hundreds of millions of dollars from the treasury in order to build up family fortunes have survived for fairly long periods without the general population ever getting a chance to act on their accumulated grievances. However, the system may run the danger of violent overthrow if large numbers of the younger political and military elites see themselves excluded from the illicit gains the top elites reserve for themselves. Nye believes that if there is wider access to "extraction" opportunities, the prevalence of corruption involving money and other "modern" inducements is likely to make elites cohere more than divide. This kind of broad-based governmental corruption is one situation in which he believes the developmental benefits of corruption exceeding the costs.

Following Merton, many of the authors perceive positive effects for social and political integration if lower-level officials and even ordinary voters are permitted to engage in small-scale corrupt practices. They believe that loss of respect for constituted authority may be more than made up for in terms not only of the material but also of the symbolic rewards that may reduce the individual's alienation from the system. Thus, the practice of giving an official a small present or bribe may reduce for the peasant the great and terrifying gap between him and the official machinery. Nepotism in government hiring is viewed as a substitute for a public works system by Bayley, who sees corruption as humanizing modern political institutions in traditional terms. He judges that it may be "better that people in developing nations misuse modern agencies to their own ends than that they reject the new because they cannot work the handles." In such a country as India stability may be maintained through the allocation of different kinds of rewards to higher and lower-level officials, with the former feeling gratified by their possession of power and moral virtue, while the latter are, in Huntington's terms, "compensated for their lack of political standing by their greater opportunity to engage in corruption." Nye, who like Huntington has looked out at the third world of the developing countries from a Harvard University observation point of Boston politics, tends to agree that a smattering of corruption may help keep the masses politically satisfied. In his cost-benefit matrix the probability that benefits may exceed costs occurs relatively often in the column that summarizes the impact on nonelites from the perspective of national integration.

Corruption, Capacity, and Legitimacy

A conventional "moralist" might accept the contention that corruption may have some beneficial effects with regard to economic growth and national integration but fall back on the argument that such benefits would be more than balanced out by the costs incurred in terms of reduced effectiveness and legitimacy by a political system that tolerates a high level of corruption. However, he would find himself challenged by revisionists who argue that corruption might even increase the effectiveness level of the governmental bureaucracy. Contending that "the corrupt are not always unable; nor are they always unpatriotic," Bayley suggests that the opportunity to increase the salaries of low officials through corruption incomes may serve as a bureaucratic recruitment inducement and actually serve to "increase the quality of public servants." If such remarks raise the blood pressure among the official guardians of civil service morality in Washington and New Delhi, Abueva's comments (in Selection 54) may well induce apoplexy. He contends that nepotism and spoils may well be the "potent stimuli" needed to convert "rigid" and "unresponsive" bureaucrats into more effective agents, and that practical exposure to corrupt practices will cause politicians who start out as popular agitators to become initiated "into the world of production and distribution," thus becoming acquainted with a "different order of rationality." As an accommodating device, corruption is credited with increasing governmental capacity by preserving a working relationship between civil servants and popular leaders that might otherwise be subject to crippling strains due to role jealousies.

While these effects may be possible in particular situations, the *Economist*'s counter-assertion that "graft beyond a certain point really does become incompatible with efficiency," seems more generally plausible. "Where money or wire pulling decides promotion, and patient merit is denied advancement, trains really do not run on time, contracts do go to the wrong contractor, research produces no discoveries, plans are not fulfilled." This line of thinking is certainly borne out at great length in the report of the Indian Santhanam Committee, which has developed perhaps the most extensive body of empirical evidence about corruption in a developing country. One of its major points is to underscore how corruption engenders accentuated centralization, precisely because the granting of discretionary authority to lower-level officials will generate corruption that will undercut the intent of government policy. As Myrdal emphasizes, "authority cannot be efficiently delegated unless those in administrative positions are incorrupt and this fact is generally recognized."

But to what extent does public knowledge of extensive corruption in the administration undermine the legitimacy of the regime? Various authors suggest that this may be affected by the visibility of the corruption and by the degree of tolerance the culture has developed toward such acts. In systems where the public came earlier to believe that officials were bound by something like the duties of office, the visibility of corruption can serve to erode legitimacy. In India the Santhanam Committee found that "corruption has increased to such an extent that people have started losing faith in the integrity of the public administration," and expressed a fear of "the deterioration in the standards of public life." The fact that corruption makes people pay several times over for the same services will naturally lead to lack of support for the political system. If the growing expectation that civil servants are corrupt is not checked it will discourage those who seek to be honest and efficient. As morale declines, it is possible for the community feeling to disintegrate into the type of amoral familism characteristic of Montegrano. To the extent that government feels less able to count upon the cooperation and support of the people it may tend to utilize more coercion, which in turn may lead to an increase in violence.

The obvious need for further research both on the incidence of corruption itself, as well as on the feedbacks generated from discussion about it, is suggested by the striking differences of opinion about the consequences engendered by various approaches to the subject. Thus Abueva depreciates the "humiliating distortions and resented abuse" generated by much Western writing about corruption in developing countries. He argues that "at a critical period in the political history of the emerging nations, supercilious criticism of the practices in question merely harass the progressive leaders and the intelligentsia and exacerbate cynicism toward the democratic system sought to be established." Myrdal retorts that "the public outcry against corruption must be regarded as a constructive force" even though some spread of cynicism may be a by-product of wider discussion of the problem. He feels that it is people like Abueva, who rationalize corruption by regarding it as an "unavoidable appendage to development," who do the most to "spread cynicism and to lower resistance to the giving and taking of bribes." But for Leff even cynicism turns out to be a phenomenon with positive aspects, and he would be content "if the cynicism caused by bureaucratic corruption leads to increased self-seeking in the rest of the society." From his point of view, "if cynicism acts as a solvent on traditional inhibitions, and increased self-seeking leads to new ambitions, economic development would be furthered."

CHAPTER ELEVEN

Assessing Effects, Toxic and Tonic

49. Towards a Grammar of Graft

THE ECONOMIST

It is curious how little notice has been taken of one of the most obvious gaps in general textbooks on economics or political science—the unwritten section on graft. Yet anyone reading the foreign, if not the home, news must be struck by the part which this basic human institution plays in affairs. One might have supposed that the economic theorist would discuss somewhere the extent to which graft, like gambling, merely transfers incomes rather than diverts resources from more to less economic forms of production. Studies abound of public taxation, direct and indirect, levied by the rulers of underdeveloped countries; why no study of the private taxation that everybody knows is levied by the same people? Again the influence of graft in forming, sustaining and undermining governments, and indeed whole regimes, is so well recognised that it is surprising that political scientists have not done more to work out a general theory of its action, toxic or tonic, in the body politic.

One reason for this neglect may be that the home of modern economic and political theory has been Britain—and Britain during and after the period of Victorian reform of public and private morality. This seems to have led to a general assumption that the elimination of graft was a necessary concomitant of the spread of democratic representative government and of increasing wealth, industrial organisation and technical progress through the world. But this, surely, has been disproved in modern times. It is clear that graft—bribery and extortion, squeeze or protection, wire-pulling and nepotism—has persisted and found its place in the most complex twentieth-century political organisations. Not only have the corrupt foreign regimes which the long arm of Victorian imperial reform failed to reach continued to flourish, but power has been given back to dependent peoples long before they have abandoned what is conveniently known as "the custom of the country." They have asserted the right to govern themselves if they can, but misgovern themselves in any event—the right, that is, of the educated and organised minority to govern or misgovern the rest.

That right has been conceded to three very cogent arguments. The first is that while the top cadre of white administrators was undoubtedly clean-handed (being well-paid), lower down the scale the persistence of poverty has left the custom of the country intact; that, indeed, the low standards and poor expectations of the clerkly class created by the British (and other imperial) administrations have provided an incentive to corruption rather than otherwise—and that therefore the administration can carry on under new management. The second argument is that there are plenty of independent nations of all shapes and sizes which run their own affairs notwithstanding lower standards than exist in Britain. The third

SOURCE: "Towards a Grammar of Graft," *The Economist,* 183 (June 15, 1957), pp. 958–959. By permission of the publisher.

is that Britain itself won an empire, developed a worldwide trade, embarked on industrialisation and defeated Napoleon when its civil service was largely an organised system of sinecures and perquisites, its parliament often largely up to auction, and commissions in its army and navy bought and sold.

These arguments have been backed by the demonstrable fact that Asian and Middle Eastern countries, where graft has certainly not been suppressed, forge ahead economically—and sometimes politically. In Africa, the recent enquiries into financial irregularities in the Gold Coast and Eastern Nigeria were followed by elections which were both won by the parties that had been indicted for those irregularities. Yet there have been other events which suggest that graft can play a very different role. The effect of corruption in discrediting and weakening the Chiang regime in China and opening the way to the communist victory is frequently cited. It played a major part in the overthrow of Farouk and the supremacy of Nasser in Egypt. It has helped the communists to win power in one Indian state. And in Africa there is the interesting case of the "disturbances" in northern Sierra Leone in 1955, when after the relaxation of control by the district commissioners as part of the policy of transferring power, the people rose against the exactions of the paramount chiefs, and the bizarre cry was raised: "Down with black government! We want white!"

It is, however, for the political theorists to impose a pattern on varied events like these; this article can do no more than raise the need for study and suggest a few starting points. One of these, surely, is that, whatever appearances may suggest, graft beyond a certain point really does become incompatible with efficiency. Where money or wirepulling decides promotion, and patient merit is denied advancement, trains really do not run to time, contracts do go to the wrong contractor, research produces no discoveries, plans are not fulfilled. Teamwork, loyalty to the job, disintegrate. The thing that sometimes disguises this in some territories is that the new and restless desire of the middle classes for money-making, which is one of the main reasons for graft, is also often in itself the main motive force behind the sudden growth of economic enterprise. Asians, Africans and others may repeat Bacon's apologia that he took bribes but never let them influence his judgment. It may serve for judges, or even for chiefs: the codification of customary payments (or "dashes") in Northern Nigeria as an attempt to apply Bacon generally. But it will not wash in engineering, contracting or the public services. When it becomes necessary to register a letter to ensure that the stamps will not be steamed off it by the postal authorities for personal use, commercial progress becomes difficult.

The next point is, surely, that so far from the growth of democracy sterilising graft, graft in the end tends to make democracy untenable. In theory, the party in opposition exposes any corruption in the party in office, and is subsequently returned to power with a mandate for reform. That this does not completely apply even in mature democracies is suggested by Belloc's lines on the general election of 1906:

> The accursed power that stands on Privilege,
> And goes with women and champagne and bridge,
> Broke, and democracy resumed her reign
> (Which goes with bridge and women and champagne.)

When democratic institutions are imposed on countries too deeply imbued with the conviction that squeeze is part of human nature, all political parties are corrupt; this means that none is more efficient in administration than others, but the total cost is far heavier. As a supporter of one South American dictator put it:

It is cheaper for the country that he should be president for life, because he has made his fortune and is satisfied. When we changed presidents every few years, the cost of presidential fortunes used to ruin us.

This is one reason why democracies as well as dynasties are superseded by dictatorships. But dictatorships of the South American or Asian type are not now the only alternative; communism offers to rid poor but ambitious countries of both graft and inefficiency. Graft is a factor in the cold war, and Marxist political scientists, if not bourgeois ones, are studying it. Much is made of the claim that communist China has a clean administration for the first time in history. But it is not so much the corruption as the impotence of a corrupt regime that communist propaganda emphasises when aimed at ardent young nationalists, frustrated in their desire alike to rise professionally and to get things done. It offers a new discipline to break the ancient matrix of loyalty to family, clan and tribe.

This by no means implies that communist countries are free of graft. There are no animals without their specialised parasites. Recent Russian literature makes this clear and Chinese self-criticism suggests that the communist claims are inflated. The "fixer," or contact man, who, for due reward, will help win the ear of authority or otherwise further his client's aims, is a prominent figure in Soviet life. In China, too, graft has seeped back under the pure surface of a puritanical regime, and senior communists have adopted a number of old habits, one of them being what the Peking newspapers prudishly term "a feudal attitude towards women." But communism has advantages over other dictatorships. Common grafting exists, but is better concealed. More important, however, is the fact that there is less need for it, because the granting of enormous differentials for the party caste produces the material results without the need for private enterprise. The party official's interest is power, not money; power gives him all he needs, and for it he ceaselessly intrigues within the party structure.

In conclusion, it may be suggested that the study of graft as a political factor must revolve round the concept of permissive limits: the limits at which graft does not detract intolerably from a country's economic progress at or which nepotism drives its growing professional and executive middle class to revolt. What a strong country like America can stand ruins a weak underdeveloped territory. And British readers should not dismiss the art of squeeze as of no relevance to them. The prospective loss of oversqueezed countries to the communist camp plainly is relevant; policy ought even to take account of it. And though the main interest for Britons may seem to be the beam in the foreigner's eye, they must always guard against being incommoded by catching a mote in their own.

50. Modernization and Corruption

SAMUEL P. HUNTINGTON

Corruption is behavior of public officials which deviates from accepted norms in order to serve private ends. Corruption obviously exists in all societies, but it is also obviously more common in some societies than in others and more common at some times in the evolution of a society than at other times. Impressionistic evidence suggests that its extent correlates reasonably well with rapid social and economic modernization. Political life in eighteenth-century America and in twentieth-century America, it would appear, was less corrupt than in nineteenth-century America. So also political life in seventeenth-century Britain and in late nineteenth-century Britain was, it would appear, less corrupt than it was in eighteenth-century Britain. Is it merely coincidence that this high point of corruption in English and American public life coincided with the impact of the industrial revolution, the development of new sources of wealth and power, and the appearance of new classes making new demands on government? In both periods political institutions suffered strain and some measure of decay. Corruption is, of course, one measure of the absence of effective political institutionalization. Public officials lack autonomy and coherence, and subordinate their institutional roles to exogenous demands. Corruption may be more prevalent in some cultures than in others but in most cultures it seems to be most prevalent during the most intense phases of modernization. The differences in the level of corruption which may exist between the modernized and politically developed societies of the Atlantic world and those of Latin America, Africa, and Asia in large part reflect their differences in political modernization and political development. When the leaders of military juntas and revolutionary movements condemn the "corruption" in their societies, they are, in effect, condemning the backwardness of their societies.

Why does modernization breed corruption? Three connections stand out. First, modernization involves a change in the basic values of the society. In particular it means the gradual acceptance by groups within the society of universalistic and achievement-based norms, the emergence of loyalties and identifications of individuals and groups with the nation-state, and the spread of the assumption that citizens have equal rights against the state and equal obligations to the state. These norms usually, of course, are first accepted by students, military officers, and others who have been exposed to them abroad. Such groups then begin to judge their own society by these new and alien norms. Behavior which was

SOURCE: Samuel P. Huntington, "Modernization and Corruption," *Political Order in Changing Societies*. New Haven, Conn.: Yale University Press, 1968, pp. 59–71. By permission of the publisher.

acceptable and legitimate according to traditional norms becomes unacceptable and corrupt when viewed through modern eyes. Corruption in a modernizing society is thus in part not so much the result of the deviance of behavior from accepted norms as it is the deviance of norms from the established patterns of behavior. New standards and criteria of what is right and wrong lead to a condemnation of at least some traditional behavior patterns as corrupt. "What Britons saw as corrupt and Hausa as oppressive," one scholar has noted of northern Nigeria, "Fulani might regard as both necessary and traditional."[1] The calling into question of old standards, moreover, tends to undermine the legitimacy of all standards. The conflict between modern and traditional norms opens opportunities for individuals to act in ways justified by neither.

Corruption requires some recognition of the difference between public role and private interest. If the culture of the society does not distinguish between the king's role as a private person and the king's role as king, it is impossible to accuse the king of corruption in the use of public monies. The distinction between the private purse and public expenditures only gradually evolved in Western Europe at the beginning of the modern period. Some notion of this distinction, however, is necessary to reach any conclusion as to whether the actions of the king are proper or corrupt. Similarly, according to traditional codes in many societies, an official had the responsibility and obligation to provide rewards and employment to members of his family. No distinction existed between obligation to the state and obligation to the family. Only when such a distinction becomes accepted by dominant groups within the society does it become possible to define such behavior as nepotism and hence corruption. Indeed, the introduction of achievement standards may stimulate greater family identification and more felt need to protect family interests against the threat posed by alien ways. Corruption is thus a product of the distinction between public welfare and private interest which comes with modernization.

Modernization also contributes to corruption by creating new sources of wealth and power, the relation of which to politics is undefined by the dominant traditional norms of the society and on which the modern norms are not yet accepted by the dominant groups within the society. Corruption in this sense is a direct product of the rise of new groups with new resources and the efforts of these groups to make themselves effective within the political sphere. Corruption may be the means of assimilating new groups into the political system by irregular means because the system has been unable to adapt sufficiently fast to provide legitimate and acceptable means for this purpose. In Africa, corruption threw "a bridge between those who hold political power and those who control wealth, enabling the two classes, markedly apart during the initial stages of African nationalist governments, to assimilate each other."[2] The new millionaires buy themselves seats in the Senate or the House of Lords and thereby become participants in the political system rather than alienated opponents of it, which might have been the case if this opportunity to corrupt the system were denied them. So also recently enfranchised masses or recently arrived immigrants use their new power of the ballot to buy themselves jobs and favors from the local political machine. There is thus the corruption of the poor and the corruption of the rich. The one trades political power for money, the other money for political power. But

1 M. G. Smith, "Historical and Cultural Conditions of Political Corruption Among the Hausa," *Comparative Studies in Society and History*, 6 (Jan. 1964), 194.

2 M. McMullan, "A Theory of Corruption," *The Sociological Review*, 9 (July 1961), 196. [See Selection 32 this volume.]

in both cases something public (a vote or an office or decision) is sold for private gain.

Modernization, thirdly, encourages corruption by the changes it produces on the output side of the political system. Modernization, particularly among the later modernizing countries, involves the expansion of governmental authority and the multiplication of the activities subjected to governmental regulation. In Northern Nigeria, "oppression and corruption tended to increase among the Hausa with political centralization and the increase of governmental tasks." All laws, as McMullan has pointed out, put some group at a disadvantage, and this group consequently becomes a potential source of corruption.[3] The multiplication of laws thus multiplies the possibilities of corruption. The extent to which this possibility is realized in practice depends in large part upon the extent to which the laws have the general support of the population, the ease with which the law can be broken without detection, and the profit to be made by breaking it. Laws affecting trade, customs, taxes plus those regulating popular and profitable activities such as gambling, prostitution, and liquor, consequently become major incentives to corruption. Hence in a society where corruption is widespread the passage of strict laws against corruption serves only to multiply the opportunities for corruption.

The initial adherence to modern values by a group in a transitional country often takes an extreme form. The ideals of honesty, probity, universalism, and merit often become so overriding that individuals and groups come to condemn as corrupt in their own society practices which are accepted as normal and even legitimate in more modern societies. The initial exposure to modernism tends to give rise to unreasonable puritanical standards even as it did among the Puritans themselves. This escalation in values leads to a denial and rejection of the bargaining and compromise essential to politics and promotes the identification of politics with corruption. To the modernizing zealot a politician's promise to build irrigation ditches for farmers in a village if he is elected seems to be just as corrupt as an offer to pay each villager for his vote before the election. Modernizing elites are nationalistic and stress the overriding preeminence of the general welfare of society as a whole. Hence in a country like Brazil, "efforts by private interests to influence public policy are considered, as in Rousseau, *inherently* 'corrupt.' By the same token government action which is fashioned in deference to particular claims and pressures from society is considered 'demagogy.' "[4] In a society like Brazil the modernizing elements condemn as corrupt ambassadorial appointments to reward friends or to appease critics and the establishment of government projects in return for interest group support. In the extreme case the antagonism to corruption may take the form of the intense fanatical puritanism characteristic of most revolutionary and some military regimes in at least their early phases. Paradoxically, this fanatical anticorruption mentality has ultimate effects similar to those of corruption itself. Both challenge the autonomy of politics: one substituting private goals for public ones and the other replacing political values with technical ones. The escalation of standards in a modernizing society and the concomitant devaluation and rejection of politics represent the victory of the values of modernity over the needs of society.

Reducing corruption in a society thus often involves both a scaling down of the norms thought appropriate for the behavior of public officials and at the same time changes in the general behavior of

3 Smith, p. 194: McMullan, pp. 190–191.

4 Nathaniel Leff, "Economic Development Through Bureaucratic Corruption," *American Behavioral Scientist*, 8 (Nov. 1964), 132; italics in original. [See Selection 52.]

such officials in the direction of those norms. The result is a greater congruence between prevalent norms and prevalent behavior at the price of some inconsistency in both. Some behavior comes to be accepted as a normal part of the process of politics, as "honest" rather than "dishonest graft," while other, similar behavior comes to be generally condemned and generally avoided. Both England and the United States went through this process: at one point the former accepted the sale of peerages but not of ambassadorships, while the latter accepted the sale of ambassadorships but not of judgeships. "The result in the U.S.A.," as one observer has noted, "is a patchwork: the scope of political patronage has been greatly reduced and the cash bribery of higher public servants largely eliminated. At the same time, large areas of public life have so far remained more or less immune to reform, and practices that in one sphere would be regarded as corrupt are almost taken for granted in another."[5] The development within a society of the ability to make this discrimination is a sign of its movement from modernization to modernity.

The functions, as well as the causes, of corruption are similar to those of violence. Both are encouraged by modernization; both are symptomatic of the weakness of political institutions; both are characteristic of what we shall subsequently call praetorian societies; both are means by which individuals and groups relate themselves to the political system and, indeed, participate in the system in ways which violate the mores of the system. Hence the society which has a high capacity for corruption also has a high capacity for violence. In some measure, one form of deviant behavior may substitute for the other, but, more often, different social forces simultaneously exploit their differing capacities for each. The prevalence of violence, however, does pose a greater threat to the functioning of the system than the prevalence of corruption. In the absence of agreement on public purposes, corruption substitutes agreement on private goals, while violence substitutes conflict over public or private ends. Both corruption and violence are illegitimate means of making demands upon the system, but corruption is also an illegitimate means of satisfying those demands. Violence is more often a symbolic gesture of protest which goes unrequited and is not designed to be requited. It is a symptom of more extreme alienation. He who corrupts a system's police officers is more likely to identify with the system than he who storms the system's police stations.

Like machine politics or clientalistic politics in general, corruption provides immediate, specific, and concrete benefits to groups which might otherwise be thoroughly alienated from society. Corruption may thus be functional to the maintenance of a political system in the same way that reform is. Corruption itself may be a substitute for reform and both corruption and reform may be substitutes for revolution. Corruption serves to reduce group pressures for policy changes, just as reform serves to reduce class pressures for structural changes. In Brazil, for instance, governmental loans to trade association leaders have caused them to give up "their associations' broader claims. Such betrayals have been an important factor in reducing class and trade association pressure upon the government."[6]

The degree of corruption which modernization produces in a society is, of course, a function of the nature of the traditional society as well as of the nature of the modernizing process. The presence of several competing value systems or cultures in a traditional society will, in itself, encourage corruption in that so-

5 Colin Leys, "What Is the Problem About Corruption?" *Journal of Modern African Studies*, 3 (1965), 230. [See Selection 1.]

6 Leff, p. 137.

ciety. Given a relatively homogeneous culture, however, the amount of corruption likely to develop during modernization would appear to be inversely related to the degree of social stratification in the traditional society. A highly articulated class or caste structure means a highly developed system of norms regulating behavior between individuals of different status. These norms are enforced both by the individual's socialization into his own group and by the expectations and potential sanctions of other groups. In such a society failure to follow the relevant norms in intergroup relations may lead to intense personal disorganization and unhappiness.

Corruption, consequently, should be less extensive in the modernization of feudal societies than it is in the modernization of centralized bureaucratic societies. It should have been less in Japan than in China and it should have been less in Hindu cultures than in Islamic ones. Impressionistic evidence suggests that these may well be the case. For Western societies, one comparative analysis shows that Australia and Great Britain have "fairly high levels of class voting" compared to the United States and Canada. Political corruption, however, appears to have been more extensive in the latter two countries than in the former, with Quebec perhaps being the most corrupt area in any of the four countries. Consequently, "the more class-polarized countries also seem to have less political corruption."[7] Similarly, in the "mulatto" countries (Panama, Cuba, Venezuela, Brazil, Dominican Repubiic, and Haiti) of Latin America, "there appears to be greater social equality and much less rigidity in the social structure" than in the Indian (Mexico, Ecuador, Guatemala, Peru, Bolivia) or *mestizo* (Chile, Colombia, El Salvador, Honduras, Nicaragua, Paraguay) countries. Correspondingly, however, the relative "absence of an entrenched upper class means also the relative absence of a governing class ethic, with its sense of noblesse oblige" and hence "there seems little doubt that it is countries in this socio-racial category in which political graft reaches its most flagrant heights." Pérez Jiménez in Venezuela, Batista in Cuba, and Trujillo in the Dominican Republic all came from non-upper-class backgrounds and all became multimillionaires in office. So also, "Brazil and Panama are notorious for more 'democratic,' more widely-distributed, graft-taking."[8] The prevalence of corruption in the African states may well be related to the general absence of rigid class divisions. "The rapid mobility from poverty to wealth and from one occupation to another," one observer has noted of Africa, "has prevented the development of class phenomena, that is, of hereditary status or class consciousness."[9] The same mobility, however, multiplies the opportunities for and the attractions of corruption. Similarly, the Philippines and Thailand, both of which have had reasonably fluid and open societies with relatively high degrees of social mobility, have been characterized by frequent reports of widespread political corruption.

In most forms corruption involves an exchange of political action for economic wealth. The particular forms that will be prevalent in a society depend upon the ease of access to one as against the other. In a society with multiple opportunities for the accumulation of wealth and few positions of political power, the dominant pattern will be the use of the former to achieve the latter. In the United States, wealth has more commonly been a road to political influence than political office has been a road to wealth. The rules against using public office to obtain

7 Robert R. Alford, *Party and Society* (Skokie, Ill., Rand McNally, 1963), p. 298.

8 Needler, *Political Development in Latin America*, chap. 6, pp. 15–16.

9 Peter C. Lloyd, "The Development of Political Parties in Western Nigeria," *American Political Science Review*, 49 (Sept. 1955), 695.

private profit are much stricter and more generally obeyed than those against using private wealth to obtain public office. That striking and yet common phenomenon of American politics, the cabinet minister or presidential assistant who feels forced to quit office *in order* to provide for his family, would be viewed with amazement and incredulity in most parts of the world. In modernizing countries, the reverse situation is usually the case. The opportunities for the accumulation of wealth through private activity are limited by traditional norms, the monopoly of economic roles by ethnic minorities, or the domination of the economy by foreign companies and investors. In such a society, politics becomes the road to wealth, and those enterprising ambitions and talents which cannot find what they want in business may yet do so in politics. It is, in many modernizing countries, easier for an able and ambitious young man to become a cabinet minister by way of politics than to become a millionaire by way of business. Consequently, contrary to American practice, modernizing countries may accept as normal widespread use of public office to obtain private wealth while at the same time taking a stricter view of the use of private wealth to obtain public office. Corruption, like violence, results when the absence of mobility opportunities outside politics, combined with weak and inflexible political institutions, channels energies into politically deviant behavior.

The prevalence of foreign business in a country in particular tends to promote corruption both because the foreigners have less scruples in violating the norms of the society and because their control of important avenues to economic well-being forces potential native entrepreneurs to attempt to make their fortunes through politics. Taylor's description of the Philippines undoubtedly has widespread application among modernizing countries: "Politics is a major industry for the Filipinos: it is a way of life. Politics is the main route to power, which, in turn, is the main route to wealth. . . . More money can be made in a shorter time with the aid of political influence than by any other means."[10] The use of political office as a way to wealth implies a subordination of political values and institutions to economic ones. The principal purpose of politics becomes not the achievement of public goals but the promotion of individual interests.

In all societies the *scale* of corruption (i.e. the average value of the private goods and public services involved in a corrupt exchange) increases as one goes up the bureaucratic hierarchy or potential ladder. The *incidence* of corruption (i.e. the frequency with which a given population group engages in corrupt acts) on a given level in the political or bureaucratic structure, however, may vary significantly from one society to another. In most political systems, the incidence of corruption is high at the lower levels of bureaucratic and political authority. In some societies, the incidence of corruption seems to remain constant or to increase as one goes up the political hierarchy. In terms of frequency as well as scale, national legislators are more corrupt than local officials; high level bureaucrats are more corrupt than low level ones; cabinet ministers are the most corrupt of all; and the president or top leader the most corrupt among them. In such societies the top leader—the Nkrumah, Sarit, San Martín, Pérez Jiménez, Trujillo—may make off with tens if not hundreds of millions of dollars. In such a system corruption tends to accentuate already existing inequalities. Those who gain access to the most political power also have the more frequent opportunities to gain access to the most wealth. Such a pattern of top-heavy corruption means a very low level of political insti-

[10] George E. Taylor, *The Philippines and the United States: Problems of Partnership* (New York, Praeger, 1964), p. 157.

tutionalization, since the top political institutions in the society which should be most independent of outside influences are in fact most susceptible to such influences. This pattern of corruption is not necessarily incompatible with political stability so long as the avenues of upward mobility through the political machine or the bureaucracy remain open. If, however, the younger generation of politicians sees itself indefinitely excluded from sharing in the gains of the older leaders, or if the colonels in the army see little hope of promotion and the chance to share in the opportunities open only to generals, the system becomes liable to violent overthrow. In such a society both political corruption and political stability depend upon vertical mobility.

The expectation of more corruption at the top is reversed in other societies. In these societies the incidence of corrupt behavior increases as one goes down the political or bureaucratic hierarchy. Low-level bureaucratic officials are more likely to be corrupt than high-level ones; state and local officials are more likely to be corrupt than national ones; the top national leadership and the national cabinet are comparatively free from corruption, while the town council and local offices are deeply involved in it. Scale and incidence of corruption are inversely related. This pattern would seem to be generally true for highly modern societies, such as the United States, and also for at least some modernizing societies, such as India. It is also probably the dominant pattern in communist states. The crucial factor in this type of society is the existence of fairly strong national political institutions which socialize rising political leaders into a code of values stressing the public responsibilities of the political leadership. National political institutions are reasonably autonomous and differentiated, while lower-level and local political individuals and organizations are more closely involved with other social forces and groups. This pattern of corruption may directly enhance the stability of the political system. The top leaders of the society remain true to the stated norms of the political culture and accept political power and moral virtue as substitutes for economic gain. Low-level officials, in turn, are compensated for their lack of political standing by their greater opportunity to engage in corruption. Their envy of the power of their leaders is tempered by the solace of their own petty graft.

Just as the corruption produced by the expansion of political participation helps to integrate new groups into the political system, so also the corruption produced by the expansion of governmental regulation may help stimulate economic development. Corruption may be one way of surmounting traditional laws or bureaucratic regulations which hamper economic expansion. In the United States during the 1870s and 1880s corruption of state legislatures and city councils by railroad, utility, and industrial corporations undoubtedly speeded the growth of the American economy. "Many economic activities would be paralyzed," Weiner observes of India, "were it not for the flexibility which *bakshish* contributes to the complex, rigid, administrative system."[11] In somewhat similar fashion, during the Kubitschek era in Brazil a high rate of economic development apparently corresponded with a high rate of parliamentary corruption, as industrializing entrepreneurs bought protection and assistance from conservative rural legislators. It has even been suggested that one result of governmental efforts to reduce corruption in societies such as Egypt is to produce additional obstacles to economic development. In terms of economic growth, the only thing worse than

[11] Myron Weiner, *The Politics of Scarcity* (Chicago, University of Chicago Press, 1962), p. 253. See in general Joseph S. Nye, "Corruption and Political Development: A Cost-Benefit Analysis," *American Political Science Review,* 61 (June 1967), 417–427.

a society with a rigid, overcentralized, dishonest bureaucracy is one with a rigid, overcentralized, honest bureaucracy. A society which is relatively uncorrupt—a traditional society for instance where traditional norms are still powerful—may find a certain amount of corruption a welcome lubricant easing the path to modernization. A developed traditional society may be improved—or at least modernized—by a little corruption; a society in which corruption is already pervasive, however, is unlikely to be improved by more corruption.

Corruption naturally tends to weaken or to perpetuate the weakness of the government bureaucracy. In this respect, it is incompatible with political development. At times, however, some forms of corruption can contribute to political development by helping to strengthen political parties. "The corruption of one government," Harrington said, ". . . is the generation of another."[12] Similarly, the corruption of one governmental organ may help the institutionalization of another. In most modernizing countries, the bureaucracy is overdeveloped in comparison with the institutions responsible for aggregating interests and handling the input side of the political system. Insofar as the governmental bureaucracy is corrupted in the interests of the political parties, political development may be helped rather than hindered. Party patronage is only a mild form of corruption, if indeed it deserves to be called that at all. For an official to award a public office in return for a payment to the official is clearly to place private interest over public interest. For an official to award a public office in return for a contribution of work or money to a party organization is to subordinate one public interest to another, more needy, public interest.

Historically strong party organizations have been built either by revolution from below or by patronage from above. The nineteenth-century experience of England and the United States is one long lesson in the use of public funds and public office to build party organization. The repetition of this pattern in the modernizing countries of today has contributed directly to the building of some of the most effective political parties and most stable political systems. In the later modernizing countries the sources of private wealth are too few and too small to make a major contribution to party building. Just as government in these countries has to play a more important role in economic development than it did in England and the United States, so also it must play a more important role in political development. In the 1920s and the 1930s, Ataturk used the resources of the Turkish government to foster the development of the Republican Peoples Party. After its creation in 1929 the Mexican Revolutionary Party similarly benefited from governmental corruption and patronage. The formation of the Democratic Republican Party in Korea in the early 1960s was directly helped by the use of governmental monies and governmental personnel. In Israel and India, governmental patronage has been a major source of strength for Mapai and Congress. The corruption in West Africa derived in part from the needs of the political parties. And, of course, in the most obvious and blatant case of all, communist parties, once they acquire power, directly subordinate governmental bureaucracies and governmental resources to their own purposes.

The rationale for corrupting the bureaucracy on behalf of the parties does not derive simply from a preference for one organization as against another. Corruption is, as we have seen, a product of modernization and particularly of the expansion of political consciousness and political participation. The reduction of corruption in the long run requires the

12 James Harrington, quoted in George Sabine, *A History of Political Theory* (rev. ed. New York, Holt, Rinehart & Winston, Inc., 1950), p. 501.

organization and structuring of that participation. Political parties are the principal institution of modern politics which can perform this function. Corruption thrives on disorganization, the absence of stable relationships among groups and of recognized patterns of authority. The development of political organizations which exercise effective authority and which give rise to organized group interests—the "machine," the "organization," the "party"—transcending those of individual and social groups reduces the opportunity for corruption. Corruption varies inversely with political organization, and to the extent that corruption builds parties, it undermines the conditions of its own existence.

Corruption is most prevalent in states which lack effective political parties, in societies where the interests of the individual, the family, the clique, or the clan predominate. In a modernizing polity the weaker and less accepted the political parites, the greater the likelihood of corruption. In countries like Thailand and Iran where parties have had a semilegality at best, corruption on behalf of individual and family interests has been widespread. In the Philippines where political parties are notoriously weak, corruption has again been widely prevalent. In Brazil, also, the weakness of political parties has been reflected in a "clientelistic" pattern of politics in which corruption has been a major factor.[13] In contrast, it would seem that the incidence of corruption in those countries where governmental resources have been diverted or "corrupted" for party-building is on the whole less than it is where parties have remained weak. The historical experience of the West also reflects this pattern. The parties which at first are the leeches on the bureaucracy in the end become the bark protecting it from more destructive locusts of clique and family. Partisanship and corruption, as Henry Jones Ford argued, "are really antagonistic principles. Partisanship tends to establish a connection based upon an avowed public obligation, while corruption consults private and individual interests which secrete themselves from view and avoid accountability of any kind. The weakness of party organization is the opportunity of corruption."[14]

13 See Leff, pp. 10–12.

14 Henry Jones Ford, *The Rise and Growth of American Politics* (New York, Macmillan, 1898), pp. 322–323.

51. Apologies for Political Corruption

ROBERT C. BROOKS

Nearly all current contributions on the subject of political corruption belong frankly to the literature of exposure and denunciation. The ends pursued by social reformers are notoriously divergent and antagonistic, but there is general agreement among them and, for that matter, among Philistines as well, that corruption is wholly perverse and dangerous. How then may one have the temerity to speak of apologies in the premises?

Certainly not, as one writer has recently done, by presenting a detailed and striking picture of the force with which the temptation to corrupt action operates upon individuals exposed to its malevolent influence. No doubt such studies are of great value in laying bare to us the hidden springs of part of our political life, the great resources, material and social, of those who are selfishly assailing the honesty of government, and the difficulties in the way of those who are sincerely struggling for better things. In the last analysis, however, all this is nothing more than a species of explanation and extenuation, which if slightly exaggerated may easily degenerate into maudlin sympathy. That men's votes or influence are cheap or dear, that their political honour can be bought for $20 or $20,000—doubtless these facts are significant as to the calibre of the men concerned and the morals of the times, but they do not amount to an apology for either.[1] If, however, it can be shown that in spite of the evil involved political corruption nevertheless has certain resultants which are advantageous, not simply to those who profit directly by crooked devices, but to society in general, the use of the term would be justified.

Four main lines of argument have been gathered from various sources as constituting the principal, if not the entire equipment of the *advocatus diaboli* to this end. These are, first, that political corruption makes business good; second, that it may be more than compensated for by the high efficiency otherwise of those who engage in it; third, that it saves us from mob rule; and fourth, that corruption is part of an evolutionary process the ends of which are presumed to be so beneficent as to more than outweigh existing evils.

I

Of these four arguments the first is most frequently presented. Few of our reputable business men would assent to it if stated baldly, or indeed in any form, but in certain lines of business the tacit accept-

SOURCE: Robert C. Brooks, *Corruption in American Politics*. New York: Dodd, Mead, 1910, pp. 3–25, 30–38. Reprinted by permission of Dodd, Mead & Company, Inc.

1 "An Apology for Graft," by Lincoln Steffens, *American Magazine,* vol. lxvi (1908), p. 120.

ance of this doctrine would seem to be implied by the political attitude of those concerned. In slightly disguised form the same consideration appeals to the whole electorate, as shown by the potency of the "full dinner-pail" slogan, and the pause which is always given to reforms demanded in the name of justice when commercial depression occurs. But while we are often told that corruption makes business good, we are seldom informed in just what ways this desirable result is brought about. One quite astounding point occasionally brought up in this connection is the favour with which a portion of the mercantile community looks upon the illegal protection of vice and gambling. A police force must sternly repress major crimes and violence. Certain sections of the city must be kept free from offence. These things understood, a "wide-open" town is held to have the advantage over "slower" neighbouring places. A great city, we are told, is not a kindergarten. Its population is composed both of the just and the unjust, and this is equally true of the many who resort to it from the surrounding country for purposes of pleasure or profit. The slow city may still continue to hold and attract the better element which seeks only legitimate business and recreation, but the wide-open town will hold and attract both the better and the worse elements. Of course, individuals of the latter class may be somewhat mulcted in dives and gambling rooms, but they will still have considerable sums left to spend in thoroughly respectable stores, and such patronage is not to be sniffed at.[2]

Ordinarily this argument stops with the consideration of spending alone. It may be strengthened somewhat by bringing in the reaction of consumption upon production. A great city prides itself upon its ceaseless rush and gaiety, its bright lights and crowded streets, its numerous places of amusement and all the evidences of material prosperity and pleasure. These may be held to be enhanced when both licit and illicit pursuits and diversions are open to its people; and further, the people themselves, under the attraction of such varied allurements, may strive to produce more that they may enjoy more. In the Philippines, it is said that the only labourers who can be relied upon to stick to their work any considerable length of time are those who have caught the gambling and cock-fighting mania. Under tropical conditions a little intermittent labour easily supplies the few needs of others, whereas the devotee of chance, driven by a consuming passion, works steadily. In the present state of a fallen humanity there are presumably many persons of similar character living under our own higher civilisation.

Strong as is the hold which the foregoing considerations have obtained upon certain limited sections of the business community it is not difficult to criticise them upon purely economic grounds. Of two neighbouring towns, one "wide-open" and the other law-abiding, the former might, indeed, prove more successful in a business way. But we have to consider not simply the material advantage in the case of two rival cities. The material welfare of the state as a whole is of greater importance, and it would be impossible to show that this was enhanced by corruptly tolerating gambling and vice anywhere within its territory. On the contrary, economists have abundantly shown the harmful effects of such practices, even when no taint of illegality attaches to them. What the "wide-open" community gains over its rival is much more than offset by what the state as a whole loses. Moreover, it may well be doubted whether the purely economic advantage of the "wide-open" city is solid and per-

2 The argument is at least as old as Plato. In the "Laws" it is put as follows: "Acquisitions which come from sources which are just and unjust indifferently are more than double those which come from just sources only." With the true Greek contempt for business, however, the Philosopher finds it an easy matter to dispose of this specious contention. *Cf.* the "Laws," bk. v, p. 125, tr. by B. Jowett, vol. v, 3d ed.

manent. Even those of its business men who are engaged in legitimate pursuits are constant sufferers from the general neglect of administrative duty, and sometimes even from the extortionate practices, of its corrupt government. They may consider it to their advantage to have gambling and vice tolerated, but only within limits. If such abuses become too open and rampant legitimate business is certain to suffer, both because of the losses and distractions suffered by the worse element in the community and because of the fear and avoidance which the prevalence of vicious conditions inspires in the better classes. Indeed cases are by no means uncommon where the better business element has risen in protest against lax and presumably corrupt police methods which permitted vice to flaunt itself so boldly on retail thoroughfares that respectable women became afraid to venture upon them. There remain, of course, the expedients of confining illicit practices to certain districts of the city, or of nicely restraining them so that, while permitting indulgence to those who desire it, they do not unduly offend the moral element in the community. But such delicate adjustments are difficult to maintain, since vice and gambling naturally seek to extend their field and their profits and, within pretty generous limits, can readily afford to make it worth while for a corrupt city administration to permit them to do so. And even if they are kept satisfactorily within bounds, the state as a whole, if not the particular community, must suffer from their pernicious economic consequences.

It has been thought worth while to go at some length into the criticism on purely economic grounds of the argument that corruption makes business good; first, because the argument itself is primarily economic in character, and secondly, because its tacit acceptance by certain hard-headed business men might lead to the belief that its refutation on material grounds was impossible. A broad view of the economic welfare of the state as a whole and business in all its forms leads, as we have seen, to the opposite conviction. And this conviction that corruption does *not* make business good in any solid and permanent way is greatly strengthened when moral and political, as well as financial, values are thrown into the scale. It is not necessary to recite in detail the ethical argument against gambling and vice in order to strengthen this point. The general duty of the state to protect the lives and health and morals of its people, even at great financial sacrifice if necessary, is beyond question. There is a possibility, as Professor Goodnow maintains,[3] that in the United States we have gone too far in attempting to suppress by police power things that are simply vicious, as distinguished from crimes; but however this may be, some regulation or repression of vice is always necessary. The real point here is that, having once drawn the line, the bribery of officials shall not be resorted to in order that vice may be permitted to flourish in certain localities. In such cases the state suffers not only from the effects of the vice but also from the disregard into which the whole fabric of law falls because of the failure to enforce it in part.

With regard to the particular plea that the life and animation and pleasures of a wide-open town stimulate its citizens to greater activity in producing wealth, it should be observed that this amounts virtually to the advocacy of the purchase of a dubious economic benefit at a high and certain moral cost. In the long run most, if not all, the vicious practices which thus find a quasi-justification directly cripple productive efficiency much more than they can possibly stimulate it indirectly. "A short life and a merry one" may serve well as a motto for a criminal career, but not as an economic maxim for a community of sane people. It may

3 Frank J. Goodnow, "City Government in the United States," New York, The Century Co., 1908, ch. ix, p. 228.

be admitted that the world is not to grow perfect in a day. Vice will persist, corruption will persist, although doubtless in less noxious forms, and business will persist with periods of greater or less prosperity under such conditions. It would be arrant folly, however, to expect business to reach its highest development with vice rampant under a corrupt police administration. A policy of repression, firmly enforced, will be best in the long run both for morals and for business. But even if honesty and prosperity were incompatible, it would still be true that it is a higher duty of the state to make men good than to make them rich. Ordinarily, however, both ends may be pursued at the same time and without conflict.

Up to this point the discussion of the argument that corruption makes business good has been confined to the forms of corruption under which vice is illegally tolerated. A dishonest government, however, is also frequently appealed to by businesses perfectly legitimate in their general character for concessions of one sort or another, ranging from the privilege to obstruct sidewalks by show windows up to the granting of public service franchises worth millions of dollars. With an open-handed distribution of such favours business is thought to flourish. Of course, all these concessions must be paid for, but only part of the money goes into the public purse, the rest falling into the hands of boodlers, contractors, and politicians. As the latter could not establish the most perfect title to the rights and franchises they sell they are often inclined to fix prices much below real values. Hence a chance for extraordinary profits to those less scrupulous business men who know the political ropes. A still more important feature of such a situation is that almost anything can be bought. In the lingo of those who are willing to engage in corrupt transactions, business men know "where they are at"; the politicians are men with whom "they can do business." With reformers in power "favours" are not to be expected. Moreover reformers differ widely among themselves with regard to the proper method of dealing with public franchises and privileges of various sorts. Under "good government" these concessions may not be attainable at all, or, if so, only at such excessive prices and under such onerous conditions designed to safeguard the public interest, that the margin of profit left is extremely small. No wonder that contributions are made by certain kinds of business men to political organisations which the contributors well know to be corrupt, and refused by the same men to reform parties. The argument is, of course, that if the rascals win it is a good stroke of policy to secure their favour in advance, where as if the reform party wins everybody will be treated alike anyway.

From a business point of view that considers immediate profits and nothing more, this reasoning is of great significance. Several deductions must be made from it, however, before the final balance is struck. It sometimes happens that corrupt organisations fix a regular tariff for privileges of all sorts. So long as the rates are low business appears to boom. But with the wide distribution of privileges the purchasers may lose any monopoly advantage which they enjoyed when the number of concessions was limited. Worse still, a corrupt gang that feels firmly entrenched in power is apt to develop a pretty fair sense of values itself, and to raise the rates for concessions to figures that prove well-nigh prohibitive. The very willingness of business interests to pay and keep quiet encourages the politicians to increase their demands and to devise new methods of levying tribute. In the end the gang may determine to assume the profits in certain lines by the formation of inside contracting rings which make all competition from the outside futile. Of course, while this process is going on the worst and most unscrupulous competitors in the businesses affected by it have a decided advantage over their fellows. Business men who complain of railroad rebates should certainly be able to recognise the destructive character of corrupt and unfair political conditions of the kind described above. Even those who most profit by alliance with the gang are apt to repent it in the end. They may have succeeded in securing all the favours which they need, and yet stand in constant terror of blackmail and strike legislation by their former political confederates or of exposure by reformers. Finally, although they may be so fortunate as to escape indictment for particular misdeeds, the general belief that a business has been corruptly managed is likely to bring about a demand for legislation affecting its conduct which, temporarily at least, may reduce its profits and the value of its securities very materially. The agitation for municipal ownership is a case in point. Quite apart from the logical weight of the arguments advanced in support of this policy, there can be no doubt that many people favour it largely because of the corrupt methods believed, although in most cases not legally proved, to have been practised by public service corporations.

II

The second argument to be considered is that corruption may be more than compensated for by the high efficiency otherwise of those who engage in it. Such a plea may be offered either for an individual or for an organisation, such as the machine. Many historical cases could be cited of statesmanlike ability of a high order and undoubted honesty on great issues coupled with a shrewd eye for the main chance whenever minor opportunities presented themselves. Even for men who are currently credited with having possessed a much larger share of guile than of ability, admiration is sometimes expressed. There are those who think that New York owes a statue to Tweed, and Pennsylvania already has a statue of Quay—if not a place for the statue.[4] The same manner of thinking prevails in other fields than politics, especially whenever graft can be made to appear as a sort of tribute levied upon a supposedly hostile social class. For example, a labour leader who extorted checks from employers by threatening and even calling strikes was defended by many of his followers on the ground that he had shown wonderful ability in organising the union and securing higher wage scales.[5]

The question is sometimes raised as to whether or not some purely personal moral obliquity should be held against a candidate for office whose qualifications otherwise are unimpeachable. A practical answer would, of course, depend largely upon the kind of evil charged against the man and the probability that it would interfere with the performance of his public duties. Even an extremist upon such an issue would have to admit that certain statesmen who have given most distinguished service to their countries have been, for example, intemperate in the use of liquor or unfaithful in the marriage relation. If in such cases we excuse and forget, why not also excuse and forget corrupt transactions that have been more than repaid by general brilliant conduct of affairs of state? No answer to this second question, however, can avoid the distinction that while certain kinds of personal immorality may affect the value of a man's public service to an infinitesimal degree only, corruption in any part of his political career strikes directly at whatever efficiency he may possess as a public servant. In the former case his sins are in a different category from his virtues, whereas in the latter case they belong to the same category. Moreover a corrupt record even on a minor point in a man's official career is

4 According to a newspaper report of October 16, 1909, the statue was finally placed in its niche in the $13,000,000 Capitol at Harrisburg.

5 This argument is presented in a very striking way in Mr. Hutchins Hapgood's "The Spirit of Labour," pp. 114, 260, 345, 369.

apt to prove a great stumbling block forever after. Usually designing persons can more readily employ their knowledge of it to force him to the commission of further and worse corrupt actions than they could hope to do had his earlier offences been of the same degree but of a purely personal character.

There is, of course, no quantitative measure whereby we can reckon exactly the efficiency and honesty of men, and, striking a joint average, definitely appraise their value for a given position in the service of the state. If there were such a measure assuredly it would seldom, if ever, register both perfect efficiency and perfect honesty. The work of government, like that of all social institutions, must be performed by relatively weak and incapable human instruments. At best we can only seek to secure the greatest attainable honesty and the greatest attainable efficiency. There may be cases where a degree of the latter amounting to positive genius may offset a serious defect in the former. Distinguished ability, however, ought to be relatively free from moral weakness. Men of more than average capacity, to say nothing of genius, should find it less necessary than others to stoop to equivocal practices in order to succeed. If no higher motives swayed such men, then at least an intelligent appreciation on their part of the risks they ran in pursuing crooked courses would serve as sufficient deterrent. It is your stupid and incapable official ordinarily who, because of moral insensibility or in order to keep pace with his abler fellows, is most easily tempted to employ shifty devices. The weakness of the second apology for corruption is thus apparent. Normally corruption and efficiency are not found together. On the contrary honesty and efficiency are common yokemates. A public sentiment which weakly excuses corruption on the ground of alleged efficiency will be deceived much more often than a public sentiment which insists upon the highest attainable standard of both.

III

The third apology for corruption is that it saves us from mob rule. In Professor Ford's felicitous phrase the appearance of corruption "instead of being the betrayal of democracy may be the diplomatic treatment of ochlocracy, restraining its dangerous tendencies and minimising its mischiefs."[6] According to this view the machine, dominated by the boss or gang, is the defender of society itself against the attacks of our internal barbarians. Tammany Hall had the brazen effrontery to assume this attitude during the New York mayoralty campaign of 1886, when it nominated Mr. Hewitt in opposiition to Henry George. "Yet it would be difficult to name a time in recent years when frauds so glaring and so tremendous in the aggregate have been employed in behalf of any candidate as were committed in behalf of Mr. Hewitt in 1886."[7] Society would seem to be in desperate straits, indeed, if it needed such defenders and such methods of defence. In favour of their employment it is sometimes said that our propertied and educated classes have grown away from the great democratic mass. Of themselves they would be quite incapable of protecting the goods, material and ideal, which are intrusted to them. The corrupt machine, seeking its own interest, it is true, nevertheless performs the invaluable social service of keeping the restless proletariat in subjection. In order to obtain the votes of ignorant and venal citizens the unscrupulous political leader is obliged to perform innumerable petty services for them, as, for example, securing jobs, both in the public service and outside, supplying or obtaining charitable relief in times of need, speaking a friendly word to the police magistrate after a neighbourhood brawl, providing recreation in the form of tickets to

6 *Political Science Quarterly,* vol. xix (1904), p. 678.

7 "The History of Tammany Hall," by Gustavus Myers, p. 323.

chowder excursions during the summer and to "pleasure club" balls during the winter. Bread and circuses being thus suppied, our higher civilisation is presumably secure. If the corrupt machine did not perform these services, it is assumed by some timorous persons that the mob would break forth, gut our shops, rob our tills, burn, and kill in unrestrained fury.

If catastrophes so great and terrible were actually impending the situation would seem not only to justify our present corrupt rulers, but might also be held sufficiently grave to induce us to establish new bosses and gangs, giving them license to graft to their heart's content, provided only that they continue their beneficent mission of saving civilisation. Dictatorship would be cheap at the price. The whole argument, however, rests primarily upon a shockingly unjust view of the real character of our proletariat class. Even if this very indefinite term be interpreted to mean only the poorest and most ignorant of our people, whether of native American or of foreign stock, the view that they need to be constantly cajoled by the corrupt politican in order to prevent them from resorting to the violent seizure of the property of others is a grotesque misconception. In the great majority of cases such persons desire nothing more than the opportunity to earn an honest and frugal living in peace. We must admit, of course, that lynching and labour riots occur with appalling frequency in the United States. No one should attempt to minimise the danger and disgrace of such outbreaks. Let us not, on the other hand, fall into the gross error of regarding them as deliberate revolutionary attacks upon the existing social order.

With such circumstances confronting us, what shall be said of the alleged utility of the corrupt machine as prime defender of social peace? If we should conclude to recognise the gang frankly in this capacity any materials for the formation of revolutionary mobs that we may possess would certainly be encouraged to increase the demands made as the price of continued quiet, and even to furnish a few sample riots from time to time as a means of enforcing their demands. In reality, however, corrupt political machines care very little for social welfare. The very essence of corruption is self-interest regardless of public interest. Familiarity with the favours bestowed by politicians is hardly the best means of encouraging quiescence among poor and ignorant recipients. It may become the first step toward idleness and crime. But besides the distribution of favours the corrupt politician has many other means of procuring power. Hired thugs, and sometimes members of the regular police force, are employed to drive honest voters from the polls, and every manner of tricky device is resorted to in order to deceive them in casting their ballots or to falsify the election returns. Do such things allay social discontent? Even the rank favouritism shown by the corrupt organisation to its servile adherents must make enemies of those who feel themselves slighted. Few forms of political evil are more dangerous than the fear sometimes displayed by mayors or governors that the vigorous employment of the police to suppress rioting may cost them votes when they come up for re-election. And there are many other consequences of corrupt rule which indirectly but none the less surely inflame the sufferers against the injustice of the existing order: insufficient and inferior school accommodations, the absence of parks and other means of rational recreation, dirty streets, impure water supply, neglect of housing reforms, poor and high-priced public utility services and so on. All things considered, the corrupt machine is the sorriest saviour of society imaginable.

Assuming, finally, for the sake of argument, that there is real danger of class war in the near future, the best defence would obviously lie in strong police, militia, and army forces. The life of the state itself would require the destruction of every vestige of corruption in these branches of its service at least. If the danger of class war were real but not imminent a thoroughgoing policy directed to the establishment of social justice and the elimination of public abuses would be imperative. Among other things, better education, sanitation, poor relief, and public services, would have to be supplied, and to get these we would have to get rid of the corrupt machine as far as possible. Under either assumption, therefore, the state threatened with social disturbance would find safety not in corruption but in honesty and efficiency. However, in exposing the hollowness of the pretence that society needs to be saved by crooked means, we should not fall into the error of assuming that the corrupt politician alone is responsible for all our social ills. We who not only tolerate his works but who tolerate many other abuses with which he has no connection whatever, should remember our own responsibility for the improvement and continued stability of society. It is the custom to castigate the rich in this connection, but the indifference, snobbishness, and narrowness of large sections of our middle classes are also very gravely at fault.[8]

IV

The fourth apology offered for corruption is that it is part of an evolutionary process, the ends of which are presumed to be so beneficent as to more than atone for existing evils attributable to it. Complaint might justly be made that this is a highly general statement, but its formulation in the broad terms used above seems necessary in order to include the various details of the argument. A similar sweeping defence might be set up for any conceivable abuse or evil—for tyranny as well as for corruption, for immorality or for crime. In all such cases, however, it would be necessary to prove—although it seems quite impossible to do so—that the ultimate beneficent end would more than repay the evil involved; and further, that no better way existed of attaining the promised goal. It must be freely conceded that we know little or nothing of the remote ends of the evolutionary process as it exhibits itself in society. Repulsive as are many of its details, there seem to be sufficient grounds for believing in wonderful ultimate achievement. An apology for contemporary corruption based on such considerations may therefore be worthy of attention, provided, however, that it does not attempt to bind us to a purely *laissez faire* attitude in the presence of admitted and immediate political evils.

From the latter point of view political corruption may be regarded as a symptom, bad in itself but valuable because it indicates the need, and in some degree the method, of cure. Like pain in the physical economy it is one of the danger signals of the social economy. Thus, as we have seen, the neglect of proper facilities for education, sanitation, poor relief and so on, particularly in our large cities, is both a resultant in part of corruption and a cause of further corruption. By providing better facilities along these lines we may, therefore, hope ultimately to improve the whole tone of our citizenship and the life of the state. A still more concrete illustration is supplied by Professor Goodnow's masterly discussion of the boss in his "Politics and Administration."[9] According to his view certain defects in our governmental organisation, notably the decentralisation and irresponsibility of much of our administrative machinery, the futile attempt to secure by popular vote the election of a large number of efficient administrative

[8] On this point *cf.* Mary E. Richmond's extremely thoughtful and sympathetic study of "The Good Neighbour in the Modern City."

[9] Particularly chs. viii and ix.

officials and the lack of a close relationship between legislation and administration, all combine to produce a situation which only a strong party organisation dominated by a boss can keep from degenerating into chaos. From this aspect it might be maintained that the evil political practices commonly associated with the boss are only incidental and in part excusable after all. Fundamentally he exists because of defects in the organisation of our government, and his activities go far to correct these defects. Even accepting this argument fully, however, some choice in bosses as Professor Goodnow points out,[10] would still be left open to the electorate. By the progressive overthrow of the worse and the selection of better aspirants for political power the boss may evolve into the leader, who will retain many of the great functions of his predecessor but will exercise them in a responsible manner and free from corruption. The practical significance of Professor Goodnow's argument, however, lies far less in the explanation it gives of the temporary ascendency of the boss and the system which he presides over than in the conviction it enforces of the necessity of certain reforms in the organisation of our government that will bring its functions into harmony with each other, and ultimately, it is hoped, make corrupt and irresponsible bosses impossible.[11] In no proper sense of the word, however, can this line of argument be considered an apology for corruption such as is usually alleged to be associated with bossism. It makes clear only that the power of the boss, under present conditions, has its uses as well as its abuses. But these uses do not justify the abuses. On the contrary the corruption associated with the great powers of the boss is a menace so great as to make necessary the most far-reaching reforms.

To sum up the four lines of apology offered for political corruption, it may be noted that only two of them are so commonly entertained at the present time as to have any large practical significance. These are the first and second, namely, that corruption makes business good, and that it may be more than compensated for by the high efficiency of those who engage in it. The two remaining arguments, dealing respectively with the danger of mob rule and the possibly beneficent effects of further evolution, are extremely interesting; but for the present, at least, they belong largely to the realm of political theory. No one is so simple as to imagine that such forms of corruption as affect our political life owe their existence to any public benefit, near or remote, which by any stretch of the imagination may be attributed to them. Primarily they exist because they are immediately profitable to certain persons who are unscrupulous enough to engage in sinister and underhanded methods of manipulation. Philosophical excuses are not thought out until later, when the magnitude and the profitableness of the malpractices involved suggest the possibility of an apparently dignified and worthy defence. Not one of the four apologies we have considered stands the test of analysis. The social advantages alleged to flow from political corruption are either illusory or minimal. On the other hand the resultant evils are great and real, although, no doubt, they have often been exaggerated by sensational writers. Whether corruption be approached from the latter side, as is commonly done, or from the side of its apologists, the social necessity of working for its limitation is manifest.

10 Goodnow, p. 195.

11 A discussion of these reforms in detail is given in ch. ix of Professor Goodnow's book.

52. Economic Development through Bureaucratic Corruption[1]

NATHANIEL H. LEFF

The bureaucratic corruption of many underdeveloped countries has been widely condemned both by domestic and foreign observers. Apart from the criticism based on moral grounds, and the technocratic impatience with inefficiency, corruption is usually assumed to have important prejudicial effects on the economic growth of these societies.[2]

Corruption is an extra-legal institution used by individuals or groups to gain influence over the actions of the bureaucracy. As such, the existence of corruption *per se* indicates only that these groups participate in the decision-making process to a greater extent than would otherwise be the case. This provides information about the effective—as opposed to the formal—political system, but in itself, tells us nothing about the content and development effects of the policies so determined. These depend on the specific orientation and interests of the groups which have gained political access. As we shall see, in the context of many underdeveloped countries, this point can be crucial. For example, if business groups are otherwise at a disadvantage in articulating their interests to the government, and if these groups are more likely to promote growth than is the government, then their enhanced participation in policy formulation can help development.

Furthermore, our discussion is limited to corruption of a particular type: namely, the practice of buying favors from the bureaucrats responsible for formulating and administering the government's economic policies. Typical examples are bribery to obtain foreign exchange, import, export, investment or production licenses, or to avoid paying taxes. Such bribes are in the nature of a tax levied on economic activity. These payments have not been legitimized by the correct political process, they are appropriated by the bureaucrat rather than the state, and they involve the subversion of the government's economic policies—hence the stigma that attaches to them. The question for us to decide is whether the net effects caused by such

1 I am grateful to Richard Eckaus, John Plank, Lucien Pye, and Myron Weiner for their comments on an earlier draft of this paper. They bear no responsibility for the remaining deficiencies.

2 But see V. O. Key, *The Techniques of Political Graft in the United States,* privately printed, 1936. Robert K. Merton, *Social Theory and Social Structure,* New York, 1959, pp. 19–85. Harold Lasswell, "Bribery," in *The Encyclopedia of the Social Sciences,* vol. 2, New York, 1930. Cf. especially, F. W. Riggs, "Bureaucrats and Political Development: A Paradoxical View," paper prepared for the Social Science Research Council Committee on Comparative Politics, Conference, January 29–February 2, 1962, to be published in a forthcoming volume edited by J. LaPalombara.

SOURCE: Nathaniel H. Leff, "Economic Development through Bureaucratic Corruption," *American Behavioral Scientist,* 8:3 (November 1964), pp. 8–14. By permission of the publisher, Sage Publications, Inc.

payments and policy redirection are likely to favor or hinder economic development.

We should also distinguish between bureaucratic corruption and bureaucratic inefficiency. Corruption refers to extra-legal influence on policy formulation or implementation. Inefficiency, on the other hand, has to do with the success or failure, or the economy of means used by the bureaucracy in attaining given goals, whether those of its political directors, or those of the grafters. Empirically, inefficiency and corruption may appear together, and may blend into each other. Both as a policy problem and for analytical purposes, however, it is important to distinguish between two essentially different things.

WHO CONDEMNS CORRUPTION?

Before proceeding to our analysis of the economic effects of bureaucratic corruption, it may be useful to make a brief detour. Any discussion of corruption must contend with the fact that the institution is almost universally condemned. Insofar as this criticism is based on moralizing—explicit or latent—self-interest, or ideology, it can be a formidable obstacle to rational analysis. Consequently, in order to gain a degree of perspective on the subject, I would like to consider the sources of the widespread prejudice against corruption. Identifying the specific sources of bias, and breaking down generalized censure to its component parts should help us to evaluate each argument on its own merits. For this purpose, let us consider the origins of the critical attitude held by such groups as foreign observers, government officials, and entrepreneurs, and by intellectuals, politicians, and businessmen in the underdeveloped countries themselves.

Foreigners living in the underdeveloped countries have been persistent critics of corruption. First, they have resented the payments of graft to which they are often subjected in the normal course of their business. Secondly, they have condemned corruption on moral grounds, and criticized it as both a cause and a characteristic of the backwardness of these countries.

A more sophisticated, and recent version of this argument derives from the new interest in promoting economic development. As economists and observers of economic development have grown aware of the enormous obstacles to spontaneous growth, they have come to assign an increasingly important role to the governments of the underdeveloped countries.

First, there has been an emphasis on the need for entrepreneurs, coupled with the fear that the underdeveloped countries may lack indigenous sources of entrepreneurship. Secondly, recent economic theory stressed the importance of indivisibilities, externalities, and other structural features that may prevent an underdeveloped economy from breaking out of a low-income equilibrium trap. In addition, there was the realization that the flow of private capital and technical skills was insufficient for promoting large-scale growth. With the ensuing flow of inter-governmental transfers, came the need for the governments of the underdeveloped countries to assume responsibility for the resources they were receiving.

Because of these reasons and political pressures, the governments of the underdeveloped countries have come to occupy a very prominent place in most visions of economic development. In a sense, economists have collected their problems, placed them in a box labelled "public policy," and turned them over to the governments of the underdeveloped countries.

In order for the governmental policies to be effective, however, the bureaucracies must actually implement them. Hence it becomes crucial that officials not be influenced, through graft, to deviate from their appointed tasks. The logic of this argument goes as follows: development—bureaucracy—efficiency—probity. This chain of reasoning is central to the whole critique of corruption, and we shall examine it carefully in the next section. Before going further, however, let us note a few important points about this argument.

First, it confuses bureaucratic inefficiency and bureaucratic redirection through dishonesty and graft. Secondly, transferring these problems to the governments and bureaucracies is hardly enough to solve them, for these institutions may not be at all likely to promote growth. Rather than leading the development process, the governments and bureaucracies may be lagging sectors. Finally, the argument implies that because the bureaucracy is so strategic an institution, an attack on bureaucratic corruption deserves high policy priority, offering relatively cheap and easy gains.

Foreign aid missions seem to have been particularly prone to draw such conclusions, for understandable reasons. The bureaucracy's performance will determine the success or failure of many other projects. Moreover, in contrast with some of the other problems facing foreign development specialists, reform of the civil service may seem a relatively straightforward matter. Furthermore, whereas in other development efforts foreign specialists may feel hampered by the lack of well tested doctrine and procedures, in restructuring the bureaucracy, they can rely on the expertise of public administration and management science. Therefore, it is not surprising that so much foreign development attention and activity have been directed toward the reform of the bureaucracies of underdeveloped countries.

In the underdeveloped countries themselves, much of the condemnation of graft has also come from interest in economic development, and from the apparent cogency of the development/bureaucracy/efficiency/probity logic. Here, moreover, the special ideological perspectives and interests of powerful and articulate groups have reinforced the criticism. Let us consider the specific perspectives that intellectuals, politicians, and businessmen in the underdeveloped countries possess.

The attitudes of intellectuals and of politicians toward corruption overlap to a certain degree. As members of the same rising elite, they condemn corruption because of the idealistic streak which often pervades radicals and reformers. Contemporary intellectuals in underdeveloped countries often emulate the Jacobins in their seeking after virtue. Moreover, as Shils has pointed out,[3] they frequently attribute sacral value to the governmental sphere: hence their hostility to the venality that would corrupt it. More generally, they may see graft as an integral part of the political culture and system of the *ancien régime* which they want to destroy.

Furthermore, they also have a direct interest in discrediting and eliminating corruption because of its functional effects. In most underdeveloped countries, interest groups are weak, and political parties rarely permit the participation of elements outside the contending cliques. Consequently, graft may be the only institution allowing other interests to achieve articulation and representation in the political process. Therefore, if the ruling elite is to maintain its exclusive control of the bureaucracy, it must cut off or control this channel of influence.[4] Such considerations apply especially when the politically disadvantaged group consists of an ethnic minority or of foreign entrepreneurs over whom the elite would like to maintain its dominance.

Entrepreneurs in underdeveloped countries have also condemned bureaucratic corruption. This is understandable,

3 Edward Shils, "Political Development in the New States," *Comparative Studies in Society and History*, 1960, p. 279.
4 Cf. Riggs, pp. 28–30.

for they must pay the bribes. Moreover, because of certain economic characteristics of graft, the discontent that it arouses probably goes far beyond the cost of the bribe alone.

It is important to realize that most of the objects of corruption are available only in fixed and limited supply. For example, at any point in time, there is only a given amount of foreign exchange or a given number of investment licenses to be allocated. Consequently, when the number of favors is small relative to the number of aspirants, entrepreneurs must bid against each other in what amounts to a clandestine and imperfect auction. With competition forcing prices up, the favors will tend to be allocated to those who can pay the highest prices. In the long run, the favors will go to the most efficient producers, for they will be able to make the highest bids which are compatible with remaining in the industry.

Marginal firms, on the other hand, will face severe pressures. Either they accept sub-normal profits, or they must make the effort to increase efficiency, so as to muster the resources necessary to bid successfully. If they drop out of the contest, they are placed in a weakened position *vis-à-vis* the other firms, which are now even more intra-marginal because of the advantages given by the bureaucratic favor.

This sort of situation, where the efficient are able to out-do the inefficient, is not generally appreciated by businessmen. It is likely to be the less popular in underdeveloped countries where—in deference to the prevalence of inefficiency, and to local ideas of equity—the more usual practice is to tax efficient producers in order to subsidize the inefficient. Moreover, as we have seen, corruption may introduce an element of competition into what is otherwise a comfortably monopolistic industry.

Furthermore, in their bidding for bureaucratic favors, businessmen may have to give up a substantial part of the profits from the favor. The economic value of the favor is equal to the return expected from the favored position it makes possible. This value constitutes the upper limit to the bids made by entrepreneurs. The actual amount paid is indeterminate, and depends on the relative bargaining skills of the bureaucrats and the businessmen. The competitive bidding between businessmen, however, may force the price to approach the upper limit. In such a case, the bureaucrat captures the lion's share of the profits expected from the favor. Competitive selling by different bureaucrats may strengthen the bargaining position of the businessmen, but in general they are probably forced to pay out a relatively large portion of their expected gains. Hence, it is not surprising that they dislike an institution which deprives them of the fruits of their enterprise.[5]

The foregoing discussion suggests that many of the negative attitudes toward corruption are based upon special viewpoints and interests. We should also realize that the background material available on the subject is both scanty and one-sided. Those who engage in corruption maintain secrecy about their operations, so that the little data available comes from declared opponents of the institution. Moreover, those who profit from corruption may themselves have no idea of the socially beneficial effects of their activities.

The widespread condemnation of corruption has come to constitute a serious obstacle to any reexamination of the subject. Indeed, the criticism has become something of a ritual and symbol-laden preamble accompanying policy discussion and statements in the underdeveloped countries. As such, it is cherished for the modicum of consensus it provides to otherwise antagonistic groups.

---

5 These processes are nicely brought out in Alexandre Kafka, "The Brazilian Exchange Auction," *The Review of Economics and Statistics,* October 1956.

POSITIVE EFFECTS OF CORRUPTION

The critique of bureaucratic corruption often seems to have in mind a picture in which the government and civil service of underdeveloped countries are working intelligently and actively to promote economic development, only to be thwarted by the efforts of grafters. Once the validity of this interpretation is disputed, the effects of corruption must also be reevaluated. This is the case if the government consists of a traditional elite which is indifferent if not hostile to development, or of a revolutionary group of intellectuals and politicians, who are primarily interested in other goals. At the same time, the propensity for investment and economic innovation may be higher outside the government than within it.

Indifference and Hostility of Government

In the first instance, the government and bureaucracy may simply be indifferent to the desires of entrepreneurs wanting to initiate or carry on economic activities. Such a situation is quite likely in the absence of effective popular pressure for economic development, or in the absence of effective participation of business interests in the policy-making process. This is especially the case when entrepreneurs are marginal groups or aliens. More generally, when the government does not attribute much value to economic pursuits or innovation, it may well be reluctant to move actively in the support of economic activity.

Even more important, the bureaucracy may be hostile to entrepreneurs, for it dislikes the emergence of a competing center of power. This is especially the case in colonial economies, where a large domestic middle class has not emerged to challenge traditional power-holders.

Governments Have Other Priorities

The foregoing relates to societies where although lip-service may be paid to the importance of economic development, the government and bureaucracy are oriented primarily to maintaining the *status quo.* It is also relevant in countries where a successful revolution against the *ancien régime* has occurred. There, the government may be proceeding dynamically, but not toward the promotion of economic development. Other goals, such as an increase in the military power available to the elite, or expansion of its control over society, may be justified in terms of economic development, however "ultimate." At the same time, the immediate effect of such policies is to impede growth.

Typically the bureaucracy plays an extensive interventionist role in the economy, and its consent or support is a *sine qua non* for the conduct of most economic enterprise. In such a situation, graft can have beneficial effects. First, it can induce the government to take a more favorable view of activities that would further economic growth. The policies or freedom sought by the entrepreneurs would help development, while those they subvert are keyed to other goals. Secondly, graft can provide the direct incentive necessary to mobilize the bureaucracy for more energetic action on behalf of the entrepreneurs. This is all the more important because of the necessity for bureaucratic help in so many areas—e.g., licenses, credit, and foreign exchange allocation—in order to get anything done.

Corruption Reduces Uncertainty and Increases Investment

Corruption can also help economic development by making possible a higher rate of investment than would otherwise be the case.

The investment decision always takes place in the midst of risk and uncertainty. As Aubrey has pointed out,[6] however,

6 H. C. Aubrey, "Investment Decisions in Underdeveloped Countries" in *Capital Formation and Economic Growth,* National Bureau of Economic Research. Princeton, 1955, pp. 404–415. Also cf. the finding of Y. Sayigh (*Entrepreneurs of Lebanon,* Cambridge, Mass. 1962, p. 117) that political conditions constituted the greatest unknown facing the entrepreneurs surveyed.

these difficulties are very much compounded in the economic and political environment of underdeveloped countries. The basic estimates of future demand and supply conditions are harder because of the lack of data and of the sharp shifts that can occur during a period of economic change. The dangers of misjudging the market are all the more serious because of the lower elasticities of substitution at low income levels.

Aside from the problems of making such economic estimates, the potential investor also faces a major political unknown—the behavior of the government. The possible dangers arising from the government's extensive role in the economy are increased because of the failure of representative government to put an effective check on arbitrary action. The personalist and irrational style of decision-making, and the frequent changes in government personnel and policies add to the risks. Consequently, if entrepreneurs are to make investments, they must have some assurance that the future will not bring harmful intervention in their affairs. We can see an illustration of these difficulties in the fact that in periods of political uncertainty and crisis, investment shrinks, and economic stagnation occurs. By enabling entrepreneurs to control and render predictable this important influence on their environment, corruption can increase the rate of investment.

Corruption and Innovation

The would-be innovator in an underdeveloped society must contend with serious opposition from existing economic interests. Unable to compete economically with the new processes or products, they will usually turn to the government for protection of their investments and future returns. If the bureaucracy supports innovation and refuses to intervene, the innovation can establish itself in the economy. In the more usual case, however, existing economic interests can depend on their long-standing associations with bureaucratic and political compadres for protection.

In this situation, graft may enable an economic innovator to introduce his innovations before he has had time to establish himself politically.[7] Economic innovators in underdeveloped countries have often supported oppositional political cliques or parties. Corruption is another, less radical way of adjusting to the same pressures and goals.

Corruption, Competition, and Efficiency

As we have seen in the previous section, bureaucratic corruption also brings an element of competition, with its attendant pressure for efficiency, to an underdeveloped economy. Since the licenses and favors available to the bureaucrats are in limited supply, they are allocated by competitive bidding among entrepreneurs. Because payment of the highest bribes is one of the principal criteria for allocation, the ability to muster revenue, either from reserves or from current operations, is put at a premium. In the long run, both of these sources are heavily dependent on efficiency in production. Hence, a tendency toward competition and efficiency is introduced into the system.

Such a pressure is all the more important in underdeveloped countries, where competition is usually absent from many sectors of the economy. In the product market, a high degree of monopoly often prevails. International competition is usually kept out by quotas, tariffs, and overvalued exchange rates. In the factor market, frictions and imperfections are common. Consequently, we can appreciate the value of introducing an element of competition, if only through the back-door.

Corruption as a Hedge against Bad Policy

Corruption also performs the valuable function of a "hedge" and a safeguard against the full losses of bad economic

7 Cf. Lasswell, p. 671.

policy. Even when the government of an underdeveloped country is proceeding actively and intelligently to promote growth, there is no assurance that its policies are well-conceived to attain its goals. In effect, it may be taking a vigorous step in the wrong direction. Corruption can reduce the losses from such mistakes, for while the government is implementing one policy, the entrepreneurs, with their sabotage, are implementing another. Like all insurance, this involves a cost—if the government's policy is correct. On the other hand, like all insurance, it is sometimes very welcome.

An underdeveloped country often stands in special need of such a safeguard. First, even when policy goals are clearly specified, competent counsel may well be divided as to the best means of achieving them. For example, the experts may differ among themselves on such basic issues as export promotion vs. import substitution, or other inter-sectoral priorities. Consequently, if the government has erred in its decision, the course made possible by corruption may well be the better one, supported by a dissenting segment of expert opinion. Moreover, the pervasive effects of government policy in an etatistic economy compound the effects of poor decisions, and increase the advantages of having some kind of safeguard against the potential consequences of a serious policy mistake. Corruption provides the insurance that if the government decides to steam full-speed in the wrong direction, all will not be lost.

Some illustrations may help clarify this point. For example, the agricultural producers whose graft sabotaged Peron's economic policies were later thanked for having maintained Argentina's capacity to import. Another example shows in more detail how this process can operate. An important element in the recent Latin American inflations has been the stagnation of food production, and the rise in food prices. In both Chile and Brazil, the governments reacted by freezing food prices, and ordering the bureaucracy to enforce these controls. In Chile, the bureaucracy acted loyally to maintain price controls, and food supplies were relatively stagnant. Inflation rose faster, supported in part by the failure of food production to increase. In Brazil, however, the bureaucracy's ineffectiveness sabotaged the enforcement of price controls, and prices received by producers were allowed to rise. Responding to this price rise, food production also increased somewhat, partially limiting the course of the inflation.[8]

In this case, we see the success of entrepreneurs and corrupted officials in producing a more effective policy than the government. Moreover, subsequent economic analysis justified this "decision," by emphasizing the price elasticity of agricultural supply, and the consequent need to allow the terms of trade to turn in favor of rural producers.

These points are perhaps strengthened when viewed with some historical perspective. As John Nef has remarked, the honesty and efficiency of the French bureaucracy were in great measure responsible for the stifling of economic innovation and progress during the 18th century.[9] By way of contrast, the laxity of the British administration permitted the subversion of Colbertism, and allowed new economic processes and activities to flourish.

ALLEGED NEGATIVE EFFECTS OF CORRUPTION

Most of the arguments concerning the negative effects of corruption are based on the assumption that development can

---

[8] I am indebted to an eminent expert in Latin American economic development for this observation.

[9] *Industry and Government in France and England: 1540–1640*. Cf. also, J. J. Spengler, "The State and Economic Growth—Summary and Interpretations," p. 368, in H. Aitken, editor, *The State and Economic Growth*, N.Y. 1959.

best proceed through the policies of an uncorrupted government and bureaucracy. As noted in the previous section, this assumes that the government really wants economic development, and that its policies would favor growth more than the activities of an unregulated private sector. Actually, the economic policies of the governments of many underdeveloped countries may be predicated on priorities other than global economic development. Even in countries where there has been a successful revolution against the colonial *ancien régime,* policy may aim primarily at advancing the economic interests of the ruling clique or of the political group on which it bases its dominance. Although the economic policies of some countries may be foolish or catastrophic from the viewpoint of development, they may be well conceived for implementing these other goals.[10]

Impeding Taxation

One version of this argument focuses on taxation. Specifically, it asserts that bureaucratic corruption may hamper development by preventing the government from obtaining the tax revenues necessary for developmental policies.

This argument probably attributes to the government an unrealistically high propensity to spend for development purposes. Economic development usually has a less compelling priority among the elites of these societies than among the westerners who observe them. Even if the dominant groups are aware and sensitive to the situation of the lower classes, they may be reluctant to bear the costs of development. Hence, the actual level of taxes collected, and their allocation in the budget may represent the decision of the ruling group as to how hard they want to press forward with economic development. In these circumstances, it is misleading to criticize the bureaucracy for the effects of its ineffective tax collection on economic growth. Of the revenues they might have collected, only a part would have gone for development rather than for the many forms of non-developmental expenditure. Moreover, when the entrepreneurs' propensity to invest is higher than the government's, the money saved from the tax collector may be a gain rather than a loss for development.

Usefulness of Government Spending

Furthermore, there is no reason to assume that the government has a high *marginal* propensity to spend for development purposes, based on a high income elasticity of demand for development. Without changes in the factors determining the average allocational propensities, increases in governmental revenue may well go for more lavish satisfaction of the same appetites. For example, as budgetary receipts rise, the military may be supplied with jet aircraft rather than with less expensive weapons.

Cynicism

Another argument has emphasized the social effects of corruption as an impediment to development. For example, it has been claimed that immorality and self-seeking of bureaucratic corruption may cause widespread cynicism and social disunity, and thus reduce the willingness to make sacrifices for the society's economic development.

This argument can be criticized on several points.

First, insofar as the disillusion is engendered among the *lower* social orders, the effects on development may not be as important as assumed. Because of economic and social conditions, these people are probably being squeezed as much as is possible, so that with all good will, they could not sacrifice any more.

Secondly, if the cynicism caused by

---

[10] Cf. Frank Golay, "Commercial Policy and Economic Nationalism," *Quarterly Journal of Economics,* 1958, and B. Glassburner, "Economic Policy-Making in Indonesia, 1950–1957," *Economic Development and Cultural Change,* January 1962.

bureaucratic corruption leads to increased self-seeking in the rest of the society, this may not be a completely bad thing for economic development. Many of the wealth-creating activities which make up economic growth depend on such atomistic egoism for their stimulus. Consequently, if cynicism acts as a solvent on traditional inhibitions, and increased self-seeking leads to new ambitions, economic development may be furthered.

Moreover, this argument also exaggerates the extent to which economic growth depends on a popular rallying-around rather than on many individual selfish activities. The implicit picture seems to be that of an "all-together" social effort, perhaps under etatistic direction. Once stated explicitly, such a model appears more like a fantasy of intellectuals rather than an accurate guide to how economic development takes place.

More generally, we should recognize that there are very good reasons for the incivism and unwillingness to make sacrifices that are often characteristic of underdeveloped societies. Mutual distrust and hostility usually have much deeper roots in cultural gaps, inequitable income distribution, and long experience of mistreatment. Rapid change, dislocating existing institutions and values, also disrupts social solidarity. In such circumstances, reduced bureaucratic corruption would make only a marginal contribution to improved public morale.

CORRUPTION AS A POLICY SYSTEM

The foregoing analysis and perspective may also be helpful in dealing with bureaucratic corruption as a policy problem.

First, we should be clear as to the nature of "the problem" that policy is attempting to solve. As we have seen, much of the criticism of corruption derives from the political, economic, and ideological interests of particular groups. Presumably the elimination of corruption is a problem only insofar as we share their specific concerns.

Aside from these special interests, however, let us consider corruption from the point of view of its effects on economic development. As we have seen, under certain conditions, the consequences of corruption for development are not as serious as is usually assumed. At the same time, it may have important positive effects that are often overlooked. Consequently, to the extent that reality approaches the conditions of our model, corruption of the type discussed in this paper may not be a problem at all. This will depend on specific conditions, and will vary between countries and between sectors.

When the conditions of our model do not obtain, however, corruption will be an important barrier to development. To the extent that corruption exists as a policy problem, it is probably wise to accept it as a particularly intractable part of an underdeveloped country. On a superficial level, we should recognize that corruption creates its own political and economic interests that will resist efforts at its eradication. More important, corruption is deeply rooted in the psychological and social structure of the countries where it exists. On the psycho-cultural plane, corruption will persist until universalistic norms predominate over particularistic attitudes. Socially, the elimination of corruption probably requires the emergence of new centers of power outside the bureaucracy, and the development of competitive politics. Such changes will come, if at all, only as the result of a long period of economic and social development.

Bureaucracy the Lagging Sector

Two conclusions emerge from this discussion. First, we should realize how illusory is the expectation that bureaucratic policy can intervene as a *deus ex machina* to overcome the other barriers to economic growth. In many underdeveloped countries, the bureaucracy may be a lagging rather than a leading sector. Secondly, it should be clear that direct policy efforts against such deeply rooted psychological and social conditions cannot hope for much short-term success. As Braibanti concludes,[11] powerful investigatory commissions may have a limited success, but one should expect the problem to be improved "more by time than by effort."

Despite the pessimistic prospects for the usual direct-action policies against corruption, certain possibilities do exist for dealing with it indirectly. The problem is perhaps best conceptualized in terms of the need to economize in the use of a particularly scarce and important resource—honest and capable administrators. Indeed, for several reasons, this shortage may be more serious than others more often cited, e.g., the lack of capital. Because of political reasons, this input into the development process cannot be imported on a large scale. Furthermore as we have noted, available domestic supplies cannot be expected to increase for a long time in most underdeveloped countries. Finally, this input is all the more crucial because of its importance for the successful deployment of other resources. If we view corruption as a problem in the allocation of scarce administrative resources, two solutions are immediately suggested.

Two Techniques

First, the available resources should be concentrated in areas where their productivity in promoting development would be greatest. Such budgeting of administrators would avoid dispersion of honest and able personnel, and make them available only for tasks of the highest priority.

A second way of economizing in the use of this scarce resource would be the use of alternative production techniques to achieve the same development results. In our context, this would mean employing measures to achieve the goals of policy without reliance on direct administration and bureaucratic regulation of the economy.

In many cases, the desired effects could be achieved either by market forces, or by indirect measures creating the necessary incentives or disincentives—i.e., with much less direct government intervention, and the consequent need to rely on the bureaucracy. For example, a government which wants to keep down the domestic price level can either institute a cumbersome system of price regulation, or it can permit a measure of competition from imports. Similarly, a straightforward currency devaluation can have many of the beneficial effects achieved by an administration-intensive regime of differential exchange rates. Admittedly, such policies may have some undesired consequences and side-effects that ideally would be avoided by more sophisticated government management of the economy. The point is, however, that when policy alternatives are evaluated, it would be better to take explicit account of how bureaucratic corruption will affect the direct management policies contemplated. This would lead to a more realistic choice between the means which can accomplish similar goals. Perhaps the best procedure would be to select a mixture of direct and of indirect management policies, taking account of the bureaucratic resources available.

By way of contrast, the more usual practice is to choose the policies that would be best *if* the whole bureaucracy were dependable, and then to deplore its corruption, and condemn it for the failure

---

[11]Ralph Braibanti, "Reflections on Bureaucratic Corruption," *Public Administration,* Winter 1962, p. 370, and p. 372.

of the policies chosen. Following the procedure suggested here, however, governments would accept corruption as an aspect of their societies, and try to optimize policy-making within this framework.

Finally, we should note that preoccupation with corruption can itself become an impediment to development. This occurs if the focus on corruption diverts attention from other political and economic deficiencies in the society, and from the measures that can be taken despite corruption. To avoid the losses from such misdirection, re-thinking of the sort suggested here may be helpful.

53. The Effects of Corruption in a Developing Nation

David H. Bayley

Studies of politics and administration in the developing nations, whether about Africa, Latin America, the Middle East, or South and Southeast Asia, almost invariably comment upon the prevalence of corruption on the part of both politicians and civil servants. Standards of public morality, we are told, are deplorably low. Local observers within these countries confirm this impression. Where the press is free, governmental corruption becomes a stock-in-trade of a great deal of journalistic commentary. Local authorities themselves sometimes take up the subject of venality in government in order to determine its extent and recommend measures for its eradication. Then groups within prominent political parties raise their voices in criticism, not just of politicians in other parties, but more impressively of the deteriorating standards of behavior within their own ranks. The conclusion, on the basis of all this smoke, must be that corruption certainly exists in many developing nations. It would probably not be too much to say that it forms a prominent, or at least not readily avoidable, feature of bureaucratic life in these nations.

Given its prevalence, whether as proven or assumed fact, it is surprising that so little attention has been given to its role and effects within the developing political situation. Western, as well as local, observers have generally been content with deploring its existence. This frequently involves taking rather perverse pleasure in dwelling upon the amount of corruption to be discovered and then asserting that elimination of corruption is a "must" for successful development. While most Western observers have manfully striven to avoid assuming a moralistic posture, they have rather uncritically assumed that the presence of corruption is an important hindrance to economic growth and progressive social change. There has been a significant absence of analysis about the effects which corruption has in fact upon economic development, nascent political institutions, and social attitudes. Unless it has been determined that a social practice, such as corruption, contributes no positive benefits, condemnation of it is really a practice at rote and is no improvement upon moralism.

The purpose of this essay is to show that corruption in developing nations is not necessarily antipathetic to the development of modern economic and social systems; that corruption serves in part at least a beneficial function in developing societies. In order to demonstrate this I shall present a list of the effects of corruption, *both* positive and negative. It will be necessary first to discuss the meaning

Source: David H. Bayley, "The Effects of Corruption in a Developing Nation," *Western Political Quarterly,* Vol. XIX, No. 4 (December 1966), pp. 719–732. By permission of the author and the publisher, the University of Utah, copyright owners.

of the word corruption, and then whether it makes sense to apply the category as defined in the West to behavior in non-Western countries. The focus of the essay will be entirely upon governmental corruption and not that within private agencies. The illustrative material will be taken overwhelmingly from Indian experience, for this is the country with which I am most familiar. I am sure, however, that the Indian situation is not atypical. Finally, it must be quite clear that in specifying the effects of corruption I am presenting hypotheses rather than proven conclusions. The arguments I make for asserting that an effect of a particular kind is present are often *a priori.* But I have carefully tried to frame my hypotheses in such a way as to highlight the empirical referents which must be studied in order to validate them.

THE DEFINITION OF CORRUPTION

Webster's Third New International Dictionary (1961) defines corruption as "inducement [as of a public official] by means of improper considerations [as bribery] to commit a violation of duty." A bribe is then defined as "a price, reward, gift or favor bestowed or promised with a view to pervert the judgment or corrupt the conduct esp. of a person in a position of trust [as a public official]." Bribery and corruption are intimately linked together, but they are not inseparable. A person bribed is a person corrupt; but a man may be corrupt who does not take bribes.[1] Corruption would surely include nepotism and misappropriation.[2] In both these cases there is "inducement by means of improper considerations." Corruption, then, while being tied particularly to the act of bribery, is a general term covering misuse of authority as a result of considerations of personal gain, which need not be monetary. This point has been well made in a recent Indian government report on corruption: "In its widest connotation, corruption includes improper and selfish exercise of power and influence attached to a public office or to the special position one occupies in public life."[3]

It is important to note that a person may be corrupt who does not in fact commit a violation of duty. Webster's definition only says that an individual must be induced to commit. The hero of the African novel, *No Longer at Ease,* which portrays the tension between the demands of traditional society and standards of a Western civil service, finally capitulates to the pressures upon him and accepts gratuities but salves his conscience with the thought that he only takes money from those whom he approves on their merits anyhow.[4] A variation of this is the civil servant who takes money from all applicants impartially but still goes ahead and decides the matter on merits. Rumor in India would have it that this is not an exceptional situation. Are such people corrupt? A strict application of Webster's definition would lead to an answer in the affirmative, and general Western usage would, I think, conform to the strict reading.

Corrupt behavior is behavior condemned and censured. "Corruption" is a pejorative term. However, applying the label to behavior on the part of public officials in many non-Western countries immediately poses a dilemma of in-

1 In this respect there has been a change in the relation between "bribery" and "corruption" from *Webster's New International Dictionary* (2d ed., 1958). In the earlier edition the definition of corruption explicitly mentioned bribery and the definition of bribery explicitly referred to corruption.

2 *Webster's Third New International Dictionary* defines (a) nepotism: "favoritism shown to nephews and other relatives (as by giving them positions because of their relationship rather than on their merits)"; (b) to misappropriate: "to appropriate dishonestly for one's own use: embezzle."

3 *Report of the Committee on Prevention of Corruption* (New Delhi: Government of India, 1964), p. 5. Known as the Santhanam Committee report, after its chairman.

4 Chinua Achebe, *No Longer at Ease* (New York: Ivan Obolensky, 1960).

triguing dimensions. The man who in many non-Western countries is corrupt in Webster's sense is not condemned at all by his own society. Indeed, he may be conforming to a pattern of behavior his peers, family, and friends strongly support and applaud. For example, in both Africa and India the man who uses his official position to obtain jobs for his relatives is not considered immoral: in traditional terms, he is only doing what every loyal member of an extended family is expected to do. He would be censured if he did not act in this way. The point is strongly made in the fictitious musings of a Delhi businessman in these words:

> Bribery and corruption! These were foreign words, it seemed to him, and the ideas behind them were also foreign. Here in India, he thought, one did not know such words. Giving presents and gratuities to government officers was an indispensable courtesy and a respectable, civilised way of carrying on business.[5]

It not infrequently happens, then, in developing non-Western societies that existing moral codes do not agree with Western norms as to what kinds of behavior by public servants should be condemned. The Western observer is faced with an uncomfortable choice. He can adhere to the Western definition, in which case he lays himself open to the charge of being censorious and he finds that he is condemning not aberrant behavior but normal, acceptable operating procedure. On the other hand, he may face up to the fact that corruption, if it requires moral censure, is culturally conditioned. He then argues that an act is corrupt if the surrounding society condemns it.[6] This usage, however, muddies communication, for it may be necessary then to assert in the same breath that an official accepts gratuities but is not corrupt or that an official gives preference in employment to his relatives but is not corrupt. Rather tedious explanations invariably must follow and people are left with the feeling that serious violence has been done to words.

Between these two alternatives the better choice, in my view, is to preserve the Western denotative meaning of corruption. This will be the meaning employed in this paper. If the Westerner chooses the culturally relevant definition, he will either end by abandoning the term altogether or will find it necessary to define it peculiarly, perhaps differently, for every non-Western country studied. This will present serious problems of communication with colleagues. There are other reasons as well for preserving the Western meaning. As Western observers we are interested in comparative findings about behavior in our own and other cultures. We are familiar with the fact that even in the West there is some disagreement about standards of propriety in the dealings of public officials. This is particularly true of the activities of politicians on behalf of their constituents. It is not entirely curious then that one may speak of an act being corrupt and not find massive social censure. This being the case it is more felicitous to say that in many non-Western countries behavior X, which in the West is called corrupt, does not attract social condemnation. Other findings, predicated on the category corruption, will be that it is

[5] Prawer Jhabvala, *The Nature of Passion* (New York: Norton, 1956), p. 56. Novels are often a forgotten key to the human problems of traditional society, and since few scholars portray social problems in intimate, biographical terms, they are indispensable sources of information to those who would seek to understand the human, motivational problems involved.

[6] This is the solution adopted by Ronald Wraith and Edgar Simpkins in *Corruption in Developing Nations* (London: G. Allen, 1963), pp. 34–35. They even go farther and say that the actor must also be afflicted with a sense of guilt. The last condition, especially, seems unduly restricting. A man may act wrongly even though he is not conscious of acting wrongly. His lack of guilt-feelings may have a bearing upon his guilt in law but surely does not affect society's definition of what constitutes improper or illicit action.

more or less prevalent than in the West, that it is or is not confined to different role players than in the West, that it serves the same or a different function, or that it is motivated by similar or rather different considerations.

The advantage of this solution is that we get rid of nonessentials, such as the element of social judgment, but keep the denotative core, i.e., the taking of bribes or employing of relatives. In this way, as the English would say, we do not throw out the baby with the bath water. Only minor adjustments are made, hence making possible comparative statements easily understood by colleagues.

There is another reason for keeping the Western denotative meaning. The intelligentsia, and especially top-level civil servants, in most underdeveloped nations are familiar with the Western label "corruption," and they apply it to their own countries. Since modernization around the world is most often Westernization, the standards the intelligentsia and opinion-leaders of these countries are trying to inculcate are Western ones. The premise of the Santhanam Committee was that "corruption," in the Western sense, should be eliminated. Similarly in Africa the conflict in the hearts of civil servants is precisely over which standard of morality should prevail, the Western or the traditional. Non-Westerners are acutely conscious of the Western meaning of corruption; they use it among themselves. And they are painfully aware that Western standards of governmental conduct condemn it. It is not unfair, therefore, to make comparative statements between West and non-West based upon Webster's definition. Such judgments will be readily understood by the nation-building elites in most developing nations.

An even more serious problem involves separating proper from improper behavior in the realm of politics whatever the country. It is easy to say that a civil servant should consider only the merits of a case. A politician, by the nature of his job, is a channel for the pressure of special groups within the country. It is an accepted part of his function that he garner public expenditures for his constituents or groups represented within his constituency; that he help them to gain access to government employment; that he influence administrators to locate a road through a town in his area rather than in an adjacent constituency. A politician is the instrument that makes government responsive to individuals. A civil servant who responded to his tribal or caste affiliation to secure jobs for young men would be accused of being nepotistic; a politician who secured government employ for the same group would be admired as an effective politician. Is there morally a difference between them? Clearly concepts of propriety, upon which the definition of corruption hinges, for the civil servant and politician are not coincidental; propriety is specific to roles to some extent. The latitude possessed by the politician is greater than that of the civil servant, and since the politician must respond to subnational pressure groups by the nature of his role, it follows that the boundary line between permissible and impermissible behavior on the part of politicians will be more hazy than that for civil servants. I shall not try to make this boundary more discernible, but will talk around the issue, realizing that even in the West there is apt to be substantial disagreement about where the duty of a politician lies as between his constituents and the larger interests of his country.

THE EXTENT OF CORRUPTION

Estimates of the extent of corruption practices in underdeveloped countries are, expectedly, very imprecise. Rumor abounds, facts are scarce. Three observations may be made:

First: in many underdeveloped countries corruption is expected by the people as a part of everyday official life. Public cynicism on this score is colossal. As the

Times of India has said, "People's acceptance of corruption as a fact of life and their general despondency need to be tackled first."[7]

Second: officials share this opinion of the people, and their opinions have at times been buttressed by government-sponsored investigations. The situation was considered sufficiently serious in India to warrant the appointment of an investigative committee by the central government. The result was the *Report of the Committee on Prevention of Corruption*, 1964, already referred to. Ronald Wraith and Edgar Simpkins in their book *Corruption in Developing Nations* cite several government studies of administrative procedures in West Africa, both under the British and after independence, which have discussed the widespread extent of corruption.

The Santhanam Committee reported that at a conservative estimate 5 per cent of the money spent during the Second Five Year Plan for construction and purchases was lost to the exchequer through corruption.[8] In discussing the granting of export/import licenses the Committee said, "It is common knowledge that *each license* fetches anything between one hundred per cent to five hundred per cent of its face-value."[9] The Government of Punjab State, India, reported that in the last four years 3000 government workers had been dismissed or punished as a result of the activities of the State Vigilance Department, which is charged with investigation of improper practices. John P. Lewis, former director of the International Development Research Center at Indiana and now A.I.D. director in India, while admitting that he cannot estimate with great accuracy the corruption at top levels in India, says that petty corruption at lower levels is immense. He also notes his impression that corruption at higher levels in India is a good deal less prevalent than in most other developing nations.[10] Read with the Santhanam Committee's assessment of the inroads corruption has made in India, this certainly does not speak well for the situation in other lands. Actually, alarming statements of the extensiveness of corrupt practices in most other developing nations could be multiplied almost indefinitely.

Wraith and Simpkins comment as follows about the African situation:

> How much is true and how much is false about corruption in high places nobody outside a small circle can ever know for certain. What *is* certain, and can be said without circumlocution, is that to wander through the corridors of power in these countries is to wander through a whispering-gallery of gossip, in which the fact of corruption at the highest levels is taken utterly for granted, and the only interest lies in capping the latest story with one that is even more startling.[11]

The same could be said of India.

Third: corruption is not confined to only a few levels of the official hierarchy, but seems to pervade the entire structure. It should also be noted that although corruption at the top attracts the most attention in public forums, and involves the largest amount of money in separate transactions, corruption at the very bottom levels is the more apparent and obvious and in total amounts of money involved may very well rival corruption at the top.

THE EFFECTS OF CORRUPTION

Corruption comes in innumerable shapes, forms, and sizes. There are as many reasons for corrupting as there are ways in which government affects individuals; there are as many avenues for corruption as there are roles to be played in govern-

7 May 10, 1964, p. 6, editorial.
8 Santhanam Committee, p. 18.
9 Santhanam Committee, p. 18, emphasis added.
10 See *Quiet Crisis in India* (New York: Doubleday, 1964), p. 145.
11 *Wraith and Simpkins,* pp. 15–16.

ment. Corruption may be involved in the issuance of export licenses, a decision to investigate in a criminal case, obtaining of a copy of court proceedings, appointment of candidates to universities, choice of men for civil service jobs, inspection of building specifications in new housing developments, avoiding of arrest by people with defective motor vehicles, granting of contracts, and in the expediting of anything. This wealth of forms would appear to make analysis of effects formidable and perhaps impossible. The solution is to distinguish and to keep firmly in mind the essential elements of a corrupt act; that is, to establish a type-form.

Elaborating upon the definition found in Webster's, a corrupt practice will be assumed to involve the following elements: (a) a decision to depart from government-established criteria for decisions of the relevant class and (b) a monetary reward benefiting either the official directly or those related to him.

In analyzing the effects of corrupt practices two categories of generalized effects may be distinguished, apart from whether the effects are good or bad. First, there are direct, unmediated effects. These are the effects that are part of the act itself. They are the effects contained in the reasons for which the favor seeker, the corruptor, initiated the act. Second, there are indirect effects, mediated through those who perceive that an act of a certain kind—in this case a corrupt one—has taken place. There are three classes of mediating actors: the corrupted, the corruptor, and the nonparticipating audience.

In the discussion that follows I shall present the harmful factors first and the beneficial ones second. No attempt has been made explicitly to locate each effect within the analytic schema just presented, but it would be possible to do so. These lists are undoubtedly incomplete; the effects presented here are the more important.

Harmful Effects of Corrupt Acts

1. A corrupt act represents a failure to achieve the objectives government sought when it established criteria for decisions of various classes. To the extent that the objectives sought were worthwhile, corrupt acts exact a cost in nonachevement. For example, if the objective in hiring government employees is the obtaining of efficiency and ability in carrying out official tasks, then corruption in appointments produces inefficiency and waste. If the issuing of permits for domestic enterprises is designed to insure that scarce resources go to projects enjoying the highest priority in terms of facilitating long-run economic development, then corruption exacts a cost by inhibiting over-all economic development. Places in universities and opportunities for foreign educational experience are severely limited in most developing nations; if corruption is present in the awards, the country fails to obtain the best result in making use of a scarce opportunity.

2. Corruption represents a rise in the price of administration. The multiple of extra cost depends on what the market will bear. The man who is both taxpayer and also forced to submit to bribing has paid several times over for the same service. Corruption is a mechanism for allocating increased amounts of resources to the performance of a single type of function, namely, government administration.

3. If corruption takes the form of a kickback, it serves to diminish the total amount expended for public purposes. It represents a diversion of resources from public purposes to private ones. For example, a civil servant may let a contract for a certain sum, but get 10 per cent back for the favor of giving the contract: 90 per cent of the allocated amount goes for the public purpose, 10 per cent goes into personal gains and acquisitions.

4. Corruption exerts a corrupting in-

fluence on other members of the administrative apparatus. This is a function of its persistence, its perceived rewards, and the impunity with which it is done. Corruption feeds upon itself and erodes the courage necessary to adhere to high standards of propriety. Morale declines, each man asking himself why he should be the sole custodian of morality.

5. Corruption in government, perceived by the people, lowers respect for constituted authority. It undercuts popular faith in government to deal even-handedly. The less a regime depends upon coercion in order to maintain itself, the more it must depend upon popular respect for it. One element in this process of legitimation is popular faith in government to deal fairly among competing claimants. Corruption weakens this element of support.

6. Politicians and civil servants constitute an elite. Their function is to give purpose to national effort. In so doing they cannot avoid setting an example others will emulate. If the elite is believed to be widely and thoroughly corrupt, the man-in-the-street will see little reason why he too should not gather what he can for himself and his loved ones. Selig Harrison has said of contemporary India:

> The old vision is gone, and there are few signs pointing to the birth of a renewed spirit of common purpose to take its place. *The mode is increasingly one of every man for himself.* This can be felt at every turn in the impatient refusal of each sector of the population to accept the disciplines of planned development. Thus a farmer who grows more food shows more determination than ever to hoard it for a time of still greater stringency or to consume it himself rather than to free it for the market in response to pleas from New Delhi. The middleman and trader reacted to the recent food price crisis by creating artificial local scarcities to push prices up, moving operations methodically from one area to another with the police one jump behind. The low-wage consumer in the cities and towns, who has been using his increase in income in recent years to buy wheat or rice instead of coarse grains, refused to shift back during the 1964 pinch despite official exhortations. All this could also have been said of earlier food crises under Nehru, but *one detected on this occasion for the first time a note of antagonism and even of contempt toward constituted authority.*[12]

Corruption among an elite not only debases standards popularly perceived, it forces people to undertake the underhanded approach out of self-defense. They feel they must resort to corrupt practices just to get their due, not to secure inordinate returns.[13] This is a classic vicious circle.

7. An important, perhaps overwhelming, problem in those nations that have sought to develop economically within a democratic political framework has been the unwillingness of politicians to take actions which are necessary for development but unpopular with the mass of the people. Taxation is the most obvious example. A corrupt official or politician is a self-centered individual. Can such a person be expected to put country before self, to jeopardize his prospects for the sake of prosperity for the whole country in the remote future? Uncommon political courage can hardly be maintained in an atmosphere of tolerance of corruption.

8. With erosion of belief in the even-handedness of public officials comes the need to cultivate special contacts, to develop enough "pull" to offset the claims of others. In many underdeveloped countries the amount of time and human energy devoted to making these contacts is immense. The effort that might otherwise be spent in enhancing credentials, in strengthening one's case objectively, goes into the necessary task of lobbying.

---

12 "Troubled India and Her Neighbors," *Foreign Affairs*, January 1965, p. 314. Emphasis added.

13 For an excellent description of this attitude see William and Charlotte Wiser, *Behind Mud Walls, 1930–1960* (Berkeley: University of California Press, 1963), pp. 128–129.

The loss in productive effort defies estimation.

9. Corruption, since it represents to the man-in-the-street institutionalized unfairness, inevitably leads to litigation, calumnous charges, and bitter grievances. Even the honest official may be blackmailed by the threat that unless he act unfairly he may be charged publicly with being corrupt. And there would be few to believe his disclaimer. The attention and energies of official and nonofficial alike are diverted into endless, unproductive wrangling.

10. Time is important in the making of most decisions, delays can be costly in monetary and human terms. The most ubiquitous form of corruption takes the form of what Indians call "speed money." The wheels of the bureaucratic machine must be oiled with money, and unless this is done nothing at all will be done. Corruption causes decisions to be weighed in terms of money, not in terms of human need. The poor man with an urgent and just request gets little if any sympathy.

Beneficial Effects of Corrupt Acts

In order to sustain the points that follow, I shall present arguments sufficient to show that the effects of corruption *may* be beneficial in nature. I do not pretend that they always are, simply that it would not be unreasonable to find that they are. Nor does it follow that because the effects are good the means are either desirable or blameless.

1. There is a common assumption that corrupt acts produce effects worse than those which would have followed from an untainted decision. This assumption is only true to the extent that the government-established—or system-established—criteria for choice are better than those served by corruption. Governments have no monopoly upon correct solutions; governments are simply one among many bureaucratic institutions which may do stupid things. Both the ends and the means served by government-constricted choices may be worse than those freely chosen and finding expression through corruption. Corruption may serve as a means for impelling better choices, even in terms of government's expressed goals. Nor do I think it necessary to say that corruption only occasionally, and by chance, operates in this direction. It could systematically do so, not perhaps across the board in all decisions but certainly in all decisions of a certain kind. For example, government may desire to build a strong fertilizer industry and toward this end may have established certain requirements for the selection of firms to receive the concession. If government economists have not selected the proper indicators of efficiency, it is not farfetched to assume that ability to offer massive bribes—bribes at least bigger than anyone else's—could be correlated with entrepreneurial efficiency. Bribes represent a peculiar element of cost, applying to all competing firms; the ability to meet it may not be unrelated to efficiency.

Corruption, then, is not an inherently defective means of arriving at decisions among competing claimants. The satisfactoriness of the inducement offered may correlate with features among claimants government would choose if it had better information or greater expertise in selecting criteria for decision-making. In order to demonstrate the effect of departing from established decision-making criteria, two general types of cases need to be analyzed, those in which the inducement is solely monetary and those in which it is something besides money such as loyalty to family, caste, tribe, and so forth. One must then ask if, for any particular group of decisions made, the absence of the extra ingredient would have made the result of the decision better? In many cases the decision probably would be unaltered; in some it might be better; but in some it could very easily have been worse. Even in the case of non-monetary inducements, it would be necessary to determine that bias across the group of decision-makers, for a particular class of choices, acted to favor persons or firms less able to carry out what government intended. It could happen that groups within a society successful in penetrating the civil service in efficient numbers to influence decisions might for this very reason have qualities instrumental for the accomplishment of activities government wants carried out. Therefore nepotistic favoritism would lead government to rely on just those groups most capable of shouldering responsibility. In underdeveloped countries the tangle of popular pressures involving traditionally antagonistic groups frequently causes government to award contracts, scholarships, privileges, and jobs according to mechanical quota systems. Since talent and ability are very often unevenly distributed through these societies, this policy is not in the direction of optimum efficiency. Corruption of the monetary and non-monetary kind might very well offset this pervasive influence.

2. Corruption, whether in the form of kickbacks or of payments originating with the briber, may result in increased allocations of resources away from consumption and into investment. Contrary to common expectations, it may be a supplemental allocative mechanism compatible with the goals of economic development. The key elements in this determination are the marginal propensities of the corrupted and the corruptor to consume and invest. In the case of kickbacks, for example, if the kickback comes from funds designed for projects contributing little to the sum total of capital investment, then diversion of some of these to an individual who will use them for investment in productive enterprises actually results in a net accretion to the stock of capital goods. This would be the case with funds diverted from famine relief or inefficient cottage industries into the hands of civil servants backing firms manufacturing tires or machine tools. A similar instance is a bribe financed by the briber himself. His marginal propensity to consume may be greater than that of the bribed. It may even be that government servants as a whole, especially at the upper levels, representing an educated elite with unique access to information about prospects for economic development, may have a greater propensity to invest in productive enterprises of a modern kind than do a cross-section of the people who seek to bribe them. It is not indubitable, then, that corruption represents a net drain from investment into consumption or even from the modern sector of enterprise into the traditional.

3. The opportunity for corruption may actually serve to increase the quality of pubic servants. If wages in government service are insufficient to meet a talented man's needs, and he has an alternate choice, he will be tempted to choose the other. On the other hand, a man anxious to serve his country through government service might opt away from non-government employment if he knew that means existed to supplement a meager salary. Even for the man with no alternative prospects for employment, security in meeting his unavoidable obligations may enhance his willingness to serve ably and loyally.

The corrupt are not always unable; nor are they always unpatriotic. These propositions seem especially true of underdeveloped countries where the rewards for government service are so piteously low. Where corruption is often necessary to provide basic necessities of life to oneself and one's family, it becomes a necessary means of ensuring a supply of able and willing public servants. Furthermore, in developing nations it is an indispensable means of reconciling insufficient wage rates with the claims of traditional society operating through extended family and clan ties. The civil servant cannot wish away these obligations. Through corruption he taxes society with preserving an important element of social continuity.

4. Nepotism in government hiring, which swells the ranks of the civil service, can be looked upon as a substitute for a public works system. It provides employment for the otherwise unemployed and by making them dependent upon government may secure a measure of support for government. Inflated civil service rolls become the price for relieving intolerable political pressure due to unemployment. To be sure, the quality of performance in government service may certainly suffer from the injection of the public works objective. The goals of each may be incompatible: relief on the one hand, efficiency in government operations on the other. But, granting the incompatibility, it is incumbent upon us to admit that to the extent that a public works program is needed corruption in hiring may serve the same end.

It is well known, for example, that in many underdeveloped countries there is a growing army of half-educated unemployed. The revolutionary potential of this mass is considerable; they gravitate to the political extremes in much greater proportions than members of other groups. In countries where the absorptive capacity of private agencies is not great enough to provide employment for the educated or half-educated, government service obtained by means of illicit considerations may provide a safety value of considerable importance.

5. Corruption provides a means of giving those persons or groups potentially disaffected as a result of exclusion from power a stake in the system. The degree to which they can be tied to the system in this way depends upon their ability and willingness to capitalize upon the opportunities for corruption. A person with money who is ideologically opposed to the regime or who dislikes the personnel at the top, may nonetheless be able to make the repugnant system work for him by means of illicit influence. He is not entirely alienated.

6. In traditional societies struggling to be Western, corruption may make the new system human in traditional terms. Corruption is an understandable means of influence in most traditional societies. A transitional people may have more faith in a system they can influence in some degree through personal action than one they do not know how to manipulate by means of the institutional mechanisms provided. The human contact provided in a corrupt act may be a necessary transitional device to insure the loyalty to the new of a tradition-bound people. Perhaps it is better that people in developing nations misuse modern agencies to their own ends than that they reject the new because they cannot work the handles. This argument particularly applies to countries trying to implant democratic institutions. The successor to the rejected democratic forms will not be hallowed traditional ones, whatever the people may wish, but a modern, impersonal system less subject to rejection.

7. Corruption provides a means for reducing the harshness of an elite-conceived plan for economic and social development. It supplements the political system by allowing the introduction of political considerations at the administrative level. Such access may be essential to the stability of the system. When political channels are clogged, corruption provides non-violent entry into government affairs and administration.

8. Among politicians corruption may act as a solvent for uncompromisable issues of ideology and/or interest. Where potential schisms based upon the claims of caste, tribe, region, religion, or language are manifold, common interest in spoils may provide cement for effective political unity, especially within a single

dominant party. In general, corruption should damp doctrinairism, no matter how predicated. It is the disheartened politician, cut off from power or perquisites, who is more likely to repair to the standard of factional rigidity or ideological extremism.

9. In developing nations, particularly where there is comparatively free play of political forces, there is often tension between the civil service and the politicians. The bureaucracy may develop considerable *esprit de corps* and feel impatient with the activities of politicians whose only thought seems to be to truckle to mass whims, hampering the orderly progress of the bureaucratic nation-building machine. Politicians, on the other hand, may find the civil service unresponsive, proud, and aloof, without the slightest understanding of the importance of the role politicians must play. Politicians accuse the bureaucrats of running a closed corporation; bureaucrats argue that politicians divert attention and resources from essential tasks.[14] The practice of corruption may lessen this potentially crippling strain. It is one means of increasing the responsiveness of bureaucrats to individual and group needs. It also links the bureaucrat and the politician in an easily discerned network of self-interest. There may be a principle here: in countries where agreement upon proper relative functions has not been fixed between bureaucrats and politicians, the less amenable planning is to political pressures—due perhaps to rigid adherence to "rational" planning criteria—the greater may be the functional importance of corruption in preserving a working relationship between civil servants and popular leaders. An alternative means to the same end could be found in the imposition of sanctions by an agency capable of disciplining both sides. In this case agreement upon functions is enforced.

CONCLUSION

Because so many incommensurables are involved in the effects of corrupt practices, it is impossible to determine firmly and precisely how the positive and negative effects combine to produce an over-all thrust along either dimension. It is clear, though, that corruption is an accommodating device. Its benefits are to be seen primarily in the realm of politics. But the analysis has also shown that the net effects of corrupt practices upon economic development are not always, or necessarily, of a baneful nature. There are serious negative effects, to be sure, and these may be assessed either in terms of economic costs or of dysfunctional attitudes being formed throughout the developing society. But even if a final balance sheet cannot be constructed, it is still abundantly clear that corruption is a social practice about which there is very little accurate theoretical analysis and even less empirical research.

Research into corruption will be difficult, but ingenuity should be able to overcome many seemingly insurmountable obstacles. Analysis of indirect or mediated effects of corruption will be easier than analysis of direct effects. Mediated effects are those which depend upon someone's perceiving that an act of this particular kind has occurred. Surveys designed to touch all three acting groups—corrupted, corruptor, audience—should be able to establish, among other things, each group's opinion about improper behavior among the other groups, concept of role in society, morale, and values operating to restrain or impel behavior of various kinds. Studies of this kind yield considerable information about the mediated effects of corruption found or believed found in others. Research into

14 For an excellent discussion of this problem in one country, Burma, see Lucien Pye's *Politics, Personality, and Nation Building* (New Haven, Conn.: Yale University Press, 1962).

the direct, unmediated effects is more difficult because it requires knowledge of how many of which kinds of people are doing what in various circumstances. Precise knowledge of actors and situations is essential. By and large the researcher will have to depend upon the results of official studies; he will not have the resources, nor would it be discreet, to undertake such a survey himself—although the researcher, especially the foreign one, may find that people are distressingly willing to speak about practices engaged in by themselves which the researcher considers corrupt but the respondents do not. This is particularly true of people still substantially enmeshed in a traditional world, with little modern education, and hence unlettered in Western standards of propriety. Generally the key to unlocking tongues is to seek information about how politics works, the amount of influence various role players possess, their tactics of maneuver, and their concept of function, carefully refraining from describing behavior in pejorative terms. It must be admitted, even so, that most knowledge will be about forms of corruption and less about extent. Nonetheless, it is still possible to analyze many of the effects of corruption. Making assumptions about who corrupts and who is corrupted, describing these actors by membership in socially defined groups, one can then collect data about consumption patterns, family size, social obligations, level of remuneration, values with respect to achievement and striving, and so forth, and thereby determine either the reasons for which corruption is undertaken or the ways in which gains from it will be utilized. Moreover, it should be possible to arrive at a description of the human predicament impelling corruption. A study of this kind would underscore the root factors in corruption and thereby provide a means of gauging its function in society.

That corruption is an accommodating device has important implications. It indicates that corrupt practices are a human response to circumstances, conditioned, to be sure, by moral codes. But it also means that corruption is to some extent a creation of the very circumstances defining political and economic underdevelopment. It becomes apparent, therefore, that considerably more than exhortation may be needed in order to eliminate venality in government. It also indicates that removal of all vestiges of corruption may not be a good thing. There are three strategies that can be employed in a transitional situation to reduce corrupt practices. First, a policy may be adopted of containing the grosser forms of corruption while waiting for changing circumstance to remove the functional utility of such practices. This strategy is essentially a passive one and may be fatally flawed by the implicit assumption that corruption will not exert such harmful consequences as to jeopardize progress to a less unstable level. Second, corruption may be rooted out without hesitancy or remorse, counting upon the power of the state to contain repercussions. Coercion is used to offset the discontinuity in social accommodation which the removal of corruption may occasion. Third, the climate of opinion may be remolded so that the temptation to corruption on the part of both briber and bribed is substantially reduced. The building of a sense of national purposefulness, sacrifice, and dedication may cause the corruptor to be shunned and the potentially corrupted to be strong. This strategy relies upon psychological change and represents the substitution of one set of operational values for another. Its defect is that unless buttressed by real social change, it quickly loses force and wastes precipitously.

These three strategies are not mutually exclusive. None of them would be employed by itself. The mix of the three depends upon the character of the regime and it should also depend upon knowledge of the function corruption plays in the particular society. Corrupt practices may be more easily eradicated by exhortation and revived national morale than many suppose; corruption may also be more resistant than realized and not yield readily to such tactics. The point is that the knowledge necessary to make this judgment is now almost wholly lacking. This situation should be rapidly transformed. And this essay has sought to provide a first step, primarily by demonstrating that corruption wears two faces and not simply one. Corruption may play a useful role in transitional societies, a role which is sufficiently important that if it was not played by this device must be played by another or the consequences might severely undermine the pace, but more importantly the character, of the development effort.

54. The Contribution of Nepotism, Spoils, and Graft to Political Development

José Veloso Abueva

In many a developing country, nepotism, spoils and graft are ubiquitous features of the governmental landscape. Leaders and intelligentsia continually deride them—with varying mixtures of sincerity, lip-service and openness. Some foreign advisers and journalists see hardly more than these, to them, perverse aberrations. And when they go home or move on to other lands they paint lurid pictures of the countries they had briefly observed. As one *Life* correspondent pontificated after a month's sojourn in an Asian country: their bureaucracy is "hopelessly inefficient and hopelessly venal." More important than just the humiliating distortions and resented abuse that are peddled around the globe about the plight of emerging nations, these judgments overlook significant aspects of the practices that are so easily condemned. Nepotism, spoils and graft in the government of many countries in Asia, South America and Africa, not to mention also in some of the more developed countries, do have vital consequences for national development.

I

Here I shall focus on the ways in which official nepotism, spoils and graft contribute to certain aspects of political development, viz. political unification and stability, popular participation in public affairs, the development of a viable party system, higher levels of political and administrative achievement of maintenance or development goals, and bureaucratic responsibility. By nepotism I mean the priority of kinship claims in the distribution of government jobs and benefits. Spoils enlarges nepotism to embrace non-kin, on the basis of other personal or partisan considerations. Graft is the illegal misappropriation of public resources—usually money, property or opportunities for personal enrichment.

To begin with, I should like to expose certain unarticulated premises of some critics, nationals and aliens alike. Whatever they wish to believe, the practices in question are not unmitigated evils, and are in fact largely good and acceptable, as perceived by a majority of the peoples of developing countries in their particular historical junctures. Had it been otherwise, these practices would not be as widespread and persistent. As a functionalist might put it, nepotism, spoils and graft perform "requisite functions" for the social system.[1] This is certainly the

Source: José Veloso Abueva, "The Contribution of Nepotism, Spoils, and Graft to Political Development," *East-West Center Review,* 3 (1966), pp. 45–54. By permission.

[1] Robert K. Merton's functional analysis of corruption and the political machine in American cities inspired my quest for the latent functions of nepotism, spoils and graft in underdeveloped countries. See his *Social Theory and Social Structure* (New York: Free Press, 1959), pp. 19–85.

reason why these modes of behavior also obtain today in varying forms and incidence in the developed countries. Until the minority among the people who now believe with our critics that the practices are dysfunctional and outright immoral have become the majority by a process of conversion impelled by a drastically changed national situation, these practices will not be materially reduced. Contrary also to the view of some critics, the rapidly changing environment in some developing countries—which has bred the present unprecedented spoils and graft—is spawning countervailing values and norms. Two or more contrasting sets of standards and behaviors coexist and interact, with puzzling outcomes, some frustrating, others gratifying.[2] This phenomenon is certainly not strange to those familiar with the history of the more economically advanced peoples.

In most developing countries strong, and in some localities almost exclusive, loyalties and commitments are owed to the family or clan. The family determines one's identity and status and affords all-around personal security. This was true when communities existed in more or less splendid isolation, which is becoming rare; this seems even more true amidst the early intrusion of strangers, goods and ideas from the modernized capitals. Beyond this kinship focus, peoples' identifications with other relatives, townmates, the ethnic community and the nation at large weaken in changing degrees. To large segments of their citizenries the concepts of "nation," "public," and "government" are all but blurred completely by the circumscribed world of daily, face-to-face relationships, governed by mutual rights and obligations defined by immemorial custom. Those with somewhat broader orientations may still view the government ambiguously as the family writ large, political leaders and bureaucrats as paternal figures; and this fact gives rise to expectations of reciprocity between the rulers and the ruled which are quite incompatible with modern government.

Various forces modify kinship values and structure. Urbanization and literacy and higher standards of living can weaken family obligations in one or two generations, depending among other things on the capacity of the cities and the towns to provide economic security for larger numbers of people, on the acceptance of the modern norms of individualism and achievement, and on inter-regional mobility. More often than not, however, the flight to the cities proceeds faster than employment opportunities can be provided there, while the painful trek back to town and village must be avoided. As a result dependency on the family continues in the cities, aggravated by the rapid rise in population. The perceived hazards to traditional family solidarity brought about by the developing modern media and by crowding in the cities may also invite new laws intended to preserve some of the age-old social ties.

Developing countries of course vary in their underdevelopedness. But without exception their bureaucracies are expanding fast in an effort to cope with new and greater demands for education, health, transportation, communications, agriculture, commerce, industry, and defense. Yet in several countries popular support and revenues for these varied demands lag considerably. While programs and agencies proliferate, even those most desired cannot expand commensurately with the demands. One consequence, where agricultural development and industrialization do not outpace population growth, is the acute scarcity of jobs, as the labor force, reshaped by an unbalanced public education, carries more unemployable persons. Inasmuch as the private sector also gives priority

---

2 Inconsistencies between ideals and realities produce tensions that could lead to salutary change. These and other sources of change are analyzed by Wilbert E. Moore, *Social Change* (Englewood Cliffs, N.J.: Prentice-Hall, 1963).

to relatives in its highly valued placements, the upshot is the enormous pressures on public employment. Given the strong kinship ties, these are largely nepotistic pressures.

In a number of the developing countries, however, the bureaucracy had been organized under colonial rule partly on the ideas of technical specialization and advancement through achievement. Despite the post-independence scramble for jobs channeled by elected officials, the bureaucracy was not wanting in defenders of its pattern of examinations, professionalization, seniority, and other official criteria and perquisites. Consequently, nepotism and the "merit system" clashed perenially, resulting in the victory of one or the other, and usually in some of the most ingenious compromises between the two. In varying degrees, democratic ideas, such as popular sovereignty, elections, equal treatment of citizens by government officials—spread by public education and electoral participation—merely intensified the conflicts.

The bureaucrats in some countries had entrenched themselves in power during colonial rule and continued to direct and control the bureaucracy after independence in more or less open defiance of the politicians. For a time at least education, wealth, social status and familiarity with the intricacies of governance favored the bureaucrats over the politicians. With some exceptions of course, one of the greatest problems of political development facing the emerging nations was the superior power of the bureaucrats and their political irresponsibility.[3] Even in those countries where the politicians held greater sway, qualifying examinations were usually obsolescent in terms of growing specialization in the government and in the society at large and of the consequent need for development-minded administrators. The personnel needs of the government often exceeded the capacity of the central personnel agency, yet bureaucrats were most reluctant to relax their rules on recruitment and staffing. Moreover, they wished to rigidly enforce the rules on transfers and seniority in promotions. As more violations of the rules occurred under political pressure, the more stringent the rules became, at least on paper and for those bureaucrats who somehow were able to enforce them. Not infrequently government rules showed up to be patently absurd, as when some of the most reputable scientists, technicians and professionals whom progressive political leaders would like to "borrow" from the universities, business, and the professions, were found "unfit" to serve in the government.

The rigid and elaborate rules concerning personnel processes were only one manifestation of the plethora of rules and cumbersome procedures that had enmeshed the whole bureaucracy, making it progressively difficult for the unknown and ignorant citizen to obtain government services. In fact the inertia of control-mindedness—an administrative hall-

[3] Edward W. Weidner observes that "The bureaucracies of the less developed countries tend to be both powerful and isolated. Their position of power encourages them in a lack of responsibility. Their isolation contributes to their lack of responsiveness." E. W. Weidner, *Technical Assistance in Public Administration Overseas: The Case for Development Administration* (Chicago, Ill.: Public Administration Service, 1964), p. 169.

Fred W. Riggs advocates the curbing of bureaucratic growth where bureaucrats wield predominant political power, and Lucian W. Pye proposes the strengthening of political institutions as a requisite to improving public administration. F. W. Riggs, "Bureaucrats and Political Development: A Paradoxical View," in Joseph LaPalombara (ed.), *Bureaucracy and Political Development* (Princeton, N.J.: Princeton University Press, 1963), pp. 120–167; and L. W. Pye, "The Political Context of National Development," in Irving Swerdlow, *Development Administration: Concepts and Problems* (Syracuse, N.Y.: Syracuse University Press, 1963), pp. 25–43. Ferrel Heady notes that "Where the bureaucracy is involved to a high degree in the political process, strategy concerning the proper guidelines for bureaucratic evolution becomes a matter of prime concern to leaders within the bureaucracy itself, to other political leaders in the country, and to those who are trying to exert influence from outside the country." "Bureaucracies in Developing Countries: Internal Roles and External Assistance," paper presented at the Conference of the Comparative Administration Group, University of Maryland, March, 1963, p. 3.

mark of law-and-order, aristocratic, minimal government[4]—had barely begun to meet the thrust of a new welfare, egalitarian and service orientation.

II

Now, in such an environment, how do nepotism and spoils contribute to political development? As it turned out, one of the remedies to the bureaucratic pathology described was the infusion of the bureaucracy with the relatives, cronies and partisans of the politicians. Too, the bureaucrats themselves could not always resist kinship pressures, and found it more and more expedient to accommodate the politicians. Critics tend to oversimplify reality by equating nepotism and spoils invariably with incompetence and irresponsibility. On the contrary, where public education had developed significantly, political proteges might be better qualified technically than those who had entered the service with minimal attainments, through infrequently-held and often irrelevant examinations. They may also be better imbued with a development-service-and-action outlook, more ambitious, and more imaginative and resourceful. Older and experienced civil servants, wrapped up in the complicated forms and procedures they have so painstakingly devised sometimes admit, albeit grudgingly, the superiority of the new knowledge and methods introduced by younger and inexperienced proteges. Moreover, the older hands may discover how insulated they had become when they suddenly, thanks to the mediation of the protege, gain access to his politician patron and a supporting interest group. In short, nepotism and spoils may very well be the potent stimuli needed by a powerful, rigid, unrealistic, outmoded, unresponsive, and irresponsible bureaucracy.

Nepotism and spoils enhance political development in still other ways. As more and more citizens find access to government jobs, services and resources, their beliefs and attitudes towards the state change. No longer is it a remote abstraction to be ignored or a proximate oppressor to be avoided. Gradually it becomes a tangible and helpful entity deserving trust and support. Involvement sparks a sense of belonging, offers the first step toward commitment. The bureaucracy becomes an important ladder for social mobility and therefore also a unifying and stabilizing force where, otherwise, social stratification and communalism, narrow loyalties and deep suspicions divide the people and impose serious limits to personal advancement and the spread of a national consciousness.

III

Nepotism and spoils derive from and strengthen the parties and their allies who represent a variety of interests. The parties may have at their base and core the dominant local leader and his relatives and those personally beholden to him, plus other leaders and their similar personal following who form a faction with him. The parties may be largely national alliances of such local leaders and factions, although in other countries they may consist mainly of individual leaders and their ideological, religious or ethnic supporters and adherents. Regardless of the composition of the parties in a competitive party system, nepotism and spoils provide the parties with much of their motivation and reward in the risky and costly rivalries for governmental power. To the extent that interest groups are organizationally and financially weak, and that parties are not mass-based and are lacking in volunteer workers, the parties have to rely mainly on nepotism and spoils and even graft for their survival as political institutions. In this set up, the opposition parties may look forward

[4] These administrative characteristics of colonial and newly independent regimes, among others, are described by E. W. Weidner, pp. 161–162.

to their turn and thus persevere *qua* opposition instead of perhaps giving up in despair, fusing with the largest party, or resorting to extremist goals and tactics. Like the bureaucracy, the parties also serve as social escalators and stabilizers.

In time inordinate nepotism, spoils and graft induce popular repudiation at the polls, or revolution, so ruling parties in competitive political systems at least must also regulate their appetites lest they be thrown out of power. In other systems military takeover or revolution have been historical alternatives, and these examples are further restraints on the operations of parties in competitive polities. Thus the more viable the parties become, partly due to spoils and graft, the more effective they would be in mobilizing the citizenry for political participation, in articulating and aggregating interests as they shape public policy, in channeling public services to citizens, in holding bureaucrats and the bureaucracy politically accountable, and in fostering national unity.

Like nepotism and spoils, graft has other functions than nourishing the parties in their critical infancy. In capital-hungry economies, which is certainly one way of characterizing all developing countries, large-scale graft which funnels capital to struggling entrepreneurs aids them in establishing essential industries.[5] When coupled with "judicious graft"—the legal discrimination in favor of successful or budding entrepreneurs—graft may actually minimize the wastage of resources by conspicuous consumers. Beginning in a few sectors, irregularities in implementing discriminatory policies also hasten the process of wresting control of trade and industry away from the alien businessmen. Undoubtedly, it has been difficult for even the most well-meaning administrators of government credit, contracts, public land, franchises and licenses, and foreign exchange to shun those who would use these scarce resources uneconomically. General poverty made starker by enclaves of affluence foment exploitation of the government as the country's wealthiest "person," the more so because "he" is a faceless, legal person, and because while graft is illegal it often is culturally acceptable. But there are quite a few politically-favored entrepreneurs who are able to enlarge, diversify, and rationalize their enterprises and eliminate the get-rich-quick operators when subsidies and controls are withdrawn.

As economic development proceeds, some politicians themselves become investors, if not also entrepreneurs. In their new roles they begin to approach law-making and administration in economizing terms. Starting as agitators during the independence movement or as manipulators of voters, fellow politicians, bureaucrats and of political financiers, politicians get initiated into the world of production and distribution and acquire a different order of rationality measured by balance sheets and the stock market.

IV

In the short run nepotism, spoils and graft look excessively wasteful and costly ingredients and concomitants of nation-building; they also appear to slow down schemes for development. Yet the view that they are unrelieved obstacles fallaciously assumes that the people, in their particular ambience, could unilaterally opt for a modern rationality marked by

[5] I had written this essay when I came upon an excellent and most relevant article by Nathaniel H. Leff, "Economic Development through Bureaucratic Corruption," *The American Behavioral Scientist,* November, 1964, pp. 8–14. Leff analyzed the positive effects of corruption for economic development under the following conditions: when the government is indifferent to the initiative of entreprenuers, being primarily interested in the *status quo*; when the government has other priorities than economic development, such as military power and social control; where there is great uncertainty regarding the behavior of the government in relation to investment; where established interests stifle competing innovators, with governmental intervention; where there is lack of economic competition and therefore little or no pressure for improving efficiency of production; where bad economic policies impel entrepreneurs to seek a way out, a "hedge" or "safeguard."

impersonality, achievement, functional specificity, and universalism. Not only are rampant nepotism, spoils and graft unavoidable, under the circumstances of most developing countries, but they may have positive, unanticipated consequences for political development. This is so because the underdeveloped countries are in varying stages of politico-administrative development and they are simultaneously seeking varied and often conflicting objectives subsumed under the grand goals of nation-building and economic and social development.[6] In the early stages of politico-administrative development, particularly where a democratic political system is consciously desired, nepotism, spoils and graft may actually promote national unification and stability, nation-wide participation in public affairs, the formation of a viable party system, and bureaucratic accountability to political institutions. At a critical period in the political history of the emerging nations, supercilious criticism of the practices in question merely harass the progressive leaders and intelligentsia and exacerbate cynicism toward the democratic system sought to be established. Given their uneven development, politically, economically and socially—not to mention their differing ideologies—it is not valid, and therefore not helpful, to simple-mindedly judge the political beliefs and styles of the emerging nations against the political beliefs and styles in vogue in the more developed Western democracies. It is instructive to recall, with Joseph LaPalombara, that "an enormous amount of national development took place in the United States and Western Europe long before the public bureaucracies achieved even the approximate degree of rational organization and behavior that characterizes them today."[7]

In view of my controversial argument, I wish to end with a personal note. I do not intend this little essay to be a brief for nepotism, spoils and graft. As teacher and writer, I have certainly spent more time pointing up the dysfunctional aspects of these familiar phenomena. By now "slighting" those drawbacks, I only wish to stress the neglected functional features in respect to some primary and urgent goals of democratic, and political development in many a developing nation.

6 Milton J. Esman has catalogued the multiple goals and tasks of developing nations and assessed the differential efficiency of various patterns of organization and action. "The Politics of Development Administration," paper presented to the Comparative Administrative Group, Boston University, revised August 20, 1963.

7 J. LaPalombara, p. 55.

55. Corruption: Its Causes and Effects

GUNNAR MYRDAL

One of the opportunistic rationalizations of the neglect of research on the problem of corruption is its alleged unimportance —or even its alleged usefulness in development under the conditions prevailing in South Asia. We believe that these unproved assumptions are totally wrong, and that corrupt practices are highly detrimental from the point of view of the value premises applied in the present study, namely, the modernization ideals.

The remnants of pre-capitalist society referred to in the preceding section represent deterrents to development. This applies to the aforementioned contrasts with Western mores and behavior patterns—namely, while markets are nonexistent or grossly imperfect in South Asia and profit motives less effective in the economic sphere, those who have public responsibility and power are more apt to use their position for private benefit. As these contrasting conditions are complementary and sustain each other to a certain extent, the prevalence of corruption provides strong inhibitions and obstacles to development.

We have referred to the fragmentation of loyalties in South Asian societies. Development efforts must attempt to modernize people's attitudes by mitigating this fragmentation, yet in a general way corruption counteracts the strivings for national consolidation, decreases respect for and allegiance to the government, and endangers political stability.[1] As we pointed out in [Selection 22], no South Asian government can be firmly in control unless it can convince its articulate groups that effective measures are being taken to purge corruption from public life.

From another point of view, corruption is one of the forces that help to preserve the "soft state" with its low degree of social discipline. Not only are politicians and administrators affected by the prevalence of corruption, but also businessmen and, in fact, the whole population. Corruption introduces an element of irrationality in plan fulfillment by influencing the actual course of development in a way that is contrary to the plan or, if such influence is foreseen, by limiting the horizon of the plan. Of particular importance is the fact that the usual method of exploiting a position of public responsibility for private gain is by threat

SOURCE: Gunnar Myrdal, "Corruption—Its Causes and Effects," in *Asian Drama: An Enquiry into the Poverty of Nations,* Vol. II. New York: The Twentieth Century Fund, 1968, pp. 951–958. By permission of the publisher.

1 "Corruption is essentially a sign of conflicting loyalties pointing primarily to a lack of positive attachment to the government and its ideals. In so far as corruption shows that the new government, with its enormous task to fulfil in the new Asian world, is not yet sufficiently integrated in society and does not evoke full sympathy, enthusiasm and unfaltering loyalty from subjects and officials, it is a sign of weakness of the present political structure." (W. F. Wertheim, *Indonesian Society in Transition,* W. van Hoeve Ltd., The Hague, 1956, p. 86.)

of obstruction or delay. Where corruption is widespread, inertia and inefficiency, as well as irrationality, impede the process of decision-making and plan fulfillment. "It was the unanimous opinion of all witnesses who appeared before us," the Santhanam Committee noted, "that administrative delays are one of the major causes of corruption. We agree with this view. We have no doubt that quite often delay is deliberately contrived so as to obtain some kind of illicit gratification."[2] The influence of corruption in slowing down the wheels of administration is particularly damaging in South Asia, where the administrative system largely retains the impediments to speed and efficiency inherited from colonial times.[3]

The Santhanam Committee report speaks of "speed money":

It is believed that the procedures and practices in the working of Government offices are cumbersome and dilatory. The anxiety to avoid delay has encouraged the growth of dishonest practices like the system of speed money. "Speed money" is reported to have become a fairly common type of corrupt practice particularly in matters relating to grant of licences, permits, etc. Generally the bribe giver does not wish, in these cases, to get anything done unlawfully, but wants to speed up the process of the movement of files and communications relating to decisions. Certain sections of the staff concerned are reported to have got into the habit of not doing anything in the matter till they are suitably persuaded. It was stated by a Secretary that even after an order had been passed, the fact of the passing of such order is communicated to the person concerned and the order itself is kept back till the unfortunate applicant has paid appropriate gratification to the subordinate concerned. Besides being a most objectionable corrupt practice, this custom of speed money has become one of the most serious causes of delay and inefficiency.[4]

The popular notion, occasionally expressed by Western students of conditions in South Asia, that corruption is a means of speeding up cumbersome administrative procedures, is palpably wrong.[5]

At the same time, when suspicion of corruption is rampant, a natural protective device is to spread and share the responsibility for decisions to the maximum extent possible. Apart from this, the most honest official will tend to shun taking personal responsibility if he works in an administrative system widely suspected of being corrupt; the present writer has often heard testimony to this effect. Paul Appleby has criticized the Indian administration for its "excessive bureaucracy," which he relates to the "timidity of public servants at all levels, making them unwilling to take responsibility for decisions, forcing decisions to be made by a slow and cumbersome process of reference and conference in which everybody finally shares dimly in the making of every de-

2 Santhanam Committee report, p. 44.

3 For India, see an excellent critique by Paul H. Appleby in *Re-examination of India's Administrative System,* Government of India Press, New Delhi, 1956.

4 Santhanam Committee report, pp. 9–10.

5 The London *Times* (August 5, 1964) reports: "Many of these instances of bribery are those in which the citizen pays in order to get what he is entitled to anyway, and some students of Indian affairs have argued that this is a necessary and not harmful lubricant for a cumbersome administration. One American writer, Mr. Myron Weiner, has put it like this: 'The system of corruption . . . is a highly stable one. It is a regularized relationship. Businessmen and agriculturalists often regard the payment of baksheesh to be as much a part of the application for government services as filling in a form. The rates of payment are generally based upon the rank of the officer, the character of the services being requested, and the financial means of the claimant. The rates are more or less predictable and on the whole (there are notable exceptions, however) moderate.' Mr. Weiner's conclusion is that this corruption is 'simply a way that citizens have found of building rewards into the administrative structure in the absence of any other appropriate incentive system.' "

The reporter comments that: "As a means of accelerating the sluggish, meandering circulation of a file within a department this might be all very well; but speed money, belying the name, actually has the effect of a brake on administration, slowing it down even further. Delay will deliberately be caused in order to invite payment of a bribe to accelerate it again."

cision," and he blames it for the fact that "not enough gets done and what gets done is done too slowly."[6] He accuses Parliament of being "the chief citadel of opposition to delegation of powers, the need for which is the worst shortcoming of Indian administration,"[7] but he could have added the press and articulate opinion generally. A situation is created that is vividly described by an Indian author:

> To avoid direct responsibility for any major policy decision, efforts are made to get as many departments and officials associated with such decisions as is considered desirable. Again, such consultations must be in writing; otherwise there would be nothing on record. Therefore a file must move—which itself requires some time—from one table to another and from one Ministry to another for comments and it is months before the decision is conveyed to the party concerned. Even where the facts make the decision obvious and involve no significant departure from the established policy, such consultations are considered necessary for "safety." The alternative is a conference of the representatives of departments or Ministries concerned. As it is thought necessary that representatives of all departments which may have even a remote interest in the question should be present, sufficient notice of the meeting has to be given and dates changed to suit conveniences of important officials even where they have little direct interest in it. Generally no action is taken on the decisions at such meetings until the minutes are approved and circulated. The increasing popularity of the conference has led to senior officials spending most of their office time in such meetings, delaying, thereby, the disposal of files.[8]

In general conformity with the taboo noted in [Selection 22], the two authors cited, like everybody else who takes part in the lively discussion about the inherited faults of the Indian administrative system and the difficulties involved in improving it, avoid relating their observations to the prevalence of corruption, the frequent allegations of corruption, and the individual official's own interest in preserving cumbersome procedures—if he is dishonest they may increase his opportunities to extract a bribe, and if he is honest they may serve to protect him from suspicion. But undoubtedly there is such a relation and it is important. Authority cannot be efficiently delegated unless those in administrative positions are incorrupt and this fact is generally recognized. In a society where corruption is prevalent, circular causation with cumulative effects operates in other ways as well. When people became convinced, rightly or wrongly, that corruption is widespread, an official's incorruptibility will tend to be weakened. And should he resist corruption, he will find it difficult to fulfill his duties. This, again, contributes to inertia and inefficiency in a society.[9]

Recognition of the very serious effects of corruption in South Asian countries raises the practical problem of what can be done to eradicate it. In all South Asian countries there have from time to time been anti-corruption drives and anti-corruption legislation. In recent years there has been, in India particularly, a growing public anxiety about corruption. The Indian Home Minister, Gulzarilal Nanda, regarded the task of eradicating corruption as his "main occupation" for some time and opened his house for daily sessions to receive complaints about corruption.

---

6 *Re-examination of India's Administrative System,* p. 42.

7 Appleby, p. 45.

8 A. C. Chhatrapati, "Planning Through Red Tape," *The Economic Weekly,* Special Number, July, 1961, pp. 1171–1173.

9 Having become friendly with the chief police officer in the district of New Delhi where he lived for a time, the writer once complained to him about the taxi drivers' habit of ignoring all traffic rules. Why didn't he order his policemen to enforce the rules? "How could I," he answered. "If one of them went up to a taxi driver, the driver might say: 'Get away, or I will tell people that you have asked me for ten rupees.' If the policeman then pointed out that he had not done it, the rejoinder of the taxi driver could be: 'Who would believe you?' "

The important Santhanam Committee report was an outgrowth of this movement. While restricted to general judgments about the actual facts of corruption and their causes and effects, based on the Committee members' own information and the testimony of numerous witnesses, the report is more specific when analyzing administrative procedures that create opportunities for malfeasance and making recommendations for reform. It urges simpler and more precise rules and procedures for political and administrative decisions that affect private persons and business enterprises and also closer supervision. A main theme of these proposals is that discretionary powers should, insofar as possible, be decreased: "While we recognize that it would not be possible to completely eliminate discretion in the exercise of powers it should be possible to devise a system of administration which would reduce to the minimum, even if there is a certain seeming loss of perfection, the need for exercise of personal discretion consistently with efficiency and speedy disposal of public business."[10] The remuneration of low-paid civil servants should be raised and their social and economic status improved and made more secure. The vigilance agencies, including special police departments, should be strengthened. The penal code and other laws and procedures should be changed so that punitive action against corrupt officials can be pursued more speedily and effectively. Measures should also be taken against those in the private sector who corrupt public servants. Among such measures the Committee proposes that income tax reports and assessments be made public and that the practice of declaring public documents confidential be limited. The Committee recognizes that ministers and legislators must be above suspicion and proposes codes of conduct for these two categories of politicians and special procedures for complaints against them. It proposes that business enterprises be forbidden to make contributions to political parties, that persons making *bona fide* complaints be protected, and that, on the other hand, newspapers be prosecuted if they make allegations without supporting evidence.

These and other proposals deserve careful study by the student of corruption in South Asia. The Committee concludes that "while it is possible to deal quickly with some forms of corruption, it is in general a long-term problem which requires firm resolve and persistent endeavour for many years to come."[11] The big questions are whether the government will take action along the lines suggested,[12] and to what extent such action will be effective within a national community when what the Committee refers to as "the entire system of moral values and of the socio-economic structure" has to be changed.

When considering the prospects of reform in countries where corruption is so embedded in institutional and attitudinal remnants of traditional society and where almost everything that happens increases incentives and opportunities for personal gain, the public outcry against corruption must be regarded as a constructive force. This holds true even when this reaction is basically only the envy of people who themselves would not hesitate to engage in corrupt practices had they a chance, and even though the common awareness of corruption is apt to

10 Santhanam Committee report, p. 45.

11 Santhanam Committee report, p. 110.

12 "On October 29, the Government of India released the text of a code it has formulated for the conduct of Ministers at the Centre and in the States. The code requires disclosure by a person taking office as Minister of the details of his and his family's assets and liabilities as well as business interests. He is also required to sever all connections with the conduct of any business." (*Indian and Foreign Review,* November 15, 1964, p. 7.) It is a hopeful sign that this was one of the proposals by the Committee in regard to the implementation of which a leading article, "Guarding the Guards," in *The Economic Weekly,* April 11, 1964, had expressed deep skepticism. Later, the eagerness for reform seems to have died down. The reports are that corruption in India has recently been increasing.

spread cynicism. As those people who can benefit personally from corrupt practices are a tiny minority, the public outcry against corruption should support a government intent on serious reforms. What the people—and the outside observer[13] —generally demand is punishment of the offenders. Resentment stems especially from the belief that ministers and high officials go unpunished.

When discussing the practical problem of how to fight corruption, knowledgeable persons in South Asia frequently point out that one should distinguish between traditional corruption on the part of petty officials, which in many cases amounts merely to the expectation of a customary fee by a person with a very low salary (though undoubtedly it often also injects an element of unnecessary delay and arbitrariness into business activity), and the extorting of big bribes by politicians and higher officials. It is usually stressed that corruption among minor officials cannot be combatted if it is not first stamped out at higher levels; this latter problem is thus given a strategic role. In some branches of public administration there is a systematic sharing of bribes between politicians and officials at different levels of responsibility. When there is not, and each takes care of his own interests, a tacit collusion often exists nevertheless, obstructing remedial action at all levels. The conclusion that it is quite hopeless to fight corruption if there is not a high degree of personal integrity at the top levels is obviously correct.

Great Britain, Holland, and the Scandinavian countries, where corruption is now quite limited, were all rife with it two hundred years ago and even later, indeed until the liberal interlude between Mercantilism (with its many vestiges of feudalism) and the modern welfare state.[14] It was during that liberal interlude that the strong state came into being. One of its characteristics was a system of politics and administration marked by a high degree of personal integrity. While the liberalization of production and trade and particularly the liquidation of the craft guild system and the arrangements protecting urban commerce, inherited from the previous era, have been closely studied, much less interest has been manifested by political and economic historians in how the corrupt state was changed into the strong, incorrupt liberal state. It was probably accomplished by a strengthening of morals, particularly in the higher strata, together with salary reforms in the lower strata, often by transforming customary bribes into legalized fees.

Undoubtedly the South Asian countries could learn something from studies of the reforms carried out a little more than a hundred years ago in these Western countries. There is, however, a fundamental difference in initial conditions. The relative integrity in politics and administration was achieved in Great Britain, Holland, and Scandinavia during a period when state activity was reduced to a minimum. When the state again intervened in the economy on a large scale, it had a political and administrative

13 "Nothing would do as much to increase the faith of the common people in their governments as the prosecution of a few of those whose unwholesome activities are unnoticed or connived at by the leaders. . . . If those in positions of authority are not above suspicion, who can blame the small man for committing similar offences? This kind of thing is infectious, and ordinary people tend to copy the conduct of those at the top." (Sydney D. Bailey, *Parliamentary Government in Southern Asia,* Institute of Pacific Relations, New York, 1953, p. 72.)

14 As noted in [Selection 22], the United States is still not as free from corruption, particularly on the state and city levels, as the countries mentioned in the text. The lag in the United States is due to many interrelated facts: the spoils system since President Jackson, the consequent relative lack of a firmly established and politically independent civli service, the heterogeneity of the population (in particular, the clustering in the cities of disadvantaged colored and immigrant groups), the rise of machine politics, and so on. However, for several decades there has been a development toward greater integrity among both politicians and administrators in the United States as part of the general movement toward closer national integration.

system whose high quality only needed to be protected and preserved. The South Asian countries, on the other hand, have to fight rampant corruption in an era of their history when the activities of the state are proliferating—and, . . . when preference, even beyond what is necessary, is being given to discretionary controls. Again, South Asia stands out as a third world of planning.

One problem of considerable importance requiring specific attention is the role of Western business interests in feeding corruption in South Asia, which we referred to in [Selection 22]. From a Western point of view—and also from the point of view of most South Asian countries—one particularly damaging effect is that Western businessmen and capitalist countries generally, already stigmatized by long association with colonialism and imperialism, appear now to South Asian intellectuals to be conspiring to undermine the integrity of their politicians and higher administrators. This damaging effect is, of course, vastly strengthened when Western government aid can be viewed in the same terms.[15]

However, a Western company that tries to maintain higher standards finds itself up against the unfair competition of companies that resort to large-scale bribery. Here Western businessmen could contribute significantly to remedial action in the South Asian countries by adhering to the stricter practices they follow at home. This would constitute a very substantial "aid" to development. At the same time it would be to the advantage of Western business interests, for collectively they have much to gain by stamping out unfair competition of this type. The Western countries might even consider putting corrupt practices by their nationals in the under-developed countries under the same legal sanctions that are applied in the home countries. The writer, in his contacts with Western businessmen, has often proposed this problem for study and action by the International Chamber of Commerce, but has met little response, even in countries where businessmen have shown more than average interest in maintaining high moral codes at home and abroad and where business concerns must suffer most from unfair competition because of their generally higher standards.

15 At the Second Afro-Asian Economic Conference in Cairo in 1960, President Nasser spoke out against "the new form of economic imperialism which is supported by the impertinent powers which are endeavoring to dominate the newly independent Asian and African countries." He pointed out that "This new imperialism is the most dangerous form of imperialism for it depends on corruption, bribes and temptation." (Quoted from *Link,* May 15, 1960, p. 20.)

56. Bureaucracy versus Kleptocracy

SINNATHAMBY RAJARATNAM

It is amazing how otherwise excellent studies on development problems in Asia and Africa avoid any serious reference to the fact of corruption. It is not that the writers do not know of its existence, but its relevance to the question of political stability and rapid economic development appear not to have been fully appreciated.

It may also be that a serious probing of the subject has been avoided lest it should offend the sensibilities of Asians. Over the years Asians and Westerners have spread the myth about a dreamy spiritual East in perpetual war with the crass materialism of the West. In fact, the more corrupt an Asian country, the greater the tendency of its leaders to glorify the spiritual life as against what they denounce as alien materialist values. So for anyone to suggest the existence of widespread corruption in a country is to challenge the myth about the spiritual East.

Because of this I confess to some difficulty as to how I should deal with the subject. There are obvious hazards in a foreign minister discussing this topic in public. He cannot, as can other students of the subject, reinforce his arguments with specific and telling data because if he does he is sure to get a protest note from a friendly country whose fair name has allegedly been brought into disrepute. As a foreign minister I am therefore constrained to talk as though a specific country is a pillar of uprighteousness. My examples must not refer to any particular country. I must assume that corruption exists everywhere and nowhere in particular. So I hope you will understand if there is a certain amount of vagueness about my discussion of the problem of corruption. Even then I might unwittingly tread on the delicate corns of friendly countries, and to safeguard myself against such misunderstanding I would like to invoke the traditional inscription that prudent novelists insert into their books and which reads generally as follows: any resemblance between characters in this book and between persons living or dead is purely coincidental.

Despite the hazards of a public discussion of corruption I think the time has come for a free, frank, and extensive study of this problem. This is necessary because I believe that corruption has not only become a serious impediment to economic growth and development in newly independent countries but also a considerable factor for increasing political instability, dangerous tensions, and conflicts in Asia. I am not saying that tensions, conflicts and economic disintegration are attributable solely to corruption, but that corruption is a significant contributory factor.

SOURCE: Manuscript of Speech given at the Second Public Services International Asian Regional Conference in Singapore, November 14, 1968. Published by permission of the author, who is minister of foreign affairs and labour of Singapore.

There are some people in both the developing countries and outside who claim that the growing alarm over corruption is somewhat exaggerated. They may regret the fact of corruption, but they do not see it as an obstacle to development or all that much of a threat to internal political stability or to peaceful relations between nations. They back this indulgent attitude toward corruption by invoking what I consider to be spurious psychology and equally spurious history. They contend that human nature being what it is, corruption is endemic in all societies. These people add insult to injury by claiming that corruption has been a time-honored tradition in Asia and has not prevented the continent from building magnificent civilizations.

First this is not true. There has been corruption in Asia and in other continents, but I submit there is a world of difference between corruption in societies and corrupt societies. In the former case what we have are lapses from what is essentially an honest society. In the latter case corruption becomes not only an essential part of the dynamics of society but also an unavoidable means for accumulation of wealth, power, influence, and even prestige in that society. In what is essentially an honest society there can be and will be scandalous instances of corruption as there will also be outbreaks of crime and violence. But such a society will make every effort to restrain, detect and punish those who attempt to deviate from the standards of honesty that it upholds and respects. It will not honour and encourage into positions of power and prestige the corrupt men who have successfully circumvented the law.

In my view, a society that is indulgent toward corruption and the successfully corrupt is not, as is often argued, a liberal sophisticated society inspired with a shrewd understanding of human nature. On the contrary it is what one sociologist has aptly termed a "kleptocracy"—a society of the corrupt, for the corrupt, by the corrupt. I am not saying that Asian societies have become full-fledged kleptocracies, but if we continue to maintain the tolerance we have shown toward corruption for the past two decades than our democracies, autocracies, and bureaucracies will become adjuncts to a kleptocracy.

In this connection I would like to say that the ideological justification for a kleptocracy has in recent years been provided by certain scholarly gentlemen from the West—a few of them, I am sorry to say, from eminent American universities. They contend that the current moralistic outbursts against corruption are based on failure to grasp the facts of history. Corruption, they contend, can create and has created dynamic societies. Bribing bureaucracies, they argue, can promote in developing countries bureaucratic efficiency, innovation and rapid economic development. This astonishing thesis was propounded, for example, by Nathanial Leff in the November 1964 issue of *The American Behavioral Scientist*. Its title made no bones about the author's viewpoint: "Economic Development through Bureaucratic Corruption." [See Selection 52.]

Another tribute to kleptocracy is contained in the January 1964 issue of the journal *Comparative Studies in Society and History,* in which an author argues that "recent experience in the so-called underdeveloped countries has most vividly brought home the fact that corruption is not a mass of incoherent phenomena, but a political system, capable of being steered with tolerable precision by those in power."[1]

Insofar as the author admits to the emergence of a kleptocracy—of corruption being institutionalised into what he calls a "political system"—I have no quarrel with him. But his contention that it can be "steered with tolerable precision" is at odds with facts that we

[1] Van Klaveren, Jacob, "Comment," *Comparative Studies in Society and History,* 6:2 (1964), p. 195.

know in Asia. A kleptocracy will steer itself into more and more corruption, and finally into economic and political chaos, whether those in power want it to or not. This has been the life cycle of societies in Asia during the past two decades. In the initial phase the successful, idealistic, and dedicated nationalists tried to work an honest democracy. There was an intolerant and puritanical attitude towards corruption. Every attempt was made to project an image of honest dedicated men working for the welfare of their people. Ministers were proud of the fact that they made do with modest homes, modest cars, and gave every appearance of trying to live on their meager ministerial pay.

But over the years their homes became not only more palatial but the ministers accustomed themselves to habits and a scale of living that was mathematically impossible to equate with their ministerial and parliamentary salaries. Politicians who lived in rented houses were renting out houses and running enterprises that they could not have possibly bought by stinting on their housekeeping money. Wives of bureaucrats were seen at official functions shimmering with jewels and gowns that in honest societies would have immediately caught the eye of income tax officials.

In most developing countries, a few years of this kind of freebooting affluence led to economic anarchy, political instability, and the eventual replacement of democracy by civilian or military autocracies. I have yet to see convincing evidence that corruption assisted economic development or strengthened political stability.

The ideologists of kleptocracy resort to history in justifying their claim that private vice can produce public good. They contend that all the affluent societies of today—Britain, America, Japan, France, to list a few—went through a corrupt phase when quick-witted but corrupt tycoons amassed vast fortunes that they used to promote development. This is spurious history. It is true that there was extensive corruption in these countries in the eighteenth and nineteenth centuries when these countries embarked upon modernization, but there is little evidence to show that without corruption there could have been no modernization. In fact, the evidence proves the contrary case. If there had been less corruption during those turbulent centuries, modernization and economic expansion in these countries could have been even more rapid, more smooth, and less violent than it had been.

I think it is monstrous for these well-intentioned and largely misguided scholars to suggest corruption as a practical and efficient instrument for rapid development in Asia and Africa. Once upon a time Westerners tried to subjugate Asia and, in particular, China, by selling opium. The current defense of kleptocracy is a new kind of opium by some Western intellectuals, devised to perpetuate Asian backwardness and degradation. I think the only people who are likely to be pleased with the contributions of these scholars are the Asian kleptocrats.

It is, I think, in the very nature of kleptocracy to progressively increase the size of its loot. For one thing, the kleptocrat can stay in power only by bringing in more and more supporters to his side, and this means that the size of his loot must increase. As the years go by, he must win over all the instruments of state power—the army, the police, the entrepreneurs, and the bureaucracy. If he must loot then he must allow his subordinates from the permanent secretary to the office boy to join in the game. It may be necessary for the sake of public appearances to allow some minor officials to be occasionally caught in the act of looting and duly prosecuted. But by and large he should maintain an air of permissive tolerance; he should manifest a humane understanding of human failings. . . .

57. Corruption, Machine Politics, and Political Change

JAMES C. SCOTT

The study of political influence in the West has for the most part focused on the process by which interest groups affect the content of legislation. To use the conceptual distinction between the input and output functions of a political system, the input process has occupied the center of attention.

Students of politics in the new states of Africa and Asia who have adopted this perspective, however, have been struck by the relative weakness both of interest structures to organize demands and of institutionalized channels through which such demands, once organized, might be communicated to decision makers. The open clash of organized interests is often conspicuously absent during the formulation of legislation in these nations. To conclude from this, however, that the public has little or no effect on the eventual "output" of government would be completely unwarranted. Between the passage of legislation and its actual implementation lies an entirely different political arena that, despite its informality and particularism, has a great effect on the execution of policy.

Much of the expression of political interests in the new states has been disregarded because Western scholars, accustomed to their own politics, have been looking in the wrong place. A large portion of indivdual demands, and even group demands, in developing nations do not reach the political system before laws are passed but rather at the enforcement stage. Influence before legislation is passed often takes the form of "pressure-group politics"; *influence at the enforcement stage often takes the form of "corruption" and has seldom been treated as the alternative means of interest articulation which in fact it is.*[1] The peasants who avoid their land taxes by making a smaller and illegal contribution to the disposable income of the revenue officer are influencing the outcome of government policy as surely as if they had formed a peasant union and agitated for the reduction of land taxes. In a similar fashion, the businessmen who protect their black-market sales by buying protection from well-placed politicians are changing the outcome of policy as effectively as if they had worked collectively through a chamber of commerce for an end to government price controls.

SOURCE: James C. Scott, "Corruption, Machine Politics, and Social Change," *American Political Science Review*, 63:4 (1969), pp. 1142–1159. By permission of publisher.

1 This process of influence, the groups which are likely to benefit from it most, and related issues are treated in much greater detail in James C. Scott, "The Analysis of Corruption in Developing Nations," *Comparative Studies in Society and History*, 11:3 (June 1969), pp. 315–341. While not all corruption occurs at the enforcement stage and not all "influence at the enforcement stage" is corrupt, the empirical referents of the two terms overlap considerably. A striking exception, of course, is the legitimate arena of "regulatory politics" that largely involves contending interpretations of statutes governing private sector activity.

Competing and complementary explanations for this prevalence of influence at the enforcement stage—usually offered as "causes of corruption"—abound in the expanding literature on this subject.[2] Among the most frequently cited factors contributing to widespread corruption in the new states are the weak legitimacy of the formal political system compared to the persuasive ties of family or ethnic background, the relative importance of government as a source of employment, the existence of wealth elites who are denied access to direct, formal influence on legislation, and the lack of strong commitments to the rule of general laws by either the elite or populace.

Implicit in each of these causes is the fundamental fact that, by nature, most political demands in transitional nations are not amenable to the legislative process. Family-centered demands—for example, a family's desire to secure a civil service post for its eldest son—are generally not expressible in legislative terms. When demands are made on behalf of a wider grouping, they are likely to refer to ethnic, linguistic, or regional blocs and only seldom can be given legislative form.[3] Thus the problem lies less with the weakness of the interest structures at the legislative stage than with the very character of loyalties in a transitional nation and the demands fostered by such loyalty patterns. Couched as it is in universalistic language, legislation is not a suitable vehicle for the expression of particularistic interests.[4] Influence at the enforcement level—whether it meets the legal definition of corruption or not—is, on the other hand, almost exclusively particularistic. It is scarcely surprising, then, that many of the narrow, parochial demands characteristic of new nations should make their weight felt during the implementation of legislation rather than during its passage. Suitable though it may be for the few groups in the modern sector organized along occupational lines, the modern legislative machinery of new nations cannot cope effectively with the host of special pleadings coming from outside the modern sector.

Despite these formal obstacles, there is one political form that has not only been able to respond to particularistic interests but has thrived on them—the urban "machine," a form that flourished in the United States around the turn of the century. Although now virtually extinct, the machine once managed to fashion a cacophony of concrete, parochial demands in immigrant-choked cities into a system of rule that was at once reasonably effective and legitimate.

The purpose of this study is to outline the contours and dynamics of the "machine model" in comparative perspective and attempt to show that the social context that fostered "machine politics" in the United States is more or less present in many of the new states. This is done by first sketching the general character of "machine politics," (2) then by suggesting a developmental model to account for the machine, (3) and finally by analyzing the decline of the machine in the United States and in less developed nations.

THE MACHINE

To abstract the basic characteristics of a political machine obviously does some

2 Among others, see Ronald Wraith and Edgar Simpkins, *Corruption in Developing Countries*. London: G. Allen, 1963; M. McMullan, "A Theory of Corruption," *The Sociological Review* (Keele, Eng.), 9 (July 1961), pp. 132–152; W. F. Wertheim, *East-West Parallels: Sociological Approaches to Modern Asia*. Chicago, Ill. Quadrangle Books, 1965, pp. 103–131; J. S. Nye, "Corruption and Political Development," *American Political Science Review*, 61:2 (June 1967), pp. 417–427; J. David Greenstone, "Corruption and Self-Interest in Kampala and Nairobi," *Comparative Studies in Society and History*, 7 (January 1966), pp. 199–210; Colin Leys, "What is the Problem About Corruption," *Journal of Modern African Studies*, 3:2 (1965), pp. 215–230.

3 Malaysia, for example, is an instance where one ethnic group, the Malays, is given explicit, constitutional preference in access to certain bureaucratic posts. Similarly, the *harijan* castes in India are accorded preferential treatment with respect to education and government employment.

4 "Pork-barrel" legislation catering to regional interests is an exception to this rule and is discussed at greater length later.

violence to the great variety of entrepreneurial talent that was devoted to creating this form. Nevertheless, as all but a few beleaguered machines have succumbed to the forces of "reform government" analysis has replaced accusation and the central features of most machines are reasonably clear.[5]

It will be recognized at the outset that the machine form can occur only in certain political settings. At a minimum, the setting of the machine requires:

1. The selection of political leaders through elections
2. Mass (usually universal) adult suffrage
3. A relatively high degree of electoral competition over time—usually between parties, but occasionally within a dominant party

These conditions reflect the fact that since machine politics represents a distinctive way of mobilizing voters, it arises only in systems where getting out the vote is essential to gaining control of the government. While these conditions are necessary for machine-style politics, they are by no means sufficient, as we shall see later.

Always applied to a political party in power, the term *machine* connotes the reliable and repetitive control it exercises within its jurisdiction. What is distinctive about the machine, however, is not so much its control as the nature of the organizational cement that makes such control feasible. The machine is not the disciplined, ideological party held together by class ties and common programs that arose in continental Europe. Neither is it typically a charismatic party, depending on a belief in the almost superhuman qualities of its leader to ensure internal cohesion. Rather, it is a nonideological organization interested less in political principle than in securing and holding office for its leaders and distributing income to those who run it and work for it.[6] It relies on what it accomplishes in a concrete way for its supporters, not on what it stands for. A machine may, in fact, be likened to a business in which all members are stockholders and where dividends are paid in accordance with what has been invested.[7]

"Patronage," "spoils," and "corruption" are inevitably associated with the urban machine as it evolved in the United States. As these terms indicate, the machine dealt almost exclusively in *particularistic, material rewards* to maintain and extend its control over its personnel. Although pork-barrel legislation provided inducements for ethnic groups as a whole, the machine did most of its favors for individuals and families. The very nature of these rewards and favors naturally meant that the machine became *specialized in organizing and allocating influence at the enforcement stage*. The corruption it fostered was not random greed but was finely organized and articulated to maximize its electoral support.

Thus the machine is best characterized by the nature of the cement that binds leaders and followers. Ties based on charisma, coercion, or ideology were occasionally minor chords of machine orchestration; the "boss" might take on some heroic proportions; he might use hired toughs or the police now and again to discourage opposition; and a populist ideological aura might accompany his acts. For the machine such bonds were definitely subsidiary to the concrete, particularistic rewards that represented its stable means of political coordination.

5 Some of the more successful efforts at careful description and analysis include: V. O. Key, Jr., *The Techniques of Political Graft in the United States*. Chicago, Ill.: University of Chicago Libraries, 1936; Seymour J. Mandelbaum, *Boss Tweed's New York*. New York: Wiley, 1965; Edward C. Banfield and James A. Wilson, *City Politics*. Cambridge, Mass.: Harvard University Press, 1965.

6 Banfield and Wilson, p. 116.

7 This analogy was made by former Liberal party president José Avelino of the Philippines in the *Manila Chronicle*, Jan. 18, 1949. Quoted in Virginia Baterina, "A Study of Money in Elections in the Philippines," *Philippine Social Sciences and Humanities Review*, 20:1 (March 1955), pp. 39–86.

It is the predominance of these reward networks—the special quality of the ties between leaders and followers—that distinguishes the machine party from the nonmachine party.

Given its principal concern for retaining office, the machine was a *responsive, informal context* within which *bargaining* based on reciprocity relationships was facilitated. Leaders of the machine were rarely in a position to dictate; those who supported them did so on the basis of value received or anticipated. For the most part the machine accepted its electoral clients as they were and responded to their needs in a manner that would elicit their support. The pragmatic, opportunistic orientation of the machine thus made it a flexible institution that could accommodate new groups and leaders in highly dynamic situations.

The applicability of this basic political form to the parties of the new states has been noted by many political analysts.[8] In his perceptive examination of the party states of West Africa, Aristide Zolberg emphasizes the limited authority of the dominant parties and explicitly suggests that they could be usefully described as political machines. "The party," he asserts "was initially a loose movement which naturally incorporated the characteristics of the society in which it grew; it was eventually transformed into a political machine but continued to reflect the state of incomplete integration of the territorial society."[9]

The particular "machine" qualities Zolberg has in mind include the flexible, bargaining character of the party that permits it to adjust demands from a heterogeneous clientele on the basis of self-interest, its capacity to respond to social change through informal mechanisms, and finally its potential for stability and popularity in a context scarcely hospitable to either.

In the West African context, at least some allowance must be made for the fact that American political machines were typically electoral machines, whereas the parties Zolberg analyzes have done their best to eliminate their dependence on winning votes. The analogy may nonetheless be valuable if it is appreciated that the tenuous authority of these parties often required that they constantly satisfy a host of particularistic interests in order to hold together their ruling coalition. The absence of acute electoral pressures, however, considerably narrows the scope of the machine pattern; beyond a certain point the regime would then resemble an oligarchy based on coercion more than a machine relying on votes. Judging from Zolberg's analysis, that point was seldom approached in the party states of West Africa.

Describing the ruling parties in the states of India, Myron Weiner also has recourse to the machine model, not only to explain what occurs, but also to recommend the machine to Indian politicians as a form to emulate. Like Zolberg, Weiner focuses on the ability of the machine to reconcile competing ethnic and particularistic claims in a manner that, while corrupt, is "a small price to pay for acculturating immigrants into a democratic society."[10]

In India's state of Orissā, for example, the dominant Congress party increasingly came to resemble a machine party as it endeavored to win elections amid the deterioration of political bonds forged during the nationalist struggle. F. G. Baily portrays the local leaders of the Congress party as machine brokers in a context where "workers and sometimes

8 Aristide R. Zolberg, *Creating Political Order: The Party States of West Africa.* Skokie, Ill.: Rand McNally, 1966, p. 123.

9 See for example, Myron Weiner, *The Politics of Scarcity*. Chicago: University of Chicago Press, 1962, pp. 70–71; Henry L. Bretton, *The Rise and Fall of Kwame Nkrumah*. New York: Praeger, 1966; Herbert Feith, *The Decline of Constitutional Democracy in Indonesia*. Ithaca: Cornell University Press, 1962.

10 Weiner, p. 71.

voters expect some tangible reward, not necessarily a bribe, but assistance of exactly the kind which brokers provide," that is, jobs, licenses, welfare payments, and so on.[11]

What all three authors have done, in effect, is to construct an analogy between the social context of political parties in Asia and Africa on the one hand, and late nineteenth- to early twentieth-century urban America on the other. In the United States, the rapid influx of new populations for whom family and ethnicity were the central identifications, when coupled with the award of important monopoly privileges (traction, electric power, and so forth) and the public payroll, provided the ideal soil for the emergence of party machines. Developing nations can be viewed as offering a social context with many of the same nutrients. New governments had in many cases only recently acquired control over the disposal of lucrative posts and privileges, and they faced electorates that included many poor, newly urbanized peasants with particularistic loyalties who could easily be swayed by concrete, material incentives. The point each writer makes is not only that the machine is a suitable and relatively democratic political form that can manage such a complex environment, but that the social context typical of most new nations tends to encourage the growth of machinelike qualities in ruling parties. For America, Burnham has summarized the argument now being applied to less-developed nations.

If the social context in which a two-party system operates is extensively fragmented along regional ethnic and other lines, its major components will tend to be overwhelmingly concerned with coalition building and internal conflict management. The need to unite for electoral [broad coalition building] purposes presupposes a corresponding need to generate consensus at what ever level consensus can be found.[12]

Given this sort of social context, so the reasoning goes, the price of effective political cooperation—at least in the short run—involves meeting narrow, particularistic demands, often through the patronage, favors, and corruption that are the hallmarks of machine politics. But why are other forms of association not feasible? What specific changes in the social context promote or undermine different styles of political collaboration? Unless the model is placed in a developmental perspective and considerably sharpened from its presently intriguing but impressionistic form, its explanatory value will remain limited.

THE SOCIAL CONTEXT OF POLITICAL TIES

The schema presented in Model 57.1 focuses on changes over time in the nature of loyalty ties that form the basis of political parties. It is tailored to a bargaining—particularly, electoral—context and is less applicable where force or threats of force are the basis of cooperation. Nothing is intended to be rigidly deterministic about the movement from phase *A* to phase *B* to phase *C*. The phases are, however, largely based on the empirical experience of the United States, England, and the new nations.

Although the phases have been separated for the purpose of conceptual clarity, they are likely to overlap considerably in the empirical experience of any nation. It is thus a question of which loyalty pattern is most common and which less common. Within new nations all three patterns typically coexist: rural villagers may remain deferential to their traditional leaders; the recent urban mi-

[11] *Politics and Social Change: Orissa in 1959.* Berkeley, Calif.: University of California Press, 1963, pp. 138–140.

[12] Walter Dean Burnham, "Party Systems and the Political Process," pp. 277–307, in William Nisbet Chambers and Walter Dean Burnham, eds., *The American Party Systems: Stages of Political Development.* New York: Oxford, 1967, p. 287. Fragment in brackets mine.

MODEL 57.1

PHASE A[1] Political ties are determined largely by traditional patterns of deference (vertical ties) to established authorities. Material, particularistic inducements to cooperation play a minor role except among a limited number of local power holders.[2]

PHASE B Deference patterns have weakened considerably in a period of rapid socioeconomic change. Vertical ties can only be maintained through a relationship of greater reciprocity.[3] Competition among leaders for support, coupled with the predominance of narrow, parochial loyalties, will encourage the widespread use of concrete, short-run, material inducements to secure cooperation. The greater the competitive electoral pressures, the wider the distribution of inducements is likely to be. Influence at enforcement stage is common.

PHASE C New loyalties have emerged in the process of economic growth that increasingly stress horizontal (functional) class or occupational ties. The nature of inducements for political support are accordingly likely to stress policy concerns or ideology. Influence at the legislative stage becomes more appropriate to the nature of the new political loyalties.

1 The broad lines of this schema were suggested by an analysis of the use of money in elections contained in Arnold Heidenheimer, "Comparative Party Finance: Notes on Practices and Toward a Theory," pp. 790–811 in Richard Rose and Arnold Heidenheimer, eds., *Comparative Studies in Political Finance: A Symposium, Journal of Politics,* 25:4 (November 1963), especially pp. 808–809. Changes in the nature of political ties influence greatly the degree to which monetary incentives are successful in electoral campaigns, and I have thus borrowed from that analysis for the broader purpose of this study.

2 Traditional ties often allow some scope for bargaining and reciprocity; the ability of clients to flee to another jurisdiction and the economic and military need for a leader to attract and keep a sizable clientele provided subordinates with some leverage. The distinctions made here in the degree of reciprocity are relative, not absolute. See, for example, Herbert P. Phillips, *Thai Peasant Personality.* Berkeley, Calif. University of California Press, 1965, p. 89, or George M. Foster, "The Dyadic Contract in Tzintzunzan, II: Patron Client Relationships," *American Anthropologist,* 65 (1963), pp. 1280–1294.

3 What appears to happen in the transitional situation is that the client is less "locked-in" to a single patron and the need for political support forces patrons to compete with one another to create larger clienteles. For a brilliant analysis of this pattern in Philippine politics see Carl H. Landé, *Leaders Factions, and Parties—The Structure of Philippine Politics.* Monograph No. 6. New Haven, Conn.: Yale University—Southeast Asia Studies. 1965, throughout.

grants may behave more as free agents seeking jobs or cash for their votes; and a small group of professionals, trade union leaders, and intellectuals may perhaps be preoccupied with ideological or class concerns. Even fully industrialized nations may contain recalcitrant, and usually isolated pockets where deference patterns have not yielded to more opportunistic modes of political expression.[13]

Prior to fuller treatment below, a brief word is in order about the process of change implied by Model 57.1. Movement from phase *A* to phase *B* involves the shaking loose of traditional deference patterns, which can occur in a variety of ways. For the United States, large-scale immigration by basically peasant populations was often the occasion for this change, while for less developed nations the economic changes introduced by colonial regimes and rapid migration from village to city has provided the catalyst. The social disorganization that resulted was often exacerbated by ethnic, linguistic, or even caste fragmentation, but similar patterns have arisen in Thailand and the Philippines—for example, amid comparatively homogeneous populations. Elections themselves have, of course, played a central role in this transformation because they placed a new political resource of some significance at the disposal of even the most humble citizens.

Movement from phase *B* to phase *C* would appear to depend on the process of industrialization as new economic ar-

13 In this context, party labels are deceptive. The existence of parties proclaiming an ideology or class position are often found in rural areas where the labels have been appropriated in toto in a continuation of traditional feuds between powerful families and their respective clienteles. The key is the nature of loyalty patterns, not the name of the organization. See Carlo Levi, *Christ Stopped at Eboli.* New York: Pocket Books, 1965.

rangements take hold and provide new focuses of identification and loyalty. As the case of the United States illustrates, however, the presence of sharp ethnic and sectional cleavage—the latter reinforced by constitutional arrangements—may considerably dilute the strength of these new bonds.

The duration of phase *B*, when the social context is most hospitable to machine-style politics, may vary widely. When the social disorganization accompanying urbanization and economic change is particularly severe and of long duration, when it is compounded by deep cultural differences, and when competitive elections with a universal suffrage are introduced early, the pressures toward machine politics will be vastly greater than when demographic change is gradual and less severe, when it occurs with a minimum of cultural cleavage, and when the electorate is restricted. The historical circumstances of both the United States and most new nations have been, in this sense, quite conducive to the development of machine politics as opposed to, say, the Western European experience.

Inducements and the Nature of Loyalty

Political parties must generally offer inducements of one kind or another to potential supporters. The pressures to enlist adherents is obviously greatest when the party faces a competitive electoral struggle, but in the absence of battles for votes merely the desire to establish a broad following among the populace will create analogous pressures.

The sort of incentives most likely to "move" people is contingent, as the phase model clearly implies, on the kinds of loyalty ties that are most salient to the potential client. In the short run, at least, parties that need supporters are more apt to respond to the incentives that motivate their clientele then to transform the nature of those incentives. Elaborating on this relationship between loyalty bonds (independent variable) and party inducements (dependent variable), Model 57.2 suggests the actual empirical patterns that are likely to occur.

Parties in the real world commonly confront all four patterns of loyalty simultaneously and fashion a mix of inducements that corresponds to the mix of loyalties.[14] Inducements, moreover, are

14 The importance of one or another pattern can, in addition, be amplified or diminished by structoral characteristics of the political system; in the U.S. federalism and local candidate selection tend to amplify geographical ties. See Theodore J. Lowi, "Party, Policy, and Constitution in America," pp. 238–276 in Chambers and Burnham.

MODEL 57.2

NATURE OF LOYALTIES	INDUCEMENT
Ties of traditional deference or of charisma	Mostly symbolic, nonmaterial inducements[1]
Community or locality orientation (also ethnic concentration)	Indivisible rewards; public works, schools, "pork-barrel" Communal inducements
Individual, family, or small-group orientation	Material rewards; patronage, favors, cash payments "corruption" Individual inducements
Occupational or class orientation	Policy commitments, tax law, subsidy programs, and soon "general legislation" Sectoral inducements[2]

1 Charismatic ties naturally involve more symbolic inducements than do ties of traditional deference in which clients are generally assured a certain minimal level of material well-being (security) by their protector or patron in return for their loyalty.
2 Term borrowed from Banfield and Wilson, p. 337.

not unifunctional; public works usually carry with them a host of jobs and contracts that can be distributed along more particularistic lines while patronage can be wielded in such a way as to actually favor an entire community or ethnic group.

With these qualifications in mind, it is suggested that, given pressure to gain support, a party will emphasize those inducements that are appropriate to the loyalty patterns among its clientele. Material inducements are as characteristic of occupational or class loyalties as they are of local or family loyalties; what is different is simply the scope and nature of the group being "bribed" by the party, not the fact of "bribery." In the case of occupational and class loyalties, the inducements can be offered as general legislation (and rationalized by ideology, too), whereas inducements at the individual or family level must often be supplied illegally ("corruptly") at the enforcement stage.[15] The classical machine faces a social context in which community and family orientations are most decisive. Responding to its environment, the machine is thus likely to become consummately skilled in both the political distribution of public works through pork-barrel legislation and in the dispensation of jobs and favors through more informal channels.

Historically, the expansion of the suffrage, together with the rupture of traditional economic and status arrangements, has signaled the rise of particularistic, material inducements. In Robert Walcott's masterful portrait of electoral politics in eighteenth-century England, this transition is vividly depicted in the contrast between the shire constituencies, where traditional landholders still commanded the allegiance of a small electorate, and the larger urban constituencies, where elections

> were notoriously venal and turbulent. Wealthy beer-barons with hireling armies of draymen battled for the representation of Southwark: while the mass of Westminster electors were marshalled out, with considerable efficiency, to vote for candidates set up by the court.[16]

Southwark and Westminster, at the time Walcott describes them, were the exception rather than the rule, and English parliamentary politics revolved around coalitions of clique leaders, each of whom was generally accepted as the "natural" representative of his constituency. The transition, however, was under way.

A similar shift from patterns of deference to patterns of short-run material inducements is evident in contemporary Philippine politics. Like the English landed proprietor in the eighteenth century, the Filippino *haciendero* could, until recently, rely on his tenant laborers and peasants indebted to him to vote as he directed. Increasingly however, the economic arrangements and traditional patron-client ties that undergird this deference are eroding, and the peasant now often requires cash or other special inducements.[17] Pork-barrel legislation is still of great electoral significance, but family and individual inducements (to the exclusion of broader sectoral demands) are the real currency of electoral struggles. As Landé describes them,

> Political parties in the Philippines, on the whole, find it unnecessary to make categorical choices between programs favoring . . . one or another social class. There are two reasons for this, the first being that Filippino voters allow their rulers to satisfy their needs particularistically. . . . The second reason

[15] Political systems vary significantly in the extent to which favors and patronage can be carried out within the law. In the United States, for example, the traditional use of postmasterships, ambassadorial posts, and a number of state jobs exempt from normal civil service requirements provides a pool of party spoils denied most Indian, Malaysian, or Nigerian politicians.

[16] Robert Walcott, Jr., *English Politics in the Early Eighteenth Century*. Cambridge, Mass.: Harvard University Press, 1956, p. 13. The coincidence between the patterns Walcott describes and contemporary Philippine politics is discussed by Carl Landé, pp. 101–107.

[17] David Wurfel. "The Philippines," pp. 757–773 in Rose and Heidenheimer, eds., p. 771.

. . . is that most Filippino voters are not much disturbed by measures that go against the collective interests of their class or category for they have learned to expect that, as individuals, they may escape the effects of these laws.[18]

Furthermore,

The ordinary voter also learns that what he does can have a direct effect upon certain substantive "outputs" of government. He knows that, rather than sell his vote for cash, he can trade it for the promise of a public works job, free medical care in a government hospital, protection against harassment by a local policeman, or exemption from the payment of taxes.[19]

As elsewhere, the decline of deference in the Philippines has encouraged the growth of machine-style politics in which a mixture of public works and, above all, more particularistic rewards provide the fuel. The necessary incentives, as the description indicates, are generally arranged by influence at the enforcement stage—reflected in the widespread corruption for which the Philippines is noted. Philippine experience, in this regard, is reminiscent of changes in the conduct of American politics that reached decisive proportions by the mid-nineteenth century. Until that time, more oligarchic patterns prevailed, which "depended on habits of deference or subordination on the part of voters toward established notables in local communities, who were recognized as natural leaders."[20] Only after such "habits of deference" had receded in the face of economic change and immigration could the machine style of particularistic, material rewards begin to thrive on a large scale.

Changes in modal patterns of loyalty help account for not only the development of machine politics but for its decline as well. In addition to other factors (discussed later), the growth of political ties in which family bonds were less important than before and in which occupational and/or class considerations played a more prominent role undercut the very foundation of the machines.[21] The specific inducements that the machine was organized to supply worked their "magic" on an increasingly smaller proportion of party workers and supporters. Instead, as businessmen and laborers each came to appreciate their broader, more long-run interest as a sector of society, they increasingly required general legislation that met their interests in return for political support. Here and there a social context tailored to the machine style remained; but the machine either reconciled itself to the new loyalties—becoming less and less a machine in the process—or was the electoral victim of social change. Parties still continued to offer palpable inducements to voters, but the new inducements were more typically embodied in general legislation whereas previously they had been particularistic and often outside the law. As Banfield and Wilson summarize the transition,

If in the old days specific material inducements were illegally given as bribes to favored individuals, now much bigger ones are legally given to a different class of favored individuals, and, in addition, general inducements are proferred in packages to every large group in the electorate and to tiny but intensely moved minorities as well.[22]

THE ECOLOGY OF MACHINE COORDINATION

The distinctive style of political coordination embodied in the machine has his-

18 Landé, p. 43.

19 Landé, p. 115.

20 William Nisbet Chambers, "Party Development and the American Mainstream," pp. 3–32 in Chambers and Burnham.

21 Family loyalties are always of significance but in the typical machine case narrow family ties become a central factor in the evaluation of government action. Occupational, much less broad civic, sentiments play a marginal or even negligible role. Most immigrants to the United States, for example, at first "took for granted that the political life of the individual would arise out of family needs. . . ." Richard Hofstadter, *The Age of Reform*, New York: Vintage Books, 1955, p. 9.

22 Banfield and Wilson, p. 340.

torically occurred in settings where, in addition to rapid social change and a competitive electoral system, (a) political power was fragmented, (b) ethnic cleavage, social disorganization or both were widespread, and (c) most of the population was poor. Drawn mostly from studies of urban machines in the United States, these features of the environment seem applicable to a large degree to the many underdeveloped nations in which political parties have begun to resemble machines.

The Fragmentation of Power

In accounting for corruption and machine politics in Chicago, Merriam lays particular stress on the multiplicity of urban authorities and jurisdictions that existed within the city. He describes eight main "governments," each with different powers, which created so many jealously guarded centers of power that a mayor faced a host of potential veto groups, any one of which could paralyze him.[23] He could secure cooperation with these authorities only by striking informal bargains—often involving patronage, contracts, franchises—and thus putting together the necessary power piece by piece.

Power was fragmented in yet another sense. Party candidates did not face one electorate but several; each ethnic group had its own special interests and demands, and a successful campaign depended on assembling a temporary coalition on the basis of inducements suited to each group. The decentralization of power created by such a heterogeneous environment meant that the "boss's" control was forever tenuous. His temporary authority rested on his continuing capacity to keep rewards flowing at the acceptable rate.

New York in the era of Boss Tweed strikingly resembles Merriam's picture of Chicago. In spite of the prodigious manipulations attributed to him, Tweed was not especially powerful and had little control over party branches that could nominate their own candidates for many posts. What he did manage to do, however, was to create, for a time, a centralized, finely articulated coalition. Carefully assessing the nature of Tweed's feat, Seymour Mandelbaum declares,

> There was only one way New York could be "bossed" in the 1860s. The lines of communication were too narrow, the patterns of deference too weak to support freely acknowledged and stable leadership. Only a universal payment of benefits—a giant payoff—could pull the city together in a common effort. The only treasury big enough to support coordination was the public till.[24]

Many leaders of developing nations might well sympathize with Tweed's difficulties. They also face a highly differentiated populace—divided not only along ethnic, religious, linguistic, or regional lines, but also representing varying stages of incorporation into the modern sector and varying degrees of loyalty or hostility in the nation state. Except in those instances where physical coercion is preferred and is sufficient to the task, rulers in the new states must reach some accommodation with enough of these interests to govern. Electoral struggles may vastly increase the pressure to reach an accommodation—for competitive elections enhance the value of popular support—but such pressures are in a sense endemic where state authority is weak. More often than not, the price of rule involves paying off each of a variety of interests in their own (usually particularistic) coin. The system of coordination thus comes to resemble machine politics.

---

23 Charles Edward Merriam, *Chicago: A More Intimate View of Urban Politics.* New York: Crowell-Collier-Macmillan, 1929, pp. 68, 90. Merriam's analysis is especially valuable as he was simultaneously political scientist and politician throughout the period he describes.

24 Seymour J. Mandebaum, p. 58. See also, Edward J. Flynn, *You're the Boss,* New York: Viking, 1947, p. 21, for a twentieth-century account of New York City politics in which a similar argument is made.

Social Fragmentation and Disorganization

The immigrants who constituted the bulk of the clientele of the American urban machine came largely from the ranks of the European peasantry. They "required the most extensive acculturation simply to come to terms with urban-industrial existence as such, much less to enter the party system as relatively independent actors."[25] If the fragmentation of power made it advantageous for the politician to offer special inducements for support, the situation of the immigrant made him eager to respond to blandishments that corresponded with his most immediate needs. Machine inducements are thus particularly compelling among disoriented new arrivals, who value greatly the quick helping hand extended to them by the party.

The dependence of machine parties on a clientele that is both unfamiliar with the contours of the political system and economically on the defensive is underscored by the character of the small pockets where vestiges of once-powerful machines still exist. One such example is the Dawson machine (really a submachine) in Chicago. This machine rests squarely on favors and patronage among the Negro population, most of which has come to Chicago from the rural south within the last generation. Deprived of even this steadily diminishing social base, the machine has elsewhere withered as the populations it assisted became acculturated and could afford the luxury of wider loyalties and more long-range political goals.

It is no coincidence, then, that machines flourished during the period of most rapid urban growth in the United States, when the sense of community was especially weak, and when social fragmentation made particularistic ties virtually the only feasible means of cooperation. The machine bound its clientele to it by virtue of the employment, legal services, economic relief, and other services it supplied for them. "For the lower strata, in return for their votes, it provided a considerable measure of primitive welfare functions, personalized help for individuals caught up in the toils of the law, and political socialization."[26]

With few qualifications, the social context that nourished machines in America matches the conditions in new nations. Rapid urban migration of rural peasantries (especially since World War II), when coupled with ethnic fragmentation, economic insecurity, and a basic unfamiliarity with the Western governmental forms adopted by most new states, has conspired to create an analogous social context. As in the United States at the turn of the century, a large clientele is available that will respond enthusiastically to short-run material incentives and to the party that provides them.

Poverty

Perhaps the most fundamental quality shared by the mass clientele of machines is poverty. Machines characteristically rely on the suffrage of poor and, naturally, prosper best when the poor are many and the middle-class few. In America, Banfield and Wilson emphasized that "Almost without exception, the lower the average income and the fewer the average years of schooling in a ward, the more dependable the ward's allegiance to the machine."[27]

Poverty shortens a man's time horizon and maximizes the effectiveness of short-run material inducements. Quite rationally he is willing to accept a job, cash, or simply the promise of assistance when he needs it, in return for his vote and that

---

25 Burnham, p. 286.

26 Burnham, p. 286, Merriam calls the precinct worker "something of a social worker not recognized by the profession," p. 173.

27 Banfield and Wilson, p. 118.

of his family. Attachments to policy goals or to an ideology implies something of a future orientation as well as wide loyalties, while poverty discounts future gains and focuses unavoidably on the here and now.

The attitudes associated with poverty that facilitate machine-style politics are not just confined to a few urban centers in less-developed nations, but typify portions of the rural population as well.[28] In such circumstances, the jobs, money, and other favors at the disposal of the government represent compelling inducements. Deployed to best advantage, these incentives are formidable weapons in building coalitions or electioneering or both. The ease with which votes are bought—individually in many urban areas and in blocs where village or ethnic cohesion is sufficient to secure collaboration—during elections in the new nations is a measure of the power of narrow material rewards in the social context of poverty. . . .[29]

THE FAILURE OF THE MACHINE IN NEW NATIONS

Looking at politics in the new nations a scant five years ago, the machine model would have seemed an increasingly practical tool of analysis. The symbolic ties of the nationalist struggle were steadily losing their strength and yet electoral procedures were still enough in evidence to reinforce the efforts of ruling parties to remain genuinely popular. Politicization of the colonial bureaucracy was often under way, and many parties were becoming adept at building support by distributing patronage and pork-barrel projects. In spite of these harbingers of machine development, very few political machines actually materialized.[30] The task, therefore, is to explain why machines failed to develop as they did in urban America. The simplest answer is, of course, that embryonic machines in new nations were generally thrown out by military coups. Beyond this truth, however, there are additional reasons why machines failed to flourish that are based on the social context of new nations and the dynamics of machine politics itself.

The decline of machine politics in America is of only limited use in accounting for what happened to rudimentary machines in the new states. After all, how does one compare the demise of two machines, one of which (in the United States) appears to die a more or less "natural" death, with a machine that is struck down by military force?

Samuel Hays explains the atrophy and disappearance of the American urban machine to

> certain rather obvious but momentous changes in American life. In the first place, a continually increasing majority of the active American electorate has moved about the poverty line. Most of this electorate is no longer bound to party through the time-honored links of patronage and the machine. Indeed, for a large number of people, politics appears to have the character of an item of luxury consumption. . . .[31]

The services that tied the client to the machine were either no longer necessary

[28] For a more extended discussion of these attitudes and their origin, see James C. Scott, *Ideology in Malaysia*. New Haven, Conn.: Yale University Press. 1968, chap. 6.

[29] Wurfel (p. 763), for example, claims that from 10 to 20 percent of Filippino voters *regularly* sell their votes.

[30] Among those new nations where ruling parties possess notable machine characteristics, one might include India, Malaysia, the Philippines, Ivory Coast, Liberia, and especially Lebanon. In the Ivory Coast and India the ruling parties still retain some of the "mass movement," ideological features that marked their earlier history.

[31] William Nisbet Chambers, p. 305. To my knowledge, no actual empirical tests of hypotheses advanced for the rise or decline of machine politics have been attempted. It would be instructive, for example, to plot the increases and decreases of machine style politics over time in a number of American cities against possible explanatory variables such as rates of in-migration, changes in per-capita income, changes in income distribution, changes in welfare measures, rates of education, and so forth. The need for this kind of empirical inquiry was suggested to me by Gary Brewer.

or were performed by other agencies than the machine. In a full-employment economy with rising wages, patronage was insufficient cement with which to organize and control a party. With aid to dependent children and old-age assistance becoming the formal responsibility of government agencies, "the precinct captain's hod of coal was a joke."[32] The protective and defensive function of the machine had simply ceased to be important political incentives.

Viewed from another angle, the machine simply destroyed its own social base. It had flourished among those who were, for one reason or another, "civic incompetents"; so when immigration slackened, when the new citizens gained a secure economic foothold, and when they developed wider loyalties, the central prop of machine politics was destroyed. Here and there, individual politicians managed to adapt to the new style and the new incentives, but the machine itself disappeared along with its social context.

The failure of machines in the new nations not only differed from the American pattern, but varied somewhat from case to case due to the special circumstances of each nation. Nevertheless, it is possible to discern a number of important factors that appear to have been significant in the demise of many such embryonic machines.

In the first place, the full development of a machine depends on its evolving capacity to create and maintain a large popular following with particularistic inducements. Typically, this capacity has developed best in the context of electoral pressures. Elections in American cities were virtually guaranteed by the fact that the city was a unit in a larger political system that sanctioned elections; machines perfected their techniques in the knowledge that they would face periodic electoral opposition. Ruling parties in new nations, however, often began with a considerable store of popularity generated in the nationalist period. As this support deteriorated, the dominant party did not necessarily have to fall back on material incentives to retain its wide support; it could alternatively abrogate elections and escape the usual machine pressures. A good many nationalist leaders—having goals of transformation in mind—were increasingly discouraged at the growth of particularistic demands from all quarters that liberal democratic forms seemed to foist on them. Not having the heart for mediating between a host of what they considered shortsighted parochial demands made of machine bosses, many concluded that liberal democracy stood in the way of long-run national goals. Both Nkrumah and Sukarno spoke feelingly in this regard, and both consciously chose to eschew machine politics for more grandiose, symbolic goals.[33]

Another factor that basicallly altered the character of machines in some cases was the predominant position of a single ethnic group. In urban America it was seldom possible for a machine to rule without being obliged to knit together a broad ethnic coalition. Where machines could be based on one dominant ethnic group in new nations, for example, pre-Ne Win Burma and, to a smaller extent, Nigeria, the excluded ethnic groups, which were often geographically concentrated, demanded at the very least

32 Chambers, p. 121.

33 In an otherwise perceptive article, Edward Feit characterizes, I think mistakenly, Nkrumah's CPP before the military coup as a political machine. He distinguishes between a political party which "aggregates demands and converts them into legislative policy" and a political machine which "exists almost exclusively to stay in power." The problem, of course, is that many regimes are motivated almost solely to stay in power, for example, the Thai military, Haiti's Duvalier, but the term machine should be reserved for civilian regimes which rest on a popular base. "Military Coups and Political Development: Some Lessons from Ghana and Nigeria," *World Politics*, 20:2 (January 1968), pp. 179–193.

more regional autonomy and launched secessionist revolts in some areas.[34] The resulting threat to the territorial integrity of the state was commonly the occasion for military takeovers.

Looking at those nations in which machines have developed with some vigor, the importance of elections and ethnic balance (or homogeneity) is manifest. Lebanon, Malaysia, and India, for example, are balanced ethnically so as to require some form of collaborative rule, while the Philippines is relatively homogeneous ethnically. All four have retained electoral forms. Beyond these two factors, however, are two broad obstacles to machine politics relating to the nature of a machine's clientele and its resource base.

Machines in American cities tended to live beyond their means and the evidence suggests that machines in new nations behave similarly.[35] As a form of rule, machines are particularly subject to what Zolberg terms "an inflationary process of demand-formation"[36] and naturally thrive best in a buoyant economy that provides them with a continually expanding store of material incentives to distribute. It is perhaps no coincidence that the high-water mark of machine politics in the new nations occurred in the mid-1950s when Korean War boom prices for primary exports underwrote high rates of growth. In addition, there were a large number of "one-time-only" rewards available to ruling parties after independence. Foreign businesses could be nationalized, new franchises and licenses could be leased, and older civil servants could be replaced by loyal party workers; but the supply of such material incentives was soon exhausted in the absence of economic expansion. Of the later cabinets before martial law was imposed in Indonesia, Feith claims,

> . . . perhaps most fundamentally, the weakness of these later cabinets stemmed from their shortage of disposable rewards. . . . Moreover, the number of material rewards and prestige roles which government was expected to provide did not decrease. . . . In sum, then, those cabinets were almost as poorly equipped to reward as to punish.[37]

It is not unreasonable to suppose that the Indonesian case is not unique. The material rewards were, finally, not sufficient to the task and, amid the ruling party's loss of support, the military—which, if it could not reward, could at least restrain and punish—stepped in.

The line of reasoning just developed suggests that perhaps the machine flourishes best at the subnational level, where it was confined in the United States. That is, the durability of this political form is maximized where there is an external guarantor of the electoral process, where the machine is a part of a larger growing economy that can afford its expensive habits, and where its bosses do not have a monopoly of coercive authority. A large measure of the instability of machines in developing nations may derive from their national rather than local character.[38]

Finally, in those nations where demand inflation was not the key factor there was some question of how well suited the social context was to machine politics. On the one hand, the machine faced opposition from a small but strategically placed middle class of civil servants, professionals, students, and above all army officers, which was less amenable to material incentives and was, like its American counterparts, profoundly alienated by machine corruption and patronage. On the other hand, the machines, particularly in Africa, faced large numbers of quite traditional folk for whom

[34] For an excellent discussion of ethnic configurations and their political implications, see Clifford Geertz, ed., *Old Societies and New States*. New York: Free Press, 1963.

[35] This fact may indicate that machine politics is not a stable form of rule.

[36] Aristide R. Zolberg, p. 149.

[37] Herbert Feith, p. 572.

[38] I am indebted to Professor Henry Hart for suggesting this.

religious and cultural issues were still important[39] and whose leaders realized that the machine threatened the ascriptive basis of their power. These populations by and large remained outside the scope of the machine and represented, at a minimum, a latent challenge to the machine's authority. Bastions of tradition were often found in areas of "indirect rule," where social and political change had been less severe, while the machine won support especially among urban migrants and in areas (often "directly" rule) where folk ways had been decisively uprooted by colonialism. The *transitional* population on which the machine relied was, in these cases, simply not large enough to sustain this form of government when it was menaced by widespread traditional recalcitrance and a powerful middle class with military allies. Machines require not only an economy that performs tolerably well but a social context that corresponds to the inducements it can give; only where both conditions have been satisfied have machines managed to survive and grow.

39 To stretch a point, one might link them with the forces in American politics that felt strongest about Sunday laws, prohibition, and so forth.

Private Vices by the dextrous Management of a skilled Politician may be turned into Publick Benefits.

—BERNARD MANDEVILLE, 1714

58. Corruption and Political Development: A Cost-Benefit Analysis

J. S. NYE

THE STUDY OF CORRUPTION IN LESS DEVELOPED COUNTRIES

Corruption, some say, is endemic in all governments.[1] Yet it has received remarkably little attention from students of government. Not only is the study of corruption prone to moralism, but it involves one of those aspects of government in which the interests of the politician and the political scientist are likely to conflict. It would probably be rather difficult to obtain (by honest means) a visa to a developing country which is to be the subject of a corruption study.

One of the first charges levelled at the previous regime by the leaders of the coup in the less developed country is "corruption." And generally the charge is accurate. One type of reaction to this among observers is highly moralistic and tends to see corruption as evil. "Throughout the fabric of public life in newly independent States," we are told in a recent work on the subject, "runs the scarlet thread of bribery and corruption . . ." which is like a weed suffocating better plants. Another description of new states informs us that "corruption and nepotism rot good intentions and retard progressive policies."[2]

Others have reacted against this moralistic approach and warn us that we must beware of basing our beliefs about the cause of coups on post-coup rationalizations, and also of judging the social consequences of an act from the motives of the individuals performing it.[3] Under some circumstances Mandeville is right that private vice can cause public benefit. Corruption has probably been, on balance, a positive factor in both Russian and American economic development. At

1 C. J. Friedrich, *Man and His Government* (New York, 1963), p. 167. See also "Political Pathology," *The Political Quarterly,* 37 (January–March 1966), 70–85.

SOURCE: J. S. Nye, "Corruption and Political Development: A Cost-Benefit Analysis." *American Political Science Review,* Vol. LXI:2 (June 1967), pp. 417–427. By permission of the author and the publisher, The American Political Science Association. The author is indebted to Samuel P. Huntington, Leon Lindberg and Robert Erwin for reading an earlier version of this paper.

2 Ronald Wraith and Edgar Simpkins, *Corruption in Developing Countries* (London, 1963), pp. 11, 12. K. T. Young, Jr., "New Politics in New States," *Foreign Affairs,* 39 (April 1961), at p. 498.

3 See, for example: Nathaniel Leff, "Economic Development Through Bureaucratic Corruption," *The American Behavioral Scientist,* 8 (November, 1964), 8–14 (See Article 52); David H. Bayley, "The Effects of Corruption in a Developing Nation," *The Western Political Quarterly,* 19 (December 1966), 719–732; J. J. Van Klaveren in a "Comment" in *Comparative Studies in Society and History,* 6 (January 1964), at p. 195, even argues that "recent experience in the so-called underdeveloped countries has most vividly brought home the fact that corruption is not a mass of incoherent phenomena, but a political system, capable of being steered with tolerable precision by those in power."

least two very important aspects of British and American political development—the establishment of the cabinet system in the 18th century and the national integration of millions of immigrants in the 19th century—were based in part on corruption. As for corruption and stability, an anthropologist has suggested that periodic scandals can sometimes "lead to the affirmation of general principles about how the country should be run, as if there were not posed impossible reconciliations of different interests. These inquiries may not alter what actually happens, but they affirm an ideal condition of unity and justice."[4] However, the "revisionists" who echo Mandeville's aphorism often underestimate tastes for moralism—concern for worthiness of causes as well as utilitarian consequences of behavior. There is always the danger for a corrupt system that someone will question what it profits to gain the world at the price of a soul. The purpose of this paper is less to settle the difference between "moralists" and "revisionists" about the general effect of corruption on development (although a tentative conclusion is presented) than to suggest a means to make the debate more fruitful. After discussing the problem in the usual general terms of possibility, we shall turn to more specific hypotheses about probability.

This paper is concerned with the *effects* of corruption, but a word should be said about causes to dispel any impression that corruption is a uniquely Afro-Asian-Latin American problem. I assume no European or American monopoly of morals. After all, Lord Bryce saw corruption as a major American flaw and noted its outbreak in "virulent form" in the new states in Europe.[5] Yet behavior that will be considered corrupt is likely to be more prominent in less developed countries because of a variety of conditions involved in their underdevelopment—great inequality in distribution of wealth; political office as the primary means of gaining access to wealth; conflict between changing moral codes; the weakness of social and governmental enforcement mechanisms; and the absence of a strong sense of national community.[6] The weakness of the legitimacy of governmental institutions is also a contributing factor, though to attribute this entirely to the prevalence of a cash nexus or the divergence of moral codes under previous colonial governments or to the mere newness of the states concerned may be inadequate in light of the experience with corruption of older, noncolonial less developed states such as Thailand or Liberia. Regardless of causes, however, the conditions of less developed countries are such that corruption is likely to have different effects than in more developed countries.

Most researchers on developing areas gather some information on corruption, and this paper will suggest hypotheses about the costs and benefits of corruption for development that may lure some of this information into the open. However, in view of the fact that generalizations about corruption and development tend to be disguised descriptions of a particular area in which the generalizer has done field work, I will state at the outset that generalizations in this paper are unevenly based on field work in East Africa and Central America and on secondary sources for other areas.

Definitions pose a problem. Indeed, if we define political development as "rational, modern, honest government," then it cannot coexist with corruption in the same time period; and if corruption is endemic in government, a politically developed society cannot exist. "Political development" is not an entirely satis-

4 Max Gluckman, *Custom and Conflict in Africa* (Oxford, 1955), p. 135.

5 James Bryce, *Modern Democracies* (New York, 1921), Vol. II, p. 509.

6 Colin Leys, "What is the Problem About Corruption?" *Journal of Modern African Studies,* 3, 2 (1965), 224–225 (See Selection 1); Ralph Braibanti, "Reflections on Bureaucratic Corruption," *Public Administration,* 40 (Winter 1962), 365–371.

factory term since it has an evaluative as well as a descriptive content. At least in the case of economic development, there is general agreement on the units and scale by which to measure (growth of per capita income). In politics, however, there is agreement neither on the units nor on a single scale to measure development.[7] Emphasis on some scales rather than others tends to reflect an author's interests.

In this author's view, the term "political development" is best used to refer to the recurring problem of relating governmental structures and processes to social change. It seems useful to use one term to refer to the type of change which seems to be occurring in our age ("modernization") and another to refer to capacity of political structures and processes to cope with social change, to the extent it exists, in any period.[8] We generally assume that this means structures and processes which are regarded as legitimate by relevant sectors of the population and effective in producing outputs desired by relevant sectors of the population. I assume that legitimacy and effectiveness are linked in the "long run" but can compensate for each other in the "short run."[9] What constitutes a relevant sector of the population will vary with the period and with social changes within a period. In the modern period we tend to assume that at least a veneer of broad participation is essential for establishing or maintaining legitimacy. In other words, in the current period, political development and political modernization may come close to involving the same things.

In this paper, political development (or decay) will mean growth (or decline) in the capacity of a society's governmental structures and processes to maintain their legitimacy over time (i.e., presumably in the face of social change). This allows us to see development as a moving equilibrium and avoid some of the limitations of equating development and modernization. Of course, this definition does not solve all the concept's problems. Unless we treat development entirely ex post facto, there will still be differences over evaluation (legitimate in whose eyes?) and measurement (national integration, administrative capacity, institutionalization?) as well as what constitutes a "long" and "short" run. Thus we will find that forms of corruption which have been beneficial effects on economic development may be detrimental for political development; or may promote one form of political development (i.e., defined one way or measured along one scale) but be detrimental to another. We shall have to continue to beware of variations in what we mean by political development. (Alternatively, those who reject the term "political development" can still read the paper as relating corruption to three problems of change discussed below.)

The definition of corruption also poses serious problems. Broadly defined as perversion or a change from good to bad, it covers a wide range of behavior from venality to ideological erosion. For instance, we might describe the revolutionary student who returns from Paris to a former French African country and accepts a (perfectly legal) overpaid civil service post as "corrupted." But used this broadly the term is more relevant to moral evaluation than political analysis. I will use a narrower definition which can be made operational. Corruption is behavior which deviates from the formal

7 Nor, by the nature of the subject, is there likely to be. In Pye's words, "no single scale can be used for measuring political development": Lucian Pye (ed.), *Communications and Political Development* (Princeton, 1963). See also Lucian Pye, "The Concept of Political Development," *The Annals,* 358 (March 1965), 1–19; Samuel Huntington, "Political Development and Political Decay," *World Politics,* 17 (April 1965), 386–430; Robert Packenham, "Political Development Doctrines in the American Foreign Aid Program," *World Politics,* 18 (January 1966), 194–235.

8 See Huntington, 389.

9 S. M. Lipset, *Political Man* (New York, 1959), 72–75.

duties of a public role because of private-regarding (personal, close family, private clique) pecuniary or status gains; or violates rules against the exercise of certain types of private-regarding influence.[10] This includes such behavior as bribery (use of a reward to pervert the judgment of a person in a position of trust); nepotism (bestowal of patronage by reason of ascriptive relationship rather than merit); and misappropriation (illegal appropriation of public resources for private-regarding uses). This definition does not include much behavior that might nonetheless be regarded as offensive to moral standards. It also excludes any consideration of whether the behavior is in the public interest, since building the study of the effects of the behavior into the definition makes analysis of the relationship between corruption and development difficult. Similarly, it avoids the question of whether non-Western societies regard the behavior as corrupt, preferring to treat that also as a separate variable. To build such relativism into the definition is to make specific behavior which can be compared between countries hard to identify. Moreover, in most less developed countries, there are two standards regarding such behavior, one indigenous and one more or less Western, and the formal duties and rules concerning most public roles tend to be expressed in terms of the latter.[11] In short, while this definition of corruption is not entirely satisfactory in terms of inclusiveness of behavior and the handling of relativity of standards, it has the merit of denoting specific behavior generally called corrupt by Western standards (which are at least partly relevant in most developing countries) and thus allowing us to ask what effects this specific behavior has under differing conditions.

10 The second part of the definition is taken from Edward C. Banfield, *Political Influence* (New York: Free Press, 1961), p. 315.

11 See, for example: M. G. Smith, "Historical and Cultural Conditions of Political Corruption Among the Hausa," *Comparative Studies in Society and History*, 6 (January 1964), at p. 194; Lloyd Fallers, "The Predicament of the Modern African Chief: An Instance from Uganda," *American Anthropologist*, 57 (1955), 290–305. I agree with Bayley on this point: 720–722.

POSSIBLE BENEFITS AND COSTS

Discussion of the relation of corruption to development tends to be phrased in general terms. Usually the argument between moralists and revisionists tends to be about the possibility that corruption (type unspecified) *can* be beneficial for development. Leaving aside questions of probability, one can argue that corruption can be beneficial to political development, as here defined, by contributing to the solution of three major problems involved: economic development, national integration, and governmental capacity.

Economic Development

If corruption helps promote economic development which is generally necessary to maintain a capacity to preserve legitimacy in the face of social change, then (by definition) it is beneficial for political development.

There seem to be at least three major ways in which some kinds of corruption might promote economic development.

Capital Formation

Where private capital is scarce and government lacks a capacity to tax a surplus out of peasants or workers openly, corruption may be an important source of capital formation. There seems to be little question about the effectiveness of this form of taxation—Trujillo reputedly accumulated $500 million and Nkrumah and relatives probably more than $10 million.[12] The real question is whether

12 A. Terry Rambo, "The Dominican Republic," in Martin Needler (ed.), *Political Systems of Latin America* (Princeton, 1964), p. 172; *New York Times*, March 5, 1966. Ayeh Kumi's quoted statement has almost certainly greatly underestimated his own assets.

the accumulated capital is then put to uses which promote economic development or winds up in Swiss banks.

Cutting Red Tape

In many new countries the association of profit with imperialism has led to a systematic bias against the market mechanism. Given inadequate administrative resources in most new states, it can be argued that corruption helps to mitigate the consequences of ideologically determined economic devices which may not be wholly appropriate for the countries concerned.[13] Even where the quality of bureaucrats is high, as in India, some observers believe that "too much checking on corruption can delay development. Trying to run a development economy with triple checking is impossible."[14] Corruption on the part of factory managers in the Soviet Union is sometimes credited with providing a flexibility that makes central planning more effective.

Entrepreneurship and Incentives

If Schumpeter is correct that the entrepreneur is a vital factor in economic growth and if there is an ideological bias against private incentives in a country, then corruption may provide one of the major means by which a developing country can make use of this factor. This becomes even more true if, as is often the case, the personal characteristics associated with entrepreneurship have a higher incidence among minority groups. Corruption may provide the means of overcoming discrimination against members of a minority group, and allow the entrepreneur from a minority to gain access to the political decisions necessary for him to provide his skills. In East Africa, for instance, corruption may be prolonging the effective life of an important economic asset—the Asian minority entrepreneur—beyond what political conditions would otherwise allow.

National Integration

It seems fair to assume that a society's political structures will be better able to cope with change and preserve their legitimacy if the members share a sense of community. Indeed, integration is sometimes used as one of the main scales for measuring political development.

Elite Integration

Corruption may help overcome divisions in a ruling elite that might otherwise result in destructive conflict. One observer believes that it helped bridge the gap between the groups based on power and those based on wealth that appeared in the early nationalist period in West Africa and allowed the groups to "assimilate each other." Certainly in Central America, corruption has been a major factor in the succession mechanism by integrating the leaders of the new coup into the existing upper class. Whether this is beneficial for political development or not is another question involving particular circumstances, different evaluation of the importance of continuity, and the question of the relevant period for measurement.

Integration of Non-Elites

Corruption may help to ease the transition from traditional life to modern. It can be argued that the man who has lived under "ascriptive, particularistic and diffuse" conditions cares far less about the rational impartiality of the government and its laws than he does about its awesomeness and seeming inhumanity. The vast gap between literate official and illiterate peasant which is often characteristic of the countryside may be bridged if the peasant approaches the official bearing traditional gifts or their (marginally corrupt) money equivalent. For the new

[13] On the economic problems of "African socialism," see Elliot Berg, "Socialism and Economic Development in Tropical Africa," *Quarterly Journal of Economics,* 78 (November 1964), 549–573.

[14] Barbara Ward, addressing the Harvard Center for International Affairs, Cambridge, Mass., March 3, 1966.

urban resident, a political machine based on corruption may provide a comprehensible point at which to relate to government by other than purely ethnic or tribal means. In McMullan's words, a degree of low-level corruption can "soften relations of officials and people" or in Shils' words it "humanizes government and makes it less awesome."[15]

However, what is integrative for one group may be disintegrative for another. The "traditional" or "transitional" man may care far more than he has a means to get *his* son out of jail that the system as a whole be incorruptible, but for "modern" groups such as students and middle classes (who have profited from achievement and universalism) the absence of honesty may destroy the legitimacy of the system. Finally, it is worth noting again Gluckman's statement that the scandals associated with corruption can sometimes have the effect of strengthening a value system as a whole.

Governmental Capacity

The capacity of the political structures of many new states to cope with change is frequently limited by the weakness of their new institutions and (often despite apparent centralization) the fragmentation of power in a country. Moreover, there is little "elasticity of power"—i.e., power does not expand or contract easily with a change of man or situation.[16]

To use a somewhat simplified scheme of motivations, one could say that the leaders in such a country have to rely (in various combinations) on ideal, coercive or material incentives to aggregate enough power to govern. Legal material incentives may have to be augmented by corrupt ones. Those who place great faith in ideal incentives (such as Wraith and Simpkins) see the use of corrupt material incentives as destructive ("these countries depend considerably on enthusiasm and on youthful pride of achievement . . .")[17] of governmental capacity. With a lower evaluation of the role of ideal incentives, however, corrupt material incentives may become a functional equivalent for violence. In Mexico, for instance, Needler has described the important role which corruption played in the transition from the violent phases of the revolution to its institutionalized form.[18] At the local level, Greenstone notes that while patronage and corruption was one factor contributing to an initial decline in governmental capacity in East Africa, corrupt material incentives may provide the glue for reassembling sufficient power to govern.[19]

Governmental capacity can be increased by the creation of supporting institutions such as political parties. Financing political parties tends to be a problem in developed as well as less developed countries, but it is a particular problem in poor countries. Broad-based mass financing is difficult to maintain after independence.[20] In some cases the major alternatives to corrupt proceeds as a means of party finance are party decay or reliance on outside funds. Needless to say, not all such investments are successful. The nearly $12 million diverted from Nigeria's Western Region Marketing Board into Action Group coffers from 1959–1962 (and probably equivalent amounts in other regions)[21] seem to have

15 M. McMullan, "A Theory of Corruption," *The Sociological Review* (Keele), 9 (July 1961), at p. 196; Edward Shils, *Political Development in the New States* (The Hague, 1962), p. 385.

16 See Herbert Werlin, "The Nairobi City Council: A Study in Comparative Local Government," *Comparative Studies in Society and History,* 7 (January 1966), at p. 185.

17 Wraith and Simpkins, p. 172.

18 Martin Needler, "The Political Development of Mexico," *American Political Science Review,* 55 (June 1961), at pp. 310–311.

19 J. David Greenstone, "Corruption and Self Interest in Kampala and Nairobi," *Comparative Studies in Society and History,* 7 (January 1966), 199–210 (See Article 47).

20 See J. S. Nye, "The Impact of Independence on Two African Nationalist Parties," in J. Butler and A. Castagno (eds.), *Boston University Papers on Africa* (New York, 1967), 224–245.

21 Richard L. Sklar, "Contradictions in the Nigerian Political System," *Journal of Modern African Studies,* 3:2 (1965), at p. 206.

been wasted in terms of institution-building; but on the other hand, investment in India's Congress Party or Mexico's *Partido Revolucionario Institucional* has been more profitable for political development.

Those who dispute the possible benefits of corruption could argue that it involves countervailing costs that interfere with the solution of each of the three problems. They could argue that corruption is economically wasteful, politically destabilizing, and destructive of governmental capacity.

Waste of Resources

Although corruption may help promote economic development, it can also hinder it or direct it in socially less desirable directions.

Capital Outflow

As we mentioned above, capital accumulated by corruption that winds up in Swiss banks is a net loss for the developing country. These costs can be considerable. For instance, one source estimates that from 1954–1959, three Latin American dictators (Peron, Perez, Jimenez, and Batista) removed a total of $1.15 billion from their countries.[22] It is no wonder that another source believes that economic development in some Latin American countries has been "checked" by corruption.[23]

Investment Distortions

Investment may be channeled into sectors such as construction not because of economic profitability, but because they are more susceptible to hiding corrupt fees through cost-plus contracts and use of suppliers' credits. This was the case, for instance, in Venezuela under Perez Jimenez and in Ghana under Nkrumah.

Waste of Skills

"If the top political elite of a country consumes its time and energy in trying to get rich by corrupt means, it is not likely that the development plans will be fulfilled."[24] Moreover, the costs in terms of time and energy spent attempting to set some limits to corruption can also be expensive. For instance, in Burma, U Nu's creation of a Bureau of Special Investigation to check corruption actually reduced administrative efficiency.[25]

Aid Foregone

Another possible wastage, the opportunity costs of aid foregone or withdrawn by outside donors because of disgust with corruption in a developing country could be a serious cost in the sense that developing countries are highly dependent on external sources of capital. Thus far, however, there has not been a marked correlation between honesty of governments and their per capita receipt of aid. If corruption is a consideration with donors (presumably it weighs more heavily with multilateral institutions), it is not yet a primary one.

Instability

By destroying the legitimacy of political structures in the eyes of those who have power to do something about the situation, corruption can contribute to instability and possible national disintegration. But it is not clear that instability is always inimical to political development.

Social Revolution

An argument can be made that a full social revolution (whatever its short-run costs) can speed the development of new political structures better able to preserve their legitimacy in the face of social change. Thus, in this view if corruption

22 Edwin Lieuwen, *Arms and Politics in Latin America* (New York, 1960), p. 149.

23 F. Benham and H. A. Holley, *A Short Introduction to the Economy of Latin America* (London, 1960), p. 10.

24 Leys, at p. 229.

25 Brian Crozier, *The Morning After: A Study of Independence* (London, 1963), p. 82.

led to social revolution, this might be a beneficial effect for political development. But it is not clear that corruption of the old regime is a primary cause of social revolution. Such revolutions are comparatively rare and often depend heavily on catalytic events (such as external wars).

Military Takeovers

If corruption causes a loss of legitimacy in the eyes of those with guns, it may be a direct cause of instability and the disintegration of existing political institutions. But the consequences for political development are again ambiguous. Much depends on differing evaluations of the ability of military regimes (which tend to comprise people and procedures oriented toward modernity) to maintain legitimacy in a democratic age either by self-transformation into political regimes or by being willing and able to foster new political institutions to which power can be returned. To the extent that this tends to be difficult, then if corruption leads to military takeover, it has hindered political development.[26]

The degree to which corruption is itself a major cause of military takeovers is, however, open to some question. Despite its prominence in post-coup rationalizations, one might suspect that it is only a secondary cause in most cases. Perhaps more significant is military leaders' total distaste for the messiness of politics—whether honest or not—and a tendency to blame civilian politicians for failures to meet overly optimistic popular aspirations which would be impossible of fulfillment even by a government of angels.[27] Indeed, to the extent that corruption contributes to governmental effectiveness in meeting these aspirations, it may enhance stability.

Crozier sees "revulsion against civilian incompetence and corruption" as a major cause of coups in several Asian countries including Burma, but he also states that the main cause of Ne Win's return to power was the Shan demand for a federal rather than unitary state.[28] Similarly, corruption is sometimes blamed for the first coup in Nigeria, but the post-electoral crisis in the Western region and the fear of permanent Northern domination was probably a more important and direct cause. In Ghana, corruption may have played a more important role in causing the coup, but not so much because of revulsion at dishonesty, as the fact that corruption had reached an extent where it contributed to an economic situation in which real wages had fallen. Nonetheless, its impact in relation to other factors should not be overestimated.[29]

Upsetting Ethnic Balances

Corruption can sometimes exacerbate problems of national integration in developing countries. If a corrupt leader must be fired, it may upset ethnic arithmetic as happened in both Kenya and Zambia in 1966. Of course this can be manipulated as a deliberate political weapon. In Western Nigeria in 1959, an anti-corruption officer was appointed but his jurisdiction was subject to approval by the cabinet, which meant that no case could be investigated "unless the party leader decided that a man needed to be challenged."[30] But as a weapon, charging corruption is a risky device. Efforts by southern politicians in Uganda to use it in 1966 precipitated a pre-emptive

---

26 In Pye's words, the military "can contribute to only a limited part of national development," *Aspects of Political Development* (Boston, 1966), p. 187.

27 "Have no fear," General Mobutu told the Congo people, "My Government is not composed of politicians." Mobutu alleged that political corruption cost the Congo $43 million: *East Africa and Rhodesia*, January 13, 1966; *Africa Report*, January 1966, 23.

28 Crozier, pp. 62, 74.

29 For two interpretations, see Martin Kilson, "Behind Nigeria's Revolts"; Immanuel Wallerstein, "Autopsy of Nkrumah's Ghana," *New Leader*, January 31, 9–12; March 14, 1966, 3–5.

30 Henry Bretton, *Power and Stability in Nigeria* (New York, 1962), p. 79.

coup by the northern Prime Minister in alliance with the predominantly northern army.

Reduction of Governmental Capacity

While it may not be the sole or major cause, corruption can contribute to the loss of governmental capacity in developing countries.

Reduction of Administrative Capacity

Corruption may alienate modern-oriented civil servants (a scarce resource) and cause them to leave a country or withdraw or reduce their efforts. In addition to the obvious costs, this may involve considerable opportunity costs in the form of restriction of government programs because of fears that a new program (for instance, administration of new taxes) might be ineffective in practice. While this is a real cost, it is worth noting that efficient bureaucracy is not always a necessary condition for economic or political development (at least in the early stages), and in some cases can even hinder it.[31]

Loss of Legitimacy

It is often alleged that corruption squanders the most important asset a new country has—the legitimacy of its government. This is a serious cost but it must be analyzed in terms of groups. As we have seen, what may enhance legitimacy for the student or civil servant may not enhance it for the tradition-oriented man. It is interesting, for instance, that there is some evidence that in Tanganyika petty corruption at low levels seems to have increased during the year following the replacement of an "illegitimate" colonial regime by a "legitimate" nationalist one.[32] Loss of legitimacy as a cost must be coupled with assessment of the power or importance of the group in whose eyes legitimacy is lost. If they are young army officers, it can be important indeed.

PROBABILITIES

Thus far I have been discussing *possible* benefits and costs. I have established that under some circumstances corruption can have beneficial effects on at least three major development problems. I have evaluated the importance of a number of frequently alleged countervailing costs. It remains to offer hypotheses about the *probabilities* of benefits outweighing costs. In general terms, such probabilities will vary with at least three conditions: (1) a tolerant culture and dominant groups; (2) a degree of security on the part of the members of the elite being corrutped; (3) the existence of societal and institutional checks and restraints on corrupt behavior.

1. Attitudes toward corruption vary greatly. In certain West African countries, observers have reported little widespread sense of indignation about corruption.[33] The Philippines, with its American colonial heritage of corruption, and appreciation of the politics of compromise, seems able to tolerate a higher level of corruption than formerly-Dutch Indonesia. According to Higgins, the Indonesian attitude to corruption (which began on a large scale only in 1954) is that it is sinful. He attributes the civil war of 1958 to corruption and argues that in the Philippines, "anomalies" are taken more for granted.[34] Not only is the general level of tolerance of corruption relevant; variations of attitude within a country can be as important (or more so) than differences between countries. Very often, traditional sectors of the populace are likely to be more tolerant

[31] Bert Hoselitz, "Levels of Economic Performance and Bureaucratic Structures," in Joseph LaPalombara (ed.), *Bureaucracy and Political Development* (Princeton, 1963), 193–195. See also Nathaniel Leff, 8–14.

[32] See *Tanganyika Standard,* May 15, 1963.

[33] McMullan, p. 195.

[34] Benjamin Higgins, *Economic Development* (New York, 1959), p. 62.

TABLE 58.1
CORRUPTION COST-BENEFIT MATRIX

Types of Corruption	Political Conditions	DEVELOPMENT PROBLEMS: 1. Economic development			2. National integration		3. Governmental capacity		General Probability that Costs Outweigh Benefits
		a. capital	b. bureaucracy	c. skills	d. elite	e. non-elite	f. effectiveness	g. legitimacy	
1. Level									
top	F	low	uncertain	uncertain/low	low	uncertain	low	low	low/uncertain
bottom	F	high	uncertain	uncertain/high	uncertain	low	high	low	high
top	U	high	high	uncertain/low	high	high	low	high	high
bottom	U	high	uncertain	uncertain/high	little relevance	high	high	high	high
2. Inducements							low/uncertain	uncertain	low/uncertain
modern	F	low	uncertain	uncertain/low	low	low	high	uncertain	high
traditional	F	high/uncertain	uncertain	high	high	uncertain	low/uncertain	high	high
modern	U	high	uncertain	uncertain/low	high	high			
traditional	U	high/uncertain	uncertain	high	high	uncertain	high	high	high
3. Deviation									
extensive	F	uncertain	high	uncertain	uncertain	low	uncertain/low	uncertain/high	high
marginal	F	uncertain	low	uncertain/low	low	low	low	low	low
extensive	U	uncertain	high	uncertain	high	high	uncertain	high	high
marginal	U	uncertain	low	uncertain/low	high	high	low	high	high

NOTES:

F	favorable political conditions (cultural tolerance, elite security, checks).
U	unfavorable political conditions
High	high probability that costs exceed benefits
Low	low probability that costs exceed benefits
Uncertain	little relationship or ambiguous relationship

of corruption than some of the modern sectors (students, army, civil service). Thus the hypothesis must take into account not only the tolerant nature of the culture, but also the relative power of groups representing more and less tolerant sub-cultures in a country. In Nigeria, tolerance was by many accounts considerable among the population at large, but not among the young army officers who overthrew the old regime.

2. Another condition which increases the probability that the benefits of corruption will outweigh the costs is a degree of security (and perception thereof) by the members of the elites indulging in corrupt practices. Too great insecurity means that any capital formed by corruption will tend to be exported rather than invested at home. In Nicaragua, for instance, it is argued that the sense of security of the Somoza family encouraged them in internal investments in economic projects and the strengthening of their political party, which led to impressive economic growth and diminished direct reliance on the army. In contrast are the numerous cases of capital outflow mentioned above. One might add that this sense of security, including the whole capitalist ethic, which is rare in less developed countries today, makes comparison with capital formation by the "robber barons" of the American 19th century of dubious relevance to less developed countries today.

3. It is probable that for the benefits of corruption to outweigh the costs depends on its being limited in various ways, much as the beneficial effects of inflation for economic growth tends to depend on limits. These limits depend upon the existence of societal or institutional restraints on corruption. These can be external to the leaders, e.g., the existence of an independent press, and honest elections; or internalized conceptions of public interest by a ruling group such as Leys argues that 18th-century English aristocrats held.[35] In Mandeville's words, "Vice is beneficial found when it's by Justice lopt and bound."[36]

Given the characteristics of less developed countries, one can see that the general probability of the presence of one or more of these conditions (and thus of benefits outweighing costs) is not high. But to conclude merely that the moralists are more right than wrong (though for the wrong reasons) is insufficient because the whole issue remains unsatisfactory if left in these general terms. Though corruption may not prove beneficial for resolution of development problems in general, it may prove to be the only means to solution of a particular problem. If a country has some overriding problem, some "obstacle to development"—for instance, if capital can be formed by no other means, or ethnic hatred threatens all legal activities aimed at its alleviation—then it is possible that corruption is beneficial for development despite the high costs and risks involved. While there are dangers in identifying "obstacles to development,"[37] and while the corruption that is beneficial to the solution of one problem may be detrimental to another, we need to get away from general statements which are difficult to test and which provide us with no means of ordering the vast number of variables involved. We are more likely to advance this argument if we distinguish the roles of different types of corruption in relation to different types of development problems.

The matrix in Table 58.1 relates three types of corruption to three types of development problems, first assuming

---

[35] Leys, p. 227. See also Eric McKitrick, "The Study of Corruption," *Political Science Quarterly*, 72 (December 1957), 502–514, for limits on corruption in urban America.

[36] Bernard Mandeville, *The Fable of the Bees*, Vol. I (Oxford: Clarendon Press, by F. B. Kaye, 1924), p. 37.

[37] See Albert O. Hirschman, "Obstacles to Development: A Classification and a Quasi-Vanishing Act," *Economic Development and Cultural Change*, 13 (July 1965), 385–393.

favorable and then assuming unfavorable conditions described above. Favorable conditions (F) means a tolerant culture or dominance of more tolerant groups, relative security of the elite corrupted, and societal/institutional checks. Unfavorable conditions (U) means intolerant culture or groups, insecure elite, and few societal/institutional checks. The development problems are those discussed above: economic development, national integration, and governmental capacity. The scores are a priori judgments that the costs of a particular type of corruption are likely to outweigh the benefits for a particular development problem or sub-problem. They represent a series of tentative hypotheses to be clarified or refuted by data. Under economic development, the specific sub-problems discussed are whether capital accumulation is promoted (benefit) without capital flight (cost); whether cutting bureaucratic red tape (benefit) outweighs distortion of rational criteria (cost); whether the attraction of unused scarce skills such as entrepreneurship (benefit) is greater than the wastage of scarce skills of, say, politicians and civil servants (cost).

Under the problem of national integration are the sub-problems of whether a particular type of corruption tends to make the elite more cohesive (benefit) or seriously splits them (cost); and whether it tends to humanize government and make national identification easier for the non-elites (benefit) or alienates them (cost). Under the problem of governmental capacity are the sub-problems of whether the additional power aggregated by corruption (benefit) outweighs possible damage to administrative efficiency (cost); and whether it enhances (benefit) or seriously weakens the governmental legitimacy (cost).

Level of Beneficiary

Shils argues that "freedom from corruption at the highest levels is a necessity for the maintenance of public respect of Government . . ." whereas a modicum of corruption at lower levels is probably not too injurious.[38] On the other hand, McMullan reports that West Africans show little sense of indignation about often fantastic stories of corruption by leaders, and impressions from Mexico indicate that petty corruption most saps morale.[39] In India, Bayley notes that "although corruption at the top attracts the most attention in public forums, and involves the largest amount of money in separate transactions, corruption at the very bottom levels is the more apparent and obvious and in total amounts of money involved may very well rival corruption at the top."[40]

The matrix in the table suggests that under unfavorable conditions neither type of corruption is likely to be beneficial in general, although top level corruption may enhance governmental power more than it weakens administrative efficiency. It also suggests that under favorable conditions, top level corruption may be beneficial but bottom level corruption probably is not (except for non-elite integration). If these judgments are accurate, it suggests that countries with favorable conditions, like India, which have considerable bottom level corruption but pride themselves on the relative honesty of the higher levels may be falling between two stools.

The rationale of the scoring is as follows: (A) Capital. Bottom level corruption with smaller size of each inducement will probably increase consumption more than capital formation. While top level corruption may represent the latter, whether it is invested productively rather than sent overseas depends on favorable political conditions. (B) Bureaucracy. Other factors seem more important in

38 Shils, p. 385.
39 McMullan, p. 195; Oscar Lewis, *The Children of Sanchez* (New York, 1961).
40 Bayley, p. 724.

determining whether expediting is more important than distortion; except that those with the power of the top levels will probably distort investment criteria considerably in conditions of uncertainty —witness the alleged selling of investment licenses under a previous government in Guatemala. (C) Skills. Whether top level corruption permits the use of more skills than it wastes depends upon their supply. Where they exist, as with Asians in East Africa or "Turcos" in Honduras, it is probably beneficial. Corruption of those at lower levels of power may be more likely to waste energies than to be important in permission of use of new skills simply because their power is limited.

(D) Elite Integration. It is difficult to see a clear relation between bottom level corruption and elite integration. At the higher levels under unfavorable conditions, e.g., a powerful intolerant part of the elite such as students or army, corruption would probably have a more divisive than cohesive effect. Under favorable conditions it might be more cohesive. (E) Non-elite Integration. Under unfavorable conditions it seems likely that both types of corruption would tend to alienate more than enhance identification, whereas under favorable conditions corruption by the lower levels that the populace deals with most frequently might have the humanizing effect mentioned above, and alienation would be slight in the tolerant culture. Top level corruption might have the same effect though the connection is less clear because of the lesser degree of direct contact.

(F) Effectiveness. Bottom level corruption is more likely to disperse rather than aggregate power by making governmental machinery less responsive than otherwise might be the case; whereas at top levels the ability to change the behavior of important power holders by corrupt inducements is likely to outweigh the loss of efficiency, even under unfavorable conditions. (G) Legitimacy. Whether corruption enhances or reduces governmental legitimacy depends more on unfavorable conditions than on level of corruption. Much depends on another factor, visibility of corrupt behavior, which does not always have a clear relationship to level of corruption.

Inducements

Another distinction which can be made between types of corruption is the nature of the inducement used, for instance the extent to which they reflect the values of the traditional society or the values of the modern sector. A traditional inducement such as status in one's clan or tribe may be more tolerable to those who share the ascriptive affinity, but others outside the ascriptive relationship would prefer the use of money which would give them equality of access to the corruptee. Weiner writes of India that "from a political point of view, equal opportunity to corrupt is often more important than the amount of corruption, and therefore . . . an increase in *bakshish* is in the long run less serious than an increase in corruption by ascriptive criteria."[41]

As scored here, our matrix suggests that under favorable political conditions (e.g., India?) Weiner's hypothesis is probably correct but would not be correct under unfavorable conditions. (A) Capital. Modern inducements (i.e., money) probably lead to capital formation (at top levels) which may be invested under favorable conditions or be sent abroad under unfavorable conditions. Traditional inducements (kin status) do not promote capital formation (and may even interfere with it) but probably have little effect on capital flight. (B) Bureaucracy. What edge modern inducements may have in expediting procedure may be offset by distortion of criteria, so the relation between type of inducement and this prob-

[41] Myron Weiner, *The Politics of Scarcity* (Chicago: University of Chicago Press, 1962), p. 236.

lem is scored as uncertain. (C) Skills. Assuming the existence of untapped skills (as above), modern inducements increase the access to power while traditional ones decrease it. (D) Elite Integration. Under favorable conditions modern inducements are unlikely to divide elites more than make them cohere, but traditional inducements tend to preserve and emphasize ethnic divisions in the elites. Under unfavorable conditions, both types of inducements tend to be divisive. (E) Non-elite Integration. Whether modern inducements promote identification or alienation varies with political conditions in the expected way, but the effect of traditional inducements is more ambiguous and probably varies from positive to negative according to the prevalence of traditional as against modern values in the particular country in question. (F) Effectiveness. Modern inducements probably give the government greater range to aggregate more sources of power than traditional inducements do. The probabilities will vary not only with political conditions but also by the opportunity costs—whether there is an efficient administrative machine to be damaged or not. (G) Legitimacy. Under favorable conditions whether traditional or modern inducements will decrease legitimacy more than they enhance it remains uncertain because it will vary with the (above mentioned) degree of existence of modern and traditional values in a society. Under unfavorable conditions, both will likely have higher costs than benefits.

Deviation

We can also distinguish types of corruption by whether the corrupt behavior involves extensive deviation from the formal duties of a public role or marginal deviation. This is not the same thing as a scale of corrupt inducements, since the size of the inducements may bear little relation to the degree of deviation. For instance, it is alleged that in one Central American country under an insecure recent regime, a business could get the government to reverse a decision for as little as $2000, whereas in a neighboring country the mere expediting of a decision cost $50,000. Such a distinction between types of corruption by extent of deviation is not uncommon among practitioners who use terms like "speed-up money" or "honest graft" in their rationalizations.[42]

(A) Capital. It is difficult to see that the extensiveness of the deviation (except insofar as it affects the scale of inducement) has much to do with the probabilities of capital formation or flight. (B) Bureaucracy. On the other hand, marginal deviations (by definition) are unlikely to involve high costs in distortion of criteria and even under unfavorable conditions may help expedite matters. Extensive deviations are likely to have high costs in terms of rational criteria regardless of conditions. (C) Skills. It is not clear that extensive deviations call forth more unused skills than they waste administrative skills; nor is the matter completely clear with marginal deviations, though the costs of administrative skills wasted may be lower because the tasks are simpler.

(D) Elite Integration. Under unfavorable conditions, the effects of corruption on elite cohesiveness are likely to be negative regardless of the extent of deviations, though they might be less negative for marginal deviations. Under favorable conditions, marginal deviations are likely to have low costs, but the effect of extensive deviations will be uncertain, varying with other factors such as existing cohesiveness of the elite and the nature of the extensive deviations. (E) Non-elite Integration. Under unfavorable conditions, corruption is likely to have more alienative than identification effects regardless of the nature of the deviations.

---

[42] Cf. William Riordan, *Plunkitt of Tammany Hall* (New York, 1948), p. 4.

Under favorable conditions, marginal deviation will not have high costs in terms of alienation, and extensive deviation may have special appeal to those who are seeking human and "reversible" government more than impartial or "rational" government. (F) Effectiveness. It is difficult to see that extensive deviations alone would increase governmental power more than weaken administrative efficiency, but with marginal deviation, the extent of the latter would be sufficiently small that the benefits would probably outweigh the costs. (G) Legitimacy. Under unfavorable conditions either type of corruption would be more likely to weaken than to enhance legitimacy, but under favorable conditions the lesser challenge to rationality might make marginal corruption less detrimental than extensive—though this would depend on the proportion and dominance of groups in society placing emphasis on modern values.

CONCLUSION

The scoring of the matrix suggests that we can refine the general statements about corruption and political development to read "it is probable that the costs of corruption in less developed countries will exceed its benefits except for top level corruption involving modern inducements and marginal deviations and except for situations where corruption provides the only solution to an important obstacle to development." As our matrix shows, corruption can provide the solution to several of the more limited problems of development. Whether this is beneficial to development as a whole depends on how important the problems are and what alternatives exist. It is also interesting to note that while the three conditions we have identified seem to be necessary for corruption to be beneficial in general terms, they are not necessary for it to be beneficial in the solution of a number of particular problems.

At this point, however, not enough information is at hand to justify great confidence in the exact conclusions reached here. More important is the suggestion of the use of this or a similar matrix to advance the discussion of the relationship between corruption and development. The matrix can be expanded or elaborated in a number of ways if the data seem to justify it. Additional development problems can be added, as can additional types of corruption (e.g., by scale, visibility, income effects, and so forth). The above categories can be made more precise by adding possibilities; for instance intermediate as well as top and bottom levels of corruption, or distinctions between politicians and civil servants at top, bottom, and intermediate levels.

Despite the problems of systematic field research on corruption in developing countries mentioned above, there is probably much more data on corruption and development gleaned during field work on other topics than we realize. What we need to advance the study of the problem is to refute and replace *specific* a priori hypotheses with propositions based on such data rather than with the generalities of the moralists. Corruption in developing countries is too important a phenomenon to be left to moralists.

Select Bibliography

ADDITIONAL STUDIES ON CORRUPTION

Braibanti, Ralph, "Reflections on Bureaucratic Corruption," *Public Administration,* 40:4 (1962), pp. 357–362.

"The Bribed Congressman's Immunity from Prosecution," *Yale Law Journal,* 75 (1965), pp. 335–350.

Bryce, James. *Modern Democracies,* 2 vols. New York: St. Martin's, 1921.

Charnay, Jean-Paul, "La Corruption," *Le Suffrage Politique en France.* Paris: Mouton, 1965, pp. 284–306.

Corpuz, Orofre D. *The Philippines.* Englewood Cliffs, N.J.: Prentice-Hall, 1965.

"Corruption in Politics," *Cyclopaedia of Political Science, Political Economy and U.S. History,* Vol. I. J. Lalor, ed. Skokie, Ill.: Rand McNally, 1882, pp. 672–674.

Dwivedi, O. P., "Bureaucratic Corruption in Developing Countries," *Asian Survey,* F/4 (1966–1967), pp. 245–253.

Dwivedy, S., and G. S. Bhargava. *Political Corruption in India.* New Delhi, 1967.

Fitzpatrick, Joseph P., "Catholics and Corruption," *Thought,* 37 (1962), pp. 379–390.

Friedrich, Carl J., "Political Pathology," *Political Quarterly,* 37 (1966), pp. 70–85.

Furnivall, James S., "Corruption," *Colonial Policy and Colonial Practice: A Comparative Study of Burma and Netherlands India.* New York: Cambridge University Press, 1948, pp. 170–177.

Goodwin, Elliot H., "Legislative Corruption," *Cyclopaedia of American Government.* New York: Appleton, 1914, pp. 476–478.

Helmore, L. M. *Corrupt and Illegal Practices: A General Survey and a Case History of an Election Petition.* London: Routledge, 1967.

Higonnet, Patrick, and Trevor B. Higonnet, "Class, Corruption and Politics in the French Chamber of Deputies, 1846–1848," *French Historical Studies,* 5:2 (1967–1968), pp. 205–224.

Jensen, Richard B., "Fraud, Corruption and Coercion," *The Winning of the Midwest: 1880–1896.* Chicago, Ill.: University of Chicago Press, 1971.

Josephson, Mathew. *The Politicos, 1865–1896.* New York: Harcourt, 1938.

Lasswell, Harold D., "Bribery," *Encyclopedia of the Social Sciences,* Vol. I. New York: Crowell-Collier-Macmillan, 1930, pp. 690–692.

Mani, Ramaswamy, "Political Corruption and Political Change." Unpublished Ph.D. dissertation (Harvard University), 1967.

McArthur, Peter, "The Science of Political Corruption," *Forum,* 47 (1912), pp. 26–33.

Mayer, Ernst, "Bekaempfung der Wahlumtriebe durch das Strafrecht," *Zeitschrift für Politik,* III (1910), pp. 10–29.

McKitrick, E. L., "The Study of Corruption," *Political Science Quarterly,* 72 (1959), pp. 502–514.

Odegard, Peter. "Political Corruption; United States," *Encyclopaedia of the Social Sciences,* Vol. IV. New York: Crowell-Collier-Macmillan, pp. 452–454.

O'Leary, Cornelius. *The Elimination of Corrupt Practices in British Elections, 1868–1911.* New York: Oxford, 1968.

Ottenberg, Simon, "Local Government and Law in Southern Nigeria," *Journal of Asian and African Studies,* Vol. 2, No. 1–2 (1967), pp. 26–43.

Prick, F., "Corruptie en Politietransactie," *Tijdschrift voor Politie.* 1959, pp. 53–56.

Proal, Lewis. *Political Crime.* New York: Appleton, 1898.

R.D.R., "Control of Non-Governmental Corruption by Criminal Legislation," *University of Pennsylvania Law Review,* 108 (1960), pp. 848–867.

Report of the Bribery and Corruption Enquiry Committee, 1940. Rangoon: official publication, 1941.

Riordon, William L. *Plunkitt of Tammany Hall.* New York: Dutton, 1963.

Schatz, Sayre P., "The Economic Effects of Corruption," Unpublished Paper Delivered at African Studies Association Meeting, Montreal, October 1969.

Scott, James C. "An Essay on the Political Functions of Corruption," *Asian Studies,* 5:3 (December 1967).

Senturia, Joseph J., "Political Corruption." *Encyclopaedia of the Social Sciences,* Vol. IV. pp. 448–452.

Shaw, G. B., "Municipal Corruption" and "State Corruption" in *Everybody's Political What's What.* New York: Dodd, Mead and Co., 1944, pp. 250–266 and 266–281.

Smith, M. G., "Historical and Cultural Conditions of Political Corruption among the Hausa," *Comparative Studies in Society and History,* 6:2 (1964), pp. 164–194.

Steffens, J. Lincoln. *The Autobiography of Lincoln Steffens.* New York: Harcourt, 1931.

Sufrin, Sidney C., "Graft: Grease for the Palm and Grease for the Wheels," *Challenge,* 13:1 (1964), pp. 30–33.

Wilson, James Q., "Corruption Is Not Always Scandalous," *New York Times Magazine* (April 28, 1968), pp. 54ff.

Venkutappiah, B., "Office—Misuse of," *International Encyclopedia Of Social Sciences,* II., New York: Free Press, 1968, pp. 272–276.

BACKGROUND SOURCES

Blau, Peter M. *Exchange and Power in Social Life.* New York: Wiley, 1964. (Esp. chap. 4, "Social Exchange.")

Burnham, Walter Dean, "Party Systems and the Political Process," W. N. Chambers and W. D. Burnham, eds. *The American Party Systems.* New York: Oxford, 1967, pp. 277–307.

Callard, Keith. "On the Ethics of Civil Servants in Great Britain and North America," C. J. Friedrich and J. K. Galbraith, eds. *Public Policy,* pp. 134–156. Harvard Graduate School of Public Administration, 1959: A Yearbook of the Graduate School of Public Administration, Harvard University.

Chalmers, David M., "The Muckrakers and the Growth of Corporate Power," *American Journal of Economics and Sociology,* 18 (1959), pp. 295–311.

Codere, Helen, "Exchange And Display," *International Encyclopedia of Social Sciences,* 5, New York: Free Press, 1968, pp. 239–244.

Eisenberg, Ralph, "Conflict of Interest Situations and Remedies," *Rutgers Law Review,* 13 (1959), pp. 666–700.

Foord, Archibald S. "The Waning of the Influence of the Crown," *English Historical Review,* 62 (1947), pp. 485–507.

Fallers, Lloyd. *Bantu Bureaucracy*. Chicago, Ill.: University of Chicago Press. 1965.

George, Henry, "Money in Politics," *North American Review,* 316 (March 1883), pp. 201–211.

Gottfried, Alex, "Political Machines," *International Encyclopedia of Social Sciences,* 12, New York: Free Press, 1968, pp. 248–252.

Greenstein, Fred J., "The Changing Pattern of Urban Party Politics," *Annals of American Academy of Political and Social Sciences,* 353 (May 1964).

Herring, E. Pendleton, "The Future of Patronage," *Virginia Quarterly Review,* 14 (1928), pp. 44–56.

Hintze, Otto, "Der Beamtenstand," *Soziologie und Geschichte*. Gottingen: Vanderhoeck and Ruprecht, 1964, pp. 66–125.

Kenny, Michael. "Patterns of Patronage in Spain," *Anthropological Quarterly,* 33 (1960), pp. 14–23.

Kern, Ernst August, "Beamter," *Handwörterbuch der Sozialwissenschaften,* Vol. I. Stuttgart: Fischer, 1960, pp. 695–704.

Kingsley, J. Donald. *Representative Democracy*. Yellow Springs, Ohio: Antioch Press, 1944.

Landé, Carl H. *Leaders, Factions and Parties: The Structure of Philippine Politics,* Monograph No. 6, South East Asia Studies, New Haven, Conn.: Yale University Press, 1965.

Lane, Robert E. *Political Ideology*. New York: Free Press, 1962.

Lasswell, Harold D., "Chicago's Old First Ward," *National Municipal Review,* 12 (March 1923), pp. 127–131.

Lee, Linda K., "Conflict of Interest: One Aspect of Congress' Problems," *George Washington Law Review,* 32 (1963–1964), pp. 954–982.

McMahon, Arthur W., "Public Office," *Encyclopedia of the Social Sciences,* Vol. VI. New York: Crowell-Collier-Macmillan, pp. 665–669.

Namier, Sir Lewis B. *The Structure of Politics at the Accession of George III*. 2d ed. New York: St. Martin's Press, 1957.

Nettl, J. P., "The State as a Conceptual Variable," *World Politics,* 20:4 (July 1968), pp. 559–592.

Rosenberg, Hans. *Bureaucracy, Aristocracy and Autocracy: The Prussian Experience, 1660–1815*. Cambridge, Mass.: Harvard University Press, 1958.

Roth, Guenther, "Personal Rulership, Patrimonialism and Empire-Building in the New States," *World Politics,* pp. 194–206. Yale Institute of International Studies, New Haven, Conn.

Rotteck-Welcker. *Staatslexikon*. Rev. ed., 1842.

Shotwell, James T., "Democracy and Political Morality," *Political Science Quarterly,* 36:1 (1921), pp. 1–8.

Sikes, Earl R. *State and Federal Corrupt-Practices Legislation*. Durham, N.C.: Duke University Press, 1928.

Silverman, Sydel F. "Patronage and Community Relationships in Central Italy," *Ethnology*, 4 (1965), pp. 172–189.

Stokes, Donald, "Parties and the Nationalization of Electoral Forces," W. N. Chambers and W. D. Burnham, eds. *The American Party Systems*. New York: Oxford, 1967, pp. 182–202.

Van Riper, Paul, "Adapting a British Political Convention to American Needs," *Public Administration,* 31 (1953), pp. 317–330.

Weber, Max. *Economy and Society,* Vol. II. New York: Bedminster Press, 1968.

Weiner, Myron. *The Politics of Scarcity*. Chicago, Ill.: University of Chicago Press, 1962.

Weingrod, Alex, "Patrons, Patronage and Political Parties," *Comparative Studies in Society and History,* 10 (July 1968), pp. 377–400.

White, Leonard D. *The Jacksonians: A Study in Administrative History, 1829–1861.* New York: Crowell-Collier-Macmillan, 1954.

Wilson, James Q., "The Economy of Patronage," *Journal of Political Economy,* 69 (1961), pp. 369–380.

Wolf, Eric R., "Kinship, Friendship, and Patron-client Relations in Complex Societies," in Michael R. Banton, *The Social Anthropology of Complex Societies.* New York: Praeger, 1966.